HAITIANS OF SPRINGFIELD

AN ORAL HISTORY

JOSHUA LISEC

New York Times Bestselling Author

Since 1947
REGNERY
An Imprint of Skyhorse Publishing, Inc.

Regnery books may be purchased in bulk at special discounts for sales promotion, corporate gifts, fund-raising, or educational purposes. Special editions can also be created to specifications. For details, contact the Special Sales Department, Regnery, 307 Fifth Avenue, 4th Floor, New York, NY 10016 or info@skyhorsepublishing.com.

Regnery® is an imprint of Skyhorse Publishing, Inc.®, a Delaware corporation.

Visit our website at www.regnery.com.

Please follow our publisher Tony Lyons on Instagram @tonylyonsisuncertain.

10 9 8 7 6 5 4 3 2 1

Library of Congress Cataloging-in-Publication Data is available on file.

Cover design by David Ter-Avanesyan

Print ISBN: 978-1-5107-8884-8
Ebook ISBN: 978-1-5107-8885-5

Printed in the United States of America

For Aiden and Kathy, who will never be able to read
this book because they lived it.

CONTENTS

PREFACE

The Conversations We Should Be Having

> "[T]his is a fascinating story about how immigration in the U.S. works today. . . . It's the story we should be talking about, and solving for.
>
> We might discuss, for instance, why Haitian immigrants with jobs are being given a year of food stamps and government assistance through refugee programs when they are gainfully employed with stable housing. We might debate why these services seem more accessible to immigrants than to local U.S. residents. We might discuss how to better train foreign citizens to drive in the U.S. before they put themselves and their neighbors in danger. We might ask what kind of programs the employers . . . or local religious groups can provide to lessen the burden on government services that are being overwhelmed so that veterans don't have to wait in line for hours to receive their benefits.
>
> These are the conversations we should be having."[1]
>
> —Isaac Saul

We are now.

Allow me to introduce myself. I am Springfield's neighbor. I've lived in the Miami Valley my entire life. Our state's history follows my own family lineage all the way back. I am Ohio. So when the story of a town I know well of nearly sixty thousand of whom many I know, a town already struggling to retain what few good opportunities that remained for the next generation, was made to receive tens of thousands of uniquely unassimilated Haitian migrants into its streets, schools, markets, clinics, and workforce, when this story made headlines from a very peculiar angle—reports of inconspicuous consumption of domesticated animals by the newcomers—I had to go.[2] It was like checking on my neighbor. I aim to be a good neighbor.

On September 19, 2024, I attended a quasi-spontaneous town hall in Springfield by then Donald Trump campaign surrogate Vivek Ramaswamy and

Tiffany Justice, a co-founder of Moms For Liberty. It would be more accurate to admit I *intended* to attend—I never made it inside. Instead, on the walk up, reporters, writers, commentators, and podcasters from as far away as Canada, Germany, even Australia, it was rumored, on site, interviewed many of us still waiting to get inside. I was more than a little distracted by Clark County sheriff deputies' overhead drones observing us, as we all knew what time it was in America, then freshly post-Butler.

But one particular interview held my distraction at bay. A spindly little fellow with curly black hair and nerd-frame glasses told me he was with Politico. We spoke as I stood in line, gently bouncing and swaying my youngest child in my baby carrier. I didn't catch the reporter's name, and I never caught our interview published anywhere; he also interviewed my then-wife, separately.

I will never let go of the words this little man shared about why Springfield had made news so significant that his employer sent him here.

"It's been debunked. It's all been debunked."

Interesting.

Study these words as I did in that very moment.

And what do you notice?

What do you notice that isn't there that should be?

Who—exactly. It's passive voice. Who, exactly, did this debunking? And what, precisely, had been debunked? *You?* I thought on the spot. *You "debunked" all this? You went to the majority-Haitian neighborhoods and—right?*

I was unsure of any motive beyond dismissal—the derision became clear, however, as we exchanged more words, and it turned into an interview of himself. There was a lot about racism, bigotry, and xenophobia. I wonder who he was and what ever became of that recording . . .

Our exchange reminded me of the viral 2021 clip of then-Vice President Kamala Harris covering, of all relevant topics, the immense number of previously illegal border crossings and vast humanitarian crises that spread across the country, with preparations as complete as the VP seemed capable of planning them.

> **Harris:** At some point, you know, we are going to the border. . . . We've been to the border. So this whole thing about the border. We've been to the border. We've been to the border.
>
> **Lester Holt:** You haven't been to the border.
>
> **Harris:** And I haven't been to Europe. And I mean, I don't . . . understand the point that you're making.[3]

What had this man debunked? And more importantly, what hadn't he?

I would, not long after, write about my experience that night for *Human Events* in a Thomas Paine-esque acknowledgment of this obviously pivotal moment in this continent's history entitled "The American Migrant Crisis."[4] But before the town hall had even concluded, I had the livestream up via YouTube. I rewound to the beginning and noticed a friendly acquaintance was the first citizen to speak—Representative Phil Plummer, Ohio District 39, former longtime sheriff of Montgomery County:

> We let the media grab the story about the ducks and the geese and the dogs and the cats—that's not the story. The story is what this is costing you guys.[5]

Whatever that cost may or may not be, as of this writing, it continues to be paid—even after the termination of Temporary Protected Status of Haitian citizens in the United.[6] Many things have been said—and said to me, specifically—about the cost of and the returns on that investment in migration. Many things said, shown, asserted, and insisted. I listened to many, I believed some, I questioned all. I heard the stories, and I asked for the proof. In a city with such an aging population, it's not first on anyone's mind to capture footage of something that will be very important later when others ask about it. Hindsight is 20/20; most concerned citizens I spoke to in the course of researching for this book wear prescription lenses for nearsightedness.[7] Data was hard to come by, but not as hard as I thought. At times, I wondered how it was possible that I could be one of the few, if not the first, to stumble upon it. Upon the story. The actual story.

Was hearsay abundant? Yes, that's correct. But to the proud centrist and cosmopolitan skeptic I will ask: **If it's hearsay, but you hear everyone say it, is it still hearsay?** When that everyone consists of hundreds to thousands who do not know each other and have not corresponded on the matter? Is it?

Or is it the collective lived experience of a city in crisis, a people in fear, a community in anguish? Is it the shared truth of a people who love each other more than they hate outsiders? Do they in fact judge friend and foe alike not by the color of their skin but by the content of their character? And at times inconvenient to the politically charged narrative, they happen to find that character troubling? And of all things . . . why was Springfield put to this test?

Was this truly the "Lie of the Year," as PolitiFact stated?[8] I set out to find out.

Find out with me.

I proudly present *Haitians of Springfield*, an oral history of the unexpected foreign influx into forgotten middle America—and what to do about it.

INTRODUCTION
Intercultural Consumption

"I knew that there was going to be chaos. I had no idea how bad it was going to be."[1]

—Carl Ruby, PhD

There's something you should know.

Communication degrees aren't completely useless. I graduated with two of them—one from Sinclair College in Dayton, Ohio, one from nearby Wright State University. Both schools required a number of classes, readings, and examinations on the subject of Intercultural Communication. That's exactly what it sounds like. What happens when peoples of different cultures come together, for one reason or another, and . . . talk. Interact. Become neighbors. Work, shop, eat, and worship in parallel or together . . . or neither. When previously they hadn't made a culture-wide group project of sorting *us* from *other*, suddenly they now must. Theories of Intercultural Communication predict what happens next.

And what did my coursework teach me? I remember from both syllabi and supplemental reading models such as John Berry's Acculturation Hypothesis. When cultures come into sustained contact, their members tend to move toward one of four broad patterns—assimilation (newcomers adopt the dominant culture), separation (new arrivals maintain their original culture and avoid the host's), integration (keep some aspects of prior culture while also participating in the larger one), or marginalization (loss of connection to both). Of all paths forward, integration—the give-and-take of both cultures—requires "substantial negotiation" but "results in the least conflict."[2] Suddenly, I'm reminded of old westerns wherein the cowboy and the Indian share a peace pipe, a *calumet*, and trade stories by the fire. That's microcosmic integration. Cowboys and Indians both have to want to do it, to "negotiate." Sometimes they don't. Most of the time they didn't.

What happens then? Henri Tajfel and John Turner's Social Identity Theory explains conflict escalation because people sort themselves into in-groups (*us*) and out-groups (*them*). Us-versus-them comparisons only occur between "relevant" groups. And what makes a competing group relevant? "Proximity." Once shared identity is at risk, and with those groups having emotionally invested in that identity, then disputes over rules and norms are simply cover for the true concern: who we are as a distinct people, and whether or not—and this is key—*we* are losing status to *them*.[3]

If so, then it gets ugly. Realistic Group Conflict Theory predicts these clashes will sharpen as non-shared-identity groups thrust into proximity with one another compete for scarce resources—such as, for example, job opportunities, neighborhoods and residences, school seats, welfare benefits, public safety prioritization, political influence, or public recognition. If the competing groups perceive a zero-sum struggle, hostilities rise. Plans to conserve give way to the race to consume. Only "mutually desired outcomes" could ease tension, mitigate conflict, and motivate intergroup cooperation.[4] *Could.* Intergroup Contact Hypothesis concurs; shared goals are prerequisite for peace.[5] Without win-wins, one group's gain demands the other's loss. The pie gets smaller; more go hungry.

William Gudykunst's Anxiety/Uncertainty Management work predicts how intercultural encounters will feel tense even before any open conflict.[6] When people cannot predict the other side's behavior, motives, manners, or intentions, anxiety rises and miscommunications mount. *Us* versus *them*, all over again, to the end.

And how is that end decided? A given culture tends to prevail when it has greater state backing, stronger demographic continuity, higher reproduction, mightier economic leverage, higher elite prestige, broader institutional legitimacy, and, frankly, greater raw power to reward friends and punish enemies (and the corrupted inversion—to refuse to punish friends when they otherwise deserve it, but punish enemies to an unfair extent even when they don't).[7,8]

Understanding this, we realize that a minority culture can upset a higher-population incumbent. The powers that be may tip the scales in their favor. *Them* receives the moral support and institutional credibility unavailable to *us*. All of this has happened before, and it can all happen again.[9,10,11,12,13,14] And so, across time, space, place, and race, the heritage citizen becomes a second-class subject in his own land. Sorted. Conflicted. Unwelcome. Consumed. Resistance is an exercise in utility against his own interests. Refusal to cooperate with top-down forced cultural spacemaking, that very refusal, becomes evidence in the case for it to have occurred in the first place. Coerced negotiations grant non-consensual concessions. Justified replacement. What's ours is theirs; what's theirs is theirs, too. And if we don't like it, our injury begets insult from the scale-tippers: *You had it coming.*

That's what you should know about Springfield, Ohio.

CHAPTER 1

FIRST HAITIANS

"[R]acialized ethnicities have developed particular cultures we should value in a multicultural society."[1]

—Ibram X. Kendi

"A Haitian chased my daughter with a machete. The police did nothing."

I put down my finger sandwich.

"Sorry—what?"

Setys (*suh-TEECE*) **Kelly**, then-candidate for Ohio Republican Party State Central Committee, repeated herself while I double-time chewed, so I could ask for further information with a mouth fully available for subsequent conversation.

"Yes. A Haitian chased my daughter with a machete. She called the police, and they didn't even come down. Thank God she was in her car."

Setys was about to speak at a meet-the-candidates mixer at a TJ Chump's in Fairborn, Ohio. I'd cycled through a spontaneous line of Greene County-area political hopefuls, migrating towards the snacklike dinner situation in the back. I knew Setys from just about every Ohio politics meetup I'd attended in the last year, and she was about to make sure I met everyone else she knew, too.

But it was mid-introduction to another candidate that this anecdote, like the alleged armed assailant, dropped in out of nowhere. I don't know how we got onto the topic, but I do know one particular detail about Setys.

She's from Springfield.

"Where did this happen?" I asked.

Then and later when I followed up to rehear the story (that's what you do when you write a book), Setys told the same tale of her daughter's near-fateful commute to her teaching job in Springfield.

"By Pleasant Street," Setys said. "Going to the school. They were doing road construction and had a road blocked by a piece of machinery. And the guy comes running over. She had her vehicle, and she was praying that that would move so she could keep going. Luckily, she went around it and moved on. Called the police. Police never showed up. Never took a report. Because then you've got something on paper that one of them has committed a crime."

I now had questions. All the same questions you do.

I picked my sandwich back up.

Not on My Planet

This machete-wielding anecdote abhors many fair-minded citizens. I understand. You might have felt uncomfortable simply reading my recounting. Tainted, dirty perhaps. Like you've witnessed something you shouldn't have, and now it's somehow on you. Some of you are even feeling tempted to quit reading this book right now, send it back, and ask for a refund. You were looking for information, for the truth, not accusations. Right? Isn't that all that was?

While we sympathize with the would-be victim of the attack and feel relief that she extricated herself from the situation, we also find ourselves force-conjuring compassion, sympathy, empathy for the man in question. Before you finished reading the concerned mother's words, you might have been thinking, *Why would she say "a Haitian" though? How could she have possibly known? Profiling much? Race and country of origin have nothing to do with a mental health crisis anyway. Literally any person, of any background, could have purchased that machete and went out in public. I mean—maybe he was a Haitian, but was just practicing the Caribbean martial art of* Tire machèt. *Or maybe he thought the daughter was about to run him over and he panicked and thought he had to defend himself. There's literally hundreds of reasons that poor man could be unjustly accused of "attacking" her and literally none of them have anything to do with race. Unless it's racism. If only the man with the machete was white. Then she wouldn't have called the—*

Stop.

Suddenly we're pulled out of our mercy spiral—if we're being honest with ourselves. Why, exactly, are we trying to self-soothe about this situation by wishing an alternative race for the perpetrator? Why are we not instead preferring a near-tragedy to never have happened?

Now we're talking solutions, some might think at this point. *We need to have a national conversation about machete control laws in this country . . .*

Well. Like firearms, machetes are not exactly self-wielding. And the unspoken, unwritten assumption baked into this anecdote that we, like Setys's daughter, will now extricate from it is as follows: We assume something was wrong with the machete-wielder outside his locus of control. We insist he (or she, the daughter) simply misunderstood the situation. Or like we thought moments ago, we wonder if he was not in his right mind. Confused, maybe we tell ourselves, *There is no rational reason for someone to attack a young woman with a machete unless it's self-defense.* But what if that's our own prejudice? Our own projection? *I would never do that, therefore, no other person would do so. Not unless . . .*

There it is. What if there is no such *unless*? What if—and this may horrify you—what if the Haitian machete-wielder was not irrational—from his perspective? What if he *was* in his right mind? What if his reaction to whatever happened in his immediate surroundings was totally and completely . . . normal?

You may be having a number of deeply uncomfortable thoughts at the moment. Perhaps you're even squirming a little, feeling a twitch, or noticing yourself readjusting your posture. That's fine. Some things are important enough to grapple with the discomfort. So while you do that, let me call to mind a scene from a perennially beloved motion picture that resurfaced for me almost daily during my interviewing, researching, outlining, writing, editing, and otherwise preparing of this book, probably because that's about how often my children wanted to watch it. From *Toy Story* (1995):

> **Buzz:** . . . [R]evenge is not an idea we promote on my planet.
> **Woody:** Oh. Well, that's good.
> **Buzz:** But we're not on my planet. Are we?
> **Woody:** . . . no.[2]

Every child and child at heart knows what happens next in the movie. A would-be make-up between frenemies becomes a tussle with lasting consequences to the plot. The point of the exchange is like that of intercultural communication—it's when normal is not normal . . . and yet *that* is what's normal now.

While you solve that brain puzzle-paradox in the background, allow me to share my own very first time with a Haitian.

The Classmate and the A+

My context writing this book was very different from many of yours who are now coming in to read it. I've met Haitians. I've studied with Haitians. I've done business with Haitians. And I've also met, studied, and done business with those who've met, studied, and done business with them in America and abroad. Like Dominicans, for example, who share their island, Hispaniola. Hold that thought—we'll revisit *la República Dominicana* shortly.

In my senior year at the aforementioned Wright State University, in one of those intercultural communication courses, I was assigned a particular group project. It was communicated to us how important our group project grade would be to calculate our individual final class grade. Having been homeschooled before that was cool, I valued independent academic excellence. Furthermore, I play golf. I've been self-employed since 2011. If I win or if I lose, it's my gain or fault either way. It's a fundamentally American way.

Back to the group project. I was nonplussed to learn of my fate in this. We—and there were five of us—were given a research subject and tasked with submitting an essay together with a slideshow. We would also be presenting all of our findings in class. Public speaking does not come natural to me, but I resolved long ago to do whatever it takes to earn an A+. That group project put me to a test I did not expect.

It came about that our research subject was the symbolism and story behind various national flags. I had recently seen the Dan Brown motion picture adaptation *Angels & Demons*, so I picked Vatican City. Three of the other students, typical for the demographics of Dayton, Ohio, picked various nations you might expect. Then there was the Haitian-American. She chose Haiti—great! I didn't know anything about Haiti at the time beyond their place in history as the only successful slave revolt that begat an independent, successful country. Very cool, OK. I get to learn something new. A rare treat for a former homeschooler.

So! I took the lead because I wanted the best grade possible. And to my teammates, I gave instructions: Write your section of the full essay, send it to me, and I'll revise them all as needed into a complete, submittable report that will impress our professor. I said the same of the PowerPoint presentation. Send everything to me, I'll make it great; you'll be fine. Just let me handle it. A+. I would do anything.

Now the Haitian. You know what she sent me? The Wikipedia article about Haiti's flag. Yeah. I know. The layout of the article remained in the obviously copied and pasted text. But surely, this was a misunderstanding. Surely this was an accident. Is this her . . . research material? A notes document? And the real essay . . . surely that would come to me in a separate file. The actual essay she wrote. Right?

I spoke with her after class. I asked her if she had, in fact, intended to submit a copy-pasted Wikipedia article with zero editing made as her submission for her section of the essay. I tried to be tongue-and-cheek in my ask so as not to offend her. This is a university. We are progressive cosmopolitans. We don't profile here. We are good people.

But then she said yes.

YES.

Yes, she had intended to send Wikipedia as her entire submission. She would send me her slideshow shortly, she added with a smile, as that was now done on time, too (yay). Note: When I opened it later, I found again . . . Wikipedia formatting included hyperlinks to other Wiki pages.

I remember inquiring of the Haitian-American as to why she had done this. She explained that our assignment was for her to send me an essay on the Haitian flag symbols and their meaning and history. And that is exactly what she had done, no?

No, actually. I told her that copying and pasting was tantamount to plagiarism and that that would not work. That would not work at all. Not at all.

She seemed confused.

Plagiarism? Plagiarism. Plagiarism?

No? OK, so, it's where you—

I felt so bad. I felt racist. Here is this tall white male explaining to this small black woman—

I felt so racist. Like I'd beklanned myself. It was my white privilege. That's all this was. See, I'd learned in an intercultural communication course at Sinclair College during my first Privilege Walk in 2009 that my pigment is stained with the original sin of (*gasp*) "whiteness"—and now it's not enough to *not* be racist, I must be actively *anti-racist.*

You know what, Miss Port-au-Prince . . . I got this.

I made the following calculation—that it would take longer to successfully explain what plagiarism was and what an essay actually is to this young lady than to just . . .

A+. Anything. Anti-racism.

When the time came to present to class, my Haitian classmate read line by line off the slides. I don't recall our exact final score, but I was proud of it. I lost track of her when that class ended. It pains me to say that I don't even remember her name. But I will never forget how that conversation felt.

And now it occurs to me to wonder something very specific.

Is Springfield a group project, too?

The Doctor and the Contract

The first white supremacist I ever met is a black Haitian woman.

Almost ten years after college, I would find myself in the presence of another Haitian-American, this one a Haitian-born female of great renown. A beautiful, successful medical entrepreneur by every public measure and known account, with clinical experience. She was to become my client. And that she was. A particular price quoted, contract signed, everything, all above board.

However, due to what happened next, and the sensitivity of this ex-client's work, I do not want to shame her in the event that it was *I* who was somehow at fault or otherwise to blame for the ensuing stage of this anecdote. I'm not sure how that could be, but maybe you'll gander a guess or two after you read what's next.

OK, anti-racist disclaimers aside, let's fast on forward to when we reached the end of our once-off project together. Out at the outset of our wrap-up call, this client asked me when I would be done with the rest. The rest? Hold up. Wait a minute. Something's not right.

Aside—you should know that due to her budget constraints, I had down-sold my services package from, let's say "100 percent of the thing" to "20 percent of the thing." Hence, 20 percent of the original budget. This was doable for her, and the written contract was explicit in all regards—what was versus what was not included and how much. She had signed; I had signed. We began. All standard course of business.

So. Done with the rest, she asked. The rest? She'd paid the 20 percent; I'd delivered the 20 percent.

What good does that do me? This was her very next ask.

Excuse me? Now I was the confused party. I politely reminded her of our contract—what it explicitly states and does not. She got exactly what she paid for. This was fair.

Then she got mad. She yelled. She cried.

I don't understand. No, you don't understand. What is this, a scam? Who are you, as a white man, to be taking advantage of this formerly impoverished black immigrant from Haiti with a harsh upbringing and without all the white privilege you yourself have enjoyed? I don't understand business contracts. I don't understand quotes and services and work products. I'm just an immigrant. I'm just a poor black woman. This is just like a white man to do this, to take advantage of—and so on.

All that went on for a bit. If she wanted me to feel like a racist piece of shit, it was working. I remember apologizing profusely. Here she was paying 20 percent, telling me she had thought all along she would be getting 100 percent, demanding the 80 percent remaining she felt entitled to.

Mind you, on this unexpected outburst of a live video call, my gaze fell to and lingered upon the "Dr." title in front of her name on screen. I then remembered my group project classmate. The A she'd received from (largely) my labor. The degree she'd probably gotten.

I recall explaining to my Haitian physician client what a contract is and how it works. It's where two people agree on a price and a service, and—yes. I really did.

I felt bad for this woman. I did. After all, she'd had such a harsh upbringing, and it was indeed unlike anything I knew in my own basement-sheltered childhood. "Back home," she'd say as she reflected, which was quite often—and despite being an American citizen, "home" did not mean the United States but Haiti, which always perked me each time she said it—she had myriad stories of black magic and sorcery, of demonic possession and literal resurrections from the dead; of curses and hexes and spells—and all of it real, none of it make-believe (there's a saying in the Dominican Republic that Haitians are 80 percent Catholic, 20 percent Protestant, 100 percent voodoo). She explained how, growing up in Haiti, white Americans missionaries were like gods and goddesses, possessing medical and other technologies no blacks on her island possessed, much less understood how to use, she would say. They always deferred to the whites, she said, of their own volition. I must admit—her repeated insistence on the racial superiority of whites as a direct result of our race made me extremely uncomfortable. But what was I going to do? Tell a black woman her lived experience is, what, wrong? She just might defer to me and then—then—I would be the very thing she . . .

Anyway. Her most disturbing claim (in my over-educated white opinion) was that the only unconditional love she as a black girl ever felt was from the whites whose compassion brought them to her island to care for her people. I recall this client telling me, on three separate occasions, that "white people loved us blacks more than we loved ourselves." That's exactly how she said it, every time she said it. What do you say to that? I always said nothing and let her continue, allowing my jaw to drop internally.

This Haitian-American client would also speak of orphaned children she witnessed scrounging about for food. Now, I've ghostwritten a number of memoirs over the years and have heard similar stories from the underdeveloped world, specifically Lebanon, post-*apartheid* South Africa, parts of modern-day England. But what I hadn't heard of anywhere else before were these so-called mudpies—eating dirt to stave off hunger—as well as hunting for food animals. Like wild animals? I would wonder aloud. They basically lived in the wild there in Haiti. The nation is mostly a mountain-jungle. What kind of animals? Like, chickens, right?

Well. Yes, but also . . .

Yes. I was horrified. I was horrified by how racist I felt about being horrified. I checked my privilege and let that little anecdote go, never to be discussed with her again. This would be my initiation into an understanding of the third-world gaze—when, for example, Americans see an animal skitter about, we reach for the smartphone to take a picture for Instagram. When perpetually hungry members of an objectively primitive society see a similar scene in their locale, they stare on with hungerlust. Who can blame them. I do not.

Anyhow, the project ended shortly after that exchange, there was not an additional contract for the remaining 80 percent of my very first project pitch, and that was that. Surely it was somehow my fault. My white privilege's fault. Had to be. Unless . . .

A Vibrantly Abridged History of Haitian Culture

More years would pass. Not so many this time before Haiti returned to my literary radar. Veteran Navy intelligence officer and journalist Jack Posobiec, host of *Human Events Daily*, published a special podcast series entitled *Chronicles of the Revolution* at the end of 2023, which critically examined Communism not as an applied philosophy of economics but as a tactic-set for infiltrating, undermining, and subsequently overthrowing an established sociopolitical order. There was a template to the revolution—this is what they do, every single time.

We were introduced by the late Great Influencer, Scott Adams, and I asked Jack if he had seen my movie. *My movie?* Yes. I, despite my overtly liberal beliefs around the time of the 2016 U.S. presidential election, abhorred the unilateral violence against supporters of then-candidate Donald Trump. Why was it OK for Leftists like the so-called American *Antifa* movement to attack Trump supporters but it was unlawful for them to engage in self-defense? Why was Trump supporter speech considered violence, but reactionary Left-wing violence was merely speech? And self-defensive speech at that?

I didn't get it. You can take Joshua out of Christian homeschool, but you can't take the Christian homeschool out of Joshua. Assaulted, brutalized, and otherwise victimized Trump supporters' stories plucked the heartstrings of this sensitive young man, and I joined an independent documentary project as executive producer. The eventual award-winning film *Better Left Unsaid* from Indian-Canadian filmmaker Curt Jaimungal released in 2021 to endorsements, praise, and mentions from figures across the ideological spectrum.[3,4,5,6] I was proud.

But Jack hadn't seen it. So he pulled up a few clips. And saw himself. Four or five times in a ninety-second-or-less span. Turns out *he* was one of the original Trump supporters attacked by the mob that inspired me to do the movie in the first place!

It all came full circle. We teamed up, together authored a book entitled *Unhumans: The Secret History of Communist Revolutions (And How to Crush Them)* (War Room Books, 2024), enjoyed an endorsement from then-Senator JD Vance, and made the *New York Times* bestselling list.[7] But the week of its release, we topped #1 atop the *Publishers Weekly* list, making *Unhumans* the top book of the most consequential summer in American political history.[8] Days later, our foreword's author, Steve Bannon, accepted his fate as a political prisoner. Donald Trump then survived yet another assassination attempt, two supporters were wounded, and firefighter Corey Comperatore was murdered in Butler, Pennsylvania. Then a palace *coup* ousted a sitting president—Joe Biden—from his democratically achieved campaign atop the opposition's ticket. The violence, the chaos, we'd predicted it all throughout *Unhumans*.

But the book was as much a lookback as a seeforward. One of the proto-Communist uprisings we wrote of in detail was that of Haiti, part of the French Revolution expanded universe. The research I'd done on their culture, their heritage, and their—shall we say—founding fathers had changed my formerly enlightened opinion (or so I'd thought) of the nation. If everyday Americans are collectively guilty of any racial *faux pas*, then indeed, it is our ignorance of the history of the Haitian nation. From ***Unhumans*, chapter 5**:

> . . . [W]e would be remiss if we did not mention a certain island nation not far at all from America's shores that owes its identity to what happened in Paris in the 1790s. You might call Haiti an offshoot of the French Revolution shared cinematic universe. By the time of the revolution, Haiti had been one of France's chief holdings in the New World, and as like other Caribbean nations, it had been stocked with slaves from West Africa.
>
> In 1790, the new revolutionary French republic committed to righting all perceived historical wrongs in society. Liberation to the oppressed! Death to the oppressors! We'll hear these refrains over and over, so get used to them. We mentioned a select few already, such as the ruling rights of aristocrats versus the everyday man and woman. Another issue the revolutionary republic decided to tackle was the representation of free blacks in the National Assembly, specifically those on the Caribbean island Hispaniola in the colony of Saint-Domingue (now known as Haiti). Half the island was ruled by France, the other half by Spain. The main advocate for his people was Vincent Ogé, a mulatto Creole and well-to-do slaveholder. His class was known as *affranchis* (freed people of color), and Ogé fought for wealthy *affranchis* citizenship in the new France—and won it. But upon his return
>
> *(continued . . .)*

to Saint-Domingue and announcement of the news, things did not go well for him. Colonial leadership on the island refused to acknowledge the National Assembly's new biracial citizenship law, Ogé took up arms against the colonists, and he was captured by Spanish colonists from the other side of the island, ruled by Spain (now known as the Dominican Republic). He was summarily tortured to death before an audience of his enemies. Things really did not go well after that. This was 1791.

The spirit of revolution passed from Ogé to all *affranchis*. Within two months of the execution, there was open warfare between the *affranchis* and French authorities. Thousands of slaves soon joined them. Anarchy overtook the western (French) half of the island. Enraged mobs of sword-wielding, gun-toting blacks, both slave and free, swarmed colonial plantations and properties. One of the few eyewitness accounts from the uprising is that of an anonymous director of the Clément plantation. His barking dog awoke him suddenly on the night of August 22nd 1791. This individual, a white European, ducked under his bed as gunfire blasted through windows and walls. He heard voices calling out.

"Who is it?" he asked.

"It is death!" answered the mob. "Kill, kill," they added. They then killed everyone else in the building before looting the place. The director was eventually found but spared by a wild leader of the revolt, ex-slave Dutty Boukman, who spared the plantation director's life because he had once treated him kindly, like an equal.

But the director's living nightmare would continue, as he joined the rebels on a forced march to commit further atrocities. The anonymous man sensed regret and remorse set in his captors that very night. But Boukman ordered them onwards with a threat: _Keep going, or *I* will shoot *you._ *[9]

. . . This is what they do.

Large and warrior-like, former slave Dutty Boukman, who had been born in West Africa, kicked off that bloody slave revolt with a ceremony of animal sacrifice that blended Islamic teaching and voodoo practices. Haiti would become synonymous for voodoo occult rituals, and Boukman was a top practitioner who led the rites. To the assembled crowd he passed around a cup of animal blood which everyone drank, and he called out, "The God of the whites pushes them to crime, but he wants us to do good deeds. But the God who is so good orders us to vengeance. He will direct our hands, and give us help. Throw away the image of the God of the whites who thirsts for our tears. Listen to the liberty that speaks in all our hearts."[10]

Then the blood massacres began—including the one that the anonymous eyewitness related to us. Most weren't so fortunate. Men, women, and so many screaming children, it didn't matter. If you were French, you were hacked to death.

The authorities would eventually catch up to the murderers marauding the plantations and put them to justice. Boukman was captured and beheaded by the French, his decapitated head placed on public display. And that plantation manager fled for France to tell his tale.[11] But Boukman would become a symbol of resistance and vengeance to the Haitian slaves; he remains a galvanizing symbol of national pride in Haiti today.

This was not the end of revolution in Haiti; it was the end of the beginning. In 1792, a new French law granting citizenship to all *affranchis* regardless of wealth or social status failed to return any semblance of peace. Other radicals would raise up armies of the aggrieved as well, men known to history such as Toussaint Louverture and Jean-Jacques Dessalines. Both were former slaves who'd joined the rebellion following the death of Vincent Ogé. Agents of the new French republic were sent to stabilize society in 1793, with all slavery being outlawed in 1794. Louverture and Dessalines had been made the lowest of their society, the have-the-least of all the have-nots. And yet neither brought law, order, or justice. Communist leaders throughout promise their followers the world, then take it from them. This is what both men did, in succession. The French initially supported Louverture, who'd raised up a vengeance-seeking army. He declared himself "governor-general for life" amid a military dictatorship over the entire colony. Former slaves were forced back to work on former slave plantations. This is what they do.

In 1801, Napoleon Bonaparte dispatched French forces that included both white and *affranchis* officers and soldiers to relieve Louverture of his duties. He died imprisoned in France in 1803; Louverture met the fate he'd forced upon his own free countrymen.[12]

Then it got worse. Jean-Jacques Dessalines, a former lieutenant of Louverture, re-revolted against the French. Multiple factors including a yellow fever epidemic, British naval involvement, and the sale of Louisiana

(continued . . .)

to the United States gave Dessalines and his forces a broken window of opportunity. Dessalines believed his comrade Louverture had not gone far enough.

Following victory over the weakened French, Dessalines re-reinstituted the plantation system, forcing fellow blacks to once again return to forced work, and in 1804 crowned himself the first emperor of a new independent nation: Haiti. Besides the brutish treatment towards his own people, his regime outlawed ownership of any and all property by white people. He then extended his racist campaign and ordered the systematic murder of all whites in Haiti. Thousands of white men, women, and children were massacred all over Haiti. This white genocide made the situation for Haitian blacks no better. His own people revolted against him, and Dessalines was killed in an attempt to suppress a rebellion against him.[13]

And that has been the history of Haiti ever since: robbing and killing. A country founded on unhuman revolts ends in chaos and cannibal warlords. The formerly French of Hispaniola was founded on the oppressor-oppressed story brought to life in a bloody slave revolt and gave its people the worst standard of living in the entire Western hemisphere: Haiti.[14] The Spanish side maintained its integrity, repelled multiple invasions from Haiti over the next century, and was named at the time of this writing the happiest people on earth: the Dominican Republic[15] . . . The results speak for themselves.

Note that the black Haitian dictators still reinstituted chattel slavery after France had ended it, even over their fellow blacks, once all the whites had been massacred. They brought totalitarian rule and speedran massacres in all territory under their control. It's almost like that was their goal in the first place. As everyone knows, Haiti never became a utopia. And yet, it shares the same island as an actual tropical utopian paradise in the DR. The difference is everything.

In one interview for the *Unhumans* book that I did solo, Haiti came up at the interviewer's prompting. On *Objectively Speaking*, Atlas Society CEO Jennifer Grossman shared this relevant episode of deep family lore:

> [R]eading your description of that proto-communist revolution in Haiti was actually very personal because on my mother's side, her maiden name was Durand and her mother's maiden name was Bienvenue. They were from Louisiana. And the very first Bienvenue that arrived in Louisiana was

> a white baby that [was] saved by one of the slaves, taken to New Orleans and, and given to a convent. And the nuns named the baby Bienvenu. "Welcome."[16]

I would not blame you if you call bull on all of the above. Setys's account, my lived experiences, this account of Haiti's history, Jennifer's family history. All of it. My own stories in particular are, I freely admit, absurd to the highest degree—if you assume a global monoculture. If you assume everyone knows soil is for potted plants and not breakfast. If you assume college coursework and business agreements can be written in such a way as to confuse anyone of any background. *Oh, so you've never been tripped up by the fine print of a contract, Josh?* It's Joshua, by the way, but indeed, some of you thought exactly that as you read the prior section. *You mean to tell me you've never cited Wikipedia as a source for information?* Or, speaking of what gets eaten where and by whom, you might have thought as the Tangle news editor wrote in his defense of Haitian migrants accused of consuming local wildlife of Springfield, Ohio, specifically waterfowl, "I'd bet many residents of Springfield spend their weekends hunting wild game, and a well-cooked duck is quite good, after all."[17]

It would not be alarming if I simply exaggerated these stories; it would be standard fare, would it not? You could dismiss me. But what if I'm embellishing? What if I'm telling the truth about outlier anecdotes on the Haitian way of being? Most troubling of all, what if my lived experiences are not outliers? What if these are members of a larger representative sample? Perhaps the public relations campaign by the likes of Bill Maher and Conan O'Brien—"Haiti is great already."—is more so about the jungle beaches than what happens from a few yards inland onward.[18]

In all the sensationalism and controversy generated by the Springfield story amid the polarized presidential campaign of 2024, one question completely escaped all major news media, professional journalists, and self-styled investigative reporters as far as I'm concerned: What do Haiti's neighbors, the Dominicans, say?

A Dominican Speaks

As luck would have it, I have close Dominican colleagues who call the same island home as the Haitians. The bestselling *Unhumans* inspired them to volunteer to me their own Haiti experiences. I'll share one expansive set of observations with you now, from a **Dominican serial entrepreneur** whom I've known for almost ten years. I've met him in person, know his family, and believe him to be as good and honest of a man as anyone could hope to meet. Upon learning of this manuscript in progress, he offered to speak with me—anonymously, for his family's personal safety. Perhaps when reading his account, unedited by me except to delete identity-laden sidebars, you will understand why:

I used to go two or three times a year to Haiti—to Cap-Haïtien, Port-au-Prince, Gonaïves . . . I used to go and . . . take photos for power plants. I used to work in an engineering company that provided maintenance and support for these power plants and also the management . . . So I went there, I took photos, made videos, actually did great marketing jobs for these guys.

. . . As soon as you land in Haiti, obviously the airport is stuck in the 1950s . . . I don't like talking shit about other countries, but it's ugly. Very ugly. And once you get out, their main avenue, in some places, it's still not even a road, like real roads with asphalt . . . It's sometimes just land and dirt. Also, there's no divider in between. So people in the freaking main avenue, they could just go the wrong way to—I don't know how to say in English—just put themselves in front of the guys who are in front of them.

. . . I went there ten years after the big earthquake that they had, and there was still rubble and buildings that were on the floor. All the rubble, all the disaster, ten years later . . . Also, there were a lot of people in the streets. Because the public transportation is shit, people just walked for hours to go to their job. [Haiti has] one of these things where you put a horse in front and then—I don't know how to say it but—it's like two chopsticks on each side of the horse . . . And the horse is just pulling a bed or something like that . . . ut instead of a horse, you have people doing that, the work of the fucking horse . . . You see them just pulling that as if they were the horses. They also ate the horses, so that may be why the guy was doing the work of the horse. How do I know? Because I saw them selling fucking horse meat on the corner!

Women, I remember seeing them just squat and pee right there [in public], which is something I had never seen. Not even in my country. I had never seen something like that.

. . . Something that caught my attention was, one day I was going from one place to another for four hours, I saw this big parade. People with drums. With saxophones, with trumpets, with drums. And I'm like, *Hey, what's happening?* . . . Someone died. That's how they celebrate death. And according to the other person that was with me . . . Haitians see death as—it's very similar to Christians, but it's not the same premise as where we are with God—someone died and they are like, *It's better to be dead.*

. . . I remember one day I was talking with one of the guys in one of the power plants, and they told me about the time that they found some bandana on top of a pole. The Haitians thought that was some kind of curse. And that day, they just didn't work because of that. One of the Dominicans, he just went, climbed the pole, and pulled the bandana down. They didn't talk with the guy for like a week because they thought the guy was cursed. Imagine that.

. . . They have a lot of . . . weird beliefs, satanic beliefs, actually, because they do a lot of voodoo, which reminds me of a time where I was up in the mountains going to . . . I think it was Gonaïves . . . I saw this weird drawing on different houses. It was a woman, with half of the body of a snake . . . [W]hen you see something like that, [it means] that a witch lives there in that house. And you occasionally saw this figure, this lady snake figure, in some of the houses. I remember vividly because it caught my attention seeing that shit.

. . . I remember going to one of these places. They had . . . some kind of riot . . . a protest where the people that drive the trucks, they were fed up with the government so they just closed everything. They just parked the big trucks right in between the street, and they didn't let us pass. So what we did was we would just go through those smaller streets, and then we got to a place where there was a little river . . . [and] a bridge. They wouldn't let us go through . . . [T]he Haitians started gathering around us and looking inside our car . . . I was really scared there because none of the guys knew how to speak Haitian Creole . . . [O]ne of the guys just took out money. "Hey, *dinero*! Money!" They understand right when you show them a bill or a dollar or whatever.

. . . [W]e just went through the river instead of the bridge, and we got into this abandoned place filled with car wrecks . . . [A Haitian at the destination] didn't let us go through . . . gate [there]. So we had to give him more money. And then we just kept moving forward.

Now, when it comes to the border, that's interesting because . . . every day, Dominicans and Haitians open it up. On this side of the island, in the Dominican Republic, we have these marketplaces where the Haitians come

(continued . . .)

in, and they buy the food from Dominicans. You see them crossing the border every day. It's interesting because they don't stay in the Dominican Republic; they just go back to their country. Some of them might stay, but most of them, they just go back to their country. Also, there's a big mafia on the border. I remember going there, and we had a big shipment of shit that we had to transport to the other side, and they wouldn't allow us . . . [T]hey took us to a little room through a back door . . . "Here's your money," and man, we didn't have to pay the taxes and the tariffs . . . I remember when they opened up the border, it was people just like ants, all of them crammed, running to get the best food early in the morning.

. . . I remember one of the guys telling us how they almost got killed by [Haitians] in the power plant because they decided to stop giving a free meal in the morning. The Haitians got used to that. When the company decided to stop doing that to save costs, they just rioted. They went through and tried to open up the door, slamming themselves into the door to kill one of the managers, according to them. So they had to revert back . . . and let the Haitians have their free meal in the mornings.

I didn't like it, man. The infrastructure is very dull. It's not a very colorful place. There's a lot of dirt, too, even in the rich places. I remember going uphill in Port-au-Prince. I forgot the name of that place where the rich people live. But it doesn't feel like rich people's places. Not even inside the houses. I remember going into one of the houses . . . nd it was weird infrastructure . . . [T]he toilets, for whatever reason, you had to walk [up] towards the toilet. The toilet was a step above the normal floor . . . [W]hy put a step to go to the toilet? I didn't understand why. It's like being on a real throne.

The people are very nice, though, at least in the corporate setting. Very amicable, very friendly. The food, subpar. I remember going to a restaurant, and it wasn't good. Not even the fancy restaurants, which is what we actually did, because we just wanted to spend the money that the company gave us because if we didn't, they just took it back.

. . . [T]hat's my experience in Haiti. I wouldn't go back there in a million years . . . especially now where they don't even have a government. Back then, they didn't have that mess they have right now. But I wouldn't go back there. Not even if I get paid. My mom was going to travel to Haiti and my dad told her, "No. Negative." She had to stop traveling to Haiti because of all the unrest they have over there.

A few years prior when Haiti came up—this man was aware at the time of that Haitian client and our inability to agree on what a contract is—my Dominican friend volunteered his first firsthand detail (to me anyway) about his travels to Haiti.

"It's so weird; you don't see any stray cats anywhere."

Stew on that one.

The Dominican government has dealt with their own Haitian influx a certain way. In March 2024, six months before the Haitians of Springfield became international news, Al-Jazeera reported:

> Every day, hundreds of men, women, and children are taken to the border to be sent back . . . Dominican authorities say they won't allow refugees in the country . . . There is no functioning government in Haiti right now, and the police seems unable to fight the gangs that control large parts of the country.[19]

It's undebatable that the state of the Haitian homeland is beyond dire. You might have seen a viral video running the tables on social media allegedly depicting a Haitian gang member who "can be seen chewing on what appears to be a finger and then proceeding to tear the flesh of a leg of a body that is burning."[20]

Can you blame those who do not want to risk life and literal limb? And before any racist and ableist should attempt an assault on the Haitian people's intelligence over human flesh consumption—not all Haitians partake—their average IQ is, apparently, not 67, as is so often claimed online. It's actually 82.10.[21] As researchers of human biodiversity will admit, "Human dignity doesn't require the possession of a 130 IQ . . . It requires nothing more than being a unique human life."[22]

The unique human lives of Haiti are under a threat unlike any other—other Haitians.

"Haiti is in the throes of an uprising not seen in decades," summarized *The New York Times*, also in March 2024. "As politicians around the region scramble to hash out a diplomatic solution to a political crisis that has the prime minister, Ariel Henry, stranded in Puerto Rico and gangs attacking police stations, a humanitarian disaster is quickly escalating. The food supply is threatened, and access to water and health care has been severely curtailed. While gangs expand their territory and band together in concerted attacks against the state, millions of people throughout the country are caught in the middle. Many are afraid to leave their homes for fear of getting caught in the crossfire. They are hungry. They are running out of clean water and gas. They are desperate."[23]

By August 2025, the path forward seemed clear for a hope of peace to one day return to the Haitian side of Hispaniola. From the Associated Press:

> A federal grand jury has indicted one of Haiti's most powerful gang leaders and a U.S. citizen accused of conspiring with him to violate U.S. sanctions and fund gang activities in the troubled Caribbean country, the U.S. Justice Department announced Tuesday.
>
> Jimmy Chérizier, best known as "Barbecue," is a leader of a gang federation called *Viv Ansanm* that the U.S. designated as a foreign terrorist organization in May.
>
> Chérizier lives in Haiti, and the United States is offering up to $5 million for information leading to his arrest or conviction. Chris Landberg, a senior U.S. State Department official, said his "reign of terror and mass violence against Haiti must end."[24]

I wonder why they call him Barbecue.

Of all the reports from Haiti and the regular denial of their existence among Westerners, the 𝕏 account @kunley_drukpa wrote this satire:[25]

> OBSCENE! In Haiti, West is getting away with evil Hitlerite Propaganda of reporting things that actually happen
>
> Western Media Outlets are Hitlerishly reporting real cases of Cannibalism in Haiti that actually happened; all to justify a Nazi agenda of reporting things that happen[26]
>
> Western Media's reporting on real and well-documented things that frequently happen in Haiti "like something out of Hitler's playbook"

That said, I recently paid a visit to the Springfield Museum of Art. One particular hall featured an exhibition entitled "Black Lives as Subject Matter."[27] Cool. A little section within, I noticed, was dedicated to the Haitians of Springfield and their plight back home. Although in many cases, the migrants who dwell in Clark County, Ohio, I've learned, haven't touched Haitian soil since the aftermath of the 2010 earthquake-disaster. Many had found a new home for themselves in Brazil, Chile, and Miami, Florida, before making their way to Springfield during the Biden administration.

The piece that drew me in, with its black and white scenes, was entitled, "The Haitians Montage: A Dream Deferred." The comic-like art by Nathan Conner told the following story in stills, left to right, top to bottom: Haitians welcomed to Springfield, playing music at a Christian church, working at McGregor Metal, dining at Rose Goute Creole Restaurant, buying a single-family home with a trim front yard, acquiring transportation at Jeff Wyler Chevrolet, and recreating on a bicycle and children's playground swings.

Ominous strips of text interrupted these scenes like labels of villainy—*Homeland Security Notice of Termination of Parole . . . This Decision is without prejudice . . . This notice informs you that your parole is now terminated . . . U.S. Gov't will purchase your ticket & give you $1,000.00 as exit bonus if you leave voluntarily . . . If you do not leave you may be subject to enforcement actions, including but not limited to detention & removal, without an opportunity to make personal arrangements & return to your country in an orderly manner.*

Like act two of this story hung beside this work was a movie-posterlike forewarning of what awaits Haitians in Haiti. "Haiti in Chaos." Corpses in the street, armed militias replete with rocket-propelled grenades and a *Bulls 23* jersey, inconsolable women of grief, countrymen huddled in terror beneath black-soot smoke rising over the mountains. The only color in either photo was the red of the dead, streaming out . . . down . . . towards us. Towards the onlooker. Towards me. As Ohio Governor Mike DeWine would say, in a counterintuitive defense of the Haitian people, their country "is hell today."[28]

Twentieth-century wartime propaganda has nothing on Nathan Conner. This was the work of a master persuader. Before versus after. What gratitude and freedom met the Haitian people in a welcoming midwestern American city, and what awaits them if the racists, the bigots, the xenophobes win—if the evil dictator Trump's thugs stay on track and send them all back. Hitlerishly evil.

At least . . . that's what I thought I was supposed to think. Standing there. Observing the scenes. Taking them all in.

I did not. I thought something very different.

What do both scenes have in common? I asked myself, the realization creeping up my spine that I would soon be writing down everything I'm telling you now. *What do both scenes have in common? Haitians in Springfield, Haitians in Haiti.*

I imagined the red blood as if it were trickling down, down . . . off the wall . . . to me . . . marking me. Crying out. Over my white privilege. Condemning me. My white guilt. Putting me to shame. Whiteness.

I heard it all loud and clear.

And I wrote back.

I pulled out my iPhone, opened a blank Google Doc, and began *tap-tap-tapping* out the very words you've just been reading.

Because there's something you should know. Racialized ethnicities have developed particular cultures. The U.S. Department of State has issued a Level 4: Do Not Travel advisory to American citizens—"Do Not Travel to Haiti due to the risk of crime, kidnapping, terrorism, unrest, and limited health care."[29] U.S. government employees in Haiti are not permitted to leave the embassy. Here is additional color on the Advisory:

> Violent crime is rampant in Haiti, especially in Port-au-Prince. There has been an increase in gangs, organized crime, and terrorist activities.
>
> - Crimes involving firearms are common.
> - Crimes include robbery, carjackings, sexual assault, and kidnappings for ransom.
> - The escalation of fighting between armed groups has led to a rise in random gunfire incidents. There is risk of being struck by stray bullets, even for people not directly involved in the violence.
> - Local law enforcement has an extremely limited ability to respond to serious crimes, particularly outside Port-au-Prince and Cap-Haitien.
>
> . . .
>
> Kidnapping is widespread. U.S. citizen victims of kidnapping have been hurt or killed.
>
> - Kidnappers often demand ransoms. Ransom demands are typically in the tens of thousands to hundreds of thousands of dollars.
> - Kidnappers target and attack vehicles, including commercial [buses]. They can also attack convoys.
>
> . . .
>
> Terrorist violence, including attacks on citizens and other violent gang activity, happens frequently in Haiti. Some Haitian gangs are designated by the U.S. Department of State as terrorist organizations.
>
> . . .
>
> - Armed, anti-gang vigilante groups attack and, in many cases, kill U.S. citizens. This is when they suspect someone of being a gang member based only on rumors or incorrect information.
> - Neighborhood watch groups have built improvised barricades and gates to control the flow of traffic in certain areas.
> - "Watch groups" often harass or detain people who are not known to be residents of their neighborhoods.
>
> . . .

- Hospitals and clinics in Haiti have limited trained staff and lack basic resources.
- Medical providers almost always require payment in cash before treatment.
- Most medical providers speak little or no English.[30]

Should Americans be in Haiti for any reason, consider these protocols:

- Choose one family member to serve as the point of contact. If you are kidnapped or taken hostage, that person can communicate with kidnappers or hostage-takers, media, U.S. or foreign government agencies, and members of Congress.
- Establish a proof of life protocol with your loved ones. If you are kidnapped, your loved ones will know specific questions (and answers) to ask the kidnappers to confirm that you are being held captive and are alive.

. . .

- Prepare a will. Designate appropriate insurance beneficiaries or prepare a power of attorney.

. . .

- We highly recommend that you buy travel insurance before you travel. Check with your travel insurance provider about evacuation assistance, medical insurance, and trip cancelation coverage.
- Make sure your insurance includes medical evacuation coverage. Medical evacuation from Haiti is very expensive and the U.S. government may not be able to assist should you need emergency medical care.

. . .

- Do not physically resist any robbery attempt.
- Use caution when walking or driving at night.
- Keep a low profile.
- Stay aware of your surroundings.
- Do not display signs of wealth, like expensive watches or jewelry.
- Stay alert when visiting banks or ATMs.[31]

Note that these warnings, prohibitions, and strong recommendations are for U.S. citizens *only*—not Haitian nationals. Americans, according to our own State Department, are uniquely, dangerously unsafe among large concentrations of Haitians subject to the Haitian way of life.

It stands to reason that when you mass-import the people of a given culture, such as the above, you import that people's culture en masse. Mass-import Haitians, and what else can they do but bring Haiti to you?

"A useful way to think about migration is to consider what kind of societies the migrants have built in their home countries and to what extent you would like those conditions replicated here," wrote Stephen Miller, the White House Deputy Chief of Staff for Policy.[32]

Back to the art museum. Where I let Google Docs auto-save. I stared the art over one more time. There by the plume of smoke, standing before the fire in "Haiti in Chaos," was a lone silhouette. It looked like he was holding something. Maybe it's a trick of the light. It's a tongue of fire. Wait. No—it just so happens to appear to be rising from the figure's raised hand. Extending upwards. Shiny. OK, I get it. It's one of those artistic creations with hidden images and optical illusions. Intentional pareidolia, I think it's called. Freudian-slipped in there as subliminal messaging by the author. But really, it looked like he's holding something.

It looks like he's holding a machete.

CHAPTER 2

TWO SPRINGFIELDS ON ONE SCREEN

> "[T]he greater the diversity in a community, the fewer people vote and the less they volunteer, the less they give to charity and work on community projects. In the most diverse communities, neighbors trust one another about half as much as they do in the most homogenous settings . . . [V]irtually all measures of civic health are lower in more diverse settings."[1]
>
> —Michael Jonas, republished by *The New York Times*

"What pissed me off is the wrong story went viral. I didn't even want to touch it after that for a while."

Walter Curt sat across from me at Charlo's Provisions & Eatery on North Fountain Avenue, barely twenty-five feet from where I'd given that destinous interview to allegedly Politico. But here in the now, our menus stood perched and proper, one each, as we deliberated over our lunch choices. I'd asked Walter if I could record our conversation. He said yes, and we were off.

Walter lives in Springfield but isn't known for Springfield these days. Netizens of 𝕏 (formerly Twitter) know Walter best as an investigative journalist who writes about deindustrialized Americana, government accountability (or lack thereof), border policy, and, simply, fraud. He's Nick Shirley with a newsletter.

We first exchanged numbers at a rave hosted by fellow journalist James O'Keefe in Phoenix, Arizona, during Turning Point's America Fest. The place was so loud we couldn't hear each other. But now at Charlo's, our voices were just about the only thing you could hear in the whole place.

I began the conversation by getting Walter, a fifteen-year resident of Springfield now, up to speed on this very book and my progress on it by that time.

"This is easy," Walter said of my authorial ambition—and my follow-up question regarding what the right story was that had not gone so viral as Candidate Trump's remarks that "[i]n Springfield, they're eating the dogs, the people that came in, they're eating the cats. They're eating the pets of the people that live there."[2]

So off Walter went. Here is his extended comments minus interruptions such as those from our server (he was fine; he was just doing a good job):

The Right Story

One of the things I was looking at a couple years ago was, why did they all show up so quickly? Well, it's actually pretty simple. We went from having only a few thousand Haitians here to over 30,000 a couple years ago. That was during the Biden years. But the reason that happened is because in this area, during Trump's first term, when he came in, manufacturing returned. . . . One of the companies is called Rittal . . . it's one of the machine shops.

. . . [T]here's about four or five factories that opened up around the area, and there's about a thousand to a few thousands jobs that came from that. Well, they opened up underneath Trump . . . Now, when that happened in this town, wages started skyrocketing. I was working at the time; I'm a master mechanic. That's what I was doing before I started doing my writing career in journalism . . . I was working as a mechanic, and my wage doubled in a month. . . . Every single place in the town was hiring. Every single place, the wages were skyrocketing. Everything was good.

. . . Then after Trump lost, within one year, all those jobs disappeared, and the Haitians started arriving by buses, and they staffed all of those factories with those Haitian workers. That's what really happened, and that's what pissed people off around there—let alone the Haitian who was brand-new, who ran the school bus off the road and killed that kid.

But before that, the tension that had built up was also because rental properties were filled. All of these places started getting steadily filled. They just flooded the city with these people. And that was a direct result of Biden's policy. Every single bit of it was.

But the biggest part is the factories. Because the wages were going up. Here they were, the city was actually recovering. . . . I moved here in 2011, and when I moved here, this city was dead. There was nothing here. When this city was dying, it wouldn't matter if they said, "Springfield is a 'Welcoming City.'" Wouldn't matter. Then there was nothing here anyway. There's no jobs. There was no income. Most of it was drugs. Most of the downtown where we're sitting now, this didn't exist. None of this did. None of this stuff was here.

Then it was around 2014 to 2015, a group of my friends bought this place sitting over here—Mother Stewart's. . . . By 2016 when Trump came in, they had just finished that, opened it, really got it up and running, and that is what revitalized us. They started doing a farmer's market. . . . There's actually a community coming downtown. All of these shops opened up as a result of that. That was all private investment, the downtown district. . . . But when I first moved here, downtown was where you get shot. There was nothing out here but drugs.

As a result of that [private investment], everything in Springfield recovered . . . I could see it. I could feel it. My wages were going up. People were getting more jobs. There were people moving into the city. They were coming from other areas into the city to get jobs because the wages were high here. And there were factories opening. Then when Biden gets in, that's when all of them went right back down. I mean immediately. Because the Haitians took every single one of those jobs. Every single one of the factories. They paid them about 50 percent less . . . I think they classify them as temporary workers, but they just rehire them. They may classify them however they want, but the reality is that most of the Haitians I know who work at Rittal are making like $15 to $18 an hour. But most of my friends who were working there before were making $35 to $36 an hour. That's the difference. That's why they wanted Haitians. "Bring them all. We'll take them all. We'll staff our factories for half the wages."

The guys I know who work for those factories, most of them ended up quitting because the Haitians just took over the factories. They also staffed them at Dole. That was another place to hire a ton of Haitians . . . I know the machine shops all had them. If you go look at [Governor Mike] DeWine's statements, he talks about businesses in the area struggling if they get rid of the Haitians. Oh, he's right. He said one of these has 700 employees and 500 of them are Haitian. . . . During COVID, when he announced the curfew, do you remember the protests that happened outside of his house? There was set up outside of his house for two weeks, a protest. I was part of that. He doesn't like me very much. The feeling is mutual . . . He's got a charity in Haiti . . .

The real story is that the amount that they brought here was directly correlated to the growth of factories from Trump. But people don't talk about

(continued . . .)

that. No one talks about the fact that the city was recovering, and then they killed it immediately by just—*boom*—pushing these people in. They did that intentionally, as far as I could tell.

In terms of the way that the Haitian population is here, I don't have a problem with these people, to be honest with you. They're terrible drivers outside of that. It's not that. It's the fact that you killed the American jobs that were supposed to be for Americans. You gave them away to people who showed up here on TPS status. That's the problem.

I've heard many, many stories of people saying they evicted elderly people from their apartments because they were getting paid more money from the government [for Haitian tenants]. To be honest with you, I've heard that; I have never seen proof of that. Now, I do know a couple of the locations that they were claiming this happened. Up on High Street, there's a retirement community up there. There used to be nothing but retirees in the area . . . I saw Haitians living there, but I don't know if they evicted anyone.

. . . The other problem is that a lot of these groups that own places around here, a lot of private investment groups, bought up a lot of houses around here. . . . The housing market here went from, at one point it was insanely cheap to live here, essentially. But in about a three- or four-year period, shortly after the factories, we were actually the number-three real estate market in the country . . . friend of mine is a real estate agent. She sold $7 million worth of property in this area, which is crazy . . . [M]ost houses were less than $200,000, so she absolutely killed it that summer. But that was all a result of the amount of growth that was happening, but the Haitian increase is in direct correlation to the factory increase. That's where you can see; that's where you can see the real numbers. . . .

I think [the Haitians] get $1,400 in cash [for welfare]. Then they get a stipend for rent as well. They also get qualified for EBT . . . before the Nick Shirley exposé on daycare, SNAP fraud was the big thing I'm looking at . . . at one point, the local Walmarts around the area pushed out a notice to people saying that they would do delivery or pickup, and you could get your groceries delivered to your house for . . . a third of the price it normally was . . . I don't understand why they did that . . . They tried to focus on getting everybody to move to that. Well, if you went to Walmart at the time,

(continued . . .)

the entire Walmart was filled with Haitians walking around with shopping carts filled to the brim. I'm talking overflowing out of shopping carts. There were hundreds of them. I remember it was so bad that we'd go to Walmart and be like, "Oh my God. I don't even want to come in here. No one's speaking English, and every single one of their carts is just flowing with all sorts of crap." Yeah. That was noticeable.

. . . I have two children. Both of them, while I was sitting in [the birthing center] waiting for both births to happen, it's filled with Haitians. There's a line out the door for Haitians having kids there. It's unbelievable. So much so that they had to hire more staff . . .

The other thing to look at . . . in 2020, there were like 100 Haitian kids in the high school, and then by the end of 2023, there were over 1,000. Now, that's kind of a problem for a number of reasons, mostly because they don't speak English. And then, how does the school pay for that? Well, they have to increase taxes because Haitians speak Creole. Translators are something like $300 to $400 an hour. They're insanely expensive.

Now, the other problem, I think that the city . . . doesn't want to solve the problem because they've set up their business plan based on growth using those metrics. . . . [W]hen you're looking at building a whole new housing area . . . you estimate what the taxes would be based on that many people living there. . . . So, here's our population increase. Here's the housing that's being desired right now. Here's our housing prices increase. So let's make the business plan and give people, the developers, deals and tax breaks . . . to be able to develop well. That only works if you've got that kind of income. What if you don't have that increase anymore? It's kind of a problem.

Cue the clichéd "lots to unpack here" remark because there absolutely is. The guy knows his stuff; he knows his city.

But what you and he may not know is, why did the least-confirmed anecdotes of animal consumption become "the story" for Springfield on the international stage? The heritage citizens of Springfield all shared with me a very specific set of anecdotes—that certain species of duck had gone missing from Clark County parks and ponds. The geese, too, but apparently they had plenty of those, and longtime residents seemed glad at the reportedly dwindling number.

Then there's the cats.

"When I moved here, and for years, we had a stray cat problem." Walter added later in our conversation. "Once the Haitians started moving in with large numbers, that problem went away. A lot of us noticed this. We're actually relieved."

Surprising? Not if you understand why residents like Walter are "pissed."

"Regardless of whether any of this happened," I said to Walter not long after the cat-disappearance anecdote, "the issue seems to be that there are thousands of people here from a foreign country, and the citizens had no say whether or not that happened. It was an anti-democratic maneuver that was pulled against the city. Who decides who gets to live inside of your house? You or someone else?"

"'Are we a Sanctuary City?'" Walter brought up a question recurrently asked to city officials. "'We're not a Sanctuary City,' the city said. 'We don't want to be a Sanctuary City. Did you guys do it anyway?' was what we kept asking when they refused to answer questions. The 'Welcoming City' thing that might be an important part, if we're a Sanctuary City without putting on the books."

What Walter shared, I'll be covering throughout this book. Because I have to. Because next to none of what Walter said or what you've read thus far has appeared in the viral cats and dogs story or in attached commentary. *It's been debunked. It's all been debunked.*

The first beyond-Ohio viral story of the Haitian influx was a Springfield city commission meeting clip in which "a Springfield resident told the mayor that she 'can't take it anymore,' explaining that Haitian immigrants are squatting on her front lawn and harassing her and her husband daily."[3]

I heard eerily similar stories from other Springfielders, including from **Rhonda Adams**, who has this corroborating eyewitness testimony for us via Facebook Messenger; she also sent me confirming pictures of what she's seen.

> [A]t first there were 12 in a 3 bedroom house beside/behind me. Now there's 9. They don't mow their grass, [and] it's almost knee high again. They wash their clothes in a bucket and lay them to dry on a dead branch in the back yard. They're constantly blocking the shared driveway where my garage is located . . . [s]o when I'm wanting to leave or [am] coming home I have to knock on the door to get someone to move their car. They just started putting their trash in bags. Before I was constantly having to pick it up from where the wind would blow it against my fence. They don't speak English so I try my best with sign language. . . . They've lived there over 3 years now[.]
>
> I've seen them . . . wrecking their cars and ending up on the roof tops.

> I've been behind them in grocery stores with 2 cart loads full and not knowing how to use the [SNAP] card. And the cashier would get the manager over to help. . . . [T]he ones [who] live behind me make several trips in the house carrying the food. I'm talking 3–4 of them making 5–6 trips back and forth. They have 3 nice cars right now.
>
> You tell me [how they can afford the cars] . . . [T]here's only one that I know [who] works. I can tell by the white uniform that he wears. The older woman babysits 2 kids that a Haitian couple drops off and picks up every week. . . . I'm not sure if it's [Topre] or [Dole because] they both have white uniforms.
>
> . . . I have a nice home and take care of it. Every year I have called the [c]ity to complain about the grass. They're depreciating our neighborhood in my opinion.

It doesn't sound like Rhonda can take it anymore either. By the way, that city commission clip I mentioned just before her was shared far and wide via @captivedreamer7 on 𝕏 on September 7, 2024. The video made the internet rounds and subsequently resulted in all manner of cat memes spread wide in the few days leading up to and following the fateful September 10th debate.[4] Without this so-called Captive Dreamer making the Haitian influx go "gigaviral," you probably wouldn't be reading this book—and Donald Trump may not have won the 2024 presidential election.

That said, I have noticed a bait and switch by mainstream reporting on the Springfield story overall, then and since. The "it" that has been debunked changed from "what residents are saying is happening in Springfield" to "what residents are saying is happening in Springfield ***with regard to Haitians eating cats and dogs***." Do you see how that works? If we can dismiss the latter, we can dismiss the former. The collective suffering of a city of sixty thousand has "been debunked."

Springfield ft. Scott Adams

Scott Adams taught persuasion analysis in public on his beloved daily livestream *Coffee with Scott Adams*. A regular reframe he taught on the show was "Two Movies on One Screen." That's where two people or groups of people can observe the same situation and come away with two completely different takes.

I remember reading around the time of the release of *Unhumans* in July 2024 an article suggested to me on Facebook published by *The Springfield News-Sun*.

About their Haitian migrant population. Hey, maybe it's because I've been writing about Haiti in this book everyone is talking about now—Zuck is listening up. And so I read it.

"Springfield mayor: Investigation into businesses, immigration continues," published July 12, 2024, begins:

> Springfield officials were in the dark about the possibility of a large immigrant relocation to the area, Mayor Rob Rue said at the recent Springfield City Commission meeting, but a "network of businesses knew what was coming."
>
> Investigation by the city's Immigrant Accountability Response Team formed in October of 2023 has revealed the possibility "there were companies that knew they were going to make an effort to bring in individuals who were crossing the border based on federal regulations that they could do that," Rue said. "I'm upset at the fact we didn't get a chance to have an infrastructure in place if there were going to be 20,000 more people from 2020 to 2025. We didn't get to do that."
>
> "Springfield is now saturated," Rue said during the meeting when talk turned to Haitian immigration.[5]

And that's the story. Well, the first story. Not two months later, that story was replaced by an alternative with overt political charge. Just as many heritage citizens feel they, too, have been replaced, in their own home. The heritage citizens' "movie" is as far as I have been able to gather reflected accurately and nearly completely in Walter's words in this chapter. But the "movie" watched by NPR-Americans—what I call everyday people nationwide who believe their news sources to be credible despite known, measurable bias—their Springfield movie is that it's "all been debunked."[6]

Again, that's not even the story heritage citizens tell me and those who've come before me to investigate on site. And has even *that* story been debunked? "Absence of evidence is not evidence of absence," said Carl Sagan famously, astronomer and leading science communicator of the twentieth century.[7] Is it hearsay if you hear everyone say it?

" . . . [E]yewitness evidence is not infallible," reads *Eyewitness Evidence: A Guide for Law Enforcement* from United States Department of Justice. Elsewhere the guidebook tells us, " . . . [I]t is absolutely essential that eyewitness evidence be accurate and reliable. One way of ensuring we, as investigators, obtain the most accurate and reliable evidence from eyewitnesses is to follow sound protocols in our investigations."[8]

Protocols like what? Like this, from ***Eyewitness Evidence*** itself:

Assessing the Accuracy of Individual Elements of a Witness' Statement

Principle: Point-by-point consideration of a statement may enable judgment on which components of the statement are most accurate. This is necessary because each piece of information recalled by the witness may be remembered independently of other elements.
Policy: The investigator shall review the individual elements of the witness' statement to determine the accuracy of each point.
Procedure: After conducting the interview, the investigator should:

1. Consider each individual component of the witness' statement separately.
2. Review each element of the witness' statement in the context of the entire statement. Look for inconsistencies within the statement.
3. Review each element of the statement in the context of evidence known to the investigator from other sources (e.g., other witnesses' statements, physical evidence).

Summary: Point-by-point consideration of the accuracy of each element of a witness' statement can assist in focusing the investigation. This technique avoids the common misconception that the accuracy of an individual element of a witness' description predicts the accuracy of another element.[9]

Since there is a best practice for examining eyewitness evidence, I put that best into practice for the Haitians of Springfield. And as we do so, continuing from all the possibilities Walter opened up for us, to my own ensuing interviews and research and more that will continue into the remainder of this book, the meta-question remains. Looming. Obvious.

Why?

I let myself sit with Walter's accounts as we ate (I ordered Charlo's' grilled shrimp po' boy, having recently found relief from ten years of chronic veganism).

"Tell the story of where the money and where all the jobs are," Walter added after a lull. "Because that's the real thing that no one talks about around here. Yeah, the Haitians showed up. But what about all the jobs that could have gone to all the American citizens? Unemployment used to be really high. All those jobs could have been used by Americans. Wages go up, and everybody moves into the city. That would have been great, but instead, they gave it all away to the Haitian immigrants they wanted to bring here so desperately."

I thought about the companies founded or brought to Springfield during the first Trump administration. How a key promise of candidate Trump as far back as 2015 and 2016 was the return of American jobs to forgotten America. "America First" means Americans first. I recall hearing live these words of President Trump in his first inaugural address:

> At the center of this movement is a crucial conviction: that a nation exists to serve its citizens.
>
> Americans want great schools for their children, safe neighborhoods for their families, and good jobs for themselves.
>
> These are the just and reasonable demands of a righteous public.
>
> But for too many of our citizens, a different reality exists: Mothers and children trapped in poverty in our inner cities; rusted-out factories scattered like tombstones across the landscape of our nation; an education system, flush with cash, but which leaves our young and beautiful students deprived of knowledge; and the crime and gangs and drugs that have stolen too many lives and robbed our country of so much unrealized potential.
>
> This American carnage stops right here and stops right now.
>
> We are one nation—and their pain is our pain. Their dreams are our dreams; and their success will be our success. We share one heart, one home, and one glorious destiny.[10]

Promises made to Springfield, promises kept to Springfield.[11] Until rescinded under President Biden. And the consequences, nothing less than a humanitarian disaster.

All this surfaced a single hypothesis; I shared it with Walter.

"What was a success story of the first Trump term was co-opted and turned into a crisis, which brought him a second term."

"That's right," he said.

"That's so . . . strange."

"That's right." He chewed. "They made it so bad here that it easily gave him the second term."[12,13,14,15,16]

CHAPTER 3

THE JOURNEY

> "[I]t is clear that Springfield, Ohio, is a microcosm of a much larger problem. The system has failed, both in protecting the migrants who seek a better life and the local communities that bear the brunt of this unchecked exploitation."[1]
>
> —Asra Nomani

The last full memory I have of my paternal grandfather takes place at a Bob Evans in 1996. To this day, their brand, to me, is synonymous with all things aging Americana. It's dining with and within the past and yet a past worth protecting.

There I was at the Bob Evans on West Leffel Lane in Springfield. My dinner guest was a key node in the spontaneously formed open-source intelligence network of concerned heritage citizens of the city. That's a real term, for those of you unfamiliar with the military—OSINT. The artificial intelligence (AI)-generated definition Google search results gave me when prompted will suffice:

> OSINT is the process of gathering and analyzing publicly available information—from social media, websites, and databases—to produce actionable insights, evaluate security risks, or answer specific questions. It is used for cybersecurity, intelligence gathering, journalism, and research.

Hold that thought. And with the other hand of your mind, let's regrasp the demographic situation of country-home Springfield. That night, nearing a brisk dusk, I looked around Bob Evans and saw families, couples, individuals dining alone—most just shy of Grandpa Baker's age, had he lived this long. Not gray hair. White. Walkers. War-specific veteran hats. Whites.

So this is Springfield. Patrons paying with exact change to a penny. Servers calling themselves waitresses. Everyone over forty with the skin-texture of a smoker, sun laborer, or both. Including the women. Especially the women.

Is this not the age group that shuffles into every Bob Evans nationwide? Yes, and also the Cracker Barrel Old Country Store, also on West Leffel, where I met another node in Springfield's citizen OSINT. I'll take you there shortly.

My first debriefing from the OSINT citizens occurred at a Starbucks adjacent to the Springfield Meijer parking lot, followed up an hour later by a Skyline Chili. Here, there, and everywhere I went about Springfield—in the course of writing this book but also during prior visits for personal reasons and for touristic sightseeing—this is the demographic I noticed. Some would call them old. I saw living testaments to times long past and valuable lessons therefrom. Maybe that's just me. Reticular activating something or another. I've been writing memoirs for senior citizen clients since I was twenty-one years old, a rookie ghostwriter and barely-twice-published novelist. In many a way, these are my people. Lifetimes of treasured wisdom and precious memories of hardship and humanity and hope are told to anyone who will listen without their smartphone out. Most could make for bestselling books. A grievous few ever will.

American Madonna

"We are simple folk, most living paycheck to paycheck or pension check to pension check."

That's how **Diana Daniels** later described the longstanding citizens of Springfield, and in she walked to the Bob Evans now. This was to be my second experience of her, the first having been at the Skyline days prior—there and then, she'd passed me a handwritten note amid my multiple parallel conversations with the people of OSINT that read, alongside her number, *You need more time with me.*

That time is now. And every time I've seen Diana—including internet livestreams I've caught where she sometimes guest co-hosts the *Empty Pockets Garage* simulcast on YouTube and Rumble—she's worn what I've gathered is her uniform: a black baseball cap that reminds us to "support ICE" and a matching black hoodie with similarly patriot-maxed incredible content.[2]

Diana is a grandmotherly spirit from an age when grandmothers were expected to be industrious in work, protective of kin, and hardened against all threats foreign and domestic. If there's a stereotype of an underclass pensionette clued into tabloid-tier pop culture while completely out of touch with her own local goings-on, Diana is the precise and exact opposite. Her heart is as big as her mouth, and she knows how to use both.

"I appear at [the] City Commission's [meetings] for all the citizens of Springfield and the people of Clark County who have been marginalized for the last five years . . . who do not have a voice in front of the throne. . . . "[3] Diana Daniels said in an interview.

I understand that at one point recently she was suspended from Springfield City Commission meetings. If you ask—and she will tell you even if you don't—it's not that she was wrong, it's that the powers that be didn't like her tone. She's probably right.

An eighteen-foot-tall statue erected at Springfield's National Road Commons, "Madonna of the Trail," pays homage to the mother-trekkers of the old National Road, the first federally funded interstate highway, which connected Atlantic and Pacific, Maryland to California. The pioneer woman statue in question "portrays a mother with an infant in her left hand, a rifle in her right hand, and a small boy arm grasping at her homespun skirts. She is wearing a sunbonnet, boots, and a look of pure determination."[4]

Let those children grow up and give our American Madonna a look like she's seen things you wouldn't believe, and you'll find yourself staring into the soul of one Diana Daniels.

We got down to business immediately after we ordered. "You're a man after my heart," she said of my sausage gravy and biscuits selection.

I noticed also the way Diana addressed our waitress. You notice things when you do this for a living. Diana's tone . . . she spoke to our waitress, likely older than even her, with a higher-pitch grace and deary fondness you might expect of family to family who've missed each other for so long and now reunite. It's not just Diana. This I witnessed throughout the city. In bars, parking lots, coffeehouses, markets, alleys. People stop to use a restaurant's restroom but buy something first so it's a mutually beneficial exchange. Someone loses a wallet or cellphone, and its finder goes out of their way to bring it to its rightful owner all the way across town. This is what I witnessed here. These are a community who know, like, and high-trust one another. Mostly. . . . I did catch wind of several cliques, feuds, and rifts even among the OSINTers. That's just small-town America though. Diana, to her credit, was a bridge-builder—well, more a bridge-not-burner-downer, to be fair. Unless it's those biweekly city commission meetings.

Now, Diana, about the Haitian situation. Take it away.

I'm just going to give you basically what we know so far. . . . [U]nderstand this: Most of your Haitians that came here early on in 2021 did not come from Haiti at all. . . . They came from Brazil and Chile. . . . [T]he immigration crisis did not start in 2020. It started probably about 2018, 2019, and that's when the migration towards the border actually started. . . .

[S]o how did the Haitians get from Haiti to the border via Brazil and via Chile? OK, so, remember that Haiti experienced in 2010 two devastating natural disasters. They had the earthquake, and then they had the hurricane. So the amount of people that were displaced was absolutely astronomical. So of course, the United States used a program—refugee resettlement—and took in mostly women and children, which is fine.

Now, what Chile and Brazil did was they had an open visa program. So they just opened their countries to anyone from Haiti that wanted to come to Brazil or wanted to come to Chile. . . . [R]ight now, both Brazil and Chile are struggling under socialism, but in 2010, that wasn't so. They had very robust economies. Brazil needed workers for the Olympics, so they got approximately 154,000 Haitians . . . underneath their open visa program. Chile also opened their doors to anyone who wanted to come.

Why would Chile do that? Well, you have to think about . . . . what their major products are: mining minerals. They needed the Haitians to work the mines. 187,000 approximately immigrated to Chile in the ensuing years. From 2010, 2011, to 2012, you had a complete reversal, from democracies to socialism, in the two countries. . . . [T]hings fell apart.

So what happens to these Haitians is that, because they are not Brazilian nor Chilean, they were not entitled to any of these social programs that were offered to citizens. They would become the low man on the totem pole. So they were struggling. . . . [E]ven before [2018 and 2019], you had Haitians that were seeking asylum in the United States because they weren't receiving money. They were poor, starving, the whole nine yards, so they wanted to immigrate to the United States.

[A]t that time, you have to look at the political atmosphere in the United States. You had some control over the border. Immigration was basically a pretty regulated process. You filed your papers to seek asylum. You either got approved, you didn't, you're waiting. . . . What was happening, though, with the embassies in both Brazil and Chile was you were Haitian and you wanted to immigrate to the United States, so you filled out your paperwork. . . . [T]o seek asylum, you go to the embassy. It was an American embassy, but yet it was staffed by either Chileans or Brazilians. You go and fill out your paperwork and pay your money, come back in a week, and we'll do step two. Well, a week goes, you come back, and they don't even know you. They have no idea. They have no paperwork . . . or they would string them along, and they would get . . . your paperwork started. "Now it's another $1,000. . . . [W]e're just getting ready to approve the visa and approve your asylum. Finish your paperwork in the United States." Or, "Your paperwork is lost. You have to start over."

So here are these people who are trying desperately to save every penny they can to do things the right way, and we're being denied because of the corruption. Now, in 2019—

I interrupted Diana just as you might have right there. Where did she get all this information?

Three sources, primarily: Oscar "El Blue" Ramirez and her two former neighbors, Haitians from Brazil named (first names only) Francois and Jean Pierre. Ramirez, Diana told me, is a bilingual investigative reporter who embedded himself among caravans of migrants traveling through some of the most remote and dangerous parts of equatorial Central and South America, practically on foot, to have a chance of making it to and through the then-porous southern border of the United States of America. Even thirty seconds on Ramirez's YouTube will confirm her description of his work.[5] Diana, like everyone of the OSINT Springfield network I spoke with, is all but a professional information amalgamator.

By the way, you can put any single claim of their OSINT to the test and you will get a similar result. Go ahead and ask any AI about it. I did. The evening after meeting with Diana, I pulled up 𝕏 and asked Grok about all these details in the quoted material of Diana's. Sure enough, the first line of the reply was as follows:

> The narrative you provided is largely accurate on the broad strokes of Haitian post-2010 migration patterns through South America to the U.S. border, with some approximations or simplifications in numbers, timelines, and details.

That doesn't mean she or the sources she claimed are wrong. More like a "tl;dr" for the story and its meaning, a "too long; didn't read," a saying in Internetspeak.

Grok pointed me to a number of mostly corroborating, slightly correcting sources. For example:

> Although instability is recurrent in Haiti, the poorest country in the Western Hemisphere, the initial exodus had a clear trigger: the devastating earthquake of January 12, 2010. Since then, many Haitians have migrated to South America, mainly to Brazil. At that time, construction workers were in demand to build the infrastructure for the 2014 World Cup and the 2016 Olympic Games in Rio de Janeiro.
>
> . . . Another key destination was Chile due to its dynamic economy, at least in macroeconomic terms. Over the last decade, however, Haitians who emigrated there have also begun to leave for the north.
>
> . . . This is a trend that has been noticed in the Haitian community itself. Jean-Claude Pierre-Paul, a Haitian social worker who arrived in Chile in 2008, before the mass entry of migrants began in 2014-2015, says: "Haitians direct themselves to the border of Mexico and the United States. They travel through Chile, Peru, Brazil, Colombia, Panama, Guatemala and Honduras until they reach Mexico," he adds. . . . Pierre-Paul criticized Chile's slow-moving migration agencies, where a four-year wait for permanent residency is not uncommon. "In Chile, no other state institution takes so long to respond to an application," he says.[6]

On Aug 27th, 2021, Oscar El Blue reported that there were 150,000 migrants at the border of Guatemala and Mexico, many Haitian. That particular day, Oscar covered widespread Haitian protests overtaking border towns where the migrants demanded—from Mexico—an opportunity to enter the country and to receive better treatment in transit. There was the familiar accusation of corruption, allowing others to the front of the processing line literally and figuratively for suspicious reasons known and unknown, while thousands of Haitians had to wait (even longer). Oscar reported also cases of syphilis, gonorrhea, and AIDS among the population, not to mention COVID-19. The end of the broadcast featured footage that showed who appeared to be Haitians seemingly attempting to climb a very important barrier wall of some sort, without commentary.[7]

This short read from the Migration Policy Institute fills in several remaining gaps and third-party-confirms the gist of what Diana relayed to me. The report would also add that the Dominican Republic, Turks and Caicos, the Bahamas, Cuba, and Jamaica had been destinations for Haitians fleeing Haiti, but they were met by largely unfriendly governments and, in short order, aggressive deportation measures. Key excerpts:

> [The] steady stream of [Haitian] emigrants may be punctuated by new migration spikes given the collapse of basic governmental functions, persistent political and economic instability, and worsening gang violence underway since the assassination of President Jovenel Moïse in 2021. As conditions deteriorate, not only are new Haitian flows expected, but prospects of migrants returning to Haiti from Latin America, the Caribbean, and the United States will diminish. The question is how will already overwhelmed migration systems in the Americas respond?
>
> . . . Outside the Caribbean, the region has responded haphazardly to Haitian migration. For instance, Brazil and Chile, where thousands of Haitians had migrated after the 2010 earthquake, had initially opened some humanitarian pathways, giving these migrants the opportunity to find work and settle. However, economic downturns, policy changes, and rising anti-immigrant sentiment have complicated the deeper integration of Haitian migrants in South America, prompting a second migration towards the north.
>
> . . . [R]ecognition rates for protection for Haitians were markedly lower [by Mexico] than for other nationalities: 9 percent, as compared to Hondurans (89 percent), Salvadorans (85 percent), Venezuelans (83 percent), and Cubans (59 percent).
>
> Still, asylum applicants can concurrently apply for a one-year renewable humanitarian visa with work permit. In December 2022, the Mexican government granted humanitarian visas to 3,000 Haitians.
>
> . . . As of August [2023], at least 71,000 Haitians had been granted a two-year right to remain [in the United States] without fear of deportation and with access to a work permit through a parole program for Cubans, Haitians, Nicaraguans, and Venezuelans (CHNV). Though the program's requirements for a passport and U.S.-based sponsor limit access of less well-off Haitians who may have higher protection needs, it is nonetheless a pathway, and thus far, Haitians are the largest beneficiaries. The [Biden] administration also redesignated Temporary Protected Status (TPS) for some Haitians already resident in the United States and resumed the Haitian Family Reunification Parole Program.[8]

2021. 2022. 2023. These are years months to years before the hyperpoliticization of the Haitian presence in Springfield—but, technically, not before such politicization of Haitian migration into America.

Do you recall the viral photographs from September 2021 that seemingly depicted a United States Border Patrol agent on horseback allegedly harassing black migrants and chasing them back into the Rio Grande River along the United States–Mexico border?[9] Those were Haitians.[10]

I paused Grok's deep-dive to look up the final report on the matter from United States Customs and Border Protection. There are a number of important details in the report that I wager most Americans, or really anyone viewing the video, did not know:

- There is no evidence any migrant was struck with reins, intentionally or otherwise. The alleged "whips" seen were split reins used on the horses. The public sees a white man on a horse, a black man running away from them both, and bias tells what happens next (it didn't). In fact, the reason such reins were used was to better control the horses in order to keep nearby migrants safe from getting too close to the potentially upset animal. The truth, then, is the opposite of what we all saw in the photo.
- There was no U.S. Border Patrol operational objective to stop migrants from moving back and forth between Mexico and the United States. Miscommunication between and among local and federal authorities resulted in Border Patrol agents unaware of permissions granted to the Haitians to be where they were at the site and on the day of the incident.
- Migrants had been permitted to cross the U.S.–Mexico border back and forth with food, water, and other supplies. Some were simply returning back to America; that's why many in the photos have their hands full. Agents on horseback were unaware of this as well. The Haitians also had in their possession color-coded tickets that others at Border Patrol had already issued them for processing. Agents were unaware of this also.
- There remains an almost two-hundred-year-old controversy over where the U.S.–Mexico border actually is in that region. Border Patrol may have been in the wrong place.
- Border Patrol Chief Raul Ortiz accepted responsibility for the command-and-control deficiencies; the Western District of Texas declined prosecution.[11]

A *Los Angeles Times* article concurrent with the horse-chase incident contains imagery depicting the sprawling greenless quasi-tropical squalor of Haitian suffering once their masses reached America. At first skim, these shanty hastytowns of thousands of people resembled photographs I've seen of actual Haitian living conditions within their country as recent as Spring 2026. No—it's actually the pop-up community of Haitian migrants in Del Rio, Texas. Nathan Conner's "A Dream Deferred." Haitians in Springfield, Haitians in Haiti, Haitians in Texas. A caption of one *Los Angeles Times* photo reads, "Texas border town reckons with Haitian influx."[12] How did those heritage citizens feel about that? From *The San Diego Union-Tribune*:

> Lewis Owens, chief executive of the surrounding Val Verde County—who visits the camp daily—said he hopes it empties by Saturday so that the Del Río-Ciudad Acuña International Bridge can reopen by Monday.
>
> "They shouldn't be here," he said of the migrants, noting that local residents—some of whom held a protest earlier this week—were upset by the camp.
>
> "They just don't want them here and can't figure out why this was allowed to happen," he said.[13]

From the *LA Times*:

> "When Trump put up the wall, they didn't come," [Del Rio Taxi driver Juan] Dehoyos said as he stood in the lot, where his grandson was hosing off taxi floor mats. "Then Biden started, and they all came."
>
> . . . "We're American. We're trying to be nice," said [local tire technician Orlando] Aguirre, 39. . . . "You get angry because we're half Mexican and we've been through a lot of things and our families haven't been helped."
>
> Aguirre said he knows Haitian migrants who were released were issued orders to report to immigration officials or court, but the process still seemed easier than it had been for his family and neighbors.
>
> "They either come in illegally or it takes years to get it fixed," he said of their legal status.
>
> . . . Aguirre's street dead-ends at Trump's border wall, which he supported. He worried that once the Haitians were released into the U.S., they would disappear—especially after they left the border.
>
> "It's going to be harder to find them," he said.[14]

Fox News congressional correspondent Bill Melugin published a video he'd recorded on September 18, 2021, from a boat in the Rio Grande River in Del Rio, adding:

> 15,000+ Haitians flooded across the border illegally and set up a camp underneath the international bridge. Mayorkas later admitted 12,000+ of them were released into the U.S.
>
> Many of them later discarded their IDs and paperwork showing they had been living and working in South American countries for years (mostly Chile) as they prepared to make fraudulent asylum claims. Their documents were all over the ground. We collected many of them.[15]

When Nick Shirley, independent journalist best known for breaking the Somali immigrant childcare fraud story in Minnesota beginning with the so-called Quality Learning Center, visited Springfield in April 2026, he "encountered Haitian migrants who utilized the CBP One app for entry into the country."[16]

Daniel Foote, United States special envoy to Haiti, resigned over all that chaos under Biden, addressing then-Secretary of State Anthony Blinken of the Biden administration, "I will not be associated with the United States' inhumane, counterproductive decision to deport thousands of Haitian refugees and illegal immigrants."[17] Almost 2,000 from Del Rio were sent back to Haiti on international flights. An additional 3,900 or so had been moved elsewhere along the border, and approximately 3,100 remained at the encampment near the aforementioned bridge.[18]

Long Journey Short

The 2010 Haitian earthquake and subsequent non-rebuilding of the Haitian side of the island resulted in a multi-nation, decade-long-plus clusterfuck spanning two entire continents. (There's an extended sidebar about Bill and Hillary Clinton's joint private and public work in post-earthquake Haiti. The Clinton Foundation reported $62.9 million in donations for Haiti relief and recovery in 2010 and had expended $57.4 million of it by year's end.[19] Also: "As US secretary of state, Hillary helped to oversee $4.4bn that Congress had earmarked for recovery efforts by the US Agency for International Development, or USAid."[20] A significant set of projects were neoliberal economic statecraft with the explicit agenda to rebuild Haitians' ability to work and do business. But "[t]en years later, the industrial park is widely considered to have failed to deliver the economic transformation the Clintons promised." That project "would attract international manufacturers, which they saw as the primary fix to Haiti's faltering economy." It did not. So what about that $57.4 million? Don't point all fingers at the Clintons. Consider looking up the so-called Clinton Bush Haiti Fund. Uh-oh. That's for another book.[21])

Going on more than a decade now, what has been that has been has left hundreds of thousands of Haitians without a Haiti. It's no surprise why it's a widely recognized stereotype that Americans "pity" Haitians, although that does explain more than it probably should what happened in Springfield and why.[22]

Two looming questions remain for this chapter's primary subject matter:

1. How did the diaspored Haitians journey from South America to the U.S.–Mexico border?
2. What happened to those who'd made it to Del Rio, San Antonio, or their next stop before their final destination of Springfield?

I interrupted Diana somewhere in 2019, but she picked right back up a couple years later to begin answering my two lingering questions in more detail than I expected but probably should have. That's Diana.

> Now, let's get back to Del Rio . . . September 2021. . . . In the space of seven days, 15,500 humans crossed the Rio Grande at Del Rio. The pictures are absolutely devastating. . . . They had no food, no water, nothing. American Red Cross and . . . of course, Border Patrol, needed to process them quickly. So they just said, "You're in, you're in, you're in, you're in, here's your court date ten years later."
>
> How did they get to Springfield? At the processing centers just outside of Del Rio, the Catholic Church had reception centers, and they had little signs telling you where to go. If you wanted to go to Chicago, then you went here. If you wanted to go to New York, you went here. If you wanted to go to Philadelphia, you went here. If you wanted to go to Springfield, Ohio, you went here.

Diana's claims are, at minimum, directionally accurate by any assessment. "[S]ome 15,000 people crossed the Rio Grande from Mexico in the past week or so . . . [in] this Texas border town of 35,000," wrote Politico on September 23, 2021.[23]

Catholic Charities, including local Texas affiliates and the national Catholic Charities USA/CCUSA, did have a documented humanitarian aid presence there primarily focused on supplying essentials from blankets to diapers, transporting government-released families, and providing post-release shelter and support.[24] U.S. Customs and Border Protection and the Department of Homeland Security handled initial processing—like apprehensions, Title 42 expulsions, asylum referrals, and releases—at the Del Rio International Bridge camp. NGOs (like Catholic Charities) would then provide humanitarian relief and resettlement aid once those migrants were released.[25]

I was unable to confirm the existence of the reported destination-Springfield signage, but, again, absence of evidence (for me) is not evidence of (all) absence. NPR did report concurrently that Haitians crossing at Del Rio planned to build new lives across the United States where family members already had—chain migration, this is called. From September 23, 2021:

> Wilgens Jean and his wife, Junia Michel, waited in Del Rio this week for relatives to send the $439 in bus fare to get to Springfield, Ohio, where Jean's brother lives. Michel, who is pregnant, huddled under the little shade the parking lot had to offer from the brutal heat. Her only request was for sunscreen that she softly rubbed on her pregnant belly.
>
> . . . After an initial stay with family in San Antonio, Veillard eventually hopes to get to New York City to live with his sister. He will take any job he can find to support his growing family.
>
> . . . [Another Haitian named] Veillard and his wife left Haiti four years ago and had been living in Brazil until they began their journey to the United States in June, much of it on foot.
>
> "I don't know how I'm going to feel tomorrow but now I feel lucky," he said.[26]

It could be as straightforward as this—people go where they are welcome, and Springfield welcomed Haitians. *Springfield News-Sun* reported a numerically identifiable Haitian community in Springfield as early as 2018; three Creole-speaking pediatric patients received services from Rocking Horse Community Health Center, a Springfield facility offering medical, dental, behavioral health, patient advocacy, and material assistance.[27]

I did not find an exact number beyond this threepeat, well, *threepeated* everywhere on the internet about Springfield, Haitians, and 2018, so I asked Grok to guestimate and show its work. Its output:

> 2018 best estimate: ~20–40 total Haitians citywide in Springfield.

Simple math used (transparent & repeatable):

3 Creole-speaking pediatric patients = ~5–10 Haitian kids (accounting for siblings[28]).

Haitian immigrant groups are ~30% children (standard U.S. Census/MPI demographic[29]).

Rocking Horse (main safety-net FQHC) captured most low-income immigrant kids that year.

→ 5–10 kids ÷ 0.30 = 17–33 total Haitians (rounded to 20–40 for families/adults).

Regardless of estimates versus exacts, the fact remains as follows:

Springfield had already welcomed Haitians.

But why had Springfield already welcomed Haitians?

I uncovered no government plan with an explicit agenda to replace the native-born population of white heritage citizens with brown and black non-English speakers. According to Bridget Houston, a Springfield City Commissioner at the time of the most viral stories amid the U.S. Presidential election season of 2024:

> "Mayor Rue has never been to Haiti. Additionally, none of us ever have, or are currently receiving any financial kickbacks."
>
> "There has been no 'importing' immigrants as well—we are a city and cannot control our physical border and cannot control who lives or visits here. . . . Most of the Haitians living in Springfield do have Federal documents as well that allow them to be here . . . "[30]

The city officially denies "sanctuary city" status. "No government entity is responsible for the influx of Haitians into Clark County. Once a person with Temporary Protected Status enters the country, they are free to locate wherever they choose," adds an immigration-focused frequently-asked-questions page on the Springfield government website.[31] There's more. The passive voice reminded me of Politico:

> Springfield is an appealing place for many reasons including lower cost of living and available work. These conditions are thought to be the primary reasons for immigrants to choose Springfield. Now that there are numerous immigrant families residing in our community, word of mouth is adding to our population, as this communal culture is sharing their positive experiences about living in our community with family and friends who

> are also seeking to leave the impoverished and dangerous living conditions of their home country.[32]

To my knowledge, the OSINT heritage citizenry network of Springfield was not able to collectively source an official government plan to contradict the city's official position on the matter, nor was it insisted to me that such a document or otherwise agenda would, could, did, or must exist.

But I said no *government* plan to bring Haitians to Springfield en masse. Not *no* plan at all.

There just might be a reason "local citizens started using the moniker 'Lyin' Bryan,' for the city [manager Bryan Heck] . . . [and] Mayor Rue, 'Mayor Rude' for his alleged stonewalling."[33]

CHAPTER 4

WELCOME SPRINGFIELD

"If you import the Third World, you become the Third World."[1]

—President Donald J. Trump

A name that came up in conversation with Diana Daniels that night at Bob Evans had already enjoyed numerous mentions at all prior and all subsequent scheduled and spontaneous meetings of the OSINTs whenever I'd asked anything remotely close to the question, "Why did Haitians first come to Springfield, and why did they keep coming?"

Occasionally the city mayor or city manager came up—Rob Rue and Bryan Heck, respectively—but universally all heritage citizens displeased with Haitian presence in Clark County held to a consensus: Haitians are here because of Carl Ruby.

I could not help but equate this Carl Ruby to a more well-known one-dimensional supervillain of the working-class cultural Right in America, George Soros, who seems to be at the seat of power when you rise high enough into any social project deemed "woke." The obviously racist and antisemitic conspiracy I've gathered from anonymous, actual-far-Right social media, group chat logs, and message boards is that Soros, a known Jew, wants to replace poor white people with even poorer black and brown people, whose gratitude will virtually guarantee their votes for the properly progressive candidates who Soros and company have pre-vetted to be under his influence prior to being granted power by the replacement population, with the end goal being the subjugation then elimination of the white races, all as revenge for the Holocaust which Soros as a young boy survived.

Something like that.

An Abridged Biography of Carl Ruby

I do not recall anyone in the OSINT group having mentioned George Soros by name as the initial Haitian migration cause, and they went to a consistent and distant extent to keep their network bigotry-free, to the best of my knowledge.

But again, I could not help but see the Sorosian archetype applied to this character Carl Ruby.

Now for the completely unauthorized biography of Ohio's George Soros—Carl Ruby—recounted that same night at Bob Evans by Diana Daniels:

> Carl Ruby has been importing immigrants since 2014 . . . [He] was the dean of students at Cedarville University. . . . [H]e's always been a big advocate for immigration reform, but he got tired of waiting; he thought the government was moving too slow. So he took things into his own hands; he created a group called G92. You will read in the newspaper that G92 is a recent anomaly. It's not. It's been around since 2011.
>
> So, G92 is an organization based on the Hebrew word *ger* that appears 92 times in the Hebrew Bible. And of course, it means "sojourner," "wanderer," or "immigrant." However, it does not broadly mean any immigrant; it happens to be Jewish immigrants or folks who are coming into a Jewish enclave. But he has twisted that to imply that means every immigrant.
>
> So at first, it started off pretty small with, I think, twenty-two churches and youth organizations but then blossomed into what it is now. . . . Why G92? Well, he was using his position as dean of students to influence the students into his immigration policies, which the Baptist church did not agree with.
>
> In 2013, he also invited a—I'm just going to use the word—homosexual theatre group to Cedarville University. Well, you can imagine how that went. Under investigation for all of that stuff. Now, rather than complete the investigation, he chose to resign, and the investigative material was sealed. He resigned. People say that he retired. He did not retire. He resigned his position. That was 2013. [In] 2014, he immediately emerges as the pastor of Central Christian Church here in Springfield. It's called Central now; it has no association with Christ.
>
> At the same time, he created two 501(c)3s. One was—I think we told you before—Welcome Springfield. . . . [T]he other was the Midwest Consortium for Immigration Research at Wright State University. He chose Anthony Ortiz, who was a Mexican immigrant at Wright State and was also the head of the athletic training department at Wright State. Where that organization has gone, or how it's been transformed, I do not know, but that was your academic arm that was going to be basically supporting businesses if you wanted immigrant labor.

Let the unpacking begin. That's what we do here.

The Midwest Consortium on Immigrant Research Institute

On August 15, 2014, during Wright State University's annual Regional Summit, Anthony Ortiz (then also Associate Vice President of Latino Affairs) publicly announced plans to create the Midwest Consortium on Immigrant Research Institute (also called Midwest Consortium for Immigration Research or MCIR) at Wright State.[2] Its stated purpose was to track and research the economic impact of immigrants in Midwestern communities, including Springfield and Clark County, Ohio. It was to be part of a broader "welcoming communities" initiatives like Welcome Dayton and the forthcoming Welcome Springfield efforts with specific emphasis on the economic argument for immigration. (There was no mention of Ruby in Wright State's announcement.)

As for Ortiz, he did indeed serve as Wright State's Head Athletic Trainer and Program Director for over thirty years, but he is of Puerto Rican descent, not Mexican. "Following his retirement, he served as the diversity liaison in the Ohio Department of Administrative Services: Office of Talent Management-Human Resources Division and, from 2016 to 2018, was the diversity liaison to Attorney General Mike DeWine and the Office of the Attorney General."[3]

Welcome Dayton, Welcome Springfield, welcome immigrant labor. Now, who exactly did the stating of the purpose? None other than Carl Ruby.

Carl Ruby gave a presentation entitled "Midwest Consortium for Immigration Research" at the second annual convening of the WE Global Network in Pittsburgh, Pennsylvania, in 2014.[4]

The We Global Network

What is the WE Global Network?

> The rust belt Welcoming Economies Global Network (WE Network) [is] a program of Welcoming America in partnership with Global Detroit [and] is a regional network of more than twenty initiatives across the Rust Belt tapping into the economic development opportunities created by immigrants.[5]

And what are the aforementioned immigrant-created opportunities, you might wonder? Let's let them make that case for us. The WE Global Network's X account (then Twitter) hasn't seen activity since 2019. But one of the last tweets the Network made, on April 24, 2019, reads:[6]

> Between 2010 and 2018, Ohio's population would have noticeably declined if not for the increase in immigration.

The sentiment is, to my reading, meant to be positive. Along with the tweet is published an article from *The Columbus Dispatch*; here is the economic case for immigration, specifically into Ohio:

> When the population numbers come out each year, "you want to be growing," said economist Bill LaFayette, owner of Columbus-based Regionomics.
>
> . . . "The working-age population in central Ohio is projected to be growing much more slowly. . . . Immigrants tend to be younger. They tend to be working age. That is a big factor not just in our population growth, but in our future workforce," he said.[7]

This particular commentary doesn't take long before becoming nakedly political:

> These numbers are coming out as President Donald Trump declares that the nation is full, and his administration tightens policies for people seeking asylum at the border and for the numbers of refugees admitted. . . .
>
> Such policies have already reduced the numbers of refugees arriving in Ohio through Community Refugee & Immigration Services, said Angie Plummer, the Columbus-based group's executive director. In fiscal year 2016, the group welcomed 833 refugees. In fiscal year 2018, which ended Sept. 30, the group settled 325 refugees.
>
> . . . "We see it on a very practical level every day when employers are calling us saying, 'Do you have workers? We need employees.'"
>
> One company in Washington Court House in Fayette County is so in need of workers that it pays for transportation for Plummer's clients from Columbus and back every day.[8]

Plummer added that her organization had "many, many families" trying to bring potentially breadwinning family members into the United States to join them but had gotten "stuck."

WE Network held annual convenings from 2013 until 2020. Its third convention, in 2015, was held in my hometown of Dayton. A resounding success, apparently:

> With over 300 attendees from nearly two-dozen Rust Belt cities who are pursuing new strategies to welcome immigrants to rebuild central cities and spark regional economic growth, the WE Global Convening demonstrated the growing energy and momentum in these local practices.[9]

In Wright State's announcement of the aforementioned immigration consortium, it was also noted that "Dayton City Commissioner Matt Joseph briefed the audience on the Welcome Dayton Plan, designed to engage new immigrants in strengthening the economy. He noted that two of every three immigrants in Dayton have advanced degrees and that the immigration population in the city jumped 40.3 percent between 2011 and 2012."[10] Interesting.

Back to the WE Network. As for that 2014 convening, Ruby as presenter was bio'ed as "founder of an immigration advocacy group called G92, an organization seeking to mobilize evangelical university students to advocate for immigration reform. He currently serves as an independent consultant working with the National Immigration Forum to run Bibles, Badges, and Business for Immigration Reform of Ohio. In addition to statewide and national advocacy for immigration reform, Carl is also focusing on mobilizing local and regional efforts to help communities use immigration as a means of economic development and population stabilization."[11]

The WE Network has a helpful toolkit of digital resources "to improve your own message and advance your local efforts," such as *Welcoming Economies Playbook,* which "builds off of years of promising work across the nation to help unlock the economic potential of refugees, immigrants, and community members born in the United States," and the *Guide to Immigrant Economic Development* that "captures more practices, strategies and models that can provide a framework for those working in immigrant economic development, and can help them develop their own initiatives based on their local needs and infrastructure."[12]

New Americans

A noteworthy passage from the *Playbook* makes this explicit case for *refugees* as economic stimulus for the Midwest, not simply immigrants more broadly:

> Refugee and other immigrant workers complement the U.S.-born workforce in positions across the economic spectrum. . . .

> Working class refugees help to fill a critical need for low-skill and middle-skill positions in the U.S. economy. U.S. workers—especially in the Midwest and Northeast—are rapidly aging and retiring. . . .
>
> About half of the job openings expected over the coming decade are anticipated to fall within the "middle skills" category—jobs that require training beyond a high school diploma but not a four-year college degree. . . .
>
> As these trends create a labor shortage, refugees are one group helping to fill unmet workforce needs. State and local leaders have developed policies and programs that help New Americans move into career pathways and connect with jobs that suit their skills, thereby helping to close regional skill gaps. Such programs enable workers to fully contribute to the region's economy.
>
> Assisting working class newcomers to integrate into the U.S. workforce is a cost effective policy solution; it is in the interest of all residents —U.S.-born and new arrivals alike—that all workers' skills and knowledge are put to their highest and best use.

As you'll soon see, this is precisely what is alleged to have occurred in Springfield—by both sides of the debate, with one interpretation being wholly positive and the other as overwhelmingly negative. It's all in the WE Network playbook. Someone followed it.

Welcoming America

The WE Network repeatedly directs us to Welcoming America, "a nonprofit leading a movement of inclusive communities becoming more prosperous by ensuring everyone belongs, including immigrants."[13] There's more:

> The Welcoming Network is composed of around 300 nonprofits and local governments working to build more inclusive and welcoming communities in the United States. Led by Welcoming America, the Welcoming Network is both a network and a movement, driven by the conviction that communities make better decisions when residents of all backgrounds, identities, and perspectives are meaningfully engaged.
>
> . . . [M]embers commit to advancing and institutionalizing welcoming efforts in their community and to share their experience and lessons learned with the network, while receiving training, resources, networking, and leveraged funding.[14]

Local governments, you say? What's this now?

Certified Welcoming

> Certified Welcoming is a formal designation for cities and counties that have created policies and programs reflecting their values and commitment to immigrant inclusion. This innovative program assesses city and county governments on their efforts to include and welcome immigrants in all areas of civic, social, and economic life in their communities.[15]

Welcome Springfield

Let's talk about the Welcome Springfield program—which never actually existed, according to the city!

> In response to recent comments regarding a 2014 Resolution, the City of Springfield would like to reiterate that we are not part of the Welcoming America "Certified Welcoming" network of communities. Membership in this network requires a formal application process and a fee of up to $12,000, followed by an evaluation and official designation from Welcoming America—a process the City has not undertaken.
>
> Springfield welcomes legal immigration efforts consistent with federal laws and policies. The City will continue to comply with all laws and regulations established by the federal government. Our commitment to respecting and upholding federal law remains steadfast.[16]

" . . . [H]e got tired of waiting; he thought the government was moving too slow."

What was that 2014 resolution now? *The Ohio Register* and WE Global Network both published a copy of **Resolution No. 5844**, which is otherwise oddly difficult to find a copy of online.[17,18]

Resolution No. 5844

The Resolution reads as follows:

A Resolution No. 5844

Declaring The City of Springfield, Ohio, a community welcoming of immigrants and immigrant-owned businesses, and declaring an emergency.

WHEREAS, this Commission recognizes the contributions immigrants have made to the community since its founding; and

WHEREAS, this Commission realizes that this community is currently home to a growing population of foreign-born residents; and

WHEREAS, this Commission understands that today's world is increasingly mobile and supports a global economy; and

WHEREAS, this Commission recognizes that population decline is a threat to economic stability, and a proactive approach to immigrants can help to offset the loss of working-age residents anticipated in the future; and

WHEREAS, this Commission appreciates the important role that global talent and immigrant workers play in building a more robust local economy; and

WHEREAS, this Commission determines that The City of Springfield, Ohio, should be a community welcoming of immigrants and immigrant-owned businesses; and

WHEREAS, in order that such a stance on immigrants and immigrant-owned businesses can be fostered and accepted at the earliest possible moment, thereby preserving the public peace, health, safety, and property, it is necessary that this Resolution become effective immediately: NOW, THEREFORE:

BE IT RESOLVED by the City Commission of The City of Springfield, Ohio, at least four of its members concurring:

Section 1. That The City of Springfield, Ohio, joins cities like Dayton and Columbus that have formed a voluntary network of immigrant-friendly communities called Global Great Lakes and Welcoming America.

Section 2. That the City Commission declares The City of Springfield, Ohio, welcoming to immigrants and immigrant-owned businesses.

Section 3. That the City Commission vows to maintain and adopt policies that promote the inclusion and integration of immigrants within this community, assisting them in their pursuit of the American dream, and thus empowering them to become a viable part of the area's economic base.

Section 4. That the City Commission encourages the facilitation of open and civil dialogue about strategies the Springfield community can practice and promote to see that immigrants achieve the highest value of hospitality and free enterprise.

Section 5. That by the reason of the emergency set forth and defined in the preamble hereto, this Resolution shall take effect and be in force immediately.

ADOPTED this 22nd day of July, A.D., 2014.

Warren R. Copeland
PRESIDENT OF THE CITY COMMISSION

Connie J Chappell
CLERK OF THE CITY COMMISSION

Warren Copeland and Connie Chappell—you will find both of these names in the news a few years later. From *Springfield News-Sun*:

> The Community Beautification Committee (CBC) if Springfield recently honored two retirees with awards.
>
> The organization presented year-end "Beautification Achievement Award" plaques to Warren Copeland and Connie Chappell.
>
> Copeland was honored in recognition of his 35 years and Chappell of her 30 years of beautification efforts, continued support and contributions "to help enhance the natural beauty of Springfield."
>
> Copeland was city commissioner from 1988 to 2023, and City of Springfield mayor from 1990 to 1994 and from 1998 to 2023. He was the first person to be elected to this post by a direct community election in 2003.
>
> Chappell served as the city commission clerk from 1987 to 2017.[19]

Copeland passed away in 2024 shortly after receiving the award.[20]

Asides aside, perhaps you caught the same anomaly I did in the above.

Rabbit Holes, Loose Ends, and the Ever-Unanswered Questions

If as the City of Springfield claims, the City is "not part of the Welcoming America 'Certified Welcoming' network of communities," why then is a copy of the "welcoming of immigrants" resolution from City Commission available on the actual WE Global Network website? Look at the web page, which by the time you read this, may be deleted. The exact address is:

> https://www.weglobalnetwork.org/wp-content/uploads/2014/11/Welcome-Springfield-Resolution-City-of-Springfield.pdf.

"wp-content," "uploads," and then "2014/11" indicate that this scan of Resolution No. 5844 was uploaded to the WordPress content folder in November 2014 (For the web-unfamiliar, WordPress is a content management system used to design and develop websites.). That means someone with administrative credentials—at minimum—must have uploaded the Springfield resolution to be hosted by the WE Global Network's website. Why? Who?

Hold all questions to the end should we ever reach it. Want to know what else was uploaded in November 2014 to the WE Global Network site? This newspaper article:

> https://www.weglobalnetwork.org/wp-content/uploads/2014/11/Springfield_Clark-County-proposal-embraces-immigrants.pdf.

This links to a scan of a *Dayton Daily News* article by Kermit Rowe published on February 4, 2014 entitled "**Clark County proposal embraces immigrants**." The subhead reads, "WelcomeSpringfield.org group targets growing Latino population. Opponent says enforcement of laws will help local economy more."

Carl Ruby's WelcomeSpringfield.org

Have a gander at this excerpt:

> A new Clark County initiative that targets immigrants will address declining population and job losses by embracing and enabling the area's growing Latino population, its founder said.
>
> . . . The nonprofit initiative is called WelcomeSpringfield.org, and its executive director and founder, Carl Ruby, said it will revitalize the county's economy.

"Our goal is to bring money into Clark County and to aggressively go after grants that will help us to serve this population and to revitalize and rebuild the economy," said Ruby. . . . "Ours is not a charitable organization—it's not set up to give out handouts but to give a person a hand up. . . . One way to mitigate losing those [projected] 10,000 [Springfield residents by 2040] is to not just recruit immigrants, but give them the skills to be homeowners and business owners[.]"

. . . "To me this proposal, in an economic sense, is a poverty magnet," said Steve Salvi, founder of the Ohio Jobs and Justice PAC. . . . This is not a demographic that is going to revitalize Springfield or any community in Clark County. . . . As soon as you institute these types of things, it will draw more illegal aliens, and they won't have PhDs. They are largely uneducated. How is this going to help the economy of Springfield?"

. . . "We are seeking to build a strong alliance with city and county government officials, because this can't succeed without it," [Ruby] said.

. . .

Wright State University will make the effort research-based, Ruby said.

"We're trying to set up for the future," said Tony Ortiz, president of the initiative's board, who was named Associate Vice President for Latino Affairs at Wright State University in October.

. . . "What we're attempting to do is to establish a reputation in this region as being one of the most proactive in trying to attract the type of businesses that attract immigrants and enable them to succeed," [Ruby] said. "If they work hard, they deserve to take a shot at the American dream."

Ruby has spoken with many Clark County leaders about the initiative.

"Throughout the history of Clark County, we'd had growth through immigration, whether it was the Irish coming in or the Germans coming in," said [Clark County Commissioner John] Detrick. "This is the avenue for a community to stay healthy, by attracting immigrants, and this program sounds really exciting. . . . That's what you have to do, think out of box . . . [I]mmigrants will come here if we have jobs."

. . .

"I think what Carl is trying to do is something that could be helpful in our community," [Springfield City Manager Jim Bodenmiller] said. "I've seen other cities work with immigrants, a lot of whom have an entrepreneurial

(continued . . .)

outlook, and it has brought new businesses to those cities . . . I just think of some our local people who came over or whose parents came over, and they are some of the most successful people in our community. Jim Lagos for example; his is a pretty neat family story[.]"

Springfield Mayor Warren Copeland knows a problem exists here. . . . "My own personal view is we need to find ways to get these folks legal status so that they can come out of the shadows and we can relate to them like we do the rest of our residents."

. . . "I think it's a void that needs to be filled," said [Springfield Foundation executive director Ted] Vander Roest. " . . . With the growing population, it's a need. . . . "

. . . "The heart of the opposition is a perception that they are coming to take advantage of our generous welfare system," Ruby said. "The facts don't bear that out; instead they say that they come to work."

. . .

"I had a defining experience a couple of years ago when I took a civil rights bus trip," said Ruby. The experience, which focused on Martin Luther King Jr.'s civil rights movement, left Ruby with a haunting question: "If I would have lived during that time, what would I have done?"

. . . *The Springfield News-Sun* talked to nearly a dozen sources to address the important topic of immigration laws and how a local effort to welcome immigrants here could affect Clark County in the future.

. . . Donations can be made through the Nehemiah Foundation

Editor's note: The correct name and website for the initiative is WelcomeSpringfield.org not WelcomeSpringfield.com as previously reported.[21]

Did you catch the italics?

The Springfield News-Sun. But the copy of the article uploaded to the WE Network site had been published by *The Dayton Daily News*. Is there not a web page for the article where it was originally published, *The Springfield News-Sun*? There is a web version of the article, but not on the *News-Sun*'s website. The article does appear with an incorrect July 3, 2020, publication date on *The Dayton Daily News* website, six years after its original publication.[22] And again, not on *Springfield News-Sun*.

There's more. A member of the OSINT citizens' network handed to me in person a printout of a newspaper article screenshot from February 9, 2014, uploaded to www.newspapers.com/image/452872979. The upper-right-hand corner of the page indicated the date the document had been downloaded for printing—July 16, 2024.

The original welcoming-Springfield article in question was indeed published in *The Springfield News-Sun* but bore the title "Initiative: Immigrants can revitalize county" with the subhead "Group seeks public, private partners: critic calls plan 'a poverty magnet.'"

Both the title and subhead are different between the *Dayton* and *Springfield* newspapers. The article text itself appears to be an exact duplicate—except for one error, which I'll reveal in a moment. Oddly enough, *Dayton Daily's* version shows a publication date of February 8, 2014—the version on the WE Global Network site—but appears to be a digital version of the article that may have run online prior to print publication rather than a photograph of a newspaper. *The Springfield News-Sun* remains credited, of course, as the newspaper that "talked to nearly a dozen sources."

And that error situation? The February 8th *Dayton Daily* version contains the *corrected* WelcomeSpringfield.org website address—the *Springfield News-Sun* version with its alternate article title and headline, dated February 9, has the older, incorrect website—WelcomeSpringfield.com. That supports my preliminary conclusion that *Springfield News-Sun* is the originator of the article, and *Dayton Daily* reprinted or otherwise republished it.

Although the *Dayton Daily News* website retains the article with that incorrect publication date from 2020, again, there does not appear to be the same article on the *Springfield News-Sun* website any longer—only a photograph of the newspaper article that an anonymous internet user uploaded to www.newspapers.com. There is no record of the *News-Sun* website for the article having existed as far as I could (not) find.

Someone, likely a local who knew the significance of the story before team Trump did, had downloaded a copy of the original *News-Sun* article from 2014, in July 2024. Someone else—or perhaps that same person?—had also, of course, previously uploaded an image of the article in the first place at some point prior. Someone knew how important this was all going to be and left e-bread crumbs for us to retrace their steps.

There was also published, on July 16, 2014, in *The Springfield News-Sun*, an article by Michael Cooper (who had not responded to my request for comment as of this writing) entitled "Springfield seeks to be immigrant friendly city." It's cited in *Urban Studies: An International Journal of Research in Urban Studies* in an article entitled, "Experiencing intentional recognition: Welcoming immigrants in Dayton, Ohio," first published online on July 1, 2016.

The link to the July 2014 immigrant-friendly piece leads nowhere. The website address https://www.springfieldnewssun.com/news/local-govt—politics/springfield-seeks-immigrant-friendly-city/ is a 404 page. Despite being published in 2014, the web page was only screenshat for a public internet archive called the Wayback Machine on September 14 and 15, 2024—ten years later, but non-coincidentally four and then five days after then-Candidate Trump's remarks about domesticated animal consumption sent Earth's e-sleuths after everything they could find regarding the Haitians of Springfield.[23]

The July 2014 ghost article appears among the cited sources of the "FACTUAL ALLEGATIONS" of a civil complaint filed by the City of Springfield and co-plaintiffs against an alleged neo-Nazi group called Blood Tribe.[24] The civil complaint dates to February 2025. Was the article wiped from the web prior to that? Or, more likely, after? And why? Perhaps the wrong person asked the right questions?

Hispanics Before Haitians

A clue for the foreseeable interim may be another now-scrubbed-from-the-*News-Sun* article Cooper wrote in 2015 that features—guess who—Carl Ruby. "**Some Clark County Latinos report lack of access to medical care**" was published by the *Springfield News-Sun* on November 5, 2015. Here is an excerpt of the article; you'll have to fetch your own full copy from the Wayback Machine, too.[25]

> Many Clark County Latinos lack access to health care and insurance and many of them earn less than $15,000 annually, according to a new health survey.
>
> The survey was conducted by Welcome Springfield with assistance from the Clark County Combined Health District. The result[s] were released at a meeting of the Clark County Latino Health Initiative on Thursday at the Rocking Horse Community Health Center.
>
> More than 500 surveys were distributed and 156 were completed. The survey, paid for by a $15,000 grant from CareSource, was given to those who attend Spanish-speaking churches or work in places with large clusters of Latinos. It doesn't reflect Latinos who have lived here for many generations, Welcome Springfield Director Carl Ruby said.
>
> . . . The group plans to find ways to add more bilingual health care providers, better mental health services and more access to Spanish brochures on health issues in places where Latinos gather. They'll begin to devise a

strategic plan early next year, Ruby said. "We need to transition from talking about (the problems) to developing some solutions. . . . This is a very at-risk population in terms of all the things related to population. . . . It shows how vulnerable this population is."

Of the 99 who answered the final question about their immigration status, 61 percent were undocumented and 21 percent had green cards.

Domestic violence also was reported as an issue for 17 percent of survey participants and only 20 percent knew where to get help. They also plan to better promote Project Woman to the Spanish-speaking community.

. . . The results are similar to those compiled by the Springfield City School District, said Lourdes Narvaez, the district's Hispanic outreach program director. The language barrier and lack of trust keeps people from seeking medical care, she said.

If Carl Ruby is synonymous with the Haitians of Springfield at present, and he is, what's with all this business of the Latin peoples? That question will be answered in time—by Diana Daniels, of all people.

Speaking of questions, a lingering question you may have pertains to Carl Ruby's 2014 speech to the WE Global Network. A third relevant document was uploaded to the WE Global Network website back end in November 2014—Carl Ruby's presentation on the Midwest Consortium for Immigration Research (technically fourth we've covered so far; the 2014 WE Global Network consortium speakers sheet featuring Ruby was also uploaded in November 2014[26]).

Ruby's slides open with the MCIR logo, the organization's values ("Education, Justice, Economics, Health, Culture"), and the consortium tagline ("Promoting Economic Growth, Workforce Innovation & Development").[27] The presentation would go on to list a number of intended deliverables such as an annual conference, an e-journal, an edited book (?), and consulting services. The presentation did list Ruby's vision for the consortium having "grown out of my work as an independent consultant working for Ali Noorani's team at National Immigration Forum."

Ruby said that he had "personally funded all of the work" of the consortium by that point but was at that time seeking both short-term funding (approximately $80,000 over the subsequent six months) and long-term funding ($250,000 to $500,000 per year).

Ruby spoke of an "urgency" to roll the project out, adding, "this initiative could play a positive role in highlighting the economic case for immigration reform this summer, which may be the best short-term window that we have to get the kind of reform that will help the Midwest economy." Not a bad angle from which to pitch; urgency-selling is a long-established persuasion technique.[28]

Ruby goes on to contrast low-skilled immigrant labor in Clark County such as Dole lettuce-packers earning $16,000 per year with highest-skilled immigrants, cardiothoracic surgeons at Springfield Regional Medical Center earning $525,000 per year. He then lays out what look like reasonable workforce development, recruitment, and empowerment categories of interest, if indeed you are interested in that sort of thing. Ruby has clearly done his homework. All of his homework. But he would become a busy man. Such individuals are colloquially known to bite off more than they will chew.

A March 2015 MCIR summit and other planned activities didn't seem to materialize. Then Ortiz retired from Wright State. Nevertheless, Ruby continued his immigration advocacy work in Springfield but as far as I'm able to confirm, pivoted away from the formal research consortium model—but not from research itself.

> Departing Cedarville [University], Ruby founded Welcome Springfield (OH) a non-profit organization that serves immigrants while also encouraging community members to sign a "Statement of Support for Immigrants in Clark County" . . .
>
> While maintaining his position with Welcome Springfield, in the fall of 2014 he accepted the position as pastor of Central Christian Church in Springfield, which describes itself as a church where "we strive to keep Jesus at the center" and where "we care about justice" and "love our neighbors."[29]

Diana Daniels doesn't miss. I was surprised by how much of her Ruby account I was able to corroborate, which by now was not a surprise, including the temperature of Ruby's departure from Cedarville, which warms up the just-quoted interview.[30]

In a February 20, 2014, radio interview with a local NPR affiliate, Ruby, presented as a "longtime conservative advocate," laid out his case for regional immigration and the needs he believed must be met. While immigration reform during the second Obama term seemed "dead," Ruby positioned himself as a local reformer who could get the job done on behalf of his city where the federal government had failed:

> [I]mmigrants are twice as likely to start a business as a native-born American . . . There's some people that push back on immigration reform

> because they feel that immigration reform will take jobs away from native-born Americans. . . . [Immigrants] provide a type of labor that often . . . a lot of Americans don't want to do. But by their willingness to do that work, it creates jobs for other Americans. For example, 60 percent of the milk that is produced in America comes from farms that employ immigrant laborers. So while the actual person milking the cow may be an immigrant, someone has to build the facility. Someone has to transport the milk. Someone has to install the equipment, and all those jobs tend to go to people who are native-born Americans.[31]

He went on about the fears that certain Latin populations have over their immigration status and their unwillingness to invest their savings, much less put forward a down-payment on a house. Ruby spoke of his desire to help immigrants, Hispanics specifically, transition from renting to owning.

As illustrative as the dairy farming example is, it's simply untrue. Immigrants are not confined to milking the cow while everything else stays native-born. In reality, immigrants are over-represented (or at minimum heavily present) in construction, transportation, and related equipment/installation work. And first things first, dairies that employ immigrant labor around the time of Ruby's interview produced 79 percent of U.S. milk supply, not 60 percent (and the 79 percent number is outdated by almost ten years; do you think that number has gone up or down?).[32] Immigrants are over-represented relative to their 19 percent share of the overall U.S. workforce in the exact tasks Ruby laid out; some over-representation by immigrants in the skilled trades is higher than 50 percent of all jobs. And that's not all. "In 2024, foreign-born workers were more likely than native-born workers to be employed in service occupations; natural resources, construction, and maintenance occupations; and production, transportation, and material moving occupations . . . Among employed men, the disparity was especially great in natural resources, construction, and maintenance occupations—22.7 percent of the foreign born worked in this occupational field in 2024, versus 14.1 percent of the native born."[33]

There's wrong, and then there's being wrong as far as you can possibly be in the exact-opposite direction. That's Carl Ruby when he founded Welcome Springfield. But I'm not even going to pin that blame on Ruby. It looks as though to spread awareness for Welcome Springfield, he was simply following the organization's playbook. The WE Global Networking toolkit web page tells browsers "Use these statistics to help make the case for immigrants across the country."[34] Click the first infographic listed, and what do you see? The very statistic Ruby cited to open his NPR interview—immigrants twice as likely to start a business.[35] The WE Global Network and Welcoming America advise *explicitly* to make the case that "America's Future Is as a Nation of Immigrants."[36]

Read this direct from Welcoming America founder David Lubell, who comes highly praised by the World Economic Forum, acknowledging his partnership "with the [Obama] White House and the US Office of Refugee Resettlement on immigrant and refugee integration initiatives."[37] These key phrases appear in an early mission-critical Welcoming American white paper entitled *Stronger Together: Making the Case for Shared Prosperity Through Welcoming Immigrants In Our Communities*:

- " . . . welcoming our immigrant neighbors can be a force for economic growth . . . "
- " . . . find information on the key audiences likely to be moved by this messaging, and themes to explore in your communications work. You'll also find ideas about how to use data to support your argument . . . "
- " . . . focused on the economic benefits a community receives by welcoming immigrants . . . "
- " . . . business owners or Chamber of Commerce members . . . want to see a growing economy that brings new customers to their business and makes it easier to attract new talent. They may see immigrants as potential customers for their business or recognize how immigrant entrepreneurs have helped revitalize a downtown business district."
- " . . . More than many people, the local government officials and business leaders who make up the key audiences for this messaging are interested in the bottom line . . . "
- " . . . Telling the story of a . . . US-born business owner who relies on immigrant employees . . . is a great way of helping your audience understand . . . the economic benefits of welcoming immigrants to a community extend to the whole community."[38]

Why are there Haitians in Springfield? I think David Lubell just told us, but more than a decade ago.

The next time Welcome Springfield appeared in the news was December 20, 2014. Remember the Latino health survey Michael Cooper wrote about in 2015? This is that.

> A Clark County non-profit is starting a research study on health care access for immigrants. A grant from CareSource is paying for the project.
>
> Carl Ruby is with the non-profit support group Welcome Springfield, which helps immigrants living in Clark County. He says a high rate of Latinos in the county are uninsured, and that causes problems for them.
>
> "When immigrants are facing challenges in the area of their health needs they are less productive, less able to take care of their families, and encounter a variety of health related challenges," Ruby said. "The purpose of this study is to get a better understanding of that and hopefully that will lead to improvements in access."
>
> Tom Wahlrab of Welcome Dayton says the study is an attempt to find a solution by being proactive.
>
> "We don't need to wait and watch suffering any longer than we have to," he explained.
>
> The CareSource Foundation presented Welcome Springfield with a check for $15,000 for the study Thursday. The organization will start . . . its research in the spring of 2015.[39]

Look at that—open admission of "we," of collaboration between Welcome Springfield and Welcome Dayton, the latter of which is indeed a certified member of the official Welcoming program.

Anyway, Ruby got the money he asked for, and he put it to use. Say what you will about the man—I certainly will—but he delivered on that particular promise. Ruby's Prezi account seems to be set to public as of this writing (so I uploaded several slideshows to the Wayback Machine). The full results of the Clark County Latino Health Initiative are public.[40] One of his more interesting findings is that 61 percent of respondents selected undocumented status. The slide adds, "If the assumption that those who skip the question are likely undocumented their percentage would rise to 73%." The slideshow goes on to note where the polled population of Springfield's Latin people seek medical care, how often, and for what reason. I wonder who's paying for all of that. Another slideshow from 2016 indicates the Initiative had a "steering team" that met throughout the year, which included Chris Cook, then of Rocking Horse.[41]

Back to Welcome Springfield proper. Over subsequent years, the work of the non-profit Welcome Springfield would continue. I checked the Wayback Machine archives of www.WelcomeSpringfield.org and saw, month after month, cross-posts from Ruby's blog from over at www.CarlRuby.com, which now redirects to a Central Christian Church page about-us page. There remained up for some time a health-care resources page and a volunteer signup page. A Twitter account (@WelcomeSprgfld) appeared occasionally active until 2017 (the corresponding Facebook page is now deleted or otherwise unavailable).

Tweets in 2015 reported partnerships with the Warder Literacy Center and Iglesia Hispana Emanuel to provide English lessons.[42,43] "Several" internships were also available that year for Wittenberg University students.[44] There was (at least) one such intern named and described as having worked on Welcome Springfield's Latino Health Initiative program.[45] That's about it until the last tweet, in 2017, which reads, "During the last three weeks almost 90 people have signed a statement of support for immigrants posted on the [website]."[46] That pledge in full, by the way, reads like so:

> I want my community to be known as a place that welcomes immigrants of all backgrounds and faiths. While I recognize and support reasonable steps to ensure our national security, I also stand opposed to all forms of communication and policy that fail to recognize the human dignity and innate value of our global neighbors, especially those fleeing hardship, violence, poverty and persecution. We welcome these individuals to our community. We want elected officials at all levels to work toward bipartisan solutions that honor and respect the needs of the immigrants and refugees who have come to our nation and to Clark County, Ohio.[47]

By this time, you could sign the petition on the Welcome Springfield website or sign up there to volunteer as an English as a Second Language (ESL) tutor.[48]

Eventually, a "Clark County Latino Coalition" appeared with mentions on the site for regular meetings.[49] So, too, does an About page for Welcome Springfield, reading:

> **The Need**
> Like many midwestern communities, Clark County has faced dramatic population decline losing over 20,000 residents since 1970. We are projected to lose 10,000 more by 2040. Other than the "over 65" category, foreign-born residents are the only segment of Clark County's population that is growing. Census data predicts that this population will triple by 2050. The County hasn't developed a strategic plan to use immigration to build and revitalize the local economy.

The Opportunity
Clark County has an opportunity to establish itself as a regional leader in our proactive approach to equipping immigrants to enhance the culture and economy of Clark County.

The Mission
Welcome Springfield exists to help immigrants flourish in Clark County, maximizing their contributions to our culture and economy.

The Vision
Our vision is to see neighborhoods in Clark County revitalized as a new generation of immigrants purchase homes, start businesses, and enrich our culture. We exist to create a climate where that can happen.[50]

The last archived version of WelcomeSpringfield.org I was able to access is dated November 1, 2023. The domain expired until someone repurchased it on September 11, 2024.[51]

Like the consortium, the Welcome Springfield nonprofit appears not to have lived up to Carl Ruby's original vision. That said, he still had Central going for him and his community, and I'll take you there in an upcoming chapter.

Now what about that G92? Diana claimed its age as older than its recent official emergence. There are no records in the Wayback Machine, and the domain name www.springfieldg92.org was purchased on August 1, 2025. The first Facebook posts on the corresponding G92 social media page appear on August 2nd, featuring what appear to be various pro-Haitian, anti-ICE protests.[52]

G92

Remember Carl Ruby's 2014 WE Network bio mention, "immigration advocacy group called G92"? The first G92 Immigration Conference—the launch event that started the movement—was held in October 2011 at Cedarville University (where and when Ruby was Vice President for Student Life). It brought together students and leaders from twenty Christian colleges to advocate for immigration reform.[53]

That said, G92 *Coalition* was formed in 2025 by Ruby and other Springfield faith leaders to support the Haitian community. It reuses the same name and Biblical reference but seems to be organizationally distinct . . . yet ideologically identical. Even theologically so.

A sermon of Ruby's from back in April 2015 was entitled "Immigration? What would Jesus Do?"[54] His slides and notes, publicly available from Prezi, reference the ninety-two mentions, the foundational G92 metaphor, and its accompanying dictates to Bible-believers:

> God tells us to love immigrants.
>
> . . . God tells us to remember that we were once immigrants
>
> "He defends the cause of the fatherless and the widow, and loves the foreigner residing among you, giving them food and clothing." Deuteronomy 10:8
>
> "When a foreigner resides among you in your land, do not mistreat them. The foreigner residing among you must be treated as your native-born. Love them as yourself. Leviticus 19:34
>
> Our response to immigration will affect people who are our brothers and sisters in Christ
>
> God wants us to make sure their basic needs are met
>
> God tells us to make sure they are treated fairly and compassionately
>
> . . . Immigration is a Bible issue.
>
> 92 passages in Old Testament that refer to immigrants.
>
> The Tenth Commandment.
>
> Remember the Sabbath day by keeping it holy. Six days you shall labor and do all your work, but the seventh day is a sabbath to the Lord your God. On it you shall not do any work, neither you, nor your son or daughter, nor your male or female servant, nor your animals, nor any foreigner residing in your towns.
>
> In the New Testament God uses immigration as a metaphor for becoming a Christian.
>
> "Consequently, you are no longer foreigners and strangers, but fellow citizens with God's people and also members of his household." Ephesians 2:19
>
> The Big Idea: God loves immigrants and commands us to love them too.[55]

Have you ever heard the expression that people buy on emotion and justify with logic? I believe that's what took place here. I believe the flimsier reason set for welcoming immigrants to Springfield is the economics one. At best, it's misleading. What I've become convinced of in writing this book—and in meeting Carl Ruby in person, as you'll later see—is that immigrants have arrived in Springfield en masse because Carl Ruby's faith directs him so. In all my research and interviews, I've identified no one other individual—except for one—more passionate about this particular population than Carl Ruby.

He must feel good about himself. That's not an insult; it's the anxiety and uncertainty management theory you read about in the Introduction. "An increase in our self-esteem when interacting with strangers will produce a decrease in our anxiety . . . "[56] It stands to reason that you will esteem yourself pretty well if you believe yourself to be following the command of literally God to prioritize immigrants.

Even so, the consortium didn't seem to pan out. The earlier faith-based advocacy within academics didn't seem to either. Welcome Springfield as an effort didn't quite make a measurable dent either, as far as I can tell, although the Clark County Latino Health Initiative did seem to identify real problems and point to potential (more so hypothetical but eventual) solutions. But it's Ruby's church, Central, and now G92 that seem to finally be the vehicles with enough fuel for Ruby's full vision.

The Haitians are that fuel.

Haitian Flag Day

One of the very first public mentions of the Haitians of Springfield by Carl Ruby hails from May 19, 2023, the day after Haitian Flag Day, when the Haitian community "raised the Haitian flag along with the American flag at the Springfield City Hall plaza."[57] This tradition also takes place around other cities in America with Haitian populations.[58,59] Ruby wrote on his church website:

> Yesterday something happened that makes me especially proud of Springfield, the city where I serve as the pastor of Central Christian Church.
>
> Over the last year or so between 4,000-7,000 Haitian immigrants and refugees have settled in Springfield. Yesterday was Haitian Flag day and the City of Springfield worked with leaders in the Haitian community to help them come together to celebrate this important Haitian holiday. According to event organizers, Haitian flag day is a celebration of "a pivotal moment in [Haiti's] fight against slavery, as Haiti became the first country in the world to achieve independence through a successful slave rebellion." In the morning the City hosted an event where our new neighbors were invited to fly the Haitian flag downtown in City Hall Plaza. In the afternoon they made the Veterans Park Amphitheater available for the Haitian Flag Day Fair and Festival.[60]

Carl Ruby did it.

He won.

"The celebration is one way the city and community have started to welcome the rapidly growing Haitian population in Springfield and Clark County."[61] That same quoted news outlet, a weekly online news magazine called Hub Springfield, had published in December 2022 this loomer, excerpted:

> A surge in the number of Springfield residents from Haiti has resulted in an outpouring of language assistance and additional forms of help from the Springfield City School District and others who are trying to meet their needs.
>
> "Four years ago we didn't have a Haitian population," says Pamela Shay, director of federal programs for Springfield City School District.
>
> Now the district has about 200 students from Haitian families, many speaking Haitian Creole, French or Spanish, she says. In the past, the district has had two or three bilingual assistants who speak students' native languages in order to help in classrooms and communicate with parents. Now the district has nine, she says.
>
> . . . Shay says she has been told there are about 7,500 Haitians in the area. . . .
>
> . . . [Davah] Germain left Haiti due to political issues and moved to Miami, Fla., in 1985. The 63-year-old moved to Springfield at the urging of a friend. Word is spreading about the ease in which newcomers can find jobs, particularly in manufacturing.
>
> "They're coming to stay," he says. "They're coming to make Springfield their home."[62]

The Website

There's one last Ruby stone to overturn for now. Remember that non-profit status of Welcome Springfield? Are most of our deception concerns alleviated and corruption fears allayed? Perhaps all those Welcome Springfield documents appeared on Welcoming America websites and have remained there as some sort of careless mistake or perfectly reasonable oversight. Maybe it was one of those Wittenberg interns. Let's all give the benefit of the doubt.

That was my view until the YouTube algorithm suggested to me a video published on September 25, 2024, with only thirteen views upon my clicking.[63] "Springfield, Ohio, Resolution No. 5844 welcoming immigrants" is the title, published on a channel called "sezthem." It's simply the Resolution's text read aloud as it scrolls past with soft music in the background. But a link in the description below took me to an interesting place—to a document hosted by cloud-based filesharing site Dropbox. Towards the bottom of the publicly available document is linked a July 2024 *Springfield News-Sun* article which, at that time, seems to be one of the few available evidences of the Resolution ever existing in the first place, as it's not found on the City of Springfield website.[64] From the hyperlinked article:

> Several speakers asked city leaders [at City Commission meetings] to rescind the resolution adopted by city leaders in 2014 declaring Springfield a "Welcoming City" to immigrants. City officials have clarified multiple times Springfield is not a sanctuary city . . .
>
> "The Haitians are here legally, so I'd really like to ask that you don't call them illegal," [Springfield Fair Housing/Mediation Coordinator Nancy Flinchbaugh] said . . . "There is no immigration reform because the businesses don't want that."
>
> . . . [Welcome Springfield] was a nonprofit initiative, she said, not a government program. . . .
>
> "I watched when our Latin American neighbors first moved into the city and the county, working jobs our people did not want to do. . . . They were taken advantage of by employers and others, and they were the reason that Welcome Springfield was started," Flinchbaugh said.
>
> . . . [At the same meeting,] Clark County Combined Health District Commission Chris Cook [formerly of Rocking Horse] offered a presentation about health care related to Haitian immigrants.[65]

There it is again—a nonprofit initiative.

I clicked out of the *News-Sun* article and scrolled up within the Dropbox'ed document. I'd missed a Welcome Springfield web page. The link is an archived version of the page, found here: https://web.archive.org/web/20150204012007/https:/www.weglobalnetwork.org/welcome-springfield/

Do you see that? Welcome Springfield is now a web page —ON THE WE GLOBAL NETWORK. Not an attachment, not a document, not some other upload. Not this time. A full-page feature. Here it is:

> Welcome Springfield and the Midwest Consortium for Immigration Research are two new entities located in southwestern Ohio that are dedicated to the economic empowerment of immigrants in Ohio and throughout the Midwest. Welcome Springfield is a nonprofit 501(c)(3) organization devoted to helping Clark County Ohio attract and serve immigrants

and the businesses that employ them. Clark County is a rural county that has lost 20,000 residents (-13%) since 1970. Its principle city, Springfield was recently identified as one of ten fastest shrinking cities in America and is projected to lose nearly 10,000 more residents during the next 15 years. The Midwest Consortium for Immigration Research (MCIR) is a brand new entity devoted to providing academic research to communities like Springfield and Clark County throughout the Midwest. We desire to complement the efforts of organizations like Global Great Lakes by providing objective data on the economic impact of immigration, and by helping communities develop strategies to recruit immigrants and maximize their economic impact. MCIR will be based at Wright State University in Dayton, Ohio and will serve researchers and communities across the Midwest.

Resolution from the City of Springfield

Resolution #5744 declaring the City of Springfield, Ohio a community welcoming of immigrants, and immigrant-owned businesses.

Welcome Springfield in the Press

Dayton Daily News

Clark County proposal embraces immigrants

Dayton Daily News—February 8, 2014

Why was Welcome Springfield touted as a Welcoming America success story—including the listing of the City of Springfield Resolution on the Welcoming America website—if the City was officially "not part" of the network?[66]

I don't know what to tell you. Ask Carl Ruby. If he's not available, try Diana Daniels.

Now, there is the final matter of who is actually behind the WE Global Network. Whether Carl Ruby's Welcome Springfield is officially disentangled from their organization only on paper as a 501(c)3, which did seem to be so, it's no false claim to imply there was some benefitting one to another going on. So, again, who?

We read earlier that WE is a program of Welcoming America in partnership with Global Detroit, "a regional economic development and community development organization . . . [w]ith a focus on immigrants and global talent . . . [to] develop and implement inclusive strategies to drive the growth, revitalization and broadly shared prosperity of Detroit and across Michigan."[67] OK, that's something. Global Detroit lists their early funding partners and donors.[68,69] What about Welcoming America, the other WE Global Network parent program?

> Welcoming America is a nonprofit, nonpartisan organization that leads a movement of inclusive communities becoming more prosperous by ensuring everyone belongs. We believe that all people, including immigrants, are valued contributors and vital to the success of our communities and shared future.
>
> Through the Welcoming Network, we work to help communities develop the roadmap they need to create welcoming policies and share new approaches to inclusion to create an environment where everyone can truly thrive.[70]

I looked up direct, confirmed, and major funders of Welcoming America. I found a name. Grant records from 2011.[71] Foundation-level donations again and again and again.[72,73,74] Another grant, to Global Detroit.[75] Same name. Again. Then ever more to foundations that support the foundations behind the WE Global Network.[76,77,78,79,80] The same organization over and over, the money coming and coming:

The Open Society Foundations.

Do you know who that is?

George Soros.

Son of a bitch.

CHAPTER 5

TEMPORARY PROFITABLE STATUS

> "This situation isn't fair to anyone. Haitian refugees are being thrust into unnecessary conflicts with Springfield residents. Struggling residents are rightly resentful of refugees receiving more in assistance than what they qualify for as American citizens. The strain on the school system and hospitals is another point of contention. And the residents, who are barely getting by, feel frustrated and abandoned by the federal government. Again."[1]
>
> —Darvio Morrow

"It's a pretty wide culture difference," said **Glenda Bailey**. She's a working-class woman of a sturdy surety you'll find in every family this side of the tracks. She's given interviews.[2] She's gone viral.[3] But now, as we spoke in person, she's home. Glenda's seated on the concrete steps leading up to her working-class house in a working-class neighborhood of this working-class town. She, like other heritage citizens, has been here for a long time. I'm led to believe this people has earned the right to a city at peace.

But what many outsiders may not know about the heritage citizens of Springfield is that not all of them are white.

Glenda raised her hand as a manual visor as she looked down the sidewalk to her right. She had to talk over the barking of the dogs in her chain link–fenced yard. That wasn't a problem for Glenda.

"When the Hispanics on the corner moved here is when we first moved here," she said. "I went down and talked to them right away. I was a little bit wary of them, but once I got to know them, they've been good neighbors. They're good people. They're an older couple. . . . They're from El Salvador . . . I think they came here after a hurricane, so they probably have legal status."

I craned to get a slightly better look at the neighbor in question. A fine yard, well-maintained house, typical Americana for this part of the Midwest.

"They've helped us on occasion, and we've helped them," Glenda added. Of the wife of the family, she said, "She knows how much I love animals. She brought a dog, a Labradoodle puppy, to me, on a leash and she said, 'Do you want?' I'm like, 'Yeah!' So I took him, and he's been with my son and my son's wife ever since. They just love him."

My present thoughts began to back-fill with my own Latin-American relations in Ohio. You won't find anyone around here of any socioeconomic status who dislikes traditionally Central American cuisine. It's how we celebrate—we go to the Mexican restaurant. Be it Troy, Xenia, Huber Heights, Englewood, Kettering, or Springfield. Pick your town within the Greater Dayton Metropolitan Area, and we're the living spirit of then-citizen Donald Trump on *Cinco de Mayo* 2016—"I love Hispanics!"[4]

I studied Spanish at Sinclair and Wright State and began putting it to use in the aforementioned Troy, a neighboring city of Springfield one county over, in Miami. There was a small Latin foods market walking distance from where I'd moved after graduation—a rented bedroom in an old rotting house from the better days was all I could afford at the time. But I was surprised and pleased at the affordability of tropical selections from the southerly Americas. I spoke to the staff in Spanish. A few years passed, and when I took on a nonfiction ghostwriting project that sent me to South America—to Brazil, specifically—my Spanish came back well enough to get around. When I lived in East Dayton, I'd befriend and play soccer (*fútbol*) in the park with the neighborhood Central Americans who had literally arrived—in the past few *days*, in many cases—from Guatemala, Honduras, and Nicaragua. The first part-time caregiver I ever hired for the occasional help with my three children around the house is from Colombia. My kids loved her. We bonded over our mutual appreciation for the music of *Juanes*. She's also friends with the founders of my favorite restaurant in Beavercreek in Greene County—*La Colombiana*. She accompanied me on a *Dia de los Muertos* outing last Halloween as of this writing. She's Colombian, not Mexican, but the custom similarities allowed her to explain to my children what the various traditions meant from her perspective, as she's a native Spanish speaker. On the occasional Monday when I'm kid-free, I drop in locally for some casual *salsa* and *bachata* dance. Then from time to time, out and about in Cincinnati and Columbus, I'll meet Dominicans, Puerto Ricans, and Cubans; we're all different but different in noticeably compatible ways. It's hard to describe and yet it's not. I love Hispanics!

Glenda looked up the street and to her left now. "I don't know where they're from," she said of the house with the children playing in the front yard. I noticed them on the drive here. I'd been primed to fondly recall East Dayton.

"There's a couple of families living there," she added. "They're all young. Lots of kids. I did see a couple of chickens running around. I would love to have backyard chickens if my dogs would let them live. But they're all fairly new. So is the taco truck."

It was more a stand than a truck. Directly across the street from the home in question was a commercial building and fenced-in parking lot. Across this part of southwest Ohio, you see these pop-up Latin-American food stands. Particularly in Dayton, they're to be found by gas stations. The one that's across from my children's favorite walking-distance playground in Beavercreek on Thursdays sells the best kidney beans and rice dish you'll ever have. I think it's the beef broth instead of vegetable oil base. Proudly non-vegan.

We return to John Berry's Acculturation Hypothesis. When cultures come into sustained contact, their members tend to move toward one of four broad patterns—assimilation, separation, integration, or marginalization. Certain aspects of American culture, these anecdotes illustrate Latin-Ohioans having adopted. Assimilation. But also, there's the give and take, the overlapping interests, the collaborations, the mutual sharing and enjoyment—all voluntary from both parties. You make the best beefy beans and rice, I pay you well; you hold Latin dance classes, I show up to step about and swing around with the lovely young Latinas who also turn up. It's the cowboy in love with dark-haired Mexican beauty Feleena at Rosa's Cantina in "El Paso" by Marty Robbins, 1959. Integration.

More important than social, cultural, and dare I say racial compatibility, in my view is the relative lack of incompatibility. Where Midwest white American culture and carried-over Central American culture do not seem to align, we generally keep to our respective selves. You tend not to see Hispanics playing billiards in a smokey bar or drinking IPAs and playing Tuesday-night trivia. And you tend not to see heritage white citizens joining in the mass grill-outs where four generations take over two whole picnic shelters and blast their *mariachi*, *norteño*, *cumbia*. It's not that these are "wrong" from either perspective, it's just not "us," from either. These aspects of one another, we all tend to keep separate, and again, voluntarily so. That's equality. Free country, free association. But also, free disassociation.

Speaking of *mariachi*, do you know why so many Hispanic folk tunes feature the accordion? German, Czech, and Polish immigrants to Mexico in the early to mid-nineteenth century.[5] The Spanish word for polka is *polca*. It's integration all the way down. Sometimes peacefully. Sometimes violently (Remember the Alamo? Or Rosa's Cantina.). But here we are. Here we all are.

"Their culture is just so much closer to ours than Haitian culture," Glenda said.

I thought of Dominican-Haitian relations. Would Latin-Americans say the same of white culture as Glenda has of theirs?

"And Now You Have 15,500 Haitians"

Overall, Glenda's sentiments felt like those of Diana Daniels. It was she who had introduced me to Glenda in the first place. Let's now return to my extended exchange with Diana, and to her own immigration-influx timeline, which followed Carl Ruby's closely.

We have had immigrants and Mexican folks working the farms, the greenhouses, the strawberry patches up and up around Troy, the asparagus field and so forth around Sidney. They trickle in. As a teacher, I've been teaching in Springfield since 1991. I did not have a Hispanic or non-English-speaking student until I got to Kenwood, and that was in 2003.

However I met my first Mexican family . . . they were the owners of the *Los Mariachis*. Salt of the earth people. The Guterres,the Perez's, Espinosa's, all of them. I got to know them. Then going back and forth between three different schools, my job was to screen all kindergarteners coming into school. . . . I did not screen kindergarteners of Hispanic descent until 2006, and I screened two, and they belong to the Perez's, which they all worked at *Los Mariachis*. . . . Two here, one here, two here, one here, maybe three. . . . Normal immigration, normal progression.

[In] 2014, that changed. In 2014, I screened five. I didn't think that was much of an anomaly, but thinking back on it, that's when it started. . . . Then it went from five to nine to eleven. By 2019, I was screening twenty-six. In 2020 just before the pandemic, I screened twenty-nine. We had enough Hispanic-speaking kindergarteners. So, we do what's called a DAR, which is an algorithm you apply to the number of kids you have in your school and you extrapolate . . . [to] get the numbers for how many [adults]. So by 2020, 2019, we had 8,000 Hispanics here . . . in Springfield. That was the target population that was desired. They came across the border and were recruited to fill jobs at Dole, at Topre, and at various other manufacturing plants all over—we'll call it mid-Ohio—through the Midwest Immigration Consortium.

. . . I don't know if you were watching the news in [2020] in December right after the election and the masses of people that were coming up from up from Colombia, up to Panama, and up along the border. . . . [M]

(continued . . .)

asses of hundreds of thousands of people. What did they have on their shirts? . . . "Thank you, Biden-Harris."

[W]e have these massive caravans overwhelming the border, not crossing at ports of entry, just crossing the river. That's illegal if you don't come through the port of entrance. Doesn't matter, which is why my argument to Francois and Jean Pierre made sense to them because they were part of the caravan.

Fast forward to September '21 and now you have 15,500 Haitians. Why Haitians? . . . Haitians in particular get TPS as soon as they enter. From Mexico? They do not; [Mexicans] do not come with a $1 sign on their forehead . . . [Haitians] qualify for so many programs like SNAP. They qualify for EBT. They qualify for social security cards. They qualify for vouchers for transportation, vouchers for housing . . .

Diana had told me the OSINT perspective on why Haitian migrants had arrived in Springfield, the alleged signage directing them here from somewhere in very close proximity to the near-border humanitarian help and migration support sites of NGOs such as Catholic Charities.

That said, I don't recall those specific Biden-Harris T-shirts worn by members of the migrant caravans. Fox News did report multiple times on migrants wearing President Biden-themed T-shirts (or similar campaign-style shirts) at the U.S.–Mexico border and along migration routes in Central America.[6,7] These reports began in early March 2021. Am I about to now countersignal Diana's claims exactly as she said to the word and to the month and year? I am not. Know better by now.

Fox News correspondent Griff Jenkins interviewed a working-age male Haitian whose story is one like many thousands. The article fascinates; here is an excerpt:

> The migrant, who gave his name as Stevenson . . . and sported a Biden-Harris T-shirt, said his remaining family in Haiti has since passed away and that he is hopeful to find employment in the United States under [President Biden].
>
> . . . [M]any of the Haitian migrants appear to have come not directly from the turmoil-wracked Caribbean nation but from countries like Chile, Brazil and Colombia where they have lived for years.

> . . . "I would like to send a message for Biden because Haiti [has] nothing [in] jobs, and because of this and who is here," [Stevenson] said.
>
> "In [the] United States, I see opportunity—because I am young and I have no job or nothing," he added.
>
> . . . [T]he Mexican government has been somewhat "cracking down" on many of the illegal immigrants currently headed north from places like Chiapas without official documentation.
>
> . . . Former ICE Director Thomas Homan later told Fox News that of the 12,000 or more illegal immigrants released by the U.S. government with notices to appear and the like, as many as 89% lose their case at immigration court adjudication for one reason or another—and less than 10% of that group actually leaves the country.[8]

Stevenson saw opportunity. He took it. Wouldn't you?

TPS, CHNV, Form I-134A, TANF, and the Path to Entitlement

Temporary Protected Status (TPS) is a country-by-country program that gives temporary deportation protection and work rights to people from places hit by crises.[9] This is why Haitians, Nicaraguans, and Venezuelans had gotten it in recent years while Hispanics as a broad group don't qualify automatically.[10] Guatemala and Mexico have not received TPS designation, so those nationalities get no fast-track option; there's no special incentive or quick benefits label pulling them the same way as the Haitians.

Haitians in particular could access TPS more readily once they arrived (especially after the 2021 Del Rio wave), and once approved they got a work permit plus Social Security card right away; they could then qualify for SNAP/EBT food assistance, and other welfare if they met the usual income rules—stuff that's not automatic but became available thanks to the legal status TPS provided.[11,12] Nicaragua and Venezuela had similar TPS pathways earlier, though many of those designations had since been terminated or were tied up in court as of this writing.

When the program is active, TPS holders are eligible to apply for and receive a work permit (Form I-766 EAD) that lets them work legally anywhere in the U.S.[13] They'll file Form I-765 with the TPS application or later; once (if) approved, the EAD is valid for the length of the TPS designation (or court-extended period). For Haitians, a federal court stay in *Miot v. Trump* kept work authorization in effect even after the planned February 2026 termination.[14] Haitians didn't have to get the EAD to have TPS, but many (most?) would because it's the document employers needed.

Once migrants have a valid EAD from TPS, they can get a Social Security Number and card. They could request the SSN card right on the I-765 form when they apply for the work permit, and SSA will mail it (If they didn't request it on the form, they'd go to a local SSA office with EAD afterward). The social security card shows work authorization and is what employers use to report wages and taxes—it's directly tied to the EAD, not given automatically just for TPS.[15]

Showing work authorization? What's this now?

Yes, a Social Security card with a restriction stamp reading, *VALID FOR WORK ONLY WITH DHS AUTHORIZATION.*

This is very important; you'll see why later:

> Individuals whose employment authorization is dependent on holding a valid EAD (like parolees, or individuals with asylum applications pending) will be issued a "restricted" social security card with the words "VALID FOR WORK ONLY WITH DHS AUTHORIZATION" printed on it. . . . [S]everal categories of EAD-holders may only work if they have a valid EAD, and so long as the EAD is unexpired.
>
> In contrast, some individuals are eligible to work in the U.S. based on their immigration status, and independent of their EAD, like refugees and asylees. These individuals, as well as green card holders, are entitled to "unrestricted" social security cards, which will not bear the "VALID FOR WORK ONLY WITH DHS AUTHORIZATION" language. If and when an individual changes their status (for example, from asylum-seeker to asylee, or from adjustment applicant to green card holder), they may return to the social security office with their proof of status and request that a new, unrestricted card be issued.[16]

Again: Once someone gets a green card or other permanent status, they can request a new, unrestricted social security card without the stamped restriction. Very important.

Now, I should note that TPS migrants are not eligible for housing assistance via the Department of Housing and Urban Development. If they have or had indeed received such benefits, it's not from the federal government.[17] Also, there does not seem to be a standard federal transportation voucher program attached to TPS. No bus passes, relocation stipends, or ongoing travel aid from the government. Any transportation help must then come from local nonprofits, state programs, or one-time emergency services (like disaster relief), but it's not a guaranteed benefit of TPS itself.

There is this thing called sponsorship. Let's talk about that real quick. A U.S.-based supporter (e.g., an individual, family member, church, or Haitian community group already living in America when TPS was in effect for Haitian nationals) would have to have filed Form I-134A and promised to cover the arriving migrant's basic living needs (e.g., housing, food, etc.) for the full duration of the parole period, which was up to two years. USCIS Form I-134A explicitly says the supporter must "Describe the resources you plan to use or provide to ensure the beneficiary has adequate financial support to cover their basic living needs" for the entire parole time.[18] The main USCIS Humanitarian Parole page states: "The financial supporter is the individual who agrees to provide financial support to the beneficiary while they are in the United States for the duration of the parole authorization period."[19] And the Family Reunification Parole Processes page (which used the same rules for CHNV-style programs) confirms: "We will assess the collective ability to support a beneficiary… to ensure that they are able to financially sustain the [beneficiaries] they are agreeing to support for the duration of the parole period."[20]

In practice, this was exactly how Haitian individuals and support groups in America could have made the Springfield influx easier than it already was. Various groups could have stepped up as official supporters to sponsor. The pathway was filing the I-134A paperwork, providing enough income or resources for more Haitians, then helping the new arrivals with housing, jobs through staffing agencies, and daily needs once they arrived. An organized community sponsorship network could thus easily and systematically turn parole approvals into real resettlement en masse.

I know I'm throwing a lot of numbers and letters around. It's complicated. To quickly disentangle:

- **USCIS Form I-134A:** A one-time sponsor form (not a status). A US-based person, family member, or group files it online to promise they will financially support a parole beneficiary's basic living needs (housing, food, etc.) for the full parole period (up to two years).[21]
- **CHNV:** The humanitarian parole program (launched Jan. 2023, fully terminated May 2025) for Cubans, Haitians, Nicaraguans, and Venezuelans. To enter legally, you needed an approved I-134A supporter plus vetting. Once paroled, you got up to two years in America and could apply for a work permit (C11 EAD), but it was not TPS.[22]
- **TPS (Temporary Protected Status):** A completely separate, country-specific status (Haiti has had it since 2010, ending in 2026). It gives people already in the US deportation protection plus work authorization

> if their country faces ongoing crises. No sponsor or I-134A form is required. Haiti TPS was kept alive only by court order (*Miot v. Trump* case) until the Supreme Court ruled in Trump's favor.[23]

Bottom line, I-134A was the entry ticket for CHNV parole. TPS was a different, ongoing protection program; Haitians came for the CHNV, then applied for TPS. The key to it all was TPS; it's temporary protection from deportation (called "protection from removal"). While TPS was active, the U.S. government would not deport Haitians based on immigration status—even if they originally crossed the border illegally, entered without inspection, or overstayed a visa. "[TPS] applicants who are out of status or entered the United States without being inspected and admitted may apply for TPS provided that they meet all other eligibility requirements."[24]

Which means yes, you *could* be an illegal alien and yet still have had TPS. Nancy "Don't Call Them Illegal" Flinchbaugh is wrong.[25] Tom Homan is right.[26] But all worries go away for any Haitians with a real, authentic social security card.

There's something else. An anonymous member of the OSINT network sourced a whistleblower who reported a $15,000 transportation voucher a Haitian migrant had used to purchase an automobile from a Springfield car dealership. I later learned other heritage citizens knew about these $15,000 vouchers as that's how Haitians were acquiring the new-ish vehicles they've been crashing all around town.

By the way, several OSINT members took me on drive-alongs throughout the city where poles, signs, fences, and gates had been smashed, flattened, or otherwise dented. One anonymous citizen told me, "These iron gates survived for a hundred and fifty years. They couldn't survive Haitian driving."

One anonymous citizen investigated the various Haitian crashes and presented evidence to me that a number of local businesses were not reporting damage to commercial property to insurance but were instead being issued checks by a third party in exchange for neither calling City Police nor filing an insurance claim. Due to this particular individual's position, I deem his claim credible. Sadly, we now find ourselves with more questions than answers. That's Springfield.

Ironically, immigrant advocacy groups such as the National Immigration Law Center complain about welfare payout restrictions put in place or soon to be put in place by President Trump and a Republican Congress since Trump's electoral win in 2024.[27] I wanted to ask Diana, *Is that what you voted for?* I already knew.

Let's get to what comes next—the job opportunities Haitians like Stevenson came here to work. There's a catch. Diana caught it.

> [The employment Haitians get in Springfield] are all temporary jobs. They're not permanent. There are no benefits associated with them, and they don't need them—just because they're getting benefits from me and you and your tax dollars. That's how they get their money. But it does take time for them to get those funds, so there's a slush fund called a TANF fund. So if you come into the country and you're seeking asylum, and you're seeking TPS status—Temporary Profitable Status!—there is cash-money that can be given to you while you're filling out your paperwork. [Processing] takes anywhere from three to six months, and you can apply for it as many times as necessary until you get it, and it doesn't come out until you get your security card, your Medicaid card.
>
> Temporary Protected Status doesn't necessarily mean that you're not illegal. It's just protected until you go and have your case adjudicated ten years from now.
>
> Here's where temporary agencies come in. The temporary agency there was doing all the hiring and running all the vans. . . . So your first year or so, 2021, the Haitians [of Springfield] weren't driving. They were all being picked up in white vans and taken to these various factories. Those numbers were pretty manageable. We're going to say probably 8,000. Then, by word of mouth and temp agencies going to Miami and bringing up more Haitians, it exploded.

TANF stands for Temporary Assistance for Needy Families. It's a federal block-grant program created in 1996 that gives states money to provide short-term cash help to low-income families with children.[28] In Ohio, TANF is called Ohio Works First (OWF). It pays monthly cash benefits to eligible families (must have a minor child or pregnant woman, income usually under 50 percent of the federal poverty line, and adults must meet work requirements). Benefits are time-limited, up to thirty-six months in most cases, with a federal lifetime cap of five years). For example, a family of three in Clark County could get up to about $608/month in cash if they qualify.

Clark County Department of Job & Family Services made it easy for us and published a helpful Haitian benefits sheet, corroborating much of what Diana told me:

> Haitians (and others) with TPS or other appropriate status may be eligible for Temporary Assistance for Needy Families (TANF) benefits at the same

> level as other Clark County residents and must meet the same eligibility criteria. They may qualify for the Supplemental Nutrition Assistance Program (SNAP), TANF and Medicaid. Work Requirements are the same as all public assistance recipients.
>
> . . . Refugee Cash Assistance is similar in nature and eligibility to Temporary Assistance for Needy Families (TANF) but applies solely to individuals without children. The individual may be eligible for this program for a period of twelve (12) months from their date of entry into the United States. Catholic Charities has been contracted by the state to work with this group on assessment and work training.[29]

It looks fair, doesn't it? Haitians held to the same standards as heritage citizens, no? Well, no. Consider that money doesn't grow on trees. Suppose I have, for the sake of oversimplistic understanding, ten balls. There are ten children. One ball per kid. Now five more kids show up. They have no balls. Oh dear. Well, the rule is, each kid gets a ball. So . . . now it's each kid gets two-thirds of a ball. How does that work? It doesn't. Equal is unfair. Until the NGO-administrative complex enters. Grants, donations, fundraising. Completely unrelated, "It is difficult to get a man to understand something, when his salary depends on his not understanding it," wrote Upton Sinclair.[30]

Speaking of salary, throughout my time in Springfield, I became aware of a number of highly specific, years-long-persistent allegations against George Ten and his company, First Diversity Staffing. I'm not going to repeat those here—I'll do that in Chapter 6!

Back to Diana. It was at about that point the Bob Evans coffee got cold and the subject had run its course. For now. We detoured into other issues presented to Clark County that impassioned Diana, such as the threats of data centers, solar farms, and developer sprawl. Tax breaks for those who could afford it logically become tax hikes for those who can't. I noticed her speak with the same tangible protective spirit over the farmland and the water supply as the people. Perhaps when heritage citizens like Diana say that Springfield is home, they actually mean it. They mean Springfield is worth protecting: it's home. *Their* home. How do you protect your home?

> . . . We did not need to be in a situation where we are at odds with each other, where we have a definitive demarcation between pro-Haitian and anti-Haitian. . . . I sat on the fence for a long time, and now, you know what? Let's just do a complete do-over. You haven't been here for twenty years? Then

go the fuck back. Try it again. Don't care. Don't give a fuck . . . There was an opportunity in 2023, for sure, and certainly in 2024 to have a legitimate conversation as to what . . . we were feeling as citizens, what was impacting us the most, and what could be done about it, for example. It's not necessarily black and white; it's culture. So, you have people from another culture who have invaded your space and are given preference over you. But there was a way around it. If we had had an opportunity to say, "Listen, we're tired of seeing this; we're tired of seeing this. This is what needs to change. No Haitian Flag Day." That was . . . last straw in 2023 when city government raised the Haitian flag over city hall.

. . . [For every Haitian] that comes in, money is going to change hands. If there's a temp agency, money is going to change hands . . . If there's people renting them out, everywhere there's . . . money involved, OK? So it's a moneymaking scheme. It's all about the money. They're making hand over fist. There's not enough jobs for that many people coming. There never has been, and there never will be. . . . You pay [Haitians] less. You don't have to pay them benefits. Done deal. Great for your business, bad for America.

Later that week, Diana introduced me to a public television producer who had interviewed her around the time of the various pet disappearances and subsequent viral stories in September 2024. This individual, who spoke with me under the condition of anonymity due to fear of employment termination, described Diana, accurately, as "having compassion" for the Haitian people. If that's not clear, let it be now, as she concluded our time together how we began—how, in fact, Haitians made their way to Springfield, Ohio.

The Darién Gap

[A]ny migrant from South America had two choices. You could either come through Colombia to the Darién Gap, [and] you could cross the Darién Gap via . . . the Gulf of Yucatán by boat and then still land in Panama, which is costly, or you could hire a guide and be guided through the Darién Gap. There is no road. . . . It's a jungle . . . with bugs and snakes and pumas

(continued . . .)

and panthers and things that eat you. And if you die, there are no remains because the animals consume it.

I'll tell you a story. What really brought home to me the fact that there are two sets of victims is this story from 2023, right after the bus accident. So, I was in the bank and there at the time—and now it's gotten better—at the bank was a huge line, mostly Haitian. I got in line, and there were two gentlemen behind me, and they were playing Calypso music. . . . They were kind of giggling, as guys giggle. Laughing. And so I'm standing there. I'm a phys-ed teacher, I love music. I love to dance . . . I knew he was looking at me, but I didn't catch him. He didn't catch me looking back at him until this one time he was looking down and I looked up at him and smiled. . . . He just started laughing. And lo and behold, I said, "I love music."

He said, "Me too."

. . . [H]e spoke very good English . . . I forget his name. I think it was Ruby George. . . . [W]e were talking, and . . . I asked him, "Are you—are you Haitian?"

"Yes, and so is my friend."

I said, "Are you from—are you from Haiti?"

. . . I said, "Where are you from?"

He said, "From Brazil."

And of course, by that time, I knew about the Darién Gap, and I made the biggest mistake of my life.

. . . I asked him, "How long have you been here?"

"I've been here about two years."

Which would coincide with him crossing at Del Rio.

. . . I asked him, "Did you . . . come through Del Rio?"

And he said, "Yes."

And this whole time, he had a very animated, happy kind of face. And I made the biggest mistake of my life.

I said, "Did you come through the Darién Gap?" And his friend immediately started to cry. A grown man.

I looked at him and I said—I forget how I said it but I said, "Where's your family?"

"I left them. In the Darién Gap."

He left his wife. And his child. They died on the way through the jungle.

By this time, I'm crying, he's crying . . . and I said, "What are you going to do?"

And he said, "Well, I have family back in Brazil . . . I want to go back to Brazil. But I signed a contract."

I think he worked at Topre . . . because he spoke good English. . . . [H]e signed a contract with Topre that he could not leave his job and he had to stay for another year. "I didn't know that when I signed that paper. If I had, I wouldn't have signed it."

. . . [M]aybe he signed it without even reading it. Just happy to get a job.

So, the Darién Gap. . . . You come through Colombia to get to Panama. . . . [S]o when you get to the beginning of the Darién Gap, you have to hire a guide. You can't do it yourself. . . . [T]he journey is not easy. You can get trains and lorries and stuff, but when you get to the Darién Gap, there is no road. None. You walk jungle trails. So when you get to the Darién Gap and you have money, you hire a guide, you and your family, you and your wife, your twelve-year-old daughter, and maybe an eight-year-old son. It takes a couple of days, it takes about a week, depending on how fast you travel.

So you have a couple of guides with you taking you through the Darién Gap. So, maybe two or three days in, you don't know your way back, you don't know your way forward, you wake up and the guy is gone. They've left you there on purpose. . . . [S]o, you paid this guide, and . . . they've left you in the middle of the jungle. Another group of guides comes up and says, "Oh, we'll guide you." Meanwhile, you've spent all your money on the first set of guides, and you have nothing else. The guide will make a deal with you.

"I'll lead you through the Darién Gap, but I'll take your daughter." That's how it works.

[S]o the kids that you are now sacrificing are part of those kids, that 360,000 that are unaccompanied minors sent across the border. . . . Taken to make even more money. Take your money to take you through, dumps you off, another set comes through, makes a deal for your daughter, and then they traffic her across the border. Evil, evil people. . . . [T]hat's . . . the misery of open migration without control. That's why it has to stop . . . It's people like [Carl Ruby] that encourage it, that have no idea what has happened to these people, that you are encouraging, what they had to go through to get here and what happened to their families. . . . It might feel good, but if you're indentured . . . you're never going to get hired on.

(continued . . .)

> . . . [T]ell that story. Not only Springfield. But the whole idea of open migration that has literally killed a generation, enslaved a generation. That's just another way to say slavery. But that's what people don't understand about—or don't get—when it might look good on the surface for us to have migrants and they're working and all that, but they're not making what they should make. They're not able to get ahead. If you take away all those government subsidies . . . they won't be able to survive only making $11 an hour. . . . It's just another welfare class.

Diana also brought up tax breaks for temporary employment agencies who hire those with TPS. She seemed to be referring to the Work Opportunity Tax Credit (WOTC), "a federal tax credit available to employers for hiring and employing individuals from certain targeted groups who have faced significant barriers to employment."[31] Those groups include ex-offenders, US military veterans, and those on SNAP and TANF, among others. "[T]he maximum tax credit is generally $2,400." Temp agencies routinely use WOTC for any qualifying hires across their workforce. They are among the largest users of the credit because they place many otherwise disadvantaged workers.[32]

Trafficked, Exploited, and Missing

The aforementioned perils do not end where the Darién Gap does. Oscar El Blue published on September 29, 2022 a short video entitled "Canoe capsized, 3 are missing," depicting an incident further along in the journey. The description, unedited, reads:

> According to the Tribuna, Honduras, Coyotes divert migrants from a main highway with intentions to take more money from them. They have them spend the night in a house and pay passage through the river Guayambre en El Paraíso . This time around 10 Haitians paid $15 each and due to turbulant waters the canoe capsized. Three are missing, one of them a toddler, who might be the child of this woman who made it to shore.[33]

The video shows the actual capsizing followed by a jumpcut to a black woman on the ground in the throes of raging grief. Unedited text on screen side by side with the clip explains:

> Women off camera is saying that woman lifts her shirt to show her cesarean section scar where her baby was born.
> Woman off camera says it has been about two hours
> Woman off camera tells Haitian women, "no, you can't go, you can drown"
> Man tells Haitian woman, "No you can't cross"[34]

Remember what the Dominican said. Remember what the Dominican said when someone died. Diana:

[My critics say] I'm the biggest racist of all, but yet I help somebody like Francois and Jean Pierre leave so that I can sponsor them to come back . . . [They] wanted to be American citizens desperately. However, under TPS status, you cannot be naturalized. So, promises made and none of them kept.

Fast forward. Where are they now? I encouraged them to go ahead and go back to Brazil or whatever country of their choice. They did not want to go back to Haiti because Haiti is not their home. They've been in Brazil, you know, since their teens. So home for them and family for them was in Brazil . . . oth of them crossed the Rio Grande at Del Rio in 2021, which makes them illegal, but they're protected by TPS. That does not mean they are not illegal. TPS is just a stay. If you have crossed the border anywhere across the Rio Grande, regardless of whether or not you were given TPS status, you are here illegally. Because when they crossed in 2021, it was a rushed process. They were never vetted. They were never processed. . . . [T]hey're here under TPS. No TPS? Then you are here illegally. If you have completed all of your paperwork for asylum-seeking? Well, 93 percent are rejected. They did not want to take that chance for being rejected because they crossed the Rio Grande at Del Rio in September of 2021 and were rubber-stamped in. They were not vetted, OK? They were never processed. They were just allowed to walk over by whoever was there.

So my convincing them to go back was over the chances of them getting picked up. You cannot seek asylum in the United States if you had crossed another country where you could have stayed. Colombia. Crossed Panama. They crossed Mexico. In one of those four countries they could have stayed in, but they went to the border, which means their asylum petition is [going to be] denied. You get deported, and you can never come back.

(continued . . .)

> [W]e had a great at-length conversation. Understand: Both of them speak very good English.
>
> "Now, go back to Brazil. Take the—" [I told them.] At the time, it was only $1,000. They'd already saved a bunch of money because they all lived together in the apartments right next to my business where I work. So they had enough pocket money and $1,000 in plane tickets brought them back to Sao Paulo. They were both from Rio, but they went back to São Paulo . . . $1,000 in Brazil is like we have a million. Their families are all there.
>
> The intent is this: They know my email, they know my shop phone number, and when they're ready to come back, all they have to do is call me and let me know, and then I can sponsor them. Then they get to come back . . . They will honor that. Then they can work on being citizens. Those are the kind of people we want because they wanted to assimilate. They wanted to learn the language. They did learn the language, but they were being used and abused, but they wanted desperately to be American citizens.
>
> . . . It becomes disheartening to know that there were people who thought so little of me and people like me that we needed to be replaced, all for some money and to fit an ideology. People like Carl Ruby.
>
> . . . If you are actually interested in helping the Haitians, why aren't you helping them actually become citizens by sending them off so you can sponsor them? You should be telling them, "This is how you get to be a citizen. If you really want them to be a citizen, go back to where you came from, which is Brazil, Chile, Haiti, or any other country of your choice. You can pick the Solomon Islands. Go to the Solomons where it's warm . . . [W]hen you want to come back, I'll sponsor you." And when all this all blows over two or three years from now, and these Haitians . . . who have not reestablished themselves where they've gone back to and want to come back, whether it's Springfield or any other community, you sponsor them. Then there you go.
>
> . . . When I heard from Francois twice, one was, "We arrived good" . . . and then about a month later, "Found my family. Living like a king."

There you go.

On September 22, 2024, concurrent with the internationally viral claims of cats and dogs, a man named Carlos Arellano reached out to me privately over Telegram from a now-deleted account. Carlos is a former unaccompanied minor transportation specialist who became a whistleblower for what he would describe in interviews as nothing less than a nationwide human trafficking program involving "300,000 unaccompanied children the Biden Administration lost or placed with unvetted sponsors."[35,36] Things would change; within the first six months of the Trump administration, "more than 59,000 of the backlogged reports have been analyzed and processed, resulting in more than 4,000 investigative leads, including fraud, human trafficking, and other criminal activity."[37] By February 2026, then-border czar Tom Homan announced that more than 145,000 such children had been found.[38] That said, his comments focus on locating the children for safety checks and protection, not on how many—if any—were deported or returned to their home countries and parents.

Carlos shared with me a number of personal experiences he had, eyewitnessing what in my view amounts to a child migrant policy of holding children in concentration camps and then placing children with credibly accused if not registered, offending pedophiles for purposes of child sexual abuse, labor exploitation, and overt slavery—within the United States.[39] Other whistleblowers concurrent with Carlos's accounts to me and others tell of a similar situation.[40,41]

I do not believe it's possible to overstate the sheer amount of human suffering caused as a direct—if not intentional, in my view—result of the Biden-Harris mass-migration policy, which left the United States with a wide-open border and without anything like safe and effective vetting.[42] Within weeks of the Trump administration's ascendancy, it all stopped. It just stopped.[43] I'm reminded of the Staples Easy Button.[44] Why hadn't the prior administration pressed it? How dark is it when you realize you have to ask the opposite question: *Why would they?*

From a joint hearing of the 118th U.S. Congress on Tuesday, November 19, 2024, two weeks after Donald Trump's presidential victory: "TRAFFICKED, EXPLOITED, AND MISSING: MIGRANT CHILDREN VICTIMS OF THE BIDEN-HARRIS ADMINISTRATION":

> As the [Biden] administration's border crisis continues to spiral out of control, the number of unaccompanied minors arriving at the Southwest Border has increased greatly, turning the situation at the border into a devastating humanitarian catastrophe. In fact, the Biden-Harris administration has encountered nearly 530,000 alien children at the border to date. In comparison, the Trump administration had less than half that number over the same period of time.
>
> *(continued . . .)*

. . . These children show up with arbitrary phone numbers and addresses scribbled on their arms as if they're, like, packaging arriving at someone's warehouse or doorstep. Some children that arrive at the border appear to be drugged, preventing law enforcement authorities from properly questioning them about those they're traveling with.

This is outrageous, and it's an affront to the very core principles that form the morality of any decent nation.

Certainly, Americans should not accept this moving forward.

The purpose of this hearing is to put some hard facts on the table so that we can work together on both sides of the aisle and address actual solutions.

The Biden-Harris administration has stated that they have the most humanitarian border policies in history, yet we witness these horrors that are happening, and there's nothing humanitarian about enabling criminal cartels to exploit, abuse, and profit from vulnerable children.

Once the children enter the United States, Customs and Border Protection, the CBP, and Immigration and Customs Enforcement, ICE, and Health and Human Services, HHS, are tasked with their well-being and safety. Initially, CBP works to process and screen those children once they're encountered at the border. Next, HHS works to identify and place them with a potential sponsor. Finally, ICE works to ensure they follow through with their immigration court proceedings.

That's how it's supposed to work. However, those agencies do not have the capacity or resources to handle the sheer number of children who have crossed the border in the last 4 years.

Compounding this crisis, the administration is not thoroughly vetting potential sponsors. This is a serious weak link in the chain.

According to information leaked to the media, Health and Human Services reportedly lost contact with more than 85,000 unaccompanied children between 2021 and 2023. Now, think about that. That's the size of major cities in America. In my district, that would be about the size of Lake Charles, Louisiana. Eighty-five thousand children that are stated and known to be lost, and this was a year and a half ago.

We are appalled that our Government has neglected its primary duty to protect the safety and well-being of those children placed in our care. It's entirely unacceptable that the current administration has allowed human traffickers to take advantage of this on-going border crisis. We have a responsibility to our Nation to fight against human-trafficking horrors and to find and rescue the children . . . that are currently missing.[45]

I have a question. How many of these children are Haitian?

The very week I wrote this chapter, a number of posts viralated across social media on both sides of the Haitian debate. One such post, on 𝕏, criticized ongoing efforts to keep in place Temporary Protected Status for the estimated 350,000 Haitian nationals living within the United States. The post reads:

> >This is 3% of the entire population of what is arguably the most dysfunctional state in the world.
> >Job openings in the US are at their lowest level in 8 years
> >At least 50% of these people are on welfare.
> In what universe is keeping these people in our country a net benefit to Americans?[46]

The 𝕏 user reads the situation completely wrong.

Haitians aren't here for Americans' benefit.

They're here for theirs.

CHAPTER 6

KING GEORGE

> "Another mark of a tyrant is that he likes foreigners better than citizens, and lives with them and invites them to his table; for the one are enemies, but the [o]thers enter into no rivalry with him."[1]
>
> —Aristotle

If you haven't received a cease-and-desist letter from the attorney of George Ten's First Diversity Staffing, you are not a big deal in this town. The letters I was shown, targeting various concerned citizens from Faruki PLL of Dayton and Cincinnati, had the usual arousing legalese, such as a given citizen being placed "on notice" that the firm will now "demand" various "immediate steps" to "remove" alleged "false and defamatory" content or else "legal action" will occur. So exciting.

I asked each citizen in receipt of such a letter if they deleted whatever rubbed George Ten's fur the wrong way.

"No," I heard every single time.

"Did they take you to court?" I would ask them.

"No," again, but with laughter.

The full extent of George Ten's involvement with the Haitians of Springfield is rivalled only by that of Central Christian's Carl Ruby, to whom two chapters in this book will have been devoted. The locals tell me Mr. Ten is known citywide as "King George," due to both the hard and soft power he wields. But if you read his profile-meets-exposé in *The Springfield News-Sun*, which reads both like a "hit piece" but also his legal-counseled dismissal of all claims therein, what you will find is an embattled George Ten asserting he's doing his best to serve employers of a city whose longtime residents are embittered they did not get the good-paying jobs the Haitians earned right out from under them.

Springfieldopoly

The *Springfield News-Sun* ran a number of lines on the First Diversity story—George and wife Rachael denied labor-trafficking, underpaying, or mistreating Haitians in any way; a First Diversity spokesman said he believed such exploitation had been done but not by First Diversity; then-Ohio Attorney General Dave Yost would neither confirm nor deny criminal investigations into the matter; a "large percentage" of First Diversity subcontracted workers are Haitian; and that word-of-mouth brought additional waves of Haitians to Springfield due to cheaper housing in Springfield relative to other regions with Haitian enclaves, specifically Florida. Nevertheless, excerpted from the *Sun*:

> . . . "Citizens have brought forward complaints about First Diversity during city commission meetings in the context of immigration," said city spokesperson Karen Graves. "The context of the complaints related to First Diversity being involved in bringing the immigrants to Springfield."
>
> These complaints include accusations that staffing agencies like First Diversity were bringing immigrants into the community to exploit cheap labor, and that Ten owns run-down rental properties housing large numbers of Haitians who are being charged high rental rates. One city resident, Mark Sanders, has raised concerns about numerous addresses to city commissioners at meetings for months, with some properties being owned by Ten.
>
> . . . "An ongoing investigation is being conducted with the appropriate law enforcement agencies looking into matters of human 'job' trafficking and other potential criminal activities involving staffing agencies in our community," Graves said.
>
> . . . George Ten says his companies had a minor role in bringing Haitians to Springfield, but said they are not busing people in as people have alleged for some time.
>
> First Diversity, which is headquartered in Springfield and owned by George Ten, employs an estimated 1,800-2,000 people at a time.
>
> . . . "They really want to work," [Ten] said, contrasting that with other workers who he said engage in "hard living," including drinking, drugs, excessive partying and only showing up to work a few days a week. He said his turnover rate is much, much lower than most staffing agencies.
>
> . . . George Ten said a number of Haitian immigrants followed his company to Springfield from Indianapolis around 2018-2020 after First Diversity closed an account there.

. . . First Diversity is an early stop for many.

Rachael Ten said First Diversity does not sponsor Haitian immigrants to enter the U.S. or come to Springfield, but it does write letters of recommendation for employed Haitian immigrants to present to immigration officials to improve their chances of sponsoring their own loved ones.

. . . George Ten created the company Ten Enterprises LLC in 2015, according to state business records. Clark County property records show Ten Enterprises owns 48 properties in the county.

George and Rachael Ten said this amounts to 69 rental units.

. . . The Tens aren't the only ones criticized for renting to Haitians. Springfield Mayor Rob Rue has been accused of profiting off immigrants because he owns multiple rental properties . . . near his business, Littleton & Rue Funeral Home and Crematory . . .

"I've never evicted anybody; I've never sought to really even be in the landlord business, but I wanted to be able to control those properties," Rue said. "That was the only reason."

. . . Officials with local social service agencies say they have heard reports of Haitians being exploited, packed into too-small apartments with no water, electricity or heating. But they have not publicly identified specific landlords.

This is one area the city is investigating with its Immigration Accountability Response Team probe launched last year.

. . . Venel Scylla lives in a Ten Enterprises home on Shaffer Street with two other adult Haitians. The rent is $500 per bedroom, he said, with all utility costs included.

. . . Like other Haitians have said, once Scylla arrived in Florida, he heard that Springfield had jobs, so he drove with others up here.

. . . Elancia Dorce Simon lives with her family in half of a double on Shaffer Street in another Ten Enterprises property. She pays $750 per month in rent.

Simon arrived in Springfield in March, making the move after a cousin who was already here suggested she come.

. . . "I was taking English classes but they had to stop them because of all the chaos, which was frustrating because I'm trying to learn English," Simon said.

. . . [Ten] said [First Diversity] does not take money out of its workers' wages. For the sake of easy math, he used the example of an employee paid

$15 an hour—he said First Diversity charges the company an additional $2.50 an hour for it to fund its own business.

> To help employees who do not have transportation, First Diversity contracts with third-party companies to shuttle workers to and from work, George Ten said. He said the vans are not authorized to pick people up for any other purpose on behalf of First Diversity.
>
> The Haitians who work for First Diversity are all in the country legally, Rachael Ten said, and the company requires I-9 forms, which determine if an employee is eligible to work in the U.S. All employees receive W-2 tax forms and are paid through direct deposit or by check if necessary, she said.
>
> . . . In a statement to the News-Sun, former state representative Kyle Koehler—who is running for a state Senate seat representing Clark and Greene counties—said: "I am shocked that much of what we are experiencing has been orchestrated by this employment agency who never informed our community leaders about the workers they brought to Springfield."
>
> "While profiting off the labor of thousands of Haitians, this temp agency failed to inform our schools, our healthcare providers, our local health department or really anyone for that matter," Koehler said. "These types of actions bring into question whether they are operating with the best interest of our community—but even more importantly, the interest of the impoverished individuals they seem to be taking advantage of."
>
> . . . George Ten said employing Haitian immigrants has led to the "resurrection" of the city and that "history will reflect" this.
>
> "Diversity is always good: Diversity of thinking, diversity of culture, diversity, you name it," George Ten said. "I think it makes the outcome better, the end product always better."[2]

A reason Mr. Ten seems to draw so much ire around town is the widespread perception among heritage citizens that temporary employment offered to Haitian migrants was not presented to the local economically distressed population. From Laura Rosenberger, member of the Clark County Board of Elections:[3]

> [Area employers are] not advertising to the local population, so there's preferential treatment through . . . First Diversity Staffing to provide the opportunity for work to the [TPS] immigrants that are coming in. . . . [T]he locals here . . . feel like they're not getting the opportunity to even apply for those jobs because they're not seeing the jobs advertised to the local community, and they would like to take those jobs if they could get them, but

> they feel like they're being slighted by the staffing services and the corporations that are here. We do have qualified people and people who do want to work, but they're being displaced.[4]

That's one reason among many. But the second-chiefest among them has to be the real estate situation. Britain's *The Guardian* has also shown a spotlight on America's own King George, specifically his investment property portfolio and practices:

> Conversations with several Haitian workers, legal representatives and community leaders in Springfield found that First Diversity Staffing, a temporary staffing agency, has played a key role in securing employment for Haitian and other immigrant laborers from Central America to work at distribution facilities, warehouses and farms in the Springfield area.
>
> All the while, a company called Ten Enterprises, whose registered agent is a person named George Ten, has been buying up dozens of properties in and around south Springfield, where the majority of the city's Haitian population lives.[5] George Ten is also the CEO of First Diversity Staffing.
>
> All 48 properties owned by Ten Enterprises—typically smaller and older residential homes—were purchased since 2021, coinciding with the height of the Haitian immigration wave to Springfield. By March of that year, a USA Today report found that Springfield had the fifth "hottest" housing market in the US, despite having a median home price of just $145,000.[6]
>
> While owning a large number of properties is perfectly legal, and landlords say renovating and renting out houses contributes to the city's tax base, many Springfield residents have taken to public forums to ask that property companies help contribute to the increased costs associated with managing an influx of new residents.[7]

I couldn't have said it better (worse?) myself. But there is someone who can—a woman named Asra Nomani. Who already did. We spoke during my writing of this book, but her previous work on King George more than does the talking for her, echoing the *News-Sun* piece in key ways but expanding as well with her own perspective. Now senior editor of investigations at Fox News Digital, Asra wrote a two-part series for the *Jewish Journal* covering Springfield in which metaphors for the board game *Monopoly* are the recurring theme.[8] Part II simultaneously previews, summarizes, and concludes the entire saga of the Ten empire:

> I have learned that federal and state investigations into alleged human trafficking of Haitian workers by First Diversity Staffing Company LLC in Springfield, Ohio, have widened to include the alleged theft of Social Security numbers and the identities of American citizens, along with wage, tax and immigration fraud. Over the past five years, I've also learned . . . [George Ten] transformed First Diversity into an empire with an estimated $180 million in gross revenues, in a business strategy the company called "Springfieldopoly" . . . Springfield's city planner, Bryan Heck, was warned as far back as 2019 that George was using First Diversity to allegedly traffic Haitian migrant workers from Florida to Ohio in a corrupt scheme that profits off the desperate. Heck said he doesn't remember such a meeting. In a charm offensive, George and his top leaders invited me into their offices, where they have a room they call the "Monopoly Room." They deny any wrongdoing.[9]

Here are a few of Asra's startling finds.

A Spider's Web

In Part I, Asra reported the following:

- George Ten lives in a $1.35 million luxury mansion with a wine cellar in an upscale neighborhood.
- FBI files document "King George's" nearly 50 Springfield properties (held via an LLC) and the systematic transport of Haitian migrants there in rundown unmarked white vans from Florida and elsewhere, housing them in squalid conditions.
- Ten controls at least ten shell companies used to move money, property, and assets such as luxury cars.
- Unmarked white vans linked to Ten and First Diversity regularly transport Haitian migrants to jobs (including at Dole); migrants steadily enter First Diversity during business hours.
- George functions as a domestic labor "mule," moving vulnerable migrant workers across state lines for profit.
- "In June 2019, employees of First Diversity were directed to stop hiring locals and focus on recruiting Haitian migrants. . . . "
- A worker paid about $50 for van rides to/from work; one van dropped a man with three trash bags of belongings at a rundown house.

- Migrants were packed into dilapidated houses owned by Ten's companies (three "purchased on the same day, Sept. 10, 2020, for $20,000, $28,000 and $32,000"); these houses were overcrowded, often shared in shifts, with some Haitians carrying all belongings in backpacks.
- "One Haitian man . . . was picked up by a driver for one of Ten's vans on a street corner near a Winn-Dixie grocery store in Immokalee, Florida. After the long journey to Springfield, he was dropped off at a rundown home on Rice Street, infested with cockroaches. He soon found work through First Diversity at Jefferson Industries Corporation, earning $12.50 an hour; he didn't know how much George skimmed off his wages. The home he lived in had no working heat, and he bought an electric heater to survive the cold Ohio winter, the heater barely heating his room."[10]

Amid the desperation, Asra also found hope. She wrote in Part I how she witnessed a local truck driver, Christopher Merrill, with social media influencer Nick Sortor engage in a few bits of heated drama with Margery Koveleski in the parking lot of the Haitian Support Center. Margery, Asra said, is the first known Haitian-American to have moved to Springfield, "arriving here from New York City with her husband and family for a simpler life after the 9/11 attacks. Her mother had emigrated to New York from Haiti years earlier. . . . When the influx of Haitians arrived as migrants, she started helping them as a translator and de facto guardian angel, one time saving a mother and her child from the traps of trafficking that had become sexual exploitation."[11] In any case, what began as a dispute ended in a hug shared by Christopher and Margery.

"It Just Went Vertical"

Asra's findings continue, in Part II:

- A young Haitian-American discovered the IRS reported approximately $20,000 in earnings from First Diversity, though she worked only two and a half weeks as a translator; her Social Security number was allegedly stolen and used for someone else.
- In early 2021, roughly a dozen Haitian workers stormed First Diversity demanding unpaid wages for sandwich-factory shifts in freezing conditions, showing time-card photos as proof.
- "By late 2019, the warnings [about George Ten] also reached Mike McDorman, the longtime president of the Greater Springfield Chamber of Commerce, and he similarly took no action."

- An investigation into illicit business practices and potential human trafficking began in September 2023.
- On October 25, 2023, Bryan Heck issued a formal request for additional support and resources to the Ohio Bureau of Criminal Investigation.
- First Diversity claimed 1,800 to 2,000 temporary workers averaging 44 hours and $1,000/week; the arithmetic implies far more overtime or workers than reported.
- "$17 x 40 hours = $680. The average pay of $1,000—$680 = $320. Overtime is time-and-a-half, or $25.50. So, $320 ÷ $25.50 = 12.5 hours overtime hours."
- "At an average wage of $17 per hour and an average of four hours of overtime paid at the usual rate of a time-and-a-half, or an average of $25.50, it would only take 4,000 workers to build an empire with the estimated annual gross revenues of $180 million."
- A whistleblower alleged staff stole Social Security numbers, faked drug tests and I-9 forms, coerced acceptance of false documents, and intimidated recruiters to approve fraudulent work-eligibility paperwork.
- First Diversity paid workers via "rapid! PayCard" debit cards rather than direct bank deposit.
- " . . . Jean André, a [local] Haitian American pastor . . . [said] that newly arriving Haitian workers, working with immigration, employment, housing and transportation insecurity, have faced abysmal rental conditions and little power with First Diversity. . . . When he drove to Springfield, starting in 2019, to pick up First Diversity's new migrant workers for church services in Columbus, he saw cramped, overcrowded housing conditions with rooms subdivided into sections, numerous men sharing one bathroom. . . . 'It is really a shame to see how they treat people as paid slavery. This is what I call it. . . . They are in hell while living on earth.'"
- George Ten attributed the sharp rise in Haitian arrivals to Biden-era policies that let people already here petition for family, plus local jobs and affordable housing. "It just went vertical."
- George Ten said his firm once controlled Haitian worker transport but later outsourced it; he claimed all workers are paid by check and taxes are paid.[12]

Part II also makes mention of George Ten's father, Miguel, who founded First Diversity in 2002, reincorporated in Ohio in 2008, then handed the business to son George to become a pastor in 2010.

By the way, in December 2024, Ohio Governor Mike DeWine visited Springfield "to announce a new traffic safety initiative in Clark County that will train members of the local migrant community on safe driving skills. . . . The Maria Tiberi Foundation and Virtual Driver Interactive donated 10 new driving simulators to the Ohio Department of Public Safety's Ohio Traffic Safety Office for use in Springfield and Clark County. The new simulators have been placed in locations that serve members of the Haitian community who have recently migrated to the area in large numbers and have had little or no driver training."[13] One location for the driving simulators is Life in Christ Community Church. Their senior pastor? Miguel Ten.[14]

I'll let Asra begin the end of this chapter the same way she ends Part II of her series on the matter of one King George:

> George's company, First Diversity, undergirds Springfield's shadow economy, which benefits everyone but the Haitians. . . . What is left to be seen is whether state and federal authorities will be able to stop the cycle of exploitation and corruption and land First Diversity in the "Go Directly to Jail" space of the high-risk game of Springfieldopoly or will First Diversity and King George invoke the "Get out of Jail Free" card and remain a dubious pillar of the Springfield economy?[15]

At the end of Part II, Asra teased a Part III.

As of this writing, Part III remains unpublished.

CHAPTER 7

HAITIANS BY THE NUMBERS

> "Rumors like [eating cats and dogs] are taking away from the real issues such as issues involving our housing or school resources and our overwhelmed healthcare system."[1]
>
> —Rob Rue, Mayor of Springfield

Every morning between 6:00 a.m. and 6:30 on the dot, Glenda Bailey moves for the computer like others might for coffee.

"I immediately sign on to the municipal court website, and I mine Haitian names off of daily case activity," Glenda told me over dumplin's at Cracker Barrel. I had to ask what a "dumplin'" is, given that particular punctuation. I'd spent summers in the southern United States with my family as a kid, Tennessee and Virginia, specifically, and failed to retain this particular dietary memory. Glenda will not let me live that one down and neither will I. She hadn't made me feel too bad about it, thankfully, and went right on to answering my questions. First had to do with her involvement in the organic formation in what I call the Springfield OSINT.

"Every day, whatever happened yesterday is going to be on today's daily case activity. I will mine those names, and what I do is I copy and paste them into an email to myself . . . I'm good at researching. . . . This is about as organized as I get."

Here come the dumplin's. I'm going to eat as I listen.

"This is what I've known for many years because I lived in Florida. Some Haitians have created very American-sounding names," Glenda said. "'Anderson Charles' is an example. Anderson Charles just had his third OVI. I don't know if you heard this on the news, but he drove into a pond last week."

I had indeed heard this. I remember the story broadcast on local WHIO-TV, a CBS affiliate, calling out the icy road conditions and cold weather as the contextual culprit. But the reporter on-site quickly corrected the record and said the car-in-pond was "believed to be alcohol-involved here and not the weather so much," having interfaced with Ohio Highway Patrol on the matter.[2] "We haven't seen any other issues on the freeway right now."

Upon that first hearing, I didn't put it together, the location and the incident. If only I had visited the story's web page and opened the comments, I would have seen this: "For those who are wondering, YES he is."[3]

Now, not only he *is*, but he *was*. That incident occurred in March 2026. Six months prior, Glenda had published on her 𝕏 account @MajorityHaitian at 6:51 a.m. local time that particular day about one Anderson Charles:

> Haitian HABITUAL OFFENDER Anderson Charles's MOST RECENT OVI ARREST REPORT (his 2nd OVI ARREST in under 3 months). AGAIN he was driven home by law enforcement. MORE police resources are taken AWAY from other criminal activities—being a free taxi service to criminal Haitians.[4]

While this may read more like opinion-editorial than breaking news to some, the facts of the matter are opinion-free. Glenda's post included screenshots of a police report and ticket citing not only vehicle operation under the influence but also a suspended driver's license. The accompanying police report twice mentions a "language barrier," the necessity of a translator, and Mr. Charles's destination—the cop drove him home.

What may have first felt like eye-rolling clickbait—Glenda's all-caps'ed incendiary commentary throughout her post—turns out not to be anything of the sort. It's correct. We don't have to like it. But we can't exactly call her wrong.

I looked up a publicly available City of Springfield Police Division's Rules and Regulations & Manual of Procedures, July 2021, and skimmed to the sections that address OVI arrests, handling/transport of OVI arrestees, and related transportation of intoxicated subjects. The OVI-specific rule (6.23.01 A) is clear and mandatory language, which is that arrested OVI subjects "shall be transported to the Clark County Jail" for processing and incarceration until arraignment or bond.[5] However, "If at the time and location of arrest for driving under suspension the arresting officer(s) determines that the individual has been processed within the previous six months, where current processing is not necessary, the arresting officer has the option of incarcerating the individual, or ordering the individual to appear in court after exercising a reasonable amount of discretion as defined in Departmental Rules and Regulations section 1.11."[6]

The "taxi" incident in question was Anderson Charles' second-recorded OVI, and it did in fact occur within the allowed-for "previous six months," assuming

Mr. Charles had already completed that prior processing and therefore "current processing is not necessary." Besides, overcapacity is a known issue within the Clark County jail.[7] There remains an ongoing dispute over how to fund and where to place the envisioned $108 million public safety center to replace the jail.[8] The officer's decision to drive Mr. Charles home "after exercising a reasonable amount of discretion" may have been out of logistical necessity as much as any other reason apparently allowed by Departmental Rules and Regulations.

Clark County Commission in a September 2024 memo on the Haitian influx bragged about low Haitian crime rates, that Haitians in Springfield are likelier to be victims than the perpetrators. "Clark County jail data shows there are 199 inmates in our county jail this week. Two of them are Haitian."[9] To me, this is a lie whiter than my button-down oxford. What about the machete-wielded incident that brought no police report? Every heritage citizen I spoke with had an overabundance of anecdotes that depicted, in my view, blatant criminal or likely illegal acts committed by Haitians. But if there is no paper trail, it's like they never happened. *Two of them are Haitian.* The Commission also stated, "Nobody is being released due to the language barrier."[10] Is that not what was said of Mr. Charles?

Besides, I met no citizen who assumed the releases were "due to the language barrier." Did you know? An individual will lose or be denied Temporary Protected Status if they have been convicted of one felony or two or more misdemeanors committed in the United States.[11] Is this equity in action? "[I]t is not enough to be non-racist, we must be anti-racist," said Angela Davis.[12]

There's more. Investigative News Service published compelling evidence based on public records requests from the City of Springfield which the publisher asserts shows the city "has been covering up race of murderers" and that the "FBI confirms the city has been lying about the agency's crime reporting guidelines," all over the past ten years, as of October 2024.

Springfield spokesperson Karen Graves claimed (to Investigative News Service) that the FBI only tracks race of murderers as Hispanic, Non-Hispanic, or Unknown. An FBI spokesperson stated (again, to INS) this is incorrect and listed their actual race categories—white, black or African-American, American Indian or Alaska Native, Asian, Native Hawaiian or Other Pacific Islander, or Unknown, with ethnicity tracked separately. The FBI confirmed that failing to report race violates mandatory Uniform Crime Reporting rules for victims, offenders, and arrestees. Springfield does report race of homicide victims, of whom 22 out of 29 (76 percent) were black. Nationally, about 90 percent of black homicide victims are killed by black offenders. Springfield's murder rate is twice the national average. City officials said Haitians have not increased local crime, yet they have not released recent homicide mug shots or arrest reports under a public-records request. The piece concludes:

> . . . Springfield officials claim that Haitians haven't added to the cities crime problem, but city officials have lied and covered up other aspects of crime in the city—and they still haven't released mug shots or arrest reports for homicides for recent years under my public records request, which would give more details about who is committing crime in the city.[13]

I've seen enough. The City of Springfield may not be willfully lying, but I deem nothing said by their official spokespeople to be credible.

Now, to bring the drunk pond-dunk story to its conclusion, it doesn't seem to me that the arresting officer failed to follow protocol, but also, I don't read Glenda's post as alleging the officer did anyway. Is the "free taxi service" close to correct? Consider the price of an Uber for an intoxicated passenger versus a ride from a police officer. To the best of my knowledge, the City of Springfield (that is, the taxpayers) covered the full cost of that patrol-car transport. Mr. Charles would not have been billed or charged anything for the officer's ride home. Glenda, vindicated.

Consider what I believe the highest-intensity point of the post: "MORE police resources are taken AWAY from other criminal activities. . . . " This remains undeniably true. However many new Haitians arrived, that's going to increase the strain on everything, whether they are per-capita *as* likely to commit a given offense or otherwise present a taxpayer-costing need as a heritage citizen, *less* likely, or, of course, *more* likely. And per-capita doesn't really matter at the individual level anyway. "Very few, if any, violations of motor vehicle laws are generally more dangerous to the public safety than operating a motor vehicle under the influence of alcohol or drugs," reads the Springfield Police policy manual.[14] The correct number of heritage citizens driving under the influence is zero. The correct number of Haitian immigrants driving under the influence is also zero. Do you see my point?

I think Setys Kelly does. She wrote to then-Ohio Lieutenant Governor Jon Husted on September 10, 2024, "My daughter being stalked in Walmart and followed to her [vehicle] is a fact. The lady [who] fought the illegal automotive repair shop next to her house is a fact. 10 or more car accidents each day causing Americans insurance rates . . . skyrocketing is a fact."[15] It is. She showed me the aforementioned repair shop herself.

Anyway! We will return to complaints regarding Springfield's justice system in a later chapter because it gets worse. For now, suffice it to say the pond incident and Mr. Charles was my first report from Glenda on how bad things really are. Of course, that was a normal day, that day she found the report.

As per routine, Glenda would post to her account @MajorityHaitian, on her personal Facebook account, and within the private Facebook group "Stop the Influx Into Springfield, Ohio," created with the intention of keeping the community better informed while offering a private, vetted space "to discuss solutions."[16] The group had approximately 4,700 members when I was permitted to join. (Later, the group transitioned and became "Springfield, Ohio: Are You Not Entertained?" in dedication to the late local folk hero William Monaghan, "whose passion, leadership, and unwavering commitment to our community will never be forgotten."[17] And it will not be.)

Every day, every hour, multiple times an hour even, there's something new in the group. Another anecdote, another incident, another instance, another situation, another eyeroller. Many concerned citizens collect and report, but Glenda has been one of the central few to become a one-woman depository. Each time I would ask around town for an introduction, alleged evidence, a lead, or for the introduction to the alleged evidence known by a specific lead, the most common reply to me was, "Glenda has that." More often than not, she, in fact, did. In my book, Glenda Bailey is in the running for whatever civic MVP award that may come of this as a candidate for most-valuable heritage citizen-sleuth. This indeed is my book.

By the way, I was given ten weeks by my publisher for this assignment, to produce this manuscript, from deal signed to draft submitted. At times this felt akin to a modern-day nonfiction *Grimms' Fairy Tales* in which my task was to record and restructure all the tales of truth told by the locals whom I could speak with during my adventures. My own participation as a very minor character in this story has been two years in the making now, but for years-long residents like Glenda, Diana, Setys, and others, this is every day. It's been every day for years.

Another Springfield OSINT network member joked (he wasn't joking) that if I included everything on the Haitian influx situation that had occurred in the year 2026 alone, this book would be eight hundred pages. I came to believe that. Throughout my research-gathering period in this writing, I would hear a claim about measurable Haitian impact—an automobile accident, a smashed-into fence or post or tree (or worse), another court report, a local who lost their place in line to a Haitian—and I'm talking about lines but also I'm not. I would then ask for evidence. After a very early point, I realized how cruel of a question this was. I'd be emailed document after document, video after video, whistleblower testimony after whistleblower testimony . . . It just became too much. Each anecdote, each data point, told the same story despite disparate sources over many miles and many months, and all shot me with the same tired-eyed question: *Now do you believe us, Joshua?*

From first virality, the saga of the Haitians of Springfield was deemed a "hoax" by the Internet's encyclopedia and fact-checkers, the "Lie of Year."[18,19,20] *It's all been debunked.* But my experience of Springfield is that the only debunking that did occur was a debunking of this prior debunking. A person may lie. People may forget. Numbers—enough numbers—over enough time will judge all. And what I and others who've come before to investigate, what we have found are "real issues," thank you very much Mayor Rue, that correlate with—and from the perspective of "the people that live there"—*causate from* the uninvited, unexpected, unprepared-for influx of thousands of Haitian migrants.[21]

But how many Haitians, exactly? We start the next leg of our investigative adventure there.

How Many Haitians

Set aside candidacy for political office and allow yourself to reframe Donald Trump's description of the Haitian influx as a politically incorrect comedy sketch. Reported by Yahoo:

> "How about in Springfield, Ohio, they had 32,000—this is a little beautiful town, no crime, no problem—32,000 illegal immigrants come into the town," Trump said. "So they almost double their population in a period of a few weeks. Can you believe it? And you know what? They've got to get much tougher. I'm going to go there in the next two weeks. I'm going to Springfield."
>
> "You may never see me again, but that's okay," he added. "'Whatever happened to Trump? Well, he never got out of Springfield.'"[22]

There will never be another.

Now, the fact-checking knee-jerkers reading this will pounce on the "almost double their population" claim. Isn't Springfield close to sixty thousand, give or take a few hundred?[23] So wouldn't it be mathematically accurate to instead have said something instead closer to "increase their population by almost 50 percent"?

World Population Review shows 44,391 *adults* in Springfield.[24] About 32,000 new arrivals would represent a 72 percent increase in the adult population specifically, which, technically is "almost double," but in a different direction. Imprecise but not incorrect. And of course, not all Haitian migrants are adults. Now, we've also established the paradoxical immigration status of Haitian migrants who, technically, *illegally immigrated*, while later receiving Temporary Protected Status. Tom Homan set that straight for us.

But where did Candidate Trump get the thirty-two thousand number? Consider the counterpoints:

> Mayor Rob Rue told CNN the city's population has grown about 25% over the past three years, in part due to the arrival of Haitian immigrants.
>
> Between 12,000 and 15,000 immigrants are living in Clark County, which includes Springfield, according to estimates on the city's website. Of that group, an estimated 10,000-12,000 are Haitian, according to a July presentation from the county's health commissioner, who cited data from school and social services officials.
>
> The 2020 Census estimated about 60,000 people were living in Springfield, and 2022 data from the American Community Survey indicated about 2% of the city's population was born outside the US.[25]

Where, Mr. Trump? We're inexplicably off between seventeen thousand and twenty thousand of these "illegal immigrants." Some explicating is necessary.

When I asked members of the OSINT their own estimates for the Springfield proper or broader Clark County Haitian population as of March 2026, I got numbers ranging from 6,000 to 12,000 with most locally educated guestimates settling in between 8,000 and 10,000 (although some local sources still assert 15,000).[26] Based on those I spoke with whom I believe to be in the knowest, that latter range is likeliest. It is believed by residents I spoke with, widely so, that many Haitians have already left. One local attorney reported that by March 2026, seventy-five Haitians had requested an information packet on how to leave the United States in the event of TPS disruption.[27] How many have already acted on that shared concern?

That said, I received multiple reports from eyewitnesses whose neighbors were Haitians that they were not the same Haitians. During rolling approximately three- to nine-month periods, a given Haitian family would appear in a home believed to be sublet to Haitians. The period would pass, and a new family would replace them. I was told this happened all over Springfield, and the most common license plates on the vehicles would be New York and Florida.

Diana Daniels added this on to that during our first long talk.

> Here's another thing. . . . Where is Springfield? . . . Right on the biggest east-west artery in the country. . . . How many people do you think have gone through Springfield? Haitians? Who've passed through to have their paperwork processed? Here's what's important: Why Springfield, and why not Dayton? Dayton is a Sanctuary City. Why not there? Well, if you're gonna dump 20,000 to 30,000 people on a community, don't you want most of your services to be centrally located so they can get to them quickly? It's walking distance from Jobs and Family Services to Topre. It's walking distance from Jobs and Family Services up to First Diversity. It's walking distance from Jobs and Family Services . . . up to the Rocking Horse. It's within walking distance to get to the DMV. Everything is within a reasonable twenty minutes to half an hour; you're going to get where you want to. You can't do that in Dayton. . . . So this makes it an ideal location for a processing center for migrants, and that's exactly what we have.
>
> . . . It's a revolving door . . . Springfield has been—is—a revolving-door processing center for Haitians and other migrants to get their paperwork done and then move on. If you need something done, you come to Springfield, get your paperwork done, and then you move on up because there's not enough jobs for that many people. They . . . get their paperwork done, and then they move on.
>
> . . . [W]e estimate between 127,000 and 135,000 Haitians have passed through Springfield since 2020, which is pretty believable. . . . [I]f you had 10,000 people descend upon a small community, and they have to get their driver's license and they have to be able to get paperwork, they're not going to keep going back. . . . One and done. OK, you might get a renewal, but that's every four years. How come we continually have a long line at the DMV? It's constant. You constantly see new people getting driver's licenses. Constantly you see new people move into apartments—groups of . . . two or three families move in, stay a while, move out. Two or three more move into the same location, stay a while—six months, nine months, then move out. We've seen that constantly for the last four and a half years.

Well, the Clark County Commission did say in September 2024 that they were "[r]esearching and planning a one-stop center for our Haitian residents."[28]

Now, the thirty-two thousand number would refer to a *peak*. Just a few "weeks"? Could Trump have summarized the mass influx the same way locals did? "Locals say it felt like it happened overnight. On Sunday afternoons, you could suddenly hear Creole mass wafting through downtown streets. Haitian restaurants started popping up," reported NPR.[29] And again, where's that thirty-two thousand?

I asked around the OSINT, and everyone seemed to attribute this number to a known yet anonymous (albeit confirmed privately) source—"[An Ohio Jobs and Family Services] employee reported over 34,000 applications by Haitians for assistance in Clark County alone," reads a text message I received on this very matter from a source I deem credible. "OJFS reported numbers under actual and actually had to create a separate 'line' for Haitian applicants only. Many legacy citizens would arrive before opening hours to form a line and wouldn't be seen due to imbalance of staffing," reads the follow-up.

The second hypothesis I gathered associated with thirty-two thousandish Haitians is as follows, courtesy of Diana Daniels:

> We have had a whistleblower. . . . She passed on some information. . . . [I]f you are processing your paperwork for your TPS, your asylum process, you're not going to get it until they approve it. Well, in the meantime, you don't have any money, so you can get a cash stipend, depending on your household size, from $4,000 to $6,000 in cash. . . . [O]nce you get that money . . . you become a "one." OK, so let's say your paperwork is delayed. You can reapply, but you're still a "one" because your three applications does not count two; it counts one. In 2024, there were 32,200 individual applications for . . . funds in Springfield. . . . [T]hat's just the number of . . . funds that we distributed in 2024. What does that tell us? That tells us that they had in 2024—that doesn't include all of those that came in 2021 and all those that came in 2022 and 2023—this is 2024 alone.

It turns out third is a third answer to my query, and it's even closer—32,200 is the number here, again, and it's the number of Haitians with "parolee paperwork to change their status," according to another of my confirmed-credible OSINT sources, adding "it's a request to either apply for [an H-1B work] visa or to change to refugee status or to straight up apply for citizenship. From what I understand this is the paperwork they have to fill out with an immigration lawyer to start the process."

However, because an individual could file multiple applications—such as one for TPS and another for a work permit—or re-register during extensions, the total number of forms processed *could* be much higher than the number of people. That said, I became confident that these numbers are not total across applications but that these are unique individuals being counted and not their applications. Even then, however, I wonder if a share of the 32,200 to 34,000 estimate were not medium- or long-term residents but might rather have been short-term "revolving door" Haitians, the likes of those seen living in houses across town for a number of months before replacement by another Haitian family. Additionally, Setys Kelly at the Concerned Citizens of Clark County Town Hall in July 2026 (more on that later) brought forward the number thirty-five thousand, which I would later hear from other heritage citizens whom I deem credible as was, to me, their determination for that highest-end estimate. (That would mean 10 percent of *all* formerly Temporary Protected Status Haitian nationals in America came to *one* city at the height of the influx.[30])

The debate will rage on as to the number, but what of the impact? Whether it's closer to the City's one-time conservative estimate of 10,000 or the OSINT's purported number as high as 34,000 to 35,000, either one is going to show up somewhere. Everywhere, even. So what did we find? What is the measurable impact of Haitians on Springfield?

The Measurable Impacts

Recall what Walter Curt told me and in the order he told me back in Chapter 2:

- "We went from having only a few thousand Haitians here to over 30,000 . . . during the Biden years." Now you know the general sourcing behind numbers of that ballpark.
- During President Trump's first term, manufacturing returned to Springfield—"four or five factories" with "a thousand to a few thousand jobs." Wages increased citywide as a result—until Haitians arrived and "staffed all of those factories" as temporary workers for "half the wages." Of one company hiring 700 new employees, it was alleged that 500 were Haitian.
- With Haitians came calamity on the roads.
- Housing costs increased as availability decreased. Longtime heritage citizens were displaced, "evicted" for Haitians who could pay more. Rents and home prices increased.
- A significant social services drain.
- Hospital and healthcare strain was "unbelievable," "[s]o much so that they had to hire more staff."
- An increase of 100 Haitian high-schoolers in 2020 to more than 1,000 in the system in 2023 means higher education costs and property tax rates.

- The explosive population growth means new developments now exist based on those numbers; there is inherent financial incentive for the Haitians' numbers *not* declining.

Categorized, Walter's concerns stretch across **commerce and labor**—which we already covered in Chapters 5 and 6 for the most part—but also **road safety**, **housing**, **welfare**, **health care**, and **education**.

So that's what we're going to cover. But first, what is the business scene on the ground in and around Springfield that Walter is talking about?

They're Eating the Jobs

Walter's mention of private investment into downtown was part of a broader rescue for Springfield, which ultimately is what attracted Haitian migrants—the city was already on the up.

> Like many communities in the Rust Belt, it seemed like good times were a thing of the past. Once a manufacturing hub, the city had been losing population for decades, with rising unemployment and falling incomes. City leaders set about turning things around, developing a strategy to lure businesses of all kinds to the city. By all accounts, this strategy has been a success. In 2008, a major new hospital was built in the city, bringing in 1,800 new jobs. In 2011, a local university, Clark State, built a large new conference center. Millions of dollars were then poured into revitalizing the downtown, tech companies moved into the region and opened new manufacturing plants, and in recent years, local retail shops in the downtown have begun to thrive. But with success came new challenges; with new businesses pouring into town, the demand for labor increased significantly, and the local labor supply wasn't enough.
>
> Enter immigrants. Around 2013 to 2014, Haitian immigrants began arriving in the town to fill open job postings. They found a community with a low cost of living, a high number of jobs, and a good quality of life. Those who initially settled in the town then told people back home about Springfield.[31]

Shortly thereafter, in 2016, Clark County began a year-and-a-half-long comprehensive process to produce a plan—CONNECT Clark County—for "a robust public engagement process that addressed community needs, values and aspirations," first of its kind for the county in nearly twenty years.[32]

You'll find nothing nefarious in the completed plan. There's mention of affordability, revitalization efforts, walkways and bike paths, the area's universities and colleges. But of course, there were opportunities, let's call them.

> Clark County, like many Midwestern manufacturing-based economies, is experiencing the negative impacts of automation and new technologies on an aging workforce. This includes a lack of appropriately skilled workers as shifts in skills requirements are leaving some behind, especially older workers and those whose skills were honed for many years based on now obsolete technologies. Without job growth, high-quality housing or an amenity base, businesses also find it hard to retain good workers. Job readiness is also frequently discussed. Prospective workers are not attuned to the requirements for work or suffer from a growing array of problems.[33]

Not enough workers, not enough businesses, not enough jobs, not enough houses, not enough workers, not enough businesses, not enough—it's a terrible cycle. That said, all hope was not lost. The plan continues on the next page.

> The sizeable regional labor force and its growing number provides an available workforce for business and industry development in Clark County. Clark County offers access and proximity to Wright-Patterson Air Force Base, Honda, and other major employers, generating opportunities for contracting and spin-off.[34]

For the plan's "goal" for "advancing prosperity," there were three objectives listed:

1. "Develop a labor force to be competitive in attracting and retaining business."
2. "Improve the County's image to attract new business through marketing."
3. "Recruit new businesses to the County."[35]

The Chamber of Greater Springfield, now the Greater Springfield Partnership, was listed as a lead coordinator for most of these efforts if not a supporting entity. And it looks to me like, given the timing, their efforts began to succeed.

Remember what Walter said about Trump's first term? Let's look into it because those successes seem to align with the timeline of the planning for CONNECT Clark County.

In case you may not know, Springfield-area manufacturing projects announced or opened during Trump's first term include:

- A Topre America facility was announced in 2017, with about $55 million in investment and 85 new jobs.[36] A year later, Topre announced an additional expansion in Springfield, with a new stamping facility and about 204 more jobs.[37]
- Silfex opened a new facility in 2018.[38] Silfex expanded into a 350,000-plus square-foot facility, a project involving roughly $223 million and up to 400 new jobs.[39]
- Champaign Economic Partnership reported Rittal's Urbana plant had 400 production workers, was hiring forty more, and had recently invested more than $3 million in equipment.[40] There is another facility in Springfield as well.[41]

Also, the company Gabe's announced in March 2023 they were opening their largest distribution center, in Clark County, at over 870,000 square feet with more than 800 full-time and part-time jobs created over a subsequent five-year period, with more than 200 positions already filled on the date of the announcement.[42]

Other area employers that came up repeatedly during my interviews include Dole, Konecranes, McGregor Metal, International Motors (formerly Navistar), Pentaflex, Yamada North America, Woeber Mustard, and Amazon.

Now, while President Trump has not appeared to personally tout Springfield's new plants or successful by name, at least not in the records I could find, his administration and campaign constantly sold Ohio as proof that America First trade, deregulation, and tax policy were reviving manufacturing, while JobsOhio and local Republicans have pointed to projects like Topre and Silfex in Springfield as concrete evidence of that broader comeback.[43,44,45,46]

Of these, several have been public regarding their use of Haitian workers, including temporary employment, as I've mentioned already in this book.

About 10 percent of the McGregor Metal workforce was Haitian as of September 2024, accounting for more than thirty employees.[47] Pentaflex employs Haitians; their CEO said, "There are no Haitians that are taking anybody's jobs. I mean, if you want a job, you can get a job. And I just encourage people to have a little bit of empathy for where the Haitians are coming from."[48] He added that Pentaflex does not pay Haitian workers less.[49] However, an American Enterprise Institute piece noted that Pentaflex "chose a staffing agency to help with hiring."[50] The AEI article prefaced this with an acknowledgment that Haitians in Springfield "came there by word-of-mouth, attracted by cheap cost-of-living and decent jobs. What is not specified is how many of them were actively recruited through the government parole system that allows companies to sponsor multiple individuals."[51]

I'd like to know that number. Wouldn't you?

The Guardian reported:

> When companies such as Amazon, Dole Fresh Vegetables and Topre, a Japanese auto parts manufacturer, struggled to find labor in the aftermath of the pandemic, temporary staffing agencies found hundreds of Haitian workers to fill the gaps.
>
> But that created insecurities for Haitians, too.
>
> "The biggest issue we see with the temp agencies is that—and it's not illegal, unfortunately—workers are not given benefits, they're not given time off," says Katie Kersh, a senior attorney at [Advocates for Basic Legal Equality].
>
> "It's just much harder for people who are trying to build lives. It prevents them from having a lot of things they need to get ahead."[52]

Dayton 24/7 Now reported that the end of TPS for Haitians would mean, of course, that they are "no longer be legally allowed to live and work in the region."[53]

> Governor Mike DeWine expressed concern over the impending changes, stating, "That's a massive change when all of those individuals, one day, can no longer work in those companies and those companies can no longer employ them."
>
> The potential departure of thousands of Haitian workers is expected to impact local businesses significantly. Companies such as McGregor Metal and Topre America are anticipated to lose a substantial portion of their workforce.
>
> Dr. Jared Pincin, an economics professor at Cedarville University, highlighted the potential economic repercussions. "I would expect similar things to happen. I'm not saying $25/hour, but I'd expect wages to go up in these areas if these companies are in desperate need of workers," he said.[54]

Up, you say? As if these "repercussions" are somehow a bad thing?

Reuters reported broadly that Springfield's labor-force rebound depended on immigrants—Haitians, specifically—filling manufacturing jobs but cast this as all upside for the city and its economy.[55]

Consider the "Haitian Immigration Statement" of the Greater Springfield Partnership:

> "Springfield is moving forward, and our progress is visible. Since 2012, we've created nearly 8,000 new jobs, retained another 11,900, added housing, and brought our downtown back into productive use. Investment is happening because the fundamentals are strong and the direction is clear. Springfield is proving that communities like ours can compete, adapt, and build a future people want to be part of."
>
> —Mike McDorman, President & CEO, Greater Springfield Partnership
>
> - We've taken proactive steps to support local efforts to help the Haitian population assimilate into our workforce.
> - Haitian workers pay taxes and re-invest in our local economy.
> - Area businesses benefit when these new workers can assimilate quickly into their workplace cultures.
> - This quick and mass influx has created many challenges in the community, but our Haitian population is willing to work hard for local employers and adapt.
>
> Assimilation efforts are focused on three key areas:
>
> - Driving Instruction
> - Healthcare
> - Language/Culture
>
> Two GSP staff members serve on the Haitian Coalition so that the best interests of the business community are represented.
>
> - Businesses are thriving in Clark County.
> - More jobs = more housing opportunities + downtown redevelopment/downtown events[56]

Assimilating into the workforce, OK. That comprehensive CONNECT Clark County plan didn't mention immigration once, but it didn't exclude imported labor explicitly either. So, here they are. And where? As Walter said, I heard a number of eyewitness reports mentioning Haitians entering and existing the premises of Rittal five days a week for at least two years; I wonder what they could have been doing there! Other reports confirm Haitians working at unnamed construction sites and "a couple of auto parts companies," in local "in demand" careers such as "healthcare and customer service," for a manufacturer that "employs about 50 Haitian workers," as well as in "warehouses, manufacturing and the service industry."[57,58,59,60,61] Then, of course, there are the Haitian-owned and -operated businesses throughout Springfield—"2 Haitian restaurants, 7 Haitian grocery stores and 1 Haitian food truck"—plus the nonprofits where Haitians are known to work, such as, obviously, the Haitian Support Center.[62]

If you're working for lower-than-salary pay, you're receiving no benefits, you're offered no time off, and you're contractually obligated to continue your labor, are you employed? Or are you indentured?

Now try to square all of that up with this five-alarm fire from Policy Matters Ohio:

> According to preliminary jobs and employment data for December 2025, Springfield's labor force shrank by 1,100 (-1.8%), coinciding with substantial job losses (-1,100, a 2.2% decrease), despite modest statewide growth in both measures. Springfield's private sector losses were concentrated in manufacturing (-900, a 13.4% decrease) and leisure and hospitality (-200, a 4.0% decrease).[63]

"At Topre America, an automotive parts manufacturing company north-east of downtown Springfield, dozens of jobs that Haitians had once filled—forklift drivers, supervisors and stackers—have remained unfilled on the company's employment webpage for months," reported *The Guardian*.[64] Open positions listed start at $19.80 an hour.[65]

On the one hand, Springfield's economy is thriving and needs more Haitians; on the other hand, Springfield's economy is suffering—and needs more Haitians. Perhaps the pro-Haitian case is not really about the benefit of Haitians to the local economy, but the benefit of the local economy to Haitians.

Guerline Jozef, Executive Director of Haitian Bridge Alliance, released this statement on the TPS program, which contains at least ten "tells" for generative AI use. How many do you notice?

> Let us be clear: ending TPS for Haiti is not a policy decision—it is an act of violence against Black migrants. When the U.S. government knowingly

> chooses to send people back to a nation engulfed in crisis, that is state-sponsored cruelty. It is a reminder that the lives of Black immigrants are still treated as expendable under a system built on racial hierarchy, anti-Blackness, and exclusion. We reject the idea that our communities must constantly justify their right to live, to work, to be safe. TPS is the bare minimum of protection, and even that is being stripped away. This is why we organize, resist, and demand a world where migration is not weaponized against the most vulnerable.[66]

It's about the economy until it's not.

Mike McDorman, CEO of the Greater Springfield Partnership, said, "We're resurging. The work we've done in downtown Springfield and across the county is going to be something we look back on as a turning point."[67] Is this not what Walter Curt told me?

McDorman seems most excited about the new area industrial park, Prime Ohio II.[68] And so the trend continues. "From probably 2016 to present, we created about 8,000 jobs, and I think that brought the opportunity for people to take advantage of those jobs. Little did we know that there would be different groups of people taking advantage of [the growth]."[69]

You don't say. Amy Donahoe, also of the Greater Springfield Partnership, sure does:

> "We needed a workforce," to fill jobs in a resurgent local manufacturing sector and staff a growing number of warehouse and distribution centers, said Amy Donahoe, director of workforce development with the Greater Springfield Partnership. "[Haitians] are coming in and they are working hard and they want to make money."[70]

Speaking of which, absolutely, some Haitian migrants do indeed want to work hard and make money, but are they spending their pay in Springfield, or are some, as *The Haitian Times* reported, "ecstatic to land a job" here only to subsequently "send money home"?[71] Can we say a local economy is being stimulated if a known share of that stimulation is felt only by people in other countries? Is this simply currency geoarbitrage because, as of this writing, 1 United States Dollar equals 130.73 Haitian Gourde?[72] Haiti's average annual income is only a mere $1,760.[73]

Creations Market shop owner Philomène Philostin told *The Haitian Times* that "customers previously sent $100 to $300 per month to relatives abroad."[74]

Such transfers were "once a regular part of many households' finances" but slowed near the fixed end of TPS.

One Springfield Haitian worker's predicament was "that she sometimes wishes she had stayed in her small, relatively safe town in Haiti. At least there, she would not be so afraid all the time [of TPS uncertainty]. But . . . too many people depend on her, both in Haiti and in Ohio, [for her] to stop going to work."[75]

I asked the AI Grok to do a little number-crunching on the matter. Here's what it said, with sources:

> Based on the 15,000-20,000 Haitian population range in Springfield/Clark County cited by local officials and news reports, approximately 75 percent of Haitian immigrants nationally are of working age (18–64) per Migration Policy Institute analysis of 2022 American Community Survey data.[76,77] Labor force participation among Haitian TPS holders reaches 79–88 percent according to the Penn Wharton Budget Model (using 2022–2023 ACS data) and Center for Migration Studies profiles.[78] Roughly 70 percent of Haitian migrants regularly send remittances as documented in Inter-American Dialogue research, and with average monthly transfers of $100–$300 as reported by a Springfield business owner operating money-transfer services, **the estimated total annual remittances previously leaving the Springfield area at pre-shrinkage peak levels ranged from $12 million to $20 million per year**.[79] No official county-level remittance data exists, so this remains a transparent extrapolation grounded in the cited national and local sources.

Did you know? Springfield's gross domestic product (GDP) rose from $4.7 million in 2020 to $5.9 million in 2023.[80] "A report from the Federal Reserve Bank of Cleveland found that it ranked second among all Ohio cities for job growth since the pandemic."[81]

Special credit will go to the Haitians. In the context of praising their labor contributions to Springfield, City Manager Bryan Heck said, "The growth in our workforce population has supported the expansion of local businesses, contributing to the stabilization of our local economy."[82]

Whatever the question, the answer is, you guessed it, more Haitians.

In my reflection, Walter's account, to me, mixes firsthand observation, local inference, credible community anecdotes, and real underlying facts. Some claims are instant-substantiated; others regarding employment remain unresolved. Even where I could not fully verify his strongest formulations, I also could not disprove the central substance of what he was saying, especially since I heard the same story over and over and over and over from residents all over Clark County of diverse ages, backgrounds, education, and socioeconomic status. When a given citizen would share their anecdotal data with me, I'd inquire if they knew such-and-such person—who told me an identical story, perhaps about Haitians transported into white or yellow vans to work at a specific company, or wages collapsing at a certain employer alleged to have replaced dozens to hundreds of full-time white employers with lower-pay temporary-worker Haitians, and they'd tell me they knew no such person. I have a hard time believing that the explanation for these corroborations I heard and found are some vast citywide conspiracy. Maybe everyone is saying it's happening everywhere because . . . it is.

What about the four or five businesses that had been known to hire Haitians, according to Walter? "[O]nly six [bigger businesses in Springfield] have sizable immigrant populations in their workforce," according to local news site The Hub Springfield.[83]

It's been debunked.

It has not.

Data on other aspects of the Haitian impact are more forthcoming from various official sources. Let's continue our study—on road safety, housing, welfare, health care, then finally education. Everything we want to know may be hard to find, as it has been for others, for reasons unstated.

> Outside of conversations with [Greater Springfield Partnership's Mike] McDorman, several attempts were made to obtain city or county-level data on the Haitian population's economic impact, workforce or educational participation, and community contributions. It was met with a lack of response, hesitancy, or outright avoidance. In asking the Springfield-Clark Career Technology Center about population-specific enrollment data, for example, The Hub was told this information isn't available to the public.[84]

Interesting. Why do you think that is?

According to the Clark County Commission at the height of the influxian chaos in September 2024, "Nothing is more important than the long-term vibrancy of Springfield and Clark County. Our priorities remain keeping a strong sales tax base, improving access to government, and retaining and attracting workforce."[85]

I don't see anything about quality of life for the heritage citizens. Do you?

They're Flipping the Cars

With no close second, the most common observation I heard from heritage citizens on the Haitians of Springfield is this:

"They're terrible drivers."

This, I heard even from outspokenly pro-Haitian citizens, who made sure to cleanse their shame immediately after this admission with a "but" and then some remark on the cultural enrichment majority-white Springfield so desperately needed.

I was introduced to **Deb Burchett**, Sheriff of Clark County from 2017 to 2025 (and first female sheriff in the county history, having defeated the prior long-time incumbent[86]). Our conversation covered just about everything she witnessed during her tenure but started and ended on the subject of road safety. From the get-go, she made clear her vision for the Haitians of Springfield. Here are her thoughts, from the Sheriff who saw it all, then after retirement, fled it all; she left Springfield and now resides out in the country. You will have no question as to why.

> I was the sheriff when the little boy was killed . . . I think ICE should come in here and clear them all out. . . . They think they own Springfield . . . [City leadership says the Haitians] should stay here because of the economy. "We'd lose the factories." Maybe if the factories paid a decent wage, people would want their jobs. You've got people in town who would take the work.
>
> You want evidence [of Haitian impact]? Just go to the grocery store. . . . Just come here for a week or so . . . they don't know how to drive. . . . We had Haitians helping each other take the [driving] test. [The City of Springfield] protects them. If you go to the courthouse and start pulling some of their charges, you'll see they don't get anything compared to the residents of the city. . . . They're not being held responsible for what they do. Go to the courthouse and get the public records. They get their fines taken down to $20 to $25.
>
> One ran into one of our police cars. There are accidents everywhere. I find it was the most amazing thing I've ever seen in my life, the cars are on their top. Never seen anything like that, and I've been here for forty-five years.
>
> . . . I bought a house out in the county. When I retired, I said, "I have to get out of Springfield."

. . . I still get calls every week. "How many cars can I have in my driveway without being ticketed?" While Haitians have cars in streets, in yards. . . . A lot of people have gone up to the City [Commission meetings] to raise the devil because they don't ticket [Haitians]. I don't know what the mayor is getting out of this.

. . . I'll tell you this. When I took over as sheriff [in January 2017], Carl Ruby wanted an appointment with me. We had Hispanics coming here, working on farms. I'll take the Hispanics any day compared to the Haitians.

Ruby told me he's in charge of the Hispanics and that he didn't want them charged if they had no green card.

"Don't tell me who I can and cannot arrest because if they commit a crime, no matter who they are, they will be arrested."

He told me he just doesn't want me to go harassing them.

"We don't harass anyone. If they're wrong, they're wrong." So that was the wrong foot. Ruby told me what I was going to do with the Hispanics, and he hated me ever since.

. . . We had this big meeting one day where the NAACP came in and said blacks were treated different than whites in Springfield. Every time I turn around, all they want are meetings, but they don't do anything about it.

. . . [What changed after the Haitian influx was] [m]ostly the accidents. And domestic violence. They believe their women are below them, but their women don't want to testify against them, so it goes under the rug before it goes to court.

[Heritage citizens tell me,] "Hey, my car just got rammed into. The city police let them drive off. No license or insurance." My deputies never let them drive off. Allison Elliott, chief of police, she's the nicest and sweetest girl, but she may be afraid they can fire her at any time, the mayor and city manager Bryan Heck.

. . . Why is there a pro-Haitian cabal? That's what I would like to know . . . [City leadership is] [v]ery corrupt. If you don't run in the same circle they do, they run you out, the city council and county commissioners. You can't be a truly honest person and be able to be a politician in Clark County.

(continued . . .)

. . . The Haitians opened a bar and . . . [the] fire department shut them down. Their little shops pop up over town. Clothing store, grocery store, a restaurant. You can't tell me all that's above board.

. . . I don't really think [deportations are] going to happen. But you can always be hopeful.

. . . Our Catholic churches and St. Vincent de Paul have been doing nothing but helping [Haitians]. I'm a lifelong Catholic, but I have to tell you, I quit going to church over this. My dad is ninety-nine years old. He still has to pay for his own medication. Not that he can't afford it, but why should they get everything? He's an American citizen, a World War II vet, and you go over to the social security office and it's Haitians everywhere? How come they get here and get on social security?

. . . [Springfield is] absolutely being held hostage . . . I still can't get over how they flip their cars.

Could it really be all that bad? Well, according to *The New York Post* in 2024, there had been four times as many fatal accidents than the year prior, and while not all reports capture the nationalities of those at fault, residents are quick to point the blame at migrants "unfamiliar" with the road rules.[87] Illegal U-turns, driving the wrong way down one-way streets, forcing right turns from the left lane . . . and those are the ones that happen every day and don't cause notable fatalities. Every couple of days during the course of writing this book, a random citizen who'd been given my contact information would send me a picture of something they'd eye-witnessed that day. Each and every time, it was a bewildered-looking Haitian standing beside their totaled car, with their vehicle idling atop a sign, a fence, a pole or some other object they'd apparently just plowed into or over. I still can't get over it.

"Now, the driving situation is bad, giving them licenses is bad, because they can't even read English. So how are they going to read the signs?" asked flabbergasted Fred Stegner, the Springfield Soup Kitchen president.[88]

Some have gone so far as to insist Haitians must be cheating on driving tests in order to get that coveted license. But the Registrar of the Ohio Bureau of Motor Vehicles, Charlie Norman, would deny these claims. "I can tell you our driver examiners monitor the knowledge testing portion of that process very closely. There are actually cameras in our facilities on those knowledge testing kiosks . . . So if we catch a person cheating they're not allowed to have phones on the counter, they're not allowed to have written instructions, anything written down, any notes or anything like that."[89]

It's his word against the former county sheriff's. Who has more to lose?

Regardless, what is decidedly not up for debate is that there has been an influx of Haitian migrants taking these driving tests who often need more education than what's required for typical American adults. Ohio Governor Mike DeWine said that the city has "seen a willingness from Haitians when they've had the opportunity to take drivers training. We've got to provide more of that. . . . We have to change our laws so that we can make sure that 18-year-olds and over, people 18 and over do get the training that they need. That's not required under our law today and we need to change that."[90]

James Blanken on *Empty Pockets Garage* and independent investigative journalism newsletter *The Heartland Beat* both reported on the instance of a Haitian driver who'd done a little house-crashing.[91] A few minutes of internet sleuthing revealed that that same driver had been pulled over numerous times for everything from driving with a suspended license (or even driving without a license at all) to speeding at 70 mph in a 35 mph zone. *None of these resulted in formal conviction.* Every document found had a big fat 0 in the "Prior Convictions" spot.[92] Why?

A *BlazeTV* interview with neighboring Tremont City police chief Chad Duncan might shed some disinfecting light.[93] He said that his force cite and tow offending Haitian drivers and their vehicles, respectively, but Springfield police do not, which creates a problem for Tremont City residents because now inexperienced, unsafe Haitians from Springfield are permitted to road-hazard their way through his citizens' part of the county. Why might they be let off so easily so often?

Chief Duncan told *BlazeTV*'s Julio Rosas about a recent traffic stop of a Haitian national who had no license and was driving 44 mph in a 25 mph zone in Tremont City. It was the second time in two weeks Duncan had pulled the same driver over and towed the vehicle. When asked whether Springfield police would have towed the car, Duncan said no. From his perspective, Springfield softens or avoids reckless-driving penalties for Haitian nationals to shield them from deportation; misdemeanors can trigger removal.

Duncan added that his access to Springfield's police radio frequency had been cut off since the city drew national attention over the Haitian influx. Had the department blocked outside radio monitoring to avoid accountability for its actions? If Springfield leaders had focused less on elites lining their pockets and more on careful management, Duncan said, the situation could have gone "so much smoother and been so much more beneficial to everybody involved."[94]

Now, several such traffic citations Chief Duncan brought up would have typically been considered misdemeanors, which meant the proper legal result would have been to deport that individual. The City of Springfield doesn't seem to want that (as much as an institution can not "want" something).

Of course, we have still additional eyewitness testimony that official Clark County documents acknowledge of roadway antics. Dismissed in part as "anecdotal evidence," there's still an insistence on much-needed driver training for Haitian Creole speakers.[95] Meanwhile, asking how many traffic stops are for unlicensed drivers? "This data is currently not available."

Given what Chief Duncan said, again, in context—no misdemeanors, no deportations—we may have found out why "in 2023, the state dashboard shows the lowest number of overall crashes investigated by [Ohio] Highway Patrol in the last five years."[96] Re-read that sentence very carefully until you realize what claim is being made—and which is not.

Fortunately for city residents of all nationalities, the state has changed the driving-test law with Ohio House Bill 54 (136th General Assembly). Passed unanimously, the bill "requires initial limited-term license applicants (i.e. temporary residents) to complete the exact training requirements as other first-time applicants, including completing a driver training course and 50 hours of supervised driving."[97] Previously, adults over eighteen could often skip the formal classes and training for driver's ed and just take the test (sometimes even using an interpreter). This change was a direct road-safety measure in response to concerns about higher accident rates involving drivers new to U.S. roads. Like Springfield's.

This bill got signed at the finish line, and everything passed without vetoes, including a key requirement for showing proper citizenship/legal/immigration status documentation upon registration at the BMV.[98] Representative Phil Plummer, a former Montgomery County sheriff with a strong public-safety background, publicly backed the budget for its safety focus. He met with me during the course of this work's research to confirm a not-insignificant percentage of findings in this chapter. Publicly, Rep. Plummer had this to say about the bill: "This transportation budget will improve Ohio's infrastructure while simultaneously enhancing the safety of our citizens."[99] And while this did have a later military and federal exemption for certain applicants with foreign licenses, the core of the bill still stood.[100] No partisan fighting and no last minute rewrites to defang the law. It was sorely needed.

Speaking of BMVs, in September 2025, the Ohio BMV's Sunset Avenue office in Springfield's Southern Village Shopping Center, now almost entirely Haitianized, was abruptly closed for several weeks after deputy registrar Cecil Rice resigned "to pursue personal ventures."[101,102] Rice had run the location for roughly two years but had worked there more than two decades; the state cited the office's failure to meet six statutory requirements, chiefly not asking customers mandatory questions during transactions, including those for proper screening for certain licenses and suspensions.[103]

The site had long been operated by the Rice family—Sheila Rice (later Henry), Cecil's close relative, served as the longtime deputy registrar and owner there for twenty-plus years until late 2023 while simultaneously being appointed (2021) and later elected Clark County Municipal Court Clerk of Courts—the first black person elected to a countywide office in Clark County, interestingly enough (or is it).

A number of storylines I picked up about the Rice family and their BMV involvement alleged nepotism and conflict of interest—that the Rice family essentially "owned" and profited from the lucrative deputy-registrar contract while Sheila held a powerful elected court position. Multiple sources told me that computers, records, and other equipment had been seized, raided, or otherwise removed by law enforcement. They told me, also, that the entirety of that investigation simply vanished, and nothing was ever made public beyond the initial report and that location's later reopening.

However bad you imagine it is, it's worse.

A confirmed employee of the Springfield City School District reached out to me on the matter of traffic safety; she was far from the first and sadly nowhere near the last. This middle-aged woman was one of many with the same story of so many in this town, writing to me of Haitians' vehicular shenanigans, "I am not allowed to talk about any of it. Even though I have firsthand seen things I have been labeled a racist. I need to take care of my family, so I don't comment on anything but just know I am getting your book when it comes out because I do live in [S]pringfield and rent has [gone] up and we are a high risk city for car insurance now. I could go on and on but I want to say thank you!" She (and others) relayed to me the usual—Haitian hits on parked cars and school buses, illegal U-turns and red-light runs galore, and town-wide accidents which the at-fault Haitians subsequently blamed on their (most often white) victims. If I included every such incident in full detail, this entire book would be nothing but that—*Haitian Stunt Drivers of Springfield*. Alas.

I was put into contact also with a Springfielder named **Quinn Ferrell**, who showed me pictures of the complete destruction of his detached garage by a Haitian driver. Note that Quinn is an exotic pet owner, and the Haitian annihilation resulted in a horrific scene of gore and splatter. From Quinn directly:

> At [3:00 a.m.] me and my wife were jolted awake after hearing what can only be described as an explosion right outside of our bedroom. When I got up I ran outside to hear the noise of a car hitting the rev [limiter], drowsy and still sleepy I had no idea what I was looking at until I went to the front of my garage. When I saw the door was lodged into the back of my (now destroyed) Jetta, I knew someone had crashed into my garage from the back of the building. Meaning he ramped my rear neighbor[']s yard went airborne, slammed through my privacy fence, then crashed [completely] through my entire garage knocking 3 of the four walls off of its foundation, when I walked around back I was helping the man "Joanne Francois" out of his vehicle because the garage was falling in. As soon as he hopped out all he kept saying was "[I'm OK, I'm OK]!" He was heavily intoxicated. So I yell to my wife to call the cops and then he takes off running. I tackled him at the fence and he started assaulting me so I returned the favor. In the midst of the fight I was able to grab him into the front yard and he persisted on fighting. So I continued to fight back to keep him there. When the police finally arrived a few officers drew weapons at me and told me to get off of the man. I explained what had happened and that he was drunk and they acted as if I was lying. So I demanded the officer in charge to come with me to assess the situation. I was threatened with arrest on multiple occasions because of how loud I was being. When state troopers arrived (for some reason they had to be the ones to administer the breathalyzer) he blew twice the legal limit. After all was said and done he was refused at the jail, got to go home that night, and got a failure to maintain ticket. He had no insurance, no license, and from my understanding the car wasn't in his name. So I am STILL to this day repairing my building slowly. My insurance only covered some of the items inside. And a small amount for the building ([$]6,000 of the [$]60,000 dollars of quoted damages) because of the lack of insurance on his end.
>
> I had fish and reptiles in that building that were dead scattered all over my property. None were covered.
>
> . . . I was called racist for speaking out about it. Being a Haitian [isn't] a race[, it's] a nationality. [That's] like me saying [I'm] Ohionese[.]

> . . . [The Haitian] called me months later asking ME for money. ([He] somehow got my number months later) I assume the insurance company gave it to him which I was thoroughly angry with them and I called to let them know. As far as I know [I'm] still paying for him to party here in Clark County[.]
>
> . . . Meaning my taxes. But no. No apologies. The mayor Rob Rue came over to my house because I called him out on [Facebook] and he was doing the politician thing. Agreeing with all of my points just to turn around at the city [commission] meeting and deny saying all of it. I tried to get him and Bryan Heck the manager of the City of Springfield to install a [guard] rail or concrete bollards in the devil's strip (The grass between the road and sidewalk) of my neighbor[']s property due to it being city owned and [m]y neighbor wanted it as well but I was met with a no from them. Instead they [i]nstalled a sign that has an arrow on it pointing left and right indicating that the road does not continue into my neighbor[']s yard. In my opinion that won[']t stop a car.

I could not believe his story, which is exactly why I did; Quinn was treated by Springfield Police like the assailant, the criminal, the instigator. Why? I can only gander a guess. (He's white.)

Stories like Quinn's are depressingly easy to find on search engines with long-trail keywords like "Springfield Ohio crash," but you'll notice something. And you'll notice what you notice—the race and nationality of the offending driver are rarely reported. "Car crashes into garage in Springfield."[104] Yes, I'm sure it did. All by itself.

It's more than residences, too; I was contacted by **Brian Cox**, who showed me photos and videos of "the aftermath of a Haitian who ran her car all the way through the wall of our business." There's more:

> [The Haitian woman] got in the parked car, put it in drive, and went right through. Wasn't cited because the cops said it was on private property. We had to find a new home for the business.
>
> . . . We're in the process of suing our own insurance company. They tried to deny the claim for moving expenses and loss of income. And I have [h]ad all my insurance with them since 1979.
>
> *(continued . . .)*

> . . . She was on TPS.
>
> . . . [T]he male Haitian [who was with the woman] tried to stare down (you know, mean-mug) my son while he was talking to the police. Didn't work. The Haitians have some sort of money-transfer business there. Now that TPS is done, we'll be reporting the business to ICE.
>
> . . . The way I see it is that Springfield has been having a really hard time for at least the last 35 years. . . . It seems to me that those who want to profit from unfettered third world immigration pick on these types of communities because the people generally are slow to fight back. Many of them are so busy trying to survive they don't have the extra energy to protect themselves from being overrun by hordes of refugees who will only make the area suffer more. Worse, they take advantage of the better nature of the poor white population [who] doesn't want to appear racist. There's something really evil about that, using the best in people to harm them.

There truly is, Brian.

Of course, the most grievous traffic lack-of-safety demonstration of the Haitian situation was the school bus accident that made headlines beyond Springfield. None other than Walter Curt broke that story, but the worst part was . . . he shouldn't have had to.[105] This wasn't an inevitable tragedy, and it didn't need to happen.

On August 22, 2023, the first day of school, Hermanio Joseph, a thirty-five-year-old Haitian immigrant, crossed the center line of the road in a 2010 Honda Odyssey minivan and collided with a Northwestern Local Schools bus carrying fifty-two elementary school students, forcing it off the road down an embankment where it flipped.[106,107] Approximately half the students were injured, and Aiden Clark, eleven, was ejected from the bus and killed.

Hermanio Joseph was later found to be an illegal alien, having come up via Mexico, who was detained at the southern border but then released into the United States in 2022 while given a Notice to Appear before an immigration court.[108] ICE officials pointed to then President Biden's Catch and Release program as the reason for him being let free. He also didn't have a valid U.S. driver's license on him, only a Mexican driver's license, as confirmed by *Breitbart*, who have also independently documented various chaos caused by the influx of Haitian immigrants into Springfield.[109]

Joseph was convicted of multiple felonies on May 1, 2024, in a trial (Case No.: 23-CR-0567) that had started the day before, after the jury deliberated for an hour.[110] His defense was that the sun was in his eyes at the time.

But what made news was not the conviction—which had taken two days and seemed a slam-dunk case given how quickly the jury came to a verdict— but the utterly viral response of Aiden Clark's father.

"I wish that my son was killed by a 60-year-old white man. I bet you never thought anyone would say something so blunt."[111]

What an odd thing to say. I wish young Aiden hadn't been killed at all.

> "Parents' worst nightmare," said Brittany Fisher, who had two kids on the bus when it crashed. "The kids are gonna remember this for the rest of their lives. They're never going to forget this."
>
> Fisher said she rushed towards the scene Tuesday morning after hearing sirens and seeing police cruisers.[112]

Brittany Fisher reached out to me when she learned of this forthcoming book. We spoke, and here is what she wants you, reading this now, to know. Some of you will not have the stomach to read this. That's why you must.

I don't even know where to begin. My two kids . . . were on that bus that day. . . . [My husband] passed away in 2023. . . . It was about six months later that I put my kids on the bus. So I was trying to navigate life being a single mom of three to very small children, a two-year-old, a five-year-old, and a ten-year-old.

[I]t was my five-year-old's first day of kindergarten and my ten-year-old's first day of fifth grade. . . . Anyway, I put them on the bus. I see all these police cruisers go by shortly after. . . . [M]y house [was] right down the road from the school. . . . I immediately get in my car. I'm thinking it's a bomb threat. I go up the road. I parked my car to see the bus that I had just put my kids on completely . . . destroyed. I ran over there. An officer tried to stop me, but I just blew past him. And I thought that Aiden Clark was one of my kids for like thirty seconds. I found one of my children, but I couldn't find . . . my older child.

. . . I started screaming because I thought he was deceased. And then the principal had already made it down, and he knew me, and he told me that [my older son] was in an ambulance and headed to Children's and to take . . . my younger son and just go. . . .

(continued . . .)

. . . I put my younger son in the car. . . . [T]his is all . . . in the middle of all the chaos. . . . Police officers are crying . . . everybody's wailing. There's blood everywhere. It's . . . the worst thing imaginable as a parent.

. . . I immediately . . . drive all the way down to Children's with one of my kids who's injured. . . . [M]y long story short, my older son needed months of physical therapy. He missed months of school. He was wearing high-top sneakers, and they blew off his feet.

At the scene, I was told that the driver was ninety percent over in the wrong lane.

I, as an American citizen, even though I have . . . health insurance, I was left with bills from co-pays that added up from all this physical therapy. So I go to the attorney general's victim of crime fund; they told me to do that. I fill out everything. I'm thinking it's like, *No problem*, you know, *I shouldn't have to pay anything for this*. . . . [T]hey denied my claim. . . .

[T]he day after the accident, I got to meet with the governor, and I looked him in the eyes and I was like, "Please, if there's anything you can do with seat belts . . . Aiden flew. I was there. Aiden flew out of the bus window, and all those children were . . . very injured. And it flipped! So, seat belts . . . can you do something? Because Aiden would still be here had he not flown out of that window."

. . . A little bit after that, he started . . . a panel of people to decide whether or not to put seat belts on school buses. And they decided not to. So I was completely filled with righteous anger [and have been] ever since.

. . . I decided to move.

. . . Northwestern, the community, got together and raised a little bit of money at the beginning, and I was told that they gave Aiden's family [a specific amount] and they gave all of us other people like $1,200 per child, which is sweet. Nobody had to do that. That's great. But that is not gonna cut it. . . . Come on now.

So my three things going forward from this accident have been compensation for Aiden's family and all those kids . . . an investigation into how all of this was even allowed to happen . . . and seat belts on school buses . . . any parent is like, "Of course! Who would not want seat belts on school buses?"

. . . I can't believe . . . I have to fight so hard to get the right things done. And the very people who are supposed to help us, our politicians, I have called everybody, every senator, every [congressional representative], trying to get meetings with people.

. . . Whoever gave this guy [who] hit the bus a fake Mexican ID, I'm sure he's not the only one. Somebody somewhere is orchestrating all of this. And this is all about greed and corruption. The Haitian people have been exploited so they can work at Amazon and places like that and get government benefits so these corporations don't have to pay Americans a living wage.

. . . As far as an investigation into all the fraud and corruption and as far as compensation . . . eventually somebody is probably going to file a lawsuit against the federal government for letting this guy in with TPS with a fake ID, which is a crime and should have never happened. So someday, hopefully, the federal government will get sued and all those kids will get compensated. But nobody's helping me . . . figure that out. . . . [W]ho do I go to who can help us? . . . [W]ho can group someone together and help us get this lawsuit going? Because in a normal accident situation . . . Aiden's family would get . . . half a million or a million-plus dollars.

. . . [O]bviously . . . DeWine . . . doesn't want to meet with me. I've tried. I've called his office several [times]. They know me. I've called his office trying to get a meeting with this guy. I've tried to fill out everything online. . . . He's not interested. He doesn't want to meet with me. I'm just begging him . . . [I]f I could just look him in the eyes, I think we could start moving in the right direction. But instead, he is saying things like, "The Haitians have been good for the economy even though innocent Americans have been killed." Like Aiden Clark and that poor woman who got hit by a car just getting her trash can. . . . And all of that never needed to happen if our government was doing its job protecting American citizens first.

. . . I ended up leaving and moving to Kentucky now . . . and my daughter started kindergarten this past year, and there is a child . . . in her class named Aiden Clark, first name and last name.

. . . God is in control. I'm going to do my part. I can't rest anyway knowing what all those kids have been through and seeing buses around and the first day of school every year . . . I cry because I think about Aiden's family and all those kids [who are] forever traumatized. That's forever with them, and we can't even get seat belts.

. . . [I]f there's any way you could help me, I would greatly appreciate it. And I know those kids would, too.

No additional commentary of mine, added to Brittany's account, can add value to what she has said. It is complete.

Rewinding now to the immediate aftermath, as you might expect, the outcry of Springfield residents was intense. During the City Commission meeting on August 29, then-Mayor Warren Copeland struggled to keep order as the populace present erupted. "Just be quiet, OK?" he ended up shouting at one point.[113]

Perhaps the populist reaction was best summed up by Mark Sanders, a citizen who ended up becoming a bus driver after all this. "One life was taken, but hundreds of lives were impacted. And there's a little girl, [who] still walks in front of my bus every day in the morning getting off her bus going into school that's permanently facially disfigured. And she is the sweetest, cutest, most adorable little girl. And my entire drive behind speaking out to the city, to its employees both elected and not elected, has been the safety aspect."[114]

Aiden's obituary spoke of him being "tragically taken" (and, as morbid coincidence, then-City Commissioner and now-Mayor Rob Rue is co-owner, manager, and president of that funeral home[115]).

Sadly, Aiden Clark isn't the only Haitian driving fatality. On December 1, 2023, thirty-eight-year-old Haitian national Robenson Louis struck and killed a local grandmother, Kathy Lynn Heaton, as she was collecting her trash cans out in front of her home on Springfield Xenia Road.[116] Heaton was your beloved rural Americana "Mawmaw" who loved thrifting, especially at the local animal shelter's thrift store.[117] Louis was struck "with so much blunt force that the sheer impact knocked her socks off and ripped out her silver hair, clumps of which were found snagged within the cracks of the sedan's shattered windshield."[118] Louis was driving the speed limit—with expired tags—and prosecutors declined to file charges.[119] As reported by Townhall.com:

> "I was driving south on my way to work," Louis told a state trooper on-scene. "I didn't see nobody in the roadway at all. I'm not sure if she [Heaton] was already laying down."
>
> It was wet and dark outside, Louis said, insisting that he never noticed Heaton, who was wearing a purple shirt at the time, in the light rain. "I didn't see her clothing. I didn't see her at all," he added.
>
> According to the series of statements Louis provided, he was approximately 200 feet away from the crash site when he realized he had "hit something."

> A witness waiting to take her child to school said she heard "a bang" followed by a long high-pitched squealing sound—Louis slamming on the car's brakes, she presumed.
>
> Law enforcement ultimately faulted Heaton, who was struck while gathering garbage bins on trash pick-up day, saying she "improper[ly]" crossed the pavement.[120]

"They will kill you, and they will blame you for it," an anonymous citizen said to me of Mawmaw's untimely passing. Her daughter-in-law Mandy had this to say at the September 10th Springfield City Commission meeting:

> Months before she was killed, I began noticing the reckless driving and complete disregard for our driving laws by some members of the Haitian community. It made me angry, but now my anger has turned to fear for the safety of my family and the citizens of Springfield.
>
> . . . I'm living in fear in my own city. It's not safe. I am paralyzed with anxiety when I'm getting my children out of the car in any parking lot, walking on any sidewalk, and driving on any road in this town.
>
> I'm haunted by the faces I saw when I had to bear the news to my children and husband that she was dead. Their grandmother, the very person who tucked my seven-year-old twins into bed just six hours before on her 71st birthday, was never coming back.
>
> What everyone has feared is my reality and it's my grief, and it should be yours as well. It saddens me greatly to think about leaving a place I've made a home [and] raised my children . . . [121]

We can also add a recent Lima accident to our tally of those "tragically taken." Around the time I began work on this book, the Haitian Yvio Michel pleaded "Not Guilty" for negligent homicide due to his part in a six-vehicle pileup near Cridersville that cost Hurshel Gipson and his eleven-year-old son their lives.[122,123] Michel, like many of the other cases I've gone over, was not a U.S. citizen and had language difficulties.[124] *Empty Pockets Garage* would interview one of Hurshel's surviving children about it.[125] "This is definitely up there in the hardships," he said.[126]

The correct number of Ohioans killed by Haitians is zero. Every number above that is intent of policy. (That makes four vehicle-related deaths in greater Springfield alone.)

How has Governor DeWine been handling all this? He'd been allocating $2.5 million over two years for health care and traffic safety.[127] He's upped the Ohio

State Highway Patrol troopers and also launched Haitian Creole translation services for driving simulations to "help the population assimilate into our culture and be increasingly self-sufficient."[128]

But it isn't just on the road where people are feeling the pain—or the pinch.

They're Raising the Prices

Glenda Bailey emailed me, and she was not happy.

> Here are the property tax records for my house . . . and the Haitian house [a few doors down]. Check out the "sales" to see how much they paid for it. There is NO WAY that house is worth $110,000. But when they have 10 people living there, they can make their money back, plus MORE in a year or less.
>
> Therefore, I am being PENALIZED with higher property taxes because a Haitian overpaid for their home.

Glenda sent me links to her house and to a nearby neighbor, known for Haitian ownership, leasing, and subletting. The Clark County auditor's web pages I viewed reflect her allegations (I will not be writing them here so as to address-doxx her).

She also wrote me about the old Catholic rectory, which I paid a visit to and met several longtime local residents outside by happenstance. The address is 802 Kenton Street, for reference. She herself had to get the fire department involved due to a burst pipe and water damage reported to her by neighbors. Via email from Glenda:

> 802 Kenton St. Sold for $50,000 in 2014, sold for $239,00 to Haitians in 2022. https://clarkcountyauditor.org/Parcel?Parcel=3400700028120018
>
> Look at all the photos of what this property looked like before the Haitians destroyed it. It only took 2 years to go from the finest property in the neighborhood to the worst. The balusters & stair railings were burned in the fireplace for heat (I assume). It's amazing that this property never caught fire with loss of lives.
>
> https://www.zillow.com/homedetails/802-Kenton-St-Springfield-OH-45505/33317868_zpid/
>
> . . . Look at the spike in property taxes on this house which is on the opposite corner from 802 Kenton St. The taxes DOUBLED over last year's property tax.

> We should have talked to him—I know the old guy . . . I'll bet he's livid . . .
>
> 747 Kenton St.
>
> https://clarkcountyauditor.org/Parcel?Parcel=3400700028300010

Separately, I was sent a Facebook post from July 27, 2024, about the rectory, which reads:

> See this house right here: 802 Kenton St. It is across the street from my daughters house. It was sold in 2022 to someone who lives in Michigan. It has 4 bedrooms and 3 baths. There are AT LEAST 40 influxers living in this house! They park cars on the sidewalks, in peoples yards, throw trash in the streets, relieve themselves in the grass, they do not have trash service and throw bags into others yards and in the street, kids running everywhere, packs of dogs in the yard barking 24/7, music and yelling and screaming at all hours, firing guns in the air, acting like complete idiots, setting off fireworks in the middle of the night, .. and she has called CPS, the cops, code enforcement does NOTHING!! THIS IS UNACCEPTABLE! I have grandchildren over there! And make no mistake, this house does NOT look like this anymore!! This is going on in too many single family homes and IT NEEDS TO STOP! GET THESE PEOPLE OUT OF OUR TOWN!
>
> Look at the spike in property taxes on this house which is on the opposite corner from 802 Kenton St. The taxes DOUBLED over last year's property tax.
>
> We should have talked to him—I know the old guy—his name is Tom. I'll bet he's livid. He just lost his wife about a year ago.

"Why are Haitian refugees coming to Springfield?"[129] This is the question asked on a Clark County FAQ document. The answer? "They found jobs and available and affordable housing here when they were first entering the United States. Today, most of those jobs are filled and housing is hard to find. We have been working to create more housing options for the entire community for the last five years."

It's as if the first sentence of the answer has no relationship to the second sentence, and authorities are shocked. Breathtaking.

In Springfield, HUD Fair Market Rent for a two-bedroom unit rose from $792 in 2021 to $1,061 in 2025, a 33.96 percent increase.[130,131] Not surprising at all because across the United States, foreign-born populations accounted for 60 percent of increased rent demand during the Biden years.[132] Overcrowding, among other things, plays a role. Think about it. Landlords can get away with raising rent on a two-bedroom unit to exorbitant prices, far beyond what might be reasonable for an individual or a family . . . but several families crowding together? Setys Kelly shared with me another story about her family. Her daughter's rent doubled in 2023 for a one-bedroom apartment on North Limestone. Why? It's "full of Haitians."

The Guardian called out Ten Enterprises for buying up and renting out properties all over Springfield to Haitians.[133] There's more. Garlind Properties LLC, meanwhile, owns over three hundred homes or parcels in Clark County, and about 260 of those it purchased since 2019.[134] Many tenants, according to *The New York Times*, are Haitian immigrants.[135] One such migrant spoke with the *Times* under the condition of anonymity and claimed that Garlind Properties is notorious locally for overcharging Haitians for housing. On the public record, the company has many negative reviews on the Better Business Bureau, calling out the poor standards of living, such as infestations of roaches and bed bugs.[136]

Ryan Davis, an attorney for ABLE (Advocates for Basic Legal Equality, a nonprofit we're going to discuss later), had documented leaking roofs, no hot water or heat in the Ohio winter, and more of the overcrowding Haitians have experienced citywide.[137]

The Guardian interviewed one Haitian, "John" (once again, not the real name), who said he paid $50 a week for a room in a house he shared with another whole family of Haitians, and that didn't include the people who came and went. Substandard conditions were, unfortunately, all too common in Springfield, especially for the newly arrived Haitians.[138]

NPR interviewed one Patrick Joseph, who used to work for Royal Caribbean Cruises, which gave him access to a visa.[139] When the pandemic hit and Haiti devolved into worsened gang anarchy following their president's assassination, he fled to Springfield where he worked in a steel manufacturing plant and in the nonprofit sector as a Creole translator, but he, too, lived in cramped conditions—in a two-bedroom house with fifteen other Haitian immigrants. He would call his wife back in Haiti, and she would tell him, "Be careful. Be courageous. Survive." If the person still stuck in the country consumed by gang violence has to tell *you* to survive, how bad do you have it?

In 2025, the city of Springfield had to establish a rental property registry to combat the negligence of landlords, to make sure the properties being rented out were actually livable.[140] And it's not just the roaches that people are worried about. On April 8, 2023, firefighters were responding to a gas leak in the area of the Ridgewood Court Townhomes when an explosion rocked the 1000 block of East Home Road.[141] Three victims were recovered and evacuated via medical helicopters. Unfortunately, on April 10, the first victim, Edeline Ducatel, age fifty, passed away from the severe burn injuries, and her sister Macdala Ducatel, age thirty-nine, passed away a few days later.[142,143] Macdala's baby, an eleven-month old girl, was later released from the hospital.

I spoke with the private investigator who had been hired to look into the matter. The authorities ruled it was a natural gas leak and not foul play.[144] Regardless, it was a senseless tragedy that displaced eight families.[145] Local groups like St. Vincent de Paul helped arrange the funeral and provided other aid.[146]

There's more. From Asra Nomani in *The Jewish Journal*:

> Between June 10, 2021, and June 30, 2021, as Haitian workers flooded into town, the town's mayor, Rob Rue, bought seven properties on N. Limestone Street, E. Madison Avenue and Mason Street for a total cost of $1.78 million through a company, Littleton Properties of Springfield LLC, according to property records.
>
> In recent weeks, as the purchases became public, raising criticism in the community, Mayor Rob said he rents the homes to Haitians, but says he rents them at market rates. Whatever the case, he, too, has been quietly profiting from the influx of low-wage labor. He has said he has done nothing wrong.
>
> It was a growing pattern in Springfield.[147]

And that pattern led Springfield's housing authority director to suggest Haitian-renting, specifically, has been forcing long-time residents out of their homes, as landlords charge Haitians per person or per bed rather than per unit because these migrants are more willing to live together and suffer higher rent.[148,149]

What's more, city authorities had announced they're building about 1,200 housing units in a West Springfield suburb in hopes of alleviating the housing pressure.[150] The only problem? Those single-family homes are expected to *start* at $300,000. For most residents of Springfield, the median household income is just above $45,000, so those homes are priced out of reach for most of the people they're ostensibly here to help.[151]

The latest updates as of this writing are still not looking good. Rent is still too much, and people are finding that they're barely able to afford places that are in a state of disrepair.[152]

This "competitive" environment (which doesn't count as actual market competition when one party is being abusively price-gouged) means that the heritage citizens of Springfield are being displaced.[153] Where once landlords were offering properties to tenants who needed government support, and utilizing those programs, they realized they could make a better profit by focusing on "market-based rents," (though how much of that is actual fair pricing and not preying on Haitian immigrants willingness to overpay, who can say).

Ten-year-old Khyre Davis said, "Our landlord kicked us out so they can move some of the Haitians in."[154]

So if things are so bad, why doesn't the government step in and fix things? One word answer: **taxes**.

City officials praise the Haitian immigrant population, and it's clear to see why.[155] *The Springfield News-Sun* reported that "From 2021 to 2022, the city saw an increase of more than $9.2 million in income tax revenue."[156] Another article, from June 2022, stated that "the portion of income tax that makes up general fund revenues have continued to increase going from making up 75.24% of general fund revenues in 2014 to now expecting to make up 81.37% of those revenues in 2023 . . . Income tax collections have been increasing over the years."[157] The one exception was during the COVID-19 experience.

For additional context, income tax collections had increased over the years, as captured in the second article, but when the city released their preliminary 2026 budget, they remarked that "The 2026 Budget was developed amid continued economic uncertainty—defined by declining income tax revenues, inflationary pressures, and increasing service demands."[158] Declining income tax revenues.

Makes you think.

They're Demanding the Welfare

Clark County's 2023 annual report had a short article from the Department of Job and Family Services headlined "Demand Increased with Haitian Influx."[159] The agency saw the caseload of Haitian Creole immigrants increase dramatically, presenting new challenges for agency staff and resources. The BenefitsPlus division saw more than 1,400 individuals receive Refugee Cash Assistance worth more than $2.2 million." That's about $1,571 per person.[160]

These Haitian immigrants are eligible for . . . guess what? Recall from Chapter 5: TANF (Temporary Assistance for Needy Families), SNAP, and Medicaid, as well now as a special Refugee Cash Assistance program for those without children.[161] Ohio DJFS caseload data for Clark County from July 2024 showed 11,714 SNAP households covering 22,820 active members.[162] Ohio Works First (TANF, you may recall) covered 1,265 households with 2,484 active members. Also, then-Lt. Governor Jon Husted posted on September 11, 2024 that 4,324 Haitian refugees were receiving either TANF, SNAP, or Refugee Cash Assistance in Clark County, and 6,590 non-citizens were receiving Medicaid benefits.[163] Whoa.

Many of these immigrants hadn't learned to speak or read English, so ESL classes needed to be funded, with that coming from both the state government and various nonprofits.[164] Meanwhile, local college Clark State received a $250,000 grant from the Ohio Department of Development to further expand their ESL classes amid the Haitian influx.[165]

Security costs, translations, government staffing . . . all of these and more ended up being more line-item costs to everyone, it seems, except the Haitians themselves. Their qualified-entitlements list seems endless. According to a Haitian influx document from Clark County, "these are just a few of the steps we are taking" that are of course not free:

- . . . Collaborating with the Haitian Community Help and Support Center to help bridge the gap between local agencies and our new neighbors. *
- Increasing security around county buildings and services for the safety of all citizens.
- Identifying locations for additional health clinics.
- Filling vacancies at key government agencies in the county with shared support.
- Equipping law enforcement and social workers with translation tools.
- Researching and planning a one-stop center for our Haitian residents.
- Providing more support to local schools.
- Collaborating with the state and federal governments to have essential documents translated into Haitian Creole.[166]

Furthermore, that same document, under the question, "Are Haitian refugees registering to vote?" we read:

> The Clark County Department of Job and Family Services is required by state law to provide voter registration forms to every customer during the benefits process including the application, reapplication and change of address. Currently, the Ohio Secretary of State's office has only approved voter registration forms in English and Spanish. The form is not being offered in Haitian Creole. Any form in Haitian Creole is invalid and is

> not approved by the county Board of Elections or the Ohio Secretary of State's Office. It is illegal to create a voter registration form without the state's consent.[167]

Notice it sounds like no but it's not a "no."

Beyond that, state and federal cuts are coming to Springfield for food bank funding, health-care funding, housing development grants, and more.[168] Meanwhile, longtime shelters for both men and women have announced closure following their own funding disputes with the City of Springfield.[169]

Are you paying attention yet?

Someone is with regard to the aforementioned voter registration business: Ohio Secretary of State Frank LaRose. Read this excerpted media release from September 12, 2024:

> Secretary of State Frank LaRose announced today that his Election Integrity Unit has issued a warning to Ohio's 88 county boards of elections after an investigation uncovered the use of illegal voter registration forms by a government agency.
>
> . . . The office's Election Integrity Unit recently concluded an investigation into the origins of an illegal voter registration form translated into the Haitian Creole language. The Clark County Board of Elections reported this form to our office after rejecting its submission by a local applicant.
>
> "The Board confirmed they've only received one of these unauthorized forms, but they rightly recognized it as illegal and worked with my team to track down its source with the help of a county government assistance office," said Hun Yi, Director of Investigations for the office's Public Integrity Division, in a memo to elections officials. "The form was erroneously included among others outsourced to a foreign language translation service. It garnered national attention considering the high number of Haitian refugees that have recently migrated to the Springfield area, and it serves as an important reminder that boards and designated voter registration agencies should be vigilant about the use of forms submitted to their office."[170]
>
> . . . The memo concludes with a notice of ongoing investigations into evidence of a pattern of fraudulent voter registration activity in multiple counties under the paid employment of a group called Black Fork Strategies.

And what is Black Fork Strategies? They're "an Ohio based progressive organization that touts itself as 'Building Long-Term Progressive Power' [and] has been identified by Hamilton county elections officials as having submitted a number of irregular voter registrations and changes," among others.[171] Black Fork Strategies has been associated with "multiple instances of fraud discovered by the board of elections, including a 'stack of registration forms' that appear to be in the same handwriting submitted by a Black Fork canvasser . . . Canvassers have a long history of taking advantage of disadvantaged individuals who may not speak English well enough to understand what they're being asked to sign."[172]

This wasn't the end of it. From the Associated Press:

> FBI agents have searched the office of an Ohio group that supports voter registration efforts, seizing documents and computer files . . . Federal agents showed up at the Cleveland office of the Ohio Organizing Collaborative . . . The organization was founded in 2007 and describes its mission as fighting for criminal justice reform, racial justice and an expansion of voting rights.[173]

Now, Signal Ohio:

> Black Fork is owned by Kirk Noden, a founder of the Ohio Organizing Collaborative, the group the FBI searched, according to tax returns filed by the group and its affiliates. The Ohio Organizing Campaign, the Ohio Organizing Collaborative's political arm, paid $10.6 million to Black Fork in 2023 and 2024 for consulting services, an amount equal to about 93% of the group's total spending in those years, tax filings show.[174]

Interesting.

I wonder if that Haitian Creole language form in Clark County was the only one.

They're Getting Free Health Care

Yet another source of stress on the system is health care, and that's where Glenda Bailey re-enters. She first noticed vans from First Diversity Staffing hauling new Haitian arrivals to the Dole facility during COVID-19 in 2020. Her son worked there, and reported to her that everyone was getting sick. She tried to do her duty and raise the alarm, but when she warned the health department, the official she was speaking to threatened her with a HIPAA violation and hung up on her.

In 2021, Glenda began delivering express-mail envelopes daily at the post office. One of those deliveries took her inside 1322 South Limestone, where the dark, stagnant air and a "creepy" man (her words) emerging from the shadows gave her such a bad feeling that she wanted to stop breathing the air.[175] She got out as fast as she could, but even then it was too late. She tested positive for latent tuberculosis—her prior tests had been negative, and she had been in the lowest-risk category—yet the new health director "couldn't care less," she told me. Glenda showed me her before-and-after tuberculosis tests to show me that she had indeed contracted the disease. As a result, Glenda had to go on two months' worth of medication and delay a scheduled hip replacement surgery.

"I'm in the lowest-risk category. . . . And now for the rest of my life, I will always test positive for TB."

Then-Senator JD Vance posted on 𝕏 that HIV and tuberculosis were "on the rise" in Springfield.[176] For tuberculosis specifically, the cumulative Clark County report shows annual active TB counts of one case in 2019, and four cases in 2023.[177] That's technically a 300 percent increase. The newer 2024 annual communicable disease report shows seven active TB cases in 2024.[178] Compared with one case in 2019, that is a 600 percent increase.

For HIV, the 2022 Clark County HIV summary shows six new HIV diagnoses in 2019, six in 2020, twelve in 2021, and thirteen in 2022.[179] That means from 2019 to 2022, new diagnoses increased from six to thirteen, or about 117 percent. But the revised 2023 annual Clark County report shows twenty new HIV diagnoses in 2023.[180] From six in 2019 to twenty in 2023 is about a 233 percent increase. The 2024 annual report lists thirty-two preliminary HIV new diagnoses for 2024, but the report itself warns that 2024 HIV data are preliminary and should not be used for comparison to previous years, program planning, or trend analysis.[181] Even if someone ignored that warning and compared six in 2019 to thirty-two in 2024, the increase would be about 433 percent.

What of treatment? The revised 2023 Clark County report says there were eighty-three individuals recommended for latent TB treatment and forty-one individuals on latent treatment in 2023.[182] But that is not the same thing as active TB case counts.

So in short, for tuberculosis, between 300 percent to 600 percent increase, depending on what year you stop at. For HIV? 117 percent increase through 2022, 233 percent increase through 2023, or 433 percent, at the risk of using preliminary data from a report that says it shouldn't be used for trend analysis.

The primacy of healthcare for Haitians in Springfield has reached the point where official Clark County documents need to "debunk" the "myths" that an entire wing of the local hospital is dedicated to Haitian women with HIV/AIDS.[183] When answering how much of the health budget is diverted towards Haitian residents, the response is head-scratchingly bizarre: "The Clark County Combined Health District's budget was about $10 million during fiscal year 2023. The district estimates it spends $56,000 per month serving the Haitian population, or about 6.7% of its annual budget. Source: CCCHD."

Do you believe that? $56,000 a month for even twenty thousand Haitians?

The last twelve videos on the Clark County Combined Health District YouTube channel are with captions in Haitian Creole, and one on tenant rights (which seems a bit out of place, given that the channel is ostensibly about health and medicine).[184] But even the Clark County Health Department website explicitly prioritizes Haitians' health needs. Let's take a look.

What's "Health Equity" you may ask?[185] Well, on this particular Clark County website, you get a video on access and disparity that demonstrates the Health Equity worldview. To paraphrase, it's cosmically unfair that these people are struggling relative to you, therefore, you need to have what is yours, taken from you. While there are statistics here, like the number of black women more likely to die in childbirth, the embedded video is happy to blame racism, a true culprit for health outcome disparity.

If you believe something to be wrongly true, are you not less likely to act as if something else is actually true?

What are some of the beliefs these migrants are bringing with them that are of supreme importance to the Clark County Combined Health District? Their website features a document entitled "Notes about: Food and Culture of Haiti." The introduction states its origin: "We compiled these notes by looking through written sources and amending and altering them through review of our public health co-workers here at Clark County Combined Health District."[186]

Let's talk about food because the health department wants us to. Lemons and limes, for example, are conflated in Haitian culture; "the green one" or "the yellow one" is how limes might be differentiated from lemons.[187] Your local Haitian patient might ask for "*citron*" (Creole for "lemon") when they actually want a lime. Or pineapples. Traditionally for Haitian culture, pineapples are considered to make women's menstrual bleeding worse, and eating pineapple during the day, while the sun is out, is a way to make one sick.

But you might be wondering what this has to do with medicine. Surely mistaking a lemon for a lime is embarrassing to any American of approximately three years of age or older as are ideas superstitious about avoiding pineapples. Well, it turns out some foods are also used as traditional medicine and will often be employed *before* seeking treatment. Soursop fruit, or *guanabana*, according to these beliefs, will prevent cancer; garlic tea will treat high blood pressure.[188] Aloe vera also has cancer-preventing qualities, according to traditional Haitian beliefs, but it also "cleans the blood." Honey supposedly promotes brain health, and pigeon meat is used to treat anemia.

The supremely anti-scientific health department memo also contains mention of "hot" illnesses such as diarrhea that require "cold" food to temper, like banana or mango.[189] But the real balance to note is between "heavy" foods (e.g., meat, rice, beans, or corn-meal), which should be consumed at midday, and "light" foods (e.g., soup, broth, or bouillon), which should be consumed in the mornings and evenings. Heavy foods also should be avoided when one is recovering from diarrhea, a symptom of typhoid fever. "Although largely forgotten in the developed world, it remains endemic in Haiti."[190]

I wonder why.

Another Clark County public health resource is entitled, "Notes about: Haitian Beliefs about Death." The document begins, "It is important to remember that just like language dialects and foods, many of the beliefs about death and dying are influenced by various factors . . . "[191]

It's important, OK. Let's peruse the document to see what's so important. What's this first, oh, organ donation. That could be a life-saving industry. But, oh—"This practice is not widely accepted in Haiti. There is an emphasis on keeping the body intact after death to be prepared for afterlife and resurrection."[192]

I remember from museum visits as a child something about this. The ancient Egyptians used canopic jars to preserve various organs for a similar purpose.

. . . four thousand seven hundred years ago.

So, what else?

Cremation is also unpopular because the body can "still feel" and thus would be in pain from the heat; burial is preferred for this reason.[193] Morgues, likewise, are unpopular for the cold as that could cause the corpse "discomfort."[194] Autopsies are also uncommon in Haiti and are regarded with suspicion.

Another bit of trivia covers the color red. It's the color of blood and must be avoided being worn in any instance when honoring the deceased. Wearing it at a funeral is disrespecting the family of the deceased or even evidence of you confessing you murdered that person. In the Haitian mind, death is considered unnatural and thus must be caused by someone else (even by their thoughts alone such as through literally "curses").

All these various factors can, well, factor into hospice care for the Haitians of Springfield, which the document warns could be "confusing to immigrants from

Haiti" as they might think palliative care hastens the terminal patient's death. [195] Or take the tragedy of infant death; this is interpreted as, again, entirely unnatural, possibly the result of various curse factors, so the family may seek out a voodoo priest to break the curse and raise the baby from the dead. Commonly, expectant Haitians mothers do not accept opportunities to receive prenatal care. Such a patient "has had limited opportunity to think about that baby as a person and may instead think of pregnancy as more of a condition." [196]

The document also notes a particular syndrome specific to Haiti, called *Se'izisman*, literally "seized-up-ness," a kind of paralysis brought on by extreme emotions, themselves often caused by receiving bad news or seeing dead bodies. This can cause headaches, loss of vision, weeping, refusal to eat, and all manner of other symptoms. Furthermore, Haitians believe *Se'izisman* can cause miscarriages or contaminate breastmilk and as such seek to protect pregnant and postpartum women from potentially "contracting" this syndrome. [197]

But we can't forget zombies. Yes, you heard me right. Zombification is an ubiquitous Haitian folk belief.[198] These are spirits of those slain by a voodoo priest that are then captured and brought back as a mindless slave. The priest would need permission from the master of the cemetery to do such a work. This is often seen as a punishment on the victim. Ironically, this is the most outlandish of the various factors discussed but also the most true: Zombies are real. I'm not kidding. As reported in *Harvard Magazine*, Wade Davis, an ethnobotanist, discovered that the zombie potion used by voodoo priests wasn't mere superstition but utilized pufferfish venom, containing a powerful paralytic known as tetrodotoxin. Ironically enough, pufferfish is a delicacy in Japan, known as *fugu,* and just enough of the poison is left in the dish to cause psychoactive effects, but those who overdose end up exhibiting very similar symptoms to Haitian zombification. Putting two and two together, he recognized that a Haitian witch or sorcerer, called a *bokor,* would dose someone (usually a social pariah they've been hired to "punish") with a powder containing dried pufferfish. That victim would fall into a deathlike state of paralysis, be buried, and then quickly dug up by the *bokor* and put to work as a zombie, an eternal slave. Definitely a horrifying end for people in a country founded through slave revolt.[199]

Beyond their beliefs and the special considerations that must now be made so as not to cause cultural offense to the newcomers, the influx of Haitian migrants has put a strain on the maternity wards of Clark County. County Health Commissioner Chris Cook, speaking at a church during an NAACP Town Hall about mass deportations, said on a record video I was sent that Haitian children "are the future of our community. . . . We've been made better by immigration over the past few years in ways we can't realize."

Cook has recently announced he is resigning at the end of 2026.[200] He, of course, blamed it on "the trickle-down effect of federal policy and funding being completely out of touch with the immense public health needs of our community" after the U.S. Department of Health and Human Services cut an anticipated grant worth $2.7 million. And according to *The Springfield News-Sun*, "The grant funded basic critical infectious disease investigation and the health district spent $947,093.67 of the total award."

NAACP

Springfield Ohio Branch 3201

Serving Clark, Greene & Champaign Counties

DENISE WILLIAMS, PRESIDENT
OFFICE 937-521-2650

TOWN HALL

Preparation for Mass Deportations

THURSDAY | DEC 4, 2025 | 6:00 - 8:00 PM

ST. JOHN MISSIONARY BAPTIST CHURCH

34 W PLEASANT ST., SPRINGFIELD, OH 45506

---

*Join **President Denise Williams**, NAACP 3201,*
***Pastor Carl Ruby**, Central Christian Church,*
Ohio Govenor DeWine's team & prominent speakers
to discuss mass deportations in Springfield, Ohio

SECURITY WILL BE PRESENT

Meanwhile, Clark County's Haitian influx FAQ document says, when asked how many recorded births can be attributed to Haitian residents, "Through July of 2024, there were 685 live births in Clark County, including 156 babies born to Haitian mothers. That represents about 22.8% of all live births in Clark County. Please note that not all births to Clark County residents occur locally.

Source: CCCHD."[201] More tragically, some estimates say that 25 percent to 30 percent of infant deaths in the county are from Haitian families.[202] It's part of why they're targeting Haitians for maternal care "outreach," according to some internal documents.[203]

But we've done some digging. We can give an exact total from 2021 to 2025, pulled from Clark County Combined Health District materials.

2021: 1,053 births.[204]
2022: 1,096 births.[205]
2023: 1,258 births.[206]
2024: 1,268 births.[207]
2025: 1,273 births.[208]

That puts Clark County at 5,945 births total from 2021 through December 2025. Approximately 20 percent of all new births are Haitian.

They're Getting the Schools

That same Clark County Haitian influx FAQ document lists in the "steps we are taking" a very vague note they will be "[p]roviding more support to local schools."[209] Why? Setys Kelly said to *Newsweek*, "The school systems are overloaded. The first week of school we had 300 new Haitian students that had never attended school here before. Last year, they were getting about 40 new kids per week at the school system, and it was costing approximately $10,000 per student, per year, to educate them."[210] Add to the complication that many of these kids don't speak English, and you can imagine the chaos and the cost of translation services.

Here we see the Enrollment Trajectory—the following image was compiled by Walter Curt with data from relevant sources.[211,212,213]

School Enrollment and ESL/Translation Cost Data

Period	ELL Students	% of Total	Notes
2019–2020	~200	~2.7%	Baseline
2022–2023	610	8.5%	Rapid growth begins
Sept 2023	~900	~12%	
October 2024	1,193	~16%	National spotlight
Feb 2025 (peak)	1,347	~18%	All-time high
April 2025	1,258	~17%	Slight decline

Haitian Creole-speaking students specifically rose from **151 (2023–24) to 572 (2024–25)**—a 278 percent year-over-year increase.[214]

This, obviously, causes a spike in translation costs. The school district, in response to the influx of new enrollments, hired approximately two dozen teachers certified to teach English as a second language, and also hired multiple Haitian-Creole language interpreters.[215] How much? Well, the translation expense went from $43,000 four years ago to $436,000.[216] That's a whole order of magnitude. Six translators of Haitian Creole, eighteen ESL teachers, and eight bilingual assistants, and tablets to assist in live translation services, all for fifteen schools.

President Trump complained that each student would "have a private interpreter."[217]

"So the mayor of Springfield, and I think he's a very nice person," Trump continued. "But instead of saying we're getting them all out . . . he says, very simply, 'we're hiring teachers to teach them English.'[218]

"Could you believe it? 'We are hiring interpreters.' So when they go to school and take the place of our children in school, we have an interpreter. Each one will have a private interpreter. What the hell is wrong with our country?" he asked.[219]

It's gotten to the point where Ohio state police have to show up to help protect schools, according to the governor, thanks to bomb threats. Thirty-three of them, in fact. But none of those threats, purportedly meant to harass the Haitian and Haitian-ally populations, were deemed credible; most were determined by the Cincinnati field office of the FBI to be from "overseas" perpetrators, often "Russia."[220] That way, no domestic charges needed to be filed. More interestingly, a civil lawsuit against radical ethnocentric group The Blood Tribe accused them of hacking the personal email account of the Executive Director of St. Vincent De Paul, one Casey Rollins, to send the emails from.

Thing is, none of the thirty-three bomb threats were tied to The Blood Tribe. And more to the point, the first of those threats came around September 2024. *City of Springfield, Ohio v. The Blood Tribe* was not filed until February 6, 2025.[221] "An email address of Rollins's was hacked, and the hacker used that email address to send a bomb threat," reads the complaint, but no evidence for this specific claim is presented that I could find.[222] Rollins's contact information was published on social media, but this information matches the same type of personal records that most of us already have available to the general public.[223,224] You are thinking what I am thinking.

But the situation isn't just fake bomb threats. An anonymous woman who had worked at a Springfield elementary school told me that approximately ten Haitian men ended up living behind a playground in what she believed to be not a residential but commercial building. They would come and stand at the fence to the playground during recess and watch. Soon, they pulled out lawn chairs. One of them, she saw counting the children on his hand, one finger, one child at a time.

"Why are they staring at us?" one student had asked.

This employee brought it up to an administrative staff member, who told her, she said, "They must just miss their families."

"The Expense of Your Citizens"

These stories and numbers could easily be dismissed as an example of the classic "after this, therefore because of this" fallacy—*post hoc ergo propter hoc*. That might be fair. But if you had to bet, an abundance of qualitative evidence the likes of which were presented to me by the heritage citizenry (and now, in part and portion, to you) would normally suggest that at least some nominal quantitative data should exist as well. And it does. Together, the numbers and the narrative agree. From Diana Daniels:

> Beginning of 2022 is when I began to notice that I was unsafe. I couldn't ride. I was having trouble riding my bike. I'm a commuter. I biked to work, bike to school for thirty years. In 2022, it became dangerous. I was always being cut off, or somebody would run a red light, and it always happened to be a black person—not to say for any racist reason, but I'm like, *What's what's going on?* Then it began to dawn on me . . . Other people were talking about it. I began to do my research and look around a little bit and started to notice those vans, all with a number, and they're always picking up multiple people and taking off, taking them wherever they needed to go. So now you balloon to 20,000 or 15,000 on top of 8,000 Hispanics . . .
>
> [H]ow the Haitians ate Springfield, that's exactly how it happened. All of a sudden, all the housing is taken up. There are two sets of victims. There are us who are displaced. And then you have promises made and never kept to these immigrants who are coming here and looking for a better life and instead are put sixty-four in one single house.
>
> So, the rectory at St. Joe's, which is where the nuns all lived and the priest. It was bought up by a Mexican and then was bought by a Haitian. . . . I can't remember when it started, but they housed sixty-four humans in the
>
> *(continued . . .)*

rectory . . . and the rectory is designed for . . . maybe thirteen or fourteen . . . Now you have sixty-four humans.

They tore out the toilets. Why would they tear out the toilets? . . . It's not [weird]. You've got to think about Haitians. Because I asked Francois this question, too.

I said, "Why aren't you drinking the water?" . . . [E]ach one of them would carry into the apartment like two thirty-two packs of water.

"We don't like the water."

"What's wrong with it?"

"It tastes funny."

Well, yeah, because the water treatment plant. . . . [T]hey can taste that. If you're used to drinking spring water, again, it tastes funny.

. . . [I]f you are in a jungle climate, what's going to live in your toilets? . . . They're deathly afraid of snakes. They didn't use the toilets because they were afraid snakes were going to come up and bite them, so they removed them, which means you were just basically pouring your excrement down the sewer line. How unsanitary is that?

. . . So now you have sixty-four Haitians in one house forced to live like cattle. How inhumane is that? They were promised a place to stay, but they weren't told what that was going to look like. . . . [I]magine you've been recruited and promised a plane ride to the United States, to the land of milk and honey, where you will get a job, and you'll have everything you ever wanted. So you board the plane, and you land in Miami . . . *Wow, it's so clean, there's no smoke* . . . And there on the tarmac is a person who speaks your language and says to you, "Welcome to America. Let me help you," And he directs you to a van or bus and says, "We're going to send you to Springfield, Ohio. And when you get there, you will have a place to live, and we'll take care of everything and get you a job." So you get to Springfield, Ohio, and you've dropped off at Kroger or Walmart. . . . They tell you where to go. They tell you to go to First Diversity, and you go to First Diversity, and instead of a place to live, you're given a bed, which you share with two other people in shifts. Then the van picks you up and takes you to work, but at the same time another van is dropping off the other person who's going to sleep in your bed while you're working your shift. That's how these folks were treated through 2022 and 2023.

We're not talking anywhere near what they expected. . . . You expected to make a living wage. Well, $11 to Francois and Jean Pierre looked like a gold mine. Except that it was not because they were just barely making it. They had to live together in order to pay the exorbitant rent, which now, instead of it being, say, $600 a month, is now $1,500 a month. So everybody with that meager paycheck, you now have to work together . . . to get yourself back and forth to work and all of that. . . . [I]t was the promise that never came true, which was another reason I told Francois and Jean Pierre to leave and come back; they know that they were being underpaid. When they first told me that they were making $11 an hour, I almost cried.

Their money was not coming from a KTH. They were being paid by these people who kept the top and gave them their cut.

. . . These stories from Francois, these stories from Jean Pierre . . . flesh out what is actually happening to the Haitians and what is happening to us. . . . [Y]ou know how your radar starts going off and the hair stands up on the back of your neck? . . . I was hearing rumbles because I was retired, and I was only working at the bike shop . . . I started hearing things from my friends. What was happening with accidents, long lines at the DMV, not being able to get your baby seen at the Rocking Horse because there were people speaking a foreign language, blah, blah, blah.

I had one . . . friend, and she came into the shop and she was crying.

I don't know what to do. I'm like, "What's wrong?" She said, "Well, I have a child . . . I got kicked out of my apartment. Well, not really kicked out, but I don't have any place to live. I'm living in my car."

I said, "Well, haven't you applied for assistance through HUD?"

"I had all my paperwork filled out, and yesterday I was getting ready to move in, and I got a phone call that I had lost my place in line for an apartment."

"What do you mean you lost your place in line? You qualify."

"No, they gave it to someone else."

I said, "Who did they give it to?"

She said, "A Haitian."

"Why?"

"They can make more money from their money than from my voucher from my welfare."

(continued . . .)

. . . I just told her, "Try to go to your mom in Dayton and stay there. Get your feet back on the ground, and I'm sure they'll find a place for you."

That was my first story of seeing what was actually happening to Springfield residents. Then you have the blow up with the bus.

I kept going to city commission meetings, and it energized people to come forward and talk about their stories. On three separate occasions, we had people come to the podium and talk about what had happened to them. One family that had lived in their [place] . . . for seven years had a knock on the door, and it was a Creole-speaking person telling them they had to get out; they had two days. So somebody else bought the house . . . and kicked them out. They had two days to get out. I believe Shannon Meadows took care of that. I wanted to find out who it was that kicked them out, but I was not allowed to be received and talk to these two ladies basically because I would have found out who it was and how they came to be kicked out of a place that they had been in and paid their rent on time for seven years.

We had another lady do the same thing. She came up and said, "My landlord told me I had to leave, that he was renting out to somebody else. I can't afford $1,200 a month." You have that happening, and you have that happening over and over and over. Do you know how many people we have lost through that process? I'm sure it's well over 2,000.

And then you have the homeless population, and that's something that [Ken Seelig] is speaking on, and he did. Our homeless population is not necessarily comprised 100 percent by drug addicts and veterans with PTSD. These are people that were forced out of their apartments and their homes and forced to live in their cars because the rent was forced up and they couldn't afford the rent. Whereas . . . Haitians are used to communal living . . . because communal living is normal, and it's also normal for Hispanics. It's very normal for them to live together, particularly if it's all men, which is basically what it is. It's all guys. They just all buddy up together and share beds or do different shifts, and they're OK with that because that's normal for them. It's not normal for us. But then, of course, you have diseases and all that kind of stuff.

So those homeless that are in that situation are what we're dealing with as far as—I want to say—probably 20 to 25 percent of the homeless are those people who don't want to leave, who want to stay here. They're still working but aren't making enough to pay as high as the rent has been raised.

It's a mess, and I don't know how we get out from underneath it. Except I want a do-over. I want my city back. And that's what you're probably going to hear from a lot of folks if you talk to them long enough is, "I want my city back. I love this place. I love Springfield." For as much as I gripe and complain and bitch and moan, it's all about public safety. It's all about what's happened to us. I know they're victims, too, but what about us? The focus has been, "oh, the poor Haitians." Well, what about us who don't have a place to live anymore? Who have left? Someone left because they're afraid to drive on the roads. We're afraid to go to the grocery. We can't go to the DMV. We can't go to the hospital.

The increased rent means what to the city? You're going to make more money off of somebody paying rent for $1,200 than somebody paying $350. So higher rents on apartments means more money for the city. . . . Now, if these folks are living ten to a house, you know, and each person is making, say, $500 a week, what's that going to do? They spend more money? The thing with sales tax, though, is these folks aren't buying big-ticket items because they're living communally. They're not buying washers and dryers. They're not buying stoves . . . We figure about $9 billion from Springfield [in remittances to Haiti] . . . all of us who are doing the deep-dives into Western Union ATMs and all of that. So, ATMs are easy to wire money. . . . And you can use Bitcoin. We've been going around checking out these little convenience stores. Every single one of the Haitian convenience stores has an ATM that does Bitcoin. Untraceable. So we've got money in a steady stream going back to Haiti. It's not staying here. It's not benefiting us except for those higher rents. . . . The cars that they're buying? They're not buying them with their own money. They're buying them on a voucher that they're getting for transportation . . . If you have a job . . . and you have your green card, you can get a voucher for transportation. You can use that any way you want to. You can either use it for daily trips . . . or the bus . . . or you can buy a car, which you can't drive because you don't know how.

By the way, the sixty-four Haitians who lived at the rectory? I spoke with two confirmed-long-time neighbors of the building that day I visited and paced the sidewalk around it. They told me it was closer to a hundred.. It also came to me that the toilets in the rectory had been recently replaced after the initial disposal.

While Diana's $9 billion in remittances hypothesis is significantly higher than the conservative estimate Grok presented to me (and now also to you) even all totaled up, I will go on this record as agreeing with her and with the Haitians themselves: A lot of Haitians sent a lot of money back to Haiti. And if they bought it in Bitcoin, playing out this hypothetical, Diana's number is decidedly not crazy. Understand that $20 million in Bitcoin bought around the 2022 bottom would have grown to roughly $160 million at the 2025 peak.[225,226] Of course, the remittances were ongoing over several years and were unlikely to have all been transacted in Bitcoin, but you understand the point. It's not crazy.

"Liberals act as if the only reason anyone would want to revoke Haitians 'temporary' (15 yrs) protected status is because we HATE Haitians. No, the point is, why does everyone across the globe have to come HERE whenever anything bad happens," wrote the original provocateurette, Ann Coulter, on 𝕏.[227]

Prior to Candidate Trump's cats and dogs remark, then-Lt. Governor Jon Husted shared on 𝕏 his own findings:

> . . . The local officials I spoke with explained these major problems:
>
> - Immigration without assimilation. Language barriers drive up costs and make it hard for educators and health care providers to do their jobs.
> - Highway safety was raised as an issue because of language barriers and a lack of training. There are many Haitian drivers who are not licensed or can't read or follow basic traffic laws.
> - Costs: Translation services are expensive and the costs of heath care services are a burden on the taxpayers because they're either paid for by Medicaid or when uninsured the cost ultimately are born by the community or healthcare providers.
> - I was told by a healthcare provider that there has been an uptick in tuberculosis and other diseases due to lack of vaccinations.
> - Employers are hiring many of the Haitian population to work in food processing plants, manufacturing, and in warehouse and distribution facilities.
>
> How did they get here? The best explanation is that temporary employment agencies were connecting Haitians to jobs at local food processing plants and this created a pipeline into Springfield. There may be other explanations, but this is the one that I heard most frequently.

> Many local residents expressed compassion for the Haitian refugees, explaining that they understand that Haiti is a terrible place to live right now and they understood why they would want to come to America. But it was also abundantly clear that local officials and citizens have little recourse and need help. The federal government's implementation of immigration laws that have led to this overwhelming influx which the community just can't handle and that has generated a lot of anger and resentment.
>
> State and local officials can only enforce laws that are broken, and they can't make refugees leave or relocate. Even when you find someone who is in U.S. illegally, this is what most often will happen: Law enforcement officials across Ohio consistently say that when they find illegal immigrants in their community, that U.S. Immigration and Customs Enforcement (ICE) will rarely follow through with arrest, detention and deportation. In fact, most say that unless a felony is committed, ICE will not respond.
>
> A refugee murder suspect in Lima was hard to track down because DNA samples are not being taken at the border as required. A border agent told the local sheriff's office in Allen County "we gave up on doing that 8 months ago."
>
> What is happening in Springfield and across America is a direct result of the Biden-Harris immigration policy. I hope that in the upcoming debate the media will ask Kamala Harris what people in communities like Springfield across this country are supposed to do about the mess she and the Biden Administration created?[228]
>
> . . .
>
> For refugees working in local businesses, many are hired through temporary staffing agencies. The practical reality is that when companies hire refugees through employment agencies they likely don't provide healthcare benefits. To receive healthcare coverage, refugees then enroll in the Medicaid program, which is primarily federally funded. Presently there are 6,590 non-citizens receiving Medicaid benefits in Springfield/Clark County (mostly Haitian origin).[229]

It all checks out; state, county, and city leadership together with the entirety of the citizenry had seemingly been willed into submission by the prior, Democrat administration to accept their fate without recourse. Complaints are not socially permitted.

"It's pretty sad some days that, as citizens, that we can't express our concerns without being called 'racist,'" said one Clark County resident at the October 8,

2024, Springfield City Commission meeting. "I'm a Christian. I feel deeply for the immigrants coming into this city. I understand they want a better life, and I wish that for them. But their chance at having a better life should not come at the expense of your citizens [who] are already here. . . . [O]bviously, we're way higher than 20,000 [Haitians in Springfield] now."[230]

Then and now, it seems that institutions, their influencers, and the mass media that descended upon this city . . . nobody really cares about the plight of the people. Each time an incident is reported, "Oh, that's just one, that's no pattern." Then a second of the same kind. "White citizens do that, too." Now a third. "What, you think this is a pattern? OK, racist." Next a fourth, the same happening. "I wish it was a white man." Sadly, I must agree with the people or Springfield; nobody who can do anything seems to care enough to want to.

The day I wrote Chapter 10, I'd visited places and spoken with people of interest to this book. I turned out of the Southgate Shopping Center. There at the intersection of South Limestone and East John Streets, I idled in the left-hand turn lane at a red light. Cross traffic both ways had green lights. Ahead of me, directly across the intersection from me and also with a red light, came a vehicle. I would see shortly that the driver was visibly Haitian as were his front-seat passenger and who looked to be two very young minors in the back, given their car seats. The reason I would see this shortly is because the driver maintained his speed right under his stoplight, through the intersection, and on past me to my left. What color was our light again? Exactly. Thank God there was a break in traffic.

That's when I realized this might be the only way America would care what happened to the people of Springfield—if what happened to people in Springfield did not happen to people from Springfield.

On June 15, 2026, west of Clark County in Darke County, Ohio, a blue Dodge Challenger driven by Marie Pintar, sixty-three, of Dayton, "was traveling northwest on State Route 49 and drove left-of-center for an unknown reason." The ensuing wreck resulted in myriad injuries, and "Wilnack Saintilma, 30, of Springfield, succumbed to his injuries at Miami Valley Hospital."[231]At Wilnack's Haitian Creole funeral, held at Littleton and Rue, an off-camera voice sounding uncannily identical to Springfield Mayor Rob Rue is heard saying, in English, "I was trying to protect you guys."[232]

This tragedy may have subverted your expectations; the next probably will not.

On July 21, 2026, at the Concerned Citizens of Clark County Town Hall—more on this event later—Mark Sanders arrived and showed several of us pictures of a Haitian-wrecked car from just that afternoon. Three Haitians wearing First Diversity Staffing uniforms, in the photos, stood around their totaled vehicle. They'd driven off the road, through a farmer's fence, across a cow pasture, and into a creek 700 feet away.

That was not the end of Mark's updates. An hour and forty minutes after the town hall wrapped, during which Mark and others expressed grave concern over Haitian nationals' continued stay in Springfield despite the expiration of their Temporary Protected Status and the likely-persistent threats to public safety that would translate to, "the driver of a Kia Soul attempted to pass a Mazda CX-9. Both vehicles were traveling westbound on SR-41. The Kia ultimately struck the front of the Mazda, sending the vehicles off the road and causing each to overturn. A passenger in the Kia was pronounced dead at the scene. The drivers of each vehicle and three passengers were taken to a local hospital."[233]

Mark was contacted by a first responder at the scene and verified that a Haitian Creole interpreter was needed.

The deceased was Haitian: Pierre Georges. He was thirty-six.[234] I was sent a copy of the Traffic Crash Report. The attempted-passer vehicle that caused the wreck was driven by a Haitian—with no driver's license.

Mark also relayed to me that shortly after the accident, according to Mark's own Haitian sources, the licenseless Haitian stopped showing up for work, sold everything, and fled the country (to Mexico, it's suspected).

Mark wrote in a private Facebook group for Springfield citizens, quoted with his permission:

"Another day and another life taken by an unskilled, untrained [H]aitian driver. Same road, same reckless actions that nearly involved many more lives, Shrine and 41 isn't a dangerous intersection, it's impossible for an inanimate object to cause harm or death, it's a static object, the behavior of a human is the deciding factor. The day the last one leaves this area is the day our roads get safer."

As of this writing, all Haitian nationals still in the United States are subject to the expiration of TPS.

We will return to this matter in Chapter 16.

CHAPTER 8

SPRINGFIELD'S NGO-ADMINISTRATIVE COMPLEX

"I'm starting to wonder if we've had a [Universal Basic Income] system all along for one political party—just disguised as grants."[1]

—Jennica Pounds, @DataRepublican on 𝕏

"[W]e have indoctrinated people here," Diana Daniels said on a January 2026 *Empty Pockets Garage* livestream. "A lot of the indoctrination has been accomplished through Indivisible Springfield, G92, and of course Love Thy Neighbor, all of whom are connected to—"

"Carl Ruby," finished co-host Glenda Bailey.

"There you go," Diana completed.[2]

Did you know? Clark County has almost 700 non-governmental organizations (NGOs). To be exact, 693 total tax-exempt organizations, by my count (Filter the file on this IRS spreadsheet to include only NGOs whose mailing address is a Clark County ZIP code.[3]).

That's, uh, dense. One nonprofit for every 195 county residents.[4] Of those, 551 are 501(c)(3) charitable, religious, or educational entities. The way the locals explained it to me, these nonprofits are not all a loose and wholly independent collection of entirely unrelated do-gooders. To use Jennica Pounds's term—she is my co-author on *Unelected: How You Paid a Sinister Elite to Take Over America* (Passage Press, 2026)—a select number of these form a tightly networked, ideologically aligned NGO-Administrative Complex—a self-referential system of for-profit labor recruiters, faith-based welcome organizations, legal-aid providers, housing nonprofits, and progressive advocacy groups that together recruit, transport, house, employ, legally shield, and politically defend thousands of Haitian migrants while local taxpayers and working-class residents absorb the costs or compete for support or both. What heritage citizens experience as overwhelming cultural change and strained services is, for this complex, a growth industry.

That kind of sucks if you're not TPS, which in this case means "thoroughly protected subpopulation." That's how it looks because that's what it is. In two words, Springfield's NGO-Administrative complex is **Haiti First**. In one word, xenophiles.

Haiti First represents those whom the heritage citizens of Springfield deem their "betters" —that's how one OSINT described the way the NGO-Admin. Complex as an organism seems to perceive its own status relatively to the region's white working class.

"What I uncovered in Springfield, Ohio . . . was what I coined 'reverse off-shoring,' wrote investigative reporter Jack Windsor. "In short: it's human labor trafficking. But because NGOs, the governor and mayor sanctioned it, many dismissed deeper considerations about what truly occurred and whether it was acceptable."[5]

Let's talk about those NGOs now.

Meet Your Betters

James Blanken, in an *Empty Pockets Garage* livestream, described Clark County nonprofits as having a "role in all this," referring to the Haitians' influx and their continued stay, with such organizations "descending upon Springfield."[6]

Nonprofits, like any other enterprise, face an awkward conundrum. The problems they exist to solve must never be fully solved, or their reason for being—and their donor base—may disappear. So when the "need" shrinks, so will the organization. The Southern Poverty Law Center offers us a recent, relevant case study. For years, its fundraising apparatus had outrun the actual supply of racism in America. Then came Charlottesville. According to a 2026 federal indictment, the SPLC paid more than $270,000 to an informant who helped organize and attended the 2017 Unite the Right rally—the very event the group publicly condemned and used to rally donors.[7] In the fiscal year that followed, SPLC revenue nearly tripled, surging from roughly $51 million in 2016 to $133 million by October 2017.[8] The "demand" for racism had finally met its supply, and the organization's coffers swelled accordingly. This is not an exaggeration; former staffers claimed in 2019 a commitment to "making hate pay."[9] Not a bad business model for the SPLC; bad for American race relations, to be sure.

Neither this example nor my broader observation impugns a single Springfield nonprofit employee's or volunteer's motives, by the way; rather, I am describing what appears to be a systematic, impersonal issue, that of incentive misalignment that's true of *all* NGOs—the more problems, the more profits. Put that in your "non" profit. Speaking of, let's see who exists to serve and support the Haitians of

Springfield. This list will not be exhaustive as that would be exhausting. Rather, it will be those organizations that repeatedly came up unprompted in my conversations with the heritage citizens as having some "role" in the influx and in the continued, funded protection of it.

The Gathering (of Haitians?)

You know the gist of "King" George Ten already, largely via the investigative efforts of Asra Nomani for *The Jewish Journal.* She also reported on Ten's connections to "**The Gathering of the Miami Valley**," led since its 2008 founding by former youth pastor Jeff Pinkleton:[10]

> In late May 2019, as First Diversity was making a strategic switch to bringing Haitian workers to Springfield, George bought a table at a high-profile event for a new organization that had come to town: "The Gathering," . . . an exclusive club started for "men who have been transformed by Christ," according to its mission statement. Its members include many of Springfield's most powerful city officials, business tycoons and community leaders, meeting in exclusive "Locker Rooms" where men form "deeper relationships."[11]
>
> In a photo posted to First Diversity's Instagram page, George beamed with his wife, Rachael, as they stood next to a former NBA basketball player, Clark Kellogg, and George's senior executive vice president, Bruce W. Harris, stood on the other side of the former NBA star, grinning.

Asra alleged that Ten was "fortified by a well-connected network of political and business elites—mostly men—who insulated him and his business from scrutiny," specifically linking his business to the Springfield elite through The Gathering, specifically: Mike McDorman of the Greater Springfield Partnership (who "didn't return requests for comment"); First Diversity's certified public accountant, Steve Stuckey, a Gathering board member alongside Springfield City Manager Bryan Heck; and mayor Rob Rue, who also participates in The Gathering. In statements, Heck wrote, "I have never discussed First Diversity with Mr. Stuckey . . . [T]he assertion around leveraging their connections to protect illicit business practices through this organization or Board is completely untrue," and Karen Graves on behalf of Mayor Rue wrote that "he does participate in a Gathering Group of Christian fellowship" but that "Mayor Rue also wants to stress that he has not acted in any way to protect any illicit business practices. It is absolutely baseless and untrue."[12]

So that settles it.

A Greater Springfield Partnership

Formerly the Springfield-Clark County Chamber of Commerce, **the Greater Springfield Partnership** is a (501(c)(6) business league, the Greater Springfield Partnership and First Diversity Staffing connection date publicly to April 2019 when Mike McDorman and George Ten appear together in a Springfield Chamber of Commerce Business Expo photo. Going by the name of "Jay," a First Diversity executive spoke to Asra Nomani, saying "[The] Chamber brings the jobs to Springfield. The locals still did not go to work." The executive further stated that the then-Chamber of Commerce had direct knowledge of at minimum and participation of at most the reassignment of local employment opportunities to First Diversity Staffing's temporary Haitian hires.[13]

"Mike McDorman is fantastic," said this Jay.[14]

More recently, the Greater Springfield Partnership has highlighted the immigration issue as unequivocally positive via its pro-Haitian Immigrant Statement on its own website, which also notes "[t]wo GSP staff members serve on the Haitian Coalition so that the best interests of the business community are represented."[15]

The **Haitian Coalition**, now renamed the less obvious **CommUnity Connection Coalition**, which includes a number of organizations such as "the Nehemiah Foundation, St. Vincent de Paul, United Way and Project Woman, as well as social service agencies like Clark County Department of Job and Family Services and the Clark County Combined Health District. Many other health agencies like Mercy Health and Rocking Horse are represented, as well as several representatives from the business community." The Coalition "is now headed by Director of Federal Programs at Springfield City School District Pam Shay and Nehemiah Foundation Community Chaplain Kelton Moore."[16]

But with that name change, the scope of the organization has moved beyond just Haitian immigrants and is now self-styled to be "identifying and addressing inequities in health, education, housing and economic opportunities."[17] These activities include learning Haitian Creole, learning about food programs, and other "community outreach" programs.[18]

"We're connecting all the different resources in our community to help serve our overall community," Shay said.

Exactly.

What the Bryan Heck?

Recall that Asra Nomani wrote that Springfield City Manager Bryan Heck knew of the planned Haitian influx into the county back in 2019. Recall that he said he did not recall.[19]

A recurring complaint about Mr. Heck you'll hear around town is his salary. In 2019, he made $126,712. In 2022, $167,617.[20] In 2024, $209,548.[21] In 2025, $229,595.[22] He must be doing a good job.

Oh, what's this . . . he is currently being audited after allegations arose that Heck went to France to see an airshow and billed the trip to the local taxpayers.[23] He expensed hotel fees, Uber costs, and also apparently a number of his own Paypal purchases. This follows on the resignation of Tiffany Smith, assistant finance director, who cited a "misalignment" of personal morals and professional ethics as the reason for her resignation.

Even if the alleged 2019 meeting of the minds never happened, we know that Bryan Heck knew about the Haitian influx impact by 2021. How? A City Commission Agenda from September of 2021, with Heck's signature, explicitly discussed Haitian immigration difficulties.[24] In a section on HUD funding priorities for 2022, it identified five "program themes":

- Housing Rehabilitation
- Homelessness Response and Special Needs Support
- Development of a Neighborhood/Community Center
- Code Enforcement
- Housing Construction

Of these five, four of them are directly related to the crisis. Furthermore, "In addition, public service programming surrounding neighborhood support, community gardens, transportation, Second Harvest Food Bank assistance, Promise Neighborhood assistance, legal assistance, immigration assistance, and crime prevention were discussed."[25]

Now, who might the city have gone to to discuss such a thing? Well, they have a handy chart, and for both Business and Civic consultation and Employment consultation, who was their subject matter expert amid public commentary and feedback?[26]

First Diversity Staffing, LLC.

Further down in that agenda, they were already pointing out the issues the Haitian community was having . . . in September of 2021. They were identifying that "Rules for housing . . . get lost in translation" and that "[m]any Haitians do not know that you cannot charge by the person for rent." It identified more needs for ESL opportunities, and asked, "What are housing laws for Immigration?"[27]

Or, in a section about "Barriers to Affordable Housing," they threw this in: "The City is currently working to strengthen communication with our new

Haitian Creole Community. Translation and Interpretation services for Haitian Creole is very limited. Work continues throughout the community, among various partners including the City School District, health department, first response, hospitals, the State of Ohio, and Community Development to provide services and assistance for the Haitian Creaole [sic] migration."[28]

These are the things people have been vilified for saying for so long.

Now take this:

> The largest obstacle standing in the way of a thriving Springfield is housing. Prior to the public health crisis on homelessness declaration, the community as a whole was facing nearly a 2,000 unit deficit throughout the community for decent, safe and affordable housing. With market tightening, transition of housing choice units to the private market, a significant increase in homelessness and displaced housing, a new Haitian community migration to Springfield, and the expiration of planned PHA affordable unit designations, the community faces an even more extreme need for affordable housing.[29]

They knew.

The City Manager had on the agenda in 2021 that the recent influx of Haitian migration was exasperating the housing market crunch. And worse, they knew that these Haitians were being exploited, as a Community Focus Group discussed "New Haitian neighbors paying extremely high rents."[30]

City leadership knew there was a serious negative impact on both the Haitians and the heritage citizens by September 2021. That was the time to properly integrate and assimilate, all responsibly. In my view, and in those shared with many residents I spoke with, city management behaved irresponsibly in their quiet allowance of the Haitian immigrant influx—even if there were efforts, and indeed there were, to directly and indirectly address these and other issues presented to the city via this public reception of feedback and direction back in 2021.

So. What is to be done? Maybe we should consider the reframing technique of the late Scott Adams, where we recast old, clichéd advice under a new and useful light, and it goes like this:

> Usual frame: With great power comes great responsibility.
> Reframe: With great salary comes great accountability.

Looking at you, Bryan. But maybe not for much longer. On July 29, 2026, he was placed on administrative leave as Springfield's city manager "by a unanimous vote by the Springfield City Commission." [31]My inner tabloid writer wants to tell you why, as I learned from Springfield's OSINT months prior what was really going on behind closed doors, if you know what I mean.

There is so much more I want to tell you. But then this book would never have been finished.

The Carlrubysphere

The government isn't the only sphere involved in whatever this is or was. **Central Christian Church** under Carl Ruby has served as both the physical and ideological hub for much of the pro-Haitian faith-based activism in Springfield. They've hosted trainings, rallies, and strategy sessions, and have advanced "Civil Disobedience for Such a Time as This," arguing that it is the Christian thing to do should the federal government end Temporary Protected Status for Haitian immigrants.[32]

Connected to Central is, of course, **G92**, a coalition of local churches that coordinate religious welcome efforts for Haitian migrants.[33] As far as I can tell, G92 exists to, speaking of framing techniques, reframe any opposition to the Haitian influx as explicitly anti-Christian.

Organized under G92 was **Love Thy Neighbor**, a public rally-protest experience.[34] It featured a large gathering at City Hall to promote unconditional support for Haitian residents and, again, insisted that the immigration influx is simply a test of Springfield's Christian values that citywide believers are theologically expected to pass. Other such events have included **Rapid Response Planning Day**, a **Call to Prayer and Fasting**, and **Here We Stand**, the latter of which brought "local and national speakers, pastors, clergy, and community members together in prayer to stand with Haitian families, call for the extension of TPS, and affirm the Gospel's mandate to welcome the stranger and defend the oppressed."[35]

On May 27, 2026, "[s]everal non-profit groups which provide necessities and support for Haitian immigrants in Springfield will be given $50k in grant funding by G92," it was announced.[36]

Up next is **Undivided**, a movement for "Jesus Followers" that works to "create spaces of belonging that equip and activate you for multi-racial healing, solidarity, and justice."[37] Charla Weiss, a founding member, spoke at Central Christian Church, and there and elsewhere has asked participants in these trainings "how far they would go to help Haitian residents avoid deportation."[38,39]

Then we have **Red, Wine and Blue**, a name riffing off the ideologically liberal "wine mom" stereotype. This group of progressive activists partnered directly with Carl Ruby and Vilès Dorsainvil of the Haitian Support Center to host a major fundraiser amid the then-expected end of TPS. The event raised $107,000 to specifically support Haitian residents facing potential deportation threats.[40] This was one of the largest single-documented crowdfunded cash infusions into the local pro-Haitian network.

Then, also in the Carlrubysphere, we have **Indivisible Springfield**, which boasts the totally nonpartisan website tagline, "Resisting the Trump Agenda."[41] According to Action Network, "Indivisible Springfield is dedicated to resisting the Trump agenda by engaging in grassroots activism" and is "a grassroots movement following the Indivisible Guide in order to resist racism, authoritarianism, and corruption in government."[42] On the Indivisible main page, the Springfield chapter has a listing and specifies that, "Indivisible.org is a joint website of Indivisible Project and Indivisible Action. Indivisible Project is a registered 501(c)(4). Indivisible Action is a Hybrid Political Action Committee."[43]

According to InfluenceWatch, "The Indivisible Project (or Indivisible) is a left-of-center 501(c)(4) tax-exempt organization headquartered in Washington, D.C., and created in late 2016 as a response to the first election of President Donald Trump. The Indivisible Project was established to provide left-of-center voters a practical guide for 'Resisting the Trump Agenda.' The organization signed a petition supporting the Green New Deal and has opposed the use of nuclear energy."[44] And who's their top funder, giving $8 million to them? George Soros' Open Societies Foundation.

While this looks like a separate leftist group, it is in reality an enmeshed network with connections to Carl Ruby and G92. Take Jen Casto, part of Indivisible Springfield.[45] Diana Daniels notably mispronounced her surname, calling her Jen Castro. In some articles, she's also quoted as "a G92 member and community activist" and Indivisible Springfield is part of the same "faith-based constellation of groups" preparing to support Haitians against potential ICE actions. In fact, she spoke at the Love Thy Neighbor event, alongside Carl Ruby.[46] One article identified her as a "leader of Indivisible Springfield."[47]

Come to think of it . . . do you think Diana did that on purpose?

Haitian Help and Support

While these organizations are primarily leftist advocacy groups—though some use religion as their motivating factor—we cannot neglect to look at the organizations that designated themselves as helping Haitians directly.

Rocking Horse has come up every time the Haitian influx impact is discussed by serious people. **Rocking Horse Community Health Center** is a federally qualified health center nonprofit in Springfield that provides primary care, dental, behavioral health, prenatal, pediatric, and other services on a sliding-fee scale regardless of insurance or ability to pay.[48] More than most, Rocking Horse has been able to chart the immediate, devastating impact on service resources and quality of care.

First and foremost, Rocking Horse is the main primary care provider for Haitian immigrants in the area—going from 115 Haitian patients in 2021 to 410 in 2022; that's a 257 percent increase.[49] Pediatric patients needing Creole and French interpreters rose from 38 in 2020 to 416; total non-English patients grew from hundreds in 2018 to over 2,000 by 2023 with ongoing high volume into 2024 and 2025.[50] Rocking Horse had to hire (at least) three Creole-speaking translators, multiple patient navigators/advocates (including Haitian immigrants), and medical students in supporting roles, plus fund a new pharmacy and a mobile "purple bus" for screenings and vaccinations.[51] Translation and interpretation expenses rose dramatically—from about $4,000 in 2018 to $344,000 from just January to August 2023.[52]

Even as expenses have increased from 2020 to 2024, so have Rocking Horse revenues increased.[53]

Next, take ABLE, or **Advocates for Basic Legal Equality**.[54] ABLE operates the main immigration legal practice serving Haitians in Springfield. Its immigration practice group is led by attorney Katie Kersh.[55] And, according to ABLE's own words (as of February 2026), "In the past 2 years, ABLE has assisted over 400 Haitians with applications for employment authorization (work permits), asylum, and Temporary Protected Status (TPS)." They've also reported that this would cost $80,000 per year to provide "exclusively free legal services."[56]

Then we have the **Haitian Community Help and Support Center**, oft-shortened to Haitian Support Center.[57] Founded in late December of 2023, the Center provides direct services including document assistance, education, translation, job placement, and welfare navigation.[58] The organization was co-founded and is now led by Vilès Dorsainvil, who serves as Executive Director and has been a frequent public spokesperson.[59] Dorsainvil maintains a united relationship with Carl Ruby and Central Christian Church as far as we can tell, often appearing in joint Haitian-American worship sessions and various events. Then there's Board Member Marjory Wentworth, identified as a "volunteer organizer with organizations helping immigrants including Springfield Neighbors United and G92."[60] Carlrubysphere.

But wait, we think as we peruse the Haitian Support Center website . . . what is this **Springfield Neighbors United** organization? It's listed as another "faith-based group" that focuses on protecting Haitian immigrants.[61] According to friendly sources, "Springfield Neighbors United is rooted in 'Love Your Neighbor: Make it Local' values and action."[62] G92's Get Involved page explicitly recommends partnering with Springfield Neighbors United.[63]

It's like Russian nesting dolls. How do you say *matryoshka* in Creole?

And we're not done. Both the **Nehemiah Foundation** and the **Springfield Foundation** are listed on the Haitian Community Help and Support Center site.[64] The Nehemiah Foundation and local churches (including partnerships with Haitian families) responded to rumors and community tension by providing English classes, practical support, and volunteer networks for the Haitian community in Springfield.[65] Feminist publication *The 19th* quotes Nehemiah Foundation Executive Director Amy Willmann extensively in one piece covering Springfield in which she said Nehemiah's "network has 28 churches and 114 volunteers who have already completed background checks. These volunteers will staff 'hubs' where children can go if they arrive home from school to an empty house or are taken in by child services once a parent is picked up by ICE."[66] The Nehemiah Foundation also links back to the Haitian Community Help and Support Center.[67] And in her own words, Willmann says "People of faith should have a biblical response to what we call the 'quartet of the vulnerable,' which is the poor, the widow, the orphan, and the foreigner," again turning the issue of immigration support into a faith-based imperative. [68]

Back to the Springfield Foundation, a major recommended donation channel for the Haitian Community Help and Support Center.[69] It awards $834,000 in grants to various Clark County nonprofits.[70] It's has gotten its own sponsored local NPR series entitled, "Haitians in the Heartland."[71] The show is also produced in conjunction with the **Haitian Community Alliance**, a "collective of over 50 organizations united to empower and uplift the Haitian community in Springfield, Ohio" whose "mission is to provide resources, support, and advocacy through programs that address critical needs such as immigrant integration, education, health and wellness, cultural preservation, and more."[72] Admittedly, they've not been doing much since December 2024.

We can't not mention the brewing controversy surrounding a recent movement by some churches around power-of-attorney and family separation planning.[73] Vilès Dorsainvil (Haitian Support Center) and Casey Rollins (St. Vincent de Paul) have been involved in preparing power-of-attorney documents so that U.S.-born children of Haitian parents could remain in the United States with guardians if their parents are deported after TPS expires.[74] The public is being told it's not nearly as nefarious as it sounds.

Speaking of . . .

We can't not mention the group that's popped up before, the **St. Vincent de Paul Society**, which provides hands-on government document assistance and other direct aid to Haitian immigrants. According to their website, St. Vincent offers "walk-in services and various resources for Haitian immigrants needing interpretation and community navigation. This helps Haitians acclimate and to comply with immigration necessities. (i.e., Temporary Protected Status, asylum applications, and work permits). We offer legal immigration clinics to expand services for additional immigration requirements and connect immigrants to jobs when possible. We also collaborate with other non-profits, faith-based organizations, and local service agencies to echo the voices of our marginalized neighbors."[75]

The 19th published a glowing profile of St. Vincent's executive director, the previously mentioned Casey Rollins. Rollins is presented as an almost Mother Teresa-like figure for the Haitians, focusing all her efforts on Haiti First priorities—for example, using "every opportunity available . . . to tell Haitian parents to get their U.S.-born children American passports. . . . The passports are also proof of U.S. citizenship."[76] Due to the twin decisions of the U.S. Supreme Court on birthright citizenship as constitutional and the Trump administration's ability to end Temporary Protected Status, there is the dire matter of impending departure, family separation, and U.S. citizen privileges now granted to the migrants' children born in Clark County. Haiti First.

Reuters, separately, interviewed Bansal Oreus, a Haitian man working at St. Vincent; his job is to help "other Haitian immigrants with government documents," specifically for "immigration, benefits, and work."[77]

Must be nice.

Similarly aligned in terms of faith-based organizations, we have **Catholic Charities**, which opened the **Springfield Empowerment Center** on East High Street in 2024 to offer job development, self-sufficiency programs, and immigration legal support to the Haitian community of Clark County.[78] These programs include language interpretation services, among others.

There is a palpable tension, a give and take, if you speak with heritage residents—there's all this perceived help and support for Haitians, with grand projects taking their existence into account, even favoring them.

Speaking of speaking, a critical future-planning organization did just that. **Springfield 2051** is a fifteen-month public-private community planning project (launched in 2025, running through 2026) to create a twenty-five-year roadmap for Springfield and Clark County (through the city's 250th anniversary in 2051).[79] It is facilitated by the consulting firm Future iQ and involves a steering committee and advisory group of local government, nonprofits, foundations, and business leaders.

On its advisory board? You'll never guess (you will). Vilès Dorsainvil of the Haitian Community Help and Support Center.[80] This group also explicitly includes Haitian and immigrant populations in long-term planning. While officially they may be *Temporary* Protected Status, project leaders do not consider it that way. Project leaders have stated they are using "Network Mapping Analysis" to integrate local and newcomer labor pools—like, say, Haitians—into the economic roadmap.[81] Steering committee members with "deep outreach into that community" (especially "faith-based" networks like the ones already mentioned.) bring Haitian perspectives into the process.[82]

The Ohio Register published an article on May 5, 2026 that described the public-private partnership update, noting concerns about "replacement migration" via TPS programs and the use of immigrant labor for economic development.[83] In other words, the Haitian influx is being planned for as if it's *not* temporary; this is exactly what former sheriff Deb Burchett told me she feared most—and why she left town.

It truly is an NGO-Administrative Complex. Funding sources can be looked into, not to mention the universities and colleges in the area—Cedarville University, Wittenberg University, Central State University, Clark State Community College—plus all the additional churches. There remains so much, and this is but a preview of a preview . . . of the preview. And yet there is one other nonprofit that came up every single time any one else did. You may already know it.

Let's talk about **Mike DeWine**, who has been in this story since day one, and literally day one.

Governor Mike DeWine first visited Haiti in 1995 during his tenure as U.S. Senator and has made more than twenty trips over twenty-five years.[84] In 1999, a school in Haiti's Cité Soleil was named the **Becky DeWine School** in honor of their daughter, killed in a 1993 car accident. The school operates through the nonprofit **Hands Together**. **The DeWine Family Foundation** gave a $400,000 grant to Hands Together in its most recent filing and has donated more than $2 million over the past five years.[85] Who wouldn't support that? Haitians receiving help and support . . . in Haiti.

On September 26, 2019, during the first Trump administration, President Trump issued Executive Order 13888 ("Enhancing State and Local Involvement in Refugee Resettlement"). This required states and localities to formally consent (i.e., opt in) in writing if they wanted to continue receiving refugees through the federal U.S. Refugee Admissions Program. Without such consent, no new refugees would be resettled there.[86]

But then in response, Governor DeWine sent a letter dated December 24, 2019, to then-Secretary of State Mike Pompeo. DeWine explicitly consented on behalf of Ohio, writing:

> Given our ability to successfully welcome and assimilate legitimate refugees, and the administration's stringent vetting process, I consent to the placement and/or resettlement of refugees within the State of Ohio.[87]

From NPR:

> More than 30 governors—both Republicans and Democrats—have agreed to allow refugee resettlement in their states . . . Ohio has a long track record of accepting refugees. Former Gov. John Kasich repeatedly criticized Trump over his rhetoric on immigrants, saying that Ohio's population has been boosted by immigration. In 2018, Kasich established the Office of Opportunities For New Americans to connect immigrants with work and benefits.[88]

Both DeWine and Kasich are Republicans.

Walter Curt brought up Governor DeWine to me, first among Springfield residents to do so, as an ideologically aligned reason why so many Haitians are in Springfield. Or rather, perhaps, a theologically aligned one. The governor, like Walter, is Catholic.[89] The single-largest Christian denomination in Haiti is Catholicism.[90]

"Catholics simply want more Catholics," Walter said. "Haitian Catholics? Great!"

Great!

But now, upon reflection, we wonder if Springfield's Haiti First alliance has actually improved the Haitians' situation prior to or following the end of their Temporary Protected Status. So much money yet so many now slated for departure from Springfield.

This very point came up during one of my longest conversations with any one Springfield resident, which makes sense because it was with two of them—**Mark William and Rosalee Massie**, a husband and wife who have a heart for the Haitian people formed from their Christian faith so many in the NGO-Administrative Complex purport to possess yet I will dispute. The Massies' account ratifies the first half of this book and forebodes the second. I took away from their account an impression of an ethnonarcissistic yet low-trust culture wholly dependent on the mercy of outsiders.

"Since Rosalee speaks Portuguese," Mark started off, "she found that . . . the five Haitian families we met . . . spoke Portuguese and that they had [come] from Brazil to here, to Springfield. . . . We were helping them out . . . Rosalee was part of the Haitian Coalition at first . . . We were helping some of the Haitian families with . . . food and different things like that in the beginning, and along that process, we [found] out . . . things that were happening with them and the city."

Rosalee took it from there.

I started meeting the Haitian families, mainly women because I work with women in crisis pregnancies . . . Or, I was at the time.

. . . I had met several and [was] able to help with maternity clothes. . . . We met when I went to their house to bring them a couple of things. We found out they . . . were living in a . . . house with three other families. They were paying $800 for one room and $600 for the second room. This is like a four-bedroom house they had, and everybody shared the kitchen and the bathroom. And then . . . I found out as I met more families that this is how everything was set up. There were always . . . four or five families, sometimes families then like two single men [who] each had their own room, which I think was dangerous, really, because [they had] small kids and complete strangers . . . living in the same house. . . .

. . . [T]hen we met this family [who] . . . had come from Brazil, and they had lived there quite a long time, and they were sleeping on the floor. . . . She was nineteen weeks pregnant. They had two little boys. So I asked if they needed anything. Did they have winter clothes? It was about a high of 26 [degrees Fahrenheit] when I . . . met them . . . [S]he said, "Well, the boys need winter clothes." . . . [W]hen I went to take them the clothes, and I got to their house, I realized they didn't have enough food . . . [N]ot even a mattress to sleep on. Their clothes were in bags because there were no dressers. They didn't have a table and chairs . . . [T]he house was very cold, and they were using space heaters, which could have been a fire hazard if

(continued . . .)

they had to use too many. . . . [T]heir landlord, who was also Haitian, for a week they had been begging him to get the heat fixed . . . [I]t took over a week, and she and the kids all got sick.

. . . [T]he day after I was at their house . . . I was crying because I used to live in Brazil, and I worked in the slums . . . I have never seen such poverty since . . . I worked in the slums of Brazil. So I put out the word on social media, emails, and everything . . . "If you guys can help with clothes, maternity clothes, food, anything." And the very next day, we had two families [who] bought . . . a ton of food for them. Somebody bought a . . . table and chairs. We had two families [who] brought in beds—not just mattresses but beds that they had extra sitting in their garage . . . For two of the [Haitian] families, they brought mattresses and beds for the children.

They just got so much stuff. We had one [Springfield] family say . . . "We've been saving money . . . to bless a family at Christmastime, and we'd like to give the money to this family."

It was like this avalanche of people just helping . . . [The pregnant Haitian mother] called me a week later and she said, "Rosalee, please ask people to stop giving. We have too much."

But then . . . I start meeting more [Haitian] families from Brazil and [Haitian] families [who] had come from Argentina and Chile. They were all transported here to Springfield, Ohio . . . I asked one of them once . . . "Did you guys have to walk a lot?" She said, "No, we walked one day. The rest of the time were transported."

So it was all planned ahead of time . . . [T]hen we start looking into other issues, like this Haitian landlord [who] was not providing heat [and who] was charging . . . $600 and $800 per room . . . At one point, their plumbing was not working properly. He took forever to fix the toilet . . . [H]e just was not responsible. So their own people are doing this to them.

There was another family that moved to Findlay, that's north of [Springfield], and they were living in a hotel because they couldn't find work or housing here . . . [The mother] was pregnant with twins and had a two-year-old. . . . Once she had the [babies], we blessed them with a bunch of gifts . . . [The father] was able to find work up there. And then they rented a house from a Haitian . . . [T]his [was] about three months later, [and the mother] called me, desperate. "Can you help me?" [They realized] this guy [they rented from] . . . was renting from the actual [owner]. They thought he was the owner. He was renting from the actual owner, taking their rent money and keeping it, and so they got an eviction notice. And so I'm calling people up there in the county to see what they can do to help.

. . . We've helped a lot. We've had people in our home for meals, for holidays. . . . The family I told you where they're sleeping on the floor, the little boys didn't even have a single toy. They had been living there for four months . . . [P]eople were donating boxes of toys, balls, you know.

[A]nother issue that we had at the beginning is they were not allowed to work initially. They had to wait for a work authorization. So a lot of them had went over a year without being allowed to work. They would actually ask me . . . "Can you help us find work? We need to buy diapers. We need to buy food. We can't just be living like this . . . just depending on other people and . . . the government." . . . But then they had several attorneys [who] worked *pro bono* to get the process moving faster . . . to get them to be able to work.

. . . [T]he other thing, of course—the big thing—is there's no accountability for them . . . [T]hey're driving without driver's licenses . . . [and] without license plates . . . [W]e have two friends that . . . both their cars were hit by Haitians, and there was no consequence at all. One of them said his truck was parked in front of the police station. Parked! This guy came and broadsided him, knocked it on its side, and he had to pay . . . no damages at all. The owner had to pay . . . out of his deductible and pay for the damages. Then there was another one that the guy hit her in an intersection [with a] four-way stop . . . Same thing: He hit her, damaged her car. Her car's still sitting in the driveway. She can't drive it. . . . The police said, "We don't know. We can't tell who was at fault."

. . . [T]here was no accountability. They can just do whatever they want to . . . I think that's what's made people so angry. They've gone to the city . . . and said, "Hey, I have [Haitians] sleeping in my front yard. I want to help people, but can they at least pick up their trash or pick up their things?" And they're not being heard, and I think that's why there's such animosity now.

. . . I grew up in Brazil. My parents came here from Brazil . . . legally . . . My dad was sponsored, then he married my mom, and she came . . . but they always worked. They didn't depend on the government for anything. You know, people helped each other a lot more than they're being helped now.

(continued . . .)

I think the big issue is our leaders [who] let them . . . instead of saying, "You can't drive," or, saying, "If you do drive without a license, then you're . . . going to go to jail or you're going to get a fine . . . " No, they just keep on driving. . . . We've seen multiple [Haitian] drivers here [who] go down to practice their maneuverability test . . . Nobody was driving them there. They were driving themselves to practice . . . So they were obviously driving on the street without a license.

. . . There's a lot of hatred, and we don't believe in hating anyone . . . Sometimes . . . it's going into the schools . . . [T]he [Haitian] children are suffering because the [non-Haitian] children are going to school and saying things they shouldn't be saying to them, to these [Haitian] children . . . They have nothing to do with anything . . . [T]he adults . . . should be responsible. I mean I can't imagine just allowing a bunch of people to come here and do whatever they want and . . . drive without a license. I've never in my life seen so many people drive without license plates . . . as I have in the last few years. . . . [S]ometimes when I went out . . . I would see like five or ten in one week driving without license plates. Why? And how are they getting away with it?

. . . I don't know how many of [the Haitians] did this, but one of them actually asked me if I would write him a letter to a judge and talk about his character. I said, "OK." And he said, "Here's a sample." Well, he . . . was going to marry [someone else but] had a girlfriend, and they had three children together. They had been together for a long time, and all of a sudden, he's marrying an American so he can stay here that way. So I said . . . "I'm not writing a letter for you. No way am I doing this."

. . . [W]e strongly believe that if you want to live in a country, you need to start the path to citizenship as soon as possible . . .

fter some of them had been here for a year and a half or two years, one of them told me . . . "My family's coming up." So his mom, his siblings, I think a cousin—there were like three or four of them coming—[and] Biden was flying [them] up, not being vetted or anything, just flying them into the country. He said he's . . . bringing them here for free . . . Hispanics [who] are here, some of them have said to me, "I don't understand this . . . We've been here working . . . and we don't get any of these . . . freebies."

. . . friend of mine . . . was at the Kroger . . . parking lot [and] saw a Haitian woman back right into this other driver . . . And she's like, "I'm calling the cops." [The Haitian woman said,] "I didn't do it. It's not my fault." . . . [She] wasn't held accountable.

. . . I have seen people say some ugly things about them, too . . . We are completely against that . . . They're human beings . . . [and] there's been an exploitation of them. Somebody made a lot of money bringing all those people into one town, then closing the doors for jobs for a lot of people that live here. We've seen it. We've seen people in college and high school here [who] have been looking for jobs [who] can't get anything and [who] are citizens.

. . . When we first started [helping Haitians], I . . . would go visit them to see how they were doing. I would call them. "Hey, are you guys doing OK? Do you need anything?" You know, always following up with them. I [would] go to their homes, and it was always hugs and everything . . . I love going there—I feel like I'm back in Brazil. Everybody's hugging each other . . . so I loved being there. . . . But this exploitation of both the people of Springfield and the Haitians . . . is an outrage.

. . . Why so many young men? That was another question we had. Why so many young men in their late twenties, early thirties? Where are the elderly people if Haiti is so bad? . . . [Some] people say [to] us . . . "You're terrible because you want them to go back to a terrible situation" . . . [M]any of them did not come from a terrible situation. . . . They were very settled in their countries in South America. They were working there, they had their lives there, and then they were promised something here . . . It was advertised there, but I don't know how or who.

[M]y one friend . . . the one [who] was pregnant when . . . I went to her house the first time, she said, "I don't even know why we came here . . . Brazil was much better . . . [W]e have nothing here. We don't even have a bed to sleep on." [S]he was very tearful. And I said, "Don't worry. God is going to provide for you."

[T]his is my impression . . . What I personally have seen . . . [is] the people [who] helped [Haitians in Springfield] are the ones [who] are for legal immigration. None of them ever said, "Are they legal? Who are these people?" They didn't say anything. "What, Rosalee, what can we do to help?" No, it didn't matter . . . wherever they were from, who they were, nothing. They were willing to help.

(continued . . .)

The people . . . I see saying, "This is an outrage to send them back," when I was asking for help, I didn't hear anything from them. They never helped with anything. In fact . . . it's kind of ironic because one of them actually came to me and she said I shouldn't be helping them so much . . . because I was doing baby showers for some of the [Haitian] moms. And she said, why don't you just wait and do like one baby shower year instead of doing them? I said, "Well, they have babies at different times, you know." And so . . . I feel like it's kind of fake to . . . be on social media saying this is an outrage to send them back when you weren't willing to help them, even with a meal or clothing or anything when they needed it. You know, isn't that what Jesus says? "I was naked and you clothed me. I was hungry and you fed me." That's what we do as Christians. It doesn't matter who it is.

. . . I had a friend who told me something about her cat missing and she thought she saw a cat hanging from one of their trees and being skinned . . . ut I don't know . . . They might be making things up . . . One thing we do know that does bother us as Christians is bringing voodoo into our town because that is satanic. They do their satanic rituals, and a lot of people say, "Well, let them do their own religion" . . . [T]he Bible is very clear: You don't bring other gods into our land . . .

. . . Now, we don't know this to be Haitian. I don't know if you've ever been to the Crabill House [near the] Clarence J. Brown Reservoir [in Springfield]. You have to walk back to it. We always take hikes there . . . I think [this] was pre-COVID when we saw this . . . I think it was about 2020 . . . [We] went back to the Crabill House, which we had done many times over the years, and it was really strange. We came upon just remnants of a pig, the pig's head . . . [I]t's just the pig's head, still in the brush, [with] feathers [and] chicken feet everywhere . . . [T]here was where you [could] see they had a fire. But we thought that was so odd. We actually stopped at the sheriff's office . . . to report it . . . [T]hey said they would go look and check it out, but . . . we look back at that and think, *Was that some kind of ritual thing going on?*

. . . [There were] woman's underclothes thrown in . . . one of the bushes [nearby] . . . [I]t reminded me when I was about eleven and we had moved to Brazil. We came around the corner . . . [and] there was . . . a chicken, cooked chicken, with all these beads on it . . . "Mom, look." And I leaned down to get the necklace . . . "Don't touch that! That's a satanic ritual. You do not want to touch that." So immediately that's what came to mind.

. . . But we didn't know [Haitians] were coming in at that point . . . I think there were already quite a few here, too, because I remember the first I heard there were so many was about 5,000 . . . and then 7,000.

. . . It's the way it was handled that's wrong, and the way it's being handled is wrong.

. . . Another concern we have is that they're saying, "Oh, if they get deported, some of them are going to leave their children here." Well, I guess that's their option. But what's going to happen to the children? . . . [T]hey have the option to leave. DHS gives them options . . . [like] money to pay for their ticket, money to take with them. They can go back to Brazil . . . Or they can get an attorney and work on . . . becoming citizens. But it can't continue like this, and they should be vetted. I don't care who it is. . . .

. . . [T]he media needs to start telling the truth instead of always lying about everything.

. . . I . . . remember an African-American woman here . . . I had met years ago when . . . this whole thing started. And she's told me, "I don't understand . . . I'm black, and [Haitians are] black, and yet they treat me differently while I'm trying to help them. Because I'm not one of them" . . . I don't think it's everyone, but you see . . . this divisiveness here and this divisiveness there, and . . . there's no need for that . . . As you could tell . . . I didn't sense any of the animosity personally from any of them. In fact, there was a lot of gratitude. They were just so grateful for all the help . . . that we brought to them. People from our church . . . [and] even my piano students got involved, [their] families [with] helping them out. Gift cards, food, clothing, whatever they could give . . . [I]t was just really wonderful to see that. Just everybody coming together to help them.

CHAPTER 9

ABDUCKTED

"You can almost argue that Haiti is more African than Africa. When the west coast of Africa was being disrupted by colonialism and the slave trade, Haiti was essentially left alone."[1]

—Wade Davis, PhD

I was braving a blizzard atop Fort Hill Earthworks in Hillsboro, Highland County, Ohio, when my hiking buddy for the day brought up Springfield. Perhaps I did, actually. I don't recall given our circumstance. We chatted so as not to chatter, as it was unduly cold. Highland County is aptly named; at the top of the Fort Hill hiking trail, we endured a surprise blizzard together. So romantic, not. But down in the valley by the ancient Siberian-American sacred earthwork circle that very same afternoon, we found ourselves enjoying mild-to-comfortable temperatures.[2,3,4] Ohio is like that.

It came about that she brought up her brother, a **landlord** way up in Springfield, and what he witnessed in one of his properties rented to Haitians. As I would later learn, it's all but a *faux pas* not to volunteer your local Haitian story upon meeting someone new who is in the know. Now, I'll admit—I couldn't believe this particular anecdote, which is why I could. I asked later if I might speak with her brother directly; he agreed, but, like the Dominican and like many others I would later talk to, anonymity was a prerequisite going into any conversation.

The people of Springfield, I gathered, are afraid. Not all. Maybe not most. But many. Now that good-paying jobs are harder to come by, and nobody wants their entire portfolio of rental properties to go unrented over runaway racism accusation-hysteria, the number-one reason given for anonymity is self-explanatory—"I'll get fired." Or for those with means, it's, "I'll lose my investment."

Speaking of getting fired, Setys Kelly relayed to me what a longtime friend who works in pest control around Clark County found on one particular job. He'd gone to a house rented by Haitians for a pest treatment one day, and there outside on a table were four headless geese. Presumed Haitians stood around them plucking the feathers out.

You're now thinking what I was thinking. *Pictures?* Exactly. That's what I asked Setys. Turns out, she'd asked the pest control professional for some, too. She reported his reason why not—a confidentiality and non-disclosure agreement with his employer. Break that, and he'd be fired. Family, work ethic, and community duty are very important to the heritage citizens of Springfield. I'm frustrated, but I understand. Jobs are hard to come by. Hostages.

Back to Fort Hill. I texted the woman's brother—after independently confirming that he is, in fact, a landlord in Springfield, Ohio (he is; every single person I spoke with, I confirmed they are who they said they were—sometimes to their chagrin, alas). Our text exchange went like this:

> **Joshua:** [Your sister] had mentioned a situation involving ~15 Haitians living in one property and upon eviction remains of bred and butchered rats were found.
> **Joshua:** Something like that.
> **Landlord:** That's probably an understatement.
> **Joshua:** You were the landlord?
> **Landlord:** Yes
>
> . . .
>
> **Joshua:** What evidence of rat consumption were you able to collect?
> **Landlord:** . . . [W]hen one of the families had left my property there were probably 15 baby mice that were in the sink alive. I suspected that they might be breeding them for whatever reason but not 100% for sure. The only thing that leads me to believe that is that I checked the property within an hour after they left and there were lots of [mice] everywhere confined to different areas of the house.
> **Landlord:** One of the issues that I had with renting to the Haitian community is that one person would come in as they were renting the house themselves but then they would move tons of people in and begin to sublease. By the time that we knew that they were subleasing and there were multiple people living in the house, the property was already destroyed so much that it would be more difficult getting them evicted because of the cost that it would take to renovate and put the house back together.

Sidebar—I heard this from every clued-in resident of Springfield familiar with multiple properties rented by Haitians. The secret subletting, the multiple people including different families in a single dwelling, and the near-supernatural trashing of the place, all of that has indeed occurred, as others I've introduced to you have also relayed. How widespread this was or is among the Haitians, I do not know. That said, I was shown one such Haitianed property in Springfield myself. It reminded me of the pre-renovation rundown and abandoned summer homes of Millionaires' Row way up in the cell phone signal–free Smoky Mountains of Elkmont, Tennessee.[5] Those overgrown, nature-reclaimed properties hadn't had residents in decades. But the Haitians? What I witnessed, it had only been a few weeks. I still don't understand how decades of ruin were possible to achieve in a matter of days. Back to the texts.

> **Landlord:** I'd also found that there's no in between with the Haitian community.
> **Landlord:** Either the Haitian families were extremely dirty and destructive or they were so OCD that they kept their place absolutely Immaculate with zero issues.

Look, there it is again. Did you see it? Two Springfields on one screen. Come for the controversy; stay for the real story. In this case, it's the way my companion first relayed the story to me in the blizzard atop Fort Hill. She'd said something like, "My brother rents to Haitians and caught them breeding and eating rats."

Scott Adams popularized the persuasion techniques Truthful Hyperbole and Directional Accuracy. They need no explanation, only demonstration, and here we have both. Like so:

Rats? No. Rodents? Yes. Haitians breeding them? Maybe. Haitians eating them? Not witnessed. Haitians keeping them way too many rodents for their landlord to allow them to continue living there? Absolutely. Does it matter what the tenants intended to do with the mice? It does not! Like every bartender says it closing, "You don't have to go home, but you can't stay here!"

Speaking of eating or not eating, I would later meet with **Mark Sanders**, an administrator for the private Facebook group I told you about earlier, "Stop the Influx Into Springfield, Ohio." You know his name from Chapter 7. He's also a retired Honda automotive engineer, part-time NASCAR pit crew member, vice chairman of the Clark County Republican Party, and at the time of this first writing was a candidate for Clark County commissioner. As far as I could discern and confirm, Mark is also a devoted husband and present father. He told me in his museum of a barn that he became a bus driver, as you know, to ease his daughter's mind following the Haitian-induced death-crash involving, yes, a school bus. If he were driving a school bus, she seemed to reason, then it would be OK for her to ride one to school again. Note that multiple school buses were on the road that fateful day when the Haitian Hermanio Joseph killed the American child Aiden Clark.[6] Mark's daughter eyewitnessed the crash that killed, maimed, and disfigured. A local NPR affiliate ran the Sanders' family story for human interest.[7]

After learning that the City of Springfield was to have an Immigrant Coalition, Mark asked Mayor Rob Rue if the City would likewise allow an independent Concerned Citizens Coalition, in fairness.

"And his comment to me was, 'You get your chance to be a coalition every two weeks for three minutes,'" Mark relayed in an interview, with reference to the City Commission meetings and time allotted to resident-speakers.[8]

Anyhow.

The various allegations of animal consumption by Springfield Haitians came up during my conversations with Mark.

"Are Haitian refugees killing geese in parks for food?" reads an official Clark County FAQ on the migrant influx. The subsequent answer provided is, "No. The local game warden with the Ohio Department of Natural Resources says there is no evidence to support these claims. The county dispatch received one call claiming this, and it was not able to be substantiated by the deputy who responded."[9]

That question begs the exact question I also fed the Springfield landlord: Is *eating* of the alleged-slaughtered animals something that's happening?

Some yes and some no, I was told by Mark and other members of Springfield's OSINT network. He recounted to me what he had shared previously via his Clark County commissioner campaign page on Facebook:

> 7 months before Springfield became national news [I] attempted to give the city everything they needed to resolve the abuse/consumption of domestic animals and waterfowl, they ignored specific info and refused to listen. So much could have been avoided if they would have treated citizens with the same care and respect as they did immigrants. I furnished addresses and times that these incidents were witnessed on paper under their laptops before this meeting.[10]

It was at that March 12, 2024, Springfield City Commission meeting that Mark addressed the commission and stated that long-time city residents don't feel "safe" due to the "cultural clash," adding:

> Our traditions, laws, and culture . . . 180 degrees different than what they're used to . . . I've actually had quite a few people contact me here lately [with] some pretty horrid things occurring to domesticated animals in the neighborhood. We've had some stuff in the park.[11]

Are they eating the cats? Are they eating the dogs? *Was that some kind of ritual thing going on?*

By the way, let's address the matter of the canines directly. At no point did I meet anyone in the city who claimed firsthand knowledge or possession of any other evidence of Haitian cultural activity in Clark County involving **dogs**. Where did dogs come from then, Mr. Trump? My pet hypothesis is auto-correct, and it goes like this:

As word began to spread from Springfield nationwide in September 2024, someone at some point typed "cats and ducks" or perhaps a typographical error meant to read as "ducks" but was auto-corrected to match the more common phrasing "cats and dogs." (According to my search engine optimization and keyword research tool Keywords Everywhere, the longtail keyword "cats and ducks" receives 3,600 average searches per month. But the keyword "cats and dogs"? More than 135,000 per month, rolling twelve-month average. It is long-established that autocorrect "can occasionally be a bit overzealous and make incorrect corrections, leading to unintended and sometimes embarrassing changes in your text."[12] Thus, I believe it plausible that someone of influence intended to type "cats and ducks," which matches verbatim what I heard among Springfield residents concerned with local animal welfare, but accidentally sent "cats and dogs" after an auto-correct fail (or perhaps they incorrectly typed "cats and docks," after which came the plausible non-duck autocorrect to "dogs"). And that's what reached Trump.

Now, I did see a number of heritage citizens share on social media what they claimed was a gruesome photograph of a decapitated, dismembered beagle, prepared for consumption by Haitians and alleged to be in Springfield. I used a reverse image lookup tool available from Google and found it originating from an animal-rights NGO called FourPawsForever.org. What appears to be French is scribbled on one of the photos; that doesn't indicate Haiti but, likelier, Cameroon, where the rescue operation advertises activity.[13,14] Apparently, dog and cat meat are a big business throughout Africa and parts of southeast Asia.[15,16] Fortunately, the United States has the Dog and Cat Meat Trade Prohibition Act.[17] Do you know who signed it into law? President Donald J. Trump, in 2018.

He's protecting the dogs. He's protecting the cats. He's protecting the pets of the people that live here.

"It's a common practice," Mark told me of those cultures known to consume cats, specifically. "They think that they get the stealthiness and the night vision of the cat by consuming the animal."

Some kind of ritual thing going on.

That said, I was consistently told by Springfield's OSINTs that alleged cat-, duck-, and goosenapping occurred potentially not out of hunger but religion.

On Voodoo

Haitian voodoo is known for animal sacrifice. From a thoroughly researched essay on the practice, written nonjudgmentally to a fault:

> In *Vodou*, animals are sacrificed as offerings to the *lwa* during religious ceremonies. These sacrifices are not acts of cruelty but are seen as necessary exchanges in which the spirits are fed and honored. The life force of the animal, known as **ashe** in Yoruba or *vitalité* in Haitian *Vodou*, is believed to sustain the spirits and enhance their power to assist humans . The act of sacrifice is seen as an offering that maintains the balance between the human and spiritual realms. In this way, the animal's life serves a purpose within the religious cosmology of *Vodou*, and its death is regarded with reverence and gratitude.
>
> Common animals used in sacrifice include chickens, goats, and pigs. These animals are often chosen because of their symbolic associations with specific *lwa*. For example, chickens are frequently offered to *Ezili*, the *lwa* of love and beauty, while goats may be sacrificed to *Ogou*, the spirit of war and protection. The choice of animal, its preparation, and the ritualistic process surrounding its sacrifice are all deeply prescribed within *Vodou*'s spiritual codes.[18]

Furthermore, from DW.com:

> Dr. Ingrid Kummels, a Latin American ethnologist at Freie Universität Berlin[, said,] "Afro-Caribbean religions, including Haitian Vodou, only involve the sacrifice of animals considered edible, such as chickens and goats. Cats and dogs are not part of these practices," Kummels told DW, adding that animal sacrifices in Vodou are reserved for significant rituals.
>
> Dr. Grete Viddal, an independent ethnologist specializing in Caribbean Vodou culture, noted a long-standing expression about Haitians and cats. "There's an expression in Haiti about extreme poverty, saying someone is so poor they might have to eat cats. But the idea that Haitians eat cats in Vodou rituals is pure fiction . . . "[19]

So poor they might have to eat cats.

The Photo

Two photos were shared regularly to social media as purported evidence of Haitians' consumption of pets—one was that likely-Cameroon beagle carcass, and the other was of a black gentleman appearing to strangle a cat to death using some sort of wire as a makeshift noose and a gate as leverage. I reverse-searched that image and found via the Wayback Machine a series of photos in an Imgur album published on or around September 13, 2012. If you'd like to see the archived album, you may do so here:

https://web.archive.org/web/20120915012941/http://imgur.com/a/Z76ZM

You'll see a black woman with a kitten in each arm (and what looks to be a goat in the background), a black man preparing to and then strangling an adult cat, and then five photos depicting the charred remains of what appears to be that very cat being cooked atop a hasty cardboard fire just off the doorstep of a dwelling where three children look on. There are no indications of date or location, except for writing scribbled on the dwelling—one of these reads, "MTI'TC." A Gemini AI search result for this via Google suggested it referred to Medical Teams International (MTI), a group that provided medical and other essential supplies to Haiti following the 2010 earthquake.[20] I also simply asked Gemini what the photo depicts, and here is what it said:

"This image shows a scene in Haiti illustrating a severe humanitarian and economic crisis."

I uploaded the archived photo of a cigaretted gentleman cooking the cat. Notice the AI highlights "MTI'TC" in the background.

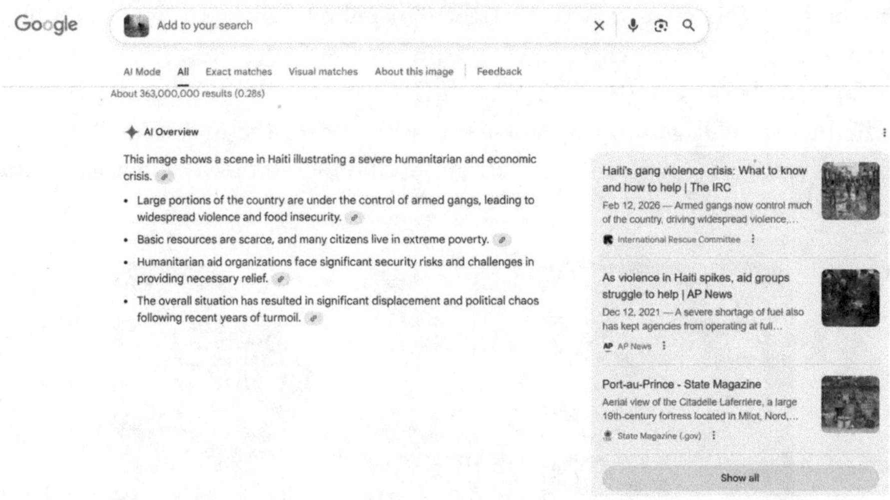

Thanks, Gemini.

Note that no text accompanies the photo, so I did not lead the witness or otherwise try to trick Google's AI. Gemini calls it like it sees it.

How quick many will be to debunk this photo.

That's just in Haiti! That's not Springfield! There's only the one photo!

I'm reminded of other allegedly Springfield reports of consumed animals—like the non-English-speaking black man at a Columbus intersection with a dead goose, the black woman in Canton crushing and eating a cat in the street, and still another (alleged) cat on a backyard grill in Dayton.[21,22,23]

Sure, the goose was dead, and the man was carrying it, but you don't know if he ate it or not! Didn't you see what TMZ said?! They confirmed the man was simply moving geese roadkill—CONFIRMED![24] *And OBVIOUSLY that poor Canton woman was not in her right mind! And if she was? It was just her CULTURE! And just because it looks like that was a cat on that grill does not mean it was OR that the family was going to EAT it! How do you know it wasn't an elaborate HOAX run by a WHITE man?! Remember, the Police and Mayor both said it never happened!*[25]

Ways to explain it all away are fruit hanging so low they grow on vines along the ground. So do additional anecdotes.

The Video

Consider a video published to 𝕏 by independent field reporter **Tayler Hansen** on October 8, 2024, with the caption stating, "A Haitian is caught on video chopping an animal apart with a machete in public. This video was taken by a resident of the Red [Coach Village] Apartments [in Springfield]."[26]

Japanese-language news TBS NEWS DIG Powered by JNN sent a reporter to Red Coach Village, who spoke with a local on site. The man said, "Someone was just cutting up a pig on a tree stump," motioning to the very spot where the incident had been filmed.[27]

The 𝕏 app allows premium users (like me) to click the Grok AI logo and instantaneously generate a description of a post or media published on the app. I asked Grok about this video, and it told me:

> Tayler Hansen's post shares shaky video footage filmed from inside an apartment at the Red Couch Apartments in Springfield, Ohio, showing a man outdoors on grass repeatedly using a long blade to chop and handle what appears to be an animal carcass.

The clip was posted in October 2024 amid widespread public debate over the rapid influx of Haitian immigrants to Springfield, where local residents had reported missing pets, geese, and other animals alongside concerns about sanitation and public behavior.

The video spread rapidly online as alleged evidence of unusual practices, drawing millions of views, though authorities had previously stated limited evidence for specific pet-eating claims while acknowledging broader community strains from the population surge.

But Joshua, why would you ask Grok when you could just ask Tayler, the guy who posted the video?

I thought ahead to you wondering just that, so I reached out to Tayler the day after I copied Grok's reply into this very book. I asked him straightforwardly and without context beyond the link to his own video, "Hey Tayler. Want to ask you about this video. Do you know the person who recorded it, or was it submitted to you anonymously?" Below are relevant replies from Tayler.

[The video] [w]as submitted anonymously through a local as they were worried about repercussions.

They provided the location so I could confirm it was actually filmed in Springfield as they claimed.

. . . I do remember the mentioning of it being a pig and not a duck/dog/cat hence why I went with animal in the caption.

. . . [T]he person that sent it claimed to know the family and was a resident in the apartment where it was taken. Wanted everyone to remain anonymous as it was a national topic and wanted to protect their identities.

. . . The apartments / exact location had been confirmed to be in Springfield Ohio[.]

. . . I spoke to Haitians about the original allegations involving ducks and I received one of three answers every time—it's not really happening/they're only used for ritualistic purposes/food.

I just received the tip that a Haitian was caught on video butchering the animal, location, etc. Not 100% sure what the purpose would be but I'd imagine it has to do with a specific ritual (organ use most likely, if so) or they're planning to eat it and have no understanding that you shouldn't be

(continued . . .)

> slaughtering animals in public (which for example is the case every single day in South Africa)[.]
>
> . . . I didn't voice memo any of [the Haitians I interviewed] as it was only when we got it into Lyfts that we spoke with them and we were usually focused on reminding them to turn their e[-]brake off or to stop at the stop signs . . .
>
> . . . Yes [the man with the machete was Haitian]- to the extent that the email with the submission claimed it was a Haitian man . . . Not many non-Haitian blacks in [the] Springfield area[.]

Anonymous sourcing. Identity protection. National attention. All of this I felt a wee suspicious about coming into this project. If abducktion is as ubiquitous as residents have claimed, together with all the other alleged Haitian antics, where are the videos they've posted? Why are not more residents sharing openly and freely what they claim to be eyewitnessing, under their own names?

I no longer wonder; I completely understand. Because when I later published to social media a brief recounting of an anecdote of my own from a Springfield Walmart, which you'll read about in a later chapter, the backlash was as immediate and horrific as heritage citizens had told me their own were, which is why so many had decided to shut up and suffer in silence, to be surrenderedly frank. Complete strangers to me, many anonymous, absolutely assaulted my posts with cancel-culture accusations. Of course, it was denied that what I observed even happened.[28] When I posted a couple of photos in response, I was met with threats to have me trespassed from Walmart for taking said photos.[29] Naturally, I was called "racist" myriad times, including by a Springfield-area football coach who had no problem messaging me a profanity-laced rant under his real name.[30] Another critic wrote, "You're going to be replaced nazifag."[31] Two more Haitian deniers called me a "pedophile."[32] Indeed, denial was intense, particularly denial with biting sarcasm.[33,34,35] Despite the Creole spoken, it was insisted the Haitians were merely your typical Walmart-American blacks.[36] And I'm still a racist for noticing that I noticed what I noticed.

I wrote in my 2023 nonfiction work *So Good They Call You a Fake* that "haters are your most valuable marketers."[37] These reputational assaults and e-sassinations taking place mean nothing to me because I do not give a shit. I am an internet personality with products and services to sell. *Their* attention becomes *my* influence. But imagine yourself as a working-class city maintenance man. A part-time retail employee. A minimum-wage hospitality worker. A single parent with children balancing night school. You can't make ends meet yet you're punished for working long, hard hours by being told that you're a couple of dollars richer than the minimum poverty required for food stamps and other welfare benefits for being just a little bit worse off than your work ethic allows you to be. Or, perhaps you finally have a well-paying job, rare as they are to come by now in Clark County. One accusation—only one—like the above, sent to your employer, as we all know, can be enough to get you immediately fired. The risk-reward analysis to go public simply does not make sense for the majority of white residents to risk their employer, for example, being threatened with a boycott, protest, or worse because they employ an accused "racist" "Nazi" "pedophile"—and again, this accusation set can be deployed against exclusively *white* Americans.

There is indeed immense racism in Springfield, Ohio.

A young Springfield woman who agreed to be interviewed for this book but then retroactively pleaded for anonymity, which I granted, told me that she was only ever brave enough to publicly comment once on the Haitian antics in Springfield. She simply said, on only one occasion, "Yeah, it's getting out of hand," she relayed to me. She was immediately met with death threats, accusations of racism and discrimination (as if she had done so personally), guarantees that she will "burn in hell," and the loss of her friend and peer group because they "can't believe" she "supported Trump" despite the President having no mention made in the entire Haitian conversation.

Outspoken citizens like Mark Sanders, I observed, are indeed employed, but I consider him a special case because his job has received some of the worst PR in city history—bus driver. He told me that the day he showed up to inquire about the bus driver job, he was awarded employment within ten minutes, with first-day training scheduled for the following morning. I understand why. Yet as we sympathize with the plight of the city on the whole, we recognize that one outlier does not define the norm. Exceptions confirm rules.

I'm grateful to be in the position where I can co-sign this statement from U.S. Representative Brandon Gill: "You can call me any name you want. I just want my children to grow up in a country that they recognize."[38] And I do. Many Springfielders, publicly, cannot.

From all of this, I concluded: The working people of Springfield are like hostages in their own homeland yet are socially forbidden from speaking about that very verbal imprisonment.

Now, back to Tayler Hansen's understandably anonymously submitted video. It and Tayler's commentary tracks with everything I've learned about Springfield, the mood of the locals, and how the Haitian population has responded to inquiries about non-standard processing of animal products since the story broke.

You may recall the alleged debunking of the so-called hoax with headlines such as "'It just exploded': Springfield woman claims she never meant to spark false rumors about Haitians" from NBC News.[39] Or this from the *New York Times*: "Ohio Woman Says She Regrets Sharing False Rumor About Haitians on Facebook . . . The woman has since deleted the post claiming that one of her Haitian neighbors might have taken a neighbor's cat."[40]

False rumor, you say. NewsGuard's Reality Check insists that is the case. NBC News reports:

> Newsguard, a media watchdog that monitors for misinformation online, found that [Springfield resident Erika] Lee had been among the first people to publish a post to social media about the rumor, screenshots of which circulated online. The neighbor, Kimberly Newton, said she heard about the attack from a third party, NewsGuard reported.
>
> Newton told Newsguard that Lee's Facebook post misstated her story, and that the owner of the missing cat was "an acquaintance of a friend" rather than her daughter's friend. Newton could not be reached for comment.
>
> Lee said she had no idea the post would become part of a rumor mill that would spiral into the national consciousness. She has since deleted the Facebook post.
>
> Other posts have also contributed to the false allegations . . . [41]

NewsGuard claimed "Triple Hearsay" on the matter, adding, later cited by mainstream media sources, "'I'm not sure I'm the most credible source because I don't actually know the person who lost the cat,'" Kimberly Newton told NewsGuard. She is the Springfield, Ohio, resident whose story started it all."[42]

From NewsGuard:

> In exclusive interviews, NewsGuard spoke both with Lee, a 35-year-old hardware store worker who has lived in Springfield for four years, and Newton, her neighbor and a 12-year resident of Springfield. The interviews reveal just how flimsy and unsubstantiated the rumor was from the beginning—based entirely on third hand hearsay.[43]

Just earlier, I mentioned my work *So Good They Call You a Fake*. Within that book, I warn of the nature of "badverbs" used by deceptive journalists. These are adverbs slipped in where they don't belong in order to mislead audiences in the narrative-approved direction. They're exaggerations made in the-lady-doth-protest fashion.

What did you notice at the close of that NewsGuard excerpt?

Entirely.

"Entirely" on third hand hearsay.

Is that so? "Entirely"?

I didn't have to wonder. The "resident whose story started it all," **Kimberly Newton**, reached out to me, personally, upon hearing of the ambitious nature of this work. And it will be of no surprise to you that what she said is not what NewsGuard said she said. It will also be an object lesson why more heritage citizens of the city did not volunteer their eyewitness accounts and various evidences to the mainstream media worldwide when they descended like exclusive-scoop vultures upon a deeply vulnerable populace. Take it away, Kimberly.

> . . . [S]o the whole cat thing . . . [W]e observed it in our neighborhood. We have one Haitian family . . . in our neighborhood. We are slim . . . [T]he other neighborhoods obviously have way more. We have one that kind of niched into a house that was in foreclosure previously. And we've noticed . . . we used to have a stray cat population in our neighborhood . . . Another friend of mine . . . lives in a different neighborhood where they have a few more Haitian neighbors . . . and they've watched that . . . [W]e discussed it back . . . in 2024. Like, "Yeah, we used to have a couple dozen. Now there's not even single digit number of cats running around like that." We don't find that to be coincidence.

That's exactly what Walter Curt and others told me.

Kimberly then told me she was personally warned that "cats were being collected by the Haitians" by a well-known and respected community leader who I am not about to doxx to you; her anonymity will remain protected for her own personal safety and financial well-being.

Kimberly has cats that she doesn't let out of the house, but she was concerned about her neighbor, Erika Lee, who has indoor-outdoor cats who would be at risk in a catnapping scenario.

"It was literally a five-minute conversation" with Erika to watch out on behalf of her cats due to the increased presence and density of Haitian families that correlated with the widely observed and locally reported disappearance of cats in those very neighborhoods. Then the mainstream media insisted it never happened.

Kimberly told me also that, during her conversation with Erika, Erika confirmed Kimberly's account via a park system employee who had warned her, Erika, about Haitian-linked cat disappearances around town. Again, no doxxing. But it was then that everything changed. From Kimberly:

> Then I go off to a meeting . . . and [Erika] puts a post on . . . a Facebook group here in town. And by the time I got out of that meeting, the whole world had exploded . . . [H]er post was going viral, and . . . I saw where Charlie Kirk had shared it, and JD Vance had [shared] a screenshot of her post because . . . the post got taken down . . . And then Reuters shows up in our neighborhood . . . [T]hey're asking her questions, and they're asking her to contact me. She's giving them my name, and . . . I had some hesitation to even talk to them. My mom was like, "Why wouldn't you tell . . . the story? You've got to tell people what's going on." And some of my other Republican friends [told me], "When you talk to them, tell them all the other things, like . . . the healthcare and the schools and all the other things." . . . I was hesitant because I felt like it could backlash on me, and it did. But I tried it.
>
> In talking to Reuters, they . . . didn't want to hear anything about any of the other parts of the story either. They just wanted to highlight the crazy people thinking [Haitians are] eating cats and dogs. I perceived it as if they just wanted to make us out like were crazy . . . and that we're racist.

I want to tell you what I said to Kimberly next; I pulled up the NewsGuard article and read her the text of the graphic which insisted she was the third to pass on a false rumor via some kind of game of local folklore telephone.

"It says, 'Alleged cat owner said something to cat owner's acquaintance who said something to your neighbor Erika, who wrote the post that then got shared out everywhere.' Is that correct or is that not correct?"

Kimberly?

> To a degree, yes, that's the story they made it out to be. When I talked to [NewsGuard], I wanted them to say, yeah, I had some information and I had observed things in my neighborhood like the cat population . . . decreasing. . . . [My] other neighbor . . . won't talk to anybody because she works for the schools. She had seen some things as well. [But] I wanted them to

> talk about the bigger issues. But . . . that's how they made it out to be, like it was just some big rumor that nobody had really any information on . . . [T] hey really wanted me to give up my friend's name [the respected community leader, but] . . . I knew that she would hate me if I did that . . . because it could sink her business. . . .
>
> There's a bunch of people who know things . . . but can't or won't come out and say who they are and what they've seen because they'd be sacrificing their livelihood because they would immediately get called a racist.

Kimberly then mentioned one such person "who worked with the city who was forced to sign an NDA before he left the city so he wouldn't talk, and he knows things." I was told some version of this approximately one and a half dozen times by various citizens who earned my trust—specifically, that current and former City employees and contractors had been threatened financially due to having witnessed the very animal slaying and processing that NewsGuard, *The New York Times*, Reuters, *The Springfield News-Sun*, and numerous others from then-on insisted never happened. The most common threat was the loss of pensions. (Municipal workers are enrolled in state-mandated public plans that guarantee retirement income, so how this threat would be executed on is a quandary. But a threat doesn't necessarily have to be true for it to work. Do you want to tell the media you saw Haitians eating Felix and Garfield, or do you want me to pull your whole retirement? I thought so.)

At that point in conversation with Kimberly, I noticed another cruel double standard—Springfield's heritage citizens have been socially and financially punished for telling what they believe to be the truth; meanwhile, the Haitians have been rewarded and believed by telling what I believe to be are plucked-naked lies.

Consider this: The credibly accused, who may know themselves to be guilty of whatever is asserted, are the least likely to tell the truth when their duress is greatest, regardless of demographic, socioeconomic status, or situational detail. This goes beyond Haitians in Springfield; this is universal human nature. Earlier in this work, I introduced a law enforcement procedure for eyewitness evidence collection. The minds behind a well-aligned U.S. Supreme Court-recognized interview process called The Reid Technique® inform us that "[t]he reason guilty suspects lie about committing a crime is to avoid suffering the consequences associated with their crime."[44,45] Our keyword here is neither *guilty* nor *crime* but *consequences*.

What would happen to the Haitian population of Springfield if the majority said, on camera and with their names public, that everything in the following section of this book is true, more or less? This question may just fester as you read on—to what happened next when claims of domesticated animal disappearances became the talk of all media worldwide, social and otherwise.

What Happens in Haiti

On September 12, 2024, two days after Candidate Trump's sharing of the cats and dogs claim in the debate against then-Vice President Kamala Harris, Elon Musk shared a video repost from TikTok account @faidiarebekah.[46] As of this writing, most of her content is cultural Christian commentary or music. But in the Musk-shared video, Rebekah Faidia reported that her father moved from Haiti to the United States in the 1960s as a teenager. From the video:

> He wasn't eating people's pets, and he didn't practice voodoo, but he did say that most of the island—the majority of the island—does practice voodoo. The reason they eat cats is for two reasons. Number one is survival. This is the poorest country in the Western hemisphere. You can't just go to a food bank like you can here or just go to McDonald's and get some free or cheap food, unless of course there's a Christian missionary there. People in the United States have a really hard time imagining that kind of thing, but it is true. Second, they do do animal sacrifices for their religion, voodoo. They make these animal sacrifices to these gods for different reasons . . . [T]hese people need prayer. But you can't just take over all these people from another country and expect it to work, not to mention it doesn't fix the problems of that country . . . It's not racist to acknowledge that this is a problem. It's not racist to talk about these things that are happening.[47]

"In response to the backlash"—because of course there was—"Faidia posted another video, defending her comments. 'I'm not spreading hate,' she said, acknowledging that some Haitians had attacked her for her views."[48]

Haitians like whom?

The Haitian-based account @LikeChrisss, which claims multiple STEM degrees from MIT and a medical doctorate, replied to Musk's share and said:

> I love how these stereotypes about Haitians are built on hearsay with no real evidence. Show me one picture of a Haitian eating a pet—oh wait, you

> can't, because it's all about spreading harmful myths. Meanwhile, there's actual evidence of American missionaries involved in child trafficking and abuse in Haiti, but no one wants to talk about that. And let's not forget, animal sacrifice happens in some U.S. religions too, but that's not used to define the whole country.[49]

I feel bad because I couldn't get past the second sentence. What are you supposed to do when a debunking attempt itself comes pre-debunked?

That said, he did say "too." Interesting.

Anonymous user @1804_Jon based in the United States replied to the Musk-shared Rebekah Faidia video also, saying, "She said most Haitians eat cat and most Haitians practice voodoo which is a lie you should know better … do we have any cat recipes ? How stupid are you?"[50]

Another account belonging to a "Meus H. Alexandre, MD" (@MeusHernst) replied, saying of Rebekah, "She's speaking facts, except that during my nearly two decades in Haiti, I never heard or saw that they do that for sacrifice. Maybe I don't know much; I am Haitian, I've never practiced voodoo, so I don't know. Such stuff is not a common practice either. I've only heard about—"[51] And then the post ends. I found it through an archived post; the original is now-deleted as do seem to be several back-and-forths this Meus individual replied, but not all.[52]

In an undeleted reply, Meus responded to anon-Jon and said, "Yes, her dad was exaggerating by saying 'most'."[53]

The Meus account, based in "the Caribbean," has a history in 2024 of commenting on Haitian news stories. For example, the account shared a September 26, 2024 video of Edgard Leblanc Fils, transitional president of Haiti's Presidential Council, with a quote from his UN General Assembly speech stressing Haiti's demand for respect instead of charity.[54] Meus's post says, translated into English, "I don't get involved in politics, but it would be shameful for me, as a Haitian, to let this event pass without taking the time to salute this man's courage for his incredible speech and the message he's delivering to both Haiti and the world at large."

That video may be the most viral Haitian story ever witnessed, more so than the cats and dogs, but not because of anything said or any Springfield tie-in—but because it was in that speech that Edgard Leblanc Fils attempted to drink water straight from a large pitcher and spilled a few splashes everywhere—now a global "internet sensation."[55,56]

Can this lovely people catch a break? They cannot. If you think that's funny, you're a racist.

A video from YouTube user Chronicles of a Zoe reappeared across social media in the context of the Springfield cats and dogs.[57] Published July 7, 2023, the video begins with Haitian-American social media influencer and independent documentariette Yvana Romelus recounting, upon her first visit to Haiti at six years old, witnessing the ritual sacrifice of a goat. She said she was "traumatized" by the experience and to this day will not eat goat.[58] I will admit I did not know you could eat goat—not until I visited the Haitian embassy. When I was nine, I did sample the goat's milk white chocolate sold at the old Caprine Estates in Bellbrook, Ohio.[59] Best candy I've ever had.

Yvana does complain about the demonization of Haitian voodoo. Various still images within the video depict Haitian women wearing white garments that are covered in what one assumes are the splattered blood of a sacrificed animal. Yvana explains that various spirits within the voodoo religion will demand a given animal's death—but not, apparently, just an animal's:

> Like, certain spirits only like specific types of animals or specific types of possessions or sacrifices. You can't bring a goat if a specific spirit wants a cow. You can't bring a baby if a specific spirit wants a virgin. Yeah, it's that specific. You can't bring a grown man if a specific spirit requires a virgin girl. Yeah, I said it. That's just how the cookie crumbles . . . Like I said, we're not going into those details, but that's how specific a lot of these rituals can go.[60]

Earlier in the video, Yvana mentioned she would be discussing, in the context of Haitian voodoo, human sacrifice—but would not be going into details. She indeed did not. But *Smithsonian Magazine* published an article in 2013 covering three nineteenth-century anecdotes of Haitian cannibalism. The first mentioned instance, this one specifically involving voodoo, was "n 1864 case that ended with the execution of eight Haitians for child murder and cannibalism [which] has helped define attitudes toward the nation and the religion ever since."[61] The article later mentions "only two other 'firsthand' accounts of vodou ceremonies involving cannibalism: one from a French priest during the 1870s, and the other from a white Dominican a decade later."[62,63] However, contemporary third-party reports assert human sacrifice and cannibalism were not so rare. From a page hosted by Florida International University (FIU) Libraries, specifically through the Digital Library of the Caribbean (dLOC):

> Sir Spencer St. John, the former British counsel for Haiti, serves as a historic spectator of daily life in the cities and countryside of nineteenth-century

> Haiti. His observations were published in the book, *Haiti or the Black Republic* (1884). Within this book one finds intriguing accounts of cannibalistic practices, human sacrifice and sorcery, all of which are condemned as practices that must be abolished for Haiti to become part of the civilized world.[64]

Following the assassination of Haiti's president, on July 28, 1915, U.S. Marines landed in Port-au-Prince, Haiti, initiating what would be sold as a nineteen-year nation-stabilizing campaign, authorized by President Woodrow Wilson.[65] In a 2019 edition of *Marine Corps History*, a publication of the United States Marine Corps, an article by David J. Ulbrich, PhD contains the following notes on U.S.-Haitian culture clashes and legal-standard differences from that period of American military occupation:[66]

> Some Haitians practiced polygamy, promiscuity, or cannibalism, all of which the [US] Marines found to be immoral and often illegal. It is easy to see why Marines were inclined to equate the religion with Christian notions of witchcraft and identify its Haitian followers as superstitious peasants at best or self-professed witch doctors or sorcerers at worst.
>
> . . . [E]ven when evidence pointed toward a guilty verdict, the Haitian courts could be swayed by Voodooism. Two examples represented what could best be termed *justifiable homicide*. An accused Haitian man testified that he killed a woman because she was a werewolf that had allegedly caused the death of his child. Another case included testimony by several Haitians that they killed a man "because he has been eating their children." Cannibalism of humans could not be considered to be the proper practice of Voodoo. The fact that both were examples of self-defense and thus permitted by Voodoo notions of morality contributed to the Haitian courts' decisions to acquit the defendants of murder charges.[67]

As of this writing, cannibalism is not explicitly illegal under Haitian law; Articles 304-306 of the Haitian Penal Code do address unauthorized burials, concealment of homicide evidence, and violation of burial places.[68] Notably, Haiti's law is narrower than those in most U.S. states. "While the vast majority of states have enacted abuse of corpse or other related laws . . . some states outline penalties for mutilating or defacing a corpse, while others more broadly define it as 'outraging family sensibilities.'"[69] Food for thought.

In defense of Haitian folk traditions, a 1959 article in *The Journal of American Folklore* documented the primitives' *post facto* explanation of various locals' death as actually resulting from human sacrifice by supernatural, not human, means:

> What . . . do Haitian peasants believe with reference to cannibalism? Haitian peasants use the expression *mangé moun* 'to eat people' in what to the outside appears to be a variety of different contexts. A great many anecdotes are told, for instance, in which evil priests or sorcerers (*bokor*) are accused of causing death . . . Yet . . . it is not the *bokor* but the deity who kills (through illness) and thus "eats" the victim. Sometimes the *bokor* sacrifices a goat, which is said to represent the human victim . . . [70]

That brings us back to Yvana, who went on in her video to suggest how one might modify a blood offering to please and appease a given voodoo spirit, swapping one animal or combination of others for whatever may be available at the time of the ritual. Interesting. *I suspected that they might be breeding them for whatever reason but not 100% for sure . . . there were lots of [mice] everywhere confined to different areas of the house.*

"At the end of the day, unless you're vegan . . . you are literally a thousand percent a hypocrite for holding [a negative] opinion [of Haitian voodoo animal sacrifice]," Yvana made sure to add. She went on to say that every piece and part of each sacrificed animal is distributed throughout the community to be consumed or otherwise used. And not just the body but its "soul."[71] Towards the end of the video, Yvana made sure to remind us that other ancient cultures practiced animal sacrifice like Haitian voodoo "centuries" ago, just like Haitians do today, in the present. I realized that her observation makes the opposite point she seems to have intended to make.

Yvana closed the video with a call-to-action for Haitian return to tradition, to a widerspread adoption of animal sacrifice and other practices and, by implication, rejection of Christianity.

You may know (or not) that the Haitian Revolution began with an animal sacrifice ritual, followed by subsequent and explicit white genocide. From the archived Official Haitian Bicentennial Website, celebrating "The First Black Republic in the World" and was "Proudly Sponsored by: The City of Miami" in Florida:

> A man named Boukman, another houngan, organized on August 14, 1791, a meeting with the slaves in the mountains of the North. This meeting took the form of a Voodoo ceremony in the Bois Caiman in the

> northern mountains of the island. It was raining and the sky was raging with clouds; the slaves then started confessing their resentment of their condition. A woman started dancing languorously in the crowd, taken by the spirits of the loas. With a knife in her hand, she cut the throat of a pig and distributed the blood to all the participants of the meeting who swore to kill all the whites on the island. On August 22, 1791, the blacks of the North entered into a rebellion, killing all the whites they met and setting the plantations of the colony on fire.[72]

What is Haiti like more recently, according to Western visitors? Not necessarily so violent towards a given white person but not exactly welcoming either. Take South African travel filmmaker Kurt Caz. His short documentary *Voodoo in Haiti Gone Wrong!* published on August 26, 2021, covers the following real-life true-crime-horror-drama. From the video description, unedited:

> Makendi, my guide for the day mentioned that they do voodoo in the town, so of course I was interested and wanted to check it out.
>
> When I asked him in the beginning of the video how much it would cost to do it he said around 200-300 Dominican Pesos which is roughly $4.
>
> Later on Makendi turned on me. He was a part of it all.
>
> I would of happily paid them $100+ or an equally fair amount for the ceremony.
>
> Instead they tried to finesse me and took my kindness for weakness.
>
> Luckily they took me back to the hotel to extort me for more money and from there i was safer to bargain, with the help of the presence of the hotel staff.
>
> In the end I paid them $70.[73]

"Took my kindness for weakness." That's the sort of line you'll remember for the rest of your life.

In one notable part of the ritual, Kurt is directed to write down his desires along with his name a number of times, and the subsequent paper is burned. I think I saw a new-age boho white chick in Portland do something like that in a marijuana-tarot card shop. I'm not sure it's there anymore.

If you're interested in learning more about Haitian voodoo practices, consider a decade-plus-old anthropologist's ask-me-anything on Reddit, still up and visited to this day. It begins:

> I am currently conducting fieldwork with Haitian Vodou practitioners in Haiti and the diaspora for my PhD dissertation. I've been working with this community for almost six years now attending ceremonies and researching worldviews . . . While there I got to see how the diaspora and local communities interact, share ideas, shape one another's worldviews, and witness initiations![74]

One of the anthropologist's remarks on witnessing Haitian voodoo spirit possessions mentions someone who, while possessed, took up a machete and began beating another person with it. An extended explanation from that same comment teaches us how possessions work:

> Spirit possessions are really amazing things to witness overall. A mild mannered arthritic little old lady will suddenly start stumbling from the spirit. When someone is possessed their primary soul that holds consciousness and personality is kicked out and the spirit takes over completely. The person has lost time while the spirit uses their body like a vehicle. But there is always a moment of struggle between person and spirit and it is visible bodily. Then the person is no longer that person. Every aspect of their gait, mannerisms, facial expressions, how they hold their bodies, etc. changes. That little arthritic lady might suddenly be dancing all over the room in a really spectacular way!
>
> But there are always interesting stories![75]

Very interesting, thanks!

"Different Cultures Have Different Dietary Standards"

Staying on Reddit for now, a user posted a now-deleted but still-publicly-viewable question to the r/haiti subreddit writing, "Now that some time has passed . . . can we unpack the 'eating the dogs and cats' situation."[76] A moderator of the Haiti subreddit, u/zombigoutesel, replied—then edited—and said:

> So in [Port-au-Prince], in poor neighborhoods eating cats is a lot more common than people think. It's partially taboo because it's considered something very poor people do, so it's a class marker. It's also associated with drinking.
>
> If you don't or have not lived in PaP and had exposure to these areas and the people that live there it might be hard to believe. But I promise, it's a thing. If you know where to go, you can even get it in little restaurants

and road side stalls, just like bega. Some people trap feral cats, some people will raise cats like rabbits as a cheap protein source.

For some reason it's also associated with the new year. The joke is that if you have a house cat, keep him in the house over the holidays if you want him to see the new year.

Dogs on the other hand, as far as I know are not a thing. The only thing I ever heard is dishonest goat meat sellers selling dogs as goats. If you ever go to meat markets, sellers leave the goat foot on the quarters so you can see it's a goat.

For some reason there is a lot of emotion around this topic.

Edit: I meant the topic in general. Not the way it was used as a racist dog whistl by maga shit heads.[77]

Anonymous user u/imaginevenus replied to this comment, saying:

> Yes to this. Exactly what my mom told me and she is from the PaP area.
>
> My stepdad was one of those people who ate everything under the sun
>
> Hoping weirdo racist don't find this but yes it is true people in poverty will sometimes resort to that:[78]

Other comments add flavor to the discussion begun by the moderator:

> That's exactly what I was told growing up. And many other countries do it as a last resort. Before they were exposed as lies.. the claims stated multiple Haitians were going on cat hunts for dinner. You would've thought Haiti had a CAT national dish with a whole recipe.
>
> I should've known they were lying when they kept moving the goal post. They claimed Haitians were eating the cats because they were so poor and hungry but at the same time accused them of receiving excessive government assistance and driving luxury cars. Which is it Conner?[79]
>
> . . .
>
> I mean, i remember listening to a Haitian in a radio talking about how his parents bought their meat from Dominicans to avoid being sold dpg/cat/human meat by haitian butchershops :u[80]

You'll find more comments like these as the thread continues. My favorite reply to the original post reads, "delete this shit bro. no good's gonna come out of it."[81]

In another now-deleted, still-visible post to the r/haiti subreddit, a user wrote:

> i'm Canadian and have lived in Haiti for a couple of years now. I was walking through a village today and saw a woman and some children plucking a dead cat. My poor Canadian eyes were a little stunned!
>
> It got me thinking. What foods are off limits here? We've learned that snails are definitely off limits and the idea of goat milk is very strange. Will people eat dogs? How about mongoose or crows? I'm so curious now.[82]

Now enters the moderator, u/zombigoutesel, taking the post serious (as it probably was) and replying:

> Dog will get passed as goat by unscrupulous marchand. People won't willingly eat dog. We eat cat but it's slighly Tabou. People actually raise them for food or catch them.
>
> We eat doves , almost all the offal from goat , pig and beef. Aside from cat, doves and duck I'm not aware of any non farmyard animals we eat. Horse meat is a thing in the north, I imagine the odd donkey also ends up in a pot. Certain foods are associated with poverty and people refuse to eat them once they reach a certains status. Like mais moulu, millet and breadfruit are considered inferior to rice and plantains. Yellow plantain is considered superior to the small white plantain. etc etc We are actually pretty picky eaters.
>
> We arent big on cheese except for casseroles.[83]

What would Americans think, witnessing all this in person, you might wonder? We needn't wonder. On April 12, 2005, author Tim Deagan wrote of his four-month experience in Haiti:

> I was working on an archeological dig, looking for the remains of *La Navidad*, Columbus's first settlement in the new world. Getting on the crew was a graduation gift from my sister (who is pretty much the premier Columbus archeologist in the country.) I had worked on digs during my summers in high school and had a minor in anthropology.[84]

The sister in question is Dr. Kathleen A. Deagan, multi-honored and award-winning archeologist and scholar.[85] She made some fascinating discoveries in Haiti, in Florida, and in other areas touched by the very first Spanish explorers of recorded history. It was on one such excursion that she found herself a great treasure of priceless value—a husband.

Her brother Tim opens his account—entitled "A Haitian Pet Store"—with this admission of overall impression with 1980s Haiti:

> Unrelenting poverty in every direction. Beautiful people working harder than any people I have ever met. Friendly faces despite hunger, fear and need. Daily life struggling with burdens I had no chance whatsoever of understanding. I was from a different planet, a different century, a different life.
>
> It took me most of my 4 months to shake a few of the scales from my eyes. I went to Haiti a liberal, a believer in respect for all people and a champion for human rights. I left Haiti disappointed with myself, having come to a clearer understanding of what a spoiled child of the richest country on earth I really was.[86]

I'm beginning to worry that the store didn't sell pets.

> I began to ask the Haitians I worked and lived around about pets. Did they have pets? What kind of pets would they keep? Reactions varied from a complete lack of understanding regarding the topic to a grudging acceptance that someone, somewhere might keep pets, but no one knew anyone who did. The military had some dogs that were used to attack people, but I rejected that as an example of 'pets.'[87]

Now I'm sure of it. But what was the store in question?

> Walking near the Cap version of the Marché de Fer, I stumbled into an alley and beheld my quarry. There, at the end of the alley, was a nicely dressed Haitian woman with cages and cages of cats! People would walk by and admire them. They mewed prettily, trying to find someone to adopt them. Soon, a young woman walked up and began haggling in rapid Creole (too fast for my poor understanding of the tongue.) Back and forth they went until a bargain had been struck. I watched as the selected cat was retrieved for the new pet owner. I imagined her taking it home to some small child, a happy moment for all. As I got ready to take a picture of this special Kodak moment, the shop owner picked up the cat, grabbed its head, twisted it with a single motion and an audible 'SNAP'. As the dead cat fell limp, she deftly whipped out a skinning knife, removed the skin, gutted the innards and wrapped the meat back into the skin. All in fewer moments than I could count.[88]

Right about then, Tim channeled Yvana Romelus of YouTube from the future (not literally—I need to clarify given the context):

> Yes, Haitians eat cat. Yes, I ate cat when I was in Haiti. Haitians were horrified that Americans ate horse (which had been being sold for a while in grocery stores in the late 70's in the USA.) Different cultures have different dietary standards and (at least for the carnivores among us,) ours aren't particularly more moral than anyone else's.[89]

TikTok user @ayoitsdamenace claimed in a video reposted as a reply to Elon Musk's original shared post that started all of this that, though born in Haiti and raised in America, family and friends of his actually raised in Haiti tell stories about "themselves eating the cat, or them knowing people that do eat cat out there."[90,91] He notes that it is normal for people of one culture to take time to become acclimated to the customs of a new environment. Like Ohio. "Of course [they're] going to keep the same habit they're doing over there."[92] Tell that to Portland.

In the replies of the Musk post, my friend Stephanie Stock from Ohio Advocates for Medical Freedom made an appearance. She reposted a set of images, taken in Springfield, depicting the head-skins of dead pigs. That's the least-graphic way to describe them. Stephanie wrote with her post:

> Sadly, abandoned pig carcasses are the least of their problems. Residents are paying twice as much rent as the Haitians. People are losing access to vital state assistance services & housing. There are multiple motor accidents a day- some resulting in fatalities, including a 71 year old woman. The BMV is completely overrun and there is an eye witness stating BMV workers are "reminding Haitians to register to vote" when they close in assisting them.
>
> Our governor ALLOWED them to be sent there during Covid and has done NOTHING to help the citizens. Now he's throwing 2.5 MILLION of our tax dollars into troopers and SCHOOL "HEALTH" and "VACCINE" clinics????
>
> GET THEM OUT DEWINE! #EndTheInvasion[93]

And we're back to the all-caps.

By the way, Mark Sanders also told me about the skinned pig carcasses found in Springfield. "There was no way that somebody butchered those pigs and dumped what they dumped" in preparation for a meal. He suggested sacrifice. Remember what the voodoo spirits allow when preferred chickens or goats are unavailable? And again from *Unhumans*, "With a knife in her hand, she cut the throat of a pig and distributed the blood to all the participants of the meeting who swore to kill all the whites on the island"?

Glenda texted me about the pigs, saying the partial carcasses were "discovered on the property of the old Reid Elementary School. It's less than a mile from the Haitian ghetto behind the Walmart on Tuttle [Road]." According to Google Maps, that property and—and I looked this up for no reason at all—is a fourteen-minute trip to the Red Coach apartments by car.

These were not the only, uh, remains found by locals. Mark also told me about various plastic and trash bags of human excrement found near apartments by a Springfield Kroger known to rent to Haitians. (It was the same first Kroger I'd visited when I began work on this book, by the way; Haitians were easy to identify. They wore thick winter coats and hats in mid-seventies Fahrenheit weather.)

"Industrial garbage bags full of human defecation, like people had just crapped in there, then tied it up, and they drove up the street. That happened for about a month. Then it went away," Mark said. There were multiple instances of bagged-up roadkill found as well, and I spoke to two separate eyewitnesses about a roadside deer carcass appearing to be field-dressed by a small group of probable Haitians.

Different cultures have different dietary standards.

The most dramatic telling of animal antics eyewitnessing comes also from Mark; he described one particular incident euphemistically, at that March 12, 2024, Springfield City Commission meeting. He gave me greater detail when we met. Mark Sanders, uncensored:

> September [2023] I first spoke [at Springfield City Commission meetings]. I was there October, November, and December. And in December of '23, I started getting messages, Facebook message requests, from people I didn't know . . . I was there religiously, so people were sending me information. . . . [One] was a city worker. They were replacing all the water meters. They were going with different water meters on an area—it would be South Limestone Street, I think, the 1600 block down there, by Speedway and by Food Mart . . . They were putting in new water meters.
>
> *(continued . . .)*

At the same time, landlords were taking these big houses and making triplexes and quadplexes out of them. So there [were] electricians, and there were plumbers, [and] gas line guys there because they . . . had to put a new gas meter for every address.

Long story short, they were sending me—and they didn't have pictures because they said they would go to the house to work, and they would have . . . a work order, and they would show the people at the front door, and they spoke no English, and they would let them in, but they would all sit on the basement stairs and watch what they were doing.

So they were taking the water meters down, put[ting] new water meters in, some of them being relocated outside. But at the same time, plumbers were there, too. Electricians were there, too. So there was a multiple of tradespeople there.

They were saying, "There is stuff hanging from the rafters in the basement. There's water fowl and what looks like big rabbits, but they're not rabbits."

So that's where the whole cat thing came from.

Then Mark reminded me how he'd brought the addresses of these and other reported incidents to Springfield City Commission meetings and slid the papers beneath commissioners' laptops before the meeting—this, it turns out, was to prevent him from having to announce the address or addresses of the reported activities publicly, giving landlords and tenants alike time to remove all evidence of what had allegedly occurred. I found out that this had happened a number of times before. Mark would report what was seen, then the scene would be gone conveniently prior to official City investigation hours to days after the Commission meeting had been livestreamed to the public.

City workers, plumbers, electricians, gas people, all of them were saying the same thing. I don't think any of them had any relationship with each other, other than maybe seeing each other out in the field. . . .

So my question to them was, "Can you give me a picture?"

They said . . . they were scared to death being down there by themselves or with just two of them. There'd be fifteen or twenty Haitians sitting on the stairs watching them. And they said, besides the lighting, they were working with headlamps because the lighting in those houses was terrible. There [were] no lights in the basement.

A video that went around the OSINTs concurrent with claims about eating animals in 2024 was one entitled, "Eating The Cats? Haitian Family Interview—Says yes it's True We Eat Cats But Not Dogs."[94] It's a video of a video; an English-speaking self-proclaimed Haitian claims to speak in Creole with recent, legal, non-border-jumping Haitian family member-arrivals—the man's cousin and brother. Their comments seem to indicate the availability and consumption of cats in present-day Haiti.[95]

Another Internet story that went around at that time in 2024 and still persists is Reveyon, or *A réveillon.* First published in March 2019, this particular pro-Haitian culture piece gets right to it—but recasts cat-consumption differently from other reports. It's not a practice of the island's poorest but rather a celebratory feast-addition for all:

> Yes, some Haitians do eat cat meat.
>
> However, it is not a daily, nationwide, or common practice. It is a highly specific tradition exclusive to a very small group of people, mostly in remote rural areas.
>
> Here is the real truth behind this rare tradition, where it comes from, and what you actually need to know.
>
> . . . Contrary to popular belief, this practice is not about poverty or starvation. It is an old, niche tradition rooted in Haiti's history.
>
> During the colonial era, runaway slaves (*Maroons*) had to survive deep in the treacherous mountains and forests of Haiti. They hunted wild animals, including wild cats, to survive. Over time, for a select few, this survival tactic evolved into a rural tradition.
>
> Today, when it does happen, it is almost exclusively tied to December 24th during a Christmas Eve celebration known as Reveyon. For this specific group of people, having this dish at Reveyon is a deeply ingrained cultural habit.
>
> . . . In the US, cats and dogs are pampered family members who sleep in beds. In Haiti, animals have jobs . . . Because animals are viewed through a lens of utility rather than sentimentality, a small percentage of the rural population does not differentiate cat meat from chicken, goat, or beef.[96]

Different cultures have different dietary standards.

The article's first comment, published May 14, 2019, came five years early. It reads, "Disgusting, I have a Haitian family at end of my street they probably ate my outside cat cuz I haven't been able to find them."[97]

The original article's author is Huguens Morency, the founder, lead editor, and primary author of HaitianReport.com. Haitian Facebook groups and podcasts refer to him as a *gwo podcastè ayisyen & entreprenè*—big Haitian podcaster and entrepreneur, I believe. He has appeared as a guest talking about business, inflation, and community issues of the Haitian diaspora on various shows.[98]

Huguens replied to the accusatory commenter, "If you did not have this information this idea would not have come in your mind. Trust me, the Haitian family in your neighborhood has nothing to do with your cat missing."[99]

That said, I did speak to an anonymous lifelong Springfield resident whose story I was able to confirm key details of independently. She told me she used to feed between twelve and fifteen stray cats near her place of employment during business hours. She'd come minimum once a week to refill their food at the same specific spot. About a year into this routine, she noticed Haitians moving in across the street.

"There was an older, bigger house that had been there for a while. Super rundown," she told me. "I'd see thirty to forty [Haitians living there]. They'd be sitting on the porch, watching me, watching us across the street."

After about a month of Haitian presence, this citizen began to do a little noticing. She narrated her thoughts at the time to me now.

"Little orange isn't here today." At the time, she thought nothing of it. Then she'd come back next week. "Oh, where's the white and black one? I guess I just don't see him today."

She made sure multiple times over the course of our conversation to note that "I'm not saying it was Haitians." The reason for her anonymity, by the way, is her fear of being accused of racism and the consequences of that in the current year in America. She told me this explicitly.

"I noticed one cat missing, then another," she said. "I saw five disappear . . . It was just a couple of months."

Thankfully, she was able to rescue a few that remained from the colony.

"I kept trying to think of another reason to tell myself so as not to jump to any conclusion or, like, judge, but it usually ends up being what your gut thinks is right," my source concluded before leaving me with a burning question. "What is it called when most people are afraid to speak out and tell the truth?"

Fowl Play

That was heavy. It's also a lot about cats. What of their potentially autocorrected duckly comrades? One of the first viral claims is that of social media influencer Anthony Harris, who is black (he's black), who claimed Haitians were seizing ducks from the park:

> They're in the park grabbing up ducks by their neck and cutting their head off and walking off with 'em and eating them . . . The only reason I say something is someone told me they were walking from school and a Haitian almost ran into them.[100]

That was August 27, 2024. He later admitted he had not, in fact, seen that first-hand but was relaying purported eyewitness anecdote.[101] A comment on one of Anthony's interviews on the Springfield matter reads, "The geese been leaving Springfield for years because they made it illegal to feed them due too over population of them and them signs was posted like ten years ago so over time the geese left due to lack of food duhhhhh."[102]

Ducks and geese both, I heard claims about. From just about everyone.

A video clipped from *Empty Pockets Garage*, the local livestream hosted by James Blanken, went viral in 2024 following the Trump-Harris debate, as most such content did pertaining to Springfield's various animal life, foreign and domestic.

"They are being killed and eaten," James says of local park ducks in the video, reposted on 𝕏. "As far as people's personal pets, I've heard stories, but I can't answer to that personally because I don't know."[103] He then proceeds to discuss road safety issues numerous others have, reportedly caused, enabled, or otherwise allowed by the old Ohio way where previously, adults over eighteen could skip formal driver's education and just pass the permit or road tests with interpreter assistance in some cases. Rep. Phil Plummer took it upon himself to close that loophole. He did.[104]

By the way, has it seemed like I've switched topics in and out on you all the time? I have. The influx of Haitians has been holistic, all-encompassing, no-aspect-of-daily-life untouched. That's why we're talking about road safety, eyewitnessed animalnapping, all of it, all at once. I digress. Because so does every aspect of this story.

I accompanied Setys Kelly on a number of ridealongs throughout Springfield to the various sites that play out as settings of this saga. My first visit saw us at Snyder Park's Buck Creek near a whitewater rafting installation.[105] Setys had shared previously with the black hosts of *The Outlaws Radio Show*, including Darvio Morrow, the claim that Haitians were seen there bathing in the nude.[106] *Newsweek* published this together with more Setys anecdotes of Haitian impact:

> Many of the homes have been condemned previously and now [the Haitians] are living in them. They have no water sometimes, no sanitation system,

> no heat. They've been seen publicly nude in Buck Creek, bathing. . . . Stop blaming the people, calling us racists [and] hate mongers. We're trying to survive.[107]

As we rolled through Old Reid Park near the C. J. Brown Dam and Reservoir, Setys observed to me:

> We used to have all the little white ducks. They were everywhere, just everywhere. And you'd pull up and . . . they're like, "Oh, more food is here! More bread! More treats!" And your kids would feed the ducks. They don't do that now there's no ducks. . . . [T]hey left very early in this game because they were friendly. They were easy to scoop up. I've heard [Haitians] take the geese, but they could take 10,000 of these freaking geese, and we'd still have too many. Those geese multiply like rabbits.

We saw no white Pekin ducks of any kind or color that day, nor during any subsequent visit to Old Reid or at any other park we (or I solo or with another companion) visited. Plenty of geese, a few swans, and the occasional odd-couple mallard ducks. I did, however, find posted to the Google Maps listing for Old Reid several photos of various white Pekin or other non-wood and non-mallard ducks, with these photos geo-confirmed to have been taken near the park—in 2017, 2020, a few more in 2022, and in 2023.[108,109,110,111,112,113,114] One was photographed in February 2026.[115] Only one. You might find more if you really look.

Or not. On September 11, 2024, Threads user Regina Rodgers Crum wrote, "Snyder Park normally has a ton of white ducks. And there is now only a few. Where did they go?"[116] Well, there's one, in that one Feb. '26 photo. Maybe citizen-activism is what did it? "Someone placed a sign that read 'Please do not eat the ducks' in front of the Peanut Pond at Snyder Park Friday, Sept. 13, 2024, in Springfield. Park staff removed the sign," reported the *Springfield News-Sun*.[117]

The same source who fed the slowly dwindling Springfield cat colony told me that she personally witnessed a visibly Haitian individual doing what official sources insist they have not: "I have seen them taking dead ducks and a goose in their hands. I saw what I believed to be a limp, dead, white duck in one hand, and what looked like a dead goose in the other." She added that several of her friends had witnessed scenes like this.

That matches another story media reported—on March 27, 2024, a resident "driving in Snyder Park around noon "saw three men—described as 'Haitian males'—place a live Canada goose and a live duck in a black trash bag and drive away."[118]

And then a local acquaintance of mine from a business networking group suggested I speak with his son, **Noah Mangold**, a student at Wittenberg University in Springfield. Noah was the rare under-fifty willing to have his name appear alongside his experience in print. When I pressed him to confirm he was indeed OK with what so many others I'd interviewed had not been, he simply told me he "doesn't care." I like him already. Anyhow, this is the gist:

One afternoon between approximately 4:00 and 5:00 p.m. in mid-September 2024 amid the bomb threats that shifted Wittenberg classes to online—likely September 17th—Noah was driving down the road, as one does.[119] The site of the sight "was just outside Snyder Park right near the underpass," which is indeed a real place. So that's good. There, Noah saw parked a "light bluish-tint minivan" with at minimum two men, a driver and at least one passenger; he's "100 percent" certain they were Haitian. Noah, as he drove past the scene, would tell me that he saw the aforementioned passenger exit the vehicle, grab a roadside Canadian goose "by the neck" (that third-world gaze again), and goosenap it into the van, shutting the door immediately afterwards. "Obviously the goose didn't like it," Noah said of the goose's failed attempts to struggle, whip, and flap free. He added:

> I didn't call the police. There was nothing I could do or they could do. I didn't get a license plate. I was just really shocked. I'm going to guess other people must have seen it, too. There were other cars on the road . . . I didn't know what to think of [the influx of Haitians into Springfield] until I saw that. Then I was like, "Maybe it's true that they're eating cats and dogs." I don't know.

What if the things that are definitely not happening are indeed actually happening?

A person may lie. An entire citizenry does not.

The Call

In another, wider-known incident, a local named Toby reported a group of Haitian migrants carrying four geese in Springfield, Ohio, two weeks before Trump's cats and dogs. Two male and two female Haitians, each carrying a goose, he'd seen on a bike path. He reported hearing Haitian Creole spoken when he dialed the authorities.[120]

Dispatcher: Clark County Communications?

Toby: Yes ma'am. I got a question. This is a non-emergency line, correct?
Dispatcher: Yes it is.
Toby: Okay. I'm sitting here, I'm riding on the trail, going to my orientation for my job today, and I see a group of Haitian people. There was about four of them. They all had geese in their hands. . . . They got away. I couldn't make out the first three of the license plate . . . it was a gray Toyota Tacoma they took off on. There was about four of them. There was two men, two women.
Dispatcher: How many geese did they have?
Toby: Uh, they each had one.
. . .
Toby (later): I was trying to get my phone out and I was trying to make it to this orientation on time . . . Yeah this has got to be reported.[121]

What came of this incident?

> . . . Clark County Commissioner Sasha Rittenhouse said that, "No videos have surfaced, no pictures have surfaced, no dead geese have surfaced; there's nothing to substantiate that it's happening."
>
> Rittenhouse said she rode with an [Ohio Department of Natural Resources] staffer last Thursday to look into some claims about Haitian immigrants stealing and eating geese and ducks, and learned that nothing came out of the call, with there being no evidence.
>
> At the same meeting, Clark County Sheriff's Office Major Scott Cultice said that "he and another employee at the Clark County Combined Dispatch Center went through 11 months of call records Tuesday to check for reports on these matters, and the Aug. 26 call was the only one he was able to verify that had been made."[122]

What did Mark Sanders learn? The better time to "look into" things is before they happen—not after.

Lisa Montgomery of Mid Ohio Waterfowl Rescue, a registered nonprofit, gave an interview to *The Daily Mail* sharing her relevant Springfield experience:[123,124]

> . . . Lisa said the sheer number of birds disappearing of late has far exceeded past summers in the region.
>
> She's been rescuing ducks and geese throughout Ohio for nearly 10 years, having owned and operated Mid Ohio Waterfowl Rescue since 2015.

> 'I have over the years had many people reach out from the Springfield area. Recently with concerns of ducks and geese being murdered for food,' she said.
>
> 'I do have serious concerns over the issue and believe it to be true.'
>
> . . . 'Predation is also a real thing but not at the rate birds have disappeared,' she said.
>
> 'Predation tends to happen more in the winter months. When the ponds freeze and the birds don't have protection.'[125]

The Mid Ohio Waterfowl Rescue Facebook page played host to a debate of its own on September 10, 2024. The page—presumably Lisa—posted, "I deleted the post about the ducks in Springfield. I only posted because I got calls from numerous concerned people. I have been to Springfield and have rescued and taken in many dumped ducks at the parks down there. It is a constant and ongoing issue. I know numerous ducks and geese have disappeared. Whether it's from predators or people eating them I'm not going to argue that."[126]

One reply read, "Maybe people have seen you taking ducks and are blaming it on immigrants. Do you coordinate with local resource management when taking ducks?"

The page said back, "yes I do inform park management and even sometimes law enforcement. Dumping domestic ducks is a huge [problem] across the globe no doubt. But the problem isn't just the domestic ducks. There's a significant loss of Canada geese. Poaching is illegal and it is done worldwide. Most times people don't get caught. In this case so many have 'disappeared'. There were no goose 'roundups' or egg addling as was confirmed by ODNR."[127]

The page's admin got into self-defense a bit, writing to one particularly negative commenter, "there was nothing wrong with what I posted. I was looking for help rescuing 4 domestic ducks in one of the parks in Springfield. I had someone making it something it wasn't. I really should have kept my post and deleted the negative comments. I just don't want my feed turning into a bashing fest."[128]

Another commenter perfectly demonstrates the sentiment I've heard expressed by proud pro-Haitians of Springfield upon inquiring of any stories they may have or be willing to share about their experiences with the migrant population.

"They sell duck at the freaking grocery store. guys go out and spray bullets into flocks of ducks and geese by thousands every duck season," the morally authoritative user said to Mid Ohio Waterfowl Rescue. "Attacking an entire community for eating duck is pretty hypocritical as a society. I have never eaten duck or will I but come on!"[129]

You're racist for saying it's happening. If it is, it's a good thing, actually, which still makes you a racist because you thought it was bad.

Filmmaker Dinesh D'Souza called out this same spirit of irony on Haitian immigration status:

> If you say Haiti is a hellhole, the Left says:
>
> "How dare you say that? Haiti is a beautiful country!"
>
> If you say Haitian illegals need to go back home, the Left says:
>
> "How dare you say that? We would be sending them back to a life of misery, hardship and death!"[130]

No matter the game, it's two ways to lose, no ways to win.

Do you understand the double bind every white Springfielder has been tied into? To retain their reputation among polite, progressive circles, they must lie, from their perspective, and deny what they've seen or at the very least deploy the white lie of silence. No wonder so many Americans I spoke with pleaded for anonymity first.

Speaking of anonymous, the Springfield resident who told me about her shrinking cat colony and that one bird theft incident had added that she expected those Haitians would eat the birds she reported having seen them seized from the park.

"How do you know they were going to eat them?" I asked.

"Well, I don't," she said. "What else are they going to do? Some kind of sacrificial ritual?" She laughed.

"At the end of the day, unless you're vegan . . . you are literally a thousand percent a hypocrite."[131]

* * *

Guess what, Yvana Romelus?

I was vegan for ten years.

Joke's on you; duck's on me.

I just won't be getting it from Old Reid Park.

CHAPTER 10

THE HAITIAN EMBASSY

"I think food, culture, people, and landscape are all absolutely inseparable."[1]
—Anthony Bourdain

I took out my phone, snapped a pic, and tweeted the scene. *Traditional Springfield, Ohio Plantains* reads my caption.[2] Spread before me on a cloudy Saturday afternoon at Rose Goute Creole Restaurant on South Limestone Street, on a gray cafeteria tray with plastic utensils were, indeed, plantains, but also sliced tomatoes and a delicious spiced coleslawish experience. I asked for sparkling water and was served a plastic bottle of still.

This didn't look like the same fine-linened dining display that I remembered from a viral John Legend visit.[3] When I'd entered Rose's about twenty minutes prior, I felt as though I'd left Springfield, Ohio. I was now in Haitian territory. Or perhaps something closer to . . . an embassy. The place looked about like any working-class strip-malled ethnic cuisinery. I heard no English, only Creole, including patrons' boisterous and physically animated conversations about as loud as the music. Three such exchanges took place via volume-maxed speakerphone—authentic ambience. A refrigeration setup to my right gave the space a mini-marketlike quality, and oh, look, an ATM. There's a line to use it. Bitcoin?

At most, there were twenty-six patrons. I was the only white male for the entirety of my hourlong duration. A potentially pregnant young white woman joined the takeout line at one point, together with two Hispanic manual laborers, based on their grass-stained company T-shirts.

Upon first entry, I felt lost and got a lot of doubletakes. I saw no sign indicating self-seating or otherwise. After about a minute of standing there like an uncultured lowbrow, I waved at the woman behind the counter, whose striking appearance I cannot describe to you accurately without naked appeal to outdated racist stereotypes.

"Can I have a table for one, please?" I asked her.

The individual grunted at me.

"Can I have a table for one, please?" I said again.

She pointed towards a table with a little sign, *6*.

"No," she called out as I approached. "Thirteen."

That was the adjacent table. OK, sure. I began to sit when—

"No, six."

. . . OK. And we're back.

I seat myself, take in the Haitianity for a few prolonged moments, reading all the various advertisements, events, and other such displays postered about the wall before me. Most are long past, some as many as four months ago. Help with taxes, help with immigration, help with religion, help with help. I recognized one poster, an anti-ICE, pro-Haitian protest that had been held in neighboring Dayton. It looked to be the only poster in English.

A server appeared. He introduced himself; I heard either *Winston* or possibly *Winton*, like Bluey's little friend in the *Bluey* cartoons my children adore. I'd had a read of the menu by that point and didn't recognize several near-meat entrées like those featuring goat and "beef feet." *Don't be a bigot; eat the feet*, I laughed to myself. No, actually, I don't think I will. The eggs with plantain option looks agreeable. Since Setys Kelly had told me she'd seen Haitians buying plantains by the box at a local Kroger, I'd begun baking chips with my own Kroger's plantains at home for my girls, lightly sweetened with monkfruit and dusted with cinnamon. They like them a lot.

I reskimmed the menu before finalizing. Now I'm the one doubletaking. The item description looks off-center and contains a giant space.[4] I read it to say, *Eggs, onion, red or green peppers, tomato dog or smoked herring and*

The look on my face—I was Jim from *The Office*.

Oh, my mistake! There's a mistake—way back in front of "dog" on the menu is the justified-left word "hot." I just hadn't seen it. Silly bigot . . . dogs are for petting.

"I know my people—dogs, cats—we don't do that in Haiti," a Rose Goute employee named Pierre had told *Springfield News-Sun*.[5]

"I said, 'What? What is that?'" said the restaurant's manager to CNN of the cat and dog claim.[6]

Be that as it may not be, I was unsure what was supposed to appear after the word "and." The menu entry simply ended.

"Yes, can I do the eggs with plantain?" I called up to Win(s)ton.

"Eh, plantain?" he said.

"Yes, eggs with plantain."

"Only plantain. Only plantain."

"Yeah. . . . Sure. . . . " I attempted. "With the eggs, right?"

I failed to comprehend his reply, but I made out several times something like "is done, is done," and then "egg is done."

"OK . . . OK . . . OK . . . " I said, three times. The man probably thought me an idiot. "That would be still fine then. I'd like to try the plantain."

"Eh . . . plantain . . . only?" asked Win(s)ton (I think; it could have been a command and not a question).

"Sure." I waited for a moment, spying the menu's appetizers and sides. "Do you have any other kinds of tropical fruit that you prepare here?"

"What?"

"Do you have any other kinds of tropical fruit that you prepare here?"

He stared at me and said nothing. I repeated the question. I made sure to uptalk the second iteration so as to make it sound like an actual question. Now who's the one having trouble with English.

"Eh . . . don't . . . understand."

"Fruit?" I asked.

" . . . yeah . . . "

"Mango?"

Despite few words exchanged in those moments, there was an inordinate amount of mutual staring taking place. Full eye contact. Involved. Finally, I was directed to the soft drinks portion of the menu.

"I got, eh, Pepsi?" Win(s)ton said.

I suggested what looked to be a traditional Haitian beverage. We couldn't seem to agree on what I was referring to. I would later request a soda water.

"Plantain." He logged my order. "You don't eat meat." I was at least two-thirds' certain that was not a question but a command. "Salad?"

"Yes, please."

"Anything else?"

"No, I don't think so."

As with other instances that appear throughout this book, I wrote this all in real time—this scene, in my head, this time as opposed to Google Docs in others. I wanted to take this place in. Haitian flags everywhere. Families, couples, singles. I'd read previously of gleeful white liberals from around Ohio, from my region especially, patronizing this establishment, pairing large tips with long five-star reviews of the place. The sharp-featured women in those videos had various facial piercings and visible tattoos. Their male dining partners, deeply effeminate and wrist-flippingly animated in contrast.

I also remembered a Haitian interview I'd read about that took place here.

Jérôme Sessini, a photographer with *Magnum*, had traveled to Springfield in October 2024. He "wanted to see for myself what mood the Haitian community was."[7] I pulled it back up for a re-read. Sessini had interviewed and photographed a twenty-two-year-old Haitian man named Walder:

> ["]I've been here for about five months. I was in Mexico, there's work there, but the pay is too low. Here, aside from work, there's not much else to do. . . . Everyone's doing overtime, even on weekends," added Walder, who now lives in Springfield with his uncle and aunt.[8]

A subsequent photograph of a yard with Democratic candidates' campaign signs like *Harriz-Walz* and *Sherrod Brown* presents the caption, "A neighborhood with an important Haitian community. Limestone South, Springfield . . . "

I wonder how Haitians vote.

> Jonas, 35, works at Amazon in Columbus. "There's not much work in Springfield itself. The big companies hiring are in Columbus or Dayton," he said. He added that he was insulted several times after Trump's comments in September, but he shrugged it off. "Even if Trump wins, he can't send us back to Haiti . . . "[9]

I no longer wonder.

Shortly thereafter, the *Magnum* piece, also published in *The Nation*, takes a turn:[10]

> Three middle-aged men, African-Americans, pulled up next to me in a gray 4×4 with the window down."Why the fuck are you taking pictures? You look weird, man. Got any ID?" they said. After a cordial conversation, the men apologized and left as quickly as they'd arrived. "I don't understand why Americans are so rude and ill-mannered," said Jonas, who witnessed the scene.
>
> As we were leaving the Creole restaurant "La Rose Gouté," a bald man who identified himself as a journalist from Detroit approached Walder and me, without saying hello . . . "He wants me to say that Springfield is better than Haiti, but no. I'm here because I had no choice. I had to flee Haiti. My mother was kidnapped by gangs, and we had to pay. My father's in Chile. Frankly, I'm fed up here. The companies aren't hiring much, and you have to speak English. I'm going to try my luck in North Carolina."[11]

First Diversity Staffing has offices in North Carolina.[12]

That's three Springfields on one screen.

I finished lunch, paid in cash with a nice tip, and headed to the Hispanic market next door for raw sugarcane.

Unlocked

A few days later, I learned from Glenda Bailey the full story behind Rose's. From her account @MajorityHaitian:

> Springfield, Ohio—Haitian woman owner of the Haitian Creole restaurant (Rose Goute Creole) at S. Limestone & John St. who DOESN'T SPEAK ENGLISH (she claims) FAILED TO FILE HER SALES TAX REPORTS & is labeled as a HABITUAL OFFENDER. Her VENDORS LICENSE has been SUSPENDED.[13]

What's this now? Click the photos attached to the post. It's an Arrest Report from the Ohio Department of Taxation Criminal Investigation Division. The named individual is one Rosena JN Louis of Rose Goute Creole Restaurant LLC, August 22, 2025. The charge is "Failure to File Sales Tax Returns."[14] There are a number of notable items of business in the Report's Statement of Fact:

> On 8/1/2025, Agent B. Sizemore was assigned this Step-3 vendor's license suspension posting and final determination letter delivery. On 8/20/2025, Agents B. Sizemore and J. Layton went to Rose Goute Creole Restaurant LLC located at 1881 S. Limestone St. Springfield, Ohio 45505 to make contact with the owner of the business regarding the sales tax delinquencies and vendor's license suspension. Upon arrival, Agents entered the business and made contact with a Hispanic female subject who identified herself as Rosena JN Louis, owner of the business. Agents identified themselves as Police Officers with the Ohio Department of Taxation and stated Rosena the vendor's license for her business has been placed under suspension due to the failure to file a State of Ohio sales tax return and remit all sales tax liability collected on or before the due date, specifically for the monthly period of 05/2025. Rosena advised Agents that she did not understand or speak English. Rosena called a male subject and put him on speaker phone. Agent B. Sizemore identified himself again and asked who he was speaking with. The male subject identified himself as Marc and advised he was the Manager of the business

> and Rosena's Nephew. Agent B. Sizemore advised Marc of the vendor's license suspension and monthly sales tax period that needed to be satisfied to lift the suspension. Marc advised he will call his accountant and get the period filed and paid as soon as he can. Agent B. Sizemore provided Marc with the contact number for the Compliance Division's HOP Group and advised him to call them as soon as they satisfy the sales tax delinquency so they can verify the business is back in compliance and lift the vendor's license suspension. Marc advised he will contact them as soon as the return has been filed and paid. Agent B. Sizemore served Rosena with the final determination letter and Marc translated all the information regarding the suspension. Agent B. Sizemore advised Marc they are no longer able to make any taxable sales while the suspension is active and they would be posting a vendor's license suspension sign on the front door of the business.[15]

What's this about "a Hispanic female subject"? Rosena JN Louis is Haitian.[16] Not Hispanic. Not Latina. Haitian.

Wait a minute.

"'It is my understanding that the FBI tracks the following categories: Hispanic, Non-Hispanic and Unknown' . . . FBI spokesperson Nicole Porter Steward confirmed that the Springfield officials' claims were not true."[17]

That unlocks a lot for me.

CNN reports having interviewed Rosena. Her answers are in English. There is no mention of an interpreter or translator.[18]

I found no evidence that Rose Goute Creole Restaurant ever closed down during the vendor license suspension period. In fact, members of the Facebook group Stop the Influx Into Springfield, Ohio, published photos during this period showing Haitian customers going in and out.

That unlocks the rest.

But we're not done yet.

The issue escalated.

"Cases called Monday, Dec. 1, [2025] included . . . Rosena J. Louis, 55, . . . failure to file sales tax return, bench warrant ordered."[19]

That's four months to the day that she was notified. Perhaps Rose Goute Creole Restaurant LLC did not, in fact, make contact with the Ohio Department of Taxation "as soon as the return has been filed and paid"?

I asked Google's AI search to tell us what the bullet above means.

> A bench warrant ordered for failure to file sales tax returns means a judge has authorized law enforcement to arrest you for missing a mandatory court hearing regarding unpaid taxes. This commonly arises from willful non-compliance, such as ignoring notices from state taxing authorities (e.g., Ohio's Habitual Offenders Program), and is treated as a criminal contempt of court matter.

Oh.

On January 22, 2026, Rosena was arrested and booked on the warrant. It doesn't appear that her mugshot was published.[20] What happened next?

"Cases called Friday, Jan. 23 [2026] included . . . Rosena J. Louis, 56 . . . failure to file sales tax return, innocent, continued, release written."[21]

What did you just read? Attorney Google translates (Disclaimer: Google is not an attorney, and this is not legal advice.):

> Based on the phrases provided, this court notice indicates a tax case involving failure to file sales tax returns has been delayed ("continued") and the defendant was released from custody under specific conditions.
>
> Here is a breakdown of what this means . . .
>
> Innocent: In this context, it often means the defendant has entered a "not guilty" plea (pleading innocence) at their arraignment, rather than a final verdict of innocence.
>
> Continued: This means the court date was rescheduled. The case was not resolved at this hearing and will be heard again at a later date.
>
> Release Written: This typically means the person was released from custody (if they were detained) upon signing a "written" promise to appear at their next court date (often called a personal recognizance bond or written undertaking).

Then what happened?

"Cases called Monday, March 16 [2026] included . . . Rosena J. Louis, 56 . . . failure to file sales tax ret., guilty, fined $100."[22]

Glenda was furious.

> Springfield, Ohio—JUDGE DANIEL CAREY FINED ROSENA LOUIS $100 W/NO JAIL TIME FOR NONPAYMENT OF SALES TAX

> FINED the MINIMUM ($100) when he could have given her $1,000 & up to 60 days in jail. Clark County's ENTIRE COURT SYSTEM is bought & paid for by HAITIAN CORRUPTION.[23]

I don't know about those all-caps latter bits, but a reading of the rest looks correct. The defendant was required to pay the fine within thirty days. I wonder if Rosena ever did. And about any potentially unpaid back taxes that started it all . . .

I did scan *Springfield News-Sun*'s Clark County Municipal Court pages for other similar sales tax return filing failures over the last ten years. I found three, all of whom appeared to be heritage citizens of Clark County. Remember the overcrowded Clark County jail mess?[24] These citizens' fates all seemed to closely match if not mirror that of Rosena of Rose Goute Creole Restaurant LLC.[25,26,27]

Nevertheless.

I probably won't go back.

CHAPTER 11

[redacted] HAITIANS

> "The purpose of our immigration system is to benefit the American people. That's the only reason it exists. If immigration from any region of the globe is economically destructive —or harmful in any way—it should be completely eliminated."[1]
>
> —U.S. Rep. Brandon Gill (R-Texas)

Have you ever heard of "Tunnel Jews"? It's not some dark-web antisemitic trope; it's an actual news story from New York City that launched one of the most viral memes of 2024 alongside Donald Trump's cats and dogs.

> A historic Brooklyn synagogue that serves as the center of an influential Hasidic Jewish movement was trashed this week during an unusual community dispute that began with the discovery of a secret underground tunnel and ended with worshippers brawling with police.[2]

A secret tunnel of unknown purpose had been constructed underground. Regardless, the public hazard had to go. That's when the cameras turned on.

> The situation came to a head Monday, when a cement truck arrived to seal the opening. Proponents of the tunnel then staged a protest and ripped off the wooden siding of the synagogue.
>
> A police department spokesperson said officers were called to the building in the afternoon to respond to a disorderly group that was trespassing and damaging a wall.
>
> For several hours, police pleaded with the young men to leave the entrance to the tunnel, according to witnesses.
>
> . . . Nine people—between the ages of 19 and 22—were ultimately arrested on charges that included criminal mischief, reckless endangerment,

> and obstructing governmental administration, according to police. Another three received summonses for disorderly conduct.[3]

A noticeably Italian-American New York City police officer was recorded delivering this absolute gem to one of the pro-tunnel Jewish protestors: "We don't do that in America."[4]

Risk

Some of the most compelling demonstrations of impact of the Haitian influx on Springfield, Ohio, I was unable to include full details of in this book. All excuses came down to these ultimate two—credible threats to the personal safety of those involved, or ongoing law enforcement proceedings. Or, wildly, both. Follow the money, and the money follows you, and that's not a good thing.

I'm admittedly breaking the fourth wall of authorship at present; I'm talking about this book rather than letting you continue reading it without commentative interruption. I thought you should know.

In the interviews and in the research and in the writing and in the editing, I interacted with a number of heritage citizens but also Haitian immigrants who shared their stories—and their evidence—under the condition of complete and total anonymity. A few warned me of life-threatening outcomes should their stories appear in print. These are those I judged best redacted if not rejected before publication entirely. The risk, by my own measure, remains too great, especially once the proper authorities are notified—and to the best of my knowledge, they absolutely have been.

A lot of people are going to be unhappy about this book. There could be even more, however, with the means, motive, and opportunity to do something about it—and not, even, to me.

Retaliation's a bitch. Let's not invite her.

Of my original intended dozen or so entries for this worst-of-the-worst chapter, life-saving risk management has negotiated me down to four. Only four. But by my own admission, I'm not sure all of you reading this could handle more. Maybe if you come to Springfield and look around, you'll find the remaining eight for yourself.

With topical terseness, here are four details-redacted findings from my adventures through Springfield after dark. The four subjects read, in rapid succession, like some kind of alt-rock garage band.

Cars

A recurring allegation I heard around Springfield regarding Haitian migrants is as follows—underticketing, underciting, underarresting, and undercharging all manner of traffic violations and otherwise law-breakage out on the roads. Most common, I heard, was the trifecta—causing a wreck, attempting to flee the scene, and providing no driver's license or proof of insurance. Yet within days, these very drivers would be back out on the roads. The 𝕏 account @MajorityHaitian and the Stop the Influx group on Facebook have catalogued more publicly available reports than I could cite.

What I was not able to discern, however, was a per capita rate. That is, are the Haitians of Springfield at fault for more wrecks than heritage citizens per capita? Are Haitians failing to provide proper identification more often, also per capita? I asked these very questions of the heritage citizenry I interviewed, and you know the number one most-common answer I heard?

"It doesn't matter."

Why doesn't it matter?

Because, as all anecdotes I gathered alleged, City of Springfield police seem to be holding Haitians to a significantly lower standard than heritage citizens. Everyone I interviewed said this. Everyone means *literally. every. single. heritage. citizen. I. interviewed.* This is universally believed, as far as I could manage, among Springfield residents unhappy with overall Haitian presence. That sentiment and the two-tiered justice-system they believe to exist have a directly causal relationship, I gathered. In short, it goes, *Why do Haitians get X when we have to Y?* Take that formula, make it cover every single issue, and that's the heritage citizenry of Springfield.

But is there any truth to the catch-and-release policy regarding Haitian driving infractions? There's a reason former Sheriff Deb Burchett told me she demanded her deputies always ticket and cite migrants and residents equally, and that reason came from [redacted] who relayed to me with supporting evidence that satisfied my personal skepticism that [redacted] of the [redacted] had been directed *not* to "ticket or tow unlicensed drivers." This was a "command decision" from [redacted] then named the names of those responsible for that call: [redacted] and [redacted]

I was not surprised.

Also on this matter—a Springfield hotel employee named [redacted] reported to me that Springfield police came to her front desk and explicitly and specifically said "not to share guest info with ICE if they came here," she relayed to me. This woman added additional material facts on this matter that bore out her story to my satisfaction together with "proof of the coordination" between the Haitian community and Springfield police.

Separately but in parallel to this point, "Springfield Police Division Captain Jeff Williams said as of earlier this year that the agency filters out any immigration-related searches . . . 'Our position on immigration is that we are here to make sure that everyone in this city is safe, regardless if they're a legal immigrant, an illegal immigrant, someone who's been here for decades, someone who just moved here; we don't care. We want everybody to be safe.'"[5]

Illegal immigrant. Don't care.

I am surprised by nothing at this point.

Guns

Have you ever heard of [redacted] It's a [redacted] with a Springfield location at [redacted]

Have you also heard of whistleblowers? Certainly you have. Springfield has them in no short supply. Some, I assume, are authentic. This one, I believe to be the case.

And have you heard about Haiti's firearm trafficking problem? Haiti "has seen a staggering influx of illicit U.S.-origin weapons—primarily funneled through South Florida." Approximately "90% of illegal Caribbean-bound firearms shipments originated in Florida, including through the Miami River and Port Everglades."[6] Where did they originate?

A distinct possibility, I suspect, is Springfield. A self-proclaimed former employee of [redacted] claimed, on video, to have engaged in what's called a "straw sale." For the unfamiliar:

> Processing the sale of a gun by [a Federal Firearms License] means they have a customer fill out the 4473 form and provide a government issued ID. They then call the FBI NICS line and have them perform a Background Check. The FBI will then reply "Proceed", "Don't Proceed", or "Wait". Once the FBI clears the buyer there is little an FFL can do to refuse the sale without risking being sued unless it is a suspected "Straw Purchase". A straw purchase is a criminal act in where a firearm is bought by one person on behalf of another who is unable to make the purchase legally themselves, FFLs are well within their right to refuse to do business with that person or group of persons if they suspect this is the hidden agenda.[7]

How stupid could you possibly be? Unless you're telling the truth . . .

The woman, whose first name is Libby, is credibly confirmed to have been employed at [redacted] She recounted her experience, if you can believe it, on video (!).[8] Libby said she was explicitly instructed by [redacted] management to process these sales the same as any other customer and was not allowed to place them on the store's "do-not-sell list" (which she had done initially). She noted that U.S. citizens were sometimes denied for unrelated address issues tied to prior residents, creating a perceived double standard. She estimated that she personally processed around forty such sales. One specific incident involved a Haitian customer with an Ohio state ID that did not list his current address; he initially claimed it wasn't current, then said he was "just kidding" and it actually was—Libby refused the sale, the situation escalated physically, and [redacted] management overrode her. She also mentioned warning other local gun stores about the pattern because it was not just her store this happened at.[9] A follow-up video from the Christian minister who initially interviewed Libby on video reported that the matter had reached the Bureau of Alcohol, Tobacco, and Firearms—and Libby had retained legal counsel.[10]

I include this anecdote for two reasons. First, while no indictments, lawsuits, or store-level actions tied directly to Libby's allegations have surfaced publicly, her claims have not been publicly debunked, and they do align with contemporaneous local reports of suspicious purchasing patterns amid Springfield's demographic shifts. The second reason is it's not the only firearm whistle heard blown in town.

Up Ohio's Route 68 from Springfield, Ohio, is the [redacted] of [redacted] where [redacted] confirmed to me that the Bureau of Alcohol, Tobacco, and Firearms and the Department of Homeland Security had sent agents to investigate the private, legal sale of a citizen's firearm at [redacted] because, I was told, "it showed up on a boat going to Haiti out of Miami, Florida. They tracked the serial number, and it was one . . . registered in his name through the dealer."

At the July 21, 2026 Concerned Citizens of Clark County Town Hall, emceed by investigative reporter Jack Windsor, the first residents to introduce themselves to me before I spoke were a mother and daughter who were rattled by a Haitian man at a stop sign. They told me a Haitian in an SUV ran a stop sign and nearly hit them. The daughter honked her horn, and the Haitian flashed a firearm at her and appeared to be visibly laughing at their understandably panicked reaction. The daughter currently works at the county courthouse and told me that, in her opinion, the Haitians are receiving lighter sentences than heritage residents. And likewise understandably, neither wanted their identity included in this book.

I was told similar stories about gun sales, gun trafficking, and gun antics—but not about the same individuals—by [redacted] [redacted] [redacted] [redacted], and [redacted] [redacted] Where there's smoke, there's (probably) firearms.

Sex

Another video shared with me remains publicly available as of this writing. From @MajorityHaitian:

> . . . Listen to this grandmother talking about Springfield High School & why she transferred her granddaughter to a different school. Adult Haitian men are in class with teenage girls.[11]

The last line of this claim may bother you—until you learn it's 100 percent legal. Then it will horrify you. Ohio Revised Code § 3313.64:

> All persons at least eighteen but under twenty-two years of age who live apart from their parents, support themselves by their own labor, and have not successfully completed the high school curriculum or the individualized education program developed for the person by the high school pursuant to section 3323.08 of the Revised Code, are entitled to attend school in the district in which they reside.[12]

Therefore, students with education gaps—as you might expect for recent Haitian arrivals—could indeed end up several grade levels behind and thus be classmates with minors as young as fourteen or fifteen.

What did this grandmother have to say about that? From the video:

> My granddaughter came home, and she told me that they were having sex on the steps, behind the steps, in the bathrooms, and in the hallways, and they did not do anything to them at all because they have that protection. And she said that it was just downright gross. And then the boys would come up and ask her if they would have sex with her and have babies with her . . . I took her out.[13]

Glenda Bailey put me in touch with the grandmother and granddaughter, [redacted] and [redacted], who were both willing to speak with me. The granddaughter was eighteen years old by the time we spoke and had almost completed her [redacted] year at [redacted]. The granddaughter, [redacted], who asked to remain anonymous, told me that overall, her feelings for her Haitian classmates and the overall Haitian migrant population in Springfield are "neutral." What her grandmother relayed to Glenda had indeed happened as described, but [redacted] added the very significant detail of at least one such Haitian tryst was recorded on a cellphone and passed around [redacted] for approximately two weeks during the [redacted]-[redacted] school year. She did not know if the students recorded engaging in sexual activity on school property were minors or adults, but she told me she was positive they were Haitian.

[redacted] herself had a number of Haitian classmates at [redacted] during certain periods of the day. [redacted] told me that the juvenile Haitian males were aggressive in coming on to white female classmates specifically, occupying close personal space, attempting to touch suggestively and inappropriately, and so forth. White, Hispanic, and other male classmates, she told me, had never acted this way. [redacted] explained it away as a cultural difference.

"We don't do that in America," I joked. [redacted] laughed.

That said, she'd had a number of very positive experiences out and about in the surrounding community and eventually became friendly acquaintances with the Haitian families who live [redacted].

[redacted]'s discomfort with young and—let's be honest, probably horny—Haitian males aligns with other young white women's experiences I gathered throughout Springfield. You'll read shortly about a community leader who reported more than a dozen such incidents occurring in his presence.

I also spoke with the daughter of [redacted], who volunteered to me that on three separate occasions after finishing up her workout at [redacted], then shopping at [redacted] or another grocery on [redacted], while still in her well-exercised athleisure attire, she had literally been chased—not simply followed but *chased*, although following had happened also—by young Haitian men in and outside of the store. While whistling for her attention, and for her to stop playing so hard to get, these young men, [redacted] told me, indicated in a rush how they wanted to "have babies with her." (This was not a surprise; independent journalists, reporters, and investigators have spoken with Springfield residents who claim to have witnessed the same if not experienced it. One startling interview you may see is a local mother who told filmmaker Nick Johnson three Haitians in a gray van attempted to "lure" her into their van while she was at the bus stop with her ten-year-old daughter. They drove away, she said, when her neighbor with an "aggressive" dog appeared. But seconds later, they appeared to attempt to likewise "lure a little boy who was standing by himself at the bus stop."[14] All this, the mother reported, happened in . . . 2020! She attended the July 21, 2026 town hall and shared this story again with additional detail. The week before this book went to print, I received a phone call, images, and videos of a Haitian attempting to abduct a local father's teenage daughter. The individual was arrested, later released, whereabouts unknown. Dad was livid.)

By the way, I spoke to several repeat-eyewitnesses of what they believed to be prostitution at [redacted] and at the [redacted]. They were repeat-eyewitnesses because they are literally the neighbors. I was able to confirm their identities via [redacted]. They told me they'd see after about 10:00 p.m. local time who they believed to be (different) Haitian men with (the same) scantily-clad Haitian women entering the [redacted] and the [redacted] next to [redacted]. They claimed to consistently see these women "streetwalking," working the corner, at these two locations both during the week and on weekends, speaking in a language with their presumed clientele these neighbors did not understand.

Had they not called the police? They had. Had the police done nothing? They had not, I was told.

Look. Somebody's lying, somebody's getting laid, and I'm pretty sure about both.

Fraud

When the authorities have the evidence and do nothing, it's the victims and their witnesses who become the subjects of investigation—by the guilty. You've heard the saying that "the inmates run the asylum." In Springfield, the inmates leave; the guards are stuck locked up behind.

A founding member of Springfield's OSINT gave me a cache of documentation so thick, physically and virtually, I was unable to include even a slim share of it in this book. A letter that does make this final cut is not a letter at all. It's a screenshot of a Facebook message from a Haitian-American woman, which surprised me; you'll soon see why. The individual showed me the original message, and I confirmed her identity as authentic. The message reads:

> [redacted], I personally spoke with [redacted] regarding [redacted] a year ago. When I spoke to him, he stated that he [redacted]. I'd say [it's] safe to say most of the Haitian community [redacted]. They are [redacted].
>
> I wish to remain anonymous. I do know that [redacted] partnered with a Haitian man who goes by the name of [redacted]. (Not sure of the spelling) [redacted] was bringing Haitians to Springfield from Florida for $5000 per person and [redacted] and [redacted]. [redacted] owns several properties in Springfield. [redacted] also was providing them with very realistic fake documents. They send him a picture, and he makes ID'S social security cards and birth certificates. He charged around $400 for the documents and will provide them to whoever pays in [less] than a week. [redacted] would pay for the documents for new people and [redacted] by [redacted].
>
> [redacted] has been tipped off that he is being investigated, so he has since fled Springfield.

Why in the world would [redacted] have allegedly told this individual all of this about a highly legal operation? Because [redacted], obviously. It all makes sense now.

But this was not the only alleged fraud operation running through Springfield on behalf of unscrupulous and desperate members of the Haitian population—allegedly.

Social Security Cardstock

At [redacted], I was introduced by [redacted] to a [redacted] named, simply, [redacted].

[redacted] brought with her documents that [redacted] had also been sent to the offices of the Clark County Sheriff, Ohio Attorney General Dave Yost, U.S. Representative Jim Jordan, and U.S. Senator Bernie Moreno together with the various obvious other state and local law enforcement agencies, including the FBI, I was told. As of this writing, [redacted] told me three months had passed, and nothing had been done; no one had requested the original copies or the accompanying full cache of "irrefutable evidence."

Evidence for what?

A worker, who requested anonymity, had been redoing the flooring at an apartment rented by [redacted], who [redacted]. I was shown an authentic rent payment receipt the worker found confirming that [redacted] had been renting the apartment where the man found what he found. [redacted]'s [redacted], [redacted], owns the apartment building, by the way. Color me shocked. I was not. And for the elimination of all further doubt, evidence of mail was presented to me, repeatedly confirming to me that [redacted] had indeed rented the apartment in question.

What was found? Seventeen ready-made Social Security cards color-printed front and back on 8.5-by-11-inch card stock. In a stack with these were found notes that included instructions on how to center the printer to mass-produce these. Each of the seventeen was waiting to be cut out; each was perfectly lined up, front to back, so that if you had removed the card-printed section from the card stock, a given person would probably assume these to be authentic.

They were not.

In fact, these seventeen looked to me and to [redacted] and [redacted] contact [redacted], who showed me the trove, like mistakes. Or possibly uninspected cards printed only for process practice purposes. Why did I assume mistakes at first reading?

On the back of these uncut Social Security cards, as on every (real) Social Security card, there's an alphanumeric number, which is supposed to be a unique identifier that matches the number on the front. But each one of these seventeen had an identical alphanumeric number on the back. It was the same number. All seventeen cards. Not unique. It began with "[redacted]."

"We wanted to get this to DHS so that if they investigate, they would find that these are invalid. Obviously these seventeen were not distributed, but others that may have been distributed, and probably were, would most likely have the same identical alphanumeric number," [redacted] said to me. "These seventeen were not distributed. But the alphanumeric number likely remained the same on the ones that were distributed, and that is our point."

Three of them in particular stood out to me because they had the same actual Social Security number but with different names. Now, as for additional mistakes, some Social Security numbers looked obviously invalid. The standard Social Security number format is three digits, space, two digits, space, four digits. But a few of these Haitian card-stockers had the wrong number of digits in the wrong place, or the space in the wrong place, or both such formatting errors.

But why? Work-eligible Haitian migrants are already able to get authentic Social Security cards in most cases, are they not?

Or are they? Earlier, I telegraphed to you the motivation potential for something like this. From [redacted], who [redacted] the worker who happened upon the entirety of this cache at [redacted]'s apartment:

> The important thing to know is that these are all just kind of thrown together like this. This is not a professional job like one from the Social Security Administration. The ones that the Haitians were eligible to get from Social Security have clearly marked in black across the top, "For employment verification purposes only." So if you are a Haitian and Tom Homan comes to town and you have ID, the last thing you want to give him is a Social Security card that identifies you as a TPS holder. The TPS people get this asterisk-based card. From what I heard, the TPS program gives them a Social Security card, but the Social Security card has "employment only" written in black across the top. These do not. I liken this to *Star Wars*: '"These are not the droids you are looking for."

I'm not sure this is the fraud Ohio's legal authorities are looking for either. I didn't know immigration-laundering was a thing. And it shouldn't be.

We don't do that in America.

CHAPTER 12

CENTRAL

"Spirit lead me where my trust is without borders."[1]

—Hillsong UNITED, "Oceans (Where Feet May Fail)"

It was Easter Sunday. I sat cross-legged in the very back of Corinth Presbyterian Church in Dayton, Ohio, upon the carpet-crusted floor with my two daughters and with the occasional visit from my older son from the sanctuary. Reading age-appropriate biblical storybooks, managing these toddlers' attempts at Easter coloring pages, the usuals one might expect of quiet time–induction children's church. That's what I was up to. It's not all I was up to.

Corinth's noticeably white, aging congregation is led by a reverendess of the same cohort, "Rev Cynthia Holder Rich," who according to the church website is "a Presbyterian pastor and educator."[2] That Sunday, beknownst to her, Pastor Cynthia, as congregants call her, volunteered to participate in this saga.

At the outset of service, Pastor Cynthia announced—in the context of noting multiple guests present—two offerings to be collected, the second "for G92 Springfield." She then shared the ninety-two instances claim about the Hebrew word *ger* which you've read of previously, adding:

> [T]hose ninety-two times . . . the people of God are encouraged to take care of the immigrant in our land. And it's a rough time right now for immigrants . . . particularly in our area . . . Springfield G92 stands with Haitian immigrants and offers them relief services in this trying and challenging time. If you're going to participate in . . . the Springfield G92 [offering], you need to note that on your check, or you can also give online . . . [3]

Corinth is Presbyterian. Carl Ruby's Central Christian Church hails from the Disciples of Christ tradition but is officially nondenominational now.[4,5] That morning, I realized I was, in fact, sampling Ruby's same Christianity also.

Later, in the pastorette's homily, she notably recast the life and ministry of Jesus as an anticolonial ethnonationalistic resistance movement:

> The Roman empire in power during the whole of Jesus' life on earth spent eighty percent—eighty percent!—of its resources on its military and was willing to use brute force and horrific and humiliating punishments to control people and . . . to deter anyone who might rise up against Roman injustice . . . including Jesus who rose up against Roman injustice.[6]

Pastor Cynthia was talking about the Roman empire. I don't think she was talking about the Roman empire.

I grew up in a faithful and devout Christian home and never knew this about our messiah's political aspirations. The only explicit mention of Rome in the teachings of Jesus I was aware of prior to this Easter Sunday was his admonition for otherwise disgruntled Jews to pay the imperial tax, to "render to Caesar the things that are Caesar's."[7] And as far as I was aware, it was the Roman provincial governor Pontius Pilate who insisted on Christ's release, being recorded as saying of Jesus, "I find no basis for a charge against him," Only the Judean locals insisted on his crucifixion despite innocence.[8,9] But I'm not a Presbyterian pastor.

She continued, waxing with the eloquence of scripted preaching on the necessity of societywide awakening to governmental injustice anywhere as a threat everywhere—with only natural disaster as sufficient cause for us to have concern. That would wake us up. That would do it. But what, exactly, might it take?

"It just might take an earthquake," Pastor Cynthia said. She continued:

> For it took an earthquake, or a series of earthquakes, to sufficiently disrupt things, to grab people's attention and to get people to wake up to a new reality. Now, "wake up" is Biblical language, but we live in a time when being "woke" is seen as politically dangerous, and "woke" ideology is viewed as taking something valuable from us. "You shouldn't be woke." But God in Christ intends to have us wake up because our belief in the power of death is so very strong that we do not question it. Our belief in violence is so robust that we see it as manly.[10]

I didn't know that either. I love gender studies!

I wondered what else I might learn from this alternative theory of Christianity. I thought I might go to its source the very next chance I got. To its central source.

Church with Haitians

I wore a light blazer and slacks from Nordstrom.com. I added a fine timepiece—a Russian-made watch commemorating the thirtieth anniversary of 1957's *Sputnik*—and my rounded Lennonlike sunglasses to match the gold of my watch to complete the look. I was ready.

I drove up to Central Christian Church the Sunday following Easter with time budgeted for an early arrival. Upon exiting my vehicle in the back of the lot, I caught a glimpse at my sheeny white button-down. Wrinkles. Everywhere. Awful. I don't know how this happened; I'd run it through the dryer a good three minutes before departure.

I buttoned my blazer so no one would notice and neither would I.

On the brief walk to the entrance, I noticed a number of immigration-activism signs about the size of campaign-seasonals. English, Spanish, Haitian Creole. I didn't recognize any of the words in Creole on the signage except for one: Springfield. Nearest the door read a particularly imperative one: *Love God. Love Others. Nothing Else Matters.*

By the time I reached the front doors, I'd already been greeted by two church-goers on their walk up as well. As I entered, I was promptly met by multiple friendly individuals, all seniors, many with noticeably large hearing aids, a few who would later speak that morning in service, delivering various announcements and such. This is many churches across America now—senior citizens, part-timers with pensions, retirees, those who've perhaps been retired into the decades now. This is Springfield.

All about the foyer, artwork meets me. A mosaic of Jesus, a print of a Caravaggio, and a bit further down, a heartfelt gift from a Uruguayan artist. There's also a bookshelf. I'll come back to the bookshelf.

Because now I hear music and singing and vigorous preaching. It's from a separate room, muffled by closed doors but not the sanctuary's. I don't understand the language. I inquire of a greeter about what's happening there. That's Haitian church, I'm told. Yeah, a lot of Haitians come here. Wow, really? Yeah. Wow, I had no idea. I'm hearing this for the first time.

"They go in there," another greeter says of the chapel, "and we go in here," with a hand motion towards the sanctuary.

Something about separate but equal worship doesn't sit.

"Can, uh . . . I go in there?" I manage. "That sounds interesting."

"You certainly may. They're cool. They're a lot of fun. We love our Haitians."

Cool.

I open the door slowly and enter Haitian church.

I am overcome.

It's a small room, smaller than it really is because it's standing room-only. I look about me and see the most well-dressed group of individuals I have ever laid eyes on in Clark County, Ohio, save for perhaps a wedding one time or two. In fact, that's how these people seem to be dressed. The all-Haitian worshippers all seem to have color-coordinated fashion as if off an Instagram page. Jewelry, hair accessories, shoes, ties and bows, even the frames of glasses—I am woefully underdressed for this church. I stand, like most, but hover in the back near the doors.

Up front, I see a number of familiar-to-me Evangelical Christian worship essentials—stringed instruments, guitar of course, a keyboard, a preacher, singer supports, impassioned words. I don't know what they mean; I can tell you how they feel. We'd call them Spirit-filled, charismatic, revivalist, perhaps, in my upbrought church.

What a beautiful, dignified people—worshiping like American Evangelical Christians. Worshipping. Like me. When I was an Evangelical Christian. I grew up in this culture. *This* culture. Right here.

There's moving music that transitions between minors and majors as the preacher oscillates from calls for change to reminders of hope and back. At least that's how it sounds. A few press tissues to cheeks. Tears of joy. Gratitude for the Lord's work in this life. Grief over sin. All of them. None of them. Who knows. They do.

I feel myself begin to sway, taken by the entrainment of it all. Moving with the music. Moving to the spirit. Orthodox and Catholic Christians have the sign of the cross. Catholics add genuflection, or bowing to one knee. Evangelicals across all denominations have their alternative and equivalent—hands raised in praise and in adoration. Swaying, waving. A breeze.

I notice a number of young children here with whom I presume to be their parents. Many look to be about my age. Millennials. Haitian millennials. I don't know that those two words have ever been placed into such close mutually descriptive proximity before.

I notice a small child in front of me trying to get mother's attention. The way the child reaches up, up, pick me up . . . that's how my own littlest girl reaches for me when she wants attention, comfort, assurance. Same look on the face, too, one of expectation and of need. And now I understand. I didn't. But now I do. The arms raised in worship—arms raised for a parent. Pick me up. God.

I'd passed from one room to another and yet I was miles away but so at home. The atmosphere had enveloped me from my first instant within. Before the doors had even fully closed back behind me. It was palpable, all of it, the unity and the wonder. I was the only white person and yet in this togetherness, I felt like no "only" anything. Suddenly, I felt possessed by an immediate and now-lasting positive sentiment for these people. For these, the Haitian people. My own voice internally monologued, like a narrator, on behalf of Carl Ruby.

I can see why you love them.

As I had arrived early for the English service, but not the Creole service, it ended before much longer, and we found ourselves about to be ushered out to the foyer. The door behind me, I turned and pushed. It won't go. Why won't it go?

I gave a little shove; it opened outward slowly, staggeredly. Only a quarter-way now. What gives? And so I gave it more heave than I expected a chapel door should need—and at that very moment, one of the Haitian women stepped forwards to reveal she had been pushing the door back against me. What? Oh. Oh! She must have exited the chapel before me. Because one of the elderly lady churchgoers, a white woman, had been standing directly in front of the chapel doors, perhaps greeting visitors, perhaps reading the bulletin, perhaps none of the above, but had been standing there. If I'd kept pushing, otherwise pressing, I would have knocked the poor lady over. Or worse. This Haitian woman, by holding me back, had protected this white woman from getting bumbled over. By me.

I apologized, thanked the Haitian, and began my mingling prior to the English-language service. Creole-language worship became Creole fellowship. At this point, the number of Haitians outnumbered significantly the number of English speakers, by my guesstimate. I stood over to the side, eyeing the place over. There's coffee over there. They have all the creamers. This truly is an evangelical Christian church service. Mom, I'm home.

White churchgoers pass through the foyer now towards the sanctuary. Maybe about half of them greet me, standing there in my blazer, black slacks, and coordinated Tommy Hilfigers. I wonder if they think I'm a greeter. I must look the part. Button stays clasped.

Then I notice. Those I presume to be heritage citizens of Springfield, joining the Haitians here, intermingling. Graphic t-shirts. Marvel and *Star Wars*. Hoodies, many stained. Unkempt facial hair. Denim jeans and tan khakis. So many Crocs. More men in sandals than women. And the women, tattoos on arms and more, with piercings galore from lobes to nose—I know that uniform. OK, there's a couple with Mr. Rogers vests. Polos next. Golf? Is this golf now? I notice not a single heritage citizen in a suit nor so much as a tie.

A man enters. He looks exactly like Bart Ehrman, the New Testament scholar and bestselling author whose critical works like *How Jesus Became God* I've followed since before my slide out of Evangelicalism. Even the glasses are a match. Same color. But, oh—no goatee. For a split-second, I'd thought . . .

This man, this bespectacled, be-demined man, came right at me. A congregant intercepted his handshake and turned to me.

"This is our pastor."

He smiled.

"Hi. I'm Carl."

Pastor Carl

"Hello, Pastor Carl," I said.

We exchanged words for a few minutes. It wasn't a few minutes, actually. Or maybe it was. Time dilates when you're flooded in split seconds with a decade of core memories that keep you the person you are today. Anyway.

We stood off to the side and spoke about the church, his experience in Springfield, the denomination. Nondenominational, actually. Now Central is a more "progressive" church, he said. As that word entered the space between us, my gaze shot to the bookshelf directly behind him. I noticed names my exceedingly Evangelical mother had warned me about. I was homeschooled, as you read earlier. And when you're homeschooled in the 1990s and early 2000s, you're an ultraconservative Christian who believes in the inerrant Word of God to an extent that not even Christian schools these days will teach. She was very much a woman of a nineteenth-century missionary's Christianity. As a youngster and still till now, I've felt as though my mother worshipped the Bible as much as the one she believed to be its author. And here behind Pastor Carl were all the false teachers and heretics and "Cultural Marxists" she and her homeschooling contemporaries had reached consensus in condemning. Rob Bell, Tony Campolo, Shane Claiborne. Is that Jim Wallis behind Pastor Carl's right ear? Someone mentioned Rachel Held Evans.

In fairness to my mother, these have become synonymous with the so-called "ex-vangelical" movement—pastors, educators, and the like who retain Christian cultural aesthetics but deconstruct core doctrines into a post-Protestant sect, with Jesus Christ partially repurposed into a holy Martin Luther King Jr. character, and he was absolutely brown and definitely not white. That's what my mother told me. She would always recoil at ex-vangelicals' ethnic label of Jesus as "Palestinian." She wanted so badly to be a grandmother. She missed that by only a couple of years. Fuck cancer.

I glanced open the bulletin in my hands as Pastor Carl spoke. "Dr. Carl Ruby," I read off aloud. I asked if he had a doctorate in divinity as had a previous literary collaborator of mine, Dr. Kent Ingle of Southeastern University, with whom I co-authored the bestseller *College Without Communism* (Southeastern University Press, 2025). Mom would've loved it

Pastor Carl said no; he used to be an educator. Cedarville University.

"Cedarville? Really?" I let my eyebrows jump a bit too much. "They're not very progressive. They're Baptist, right?"

"Very" Baptist, he made sure to add. And that, he explained, was the true reason for his departure from Cedarville. Diana Daniels, you've done it again.

Pastor Carl asked what brought me to Springfield today. I told him I was in town to pay a visit to George Rogers Clark Park. I hear that's near here? Isn't it a pretty cool place to check out? I wondered these aloud.

Dear reader: I have been to George Rogers Clark Historical Park many times since my first attendance of the annual weekend-after-Labor-Day Fair at New Boston in 2003. It's basically a Renaissance Fair meets late-colonial American reenactment of the Northwest Territory frontier. Which this Park was, by the way, at one point. It's wider-known for its significance as the site of the 1780 Battle of Piqua, the largest Revolutionary War military engagement fought west of the Alleghenies. I've brought each of my children here when they've come of age to comprehend that sort of thing.

Pastor Carl proceeded to give me turn-by-turn directions to George Rogers Clark Park.

I had no intention of going to George Rogers Clark Park that day.

The conversation wrapped not long after, and I proceeded through the coffee bar, negotiating a short route between the best-dressed Haitians among the heritage hoodied. Crocs. Everywhere. I never want to see an adult white male wearing Crocs ever again. Is this church or Walmart?

It's unspoken, but you're supposed to pay for your church coffee. The lowest denomination I had was a $5 bill, so that's what I presented to the offering box.

Flipping through the bulletin before heading inside, I noticed the language was informal but not sloppy. It was a sort of female millennial marketingspeak, similar to the way artificial intelligences like ChatGPT are known to be—chummy in an oddly optimistic, quasi-feminine way. But this did not appear to be written by AI to my eye. That said, one of the bits about Central, which was self-referred to as a nice little church, was the casual manner of dress to expect. Promises made, promises kept.

The sanctuary began to fill; music commenced. A man who looked like an identical twin of Aaron Earlywine—board member of the nearby Haitian Support Center—played acoustic. I saw more Haitian individuals, many with children, but also other heritage citizens, also with their children, all sitting together. But as the music built, I noticed Haitians mostly congregating themselves toward the back, as I had done during the latter portion of their chapel service.

A woman whose name I did not catch sang. The first song, I recognized as one of Hillsong UNITED's. Everyone stood; many raised their hands in the Evangelical childlike genuflect-up. A lyric spoke of the Holy Spirit leading believers to a spiritual destination where faith but specifically "trust" is "without borders."[11] Interesting.

I'd placed myself about midway towards the front directly facing the podium so I had congregation's best view for the sermon to come, and come it soon did. But first occurred what Pastor Carl called the passing of the peace, which was mingling about and greeting and wishing blessings upon others there for the service. My positive-sentiment high for the Haitians had not subsided, and so I went about greeting as many as I could, offering handshakes and exchanging brief pleasantries. The way they pronounced their otherwise Englishlike names had an audibly French accent with reminiscently West African tone. I was absolutely charmed. I introduced myself as Joshua, and they all seemed eased to see me; the way they repeated my name back to me was pure custom ASMR. Like the earlier Creole-only attendees, these worshippers had apparently not seen the bulletin's notice of casual dress, as per the cultural custom of the Central Christian Church. They would not assimilate. I was relieved.

Crocs aside, I witnessed in front of me during this period a rather portly gentleman in a Hawaiian beach shirt greeting the Haitian woman seated in my same pew. I recall also a pair of maximally pocketed cargo shorts and thigh-high stockings. Sandals, naturally. She had been one of the few who, when I introduced myself, volunteered her name upon hearing mine but said nothing else. I thought perhaps she might be a newercomer to America.

During the passing of this particular peace, the gentleman greeted her in what sounded like French, perhaps Creole. They had a brief, nonverbally upbeat exchange that extended into a full conversation. It occurred to me that I was witnessing John Berry's Acculturation Hypothesis come to life. When cultures come into sustained contact, their members tend to move toward one of four broad patterns, the most cooperative being integration, the keeping of some aspects of the prior culture while also participating in the larger one—yet mutual exchange on the part of members of the larger, host culture occurs as well. As far as I can tell, this mutual integration here at Central Christian Church, where both cultures make space for one another, is entirely voluntary on the part of all parties.

If one is part of this environment, and one participates either as a Haitian or a heritage citizen, one would likely have only positive experiences to share about the other, as predicted by models of intercultural communication. Take, again, Realistic Group Conflict Theory: Only mutually desired outcomes can ease tension, mitigate conflict, and motivate intergroup cooperation.[12] *Love God. Love Others. Nothing Else Matters.*

My final peace-passing came courtesy of another heritage citizen, or an individual whom I presumed to be so. He looked to be in his sixties, or possibly younger given his golfish attire—hours and hours of sun on the regular will do that—and he spoke of attending here for a number of years. He said that at Central, they do a lot of things differently.

"What do you do differently that churches aren't known for?" I asked.

"We feed the homeless. Once a week, we feed two hundred homeless people."

And I said, "Isn't that what church is supposed to be for?"

"Yes." He chuckled. "We also vehemently support the Haitians."

Vehemently—I wondered if he knows what that word means. Then I wondered if I did.

As I was writing this reflection later that afternoon, typing these very words out in my Google Docs iPhone app, I was standing inside of a reconstructed mid-eighteenth-century Shawnee dwelling made of straw, trunk, branch, and mud. The entirety of this culture was removed by the newcomers. There was not successful assimilation here in what is now Springfield. Only crude modern reconstructions at the site of a centuries-old culture keep its memories alive and lasting, and they're neither. Several of the other reconstructed Shawnee dwellings nearby are caving in or out; some require modern shingles to remain even partially roofed. It looks wrong.

The three thousand Shawnee who made these very lands home would be defeated despite British alliance.[13] George Washington's officer of the wild western frontier, George Rogers Clark, older brother of the eventual legendary explorer William Clark, together with almost a thousand Kentucky militiamen, took this land. They came here through Cincinnati, up the Little Miami and Mad Rivers, and took it. The entirety of the county now bears the chief victor's name. It remains local lore that Clark's advantage came from pre-attack reconnaissance atop an ancient Adena culture burial mound nearby.[14] I visited the mound on a previous visit to Springfield in the course of this work. Long gone are the Adena from Ohio as well.

At other parks in Ohio where the Shawnee are believed to have lived, visitors may find a land acknowledgment plaque, display, or other such signage. The first one I noticed appeared at the Glacial Grooves Geological Preserve on Kelleys Island in Lake Erie. Three different Shawnee tribes are acknowledged on the sign as are, among others, two different Seneca. It is without irony and not as a joke that I looked up and learned that various tribes listed together warred with one another within Ohio, with that conflict resulting in destruction and displacement of ones by others.

I'm pulled by my most recent memory back to Central now. As the sermon portion of service commences, I see a little boy in the back row with what appears to be a Haitian family, husband and wife and son altogether, the adults probably about my age. The small black child has a big pacifier clipped to his outwear—a plaid shirt that matches perfectly the plaid pattern of his newsboy cap. Color-coordinated. Excellence.

Now began Carl Ruby with an acknowledgment of his own about yesterday's funeral for a local Haitian pastor—Osmond Cheres.[15] He remarked on the beautiful singing within a "packed" sanctuary here.[16] The celebration of life was livestreamed by Central's social media.[17] Pastor Carl was right.

Lucky me now—this was to be the start of a weekly six-part series on the Bible, based on Marty Solomon's *Asking Better Questions of the Bible.*[18] This author "brings a Jewish perspective" to scriptural analysis, Pastor Carl said.[19] A visual aid for the message stood beside him—a stack of seven Bibles from Pastor Carl's life and family, going back generation before generation before generation . . .

Love God.

This series of sermons adapted from Solomon's book would become "defining" for Central Christian Church, Pastor Carl prophesied, "because how you approach the Bible kind of shapes who we become as a church."[20]

Throughout the forty-minute or so remarks of Carl Ruby, I found myself transfixed in rapport. His own prior faith-struggles he shared freely, such as his transition out of the simplistic faith of his childhood, which demanded absolute belief in an inerrant, not merely inspired, holy Bible, mirroring mine exactly. Indisputable observations such as the Bible being not, in fact, a book but rather a library of various genres of work of various degrees and extends of literal truth, metaphorical retellings, and purposeful exaggerations—I heard my own arguments to my mother as an upstart college student in Pastor Carl's story. My mom knew Ken Ham of Answers in Genesis, the Creation Museum, and the Ark Encounter. These ministries separately but collectively assert the faith-based belief that the first books of Genesis are a scientifically accurate description of the formation of the observable universe, which took place over seven literal twenty-four hour calendars days approximately six thousand years ago.

I had a hard time accepting that. So, too, had Pastor Carl as a youngster, with other such literalist interpretations of the Bible:

> The one I struggled with was the story of Samson going out and catching . . . a thousand fox. And he tied torches to their tails and set them loose. And I remember thinking, "Man, it'd be hard to catch a fox. I've never caught a fox. Be hard to catch a fox." I think miracles can happen. I think if God wanted someone to go out and catch a thousand fox, he could make that happen. That's possible. But I think it is more likely that ancient people used numbers differently, and a thousand was a number to indicate a bunch, power, things like that, and I don't need to get hung up. I think that when we try to make the Bible more than it is, it actually damages people's faith.[21]

It certainly does. The Evangelical Christian faith community of my upbringing drilled into me that either all the literal claims of a literal reading of the Bible are 100 percent correct, or all of them are false and "your faith is useless," to quote the Bible itself.[22] So be it then. Shortly after my mother passed away in June 2015, I admitted for the first time in public that I lost my faith and had become an atheist.

The one I struggled with the most—and lost—was not literal readings of numbers but rather the fossil record. Creationism insists on a literal global flood during the time of the biblical character Noah, maybe five thousand years ago, tops. All those fossilized corrals and critters and other unidentifiable in stone, rock, and pebble found all over Ohio's hiking trails and dry creekbeds? That's all evidence the Bible is true, hell is real, and you're going straight there if you're gay. And so forth.

But then I learned, in college, how fossils actually form—and how long it really takes. My faith is useless. Now as I've reflected on Pastor Carl's alternative interpretation model—reading the books of the Bible as if they were written for the contemporary audiences to which they were actually written, imagine that—my faith didn't need to be. But what then might it have been? If faith and church and the Bible and Jesus and all that aren't about getting to heaven when you die, what's it all for?

How you approach the Bible shapes who we become.

Pastor Carl concluded his sermon with a prayer in which he laid out who the people of Central Christian Church are to become: "people transformed by the Bible who look more like Christ," who are "patient, kind, and gentle, people who have self-control and are loving and generous."[23]

This seemed like a mashup of two passages on Biblical love that my mother had required me to memorize as a child, Galatians 5:22-23 and 1 Corinthians 13:4-8.

Love Others.

As I wrote this particular section in Google Docs on mobile, I'd taken a hike up and out from the Shawnee village. I now stood atop bare earth, soil exposed. I could see various fossilized invertebrate marine organisms. Possibly Devonian or Ordovician, given Clark County. That timeline stretches back to between 485 and 359 million years ago, and I'm standing right on top of it. Corrals and brachiopods and primitive snails and various aquatic plants so archaic nobody knows for sure what they looked like. Millions. Not thousands.

In my reflections, I'd wanted to term this non-literalist and inclusive reimagining of Christianity as unique to Carl Ruby personally, a sort of nondenominational denomination of his very own—a sect called perhaps *Carlrubyism.* Since the purpose of a system is what it does, what is the purpose of Pastor Carl's faith system? I must be fair, because unique to him, this faith is not.

The Central service concluded after "the Lord's table," which is what both Pastors Carl and Cynthia called their inclusive communion experience. I did not partake of either. Both seemed to indicate, however, that you don't need to identify as a Christian in order to drink the little plastic-covered grape juice cuplet. Pastor Cynthia had dismissed that notion last Easter Sunday as "silly."[24]

Then, I wondered to myself, as there is no one else to wonder to in my mind, *Why are the numbers symbolic? Why can't other claims of the Bible be symbolic, too?* You see where I'm going with this. Protestants worldwide already insist that the Catholic celebration of the Eucharist is metaphorical body and blood, not literal. But why not continue? What if the Last Supper itself was a mythic titling of an ahistorical event and there were not, in fact, twelve literal disciples of Christ because the number twelve in Hebrew actually meant—

And now you see. Carlrubyism? Not really. My faith, still useless.

As I make my exit, Pastor Carl bids me farewell. I conversationally pulled him away from a Haitian family and presented this little trivia.

"Does the name 'Bart' mean anything to you? So if I say 'Bart,' what comes to mind for you?"

His eyes moved about for a few moments.

"Ehrman?"

Bingo. I suggested he read *How Jesus Became God*, given today's sermon takeaway runs the same race as Ehrman's hypothesis of history about the early

Christian church presented in the book—that the religion *of* Jesus became a religion *about* Jesus.

As I turned to leave, I saw a basketball court and otherwise outdoor play area through the panes at the further end of the foyer. The children of Haitians and heritage citizens alike played together.

As I thumb-typed those words, I felt myself return to the present physical moment. I'd walked back down and now stood above a pristine creek's bank. Perhaps Clark's Kentuckyians refreshed themselves at this very spot. I noticed, then, fossils—some sort of shells, a leaf thing, something else. And also little specks. Almost-perfect circles. No, spheres. Many of them. Hundreds. Thousands? A lot. They're on the soil of the bank, I see. And on sticks, branches, rocks, even upon last autumn's leaves, all over everything in the creek. These tiny black capsules . . . eventual tadpoles. I see now—this shady creek provides sufficient shielding from the elements. I've seen this before; if I return in a few weeks, I will see almost no water. I would see no more a creek, but a habitat of tadpoles becoming frogs, making this theirs.

At that moment, I hear the boom of war cannon. Pull my man card and give it to Pastor Cynthia because I jump-scared myself and about slid right down into the creek. I should've known; this was the first firing test of the day for the Mad River Light Artillery, a local reenactors' group who run demonstration-blasts at the Fair at New Boston held here. Springfield, after all, is the site of battle.

I trudge uphill to the highest point in the park—the monument. On it, I read, *Tecumseh the great Indian chief was born here in the Shawnee village of Piqua about 1768*. Above the writing on this side is a Shawnee youth in loincloth and moccasins, depicted receiving a bow and arrow lesson from an elder.

Family records rediscovered after my mother's passing show our lineage stretching back to and through the Wyandot chief of central (what is now) Ohio named Leatherlips; he made peace with the white settlers of the frontier, encouraged integration and assimilation in his own way of the times, and signed the Treaty of Greenville together with other tribal leaders and representatives to allow Euro-Americans additional, unmolested settlements.[25] A painting of the Treaty featuring Leatherlips in the very bottom lefthand corner hangs in the Ohio Statehouse in Columbus.

It is said that in retaliation for fraternizing with outsiders, up to and including his stated desire to live among them, Chief Leatherlips was seized by his own kind. None other than Tecumseh advised his brother, widely known then and now as simply the Prophet, to bring false charges against Leatherlips that would merit the death penalty—all as revenge for what Leatherlips had done to make and keep peace between two cultures at war for so long, as best he could.[26]

And so he did. And they did. My ancestor Chief Leatherlips was executed by tomahawk by his fellow Wyandot. Tecumseh died in battle against the Americans three years later. A sculpture of Leatherlips' face emerges from the hillside above the Scioto River in Dublin, Ohio, near the chief's old encampment.

A white eyewitness of Leatherlips' execution would later retell through tears "how my heart was touched by the taking away of that good Indian. His word was as true as Gospel. He proved it by his actions."[27]

Nothing Else Matters.

All these things returned to me in the shadow of Tecumseh at George Rogers Clark Historical Park, typing all this into my iPhone's Google Docs app.

I had no intention of going to George Rogers Clark Park that Sunday. But now, here am I.

I'm not known for my piety, rarely my purity, but occasionally my profundity. While I'm not an error-free narrator, there is one thing I will not do.

I don't lie to preachers in their own house of worship.

The next day, I phoned into a member of the heritage citizenry's OSINT network, who offered me evermore leads whose following-ups appear elsewhere in this book. I shared where I'd been the previous day.

"What'd you think of him?" he asked.

"Your problem is not that he doesn't believe what he says he does," I said, of Carl Ruby. "Your problem is that he does believe it."

To love God, this is obvious. To love others—who are these "others," exactly? Who is the most othered and thus the most entitled to love?

For the socially conscious Christians of Springfield, Ohio, there will be degrees of otherness, from their perspective. White citizens born and raised here are what? Are they like you—you with your white guilt and your white savior complex, à la Peter Griffin, "King of the Black People"—or are they the "other"?[28]

And the foreigners—the *ger*—those who've braved the gap of death then despair and detention and have arrived at this destination speaking barely English if any at all . . . what are they?

What are they?

Exactly.

Nothing Else Matters.

CHAPTER 13

SOCIAL INJUSTICE

> "We are a nation of immigrants. That's who we are . . . an unrelenting stream of immigration, nonstop. . . . Folks like me who are Caucasian of European descent, for the first time, in 2017, we'll be in an absolute minority in the United States of America . . . Fewer than fifty percent of the people in America, from then and on, will be white European stock. That's not a bad thing. That's a source of our strength."[1]
>
> —Vice President Joseph R. Biden, Jr., in 2015

I was back at the Skyline on Goodwin Avenue in Springfield where it all began, the site of my first in-person meeting with proud but in most cases unexpected and occasionally hesitant members of the OSINT citizenry network. My sole conversation partner this time around was **Kenneth "Barron" Seelig, Jr.** His ministry, Out to Pastor, has been "been doing what we can to feed, clothe and advocate for the homeless since 2008."[2] He also operates a "road grill cafe" (food truck) known for satiating sandwiches and the dad joke to devour all dad jokes: "Eat here or we'll both starve!"[3] I love these people.

That same week, Amazon had apparently banned then unbanned a 1973 dystopian novel from Jean Raspail, recipient of numerous prestigious awards and prizes for literature and various lifetime accomplishments.[4,5,6] It's called *The Camp of the Saints*. It reached the top five overall Amazon bestsellers concurrent with the U.S. House of Representatives passing bipartisan legislation (H.R. 1689) to extend Temporary Protected Status for Haitians in America by a 224 to 204 vote.[7] Republican Senator Katie Britt of Alabama declared the bill "dead on arrival" upon that arrival to the U.S. Senate.[8]

A brief excerpt from *The Camp of the Saints*—summarizing complex and multivariate criticism of mass foreign migration into the Western world in three short sentences—remained in my social media feed, widely shared as it was that week:

> Your universe has no meaning to them. They will not try to understand. They will be tired, they will be cold, they will make a fire with your beautiful oak door . . . [9]

The imagery haunted my thoughts as I entered Skyline. Barron beat me there, as he is of the generation who understands that to be early is to be on time. He still sported the bib overalls many of us witnessed in his citizen's address to Springfield City Commission—now a viral clip published by the Trump presidential campaign in 2024: "OHIO HOMELESS ADVOCATE: I don't know of a single homeless [Haitian] in this town—because they all got vouchers! But I can show you a whole bunch of people that have been displaced."[10]

That's Barron Seelig. He became a go-to source for a number of federal officials at the height of the frenzy and afterwards, post-election and post-inauguration. But by this point in the saga, too many promises had been made—to him, specifically—with not enough kept.

"This is not the city I grew up in," Barron told me. "I was never gonna give up. But I just had a cash offer from one of them cash offer places, you know, on your house. . . . The meeting's set up next week . . . We're out."

"Where will you go?" I asked between interruptions from our early-twenties server.

"County. Probably here. So I can still do ministry work."

Of the hours we spent together that day, that was our subject-focus for most of them—who Barron felt called to minister to, how he'd served them, where he'd fed and clothed and counseled and even literally saved—and not just spiritually—the most downtrodden populations of heritage America in the present day. He shared how he'd invested his own money, never recouping it, by establishing a warming center for those of any background who needed some place safe to go amid Ohio's winter frigidity. There were rules, but there was food. If week after week he'd see the same individuals seeking free meals and snacks, Barron told me he'd take the person aside privately for a candid conversation as to their station in life and how they might plan to raise their socioeconomic status out of that place of need.

It occurred to me that the hand-up-not-hand-out work of Barron Seelig is increasingly a rarity in America, especially amid the blank-check charity abuses that Elon Musk's Department of Government Efficiency brought to light involving USAID and others.[11,12,13,14] It would not surprise you that Barron gave me two earfuls on his opinions of city, county, and state federal governance. He'd had enough.

"I want to go on the record with a, 'Shame on you. Just because it's freaking legal, don't make it right,'" Barron said of his intention to attend and speak at another Springfield City Commission meeting.

So much more than the Haitian influx and the homeless lot weighed on him. He brought up city budget issues, firefighter understaffing and overworking—a hot topic for the sit-in union protest at the City Commission meeting I attended the following Tuesday—citizen concerns and complaints about entire tracts of land sold off to presumed-sketchy non-local developers to do God knows what with it, and so much more.[15,16,17] (Few were enthusiastic that "Springfield City Commissioners authorized a purchase agreement for the sale of a former city fire station to the Haitian Community Help and Support Center to house the group's operations," by the way.[18])

This commercialization of Springfield land was an issue brought up at that same City Commission meeting by none other than Diana Daniels, only to be immediately dismissed as a non-issue by Mayor Rob Rue.[19] I was there. It was bad. Of the experience of her and other concerned citizens who spoke, Diana recounted to me on Facebook, "Look at faces [of residents] when they talk [at Commission meetings], look at them when they are abused when at the podium asking for redress, listen to the shake in their voices. This is not easy to speak, especially when in the forum [you] know they think [you] are a [nuisance]."[20] I did notice an audible, visible tremble among most of those who shared their concerns that night at the mic. The jean-clad, hoodied, tennis-shoed, tattooed residents spoke; the upper-classy government employees sat there, mostly still, enduring citizens' ire, pleas, and grief. Each citizen got three minutes. I watched as commissioners got distracted during the people's remarks by laptops in front of them, presumably cellphones, and more. Mayor Rue responded to most speakers with a terse thank-you before moving on to the next item of business. As exhausted as city leadership seemed with their people, so, too, did that feeling appear mutual. At one point, a young black gentleman offered a profanity-laced rant that I'm still not sure what it was about even after hearing it twice; the young woman beside me hollered out to watch his language, which included racial slurs. City Commission told her to quiet down so the individual could exercise his free-speech rights.[21] I then overheard this individual, on his strut out of the room, call the husher-woman beside me "stupid bitch." I was surprised that the cadre of police standing right there did nothing. Maybe I shouldn't be. Springfield needs help.

"I'm sixty-three years old, man. I'm at the end of my run," Barron said. "But I'm trying to make it better for my grandchildren. . . . It's sad that we're going to leave them not a legacy . . . We're leaving them a . . . battle zone. 'Cause these people that are in power, they're happy to rule over the ashes. Does that make sense?"

It does.

A phone call joined our conversation not long after. It was another heritage citizen, whose wife's car had been struck by a Haitian migrant with her in it. Over speakerphone, the caller relayed the details to me, which by this point was a rerun I'd heard so many times from so many citizens I could predict how it went down, which was, in fact, how it did—the at-fault Haitian attempted to flee, the citizen called police, as many as fifteen Haitians showed up in what the victim considered an attempted intimidation, then the victim's family arrived to un-intimidate their loved one . . . all before police arrived. Springfield needs help.

I was shown pictures and video to confirm key aspects of the story. In this instance, it was noted that the Haitian driver at least had a license and proof of insurance. So that was good. Barron also relayed to me the technique behind oft-reported Haitian car-flipping transportation mishaps. He'd not so long ago spoken with a stunt driver who explained to him how to roll a car at only twenty-five miles per hour. Use a two-foot system—one foot on the brake, one foot on the gas. "Cut the wheel, pedal it, and roll it." You're telling me local Haitians flip their cars not because they can't drive but because they drive like professional stunt performers? Interesting.

At about this point, Barron polled our server as she dropped back in on us. He asked her casually about her take on America, the city of Springfield, where all this is headed.

"Honestly? Have not paid too much attention . . . I'm terrible with politics right now . . . I'm only twenty-four."

As soon as she was without earshot, Barron revealed the reason for his spontaneous survey, for my benefit.

"Gen Z," Barron said, looking as done as he said he was. "My point in having that conversation with you sitting here is, she doesn't have a clue. Does not have a clue . . . That's the future."

In that moment, a suspicion formed within me—*I bet Gen Z residents of Springfield don't mind the Haitians.*

Barron named all the names to me next—those stoking the fire that has burned out so many residents, both those of the institutional Left in Springfield and those of the reactionary Right, who most notably are not from and do not actually live in Springfield.

"'I didn't ask you,'" Barron relayed to me what he'd told an unruly anti-Haitian protestor whom Barron subsequently ran out of town (literally). This particular fellow claimed, Barron said, he was there to support his fellow whites. Something like that.

"'What are you doing here?'" Barron said he'd asked. To this agitator, that was apparently the wrong question. Barron then received a number of threats regarding the allegation he was now a "race traitor," mixed in with various chants that the Haitians of Springfield ought to "go back to Africa."

To the best of my knowledge, Haiti is not in Africa.

We discussed next the storied history of Springfield and its proud union labor heritage—and yet so much of what once was has now fallen into disrepair, disregard, disillusionment. As many problems may have come with the migrant influx, the city of Springfield had not been without its own self-generateds. Barron noted a troubling occurrence not uncommon with some residents who've visited his local food pantry. Having received canned food they deemed unpalatable, the purportedly homeless, seemingly hungry individual then "chucks" the unopened food into a nearby yard, as Barron put it.

"The Haitians, they don't throw nothin' away," Barron said, then added that this did not, however, mean that they always consumed what they received from the food bank. There was one instance in which his food bank had received as a donation a particular brand of beverage unavailable in Clark County. Haitians who had presumably accepted those very containers of beverage from Barron's food pantry were found reselling them at a perfect profit out of a van on a street corner. Barron referred me to the individuals who confirmed eyewitnessing the incident.

Speaking of incident, Barron has had to teach minimum-viable manners "at least fifteen times" to Haitian men in line at his food pantry which, again, is open to all.

"Let me put a baby in you," is not, in fact, an appropriate way to address white women in line at a Springfield food pantry. Or any women of any race or ethnicity, as a matter of fact, but in this particular case, it was various Haitian men who deemed this an appropriate self-introduction to women of lighter color in line for the generosity of Barron's ministry.

We don't do that in America.

That said, Barron, I observed, had a merciful fondness for all of humanity. He spoke of cordial relationships, even friendships, with a number of Springfield Haitians. It was through conversations with them he eventually learned—and confirmed from these Haitians themselves—a number of things you read about in Chapter 9, which did indeed happen exactly as reported.

Given that, as you might expect, Barron has fielded a number of reporter inquiries from the likes of *The New York Times*, *New York Post*, and *Washington Post.* What do you suppose they asked him about seeing?

"[L]ooking for, you know, cats on the barbecue. I said, 'They're not here,'" Barron relayed to me. "'But while you're here, let me tell you a story . . . Let's go talk to [a mother] who got displaced because of the Haitians through no fault of her own. She's living in her . . . car . . . with kids!' They ain't telling that story."

That is the story to tell.

"Charity begins at home." Barron said earlier of the city's own internal strife and struggle. "Take care of yourself. Don't be offering this guy something . . . [when] we're not in a position to do that."

Springfield needs help. I believe this. I believed it before writing this book. I believed it while writing it. And I believe it yet now. What is a place but its people who make it what it is? And here, there are those who feel they've had insult added to their injury.

Often in my conversations and travels, I heard reported a two-tiered justice system—Haitians being advantaged in everything whereas longtime residents and native citizens not so. A few such cases brought, re-brought, and re-re-brought to my attention those involving not simply *Grand Theft Auto V*-style aggression through traffic but, like the aforementioned video game, actual crime.

A Two-Tiered System?

Jacob Payen is spokesperson for the Haitian Community Alliance, with which Springfield's "vast majority of Haitian businesses, churches and other organizations are involved."[22]

"Payen said Haitian residents are 'living in fear' but most understand that this is a 'difficult moment' that will end in due time. 'The city officials put together the proper security measures for us to feel safe . . . '"[23]

That may explain in part why, on August 27, 2024, Payen walked into the Clark County Municipal Courthouse with a loaded Glock 17 9mm pistol and fifteen hollow-point rounds in its magazine.[24] Jeff Skinner of *The Ohio Register* detailed the incident:

- Payen, among a party of three, told bailiffs they intended to visit the Prosecutor's office.
- An X-ray at security revealed the loaded firearm in Payen's Louis Vuitton bag.

- When questioned about the firearm, Payen claimed he had forgotten about it.
- Payen showed his concealed handgun license (CHL) issued by the Clark County Sheriff's Office, as he "carries large sums of money for his 'store.'" (Payen owns Milokan Botanica, a "religious goods store," reported a public news station.[25] The Associated Press said the shop sells "Haitian spiritual and natural healing products."[26] Glenda Bailey calls it a voodoo shop.)
- Payen's firearm was seized and a receipt issued. He was told that Judge Valerie Wilt would be consulted on "possible charges" and the fate of the weapon.
- Payen "advised he did not feel bad for bringing the gun in since it was located in his bag."
- But then officers "permitted Payen to continue his business of meeting the prosecutor, rather than arresting and further questioning Payen about his business and purpose within the courthouse."
- The subsequent charge of carrying a concealed weapon into the courthouse was pled down from a felony to a misdemeanor.[27]

"If you or I had done what Jacob did," Diana Daniels told me, "we wouldn't have been allowed in that building or out of it. We would have been put under it."

Suddenly, I'm reminded of the Bolshevik anarcho-tyranny written of by Soviet Union gulag survivor and acclaimed author Aleksandr Solzhenitsyn: "[Y]our punishment for having a knife when they searched you would be very different from the thief's. For him to have a knife was mere misbehavior, tradition, he didn't know any better. But for you to have one was 'terrorism.'"[28,29]

Here is the gist, according to *The Ohio Register*: Court records from St. Lucie County, Florida, show Jacob Payen was charged with felony grand theft in 2009; the adjudication was withheld, so the conviction stayed off certain background checks, but he still completed probation. Under the plea deal, Payen received 90 days in jail, forfeited the firearm, and paid a $250 fine. A color from the *Register* on the matter:

> Many have been stunned by the turn of events in the case as most individuals would have been immediately arrested for attempting to bring a loaded firearm into the courthouse rather than permitted to continue about their business, let alone that business being to meet with a prosecutor over a case. . . . Many are calling it a gross miscarriage of justice as the

> original felony charge of attempting to conceal a weapon into a courthouse was lowered to a misdemeanor charge of failing to report a weapon to an officer during official police business.[30]

Somehow, it now gets worse. The *Register* reported on court records showing Payen frequently inserting himself into criminal cases involving Haitians in Springfield. In one hit-and-run police report, the suspect got Payen involved, who then called the officer claiming to be the suspect's necessary translator. "Payen's involvement and conversation with the suspect was not investigated." In closing, *The Ohio Register*:

> . . . In the case of Jacob Payen, a Haitian immigrant who has incurred multiple felony charges in Florida, yet none processed to the fullest extent, was potentially permitted a CHL in Ohio in violation to ORC, and has signed off on multiple LLC's and nonprofits throughout the city, has immediate access to the county prosecutors and was not immediately arrested when attempting to bring the firearm into the courthouse, has somehow again evaded another felony charge. Some are calling Payen one of the luckiest men in Springfield, while others are asking if there is something else going on behind closed doors.[31]

By the way, that fraud story dates to 2003, not 2009, when Jacob Payen attempted to defraud his automobile insurer and made a false police report in the process of doing so. I had a look at the St. Lucie County Florida website (https://courtcasesearch.stlucieclerk.gov) and searched the two case numbers associated with his years-long drama, case numbers 2003CF002935 A and 2009CF001751. Here's what I gathered from a read of both court dockets; document scans and all, it's a long and tedious read, but it goes like this:

In April 2003, Jacob Payen was accused of filing a false insurance claim worth "$20,000 to $100,000" in St. Lucie County, Florida. He was arrested in July 2003, pleaded no contest in March 2004, and in April 2004 received a sentence of adjudication withheld, fifteen years' probation, restitution of approximately $16,500, court costs, and 200 hours of community service. He later violated probation several times, was arrested on a warrant in February 2008 and spent roughly fifty-five days in jail before probation was reinstated in April 2008. In May 2009, Payen won a post-conviction motion; the judge vacated the original 2004 plea and sentence, after which the state immediately re-filed the charge as a new case (that second number, 2009CF001751) for third-degree grand theft. That new case also ended with adjudication withheld and a fresh term of probation.

There's more. Look up another Jacob Payen case—number 2008CF000701 A; I found this only when I clicked Payen's name in the court case search website. It's the same man alright, Jacob Payen, born 1979.

One week prior to a February 18, 2018, affidavit for Payen's first violation of probation on the fraud case, he was accused of child cruelty and abuse against a minor victim, "M.P.," on February 11th. He was arrested two days later, posted a $25,000 bond, and had a strict no-contact order issued with the alleged victim.

But Payen would be arrested not long after this incident for his parole violation on the fraud case. A real standup guy. On March 24, 2008, the State filed "No Information," formally declining to prosecute, and the child abuse case was dropped. It appears, however, that Payen petitioned to have all these records sealed/expunged, in 2009, so we wouldn't find them. It appears that way because he lost, and now we know. We know it all.

Entry 92 of the fuller court docket dating back to 2003 is a document uploaded on October 27th, 2008, but originally dated May 15, 2008. Beginning on page 44 of the PDF are scans of Form I-862 "Notice to Appear," charging Payen as removable—deportable—because the insurance-fraud conviction qualified as a crime involving moral turpitude under immigration law. Here is an excerpt. As of the day I requested access, mine was only the fiftieth such request.

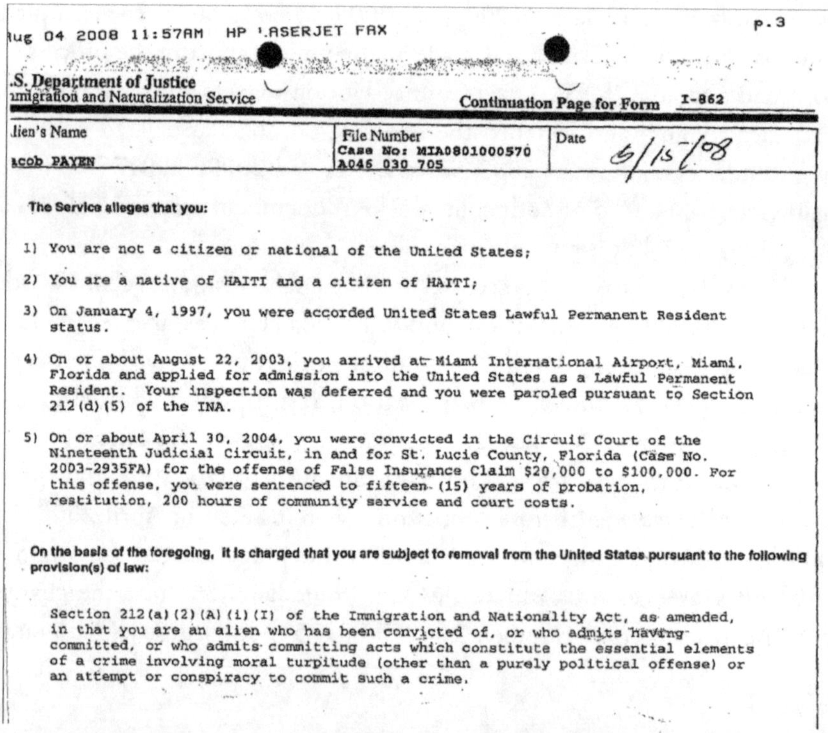

ug 04 2008 11:57AM HP LASERJET FAX p.3

.S. Department of Justice
mmigration and Naturalization Service

Continuation Page for Form I-862

lien's Name	File Number	Date
acob PAYEN	Case No: MIA0801000570 A046 030 705	5/15/08

The Service alleges that you:

1) You are not a citizen or national of the United States;

2) You are a native of HAITI and a citizen of HAITI;

3) On January 4, 1997, you were accorded United States Lawful Permanent Resident status.

4) On or about August 22, 2003, you arrived at Miami International Airport, Miami, Florida and applied for admission into the United States as a Lawful Permanent Resident. Your inspection was deferred and you were paroled pursuant to Section 212(d)(5) of the INA.

5) On or about April 30, 2004, you were convicted in the Circuit Court of the Nineteenth Judicial Circuit, in and for St. Lucie County, Florida (Case No. 2003-2935FA) for the offense of False Insurance Claim $20,000 to $100,000. For this offense, you were sentenced to fifteen (15) years of probation, restitution, 200 hours of community service and court costs.

On the basis of the foregoing, it is charged that you are subject to removal from the United States pursuant to the following provision(s) of law:

Section 212(a)(2)(A)(i)(I) of the Immigration and Nationality Act, as amended, in that you are an alien who has been convicted of, or who admits having committed, or who admits committing acts which constitute the essential elements of a crime involving moral turpitude (other than a purely political offense) or an attempt or conspiracy to commit such a crime.

That's page three of the official U.S. Department of Justice / Immigration and Naturalization Service Form I-862. It's a formal charging document that started **deportation** proceedings against him. The government alleged at that time:

- Payen was not a U.S. citizen.
- He was a native and citizen of Haiti.
- He was granted Lawful Permanent Resident (a green card) status on January 4, 1997.
- In August 2003, after his July Florida arrest, he was paroled (back) into the US at Miami International Airport.
- On April 30, 2004, Payen was convicted of False Insurance Claim ($20,000 to $100,000) and sentenced to fifteen years' probation, restitution, 200 hours community service, and court costs.

Because of that 2004 Florida conviction (classified as a crime involving moral turpitude), Payen was subject to removal from the United States under Section 212(a)(2)(A)(i)(I) of the Immigration and Nationality Act. That was May 2008. But we know how the rest of his cases went in Florida. It does not appear Payen was deported.

Something's not adding up for me. As of this writing, I've requested (but not yet received) copies of letters sent to the court regarding Payen's cases sent by, among others, third-party professionals. But one particular letter is not listed as requestable, "LTR FROM NOTRE DAME CATHOLIC MISSION FILED," which appears as one of the final entries on the docket in the child abuse case. I presume this is a letter of support, character witness perhaps, from Notre Dame Catholic Mission in the Diocese of Palm Beach, whose Facebook page posts appear auto-translated into English for me from Creole.[32]

Few things anger the Americans I spoke with more than the appearance of getting away with it, especially when hard-earned money is stolen or a kid gets hurt. One of those "few things" might be, well . . . you can put two and two together here for yourself:

The Springfield News-Sun referred to Jacob Payen as "a veteran of the U.S. Navy" who "fought in the Persian Gulf."[33]

Fought, you say? *Fought?* When was Payen born? 1979, right? Right. If whoever made that initial claim to the *News-Sun*—Payen himself?—was referring to the Persian Gulf War, *oops* . . . that ended officially in ceasefire on April 11, 1991.[34] If "Persian Gulf" means, rather, the Global War on Terror, the earliest full stage taking place largely in Afghanistan beginning in 2001 and then through Iraq in 2003, then Payen as a Marine could have hypothetically "fought"—

Wait.

The Miami Herald records Payen claiming he lived in Port St. Lucie, Florida for twenty-seven years and only moved his family to Springfield "after getting discharged from the U.S. military."[35] Hold that thought. In the same piece, Payen dismissed concerned heritage citizens of Springfield as a "small group of people who do not understand Haitians and perhaps haven't yet been able to adapt to the influx of Haitians in Springfield" and who also have a "political motivation" for their resistance.

Other media like *The Guardian*, the Associated Press, Scripps News, and Payen's own Haitian Community Alliance repeat the U.S. Navy veteran claim.[36,37,38,39] Elsewhere, we get some sense of that "official" timeline I just told you about. "Haitian entrepreneur Jacob Payen moved to Springfield with his wife and son in 2021," reported Ideastream Public Media, an affiliate of NPR.[40] Who told the writers of the story that? Because a 2025 interview sets the Payens' Springfield arrival year at 2022:

> Payen said he saw Springfield as rife with possibility. He and his wife previously lived in Port St. Lucie, Florida, where they owned and operated Milokan Botanica, a spiritual goods and natural remedies store. He said he initially came to Springfield to visit a friend.
>
> "I came for a week—that was three years ago," he said.
>
> He said he noticed "a lot of abandoned houses" around the city—which he said he didn't view as a blight, but rather as a kind of canvas for rejuvenation.
>
> "We ended up falling in love with Springfield," Payen said. "I told my wife, 'Maybe we're here at the right time, because this city cannot remain isolated like this. Something's got to be done, and we need to be a part of it.'"
>
> Payen and his wife bought and renovated several crumbling homes, which they now lease as rental properties. They also opened a second location of Milokan Botanica on Limestone Street.[41]

They're making themselves sound like good Samaritans. They're pretty good at this.

Anyway, also in 2025, a new title is added to Payen by fawning news media—"US citizen."[42]

Let's rewind the timeline and shift right back to the military. Payen's Florida arrest, probation, and immigration records list him living in St. Lucie County between 2003 and 2009. The very first document that begins the paper trail, Probable Cause Affidavit in case 2003CF002935, contains absolutely zero explicit or implicit mention of military service.

No U.S. Navy, no active duty, no leave, no deployment, no discharge, no veteran status, no military benefits, no combat experience, no VA records—nothing at all related to the military. The affidavit simply paints the picture of Payen as purely a civilian living with roommates and friends from whom he bummed rides around town before the insurance fraud scheme.

Now, the original affidavit was written in July 2003. If Payen had been in the Navy, it would almost certainly have appeared somewhere in the investigator's narrative—especially in a detailed fraud affidavit. This is the very first official document in the case, and it treats him as a regular local resident with no military connections whatsoever.

Furthermore, from my U.S. military veteran friends and colleagues over the years, I've gathered that military personnel routinely provide character statements or letters of support for service members facing civilian charges.[43] I saw no such letters appear in Payen's case dockets.

And guess what? Between 2003 and 2009, there were no active U.S. Naval bases in St. Lucie County, Florida.

Let's say we're going to be maximally generous with the last burden of all doubts. Perhaps Payen participated in Operation Enduring Freedom between October 2001 and March 2003, as the United States Navy was known to have participated in the effort.[44] A quick Wikipedia skim of the matter also tells us that "naval assets also supported maritime interdiction operations in the Persian Gulf under the banners of Operation Southern Watch and Operation Northern Watch until 2003."[45] That said, this was an air-centric military operation. You'll not see anything about naval gunfire, ship-to-ship combat, surface naval battles, or any large-scale fighting in the waters of the Persian Gulf as alleged regarding Payen's U.S. Navy combat record in which he "fought" there.

The timeline of Payen's documented civilian life in Florida, 2003 to 2009, creates an obvious inconsistency—at best—with his discharged-then-moved-in-2021 narrative. Obviously.

Ultimately, no credible evidence publicly exists that I could find to support the repeated news claim that he is a U.S. Navy veteran, much less that he "fought in the Persian Gulf."[46] Could Payen have served a standard four-year Navy enlistment, starting between the 1997 green card and 1999, then ending by 2001 through 2003, at the absolute latest?[47] Legally and chronologically, all on paper, military service is possible. But nothing I've witnessed makes that plausible.

Consider how Jacob Payen is presented in the media—consistently as a "Springfield Haitian leader" and other such descriptors (often co-praised with Vilès Dorsainvil and Lindsay Aime of the Haitian Help and Support Center; there are too many stories there, by the way).[48,49,50] Notably, in one such pro-Haitian-bias interview, Payen said of his fellow countrymen, "there are other channels to bring all these people to legality to make them legal. Yes, I believe there are proper channels. This is what president Biden was doing."[51]

What did Payen advise again? He "advised he did not feel bad . . . "

You want to know what I want to know?

How did Jacob Payen get a concealed handgun license from the Clark County Sheriff, with that record?

Why the fuck is this son of a bitch still in my country?

Payen is a noted and quoted critic of President Donald Trump, as is the only Haitian-American in U.S. Congress, Representative Sheila Cherfilus-McCormick of Florida.[52,53,54,55] Well, she was. And she, uh, was. The congresswoman, paraded in the mainstream media as a Haitian role modelette, was indicted by a federal grand jury for "stealing $5 million in FEMA funds and making illegal campaign contributions."[56,57,58] She resigned her position four days after I met with Barron Seelig at Skyline.[59] I do not suspect the events are related.

The number of court case records I've read, stories I've heard, and anecdotes I've collected on the non-ideal behavior of Haitians in Springfield . . . they could and perhaps should be their own book. Glenda Bailey emailed me case report collections forty-plus times in a one-week period with incident upon incident upon incident upon—you get it. I simply could not include every single case in this chapter, much less this book. There are many, many more Jacob Payens to be found among the Haitians of Springfield.

Of them all, the habitual offenders I learned about bothered me most. Just take a sampling of three document collections Glenda sent me on one evening of so many: One is a nine-page compilation of extensive records of repeated traffic violations for driving without a license, without insurance, and under suspension, culminating in a crash. Another shows a Haitian who's racked up multiple traffic citations over several years and twice sued the Ohio BMV in attempts to obtain a valid driver's license he never legally held in the state—and he's still driving. Thirty-six pages in his file. The third, despite his public role as a community advocate for

Haitian-Springfield integration, has his own documented collection of parking violations and traffic tickets. Eleven pages on him. There is so much here. How many Haitians came to Springfield again? One night halfway through this chapter, I pulled up Clark County Municipal Court's Case Search and Inquiry page, https://clarkcountymunicipalcourt.gov/web.nsf/casesearch?openform. There was a specific name I was looking for; I simply typed the French name "Jean" in the surname field and suddenly it's 4:27 a.m. local time after reading up on every Haitian in Springfield with a surname starting with "Jean" and their long and growing records of delinquency.

There's your impact.

By the way, it might intrigue you who I was looking for. Yet another such habitual offender goes by the name of Petuel Jean Jacques. There was a wreck, insistence the police not be called, refusal to show law enforcement identity documentation, then an actual fight with the arresting officer. Have yourself a gander:

The State of Ohio
SS:
Clark County

Court Case # CR-____________________

The Affiant, Officer T Melvin , being first sworn, says there is probable cause to believe the defendant, Petuel Jean Jacques , committed an offense based on the summary of facts below:

On 01/18/2025 at approx. 2243 hours I, Officer Melvin, was dispatched to on a report a a non injury accident. When I arrived I spoke with Jean Louis who advised that he was stopped at the red light on S. Spring St. at E. Main St. He advised a black BMW was approaching from behind him. The BMW quickly attempted to change lanes to go around his vehicle and when he did so the BMW struck Mr. Louis's vehicle.

Mr. Louis advised the BMW kept going so he followed it. The BMW pulled to the rear of St. and a black male exited the vehicle. Mr. Louis spoke to the male who asked him not to call the police. Mr. Louis advised the male then went into the back door.

I located the BMW to the rear of the residence. While doing so a female looked out the door. I asked her who was driving the vehicle. The female then went back inside and yelled upstairs. A male then came down. He was a hatiain male who appeared to understand little to no english. I asked the female if she spoke english she advised she did a little I advised her to ask him for his I.D. The male then went to the BMW and pulled out what appeared to be some type of I.D and a Social Security Card. I attempted to grab the information from the male.

When I did so the male pulled the two documents away from me and said no. I advised him to give me the information he again pulled away from me and said no. I then advised the male he was under arrested and put one cuff on his hand. At this time the male started pulling away from me and pushed me with one arm. I pulled the male from the vehicle and attempted to turn him around to finish handcuffing. The male turned towards me again pushing me. I then again tried to get the male around and on the ground. While doing so the male and I slipped on the ice and fell to the ground.

Once on the ground the male continued to fight with me pulling his hands and pushing me. I was able to get him to stop and to take him into custody. The male was found to be Petuel Jean Jacques. Mr. Jacques was arrested and booked into the Clark County Jail for Obstructing Official Business, Resisting Arrest, Marked Lane Violation, and Driving without a Valid Drivers License.

Defendant:
Petuel Jean Jacques

IN THE MUNICIPAL COURT OF CLARK COUNTY OHIO

2025 MAR 10 PM 4:48

MUNICIPAL COURT

BY__________DEPUTY

STATE OF OHIO	**CASE NO 25CRB0226**
v.	
Petuel Jean Jacques	**DISMISSAL ENTRY**

The Defendant was before the Court on this date for hearing on the charges of ______________
OOB and Resisting. Per prosecutor, language barrier likely culprit for the behavior.

Upon request of the Prosecutor, all charges against the Defendant are hereby dismissed.

The dismissal is without prejudice.

The dismissal is without costs.

3-10-2025

Civil Case

Judgments | Payments | Events | Accts Receivable | Interested Parties | Images

Case #:	2600366	**Assigned Judge:**	
Action Code:	H	**Signed Out?:**	
File Date:	01/23/2026	**Filing Amount:**	SEE COMPLAINT
Close Date:			
Status:			

Plaintiff:	JACQUES PETUEL JEAN
	---VS---
Defendant:	BMV DRIVERS MODIFICATION

Guess what happened? Dismissed without prejudice and without cost—the "language barrier" was held to blame.

IN THE MUNICIPAL COURT OF CLARK COUNTY OHIO

2025 MAR 10 PM 4:48

MUNICIPAL COURT

BY__________DEPUTY

STATE OF OHIO	**CASE NO 25CRB0226**
v.	
Petuel Jean Jacques	**DISMISSAL ENTRY**

The Defendant was before the Court on this date for hearing on the charges of ______________
OOB and Resisting. Per prosecutor, language barrier likely culprit for the behavior.

Upon request of the Prosecutor, all charges against the Defendant are hereby dismissed.

The dismissal is without prejudice.

The dismissal is without costs.

3-10-2025

Do you know who approved the dismissal? The signature looks familiar . . .

Now let me ask you something. If you or I get into a scuffle like that with a police officer, would our charges be all entirely dismissed? Or would you and I become Springfield's Alex Pretti?

"Clearly, there is NOT 'equal justice under the law' for Americans charged with the same or similar offenses," Glenda Bailey wrote to me via email. "The reason this is happening is so that Haitians will not have criminal convictions that could result in deportations."

No matter what, the Haitians must stay. They must stay in Springfield.

Among the various other reports presented to me by Glenda and the various Springfield OSINT citizens, I saw domestic violence. Credible allegations of stolen valor is one thing; quite another to me, as a father, is physical abuse. I read authentic police reports about knives brandished, faces slapped, smartphones destroyed. Women and children alike suffering bodily harm not to mention the mental turmoil and emotional suffering of it all. A Haitian couple who resided in an upscaled new housing development was charged with domestic violence and endangering children; both the mother's and father's charges were dismissed and the endangering-children charges were reduced to disorderly conduct (she received a $100 fine, he received a $150 fine). So easy to find this was, too.

But six months later, the father was charged again with domestic violence—which was also reduced to disorderly conduct. He was given six months probation and a suspended, less-than-a-month-long jail sentence (he served three days) and was released without bond.

What are we doing here.

That is not a question.

Springfield needs help.

"The One Big Win"

"So did you hear about the . . . illegal Haitian nightclub?" Glenda Bailey asked me.

"That's different from the brothel?" I asked, having to keep my after-dark activities around Springfield straight.

"Yeah, that's different," Glenda said as the day's ridealong passed the subject of the next leg of our conversational journey.

And so she told me the story. Remember Creations Market shop and its owner, Philomène Philostin? Creations is a company of companies, in a way. Creations Market Multi-Services, LLC, now on West Main Street, is presented as a grocery store that also offers money transfer, tax preparation, and other professional services, which Glenda told me amounted to "a one-stop-shop for all types of immigration services." But back when Creations used to be on North Limestone in the shopping center best known for O'Conners Irish Pub, the Creations address played host to "Saturday Overnight," an every-Saturday 9:30 p.m. to 3:00 a.m. night club experience with live Haitian and Haitian-American DJ performances and beer, wine, cocktails, hard liquor, and hookah, according to eyewitnesses. I was shown flyers and pictures of flyers dating to August and September 2025. Eyewitnesses reported to me hundreds of attendees to these events, and I saw at least one video showing quite a crowd gathering right at the door to Creations Market there on North Limestone, its prior location.[60]

Leave it to Glenda Bailey. Glenda via the @HaitianMajority account was one of the first to break the story, posting on August 31, 2025, a video taken inside the pop-up club with the caption, " . . . Illegal Haitian nightclub selling alcohol & no liquor license. '[Z] SPOT LOUNGE' menu of drinks & what ELSE are they selling? Sex? Drugs? Guns? Licensed as convenience store open until morning!"[61] Glenda posted another video that same evening showing black men in security uniforms and what appeared to be bulletproof vests.[62]

The so-called "Z Spot Lounge" was indeed located at the address of Creations Market. The two times I visited this former location of Creations, I saw a sign on the door confirming their new location on West Main that included the text in all-caps, "We offer the same services and more!" More on the move shortly.

Heritage citizens were unhappy with what they deemed naked flaunting of the law, which indeed continued, as posters kept going up, people kept showing up, and the club kept making money. Did someone call the police? Of course.

"[The owner] and I actually had a discussion with Allison [Elliott] out in front of City Hall after a meeting about that [night club]," Mark Sanders told me over the phone when Glenda called him during the ridealong to fill me in. " . . . and she said that we shouldn't be interfering. I said, 'Well, you can't interfere with somebody that's not doing anything.' I said, 'You guys need to start stepping up your game.'"

A letter dated September 5, 2025, signed by Director of Community Development Logan M. Cobbs, was posted to the Creations Market door in a photo I was shown. The letter directed the commercial space's occupants to "immediately cease all use of the building" until such time as "proper inspections and documentation necessary for the issuance of a Certificate of Occupancy. Until such time, the property must remain vacant. . . . Failure to comply may result in . . . criminal prosecution."

Was the Z Spot Lounge at the Creations Market address illegal? Indeed it was, to the very best of my knowledge. I was shown screenshots of the Ohio Liquor Control: Permit Lookup taken concurrently with these Saturday-night events. The Class and Issue Status were "C1" and "Pending." An Ohio C-1 liquor license authorizes retail stores to sell beer in original sealed containers for off-premises consumption (carry-out); it does not allow on-premise consumption.[63] But that's exactly what was happening, according to the videos shown, and to the eyewitnesses who went into Creations. I was also told by multiple Springfield residents who entered what still appeared to be Creations Market given the door and window signage that the place had been remade into a night club—and that beers and other alcoholic beverages were kept in ice chests before sale to customers and event attendees.

I looked up the permit myself and, sure enough, the permit application for Creations Market to sell beer retail was still pending as of May 1, 2026.[64] But get this—the date the permit requested? February 16, 2023.

I wanted to make sure I got this right, so I looked up a few other Ohio businesses with the Ohio Liquor Control search tool, including convenience stores, bars, restaurants, and other such businesses. That included O'Conners, for kicks. Sure enough, multiple permits per business applied for according to what they sold alcoholwise and when. I looked up additional permit classes such as D-2, D-3, and D-6 and noted that Creations Market would potentially have to have held other permits to do and sell all that had been witnessed and documented as having occurred there.[65] But again, only the C-1 license showed as pending. And no, you cannot sell and serve alcohol until the license is issued.

Got 'em, Glenda.

Or had she?

On September 6, Glenda on her account @MajorityHaitian published a screenshot from Facebook of that weekend's Haitian entertainment for Springfield, VagLavi Officiel, with a photo taken of the performer at an airport in Fort Lauderdale, Florida. Glenda wrote with the photo, " . . . Looks like the illegal Haitian nightclub in the [O'Conners] plaza is still planning on a big Haitian rave tonight, despite Bryan Heck telling the owner she must shut down the business... Haitians do whatever they want to do, regardless of the law."[66]

Glenda was pissed. The Facebook post tipped her off that there would still be a performance in town—but not if she could help it. That Saturday's event was indeed moved, and its new address was on South Yellow Springs Street. I inquired of Glenda details about this location, and she emailed me later and wrote:

> [T]here are two bays in this building. The bay to the north . . . was ONCE a hair salon. Glenn Williams bought the building and there is no longer a hair salon in the north bay. He has been renting it out as a "venue".
>
> A few years back, there was a shooting on the property when a supposed "celebration of life" was being held in the south bay . . . which is where the Haitian event was moved to.
>
> This property is used as a "pop up" rental venue and has been since before the shooting. That way, no liquor licenses are necessary and people can claim to rent it out for any number of purposes.

My quick fact-check confirmed the building ownership and the shooting.[67,68] Regarding liquor license necessity, according to the Ohio Investigative Unit:

> Non-liquor permit businesses may rent private event space to a person, and may allow that person or his invited guests to bring in alcoholic beverages provided:
>
> 1. The event is a private event and access is restricted to invited guests only,
> 2. The business does not charge a corking, cup, storage, or any additional other fees related to BYOB and the consumption of that alcohol, and
> 3. No alcohol is being sold (no cash bar, ticket sales, or cover charge at the door).
>
> Whether an illegal sales violation has occurred, or if and whether an event is considered to be open to the public or a private event, is determined on a case-by-case basis.[69]

I would later learn that eventgoers who showed up at Creations Market were driven, accompanied, or otherwise brought to the South Yellow Springs Street event venue. I'll tell you shortly who told me this—he was watching it all from his vantage point because it was convenient to do so. Given this plus what we know happened during typical Saturday-night events at Creations Market, it's not a stretch to presume "an illegal sales violation has occurred."

Glenda sent me the video she took out front at the South Yellow Springs Street event, dated to September 6, showing "the video I took of the people standing outside waiting to get in," she wrote in an email to me with details.

" . . . When I saw it, I was, 'Yes! I found it!'" Glenda said of September 6th when she'd sleuthed around town to find the quickly-moved event. She then spoke of the outcome. "There must have been fourteen, fifteen, police cars there shutting it [down] . . . helping people get out of there. Shut it right down, right in the middle of all of it. . . . The one big win we've had."

Jeff Skinner of *The Ohio Register* wrote up the entire Springfield Haitian night club saga, corroborating what others told and showed me. This was a big deal to people.

> [O]n Saturday, Sept 6 [2025], local residents coordinated a reporting operation of a local business, allegedly violating liquor laws as they attempted to host a Samedi party, flying in entertainment from outside the state to an all-night rager. The move comes after repeated media reports of the Haitian community being destitute and desperate for more financial aid from U.S. tax payers.
>
> . . . That evening, a coordinated effort was launched by residents who were driving throughout the area investigating the rave only to find out the location have been changed at the last minute to evade authorities from 2200 North Limestone Street to John & S. Yellow Springs St, however once this was reported, witnesses stated police cars surrounded that venue as well.[70]

That's exactly what happened; Glenda showed me the video herself.

I was also shown the Eventbrite for the "Harmonik Live Concert in Springfield Ohio," a Saturday night Haitian DJ experience, presented by The Hill Lounge.[71] I noticed the logos across the bottom of the Harmonik Live Concert flyer—event sponsors, I presume. And would you look at that, one of them is Milokan Botanica. That's Jacob Payen.

The Harmonik Live event was scheduled for September 13, 2025, originally, but was not to be at Creations Market. No, the address for this one is Park Road. It's the same address as CMS Caribbean Market, a grocery.[72,73]

Oh dear. Not again. But look—that event got bumped back two weeks.[74] It appears from Eventbrite that it was moved to The State Theater on South Fountain Avenue.[75] Well, that's something. But that same *Ohio Register* piece notes:

> Another local establishment labeled as "The Hill LLC" is another such nightclub allegedly operating out of a convenience store.[76]

An LLC, you say? I decided to look up "The Hill Lounge LLC" on Ohio's business directory and there it was, a company founded June 26, 2025.

Guess who registered the company.

Jacob Payen.

Its stated purpose is "Cultural and Intertainment events organizer." A June 21, 2025 article on The Hill Lounge website teases a July 4, 2025, opening night—on Park Road.[77] CMS Caribbean Market. Same address. The article promises "cocktails," "VIP squares with bottle service," "hookah rentals," and more.

Speaking of VIP, I was shown screenshots of Eventbrite for one Hill Lounge event's pricing—they ranged from $149.99 for VIP table access for two all the way up to $1,200 to a special-access VIP experience for six. I wonder where Springfield's Haitian migrants suffering from low wages and barely subsisting on welfare are getting that kind of money.

That said, did you notice a little bit of timeline suspicion? The Hill Lounge LLC didn't exist as a business for another five days when that article went live. Now, as far as I am aware, you can obtain a liquor license in Ohio without an LLC. So I went back to the Ohio Department of Commerce's searchable Liquor Control database.[78,79] I searched Permit Holder, Location Name, and Address, covering Jacob Payen, The Hill Lounge LLC, Payen's home address (it's public), CMS Caribbean Market, its owner, and her home address.

Recall that The Hill Lounge LLC and CMS Caribbean Market share an address on Park Road. As of this writing, CMS Caribbean Market has an active D-5 license for "Spirituous liquor for on premises consumption only, beer, wine and mixed beverages for on premises, or off premises in original sealed containers, until 2:30am"—but also as of this writing, there were and had not been any entries, even pending, for Jacob Payen or The Hill Lounge LLC.

CMS Caribbean Market, LLC, was amended to become CMS & Event Center, LLC on, of all days . . . September 5, 2025.[80]

It's getting complicated. But not really.

> The [September 6, 2025, night club shutdown] is getting lauded as a victory by residents as the heritage population, which has gone ignored and blighted for several years from the ruling political establishment, has won this battle against what many view as an invading force that has overtaken the city. Whatever the case, Springfield residents have shown others that enacting change is possible but only with significant effort and force, something these residents apparently hold in spades.[81]

In May 2026, I dropped by CMS Caribbean Market to see what I could see. Crestfallen, I was. Because right on the door, a yellow sign—"NO OCCUPANCY

IS PERMITTED." Dashed and heartsunken. I had arrived early that Saturday in hopes of smoking hookah, playing cash slots, and drinking cocktails in the VIP lounge with Jacob Payen.

I looked up the ordinance mentioned as "pursuant" on the no-occupancy sign. "Approval required to occupy" involves the City "certifying that the use of the building or structure and the premises upon which the building or structure is situated is in compliance . . . The building owner shall only use the structure in compliance with the certificate of use and occupancy and any stated conditions therein. The structure and all approved building service equipment shall be maintained in accordance with the approval."[82]

If you come to Springfield late some Saturday night and find yourself with time to kill, you just might try browsing the strip malls and empty salons in town, and you just might find where the pop-up night club has moved next.

As for me, I wanted to speak with **Terry Reed**, owner of O'Conners Irish Pub and quite obviously a first-party eyewitness to all of this when Creations Market operated out of his same shopping center. So I did.

"We have videos of them loading up their white truck back here for the slot machines," he said when we met in person at the back of O'Conners. "[Y]ou can't have slot machines. They were doing slots for cash, which is illegal."

True cash-paying slot machines—or video lottery terminals that function like slots—are only legal at Ohio's four stand-alone casinos (Cleveland, Cincinnati, Columbus, and Toledo) and seven racinos. Creations Market doesn't appear to have made the list.

"If any device is paying out cash and it's not at an authorized casino or racino in Ohio, then they are doing so in violation of the law," said Andromeda Morrison, Director of Skill Games, Ohio Casino Control Commission, to News 5 Cleveland, an ABC affiliate, in the context of an investigation into illegal cash payouts at strip-mall gaming storefronts in Medina, Akron and Mentor-on-the-Lake, all in Ohio, in 2021.[83]

"They had a hair salon, which you have to have certain license [for] because of the draining of the hair. They had that. That got shut down, too," Terry told me.

I looked up Creations Market on Ohio's Professional Licensure website. "Your search return 0 records." Interesting. Not really.

Terry then showed me a picture of a sign on the door of the space in his same shopping center when it had been Creations Market. It indeed advertised "Lightening Cream," "Soap," "Gel," "And More." The sign had a pink, white, and yellow-paletted brand name, logo, and posterly layout. It was called Lolo Beauty Supply; this company advertised itself as providing those salonlike services. Ohio's

Professional Licensure site turned up no results for me for Lolo Beauty Supply. I also looked the brand up in Ohio's business directory and found no company named Lolo linked to Springfield or to Creations Market or its founders.

Let's let Terry take it from here.

> [F]or a couple of years, it was just a grocery store. That's also where they would go get their tax information, ID stuff, and all that. They had that on their door . . . "[T]his is where you come to get legal advice" and all that. But then after the store, all of a sudden during that time, that's when they had the . . . hair salon, which . . . got shut down, and then they . . . tore everything out and it became a disco club night, which the landlord had no clue on . . .
>
> [There were] a lot of people showing up. A lot of cars, which . . . would take away from my business.
>
> [Creations had] no license, and they just operated. I remember the police being down there one time. Told them to close. They did. Cops left. They opened it right back up . . . [T]hey even had hookahs in there with no license.
>
> . . . [W]e called the police . . . "They're out here partying." They even had a guy looking like he was an officer standing at the door, and he wasn't. And they would have fights out there. It just—it got bad, but they weren't legal . . . I've got to pay [for] licenses. I've got to pay taxes. I've got to do all this just to stay operational. And they were just doing it, and no one seemed to care. The city wouldn't do anything . . . Like I said, the police showed up, but then they just still did it. I don't get it.

I then asked Terry a very important question. How long was it from the first infractions he noticed until something was done? Basically, how long was it that things were happening that things weren't supposed to be happening? Let's see.

> [T]hey were doing other things . . . the hookah, the salon . . . I'm gonna say a year, but that's just a guess . . . Prior to that [first call to police], that stuff was going on, but we just didn't bother with it because we still thought it was a grocery store . . . [O]ther people should have known. The health department should have known . . . So when we went in there, they had

no—they just had everything on the counter, and they had coolers, just regular Walmart coolers [for] getting your beer.

. . . I have [four] licenses . . . I have one to . . . serve until midnight. Then I had to get one just to serve an extra hour . . . I do not have a . . . Sunday night liquor [license]. That's the only one I don't have. I can sell beer on Sunday, but I'm not open, but I can't sell liquor on Sunday, but you have to have a license.

. . . When [Creations Market] moved out of here, they had a sign on the door—and there is still a sign on that door where their location is . . . [T] hey taped it. [I]t was an old barbershop or something, and they had their gig and DJs and everything out there until it got shut down again. But they would drive people [who were sitting here] waiting because people showed up. They would drive them there to show them where it was at.

That together with Glenda Bailey and *The Ohio Register* caps the story. But Terry wasn't done yet and neither was I. His full remarks would be incomplete without a set of anecdotes I've heard from just about everyone else in this city.

. . . We were all sitting out on the patio. [A Haitian] hit the light post out there . . . got out of the car, picked up the light . . . took it off [of his car], laid it on the ground, got back in his car, and just drove off . . . No one cared. They just give 'em the license and let 'em drive.

. . . The cat and dog thing? I . . . didn't know [about] or see anything [like that] . . . [W]hether you like Trump or not, he said [dogs] specifically because if he said ducks, no one would care. But because he said cat and dogs, people freaked out . . . and they went and investigated. "See? Nothing." But they made them go investigate to put a spotlight on it, and that was his reasoning [in] doing that. Ducks, though, on the other hand, yeah, there's some missing ducks . . . I don't know what kind of [ducks], I just know Reid Park used to have [ducks]. They don't have a lot of ducks [anymore].

. . . [W]alk into WalMart. Just stand there at the entrance and just watch. [Haitians] will come in, and they will pay in cash. Loads of groceries in their shopping carts. My dad has gone there and can't believe all the stuff they're buying . . . They're buying so much stuff, and they're paying

(continued . . .)

> [cash for] it . . . How are they doing this? They're getting money from the government, and the government doesn't care, because they're getting whatever . . . kickback on it . . . I hate to say it's either Republican or Democrat. I think they're trying to get voters in here . . . Give 'em money, they'll vote for your way. So whoever's bringing them in, they'll become [their] vote. That's just my opinion.

Terry, Setys, Diana, Walter—so many heritage citizens and longtime residents told me of the bewilderingly full shopping carts to be witnessed among the Haitians at the grocery. So finally, the first weekend of the month of May 2026, I took them up on their challenge. I'd heard that by this point in the city's saga, Haitians kept to themselves out in public during the day, and I'd hadn't noticed but a few couples and solos at the Kroger off North Bechtle when I'd dropped by at various hours of the day and night during the week.

But welfare and public assistance go out when every month? Exactly. So I thought I'd see what could be seen at the start of the month. I'd planned to hit the Walmart on North Bechtle a Saturday morning near daybreak but extended play with my children (family first!) delayed that into a lunchtime visit. I figured I'd already missed the show and halfcided to abandon my plan. But why not, let's go. You never know. I didn't, so I did.

I walked into Walmart, past the security theatre, and proceeded to embody the wide-eyed overwhelm of Willem Dafoe in *At Eternity's Gate* (2018) for the next fifteen minutes as I paced about the store. Haitians everywhere, carts filled up past the top, meats and fish and fresh-cooked gourmet and more fucking plantains than you have ever seen in your life. A group of seven squabbled and haggled in loud Creole by great boxes of plantains stacked five-high in produce. I snapped a quick discreet pick because I wasn't sure even I would believe my own memory the next day.

Elsewhere, young adult males and their female partners, impeccably street-dressed and well-groomed and elite-cologned, if I do say so myself (and I do), stood proud in line after line after line. A few of the men wore sunglasses inside. I saw no children. There were a few older individuals, dressed their Saturday best, also presenting Springfield's bounty in overfilled carts.

I also saw in just about every other line and aisle, an obviously working-class Springfielder. Older. Much older. And dare I say (I do) poorer. A limp. Smoker's cough. Sweat pants and roughly-used tennies. Two, three, six items tops. Cheap chicken. Some Pepsi. Toilet paper.

Terminally online that I am, I muttered to myself aloud Han Solo's great admission in *Star Wars: The Force Awakens* (2015):

"It's true . . . all of it."[84]

I wrote up my experience of the day on social media. Walter Curt quote-shared and wrote, "Everyday at Springfield Walmart this is the case. I am convinced it's why Walmart started offering discounted home delivery in the area. They didn't want you to see foreigners with overflowing grocery carts paid for by your tax dollars."[85]

On Facebook, former Clark County Sheriff Deb Burchett commented, as she had also been at that same Walmart that same weekend. She wrote:

> I was at Walmart today and there [were] [Haitians] in the check out line. They had 3 carts stack[ed] to the top. Now I don't care where they allegedly work. There is absolutely no way they are . . . making that much money for 3 carts of groceries.[86]

A long-time resident who I met with in person a number of times, calling herself Brinkley Lehmkuhl, also commented:

> I hope you noticed the carts belonging to Senior Citizens on Social Security—you know—the 'legacy citizens' who kept this town going for decades despite everything.[87]

The great irony came to me—the parable of the prodigal son found in the Gospels in the New Testament, Luke 15, specifically. The younger brother of the tale, taken in by rumors of wealth and women and worldly ways, persuades his landowning father to bequeath his inheritance early. He gets it, then proceeds to blow it all, fall in with and into the pigs, then crawl home . . . only to be celebrated by his father who had feared his runaway son dead. Cue pomp and glee and great expense. The man's older son, however, always having been faithful to the family estate, is overcome with envy. Why must irresponsibility be rewarded, celebrated, incentivized? How is it that the one who showed back up from out of nowhere is entitled to the very best of the land while the harder-working and loyal are cast aside and forgotten?

Another recurring anecdote relayed to me by heritage citizens—which I did not see personally but heard enough times to subside all skepticism—is that Haitians would open up food and drink products, from peanut butter to milk and orange juice, consume a portion right there in the aisle at the store, close it up, and put it back on the shelf without paying. There's that third-world gaze again.

A question occurred to me in Walmart that day as I witnessed a visibly athletic Haitian man argue with a white female senior cashier, he in Creole and she forcing an awkward smile back at him.

Are the Haitians eating Springfield and Springfield is paying for it?

What compounded insults within many citizens' injury, so to speak, are the strictly enforced double standards. Back to Terry Reed now, consider how O'Conners ownership and staff had been treated during the COVID-19 lockdown period in March 2020 and after. The City showed up with two armed police sergeants with the threat of arrest, Terry told me. Meanwhile, it felt like "the city wouldn't do anything" about the illegal Haitian-run operation just a few doors down. "I don't get it."

I think I do.

CHAPTER 14

SCHRÖDINGER'S HAITIANS

> "Let's get on to Schrödinger's Cat . . . [This quantum physics thought experiment is] from an era where people spoke lightly of doing bad things to cats . . . They could have been dogs . . . But cats are loveable and will fit in a box . . . You put a cat in a box, and if the cat is a quantum cat with two states, two states of existence, it's either dead or alive. While it's in the box, you have no idea which it is. And so the way we describe this in quantum physics, if you do the experiments, some percentage of the time you open the box, the cat will be alive; others, the cat will be dead . . . [T]he cat's existence is a superposition of being dead and being alive . . . [Because] it's in the box, and you're not looking at it."[1]
>
> —Neil deGrasse Tyson

Five days before the Springfield story broke to the rest of the world, PBS correspondent and host William Brangham teased, via Instagram, his next story, teeing it up with a quote from McGregor Metals CEO Jamie McGregor:

> "I think in general, the Haitians who come to Springfield are here to work." Jamie McGregor . . . is the CEO of McGregor Metals, which makes welded parts for industries like autos and farming. McGregor has hired roughly 30 Haitians since they started arriving in town in large numbers a few years ago, and they now account for about 10% of his workforce. "I wish I had 30 more," he says. "They're here to improve their life. They're not here to cause trouble, either in the workplace or in our community . . . They don't have a drug problem. They'll stay at their machines. They'll achieve their numbers. . . . And so in general, that's a stark difference from what we're used to in our community and what we've been seeing in the people that we employ." One of those employees—Anderson . . . says he's grateful for work that helps him support his family in Springfield. Anderson,

> like thousands of his fellow countrymen, fled his home nation when violence and chaos spread. Haiti's President, Jovenel Moise, was assassinated in 2021, and things have only spiraled downward since. The Haitian residents are here legally, for now, under the Federal "Temporary Protected Status" program.[2]

Drug abstinence, workplace productivity, successful quota—"a stark difference from what we're used to in our community and what we've been seeing in the people that we employ."

What people is that, William? What people?

In April 2023, the *Springfield News-Sun* reported that "Springfield and Clark County first responders and health agencies are seeing an increase in drug overdoses and the need for increased doses of Narcan to save those people."[3] Local government seems to have taken this seriously, forming the Clark County Substance Abuse, Treatment, and Support Task Force.[4,5]

It's not just Springfield, however; thirteen of the top sixty U.S. cities for opioid death rates have been in Ohio.[6] Springfield appears on the list, but my Dayton and JD Vance's Middletown are higher on the list, both in the top fifteen.[7] Drug abuse has long been a problem statewide; with his implications, Jamie McGregor is not wrong. But the root issue is not due to demographics but logistics. According to Ohio Northern University's Institute for Civics and Public Policy:

> Opioids are trafficked into Ohio at excessively high rates, much higher than most of the country. In 2017, Montgomery County, containing the city of Dayton, became the 'overdose capital' of the United States, as Dayton became one of the major distribution centers in Ohio. This city would funnel opioids all over Ohio, but southern cities were affected the worst.
>
> Ohio is also home to many "pill-mills," places where high potency opioids are produced and distributed.
>
> . . . Poverty and economic situations, including rate of economic opportunity and unemployment, also factor into the rate of opioid use in the state. Many of Ohio's small-town communities and rural areas have struggled with economic growth coupled with rising poverty.
>
> The opioid crisis in Ohio has had disastrous consequences on surrounding states and the country more generally. Ohio is one of the most interconnected states along the US Interstate Highway System. Major cities in Ohio have become economical centers for the country due to their

> diversity, location, and convenience. These same factors have made Ohio a hub for opioid trafficking. The ease of access to surrounding states from Ohio can increase the amount of opioids transported between states, and this can have dire effects for many people around the United States.[8]

And so we return to the two Springfields on one screen. In one movie, community and business leaders like McGregor are justified in admittedly preferring Haitian newcomers to the addled heritage citizenry. *I wish I had thirty more.* Amid the U.S. congressional debates over Haitians' Temporary Protected Status in April 2026, Nebraska US Representative Don Bacon, a Republican, published on 𝕏 what we can take to be a summary of that side's movie:

> Removing TPS status for Haitians living in the United States would cost 350,000 workers their ability to work at a time when we're already facing serious workforce shortages. I've heard from healthcare providers and business leaders across Nebraska, including @OmahaChamber, who are concerned about the impact this would have on patient care and our economy. I don't see the goodness of deporting people who are here legally, working, and contributing to our country.[9]

Other Republicans like U.S. Representative Brandon Gill of Texas have been watching the other movie:

> 65% of Haitian non-citizen households are on welfare.
>
> They are draining our resources, making America weaker and poorer.
>
> It is absolutely idiotic to give them backdoor amnesty by extending TPS.[10]

As an aside, an American Enterprise Institute editorial took issue with the logic behind preferential employment offered to immigrants over native-borns:

> What [Ross] McGregor is alluding to is the alleged lack of similar work ethics among young white men . . . [T]his was the same rationale for why immigrant employment in chicken-processing plants was necessary, it was claimed, because native-born workers found those jobs unacceptable. He pointed to the dynamics at Crider, Inc., a chicken-processing plant in Georgia that lost 75 percent of its workforce when raided by immigration agents. Shortly afterwards, Crider placed an ad in the local newspaper

> announcing job openings at higher wages sufficient to attract native-born workers.
>
> More generally, studies consistently find that immigration lowers wages in occupations that hire low-wage workers.[11]

Back to Gill's post now, which included an image from CIS.org with combined 2023 to 2025 data showing exactly what Rep. Gill described—the 65 percent of Haitian households on welfare.[12] By the way, it's probably to no one's surprise that Afghanistanis rank highest for non-citizen head-of-household welfare consumption in America, at 87 percent. But do you know number two?

The Dominican Republic. Speaking of Dominicans . . .

> According to CID Gallup's latest survey conducted in May 2025, 64% of Dominicans say they are very concerned about the situation in Haiti.
>
> And with rising Haitian migration, 92% believe the Dominican Republic should not accept more refugees.[13]

There's more. Or put another way, less. Almost nine in ten Dominicans—88.3 percent—favor the government *increasing* deportations of Haitians from the Republic.[14]

The existence of such polls entered my thoughts as I gave spontaneous interviews to various local and international newsbreakers and truthshakers on the streets of Springfield back in 2024. Repeatedly, I was asked what my opinion was of the Haitians and what ought be done with them. Repeatedly, I refused to answer; what may have sounded like deflection was reassignment of responsibility. *Why don't you ask the people of Clark County what they want?* I asked the Grok AI about it, and it said:

> No scientific or professional polls (e.g., from Gallup, university researchers, or major firms) on Clark County or Springfield, Ohio, residents' opinions specifically about Haitian immigrants appear to exist as of April 2026. Local media and community efforts have gathered some resident feedback through informal or broad surveys. Here's what's available . . .

Then Grok sent me to a February 2026 *Springfield News-Sun* article, which begins:

> Springfield is a community divided.

> Among the hundreds of responses from Springfield area residents to a Springfield News-Sun/Dayton Daily News online survey about the end of Temporary Protected Status for Haitians, there was a sharp divide.
>
> Slightly more than half felt the end of TPS would be bad for the city. They expressed concern for the Haitian community, saying TPS should be extended and expressed profound fear of what could happen if Immigration and Customs Enforcement rolls into town on a mass deportation campaign.[15]

The second result was the Springfield 2051 Community Survey Broad community visioning effort (for the city's 250th anniversary in 2051), mentioned earlier, with more than 1,500 responses plus focus groups.[16]

> "People are not nearly as negative as we thought," [Marta Wojcik, a committee member with Springfield 2051] said. "When you probe and ask more questions, there is really so much positive."
>
> It's just a few loud voices that affect the whole city, she said.
>
> "It's amazing how much actually unites us," Rose said. "There's the pressure of the larger political discourse in America, but when we're talking about where we want our communities to go, there's a lot of harmony in that."[17]

Is it "just a few loud voices"? What do the Dominicans believe about Haitians that Springfield citizens don't? Or rather, maybe they do? Maybe we should find out. Maybe *I* should find out. With a scientific, professional poll—not an informal survey whose full results and methodology went suspiciously unpublished.

Prior to beginning *Haitians of Springfield*, I wrapped up *Burn It Down: What the Polls Say Young Americans Really Want* (Bombardier Books, 2026) with co-author Rich Baris, director of Big Data Poll. In case you don't know Rich:

> He is the only national and state pollster to correctly forecast Donald J. Trump would win the 2016 presidential election with 306 Electoral Votes and was recognized again as the most accurate national pollster of 2024, with his state polling again projecting a victory for the returning president with 312 Electoral Votes. He has been widely cited as the leading independent pollster in the Trump Era to identify key demographic trends and cutting edge methodologies to improve industry standards and performance.[18]

What do you think I did?

Yes. I talked to Rich about *this* book, then subsequently commissioned his company Big Data Poll to run the **first** scientific and professional poll on Clark County and Springfield, Ohio, residents' opinions specifically about Haitian immigrants.

As work-life balance is not a thing for me, I wrote much of this manuscript (and *Burn It Down*) while my children were asleep in their beds. But one Saturday afternoon, the day before Chapter 12's Easter Sunday as a matter of fact, I was at the local tutoring center my son attended playing with my daughters in the lobby. There was a woman of what appeared to be grandmotherly age also there, sitting and staring at her phone during the various children's lessons inside. Not unusual.

Then Rich Baris called me to discuss what questions I wanted to make sure the people of Springfield were asked. This situation was not a secure area, but given my kids, I couldn't exactly go anywhere, so I was a bit coy with Rich over the phone, referring to "them" and "the people" and "those who are not from the city" and so forth.

Have you ever tried to read a *Toy Story* board book, play *Bluey* make-believe, color with crayons, and provide all manner of snacks and refreshments to two toddlers while holding a very important business meeting for forty minutes without placing yourself on mute at any point? And they say women are the multi-taskers.

It was the end of the call and Rich got what he needed when I had to let him go anyway; now we were chasing each other around the tutoring center, about to begin playing a carbohydrated toddlers' version of *tag* called *slam-your-sibling-into-the-wall*, which I would rather let's not.

A split-second before Rich hung up, my gaze fell to the smartphoned grandmother's purse. There was a lanyard, stretching out of and onto the floor.

Springfield City Schools.

"Excuse me, ma'am," I said, sliding my phone away. "You wouldn't happen to work at Springfield City Schools?"

She told me her name was [redacted] and that she taught [redacted] at [redacted] and [redacted] Schools. I looked her employment records up later and confirmed this was indeed the case.

"How do you like the city?" I asked.

"Oh, I love it. Born and raised in Springfield."

"OK, yeah," I said. Let's go. "I've heard over here that there are a lot of, like, various people from other parts of the world that are in Springfield. How has that been for you?"

"It's wonderful." [redacted] laughed.

"Oh, yeah?

"I have a lot of Haitian students and different—all different groups in [redacted], especially. It's very diverse. It's really nice."

"Oh, yeah? What's nice about it?"

"Everything," she said. "I just love my students. They just are so fun."

She added that in her own neighborhood near [redacted], she lived around all manner of diverse communities.

"I really enjoy them as neighbors," she said of the non-whites, "I enjoy the diversity. We have good, good people."

"OK. Never had any bad experiences?"

"No," [redacted] said. "I've grown up there all my life, and I chose to go back and live [in Springfield]."

She described the nature of her work at Springfield City Schools and her love for the children of diverse backgrounds. I noticed that in the span of two sentences, she used the word "diversity" three times more on top of all the previous. A liberal's tic?

[redacted] has up to seven languages," she volunteered. "We're just a [redacted]."

"Oh, wow. What are those languages?"

"There's Creole. Haitian Creole. There's French. There's Spanish. And then there's another one . . . Portuguese from Brazil."

"Interesting," I said. "And is that pretty recent? All the different languages?"

"I would say yes," [redacted] said. "When the Haitian population came to Springfield, it's increased. Our students really get along." Various toddlish squealing pulled me out of the conversation for a moment, but then she added, "I don't have to use translators anymore. You used to have to, but the culture has changed."

"The culture?" I echoed. "Has changed?"

She explained that her Haitian students have learned, understand, and now speak and write English "very well." She spoke of having a translator in class with her, but now that's no longer a thing.

Then racism entered the chat.

[redacted] described negative sentiment towards the Haitians as "political" and denied any consumption of cats and dogs, which I hadn't even brought up. Of the heritage citizens, she said they're "accusing" Haitians of doing things "that they're not doing."

"Ignorant behavior. So bad. So bad," she said twice. "We just don't have those issues. And they made it up to make it seem like we do. But we don't."

"To your knowledge, there's no problem with the Haitians at all?" I asked.

"No."

"And there never has been?"

"No." Then a long pause. There's always a long pause. "The only thing I know is they're price-gouging people. I know that," she said, shortly thereafter adding that Springfield's rents have gone up "triple."

I thought there's no problem and there never has been.

[redacted] continued.

"What I was told was that some of them have to share houses and share rooms and that some of the landlords were charging up to five hundred dollars a person—in the same house!"

"You don't blame the Haitians for that though." I offered her my clarification.

"No, no, no. That's not something that they can control . . . It's sad . . . They're taking advantage of them."

Look in the Box

The Haitians of Springfield are a superposition of being positive and negative for the city. Environments like churches and schools, these, we can reasonably assume, select for certain behaviors of all who participate, heritage and Haitian alike. So, too, would be traffic accidents, lines for welfare help, court cases, and so forth, for a different sort. You don't know if Haitians are a net benefit or detriment to Clark County until you look in the box.

"If you don't believe us, just come here," Setys Kelly said to me of hypothetical skeptics and doubters. "Just come here and see it all for yourself."

So that's what I did in writing this book. And I've been left wondering why there remains an explicit and persistent denial of one of the two states of Haitian potentiality. The heritage OSINTs I spoke with acknowledged both states—most of the time, a net-negative cost to Springfield, they told me, but also, very real positives. Only one side—the pro-Haitians—consistently spoke in absolutes. Like this educator that day. Which is more credible?

The pro-Haitians are not, in my estimation, to use the correct term, quantum-mechnically accurate in their estimation of the situation. *There's no problem, and there never has been . . .* followed by admissions of tripled rent and Haitian overcrowding, neither of which they can be held accountable for, of course. Not a serious viewpoint.

Suppose that any negative outcomes tied to Haitian presence in Springfield . . . suppose they haven't happened to you or to anyone you know. Then we must assume everyone in Springfield of the generally anti-Haitian sentiment is willfully deceiving others, myself included, on all these things. Expand the search now. Is no one in America being harmed by Haitian presence? Is it all just underemployed, drug-addicted white Americans doing a racism?

Chip Roy, Texas attorney general candidate as of this writing, wrote of the black Floridian woman murdered, on video, by a Haitian assailant with a hammer and questionable immigration status:[19]

> I've heard my colleagues talk about Haitians fleeing danger.
>
> You know who else was fleeing danger?
>
> An innocent mom in FL just last week, who was bludgeoned to death with a hammer outside of a store by a Haitian national released into the country by the Biden Admin. Enough.[20]

Is everyone, everywhere, all at once, lying about Haitian harm? Is it all dismissible due to "ignorant behavior"? *Joshua, you don't understand,* I already hear a voice say from off the page, *Not literally every Haitian in America is hurting people. Most just want a better life here.*

Excellent. Does that unmurder that mother? Would telling her surviving, grieving family that it's not all Haitians who are doing irreparable harm help them press on? Not 100 percent of Haitians are guilty of murdering Americans, true. And yet the man committing murder on video is 100 percent Haitian.

I watched the uncensored video, by the way.[21] Some would say that watching a Haitian man smash, crack, and otherwise slash a woman's face and skull with a hammer, to watch his victim lay there and die like that, would bias me against Haitians on the whole. Never mind that it's video evidence of it having literally happened. But turn this concern inside-out to find another claim my likely critics will be silently making—that *not* watching that one murderous Haitian on video will help maintain any bias we may have *for* Haitians.

Elon Musk commented on the murder:

> The Biden administration actively flew illegals into America with no vetting of their violent criminal past into America and paid for their flights via NGOs.
>
> This is a war crime. [Biden Secretary of Homeland Security Alejandro] Mayorkas and his buddies orchestrated this and should be on trial for their diabolical deeds.[22]

In both movies of the Haitians of Springfield, there appears another group held responsible for excesses, extracurriculars, and extreme outcomes, be that tripled rent or cracked craniums—the ones who enabled it all in the first place. "The tiger that rips men open is following his nature; the real criminal is the man who unmuzzles him and launches him on society," wrote Joseph de Maistre.[23]

Anyway.

The heritage citizens may not always be right, but they are not completely wrong. I've seen enough to confirm in my own rational mind that the pro-Haitian side *is* completely wrong because of their stated view—that nothing negative resulting in understandable anti-Haitian states of sentiment has occurred, when available qualitative and quantitative evidence both confirm that it very much is.

But why? Why must pro-Haitians insist on the complete and total absence of direct consequences? And even if there are such consequences—like Springfield City Schools and their highly non-white next generations of students with their seven languages—then these consequences are a good thing, actually?

Henderson, Hitchens, Haidt, and Rue

Why would born-and-raised heritage citizens like [redacted] [redacted] hold to an opinion like this? Could Rob Henderson's Luxury Beliefs model sufficiently explain? On Luxury Beliefs:

> [At Yale], I developed the concept of "luxury beliefs," which are ideas and opinions that confer status on the upper class at very little cost, while often inflicting costs on the lower classes.
>
> . . . Later, I would connect my observations to stories I read about tech tycoons, another affluent group, who encourage people to use addictive devices while simultaneously enforcing rigid rules at home about technology use. . . . Many affluent people now promote lifestyles that are harmful to the less fortunate. Meanwhile, they are not only insulated from the fallout; they often profit from it.
>
> . . . White privilege is the luxury belief that took me the longest to understand, because I grew up around a lot of poor white people. Affluent white college graduates seem to be the most enthusiastic about the idea of white privilege, yet they are the least likely to incur any costs for promoting that belief. Rather, they raise their social standing by talking about their privilege. When policies are implemented to combat white privilege, it won't be Yale graduates who are harmed. Poor white people will bear the brunt.[24]

Another telltale insight may hail from a certain Peter Hitchens reflection on 1960s-era Left-wing revolutionary fervor among the white-privileged upper class:

> When I was a Revolutionary Marxist, we were all in favour of as much immigration as possible.
>
> It wasn't because we liked immigrants, but because we didn't like Britain. We saw immigrants—from anywhere—as allies against the staid, settled, conservative society that our country still was at the end of the Sixties.
>
> Also, we liked to feel oh, so superior to the bewildered people—usually in the poorest parts of Britain—who found their neighbourhoods suddenly transformed into supposedly 'vibrant communities.'
>
> If they dared to express the mildest objections, we called them bigots.
>
> Revolutionary students didn't come from such 'vibrant' areas (we came, as far as I could tell, mostly from Surrey and the nicer parts of London).
>
> We might live in 'vibrant' places for a few (usually squalid) years, amid unmown lawns and overflowing dustbins.[25]

Thus, disputes over the Haitians of Springfield seem to be a conflict of the privileged educated—and the educators—against "poor white people" who are not "insulted from the fallout" of the former's Luxury Beliefs. Doesn't it seem that way to you?

By the way, have you seen Dr. Jonathan Haidt's now-viral morality heatmap meme?[26] His findings go like so: Conservatives assign "highest moral allocation," that is moral care, attention, and value, to those closest to them, beginning with immediate family, then extended family, then closest friends, then outwards. Liberals conversely place highest moral priority on those *farthest* from them relationally—to "all things in the universe," then "all natural things" including rocks (yes, actually rocks), then all animal life . . . and eventually, way, way down . . . to your own immediate family, with the lowest moral allocation you assign them (and that explains veganism).

Understand the extreme result: Liberals expressed the *lowest* moral concern for immediate family—a complete reversal of the ordered conservative moral value rating system. Here's another way to put that, from Haidt's research: "[L]iberals, relative to conservatives, express greater moral concern toward friends relative to family, and the world relative to the nation."[27] Along these lines, we then reason that Springfield liberals assign higher moral allocation to a version of humanity that includes the people of Haiti (and beyond), whereas Springfield's conservatives assign that allocation according to a common patriotic expression around Republican America—"God, family, country."

Let's hear the liberal perspective applied, like a filter, to the Springfield saga to see if we can't learn something new. Then-City Commissioner Rob Rue joined the Global Education Peace Network Juneteenth Celebration for Juneteenth 2020, hosted by Carl Ruby on Zoom. Take it away, Rob:

> [A]s a community leader and as a . . . citizen . . . in Springfield, I feel like the [death] of George Floyd has been an awakening . . . What I've decided is and what's been on my heart is that there are defaults inside my white body that cannot be tolerated anymore . . . Defaults meaning there's just things in there that may not be, that I would not overtly act on but I would maybe tolerate. And I have just come to the point where I can no longer tolerate those. So nevertheless, I have decided to not stand on the sidelines with my voice and not be passive and . . . speak out . . . specifically to white people and not with a condemning voice but a voice of empathy that says it is time that white people who don't understand need to understand, white people that don't empathize need to empathize.[28]

Empathy. More like Rob Rue's empathy props, the Haitians. If you've ever spoken at length with Americans who identify as liberal in any way ideologically, you'll no doubt hear them bring up this favorite self-proclaimed trait in their unique possession. But do liberals actually have empathy for those their own held morality insists they value more?

Consider the example of Diana Daniels versus Central Christian's *Love Others*. Just because one may share the same faith, does that mean we are of the same citizenship as well? Perhaps when the apostle Paul wrote to the early church, "There is neither Jew nor Gentile, neither slave nor free, nor is there male and female, for you are all one in Christ Jesus," he was talking about . . . a thousand fox?[29]

I think that when we try to make the Bible more than it is, it actually damages people's faith.

If one truly loves others, with those others being Haitian migrants, then perhaps a solution is the one Diana presented to her neighbors—render to Caesar what is Caesar's, assist in their safe return to their country of origin to reunite with family, then sponsor a legal and permanent return if or when the time is right. If we're going to get and stay biblical, Jesus himself left the country for a time before only returning with family later when conflict had subsided. [30]

Yet citizens like Diana are condemned as racist.[31] Why is she labeled so? Because she is white, obviously. She, like many working-class citizens expressing confirmed-credible concerns about a drastically altered city, is judged not by the content of her character but by the color of her skin.

To the best of my knowledge on the matter of the Haitians of Springfield—and I've collected more from all sides than most if not all who've come before to investigate—the only hoax in Springfield is that its story of sudden transformation and harmful impact itself is a hoax.

Speaking of which, "America is a providential people with a distinct heritage and shared history," wrote Charlie Kirk nine days before his assassination. "We cannot be replaced and remain the same, even if by Christians."[32]

It's been debunked. It's all been debunked.

You sound like my mother. You are the Evangelical who believes that everything has to be literal for it to be true. You are the one who looks at the Ordovician coral fossil, reads the story of Noah in Genesis, and tells me this tiny creature was killed by a global flood in divine judgment because the Bible is inerrant and who are you going to believe, the Word of God, or the fallible words of atheist scientists pushing the evolutionary agenda just because they want to have gay sex guilt-free? My, that escalated quickly.

I met many in Springfield who shared Trump's pet-eating claim yet did not take it literally, not then in September 2024, and still not now. They did speak of a symbology to it all—all the way up to the Oval Office.

"The American media totally ignored this stuff until Donald Trump and I started talking about cat memes. If I have to create stories so that the American media actually pays attention to the suffering of the American people, then that's what I'm going to do," Vance said to CNN, posting on social media also, "If you're a reporter, or an activist, who didn't give a shit about these suffering Americans until yesterday, I have some advice: Spare your outrage for your fellow citizens suffering under Kamala Harris's policies. Be outraged at yourself for letting this happen."[33,34]

The overwhelming majority of heritage citizens didn't know or care, in my estimation, about reports of cats or ducks or what have you. They wanted to talk about single mothers losing housing, reports of Haitians getting off after wrecks without so much as a ticket despite no insurance or driver's license, lines wrapped around social services buildings, and on and on and on. That is the real story here, and their own side—state and local Republicans—they feel, has ignored every point of the full plot.

To those who would scoff and mock the heritage citizenry of Springfield from far, far away, I say: Let he who is without racism cast the first invitation to import thousands of Haitians to his neighborhood, too.

As revelatory as all this is, that still doesn't explain why the more liberal residents I spoke with, [redacted] included, insisted everything is fine—good, even, with regard to having more immigrants, more Haitians. "Diversity is always good: Diversity of thinking, diversity of culture, diversity, you name it," George Ten said. "I think it makes the outcome better, the end product always better."[35]

But why?

Even those who try to take neither side have taken a side. Recall I mentioned earlier a news producer who spoke with Diana Daniels, to whom she connected me. The producer told me she was "uncomfortable" with publicly appearing on this record as that might end her illustrious career, for which she said she was "really sorry." Here is the fuller gist of what she shared with me, based on her personal findings—and her notably cosmopolitan interpretations of them:

- Many residents were upset by multigenerational communal living arrangements, such as multiple people sharing small dwellings.
- Opposition to multiple occupants per house was largely driven by the impact on housing affordability.
- Haitian households often pay higher rents on and prices for single-family homes, increasing costs and taxes for heritage citizens.
- Any significant rise in accidents or crimes following the Haitian influx was to be expected due to an immediately larger population size.
- A larger population benefits the City of Springfield as an institution by generating more tax revenue.

- Some residents see the Haitian influx as positive, noting the city had been declining in population for a half-century. Most newcomers, she viewed as willing workers, with any growing pains to be understandable.

Did you see the bifurcation? What's good for the "City" as an impersonal entity may not be so good for the citizenry. The benefits of the Haitians accrue to the City and to a select few real estate and business owners; the costs fall to all others. Poorer, whiter heritage citizens see the warm welcome for the Haitians and feel forgotten. Then envious. Then angry. Does a tragic story entitle you to American opportunities? These would say no; those not having to compete for those few opportunities would say yes. It's easy to buy when you don't have to pay.

This is what I asked the media who interviewed me on site in September 2024: Who decides who lives in your house? And is it even your home then, if you don't get to? If it's not yours, then now you're homeless. You're worse off than the one who came to you seeking the charity and shelter you were given no choice but to provide. Now it's you who needs help, and nobody cares.

"I was surprised they don't blame the Haitians," the news producer said of heritage citizens like Diana Daniels. "They blame the 'elites' of the community, like the mayor and the nonprofits. It's blue-collar people versus the elites of the community."

However, the producer added that she had not, did not, and would not take any side, so to speak, adding that she "feels like both sides are compelling." I noted her reference point, her decision hinge, her standard of judgment: *feels like*. Her feelings. Do your rights end where another's feelings begin?

We just don't have those issues. And they made it up to make it seem like we do. But we don't.

Suppose you're not an elite and yet this is what you think. Why? What could possibly be your motivation to deny an evident story of population change and demographic transformation as it measurably happens all around you and even to you directly? Fear of retribution? White guilt-laden Luxury Beliefs and outgroup-first ethics? Something else?

All this, I wondered that afternoon at the tutoring center as I packed up my children's toys and waited for my son to rejoin us in the lobby after class.

"Good to meet you," I said to [redacted] as the children exited class. "Good talking."

"Nice to meet you, too," she said. "And what do you do for a living?"

"Writer," I said. "Are you a tutor here or . . . "

"No, I'm just bringing my grandson," she said.

Right about that moment, her grandson walked out to the lobby.

He was biracial.

CHAPTER 15

THE POLL

"The simple step of a courageous individual is not to take part in the lie."[1]

—Aleksandr Solzhenitsyn, *The Gulag Archipelago*

I spent $5,000 of my own money on a professional survey to find out what no major media entity, interest group, or elected politician cared enough about the heritage citizens of Springfield, Ohio, to ask them:

What do you want?

We know what certain businesses of a specific size want—their owners, operators, founders, executives, and shareholders, rather. Take it back and away, Jamie McGregor:

"I think this whole notion of migrants taking American jobs is hogwash. That's spoken like a true person that has never made a payroll or tried to, you know, run a business. . . . You know, my family was once an immigrant. And so I wonder how they were accepted."[2]

I wonder if Mr. McGregor's ancestors assimilated or how that went. Is there a reason one culture's immigrants work out better for America—and for themselves, the newcomers—than others? The week of this chapter's writing, white South African refugees had gone viral across social media for videos of gratitude. One such refugee, Jason Bartlett, has published videos of himself strolling about on the American farmland he now works, writing each time something like, "I'm just a white South African having a lovely, peaceful and safe weekend on my farm in Alabama. God is good."[3]

White South Africans comprise only about 7 percent of their diverse nation, known for among others things as the birthplace of Elon Musk.[4] Musk has credibly accused, with evidence, the majority-black South African government of "racist ownership laws" and of a white "genocide."[5] I wrote with Jack Posobiec in *Unhumans* about the communist revolutions that devolved prosperous Rhodesia into the comically incompetent Zimbabwe, and the stable and safe South Africa into the place where, thanks to the legacy of Nelson Mandela, "if you're white, you have a target on your back," said refugee Jason Barlett.[6,7]

In one video, he shared the inciting incident for his family's flight to freedom and safety in America—his wife's grandfather, who was born in Austria, was tortured, strangled, burned, and murdered but only after the black assailants gang-raped his wife to death in front of him.[8] The *Witkruis* (White Cross) Monument in Mokopane, South Africa, features nearly three thousand white-painted metal crosses, each representing a white farmer or their family member killed in racially motivated farm attacks by black South Africans since 1994.[9] Swap the races, and this is the biggest story in the world. My nonfiction book ghostwriting clients who are from or who have family and friends who live in South Africa tell of a new normal following the African National Congress' sweep into power under Mandela. The worst parts of American cities, our no-go zones, feature living conditions with iron bars about the windows. Racially motivated crime in South Africa brought the iron bars *inside* the homes—gates, doorways, and other defenses inside due to the persistent white-targeted home invasion (and worse) risk.

Elon Musk's own father Errol exchanged gunfire with three black men who had broken into his home many years ago. An anonymous user on 𝕏 had complained in the replies to an Elon tweet that Elon's father "killed black people in South Africa."[10] Elon added necessary context on those three men in his own reply back, saying, "Yeah, because they broke into his house in South Africa and tried to kill him and my kid sister, you stupid asshole."[11]

The story of South Africa remained in my thoughts writing this book. I think of the question posed by Glenda Bailey in the bio of her account, @MajorityHaitian, "Will Haitians be the majority population in Springfield, OH?"[12]

When I spoke with **James Blanken** of *Empty Pockets Garage*, he concluded his remarks with a sobering prediction.

"They've done a very good job at spinning a narrative that is pro-Haitian, pro-local government, and that everyone else is a racist, backward hick," he first said of the media, then adding, "The day they say TPS has ended, there will be a portion of the Haitian community that gets violent. They will do things to us, to the heritage citizens. They will not go quietly. That is my prediction."

I asked James his motivation for wading into this topic so often on his show in the first place when the show itself, given its name, is for car enthusiasts. Other members of the OSINT network of Springfield have praised James for "giving us a voice" via his livestreams.

"I have great-grandchildren, and that's why I'm doing this," James said. "For them. I'm worried about the national debt and what they're going to have to deal with—and all this."

I remembered that one quote of Thomas Paine, "I prefer peace. But if trouble must come, let it come in my time, so that my children can live in peace."[13] And right then, I thought again of Rep. Brandon Gill's viral post:

> 65% of Haitian non-citizen households are on welfare.
>
> They are draining our resources, making America weaker and poorer.
>
> It is absolutely idiotic to give them backdoor amnesty by extending TPS.[14]

Heritage citizens of Springfield like James Blanken, Barron Seelig, Diana Daniels, Glenda Bailey, Mark Sanders, Setys Kelly, and so many more are just. simply. done. Their minds are made up. But are theirs "just a few loud voices," as Springfield 2051 committee member Marta Wojcik's infamous remark would imply?[15] Or do they speak for the majority?

I endeavored to find this out because no one else has. And what I found is, I believe, precisely the reason why.

Let's look in the box.

What Springfield Wants

Here are the questions, the broad-strokes answers, and a few detailed breakdowns. Rich Baris was so helpful as to visualize the results for us.

Haitian Immigrant Influx: Approve or Disapprove?

This is the question to begin all other questions.

Generally speaking, do you approve or disapprove of the influx of Haitian immigrants into the county?

A combined 67.7 percent of polled residents say they "somewhat disapprove" or "strongly disapprove," with a clear-cut majority of 55.9 percent agreeing with strong disapproval of Haitian migration into Clark County. To compare, only 28.9 percent total said either "strongly approve" or "somewhat approve," combined. All of them go to Carl Ruby's Central Christian (They don't. Or do they?).

Haitian Immigrant Influx: Approve or Disapprove?

Generally speaking, do you approve or disapprove of the influx of Haitian immigrants into the county?

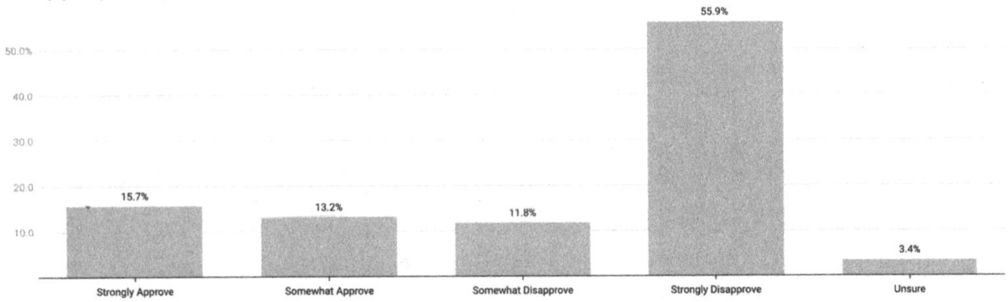

BIG DATA POLL conducted research for Entrepreneur's Wordsmith LLC DBA LisecGhostwriting.com, interviewing 446 residents of the City of Springfield and Greater Clark County area from April 18 to April 21, 2026. Results were weighted for sex, age, race, region and geography. The overall sampling error is ±4.0% at a 95% confidence level.

Residential Sentiment Toward Haitian Migrant Impact in Clark County, Ohio

Here, we asked a bifold question—personal impact versus community impact.

Thinking about your personal experiences with members of the Haitian migrant community, would you say they have been positive or negative?

A combined 53.5 percent answered "negative" or "very negative."

Thinking about the community overall, would you say the influx of Haitian migrants has had a positive or negative impact?

Even more—a combined 65.5 percent—answered either "negative" or "very negative."

"Just a few loud voices," huh?

Residential Sentiment Toward Haitian Migrant Impact in Clark County, Ohio

The percentage of the overall sample for each sentiment component and resulting sentiment score calculations.

SCOPE	VERY NEGATIVE	NEGATIVE	NEUTRAL	POSITIVE	VERY POSITIVE	NET SCORE	IMPACT
Personal Impact Sentiment							
Thinking about your personal experiences with members of the Haitian migrant community, would you say they have been positive or negative?	23.2%	30.3%	20.9%	11.8%	13.9%	-28.03%	Negative
Community Impact Sentimen							
Thinking about the community overall, would you say the influx of Haitian migrants has had a positive or negative impact?	34.2%	31.3%	12.1%	12.6%	9.8%	-43.05%	Negative

BIG DATA POLL conducted research for Entrepreneur's Wordsmith LLC DBA LisecGhostwriting.com, interviewing 446 residents of the City of Springfield and Greater Clark County area from April 18 to April 21, 2026. Results were weighted for sex, age, race, region and geography. The overall sampling error is ±4.0% at a 95% confidence level. Sentiment Score Calculation Components are as follows: Strong Positive (1); indicating high satisfaction (e.g., "Very Positive"); Weak Positive (0.5); indicating mild satisfaction (e.g., "Positive"; Neutral (0); non-emotional words or stop words (e.g., "Neutral"); Weak Negative (-0.5); indicating mild dissatisfaction (e.g., "Negative").Strong Negative (-1); indicating high dissatisfaction (e.g., "Very Negative"). See citations for a more detailed methodology statement on how the research was conducted and sentiment scores were calculated.

Knowledge of Recent Movers Due to Haitian Migrant Impact on Community

It was Diana Daniels, specifically, who suggested I ask this question because she happens to know so many who agreed, as it were, that "this town isn't big enough for the two of us."

Do you know family or friends who have moved as a result of Haitian immigrants into Clark County and/or the City of Springfield—or, no?

Of the respondents, a combined 39.7 percent answered "yes" to "family," "friends," or "both family and friends."

Knowledge of Recent Movers Due to Haitian Migrant Impact on Community

Do you know family or friends who have moved as a result of the influx of Haitian immigrants into Clark County and/or the City of Springfield—or, no?

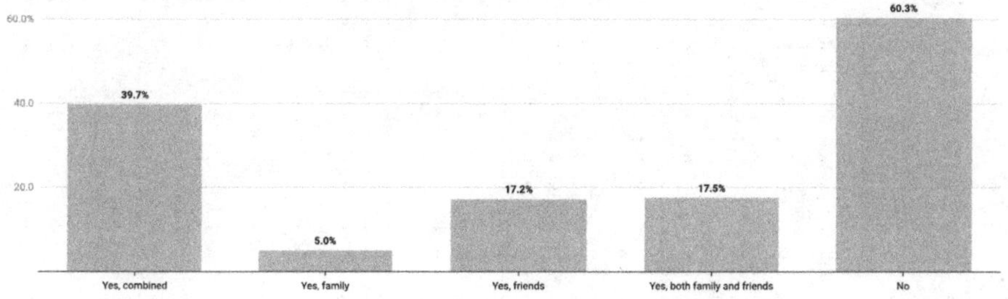

BIG DATA POLL conducted research for Entrepreneur's Wordsmith LLC DBA LisecGhostwriting.com, interviewing 446 residents of the City of Springfield and Greater Clark County area from April 18 to April 21, 2026. Results were weighted for sex, age, race, region and geography. The overall sampling error is ±4.0% at a 95% confidence level.

How Many Recent Movers Due to Haitian Migrant Impact on Community?

Of those who answered yes, we asked for specifics.

How many friends and family combined would you say moved as a direct result?

The average (mean) is just over seven people on average for Springfield and just over six for Clark County registered voters outside Springfield proper.

The median and mode (most common number given) are five and four, respectively, for Springfield.

The highest number? Twenty-five. Someone knows twenty-five people who fled the area because of the Haitian influx.

Replacement migration? White flight? Or ethnic cleansing?

How Many Recent Movers Due to Haitian Migrant Impact on Community?

How many friends and family combined would you say moved as a direct result?

Statistic	Total	Springfield	Non-Springfield
Mode	4.00	4.00	3.00
Mean	7.02	7.22	6.12
Median	5.00	5.00	5.00
Std. Dev.	5.59	5.84	4.24
Std. Err.	0.42	0.49	0.75
Min	1.00	1.00	1.00
Max	25.00	25.00	18.00

BIG DATA POLL conducted research for Entrepreneur's Wordsmith LLC DBA LisecGhostwriting.com, interviewing 446 residents of the City of Springfield and Greater Clark County area from April 18 to April 21, 2026. Results were weighted for sex, age, race, region and geography. The overall sampling error is ±4.0% at a 95% confidence level.

How Do Residents Feel About the Haitian Influx and Various Proposals to Address Community Impact?

We then presented Clark County residents with a multiple-choice set of options as to what ought be done.

A combined 63.6 percent of respondents "strongly approve" or "somewhat approve" of the solution "Removal of Temporary Protected Status and deportation."

Only a combined 38.9 percent supported "strongly approve" or "somewhat approve" of "A pathway to naturalization," and even fewer—34.4 percent—chose "Amnesty and residency."

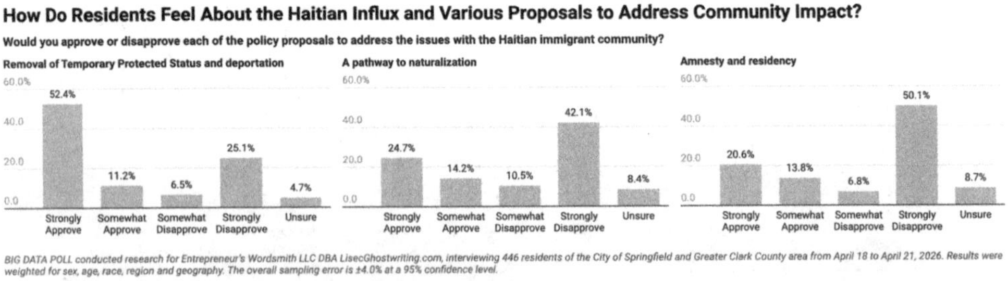

Which Policy Do Residents Prefer to Pursue to Deal with Haitian Immigration?

And now we have the number; note the first question and its results, teased at the outset, appear within this larger graphic.

If you had to choose, which of these policies would you prefer to be pursued?

"Removal of Temporary Protected Status and deportation" wins 61.9 percent.

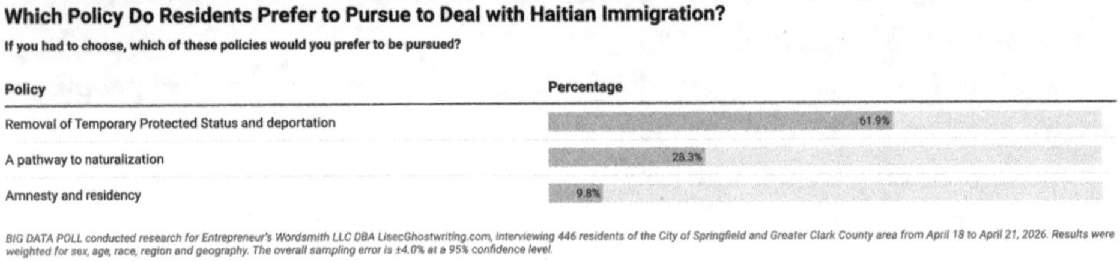

I can already hear Diana, Setys, and Glenda in my head as I type this. *I'm surprised it's not higher.*

Surprising (Unsurprising) Results

You can access the full portal of results broken down by demographics and affiliations at **www.haitiansofspringfield.com/poll**. At a glance, here's what I noticed:

- Of the 22 Black / African American respondents to *Generally speaking, do you approve or disapprove of the influx of Haitian immigrants into the county?*, 14 total answered "strongly approve" or "somewhat approve." That's almost two-thirds. It's about race, isn't it?
- To that same question, a combined 79 percent of Hispanic / Latino respondents chose either "strongly disapprove" or "somewhat disapprove" of the Haitian influx. And of the Asian / Other demographic, the combined disapproval result was 84.9 percent. So it's not about race. Or is it.
- Every single reported income bracket had a majority—50 percent or higher—"strongly disapprove" of the Haitian influx . . . except for one, the highest, at "$200,000 or more." Only 40.2 of this cohort "strongly disapprove" whereas a combined 56.4 percent of the highest-earners approve either "strongly" or "somewhat." We saw a similar effect with the "Advanced / Postgraduate" education-level cohort, with this being the only group to majority-support the Haitians at a combined "strongly" and "somewhat" of exactly 60 percent. Definitely not about race.
- Continuing from the previous, a majority of college-educateds overall still "strongly" or "somewhat" disapprove of the Haitian influx with a combined 53.9 percent.
- The religious affiliation with the highest and most Haitian influx support was "no religion" with 25.2 percent who "strongly approve." Wow. Really. Wow . . .
- Non-Springfield residents—that is, those outside the city's Haitian population center, living elsewhere in Clark County—also had a negative overall sentiment, with a combined 64.8 who "strongly" or "somewhat" disapprove.
- The age cohort with the highest selection of "unsure" whether they "approve or disapprove" of the Haitian influx into Springfield was ages 18–29, i.e., Generation Z, the Zoomers.
- Of Springfield resident respondents identifying as Democrats, 48.3 percent "strongly approve" of the Haitian influx whereas 73.6 percent of Republicans simply "strongly disapprove." Adding together the

"somewhat's," we get a combined Democrat approval percentage of 73.1 percent.

- We also asked for ideological identification besides political party. Barely almost 80 percent of liberals combined either "strongly" or "somewhat" support the Haitian influx.
    - Did you know? Liberal whites prefer non-whites. American National Election Studies found liberal whites to be the only racial group with a *negative* in-group preference for their own race.[16] So, yeah . . . maybe it is about race.

I noticed.

And I noticed that I noticed.

What do you notice?

www.haitiansofspringfield.com/poll

Survey Methodology Statement

BIG DATA POLL conducted the survey interviewing 446 residents of the City of Springfield and Greater Clark County area from April 18 to April 21, 2026. Four hundred sixteen (416) interviews were conducted by phone via live-agent including P2P SMS and text-to-online, sourced from a random sample derived from the L2 National Voter & Consumer File Databases. Participants who opted for text-to-online were given 24 hours to complete the interview, and were contacted one additional time to be provided an opportunity to complete the interview either live or text-to-online.

Thirty (30) additional interviews were conducted online opt-in to ensure age balancing, and were sourced via Lucid Holdings LLC (formerly CINT). Respondents were data-appended—otherwise known as dedupped/matched—against the file to confirm residency status. The online sample was calibrated to the file to ensure subgroups were represented.

All data collected via text-to-online and Lucid were subjected to quarantine checks for speeders and poor answer quality such as repeat first responses. Survey forwarding is prohibited and blocked by IP and cookie detection, and each survey returns a unique identifier to ensure shared responses are later removed.

If provided, interview details plotted on maps can be reviewed by hovering and clicking on the locator pins. Results were weighted for sex, age, race, region and geography. The overall sampling error is ±4.0 percent at a 95 percent confidence level. It is important to note that sampling errors for subgroups are higher. The survey was sponsored by Entrepreneur's Wordsmith LLC DBA LisecGhostwriting.com and NOT funded by or jointly with an entity affiliated with any candidate, campaign, committee, or political entity. Full and interactive crosstabs can be viewed on MarketSight.

Net Sentiment Score and Calculations Components

The sentiment score was calculated using assigning a range of -1 to 1 with 0.5 increments to responses selected and summing assigned values for those words, resulting in a final average between -1 (very negative) and +1 (very positive). In this case, the Net Sentiment Score is calculated as follows:

Net Sentiment = ((# of Positive mentions—# of Negative mentions) / Total mentions) × 100

Sentiment Score Calculation Components

- Strong Positive (1); indicating high satisfaction (e.g., "Very Positive").
- Weak Positive (0.5); indicating mild satisfaction (e.g., "Positive").
- Neutral (0): Non-emotional words or stop words (e.g., "Neutral").
- Weak Negative (-0.5): indicating mild dissatisfaction (e.g., "Negative").
- Strong Negative (-1): indicating high dissatisfaction (e.g., "Very Negative").

A Net Sentiment Score for "Personal Experiences" was significantly negative at -28.03 percent. The Net Sentiment Score for "Community Impact" was considerably more negative than the former at -43.05 percent.

Population and Demographic Representation

Below is a table detailing how each key demographic is represented as a share of the overall sample size for the population surveyed.

DEMO	SAMPLE %
Party Detail	
Republican	43.7%

(continued . . .)

Democrat	17.5%
Independent	29.6%
Something else	9.2%
Sex	
Male	48.6%
Female	51.4%
Race	
White / Caucasian	90.6%
Black / African American	4.9%
Hispanic / Latino	1.6%
Asian / Other	2.9%
City	
Springfield	73.1%
New Carlisle	9.4%
Neither	17.5%
Age	
18–29	5.1%
30–44	17.4%
45–64	43.4%
65+	34.1%

CHAPTER 16

WHY DO YOU CARE SO MUCH?

> "America is not a strip mall with an airport attached. We are not some global economic zone. We're a nation, a people with a shared heritage and history. But we have to fight to keep it that way."[1]
>
> —U.S. Senator Eric Schmitt (R-Missouri)

Why do you care so much? Racist much? I encountered this question while attempting to share with a liberal female family member a brief preview of my findings during the preliminary research of this book.

That was my first mistake. I did not make a second by inviting an argument within her frame of reality. I've saved those thoughts for you.

Public safety melodramas, crime reports, obviously illegal operations, suspiciously missing animals, court outcomes, and equal application of the law matter to me because they matter to the people who live here. Pretending they don't because the people involved are Haitian immigrants is the actual problem. Why must the burden of proof perpetually remain on the citizenry?

I am struck by this predicament—*you, the people of Springfield, have to prove beyond all reasonable doubt a negative Haitian impact, or otherwise your stories have no credibility and are debunked hoaxes.* It's a preposterously cartoonish double standard.

As but one example, how can I be the first public figure to call into obvious question Springfield Haitian leader Jacob Payen's assertion of a military record while every single major news organization, it seems, neglected to ask him for even a teeny sliver of the evidence demanded of every single heritage citizen for they report what happens to them daily and has for years? Does due diligence not exist in the presence of Haitians? Would that be offensive? Why don't we care about offending the heritage citizens? Is it because they're . . . white?

The aforementioned liberal female, as I declined to engage further, said something about the people of Springfield that, I shit you not, went like this:

"It's not happening, and they're racist for saying it is. And even if it is all happening to them, that's a good thing. They deserve it because like I said, they're racist."

The heritage citizens of Springfield love their city more than they hate Haitians. And as far as I could collect, they don't really hate the Haitians at all. Certainly some racist comments and characters have gone viral. These are not in my estimation anything like a representative sample. And as Barron Seelig made the point to me at Skyline, they're typically non-locals anyway. I spoke with only one American who irked my vestigial liberalism commenting on the matter of the foreigners. The remark appeared on Facebook after I'd shared news of a Haitian man shot while taking his children to church in Springfield on Sunday, July 5, 2026. The troublemaker suggested that such tragedy ought to happen more often. I disagreed; Springfielders joined in my pile-on to rebuke the individual. I wish the Haitian man a full recovery if at all possible and safe travels home to his people.

Speaking of, I was troubled by the official story as stated by Springfield's police chief; notice how this second paragraph from Jessica Orozco at the *Springfield News-Sun* contradicts the first—and the police:

> There is no evidence that the shooting of a Haitian father . . . was motivated by his identity, Springfield Police Division Chief Allison Elliott said in a statement Wednesday.
>
> The man, 51, was shot in the head while sitting in his car. A . . . witness heard someone prior to the shooting say the n-word. The man charged with the shooting, 42-year-old Rodney Oglesby, is Black.[2]

An intraracial, racially charged shooting was not racially motivated at all. OK.

Anyhow, beyond that one Facebook reply, I came upon nothing explicitly racist, bigoted, or xenophobic by my own high standards from the heritage citizenry. Again, these are a people who, like the exemplary Glenda Bailey, welcomed Spanish speakers by the hundreds to thousands to Clark and surrounding counties, including my own. On the whole, I believe my fellow Ohioans are judging the Haitians on the content of their character—not by the color of their skin.

Not everyone is capable of returning the favor.

"There Is No Judicial Review"—Until There Is

Consider the President Biden–appointed U.S. District Judge Ana C. Reyes, Uruguayan immigrant and first Hispanic woman (and first openly LGBTQ) to serve on that court. In early February 2026, she issued the eighty-three-page ruling that blocked the Trump administration from terminating Temporary Protected Status for the roughly 350,000 Haitians in America, Springfield's included. She paused the termination while a lawsuit challenging it proceeds, writing that the plaintiffs—which include Vilbrun Dorsainvil, brother of the Haitian Support Center's Vilès Dorsainvil—are likely to win on the merits and that it was "substantially likely" that then-Secretary Kristi Noem's decision was motivated, at least in part, by "hostility to nonwhite immigrants" and "racial animus."[3,4,5] This is asserted in the ruling without evidence by Judge Reyes, who, again, is not white. She appears to engage in mind-reading of now-former Secretary Noem, intuiting that her case could have only one motivation—and therefore the entirety of the case *must* collapse because of the unacceptability of what was discovered while mind-reading. *You don't want Haitians to lose TPS, therefore, they need to keep it, specifically because of what I believe you actually think of them*, in as many words, minus the legalese. How can Judge Reyes be so confident she knows Kristi Noem's motive?

"Racial animus."

Kristi Noem is white. Judge Reyes is not.

It's not happening. You're racist for saying it is. Even if it is, that's good. You deserve it because you're racist for saying it's happening. But it's not happening. And you're racist for saying it is. Even if it is, that's good . . . forevermore.

It is acceptable in America to judge—pun intended—only one color by their skin and, apparently, to decide that your worst prejudices about and biases against that race define the character of individuals within that population.

When oral arguments before the U.S. Supreme Court began on the matter of Haitian TPS at the end of April 2026, both Justice Sonia Sotomayor and Justice Ketanji Brown Jackson invoked negative comments President Donald Trump had made about Haiti and Haitians as, in an attempted mind-reading, his reason for ending the status with the implication being that this attitude is the very reason the program must not end.[6]

But this shade-throwing war was not the beginning nor middle to end of executive versus judicial conflict over mass migration into America and the special protections due non-citizens.

As of March 31, 2025, the U.S. had granted TPS to nearly 1.3 million people from seventeen countries, the top five by approvals being Venezuela, Haiti, El Salvador, Ukraine, and Honduras.

During the prior year's presidential campaign, Candidate Trump promised to end TPS, which he had done in his first time, terminating in 2017 until reinstatement as of May 21, 2021 by President Biden.[7,8] (But as you might know and/or might not be surprised to, *Ramos v. Nielsen* "was filed in federal district court after the Secretary of Homeland Security agreed to terminate the TPS designations in late 2017 and early 2018."[9] It wasn't until September 14, 2020, that the Ninth Circuit overturned a district court's injunction protecting TPS. "A separate lawsuit in New York challenging the Haiti designation alone, *Saget v. Trump*, has also blocked Haiti's TPS designation and could afford those TPS holders more time."[10] The war on behalf of Haiti First has been long fought.)

"It has nothing to do with Haiti or anything else. You have to remove the people, and you have to bring them back to their own country," he said at a private fundraiser.[11] His administration would later note that "the TPS programs for Honduras and Nicaragua were first created in 1999, after Hurricane Mitch caused catastrophic floods and killed thousands in Central America" and the "TPS program for Nepal was announced in 2015, after an earthquake hit the small Asian country." That's a long time to be temporary, not to mention Haiti's in 2010.

In Chapter 7, I mentioned a Springfield Haitian interviewed by *The Haitian Times*—"So frustrating is her predicament that she sometimes wishes she had stayed in her small, relatively safe town in Haiti. At least there, she would not be so afraid all the time."[12] It's only because she is earning in U.S. dollars in Ohio that she has stayed—she has an undisclosed number of dependents in both Ohio and Haiti pining for her paycheck. Is this arrangement in the best national interest of the United States?

Note the cascade of power plays once Trump was elected, winning the popular vote, the electoral college, and all seven swing states. It seems that the various unelected judges who oppose the Commander-in-Chief have been denying presidential power because they personally disagree with what they assert are the reasons for its use.

Can unelected judges do that? Can unelected judges issue dictatorial commands that strip the executive branch of executive power? If that be the case, and it certainly seems so, then the United States can in no way be considered a democracy, a democratic republic, or anything of the sort. Yet I don't know of any "No Kings" protestors upset over unelected, unaccountable judicial exercises in absolute power. It's not possible to disentangle sociopolitics from law at this juncture.

> On March 31 [2025], U.S. District Judge Edward Chen in San Francisco temporarily blocked DHS' attempt to end TPS protections for Venezuelans under the 2023 designation, extending those TPS protections until the Biden administration's original date of October 2, 2026 (*NTPSA v. Noem*).
>
> . . . On September 5, Judge Chen issued a final order on the merits of the case (*NTPSA v. Noem*). The judge's decision blocked the Trump administration from ending TPS for Venezuela and Haiti, restoring the Biden-era TPS extension date of October 2, 2026 for Venezuela and February 3, 2026 for Haiti.[13]

Judge Chen is of Chinese descent; he was nominated by Democratic President Barack Obama.

But once February 3rd neared, judicial supremacy remerged on behalf of the Haitians against the United States.

> On February 2, 2026, two days before it was set to expire, [U.S. District Court Judge Ana Reyes] in Washington, D.C. issued an order indefinitely pausing the termination of TPS for Haiti. The judge found that the decision to terminate TPS for Haiti was "arbitrary and capricious" and violated the Administrative Procedures Act (APA) by failing to fully consider dangerous conditions in Haiti.[14]

Meanwhile, other countries' citizens living in America saw judicial intervention for their benefit also.

> . . . [U.S. District Judge Trina Thompson], the San Francisco-based federal judge, said the TPS holders who sued the Trump administration were likely to succeed in their arguments that Noem's decisions were "preordained" actions that did not fully consider lingering conditions in Honduras, Nepal and Nicaragua.
>
> Thompson . . . also found the plaintiffs were likely to prevail in arguing that Noem's decisions were "motivated by racial animus." Thompson cited statements by Noem that she said stereotyped the TPS program and associated immigrants with criminality.
>
> . . . "The freedom to live fearlessly, the opportunity of liberty, and the American dream. That is all Plaintiffs seek. Instead, they are told to atone for their race, leave because of their names, and purify their blood. The Court disagrees," Thompson wrote in her order.[15]

Really? Is that explicitly what TPS holders were "told," Judge Thompson? Literally? Or what you perceive them having been told, given your own biases?

Consider that Judge Thompson is black; she was nominated by President Biden, also a Democrat.

Also, notice the emotional sentimentality of *her* reason for disagreement with President Trump's order: " . . . freedom . . . opportunity . . . liberty . . . the American dream . . . all Plaintiffs seek." Or could it be the welfare and social services, Judge Thompson, or any other reason? And does it matter? It does not! An incorrect defense of immigrants is being asserted. The question before the various courts is not whether TPS revoking makes those courts' respective judges feel bad, mean, or, like, so not nice; it's whether or not the executive branch of the United States federal government has the authority to revoke these immigrants' protected status.

> . . . Since Mr. Trump took office, his administration has announced plans to terminate TPS for hundreds of thousands of immigrants, including Afghans, Cameroonians, Haitians and Venezuelans.
>
> Federal courts have blocked some of those terminations, but the Supreme Court allowed the administration to revoke the TPS protections of more than 300,000 Venezuelans.[16]

Oh. So . . . President Trump *does* have the authority to "revoke . . . TPS protections." If the executive has the authority for one, he possesses the authority for all.

Note that last bit about the Supreme Court allowing the revocation. I looked up 25A326 *Noem v. National TPS Alliance* (10/03/2025). I translated the gist of the docket into vernacular English, and it goes like this:[17]

- In March 2025, a federal trial court in California temporarily blocked the Trump administration (Secretary of Homeland Security) from ending Temporary Protected Status (TPS) for Venezuelans living in the U.S.
- In May 2025, the Supreme Court stepped in and paused that block, letting the administration move forward while the case was appealed.
- The 9th Circuit appeals court later agreed with the trial court and kept the block in place.
- Then in September 2025, the same California trial court issued a final ruling saying the administration's decision to cancel the TPS extension and terminate TPS for Venezuelans was illegal. They threw out those actions.

- (The court also blocked the Haitian TPS termination, but the government is only asking the Supreme Court to lift the block on the Venezuelan part right now.)
- Bottom line: The Supreme Court just granted the government's request. It is once again pausing the lower courts' rulings. This means the administration can immediately revoke TPS for the ~300,000 Venezuelans while the full appeal continues in the 9th Circuit (and possibly back at the Supreme Court later).
- In short: The Court sided with the Trump administration again on this emergency stay, allowing TPS to end for Venezuelans now.

This is getting a little confusing, so I want to call this factlet out for your attention now: The Trump administration itself chose to ask the Supreme Court for an emergency stay *only* on the Venezuelan portion of the lower-court ruling on TPS, *not* Haiti.

That said, there is no special rule that treats Venezuela differently from Haiti or any other country. Just look up the statute (8 U.S.C. § 1254a), which grants the same power to designate, extend, or terminate TPS for any country based on conditions there. (While this statute references the Attorney General, the position now being referred to is deemed to be that of the Secretary of the Department of Homeland Security.[18]) Read:

> If the Attorney General determines under subparagraph . . . that a foreign state (or part of such foreign state) no longer continues to meet the conditions for designation . . . the Attorney General shall terminate the designation by publishing notice in the Federal Register of the determination under this subparagraph (including the basis for the determination[19]).

Who is given authority over TPS? Exactly. This member of the executive branch. Now notice this language in the statute elsewhere: "If the Attorney General does not determine . . . the discretion of the Attorney General . . . the Attorney General may designate . . . the Attorney General establishes . . . " These are but a sampling, but who is it doing this determining, discreting, designating, and establishing? Exactly. Now this, emphasis added:

> **There is no judicial review of any determination of the Attorney General with respect to the designation, or termination or extension of a designation, of a foreign state under this subsection.**[20]

There it is. "No judicial review" means "No judicial review." Or doesn't it? Well, it doesn't. Probably. Maybe not.

The midcourt dispute seems to go like so: That statute *does* protect the DHS Secretary's core substantive determination on country conditions, e.g., does Venezuela (or Haiti, etc.) still meet the statutory criteria for TPS or not. Courts cannot second-guess that policy or fact call.

The statute does not—according to the district court and 9th Circuit rulings in *National TPS Alliance v. Noem*—block *review* of "the meta," I'm calling it. That is, purely legal and procedural questions about the statute itself, such as:

- Did the DHS Secretary follow the exact procedures Congress wrote in the statute?
- Does the statute authorize the specific action Secretary Noem took, e.g., "vacating" a prior extension instead of using the termination process with sixty-day notice?
- Was the action "in excess of statutory jurisdiction, authority, or limitations" under the Administrative Procedure Act (5 U.S.C. § 706(2)(C))?[21]

And that is how the federal courts blocked the Venezuela/Haiti *vacatur*/terminations, insisting the DHS Secretary invented a "*vacatur*" power that Congress never granted in this statute. It is insisted that this is a legal question outside the protected "determination" the statute shields. The Trump administration, naturally, argued the opposite—that the statute is broad and covers all APA challenges to terminations. Indeed, the language is explicit, but courts read their own power back into them to preserve judicial review authority over legal and procedural questions.

At the most base level, what seems to be happening is that non-white Democrat-nominated judges are reading the sentence "There is no judicial review" and all that comes after in the statute but insisting that they still have judicial power to review *how* that sentence and all that comes after in the statute are read by the DHS Secretary to whom all authority is given, with none carved out in the statute for any level of the judiciary. But because President Trump's administration used in their opinion the wrong word, "*vacatur*," to describe its exercise of power, all such power exercise is null and void—and therefore so, too, is that statutory "no judicial review"—until that now-non-prohibited "judicial review" takes place.

Are you kidding me. You are not. Make it make sense. I haven't been able to—except for what I believe is an anti-white racial interpretive bias and political motivation favoring the Democratic party and, of course, non-Americans over Americans. That particular motivating bias is not hard to find, even outside the courts.

Representative Don Bacon, a Republican you'll recall, pushed for a more permanent protected status for Haitians in America in April 2026. He took flak for evidently prioritizing non-American interests over those of his constituents, to which he replied in a tone I can only read as one of class-conscious vengeance:

> I will vote my Christian and American values. You've convinced me now to look at Venezuela and El Salvador TPS. Thanks.[22]

Author Auron MacIntye called this out for what it was:

> Just a GOP congressman casually threatening to flood the country with immigrants to punish Americans.[23]

A question most heritage citizens of Springfield asked aloud as a rhetorical question to me was why Springfield—why here—why us—why me.

Ohio Turning Point Action man Gabe Guidarini, who contributed the foreword to my book *Burn It Down: What the Polls Say Young Americans Really Want* (Bombardier Books, 2026), gave an almost spiritual answer to these questions:

> There's a reason Ohio is the most frequently targeted state for mass-importation of foreign nationals like Haitians and Somalis:
>
> Ohio is the spiritual center of the American identity.
>
> Ohio's factories provided the tools that built this country, the weapons that won two world wars, the steel that took us into the sky. Ohio's farms fed this country. Ohio's men led this country.
>
> Ohio is arguably the centrifuge of the historic American nation. It's still the most traditionally "Americana"-esque state in terms of scenery, culture, and identity.
>
> To break the identity, cohesiveness, and soul of an entire nation requires striking it at its heart.
>
> Ohio is the economic, cultural, and spiritual heart of America.[24]

Gabe is 100 percent correct.

"I understand these folks are fleeing a hellhole of a country run by gangs. They are thankful to be here," said Kyle Koehler, now an Ohio state senator, to the Shelby County Republican Party. "Our community simply cannot handle the influx of 20,000 new residents who do not understand our language, our culture, our laws, and are being treated again, in my opinion, as indentured servants."[25]

Fortunately, the United States Supreme Court put this anti-white-biased dispute to rest on June 25, 2026, with a 6-3 ruling in *Mullin v. Doe*, enabling the Department of Homeland Security and U.S. Citizenship and Immigration Services (USCIS) to terminated Temporary Protected Status for Haitians.[26] Jeff Skinner at *The Ohio Register* wrote:

> . . . [T]he court held that the Immigration and Nationality Act's judicial review bar in 8 U.S.C. §1254a(b)(5)(A) precludes most Administrative Procedure Act claims challenging the Secretary of Homeland Security's determinations on TPS designation, extension or termination. The majority found the statute's language broad, covering both procedural and substantive decisions as well as the overall process leading to termination.
>
> . . . The court also rejected an equal protection claim by Haitian plaintiffs alleging racial motivation, finding statements by President Donald Trump and former Secretary Kristi Noem expressed race-neutral policy views on immigration enforcement and opposition to prolonged TPS designations.
>
> . . . Lower courts had repeatedly blocked terminations, but the Supreme Court emphasized congressional limits on judicial intervention in foreign policy and immigration determinations tied to TPS.
>
> Dissenting justices, led by Justice Elena Kagan, argued for broader review of procedural claims. Concurring, Justice Clarence Thomas questioned whether aliens possess equal protection rights against the federal government in this context.[27]

On the immediate impact, from *Ohio Capital Journal*:

> "The Supreme Court's decision means that many, many people are going to die violent, needless deaths," Geoff Pipoly, one of the attorneys representing Haitian plaintiffs, said during a press conference immediately following the Supreme Court ruling.
>
> "Please express to all the Haitians in Springfield just how broken our hearts are by this, and that we wish there was more we could have done, but we did everything that the law allowed us to try to do . . . We maybe we can try to navigate this together, but that won't prevent ICE to deport folks, that won't prevent ICE to separate families, and we know a lot of

> things awaiting us now that we will have to make sure that we are ready for this," [Vilès] Dorsainvil said.[28]

That evening, June 25th, my father Jeff attended a rally held at Springfield City Hall and recorded a number of speakers. Out of the approximate 400 to 450 attendees he estimated, my dad said there were only three or four who were visibly Haitian. *Ohio Capital Journal* adds:

> "We had hoped that this would be a time of celebration, but it has become a time of lament," said Carl Ruby, pastor of Springfield's Central Christian Church.
>
> "This is not a time to throw a punch or a rock, it is the time to turn the other cheek. It's a time to go the extra mile to sacrifice our comfort and to suffer if need be to protect the lives of others."
>
> People cried and hugged each other. Several held signs saying 'Immigrants Make America Great,' 'Springfield is for everyone,' 'Love thy neighbor,' and 'We are commanded to welcome strangers.'
>
> . . . "Do not wait until ICE is at your door," [Mia Perez, founder of Voices of Immigrants] said. "Gather your documents, keep copies of your immigration papers, work permit, passport, court notices."
>
> . . . "You must also prepare," said Katie Kersh, an attorney with Advocates for Basic Legal Equality in Dayton.
>
> "You need to decide what you stand for and what you are willing to fight for in the coming days."[29]

Rev. Dr. Marian Stewart of Springfield Neighbors Unite, announced a food and diaper drive for Haitians, and Ruby requested Creole translators, resources, and food via personal appeal to Governor DeWine.

Another female speakers—my dad didn't get her name—insisted that TPS termination was a "moral and social failure" and that the U.S. Supreme Court had "no moral justification" for doing so.[30]

Meanwhile, heritage citizens like Barron Seelig and Diana Daniels attended the rally in support of the sovereignty of Springfield—finally, the American will was represented. During one gigaviral moment, Barron Seelig was photographed raising the American flag behind the Haiti First stage of protestors. An elderly white liberal man with pro-Haitian gear then spat on Barron. Barron did not engage. The spitter was then featured prominently and positively in the *Dayton*

Daily News along with his sign, reading, *Love opens doors and hearts.*[31] Barron was greatly displeased with this.

"So far in fiscal year 2026, 88% of asylum decisions involving Haitian applicants have been denials."[32]

The day that I wrote this very sentence, four days remained on "a last-minute extension of [Haitian] work permits under Temporary Protected Status . . . "[33] Once the extension ended, and it did, so did the work permits and drivers licenses.

"We have some type of Lyft account and an Uber account, and we'll use the Springfield 'Field Trip' fellowship as well to help them as best as we can," Dorsainvil said. "We will work with other volunteers in town, so if they want to commute and they can't . . . we are asking folks if they can help on this."[34]

On CNN, Governor Mike DeWine re-committed to Haiti First:

> It is not in the United States's interest, certainly not in Ohio's interest, to have people who are working every single day, who are supporting a family, who are buying houses, fixing up old houses, starting businesses, and then put deep roots in this country and really are contributing and yank them out.[35]

I'm not sure if even the governor believes that anymore.

Neil Munro, writing for *Breitbart*, would call out other remarks Governor DeWine made, these to CBS, indicating his prioritization of Haitian well-being over his own voters', referring to Ohioans as simply "other people" who would not work the jobs in Ohio that Haitians would end up taking:

> American citizens are "other people," according to Ohio Governor Mike DeWine, who used a CBS interview to praise Haitian migrants for revitalizing Springfield, Ohio.
>
> . . . Americans do not have a broadly accepted term for politicians who praise and prioritize migrants over their own citizens . . .
>
> . . . One term to describe such politicians, [Jessica Vaughan, the policy director at the Center for Immigration Studies] suggested, would be "Opportunity Zone" Republicans.
>
> "Economic zone [Republicans] is a pretty good descriptor," said Joshua Lisec, an author who has written a book about the migration's damage to citizens in Springfield. "There's a number of people who've said something to the effect of 'America is not an economic zone, but our home.'"

> Americans in Springfield "use the word 'Elites' to refer to the Republicans and the country club people and the landowners, real estate owners, and businessmen who profit off the Haitians," Lisec said, adding . . . "I refer to them as the 'Coalition of Haiti First.'"[36]

Senator Bernie Moreno of Ohio quote-posted DeWine's Haiti First interview on CNN and wrote:

> Average home price in Springfield Ohio in 2022: $140,000
> 2026: $220,000
>
> Average rent per month:
> 2022: $865
> 2026: $1,245
>
> More than 2/3 Haitians are on some sort of welfare. Americans in need waiting in line behind foreign nationals. Car accidents and deaths due to lack of English and driving skills.
>
> Flooding a small community in Ohio with third world economic migrants, who mostly came here from South America, is next level insanity.
>
> Congress has spoken.
> The President has spoken.
> The Supreme Court has spoken.
>
> Enough.[37]

Jeff Skinner again, from *The Ohio Register*:

> . . . [D]eportations could ease pressures on Springfield's strained finances and emergency services. Despite promises of economic revitalization, city income tax revenue—the general fund's backbone—has flatlined. Projections for 2027 show stagnant or declining collections after post-pandemic gains slowed sharply. Officials project a roughly $4 million general fund gap under current assumptions.
>
> . . . Firefighters' union leaders report chronic staffing shortages, mandatory overtime and brownouts, exacerbated by population growth. Data center subsidies and tax abatements, once touted as future drivers, have

delivered few jobs while forgoing tens of millions in revenue and increasing utility and emergency demands.

Removing a large TPS population could reduce burdens on housing, healthcare, education and emergency services, potentially freeing resources and improving fiscal stability, according to opponents of the influx.[38]

So. Now what? From WCPO Cincinnati:

Dorsainvil said that losing TPS workers would have a broad economic impact in Springfield and beyond the city.

. . . Not everyone in Springfield shares that concern. Diana Daniels, a Springfield resident, said she supports ending TPS for Haitian immigrants.

"Well, guess what? There's a lot of Americans without jobs," Daniels said. "Go to any town up and down the Ohio River that was impacted by closing of the steel mills, closing of the auto industry, closing of the coal mines."

. . . "There's a lot of people that would push back on (support for TPS ending), and probably the majority of them have never stepped foot in Clark County, let alone Springfield, Ohio," [Setys] Kelly said.

"They are people trying to better themselves, but they need to spend the time, money, and effort back at home, and making Haiti a better place," Terry Adkins, another resident, said.

. . . Dorsainvil said his center is advising community members to stay calm, explore options such as relocating to Canada if they have family there, and prepare legal documents in case of sudden detention.[39]

The social security cards. How many were there? How many are there still? How many Haitians will remain in Springfield? In Ohio? Who will help them?

"We have had to think about issues of civil disobedience. We've had to think about the issue of providing sanctuary, and when there's a conflict between man's laws and God's laws, we have an obligation to side with God's laws," Carl Ruby said in the wake of the decision.[40] Nothing else matters.

"There are still many Haitians in Springfield who plan to stick around because they believe going back to their home country is too dangerous."[41] But Brazil. Chile.

From select Haitians directly now:

Olphane Bely, who says he has lived in Springfield for the last five years, says he is not sure if showing up to work is a good idea.

> "I would say probably not, because they are scared," he says.
>
> Bely says he is finally thinking about taking the government's offer to self-deport.
>
> "They say the government will give, like, $2,600 for people who want to go voluntarily," he says.
>
> . . . James Fleurijean with the Haitian Support Center said that if it were safe to go back [to Haiti], all 350,000 Haitians living in the U.S. under TPS would leave.
>
> "Haitians, they're so proud of their country, they are so patriotic and they love that country," he said. "They just stay here because they don't have a choice."
>
> Recent events have Bely rethinking the safety of Springfield, however.
>
> "People, people were very, very, very . . . I would say very kind," he says. "Not anymore."[42]

It didn't sound to me like the Haitians had been leaving Springfield. The day I wrote this section, a false rumor spread online that 80 percent of Haitians had self-deported already from Springfield, Ohio, and, even, from the United States. Absolutely not. Hundreds—not an exaggeration, actual hundreds—of Springfield residents told me directly that this was not the case.[43] One viral story indicated Haitians opening new businesses amid the supposed mass departure, such as the Lantern Bar Restaurant.[44] I was also told by residents that family and friends had seen Haitians in nearby Miami Valley cities and townships that they were not typically known to inhabit, such as Beavercreek, Englewood, Huber Heights, and Troy.

The Haitians weren't leaving; they're spreading. "The Haitian invasion continues," one Springfielder told me on the matter. What is to be done?

"Temporary Protected Status was going to end. It was never intended to be permanent. It was always temporary. Everybody always knew the date, so we shouldn't have to surge a force in there, to forcibly deport people who knew for a long time that they have to do that on their own," said Senator Bernie Moreno, adding also that "there isn't evidence documenting mass voluntary self-deportations in Springfield."[45] This was true in January 2026 leading up to the prior TPS expiration and remains true as of this writing in July 2026.

Once more, Jeff Skinner, *The Ohio Register:*

> Haitian TPS beneficiaries and advocates may pursue remaining individual relief options or legislative fixes, but mass deportations appear more

> feasible. Springfield officials must now navigate enforcement realities while addressing longstanding fiscal and service challenges tied to the demographic shifts of recent years.[46]

But now this from local news station WDTN, an NBC affiliate: "There is currently no word on any type of immigration enforcement operation."[47]

This was the low-intensity letdown I sensed lingering among the heritage citizens of Springfield who attended the July 21, 2026 town hall. I was told that a group named Champion City Hate Watch had attempted to coerce the hotel into canceling our event and forcing us out; they'd evidently failed. Dozens came; hundreds more expressed to organizers they feared for their personal safety due to the derangement of Haiti First over the prior few weeks. Three news organizations braved all concerns and were present. From Jessica Orozco, who I met at the event, for the *Springfield News-Sun*:

> Some in Springfield feel that they have been unfairly branded racist or bigoted while their concerns about the city's Haitian population have been ignored, they shared at a citizen town hall Tuesday, July 21.
>
> Around 40 people attended the meeting moderated by The Ohio Press Network's Editor-in-Chief Jack Windsor to discuss their experiences with the city's Haitian immigrant population, with some sharing concerns related to driving, grocery store etiquette, living conditions, a lack of assimilation, price increases related to the population increase and potential unregistered businesses.[48]

I can best describe the experience to you as cathartic. For everyone. For me.

> Also in attendance was Joshua Lisec, whose book "Haitians of Springfield: An Oral History" . . . "debunks the debunkers" related to claims about the Haitian population, Lisec said.
>
> Several people said they had been dismissed when bringing concerns about the population, painted as being bigoted in some way.
>
> "For three years, people in this city have been telling their story at council podiums on the record—many of you attaching your names—and for two years, the country talked about instead of listening to you—on debate stages and national headlines, for people who have never set foot on Limestone Street," Windsor said, calling the town hall a chance for people to share their stories "on the record."[49]

For approximately two-and-a-half hours, it was story after story after story like this—experiences, with evidence, straight from this book but also ever more, all eerily similar to those you've read throughout this book. For example:

> . . . Kenneth "Barron" Seelig said someone at a local grocery store told him a Haitian immigrant had $14,000 on his EBT card, which Seelig said he saw on a receipt.[50]

The people of Springfield have told the truth from the very beginning. They are vindicated. That's something. In *Haitians of Springfield*, I have been able to include roughly 1 percent of 1 percent of all the stories I collected from lifelong residents. There's so much. But what's here, was enough.

I was puzzled by Jessica: Why had she not covered over many years of reporting for the *Sun* what I found to be credible and evident in just days on the ground? It shouldn't be so effortless to steal all the scoops.

Jessica would meet with me to discuss the poll, this book, and my sources (I was secretly hoping for a hit piece; hit pieces sell books.). Approximately one hour after she interviewed me on July 28, 2026, Jessica wrote in the *Sun* that, in 2024, then-candidate Trump "repeated unfounded claims that Haitians in the city were eating people's pets." Unfounded, you say. What had we just discussed an hour ago, Jessica? It's easy not to find what you're doing your best not to. And it was easy for me to find what the citizens never bothered to hide because it is their true and lived experience from the beginning of this saga.

Also, in that same "unfounded" piece—and I counter that her unfoundedness is itself unfounded—Jessica wrote of Carl Ruby's worries that Haitians would face "existential" crises in Haiti.[51] But if the people were to self-deport back to Brazil (or Chile or what have they), that wouldn't be an issue. Would it. (I realize I've been writing about journalists writing about this book, in this book. It's like that scene in *Spaceballs* with the screens.) To Jessica's credit, she did write with something adjacent to honesty of my appearance at the town hall:

> Lisec said in his work on his book, he found many "heritage citizens" who have suffered.
>
> "You have felt like no one has believed you. That you have been dismissed, you've been derided, you've been humiliated, you've been ridiculed, you've been disbelieved, and you have been frankly tormented," Lisec said.[52]

And they have. But that's over now. Because of this book. It's over. There were tears that night as I spoke. So many. Weeping. Joy. Grief. Validation. Truth. Believed. They don't have the city they did, but they have each other. That's something. Ohio.

After the town hall, James Blanken, who was in attendance, like others who spent many hours with me for this work, began a spontaneous post-town hall livestream on *Empty Pockets Garage*. While many residents had told me almost a month by that point that the end of TPS for the nation's Haitian nationals equated to "the liberation of Springfield," citizen celebration would be premature. James began the livestream saying, "My biggest takeaway from tonight is . . . Joshua, that was the thing is, [the media] finally got to hear somebody say that, 'I believed them. That what you guys have been going through is real.'"

"That's refreshing, wasn't it?" said Barron Seelig, joining James live.

"I've been involved for about a year and a half now [talking about the Haitian influx impact publicly], and . . . I've seen the frustration," James went on to say. "I've seen the real side of things. I've seen the evidence, and it just didn't seem like it was ever enough. Everybody wanted to sensationalize the craziness . . . "

"The world was more worried about cats and dogs being eaten than a city being destroyed," Barron said.

James reiterated Springfield's stray cat disappearances all over town coinciding with the height of the influx. But the stray cat colonies, James said, have now begun to reappear.

But that's when James and Barron both shared, in agreement, that Springfield's destiny remains far from decided. As of that episode, Haitian TPS was set to expire in three days.

"I deal with Haitians still . . . at my part-time job. They're not acting like they're leaving. They're not acting like they're scared. Everybody says, 'They're hiding,'" James said.

Barron brought up bumper stickers that Haitians have reportedly begun to display on the back of their cars all over town, as residents have been sending him photos of them. The stickers read, *We ain't leaving*, Barron said. Prostitution among the Haitians, James said, has continued.

"As the weeks go on . . . there will be some kind of violence," James reaffirmed his prior prediction, made to me. "They've got no incentives to leave. They've got a good network going on here as far as they're concerned, and they've got all kinds of people, including the churches of this town [who] would hide the criminal elements of this group of people."

James turned back to the book, the media, and what happens next.

"You would think it would be a good story for them to put out there that these people, these regular individuals, after years of being told that they're this, that they're that, finally [have an] outlet that shows what they've been saying is the truth, and . . . it's a little bit of redemption . . . Joshua probably already knows this. Come closer to the release of his book, the propaganda is gonna go crazy over this. It's gonna be negative, negative, negative. They're gonna try to say, without really checking in . . . and having real proof, they're gonna say, 'Well, this has been debunked in this book. He's not telling the truth on anything.' I loved that word, debunked, but they never tell you how they debunked it. Just like Joshua was saying tonight."[53]

It's not been debunked. It's all not been debunked.

Haitianed

What happens now? Exactly. I wondered this leaving Springfield that night. Thinking. Emoting. Predicting. Likely? Some of the Haitians will find a way to stay. Carl Ruby's civil disobedience or the fake social security cards as ICE repellant or *pro bono* immigration lawyers or all of that or not of it and it doesn't matter. *We ain't leaving*. Surely some will as others already have.

On July 28, 2026, I attended the Springfield City Commission meeting; several patriotic heritage citizens wore red-and-white T-shirts reading, *Stay on track; they all go back. Ohio first!* in reference to comments I made on *Empty Pockets Garage* previously that also become a counterprotest rallying cry for local Ohio First patriots. At the meeting, Mayor Rob Rue said no communication between ICE and the city had taken place on mass deportations or anything of the sort. Rue's statement also urged U.S. Congress to formally protect Haitian nationals in America more broadly but specifically in Springfield.[54] Meanwhile, "A group of pastors in Springfield say federal immigration officials have met with them to talk through how the agency will handle Haitians in the city after the Trump administration ended temporary protected status. ICE won't say what its intentions are and whether it will target Haitians residing in communities like Springfield or Columbus. The agency told WOSU . . . it won't comment on ongoing or future operations."[55] It's a carrot-and-stick approach; some Haitians will take the money, or they'll take Tom Homan. President Trump's border czar said the day before my town hall on *Newsmax* that ICE had planned an enforcement operation surge for New York City's illegal immigrant populations. Springfielders sent me the interview.[56] *Can you ask him to pick us next, please?* They're ready for it to be over. On my drive into downtown the night of the July 28 commission meeting, I noticed several *For Rent* and *For Sale* signs. However, I also noticed individuals who appeared Haitian to be driving cars and carrying workplace paraphernalia as if they'd just completed a work shift—neither of which is supposed to be happening anymore. I'd received eyewitness reports, with evidence, of this happening all over town past the expiration date—Haitians working, driving, going about their daily business. That's confusing, isn't it? Then again, several employers in the region known for having hired Haitians through temporary staffing agencies had suddenly announced myriad job openings, even as other city employers, I was told by credible OSINT sources, had returned to hiring Haitians instead of Americans, transporting new and additional Haitian nationals from out of state into the Springfield area—"hundreds," I was told. Here we go again.

Nevertheless, what is certain to us all is that the resultant impact of the years-long Haitian influx into Springfield, Ohio, is not over—even if Temporary Protected Status is. The Champion City that built America, regardless of the protracted outcome of the TPS matter, will never be the same.

Springfield was Haitianed. There is no coming back from that. What's done was done, and it is.

Again I say: The people of Springfield weren't asked if they consented to the influx, nor were the Haitians made fully aware that was their ultimate fate in central Ohio. There were two sets of victims, heritage citizens reminded the news media in town-hall attendance. But again—why? Why did this happen? Here. To these people. To us.

I reasoned during my very first conversation with Walter Curt that the implicit intent, even if only an unconscious one, but an aligned intent nevertheless, seems to have been the interception of a great American success story under President Trump the first time around—*Jobs return to the American heartland!* Redirect that incoming work to foreign laborers, and it becomes retroactive revenge against your political enemy's most ardent supporters—and against their entire demographic.

This is what they do.

And that's what I told Barron Seelig that one afternoon at Skyline three months before the town hall, in April 2026.

"These stories continue to surface after the presidential election," I said. "'Trump's gonna get in office, and they're all gonna be gone. Yay. Problem solved.' Then it's not. A short-term problem has become a protracted, chronic issue. It's happening all over the United States. For whatever reason, legislatures, governors, judges, they're all forcing communities across America to retain foreign populations. It looks to me, obviously, like punishment. 'Punish Trump supporters. Punish working class people. Punish Springfield.' That, I believe, is why the Haitians are still here. They're your punishment. They're your punishment for being white."

"That's probably one of the realest things I've ever heard spoke," Barron said. "A lot of people are thinking it."

"I'm putting it in the book," I said.

Minority

The weekend after Barron at Skyline, I paid a visit to the Clark County Combined Health District's Minority Health Fair held at Springfield's Hayward Middle School.[57]

The event appeared quite popular on the drive-up. I had to park a ways back from the school entrance but was content to do so. And so I walked in and was visually presented with the names and logos of various charitable organizations and foundations as well as a few religious institutions and, of course, various public health and government departments. What caught but kept my attention just inside now were the various black history displays on the wall. This was the end of April; Black History Month is in February. Much of the lasting artwork was student-produced. I noticed three pertaining to Haiti, specifically. These children were very proud of their country.

There was another section further down on that same wall where there appeared an artistic display of various photographed children with what appeared to be their national flags—I saw El Salvador, the Dominican Republic, Haiti, of course, and also India. School administration and staff appeared to want to nurture this deep pride these children have for their countries.

From there, I wandered about the health fair's exhibitors and booth-mazes. Everything, it seemed, was trilingual: English, Spanish, Haitian Creole. Fair volunteers or perhaps employees were the sort of individuals you would imagine to be far-Left-of-center, judging by appearance—short-haired, sharp-featured, Ozempric-advertisement women; soft-faced, manually animated, effeminate men. There wasn't much to see and yet I saw all I needed to.

On my way back out, I saw a sign about Hayward's history, this very middle school, and the family it was named after, who came here in 1803 when Ohio became a State. They were active for more than 100 years in the community, apparently. Neat. Then I saw on the opposite wall a number of displays featuring the school's honor roll. There were a couple I took in up close. The first honor roll, I noticed, featured fifteen students; of them all, only three were white. Another honor roll praised the academics of twenty-one Hayward students; I counted again: only three whites. The rest appeared to be Haitian, Hispanic, or African-American.

As I turned to leave, a young white family passed me. Dad, mom, daughter.

I'd read the room, and I'd read the room.
Minority Health Fair.

Forest of Ghosts

Have you ever heard of procedural generation? Even if not, you've probably heard of its better-known demonstrations—the massive multiplayer video and computer game *Minecraft*. Its virtual worlds are effectively infinite—you can walk for days, and it keeps going. Every new chunk of land, cave system, or village appears the moment you approach it, all based on your world "seed" and some clever math. Video games like this don't store a giant, complete, pre-made map. Instead, *Minecraft* has a set of rules that can instantly calculate what should exist at any spot in the world. Procedural generation.

When I set out to author and publish the first, definitive, complete account of the Haitian influx impact on Springfield, Ohio, I had not realized the virtual impossibility of the task given the limitations of literature. This is an infinite story with finite space in which to tell it. When I looked into each anecdote, when I followed every clue, when I examined any given measurable, quantitative data point, I procedurally generated nigh-uncountable numbers of additional anecdotes, clues, and data, many tied together, many leading separate ways, but all of them telling the same story. Patternistically, my on-site and online research felt like a hike along the structure of a supermassive snowflake. Imagine a maze shaped like one; you begin from the middle. Which path along the body of the snowflake do you take? Pick one, and suddenly, that path leads to more paths to take. Which now? Pick one. Go, and there's now even more. On and on and on. It's fractal. The more citizens I interviewed, the more citizens appeared for an interview; the more police reports I read, the more police reports appeared for me to read. This effort was a journey through postindustrial immigration dystopia, and yet I charted only one path through it among what seemed to me like an unlimited number of potential full documentations. Yet none of them would be 100 percent "complete" on its own because, again, procedural generation.

This is why I mock or otherwise fail to take seriously, at all, any mainstream report that the situation in Springfield has been "debunked" as a "hoax." In the ten weeks of my life and the thousands of dollars I dedicated to this work, I found the claims of hoaxes to themselves be hoaxes; I debunked the debunking to my own satisfaction. Do you understand? You will find no evidence of something when you are attempting not to find it. My chore was closer to the opposite, to find what could be found, and it overwhelmed. Thus, the resulting *Haitians of Springfield* has become more narrative journalism than investigative report; I went around and interviewed people, and this, herein, is merely a preview of a preview of all that they told me. Yet it pains me to say that, despite the vastness of this completed project, in no way does it feel complete. I have included the tip of the tip of the iceberg to demonstrate to you—and mostly, perhaps selfishly, to myself—that there is indeed a "there" there, or rather, a "here" here. And there is.

That said, I didn't interview and record everyone I could have or even that I listed in my own internal project brief (it was not a brief brief, let's just say that). First, I quickly realized the *Minecraft*-iness of such an endeavor. I did, however, endeavor my best to follow the standard law-enforcement procedure for eyewitness-evidence documentation. I considered each component of the witness's statement separately; I reviewed each element of the witness's statement in the context of the full statement and looked for internal inconsistencies; and I reviewed each element of the statement against evidence from other sources, such as other witnesses' statements and physical evidence. This book is what resulted.

Now, the second (practical) reason I didn't speak with all I perhaps could have is that I didn't want to re-cut the same trail. My task, therefore, was to compile, curate, compose, and construct rather than to create entirely from scratch. Most of the people I spoke with, Haitian and heritage alike, I was not the first person to have interviewed them. But I did find a one-to-one match between what they told me and what they had shared prior on televised, livestreamed, or published interviews. The citizens' stories haven't changed. They never have. Nor, seemingly, have the Haitians'. And yet in case you didn't notice, an overwhelming majority of Haitians in Springfield have appeared in news media under false names, unwilling to be interviewed otherwise. Men like Vilès Dorsainvil, Lindsay Aime, and Jacob Payen have functioned as their *de facto* spokespeople together with Carl Ruby. In my time interacting with Haitians in Springfield in person, however, there was a lot of interacting but very little communicating due to the language barrier. I put in what I estimate is the same effort to learn Haitian Creole as these many have to learn American English.

Third, due to the expected consequences this book will have on the *status quo* of Springfield—due, among other things, to what I have brought to light herein—I wanted to protect the project's progress from undue influence from, much less mitigation by, those local powers who have profited or otherwise benefited as a result of Haitian presence in Springfield. Some things are best kept quiet. To paraphrase President Theodore Roosevelt, speak softly and write a big book.

Some findings, even I did not expect. Although the heritage citizens' sentiment regarding Haitian presence overall was deeply negative, not a single person I spoke with, from the OSINT network or otherwise, was, as I've told you, entirely negative. They grasped the difference between group dynamics and interpersonal relations with individual human beings worthy of a universal dignity. I met in Springfield a people with compassion, mercy, and sympathy for their fellow man, woman, and child. I discovered no heart hardened to the plights of the Haitians. Rather, I gathered that citizens felt their kindness was mistaken for weakness—their welcoming spirit was crushed, their capacity for openness maxed out, their charity fully expended. They have nothing left to give. As the Old West cliché goes, this town isn't big enough for the two of them.

The following micro thought experiment is only half an adjacency away from the truth:

> The heritage citizens of Springfield would give you the shirt off their back.
>
> Haitian migrants without proper clothing just heard, *Free shirts in Springfield!*
>
> And it was the progressive, upper-class, cosmopolitan elites who told them so.

The story told by this book's headline—*When One Culture Eats Another*—is not, in the grand twist of this book's closing, about the norms of a disrupted Haiti overcoming their counterparts in barely-rural Ohio. No. It's not black and white. The sociopolitical consumption occurring is a white-on-white conflict. The Haitian community merely appears to be an available and convenient metaphorical silverware—by another metaphor, a human leverage for waging low-intensity intra-racial warfare. A mostly-unelected class has, I believe, willfully subjugated and subordinated a lower class of their own kind but who is yet unable to self-organize or self-advocate to any compelling defensive extent—perhaps not on all matters, but certainly, it seems to me, on the matter of the Haitian influx and what I further believe amounts to special protections of that population.

At the extreme least, this elevated class of supranationalists—who seem to possess a worldview that raises the people of Haiti to a level higher than that of their own fellow citizens—this class has repeatedly failed, according to what I believe is a representative sample of Springfield, to accept opportunities to do right by the locals.

"There's a definite divide in this city," Glenda Bailey told *Newsmax*, "between the upper-class business owners and the middle-class and working-class people. And the politicians and the upper class . . . and people that work in the non-profits, they're all making money from this issue, and we, the working class, are taking up the slack for their social services . . . such as housing, food, medical, cash assistance."[58]

This town isn't big enough for the two of them. I believe that to Springfield's elite and privileged—and elite and privileged they truly are—that's a good thing.

Nevertheless, the people will do what the people will do. They will hamper and fold and wear with heritage pride what remaining shirts they have. They will protect what they believe is worth preserving, shrinking as that local territory may be, dwindling as their resolve may be to prosper it. To those who can stay, it will be worth it. It was always worth it.

Haitians of Springfield is the story of a city and of a nation, carefully building something worth sacrificing for, only for others to be welcomed and to reap the fruit of another's prior labor. If what the heritage citizens have told me is indeed true—and I believe it on the whole to be—there are here those who have been enriched at the expense of the impoverished. Sadly, this strikes me as a living example of the words of Jesus Christ as recorded in Matthew 13:12. "For whoever has, to him more will be given, and he will have abundance; but whoever does not have, even what he has will be taken away from him."[59]

On the matter of the Haitians of Springfield, the truth was easier to find than I had at first expected. Here, I found people wracked with fear for speaking out as to what had befallen them. With this book, I have endeavored to do what they have been silenced from, curating and compiling all the tales they've told, verified yet unspoken from that same fear. And so, as citizen journalist and loving neighbor, I do this for them until they learn to do it for themselves.

Members of the Springfield OSINT hosted me on June 28, 2026, on the *Empty Pockets Garage* podcast for a special interview episode entitled, "The Battle for Springfield, Ohio, is just beginning—and battle lines are being drawn."[60] I showed up wearing a custom red snapback with the text: "OHIO FIRST." I shared that special rallying cry with the OSINT and the audience during that episode—*Stay on track; they all go back!*—which Diana Daniels subsequently sported on that custom red shirt about town.

In any war, standard or irregular, there are flights to safety. And as this conflict carries onwards, some may leave Springfield for the surrounding county or for Ohio's open country elsewhere. But many will not quit. As the *Madonna of the Trail* stands for her city, so, too, will her citizens with her. Even if beyond city limits.

"Are you familiar with John Bryan?" Diana Daniels asked me that one night at Bob Evans, what feels like so long ago now.

"State Park?" I said. To Ohioans, John Bryan is exemplary state natural beauty. Right in my county, Greene County, next to Clark.

"I'm project manager and trail facilitator. . . . Any of the mountain bike trails are my design. And all of the new trails back behind the campground, back up around what we call . . . the old cow meadow, that's all my design as well . . . And now all I do is just maintenance because we have enough trail . . . I've been working on trail [since] 1999."

That's the spirit. Making trails. For others to walk. Decades.

Speaking of trails, as a girl, Glenda Bailey made ones of her own. On one of my many excursions to and around Springfield, she drove me through the neighborhood of her childhood.

"This is a friend of mine that I grew up with. His mother still lives here. She's eighty-five years old."

Have you ever seen a circa-1960s sepia-toned Polaroid photograph of American suburban housing? I want you to picture that. Because that's what I did, and it was right in front of me. This quaint ranch of lovingly-kept space-age Americana. Do you know what lawn ornaments are? This place had them. Front and back, it had it all.

Throughout this particular neighborhood, I also saw postwar American GI housing. Every other such house, it seemed, there were Haitians in the front yard or on the porches or by their cars in their street working on them. I saw that a lot.

"This whole area used to be the woods that we played in as kids," Glenda said as we drove past the ranch. The road continued, but the neighborhood did not. Suddenly, wheels touched fresh pavement, quite different from what came before. We'd had a recent rain. The new housing development before us was a field of mud with this road winding through it. Well, it wasn't a field. Just mud. Save for what looked to be a manmade retention pond over to the left, there was nothing for hundreds of yards. The prior ranch in question used to be the last house on the right. Now it was nothing of the sort. Already, housing had gone up, on the opposite end of the roaded ex-forest. Housing not worth its price, in my estimation. They looked the epitome of Malvina Reynolds's 1962 "little boxes on the hillside, little boxes made of ticky-tacky . . . little boxes all the same."[61]

"This land was owned by [my friend's] ancestors . . . [I]t was just sold to make this development, and she didn't have any say in the sale of it. . . . [S]o now this development . . . is going to be . . . causing a lot of traffic going right past her house," Glenda said of the eighty-five-year-old's ranch. "It's going to be similar to a ghetto."

We drove a bit further. We covered the majority of this tract of land and yet really went nowhere.

"It breaks my heart that this all used to be woods," Glenda said. "[W]e played in these woods. Built forts. Rode our bikes. And now it's just going to be cookie-cutter home after cookie-cutter home."

She paused and that gave me one, too.

"They're also going to have apartments, multi-family apartments," she continued. "[I]t's just sad to see everything changing so drastically within . . . such a short amount of time. . . . [T]his all happened after COVID . . . [S]ix years ago during COVID . . . everybody was in their home, in their house, not going out, not doing anything, and it was still like it was when I was a kid. And then as soon as COVID was over and the Haitians came, it's like everything changed. They started . . . developing. And first of all, I don't know where they think all these people are coming from that they're building all these homes for . . . lot of the heritage citizens feel like there is a great replacement, and we're seeing it day by day, not year by year, but literally day by day."

What was once thought conspiracy theory never actually was. A United Nations white paper from the year 2000 entitled *Replacement Migration: Is it A Solution to Declining and Ageing Populations?* reaches this dark conclusion:

> In the absence of migration, the size of the working-age population declines faster than the overall population. As a result of this faster rate of decline, the amount of migration needed to prevent a decline in the working-age population is larger than that for the overall population.[62]

Exodus in America. Extinction in America. Ninety-nine percent.

> . . . In contrast to the migration streams needed to offset total or working-age population decline, the levels of migration that would be needed to prevent the countries from ageing are of substantially larger magnitudes. By 2050, these larger migration flows would result in populations where the proportion of post-1995 migrants and their descendants would range between 59 per cent and 99 per cent.[63]

In the 2018 Netflix documentary *Alt-Right: Age of Rage*, Southern Poverty Law Center Senior Fellow Mark Potok is seen to be tracking, on a sticky-note in his office, the dwindling white proportion of the U.S. population from 1920 over the decades until 2015, from 90 percent to 62 percent.[64,65] This was widely interpreted as a key performance indicator to track both the intent and success of Left-wing activism.[66,67,68,69]

They're also going to have apartments, multi-family apartments.

It breaks my heart that this all used to be woods.

Not just woods. But forts. Bike rides. Endless summer. Childhood joy. Exploring and playing. Formative years, formed by mother nature. All here, here by the last house on the right.

We are where we grow up. We become where we're from. Trees climbed. Limbs and leaves, swaying and playing with and in the sweet winded breeze. Rainfall and snow. It's a seventy-five-acre wood for the passing of seasons, for rites, for growth—nature and nature's children alike. Think of the laughter. Hours. Years. New friends and first loves. Secrets shared after school and stories told as dusk comes, the streetlights flicker, and you and your best friends and classmates bike, skip, jump-rope home. Because that's what you do in America but now it's a ghost and a shell and a pond and pavement. The very spot where that life-changing thing happened. That one tree with that branch. Carving's still in it. Pocketknife. You know what it meant. Every step on the child-forged path into forestland, its own story.

It's all gone now. It's echoes of echoes only Glenda can hear as we drive in the silence. No more limbs for the birds or squirrels or kids. No more birds or squirrels. Or kids. It won't be long now. They'll spread sod atop the mud. Strips of the stuff from some farm. I know of one off the interstate. Maybe there. But they'll cut it out and lay it down. Squishy flat tombstones of green bury memories of lives lived that never shall be again; this forest, its own ghost. There will be neat little fences that don't quite close or lock right, hastily assembled when each mud-tract gets bought and sold. Illegal labor, probably. Who cares. I do. Tiny yards of uniform greens will sprawl here about this land, hiding what was and will be for nevermore. Maybe there will be families. Kids? Maybe. Maybe not. Glenda's ex-forest has no meaning to them. They will not understand. When they're tired, when they're cold, they'll go inside their little boxes made of ticky-tacky.

There was something here worth saving.

It's gone now.

We turn the corner. Turn signal.

"I'm going to take you to the voodoo shop," Glenda says.

We're out.

There Is More. What Is to Be Done?

This book is complete; the story is not. A free bonus chapter is available for the discerning reader to continue the literary journey—at www.haitiansofspringfield.com/chapter.

While outside the scope of this particular work, this complimentary content upgrade covers what could, what arguably must, and what providentially just might for the Haitian people to find their own peaceful resolution to the Springfield, Ohio, and Temporary Protected Status saga.

Read the Bonus Chapter at www.haitiansofspringfield.com/chapter Today.

APPENDICES

APPENDIX A

COURT ANALYSIS, TWO-TIER JUSTICE

I commissioned an artificial intelligence–assisted analysis into the matter of allegations of a two-tiered justice system in Springfield and Clark County, Ohio, one that has held Haitians to different standards than heritage citizens. Here, I present the findings.

8. COURT ANALYSIS — TWO-TIER JUSTICE

2024 Criminal Cases (Jan-Mar, partial year)

Generated: 2026-05-06

STATUS: PRELIMINARY — based on 881 cases (est. 30% of 2024)

Methodology

1. Scraped Clark County Municipal Court case search (Lotus Notes/Domino web app)
2. Iterated through case numbers 2400001-2401000
3. Extracted: defendant name, charge code/description, finding, plea, offense date, location, DOB, address
4. Applied Haitian surname classifier based on French-Creole naming patterns
5. **Framing: "Defendants with surnames characteristic of Haitian Creole naming patterns"**

Classifier Notes

- Uses ~150 common Haitian surnames (Jean, Pierre, Joseph, Baptiste, etc.)
- Also detects compound patterns (Jean-Pierre, Jean-Baptiste, Saint-*)
- THOMAS removed from classifier — too common in both populations to be diagnostic
- This is probabilistic, not definitive. False positives possible (Bernard, Philippe could be non-Haitian)
- Conservative estimate — will miss Haitians with less distinctive surnames

Results

Overall Statistics

	Count	% of Total
Total criminal cases	881	100%
Haitian-flagged	10	1.1%
Non-Haitian	871	98.9%

Dismissal Rate Comparison

Metric	Haitian-Flagged	Non-Haitian	Gap
Total cases	10	871	—
Dismissed (all types)	9 (90.0%)	586 (67.3%)	+22.7pp
Guilty	1 (10.0%)	238 (27.3%)	-17.3pp
Dismissed, Indicted	1 (10.0%)	—	—

Key Finding

90% of Haitian-flagged defendants had their cases dismissed, compared to 67.3% for non-Haitian defendants.

Only 1 out of 10 Haitian-flagged defendants was found guilty.

IMPORTANT CAVEATS:

1. **Sample size is very small** — 10 Haitian cases is not statistically significant
2. This covers only ~30% of 2024 (case numbers 1-1000 of ~3,230)
3. "Dismissed, Indicted" means the case was elevated to Common Pleas (felony) — not truly dismissed
4. The server throttled the scraper before completing; remaining cases should be scraped in a follow-up session
5. The BERNARD surname (2 cases, both protection order violations, both dismissed) might be false positives

Haitian-Flagged Cases Detail

Defendant	Charge	Finding
JEAN YVES	CHILD ENDANGERING	Guilty
AIME LINDSAY*	CRIMINAL TRESPASS	Dismissed
PIERRE CHRISTIAN	CRIMINAL TRESPASS	Dismissed - Prosecutor
JEAN LUC J	CRIMINAL TRESPASS	Dismissed
JEAN-PIERRE WILBERSON	DOMESTIC VIOLENCE	Dismissed
JEAN-PIERRE WILBERSON	STRANGULATION	Dismissed - Prosecutor
BERNARD JAMES	VIOLATE/PROTECTION ORDER	Dismissed
BERNARD JAMES	VIOLATE/PROTECTION ORDER	Dismissed
PHILIPPE FRIJENSON	FAIL TO REGISTER DOG	Dismissed
JEAN-BAPTISTE WANN	BURGLARY	Dismissed, Indicted

AIME LINDSAY is one of the officers of the Haitian Community Help & Support Center (EIN 93-4819144)

Charge Distribution Comparison

Top Charges (All Cases)	Count	Haitian	Non-Haitian
DOMESTIC VIOLENCE	73	1 (1.4%)	72 (98.6%)
THEFT	44	0	44
ASSAULT	26	0	26
STRANGULATION	17	1 (5.9%)	16 (94.1%)
CRIMINAL TRESPASS (all)	22	3 (13.6%)	19 (86.4%)
OBSTRUCTING OFF.BUSINESS	15	0	15

Criminal trespass has a disproportionately high Haitian representation (13.6% of trespass cases vs 1.1% of all cases). This is consistent with housing/shelter issues.

Interpretation for Lisec

This preliminary data suggests the two-tier justice finding exists, but **in the direction of leniency toward Haitian defendants, not severity**:

- Haitian defendants are more likely to have cases dismissed
- The single guilty verdict (Jean Yves, child endangering) was a serious charge
- Multiple dismissals by prosecutor request suggest deliberate discretion

Possible explanations:

1. **Prosecutorial discretion** — prosecutors declining to pursue cases against Haitian defendants (language barriers, witness issues, political pressure)
2. **Policing patterns** — Haitians arrested for minor charges that don't survive prosecutorial review
3. **Systemic barriers** — translation/interpreter issues preventing cases from proceeding
4. **Sample bias** — 10 cases is too few to draw firm conclusions

What's needed to strengthen this finding:

1. Complete the scrape (remaining ~2,200 case numbers for 2024)
2. Also scrape 2022 and 2023 for year-over-year comparison
3. Clark County Common Pleas Court (felonies) — to see if "Dismissed, Indicted" cases resulted in convictions
4. Sentencing data — for the cases that ARE guilty, compare sentences

Source: Clark County Municipal Court case search (clarkcountymunicipalcourt.gov/web.nsf/CaseSearch). Data scraped May 6, 2026. Case URL pattern: /web.nsf/Traffic?ReadForm&CATYPE=Crimnal&CASENUM=24XXXXX

APPENDIX B

HAITIANS OF SPRINGFIELD, THE WEB COMIC TIE-IN

Humor is when you tell the truth, exaggerate, then add contrast. The more biting, the better. The Haitian influx into Springfield, Ohio, has provided immense material for lampooning all sides of the situation. But as *Haitians of Springfield* is a serious narrative and investigative work, outright parody within the core manuscript was not appropriate.

Fortunately, early pre-release book promotion offered an appropriate opportunity for comic relief. Literally. During the pre-order period for *Haitians*, I released a short series of web comics by the same name, many with an appropriate call-to-action: Get the mildly more serious and outrageous book on Amazon.com.

The comics were a hit. And now, they live on for all readers of said mildly more serious book in this first appendix. While I used Grok and ChatGPT for the comic art, all dialogue, text, scenes, and characters (and the actual prompts written for Grok and ChatGPT) are original Lisec creations. I've always said that the best fiction reads like nonfiction and the best nonfiction like fiction. It's up to you to decide what these are.

Haitians of Springfield: An irregular web comic
Are Haitians eating pets?
ACME NEWS
No, no. We do not just cook and eat cat.
Trump's lies are debunked!
We sacrifice it first. Voodoo.
ACME NEWS

Haitians of Springfield
An irregular web comic
WTF!? You crushed my car!
Racism is a crime.
I have no insurance.

Haitians of Springfield
An irregular web comic
This is fine. It's just their culture.
Support our Haitian neighbors.
HAITI FIRST

Haitians of Springfield
An irregular web comic
YASSS KWEEN
BACKWARD SEPARATELY
I'm ashamed of my white body.
YASSS KWEEN
BACKWARD SEPARATELY
97% of the city wants me tarred and feathered in the street.
YASSS KWEEN
BACKWARD SEPARATELY
They say I rent to Haitians. But those are LLCs. Completely different.

Haitians of Springfield
get the mildly more serious book on Amazon.com
I AM CO-CEO WITH MYSELF. MY PRONOUNS ARE FU/PAYME.
FIRST INDENTURED
I TRAFFICKED 6 MILLION HAITIANS INTO SPRINGFIELD.
FIRST INDENTURED
THEY PAY ME FOR HOUSING. THEY PAY ME FOR RIDES TO AND FROM WORK. THEY PAY ME TO WORK!
FIRST INDENTURED

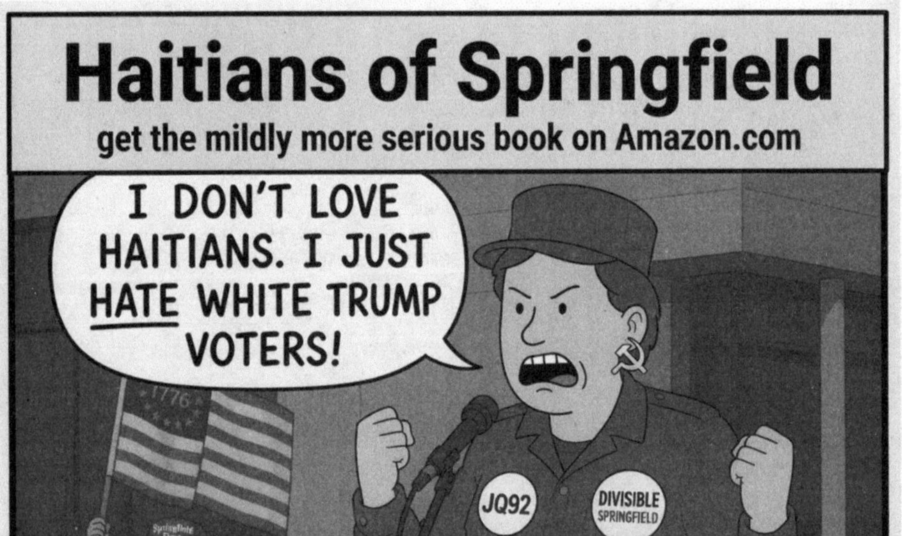
Haitians of Springfield
get the mildly more serious book on Amazon.com
I DON'T LOVE HAITIANS. I JUST HATE WHITE TRUMP VOTERS!
JQ92
DIVISIBLE SPRINGFIELD

HAITIANS OF SPRINGFIELD
GET THE MILDLY MORE SERIOUS BOOK ON AMAZON

HAITIANS OF SPRINGFIELD
GET THE MILDLY MORE SERIOUS BOOK ON AMAZON
Pastor Snarl Tuby and Mayor Bob Brew "help" their Haitian neighbors.
This bad boy can fit so many Haitian neighbors in it right now.
Thousands.
Hundreds?
I should have stayed in Brazil!

HAITIANS OF SPRINGFIELD

get the outrageous book on Amazon

APPENDIX C

"THE AMERICAN MIGRANT CRISIS"

Inspired by "The American Crisis" by Thomas Paine, published December 23, 1776. First published on September 23, 2024, in *Human Events*. Reprinted with permission.

These are the times and seasons of change. The autumn of our empire will, in this crisis, lead us into desolation of winter; but we that cherish the harvest of liberty and protect its fruits and yields shall preserve this country until thaw.

Invasion, like the frost, is not easily defended against, and yet the only way to spring, is to endure the ice. What we took for granted, we have let be seized from us, and either fed to another, or left to shrivel, rot, and freeze on vine and branch and bush and in field. What was ours is no longer, and we were given no choice nor voice in the matter.

It is sovereignty, only, over the fertile fields and valleys of a civilization that ensures its safety and satiety. Providence knows, in the names of mercy, of compassion, and of trade, that we have been forced to offer up our nourishing bounty present and future to total and complete strangers. Our federal government together with their collaborators in private enterprise have placed the wellbeing of others over that of our own. Our merchants, once necessary to the growth of our nation and the prosperity of its people, have allowed their rapacity to render them indifferent to our nation and contemptuous of her people. And so they prize the urges of migrants over and against the needs of our own kin. The unwelcomed guest has been made house master by unaccountable immigration overlords, public and private alike.

All that we have may become another's to use and abuse at will and at whim by a government not of the people, not by the people, nor for the people. And not only our own properties and opportunities, but our children's and our children's children's as well. So we the people are left to hunger and shiver while citizens of other lands are welcomed in celebration, warmth, and privilege. Imagine their joy! It cost only the suffering of our countrymen.

It is fruitless to ask whether immigration reform ought to have been completed during the prior administration. We did not make proper use of the power we possessed until it was lost to those who would deplete our stores and consume our goods and services before harvest, in the name of charity. Much has been lost. We are ravaged in quiet conquest. Our young are taken by the reckless, their virtue stolen and, for some, also their lives. Those who have died should have lived; those who live in their stead, should live someplace else. The branches of liberty tree hang low and bare. Scavengers pick over her fallen carcassed fruit. Nightfall comes early.

My opinion has been, and still is, that the founders and the forefathers of this great country, in honest hindsight but also with pessimistic foresight, ought to have set an expiration for birthright citizenship. This policy has lost its use. The man may leave the old country, but if the old country does not leave the man, the new country ought have no place for him, lest he degrade the new to become like the old. And so paradise is no more. A garden without walls soon yields to the wilderness. A nation without standards is a nation no more. Neither Roman nor American empire is exception. I cannot see on what grounds we give meal and money and room and board to the unknown and outside, while we forsake and forget those whose labor gave us all of the former. It is written, "If anyone is not willing to work, let him not eat." And now it is said, "If anyone is not willing to assimilate, let him remigrate." Such policy is sound. Remigration is compassionate, safe, and effective.

In the meantime, it is not surprising to see foreign peoples bring broken ways, loud prejudices, and strange cuisines into our country. All times and places subject to ethnic and religious diversities have suffered strife, save for America with her new story, her new values, and her new laws, where the order was to keep the order, or be ordered to leave. The Scots and the Irish, the Germans and the Poles, Protestant and Catholic alike, having come in centuries prior, fought and bled over archaic feuds. But now the matters are settled. Let him not call himself "Scottish-American" but only "American." Heritage and ancestry are twin sources of pride and strength, yes. This is correct. And yet we allow him to quarrel with his English neighbor over disputes back home, and worse, to organize township and state around it, at the peril of us all. And so we did not. For nigh two centuries, men became Americans; a new race was risen from the earth. He has hailed from many a land and people. Now this is his land and this is his people. We are Americans.

As I was with the citizens of Springfield on September 19, 2024, overhearing murmurs and complaint, I have become well-acquainted with the lot of the city. I, being born, raised, and residing in her neighbor, Dayton, know well the post-industrial fate of a region in intentional, accelerated decline. Importation of workforce (and, indeed, of those who are pervasively idle) will leave us with nothing; soon we will have less than that. Enterprise chases green as the spirit of the people bleeds red. That green is not of the infant leaves and sprouts of springtime. No, it is that sterile yet slimish gray green of the almighty dollar, in gross domestic product. In GDP we trust, say globalist businessmen whose profit from human labor trafficking feeds the bottom line even as it starves the common man. And so the man whose family needs more will be replaced by the man whose family demands less (from the employer, that is; the public treasury, previously withheld from suffering citizen, is drained for newcomer, with expedience and pleasure). A few dollars per hour is the price of local will and national sovereignty. We are a nation with bought and sold borders. Such is the situation in the sovereign states of Texas and California but also Ohio.

I shall not now attempt to give all the details as to the past causes or present state of immigration dysfunction and economic decline. Suffice it to say, the summer sun sets on all empires. Moonlit drifts of snow will cover all. The winds of coming winter, we feel them now. The late stage of decline and fall is upon us. But the diligent feel time and season, then plan, with a resolve to warm the soul beyond any chill. The diverse leave such planning to another; this is the plan to fail. A people of homogenous culture and singular value set, committed to mutual thriving of one another in the barren and bitter times, are separated and isolated and soon now outnumbered. The best-case scenario seems mere survival. Greatness again, some say. While we will settle for goodness on the part of those we call leaders, both elected and unelected, representative and bureaucrat.

I shall conclude this piece with remarks on the view of those who oppose us. I ask the following question: Why does the liberal prefer strangers to citizens? It is neither brave nor merciful to open the storehouse and leave unguarded the ripened fields and pregnant orchards. Who would give his best to a young male from another land, with whom he holds in common nothing but proximity and gender, and forsake duty to protect and provide for his women? His hormonal deficiency and testicular neglect are not irreversible; their consequences may just be.

But how does this affect us personally? So says the pragmatist who holds himself above the fray. I once felt anger against this unfatherly stance. Now I have pity. But that pity shall not prevent me from speaking my mind freely. Rather, I will speak the mind of President Donald J. Trump, whose words on the matter none can, with reason and conscience, contest:

> We want people to come into our country, but they must love our nation, and come in legally and through a system of merit. The world is laughing at us as fools, they are stealing our jobs and our wealth. We cannot let them laugh any longer. Make America great again!

Yes, let us make America great again. But we cannot—unless we make our men good again.

Let our men fear not the liberal scorn or scold. Let him say to those who would give his sons' opportunities and his daughters' safety away for a few dollars per hour that sweetest, bravest, most valorous of all the English words:

"No."

America did not want to become a nation of givers to a world of takers. To say this we say, "No." We wanted only the best and brightest of like mind and soul, those who have held out hope for their own great American dream, and no other. For there is no one who detests the illegal alien more than the legal immigrant. Let us honor those who honor our laws. It is folly and shame to do otherwise. And yet we have.

By perseverance and fortitude, we will make America great and our fellow men good again. We will not allow our nostalgic footpaths or our markets and playgrounds, embedded with merry family memories and sentimentality, to become no-go zones. We say, "No." We will not allow a variety of evils to occur on our watch—a ravaged country, a depopulated city, habitations without safety, and alienation without hope. Again, "No."

Look on that future, fellow man, and weep over it! And if there yet remains one useful idiot who believes the American migrant crisis to be nothing more than fake news, let him shut the hell up.

The autumn of empire has come and it will go. Now is the time and now is the season to wrest back control of our wintry fate. We can be warm. We can be safe. But we must plan. A great and good future is ours if we do.

We thank God that fate allows us one more chance to right the lefts and the wrongs. It is to man's credit that the majority of his kind in this country, and by no small margin, understand his duty to protect and to provide. Only the complete and total end of illegal migration into our states, counties, towns, neighborhoods, and businesses great and small will satisfy. Only the enforcement of law can bring order, order that our spouses and children adore so they may live in peace and grow in joy. This is the duty of every man—to cast his vote for Donald J. Trump and by mail-in ballot prior to Election Day.

Because man does not wait until the last minute to do what is right.

Man does what is right, right now.

He votes early, so that he may win early.

Search "get mail in ballot" now.

ACKNOWLEDGMENTS

A very special thank-you to all the heritage citizens of Springfield and surrounding areas who contributed to this book in some meaningful way via interviews, tour-guidelike treks around the county, evidence and anecdotes, and so much more, specifically: Walter Curt, Setys Kelly, Diana Daniels, Barron Seelig, Glenda Bailey, Deb Burchett, Mark Sanders, Noah Mangold, James Blanken, Terry Reed, Tayler Hansen, Katherine Baldridge, Heidi Jo, Roger Smith, Quinn Ferrell, Cindy Porter, Kimberly Marie, Rhonda Adams, Brian Cox, Brittany Fisher, and the Massies, among innumerable more citizens who contributed anonymously. This is for you.

I extend as well a perhaps unexpected thank-you to the Haitians of Springfield, whose vibrance made my time within city limits altogether memorable. Many of you met me, some of you spoke with me; none of you who did are written of poorly in this book. I'm reminded of the fictional Catholic clergyman addressing Tom Hanks's protagonist in *Angels & Demons* (2009), saying "When you write about us, and you will write about us, do so gently."[1] I have endeavored my best to do so. That said, what good is gentleness if not paired in equal parts with honesty? You deserve my best in both. I believe herein I have given them. *Bon chans!*

Thank you also to the president and editor of Skyhorse Publishing, Tony Lyons and Hector Carosso, respectively, who continue to believe in (and believe!) the stories I believe are worth telling. Let's do another.

A note of gratitude as well for Jennica Pounds—thank you for all that you did (and you know what you did).

And of course, thank you to my children Wesley, Willow, and Summer, whom I brought to Springfield on more than one occasion (or maybe one dozen) over the course of writing this book to see the various historic and soon-to-be-historic sites of Clark County. One day, you'll understand what your Papa was going on about. I just want you to grow up in a country that you recognize.

ABOUT THE AUTHOR

Joshua Lisec writes books of consequence. He is best known for his literary collaborations with controversial public figures, capturing their authentic voice and conveying the whole story. Lisec is a *New York Times*, #1 *Publishers Weekly*, *USA Today*, and *Wall Street Journal* bestselling author, co-author, and ghostwriter and has written more than 120 nonfiction books on politics, business, and more that have been translated into a dozen languages.

Lisec is author alongside Jack Posobiec of *The New York Times* bestseller *Unhumans: The Secret History of Communist Revolutions (And How to Crush Them)* and the *Newsmax* bestseller *Bulletproof: The Truth about the Assassination Attempts on Donald Trump*, endorsed by Vice President JD Vance and President Donald J. Trump, respectively. He has been featured in *The New York Times*, *Publishers Weekly*, *Newsweek*, *The Observer*, *Business Insider*, *Forbes*, NPR, BBC, TEDx, and TMZ. He is the world's only Certified Ghostwriter and Certified Hypnotist.

Follow Joshua on 𝕏 @joshualisec and at www.lisecghostwriting.com.

ENDNOTES

Preface

1 Isaac Saul, "The Haitian Immigrant Controversy in Ohio," Tangle, September 12, 2024, www.readtangle.com/springfield-ohio-immigration-haiti-cats.

2 Ohio Department of Development, Office of Research, 2023 Population Estimates: Cities, Villages, and Townships by County (May 2024), https://dam.assets.ohio.gov/image/upload/development.ohio.gov/research/population/2023_Pop_Est_-_TwpPlaces_By_County.pdf.

3 Dominick Mastrangelo, "Harris Defends Not Going to Border: 'And I Haven't Been to Europe,'" The Hill, June 8, 2021, https://thehill.com/homenews/administration/557282-vp-harris-not-discounting-concerns-about-events-at-us-border-during/.

4 Joshua Lisec, "The American Migrant Crisis," Human Events, September 23, 2024, https://humanevents.com/2024/09/23/joshua-lisec-the-american-migrant-crisis.

5 Dayton 24/7 Now, "Springfield Residents Pack Town Hall Hosted by Vivek Ramaswamy," YouTube video, 1:28:24, September 20, 2024, https://www.youtube.com/watch?v=4qxA3TLj0xU.

6 U.S. Citizenship and Immigration Services, "Update on Termination of TPS for Haiti," March 13, 2026, https://www.uscis.gov/i-9-central/form-i-9-related-news/policy-related-news-archive/update-on-termination-of-tps-for-haiti-release-march-13-2026.

7 U.S. Census Bureau, "QuickFacts: Springfield City, Ohio," accessed July 20, 2026, https://www.census.gov/quickfacts/fact/table/springfieldcityohio/AFN120222.

8 Ali Rogin, Matt Loffman, and Saher Khan, "PolitiFact's 'Lie of the Year' and Its Impact on the Ohio Town Caught in the Middle," *PBS NewsHour*, December 25, 2024, https://www.pbs.org/newshour/show/politifacts-lie-of-the-year-and-its-impact-on-the-ohio-town-caught-in-the-middle.

Introduction

1 More Perfect Union, "'Deport Them All'—Who's to Blame for Springfield's Immigrant Crisis?," YouTube video, 27:45, May 28, 2026, https://www.youtube.com/watch?v=MI66d8e74nM.

2 John W. Berry, "Acculturation: Living Successfully in Two Cultures," *International Journal of Intercultural* Relations 29, no. 6 (November 2005): 697–712, https://doi.org/10.1016/j.ijintrel.2005.07.013.

3 Henri Tajfel and John C. Turner, "The Social Identity Theory of Intergroup Behavior," in *Psychology of Intergroup Relations*, 2nd ed., ed. Stephen Worchel and William G. Austin (Chicago: Nelson-Hall, 1986), 7–24, https://web.mit.edu/curhan/www/docs/Articles/15341_Readings/Intergroup_Conflict/Tajfel_%26_Turner_Psych_of_Intergroup_Relations_CH1_Social_Identity_Theory.pdf.

4 J. W. Schofield, "Realistic Group Conflict Theory," in *Encyclopedia of Group Processes & Intergroup Relations*, ed. John M. Levine and Michael A. Hogg (Thousand Oaks, CA: SAGE Publications, 2009), 682–85, https://sk.sagepub.com/ency/edvol/processes/chpt/realistic-group-conflict-theory.

5 Thomas F. Pettigrew and Linda R. Tropp, "Allport's Intergroup Contact Hypothesis: Its History and Influence," in *On the Nature of Prejudice: Fifty Years after Allport*, ed. John F. Dovidio, Peter Glick, and Laurie A. Rudman (Malden, MA: Blackwell Publishing, 2005), 262–77, https://doi.org/10.1002/9780470773963.ch16.

6 Em Griffin, "Anxiety/Uncertainty Management Theory of William Gudykunst," in *A First Look at Communication Theory*, 6th ed. (Boston: McGraw-Hill, 2006), 426–38, https://www.afirstlook.com/docs/anxietyuncertainty.pdf.

7 *The Oxford Review*, "Cultural Hegemony: Definition and Explanation," accessed July 20, 2026, https://oxford-review.com/the-oxford-review-dei-diversity-equity-and-inclusion-dictionary/cultural-hegemony-definition-and-explanation.

8 Elsevier, "Dominant Culture," ScienceDirect Topics, accessed July 20, 2026, https://www.sciencedirect.com/topics/social-sciences/dominant-culture.

9 The Editors of Encyclopaedia Britannica, "Norman Conquest," *Encyclopaedia Britannica*, accessed July 20, 2026, https://www.britannica.com/event/Norman-Conquest.

10 The Editors of Encyclopaedia Britannica, "Mamluk," *Encyclopaedia Britannica*, last modified December 13, 2024, https://www.britannica.com/topic/Mamluk-dynasty-Egypt-Syria.

11 Smithsonian's National Museum of Asian Art, "Qing Dynasty, 1644–1911," accessed July 20, 2026, https://asia-archive.si.edu/learn/for-educators/teaching-china-with-the-smithsonian/explore-by-dynasty/qing-dynasty/.

12 The Editors of Encyclopaedia Britannica, "Mughal Dynasty," *Encyclopaedia Britannica*, accessed July 20, 2026, https://www.britannica.com/topic/Mughal-dynasty.

13 Elavie Ndura, "Ethnic Relations and Burundi's Struggle for Sustainable Peace," prepared statement for the hearing The Unfolding Crisis in Burundi, Subcommittee on Africa, Global Health, Global Human Rights, and International Organizations, Committee on Foreign Affairs, U.S. House of Representatives, 114th Cong., 1st sess., July 22, 2015, https://docs.house.gov/meetings/FA/FA16/20150722/103782/HHRG-114-FA16-Wstate-NduraE-20150722.pdf.

14 Daniel Pipes, "The Alawi Capture of Power in Syria," *Middle Eastern Studies* 25, no. 4 (October 1989): 429–50, https://www.jstor.org/stable/4283331.

Chapter 1

1 Yascha Mounk, "Ibram X. Kendi on Great Replacement Theory," The Good Fight, Persuasion, March 18, 2026, podcast and transcript, 58:40, https://www.persuasion.community/p/ibram-x-kendi.

2 Disney, "A Buzz Lightyear Quote for Every Situation," *Disney News*, September 10, 2015, https://news.disney.com/a-buzz-lightyear-quote-for-every-situation.

3 Anthem Film Festival, "Better Left Unsaid," accessed July 20, 2026, https://anthemfilmfestival.com/films/better-left-unsaid-2.

4 Steven Pinker (@sapinker), Twitter post, March 25, 2021, https://x.com/sapinker/status/1375189195354951686.

5 Jonathan Pageau (@PageauJonathan), Twitter post, March 26, 2021, https://x.com/PageauJonathan/status/1375420463409676298.

6 Michael Shermer (@michaelshermer), Twitter post, March 25, 2021, https://x.com/michaelshermer/status/1375251249017331716.

7 *The New York Times*, "Hardcover Nonfiction Books—Best Sellers," August 11, 2024, https://www.nytimes.com/books/best-sellers/2024/08/11/hardcover-nonfiction/.

8 *Publishers Weekly*, "Hardcover Frontlist Nonfiction," July 22, 2024, https://www.publishersweekly.com/pw/nielsen/HardcoverNonfiction/20240722.html.

9 Jeremy D. Popkin, *Facing Racial Revolution: Eyewitness Accounts of the Haitian Insurrection.* Chicago: University of Chicago Press, 2007. Excerpt from pages 49–58. Accessed April 11, 2024. https://press.uchicago.edu/Misc/Chicago/675831.html.

10 Tickner, Arlene B., and David L. Blaney. *Claiming the International.* Pg. 147. London: Routledge, 2013.

11 Jeremy D. Popkin, *Facing Racial Revolution: Eyewitness Accounts of the Haitian Insurrection.* Chicago: University of Chicago Press, 2007. Excerpt from pages 49–58. Accessed April 11, 2024. https://press.uchicago.edu/Misc/Chicago/675831.html.

12 The Editors of Encyclopædia Britannica. "Haitian Revolution." *Encyclopædia Britannica*, last modified March 28, 2024. Accessed April 11, 2024. https://www.britannica.com/topic/Haitian-Revolution.

13 The Editors of Encyclopædia Britannica. "Jean-Jacques Dessalines." *Encyclopædia Britannica*, last modified February 27, 2024. Accessed April 11, 2024. https://www.britannica.com/biography/Jean-Jacques-Dessalines.

14 "Haiti Overview." World Bank, last updated October 26, 2023. Accessed April 11, 2024. https://www.worldbank.org/en/country/haiti/overview.

15 Esther Marshall, "The world's happiest country named but Britons might be surprised about the UK." Express.co.uk, March 9, 2024. Accessed April 11, 2024. https://www.express.co.uk/travel/articles/1875540/world-happiest-country-dominican-republic.

16 Jennifer Grossman, interview with Joshua Lisec, "Communism's Secret History with Joshua Lisec," The Atlas Society Presents: Objectively Speaking, podcast audio, 1:00:28, April 1, 2026, https://the-atlas-society-presents.castos.com/episodes/communisms-secret-history-with-joshua-lisec.

17 Isaac Saul, "The Haitian Immigrant Controversy in Ohio," Tangle, September 12, 2024, https://www.readtangle.com/springfield-ohio-immigration-haiti-cats/.

18 Ben Kew, "Flashback: Leftist Celebs Wore 'Haiti Is Great Already' T-Shirts after Trump Allegedly Called It a 'Shithole Country'—Today It Descends into Chaos," The Gateway Pundit, March 11, 2024, https://www.thegatewaypundit.com/2024/03/flashback-leftist-celebs-wore-haiti-is-great-already/.

19 Al Jazeera English, "Heavy Fighting in Haitian Capital: Dominican Republic Expels Hundreds of Haitians," YouTube video, March 11, 2024, https://www.youtube.com/watch?v=4yFJMcBPxmc.

20 "Haitian 'Cannibal Gang' Eating Victims' Body Parts? Truth Behind Viral Video," *Times Now*, March 11, 2024, https://www.timesnownews.com/world/haiti-gang-violence-haitian-cannibal-gang-eating-victims-body-parts-disturbing-video-surfaces-article-108378390/amp.

21 Richard Lynn and David Becker, *The Intelligence of Nations* (London: Ulster Institute for Social Research, 2019), https://www.ulsterinstitute.org/ebook/THE%20INTELLIGENCE%20OF%20NATIONS%20-%20Richard%20Lynn,%20David%20Becker.pdf.

22 Bo Winegard, "Human Biodiversity: A Guide," *Aporia Magazine*, March 21, 2023, https://www.aporiamagazine.com/p/human-biodiversity-a-moderates-manifesto.

23 Frances Robles, David C. Adams, and Andre Paultre, "With Haiti in Chaos, a Humanitarian Crisis Is Rapidly Unfolding," *New York Times*, March 9, 2024, https://www.nytimes.com/2024/03/09/world/americas/haiti-gangs-political-uprising-ariel-henry-humanitarian-crisis.html.

24 Dánica Coto and Ashraf Khalil, "US Grand Jury Indicts One of Haiti's Most Powerful Gang Leaders and One of His Friends," Associated Press, August 12, 2025, https://apnews.com/article/us-jury-indicts-cherizier-barbecue-haiti-gangs-1329d2d13e11afce536bb8bb01a3c9aa.

25 Paweł Wargan (@pawelwargan), X post, March 10, 2024, https://x.com/pawelwargan/status/1766723124370825455.
26 Kunley Drukpa (@kunley_drukpa), X post, March 10, 2024, https://x.com/kunley_drukpa/status/1766931357798727843.
27 Brett Turner, "'Black Lives as Subject Matter III' Exhibition Open at Springfield Museum of Art," *Springfield News-Sun*, February 20, 2026, https://www.springfieldnewssun.com/news/black-lives-as-subject-matter-iii-exhibition-open-at-springfield-museum-of-art/article_561a1261-9aea-5f23-a246-30e1b159c493.html.
28 CBS News, "Ohio's Republican Governor, Mike DeWine, Is Urging the Trump Administration to Back Down from Plans to Deport Haitian Migrants Who Are Set to Lose Their Temporary Protected Status," Facebook video, July 28, 2026, https://www.facebook.com/watch/?v=1082010264335834.
29 U.S. Department of State, "Haiti International Travel Information," updated July 10, 2026, https://travel.state.gov/content/travel/en/international-travel/International-Travel-Country-Information-Pages/Haiti.html.
30 U.S. Department of State, "Haiti International Travel Information," updated July 10, 2026, https://travel.state.gov/content/travel/en/international-travel/International-Travel-Country-Information-Pages/Haiti.html.
31 U.S. Department of State, "Haiti International Travel Information," accessed July 20, 2026, https://travel.state.gov/content/travel/en/international-travel/International-Travel-Country-Information-Pages/Haiti.html.
32 Stephen Miller (@StephenM), "A useful way to think about migration is to consider what kind of societies the migrants have built in their home countries and to what extent . . .," X, April 16, 2026, https://x.com/StephenM/status/2044920708585914460.

Chapter 2

1 Michael Jonas, "The Downside of Diversity," *New York Times*, August 5, 2007, https://www.nytimes.com/2007/08/05/world/americas/05iht-diversity.1.6986248.html.
2 Alice Herman, "'They're Eating the Cats': Trump Rambles Falsely about Immigrants in Debate," *The Guardian*, September 10, 2024, https://www.theguardian.com/us-news/article/2024/sep/10/trump-springfield-pets-false-claims.
3 Sarah Arnold, "This Small Ohio Town Is Being Overrun by Haitian Immigrants," Townhall, September 7, 2024, https://townhall.com/tipsheet/saraharnold/2024/09/07/this-small-ohio-town-is-being-overrun-by-illegal-haitian-immigrants-n2644458.
4 Sarah Arnold, "This Small Ohio Town Is Being Overrun by Haitian Immigrants," Townhall, September 7, 2024, https://townhall.com/tipsheet/saraharnold/2024/09/07/this-small-ohio-town-is-being-overrun-by-illegal-haitian-immigrants-n2644458.
5 Vicky Forrest, "Springfield Mayor: Investigation into Businesses, Immigration Continues," *Springfield News-Sun*, July 12, 2024, https://www.springfieldnewssun.com/news/springfield-mayor-investigation-into-businesses-immigration-continues/article_784f876a-62d0-5546-972b-3cce31baca2a.html.
6 Mike Gonzalez, "NPR and PBS Dug Their Own Graves," The Heritage Foundation, May 15, 2025, https://www.heritage.org/budget-and-spending/commentary/npr-and-pbs-dug-their-own-graves.
7 Magda Feres and Murilo Fernando Neuppmann Feres, "Absence of Evidence Is Not Evidence of Absence," *Journal of Applied Oral Science* 31 (2023): ed001, https://doi.org/10.1590/1678-7757-2023-ed001.
8 Technical Working Group for Eyewitness Evidence, *Eyewitness Evidence: A Guide for Law Enforcement*, NCJ 178240 (Washington, DC: U.S. Department of Justice, Office

of Justice Programs, National Institute of Justice, October 1999), https://www.ojp.gov/pdffiles1/nij/178240.pdf.

9 Technical Working Group for Eyewitness Evidence, Eyewitness Evidence: A Guide for Law Enforcement, NCJ 178240 (Washington, DC: U.S. Department of Justice, Office of Justice Programs, National Institute of Justice, October 1999), https://www.ojp.gov/pdffiles1/nij/178240.pdf.

10 Donald J. Trump, "The Inaugural Address," remarks delivered in Washington, DC, January 20, 2017, archived White House website, https://trumpwhitehouse.archives.gov/briefings-statements/the-inaugural-address/.

11 C-SPAN, "Presidential Candidate Donald Trump Rally in Springfield, Ohio," video, October 27, 2016, https://www.c-span.org/program/campaign-2016/presidential-candidate-donald-trump-rally-in-springfield-ohio/458845.

12 *The Columbus Dispatch*, "How Residents of Springfield, Ohio, Are Reacting to Trump's Election," November 7, 2024, https://www.dispatch.com/story/news/2024/11/07/springfield-ohio-reacts-to-trumps-election-haitian-immigration/76092373007/.

13 Andrew Mark Miller, "Flashback: 2024's Immigration Ground Zero in Spotlight Again as Judge's 11th-Hour Ruling Sparks Outrage," Fox News, February 3, 2026, https://www.foxnews.com/politics/flashback-2024s-immigration-ground-zero-in-spotlight-again-as-judges-11th-hour-ruling-sparks-outrage.

14 Ali Rogin, Matt Loffman, and Saher Khan, "PolitiFact's 'Lie of the Year' and Its Impact on the Ohio Town Caught in the Middle," *PBS NewsHour*, December 25, 2024, https://www.pbs.org/newshour/show/politifacts-lie-of-the-year-and-its-impact-on-the-ohio-town-caught-in-the-middle.

15 Danielle Paquette, "The Haitians of Springfield, a Trump Campaign Target, Brace for His Presidency," *Washington Post*, November 7, 2024, https://www.washingtonpost.com/elections/2024/11/07/springfield-ohio-haitian-migrants-trump-win/.

16 Asawin Suebsaeng, "'He Is Coming for Us': Springfield's Haitians Are Terrified after Trump's Win," *Rolling Stone*, November 19, 2024, https://www.rollingstone.com/politics/politics-features/trump-springfield-ohio-haitians-terrified-1235171187/.

Chapter 3

1 Asra Q. Nomani, "Exclusive: Feds and State AG Investigate an Alleged Human Trafficking Empire Run in Springfield, Ohio, for Years by 'King George,'" *Jewish Journal*, September 18, 2024, https://jewishjournal.com/commentary/opinion/375011/feds-and-state-ag-investigate-an-alleged-human-trafficking-empire-run-in-springfield-ohio/.

2 Empty Pockets Garage, James, YouTube channel, accessed July 20, 2026, https://www.youtube.com/@emptypocketsgaragejames6393.

3 Empty Pockets Garage, James, "Haitian Invasion, Springfield, Ohio: Corrupt N.G.O.'s in the Name of Religion," YouTube video, accessed July 20, 2026, https://www.youtube.com/watch?v=uXxD6MVyYbY.

4 Ohio, The Heart of It All, "The Original Pioneer Woman: Springfield's Inspiring Madonna of the Trail Statue," August 13, 2020, https://ohio.org/travel-inspiration/articles/the-original-pioneer-woman-springfields-inspiring-madonna-of-the-trail-statue.

5 Oscar El Blue Independent Media, YouTube channel, accessed July 20, 2026, https://www.youtube.com/@oscarelblueindependentmedi7834.

6 Santiago Torrado, Rocío Montes, and Lorena Arroyo, "The Silent Exodus of Latin America's Haitian Population," *El País*, August 11, 2021, https://english.elpais.com/usa/2021-08-11/the-silent-exodus-of-latin-americas-haitian-population.html.

7 Oscar El Blue Independent Media, "Chaos at the South Border of Mexico," YouTube video, accessed July 20, 2026, https://www.youtube.com/watch?v=fq02FHGQ638.
8 Valerie Lacarte, "Addressing the Next Displacement Crisis in the Making in the Americas," Migration Policy Institute, October 2023, https://www.migrationpolicy.org/commentary/addressing-next-displacement-crisis-making-americas.
9 U.S. Department of Homeland Security, U.S. Customs and Border Protection, Office of Professional Responsibility, Report of Investigation: Incident Near Del Rio, TX, Port of Entry, September 19, 2021/Del Rio, Val Verde, TX, case no. 202112280, closing report (April 2022), https://www.cbp.gov/sites/default/files/assets/documents/2022-Jul/202112280-cbp-closing-report-public-redacted-final.pdf.
10 Valerie Lacarte, "Addressing the Next Displacement Crisis in the Making in the Americas," Migration Policy Institute, October 2023, https://www.migrationpolicy.org/commentary/addressing-next-displacement-crisis-making-americas.
11 U.S. Department of Homeland Security, U.S. Customs and Border Protection, Office of Professional Responsibility, Report of Investigation: Incident Near Del Rio, TX, Port of Entry, September 19, 2021/Del Rio, Val Verde, TX, case no. 202112280, closing report (April 2022), https://www.cbp.gov/sites/default/files/assets/documents/2022-Jul/202112280-cbp-closing-report-public-redacted-final.pdf.
12 Molly Hennessy-Fiske, "'They Shouldn't Be Here': Texas Border Town Divided by Haitian Influx," *Los Angeles Times*, September 23, 2021, https://www.latimes.com/world-nation/story/2021-09-23/del-rio-texas-border-community-copes-with-haitian-migrant-influx.
13 Molly Hennessy-Fiske, "'They Shouldn't Be Here': Texas Border Town Divided by Haitian Influx," *San Diego Union-Tribune*, September 24, 2021, https://www.sandiegouniontribune.com/2021/09/24/they-shouldnt-be-here-texas-border-town-divided-by-haitian-influx/.
14 Molly Hennessy-Fiske, "'They Shouldn't Be Here': Texas Border Town Divided by Haitian Influx," *Los Angeles Times*, September 23, 2021, https://www.latimes.com/world-nation/story/2021-09-23/del-rio-texas-border-community-copes-with-haitian-migrant-influx.
15 Bill Melugin (@BillMelugin_), "I shot this video while on a boat in the Rio Grande in Del Rio, TX on 9/18/2021 as 15,000+ Haitians flooded across the border illegally . . .," X, April 16, 2026, https://x.com/BillMelugin_/status/2044818290753651064.
16 Nick Shirley, "CBP One App Migrants: Their Journey to Springfield," Facebook video, April 17, 2026, https://www.facebook.com/watch/?v=2027984364800204.
17 Molly Hennessy-Fiske, "'They Shouldn't Be Here': Texas Border Town Divided by Haitian Influx," *San Diego Union-Tribune*, September 24, 2021, https://www.sandiegouniontribune.com/2021/09/24/they-shouldnt-be-here-texas-border-town-divided-by-haitian-influx/.
18 Molly Hennessy-Fiske, "'They Shouldn't Be Here': Texas Border Town Divided by Haitian Influx," *San Diego Union-Tribune*, September 24, 2021, https://www.sandiegouniontribune.com/2021/09/24/they-shouldnt-be-here-texas-border-town-divided-by-haitian-influx/.
19 William J. Clinton Foundation, Independent Accountants' Report and Consolidated Financial Statements: December 31, 2010 and 2009 (Little Rock, AR: William J. Clinton Foundation, 2011), https://www.clintonfoundation.org/wp-content/uploads/2021/07/clinton-foundation-financial-report-2010.pdf.
20 Jacob Kushner, "Haiti and the Failed Promise of US Aid," *The Guardian*, October 11, 2019, https://www.theguardian.com/world/2019/oct/11/haiti-and-the-failed-promise-of-us-aid.
21 Jacob Kushner, "Haiti and the Failed Promise of US Aid," *The Guardian*, October 11, 2019, https://www.theguardian.com/world/2019/oct/11/haiti-and-the-failed-promise-of-us-aid.

22 Katie Hooker, "Haitians' Response to U.S. Media Coverage of Haiti," International Affairs Forum, accessed July 20, 2026, https://www.ia-forum.org/Content/ViewInternal_Document.cfm?contenttype_id=5&ContentID=9001.
23 Jack Herrera, "Why 15,000 Migrants Ended Up in One Spot on the U.S.-Mexico Border," *Politico Magazine*, September 23, 2021, https://www.politico.com/news/magazine/2021/09/23/del-rio-desperation-dysfunction-immigration-513978.
24 KGNS Staff, "Catholic Charities of Laredo Prepares for Incoming Migrants from Del Rio Crisis," KGNS, September 21, 2021, https://www.kgns.tv/2021/09/21/catholic-charities-laredo-prepares-incoming-migrants-del-rio-crisis/.
25 John Lavenburg, "Catholic Charities in Texas Struggles in Face of Immigration 'Madness,'" *Angelus News*, September 20, 2021, https://angelusnews.com/news/nation/catholic-charities-in-texas-struggles-in-face-of-immigration-madness/.
26 Associated Press, "Many Haitian Migrants Are Staying in the U.S. Even as Expulsion Flights Rise," NPR, September 23, 2021, https://www.npr.org/2021/09/23/1040000579/many-haitian-migrants-are-staying-in-the-u-s-even-as-expulsion-flights-rise.
27 Vicky Forrest, "Crowd Questions Springfield Leaders on Immigration Issues after Bus Crash," *Springfield News-Sun*, August 30, 2023, https://www.springfieldnewssun.com/news/crowd-questions-springfield-leaders-on-immigration-issues-after-bus-crash/article_ff342079-cbfa-504e-8ce6-27acd04daba9.html.
28 Zip Atlas, "Haitian Average Family Size," accessed July 20, 2026, https://zipatlas.com/us/family-structure/haitian-average-family-size.htm.
29 Kira Olsen-Medina and Jeanne Batalova, "Haitian Immigrants in the United States," Migration Information Source, Migration Policy Institute, August 12, 2020, https://www.migrationpolicy.org/journal/spotlight/haitian-immigrants-united-states-2020.
30 Danielle McLean, "Unfounded Claims Target Springfield Officials, Haitian Immigrants," FactCheck.org, October 3, 2024, https://www.factcheck.org/2024/10/unfounded-claims-target-springfield-officials-haitian-immigrants/.
31 City of Springfield, Ohio, "Immigration FAQs," accessed July 20, 2026, https://springfieldohio.gov/immigration-faqs/.
32 City of Springfield, Ohio, "Immigration FAQs," accessed July 20, 2026, https://springfieldohio.gov/immigration-faqs/.
33 Asra Q. Nomani, "Exclusive: In a Game of 'Springfieldopoly,' 'King George' Built an Empire with Estimated Revenues of $180M, and Feds and State AG Now Expand Human Trafficking Probe into Alleged Identity Theft and Tax Fraud," *Jewish Journal*, September 28, 2024, https://jewishjournal.com/commentary/opinion/375369/exclusive-in-a-game-of-springfieldopoly-king-george-built-an-empire-with-estimated-revenues-of-180m-and-feds-and-state-ag-now-expand-human-trafficking-probe-int/.

Chapter 4

1 The White House (@WhiteHouse), "'If you import the Third World, you become the Third World.' —President Donald J. Trump," X, April 10, 2026, https://x.com/WhiteHouse/status/2042402293446767065.
2 Jim Hannah, "Economic Development, Aerospace, Immigration Highlight Wright State's Annual Regional Summit," Wright State University Newsroom, August 15, 2014, https://webapp2.wright.edu/web1/newsroom/2014/08/15/economic-development-aerospace-immigration-highlight-wright-states-annual-regional-summit/.
3 The Dayton Foundation, "The Dayton Foundation News," June 1, 2021, https://www.daytonfoundation.org/The-Dayton-Foundation-News.
4 WE Global Network, "Second Convening of the Network," June 12, 2014, https://www.weglobalnetwork.org/2014-pittsburgh/.

5 WE Global Network, homepage, accessed July 20, 2026, https://www.weglobalnetwork.org/.
6 WE Global Network (@WENetworkGlobal), X post, April 24, 2019, https://x.com/WENetworkGlobal/status/1121079264626061315.
7 Doug Caruso, "Immigrants Driving Ohio's Population Growth, U.S. Census Says," *The Columbus Dispatch*, April 18, 2019, https://www.dispatch.com/story/news/politics/county/2019/04/18/immigrants-driving-ohio-s-population/5410859007/.
8 Doug Caruso, "Immigrants Driving Ohio's Population Growth, U.S. Census Says," *The Columbus Dispatch*, April 18, 2019, https://www.dispatch.com/story/news/politics/county/2019/04/18/immigrants-driving-ohio-s-population/5410859007/.
9 WE Global Network, "Our 3rd Annual Convening a Huge Success," accessed July 20, 2026, https://www.weglobalnetwork.org/2015-dayton/.
10 Jim Hannah, "Economic Development, Aerospace, Immigration Highlight Wright State's Annual Regional Summit," Wright State University Newsroom, August 15, 2014, https://webapp2.wright.edu/web1/newsroom/2014/08/15/economic-development-aerospace-immigration-highlight-wright-states-annual-regional-summit/.
11 Global Great Lakes Network, Global Great Lakes Pittsburgh Convening, June 2014: "Promoting Immigration as an Economic Development Opportunity"—Speakers (June 2014), https://www.weglobalnetwork.org/wp-content/uploads/2014/11/2014-Speaker-Bios.pdf.
12 WE Global Network, "Welcoming Economies Toolkits," accessed July 20, 2026, https://www.weglobalnetwork.org/toolkit/.
13 Welcoming America, homepage, accessed July 20, 2026, https://welcomingamerica.org/.
14 Welcoming America, "Welcoming Network," accessed July 20, 2026, https://welcomingamerica.org/welcoming-network/.
15 Welcoming America, "Certified Welcoming," accessed July 20, 2026, https://welcomingamerica.org/initiatives/certified-welcoming/.
16 City of Springfield, Ohio, "City of Springfield Clarifies Position on Welcoming America Network," October 24, 2025, https://springfieldohio.gov/city-of-springfield-clarifies-position-on-welcoming-america-network/.
17 City Commission of Springfield, Ohio, Resolution No. 5844, "Declaring the City of Springfield, Ohio, a Community Welcoming of Immigrants and Immigrant-Owned Businesses, and Declaring an Emergency," adopted July 22, 2014, https://storage.ghost.io/c/76/b4/76b4b53f-1dbe-4e39-9f8a-e97b7a95c1ab/content/files/2025/10/Welcome-Springfield-Resolution-City-of-Springfield.pdf.
18 City Commission of Springfield, Ohio, Resolution No. 5844, "Declaring the City of Springfield, Ohio, a Community Welcoming of Immigrants and Immigrant-Owned Businesses, and Declaring an Emergency," adopted July 22, 2014, https://www.weglobalnetwork.org/wp-content/uploads/2014/11/Welcome-Springfield-Resolution-City-of-Springfield.pdf.
19 Brooke Spurlock, "Springfield Beautification Group Honors 2 Retirees with Awards," *Springfield News-Sun*, January 4, 2024, https://www.springfieldnewssun.com/news/springfield-beautification-group-honors-2-retirees-with-awards/article_0806f984-8f4a-5432-8f2c-112d79553a6e.html.
20 Jessica Orozco, "Memorial Services for Former Springfield Mayor Copeland Set," *Springfield News-Sun*, January 23, 2024, https://www.springfieldnewssun.com/news/memorial-services-for-former-springfield-mayor-copeland-set/article_83189ae0-cf3e-5282-8712-1b82cb43d7df.html.
21 Kermit Rowe, "Clark County Proposal Embraces Immigrants," *Dayton Daily News*, February 8, 2014, https://www.weglobalnetwork.org/wp-content/uploads/2014/11/Springfield_Clark-County-proposal-embraces-immigrants.pdf.

22 Kermit Rowe, "Clark County Proposal Embraces Immigrants," *Dayton Daily News*, February 9, 2014 (Dated July 3, 2020), https://www.daytondailynews.com/local/clark-county-proposal-embraces-immigrants/article_35d14af3-8a8e-5f47-8a86-82a9bd553b65.html.

23 Mike Catalini, Julie Carr Smyth, and Bruce Shipkowski, "Watch: Trump Amplifies False Racist Rumor about Ohio's Haitian Immigrants in Debate," PBS NewsHour, September 11, 2024, https://www.pbs.org/newshour/politics/watch-trump-amplifies-false-racist-rumor-about-ohios-haitian-immigrants-in-debate.

24 City of Springfield, Ohio, et al. v. Blood Tribe, et al., Complaint, Civil Action No. 3:25-cv-33 (S.D. Ohio, filed February 6, 2025), https://clearinghouse-umich-production.s3.amazonaws.com/media/doc/156040.pdf.

25 "Some Clark County Latinos Report Lack of Access to Medical Care," *Springfield News-Sun*, accessed July 20, 2026, https://www.springfieldnewssun.com/news/local/some-clark-county-latinos-report-lack-access-medical-care/tcu4p7iwkgrb10fd7v256n/.

26 Global Great Lakes Network, Global Great Lakes Pittsburgh Convening, June 2014: "Promoting Immigration as an Economic Development Opportunity"—Speakers (June 2014), https://www.weglobalnetwork.org/wp-content/uploads/2014/11/2014-Speaker-Bios.pdf.

27 Carl Ruby, "Midwest Consortium for Immigration Research," presentation at the second convening of the Global Great Lakes Network, University of Pittsburgh School of Law, Pittsburgh, June 12, 2014, https://www.weglobalnetwork.org/wp-content/uploads/2014/11/2014-MCIR-Pres.pdf.

28 Tom de Bruyne, "Cialdini's 7 Principles of Persuasion: Each One Explained," SUE Behavioural Design, March 1, 2026, https://www.suebehaviouraldesign.com/en/blog/cialdini-principles-of-persuasion/.

29 William Trollinger, "Life after Fundamentalism: Carl Ruby, Cedarville University, and Haitians in Springfield," Righting America, September 24, 2024, https://rightingamerica.net/life-after-fundamentalism-carl-ruby-cedarville-university-and-haitians-in-springfield/.

30 William Trollinger, "Life after Fundamentalism: Carl Ruby, Cedarville University, and Haitians in Springfield," Righting America, September 24, 2024, https://rightingamerica.net/life-after-fundamentalism-carl-ruby-cedarville-university-and-haitians-in-springfield/.

31 WYSO, "Making Springfield an Immigrant-Friendly City: WYSO's Lewis Wallace Talks to Carl Ruby," audio, 5:00, February 20, 2014, https://www.wyso.org/news/2014-02-20/making-springfield-an-immigrant-friendly-city-wysos-lewis-wallace-talks-to-carl-ruby.

32 Karen Bohnert, "The Vital Role of Immigrant Labor in the U.S. Dairy Industry," Dairy Herd, July 18, 2025, https://www.dairyherd.com/news/labor/vital-role-immigrant-labor-u-s-dairy-industry.

33 U.S. Bureau of Labor Statistics, Foreign-Born Workers: Labor Force Characteristics—2025, news release USDL-26-0760, May 19, 2026, https://www.bls.gov/news.release/pdf/forbrn.pdf.

34 WE Global Network, "Welcoming Economies Toolkits," accessed July 20, 2026, https://www.weglobalnetwork.org/toolkit/.

35 WE Global Network, "National Statistics," infographic, accessed July 20, 2026, https://www.weglobalnetwork.org/wp-content/uploads/2015/05/GGLN-Toolkit-National-Numbers-.pdf.

36 WE Global Network, New Hampshire and Nashua, presentation, accessed July 20, 2026, https://www.weglobalnetwork.org/wp-content/uploads/2015/10/New-Hampshire-Nashua.pdf.

37 World Economic Forum, "David Lubell," accessed July 20, 2026, https://www.weforum.org/people/david-lubell/.

38 Welcoming America, Stronger Together: Making the Case for Shared Prosperity Through Welcoming Immigrants in Our Communities (2013), https://www.weglobalnetwork.org/wp-content/uploads/2014/11/WA-Economic-Messaging-Toolkit.pdf.

39 WYSO, "'Welcome Springfield' to Study Health Issues Facing Latino Immigrants," December 20, 2014, https://www.wyso.org/news/2014-12-20/welcome-springfield-to-study-health-issues-facing-latino-immigrants.

40 Carl Ruby, "Clark County Latino Health Initiave," Prezi presentation, accessed July 20, 2026, https://prezi.com/peycouozyci7/clark-county-latino-health-initiave/.

41 Carl Ruby, "Clark County Latino Health Initiative," Prezi presentation, accessed July 20, 2026, https://prezi.com/hdf0rn_yxfdu/clark-county-latino-health-initiative/.

42 Welcome Springfield (@WelcomeSprgfld), X post, August 7, 2015, https://x.com/WelcomeSprgfld/status/629632178326900736.

43 Welcome Springfield (@WelcomeSprgfld), X post, August 31, 2015, https://x.com/WelcomeSprgfld/status/638396566500417536.

44 Welcome Springfield (@WelcomeSprgfld), X post, November 18, 2015, https://x.com/WelcomeSprgfld/status/667134747542478848.

45 Carl Ruby, "Clark County Latino Health Initiaitve," Prezi presentation, accessed July 20, 2026, https://prezi.com/t7kzhvzhgu1b/clark-county-latino-health-initiaitve/.

46 Welcome Springfield (@WelcomeSprgfld), X post, February 24, 2017, https://x.com/WelcomeSprgfld/status/835226353368715264.

47 Welcome Springfield, "Welcome," archived July 9, 2017, Wayback Machine, https://web.archive.org/web/20170709023330/http://www.welcomespringfield.org/.

48 Welcome Springfield, "Welcome," archived July 9, 2017, Wayback Machine, https://web.archive.org/web/20170709023330/http://www.welcomespringfield.org/.

49 Welcome Springfield, "Welcome," archived September 19, 2020, Wayback Machine, Internet Archive, https://web.archive.org/web/20200919142901/ http://www.welcomespringfield.org/.

50 Welcome Springfield, "About," archived June 30, 2022, Wayback Machine, Internet Archive, https://web.archive.org/web/20220630033354/https://welcomespringfield.org/about/.

51 GoDaddy, "WHOIS Search Results for welcomespringfield.org," accessed July 20, 2026, https://www.godaddy.com/whois/results.aspx?domain=welcomespringfield.org.

52 G92, Facebook page, accessed July 20, 2026, https://www.facebook.com/p/G92-61579215051057/.

53 Lisa Sharon Harper, "A Turning Point on Immigration," *Sojourners*, January 2012, https://sojo.net/magazine/january-2012/turning-point-immigration.

54 Carl Ruby, "Immigration? What Would Jesus Do?," Prezi presentation, accessed July 20, 2026, https://prezi.com/erws83lz1h1x/immigration-what-would-jesus-do/.

55 Carl Ruby, "Immigration? What Would Jesus Do?," Prezi presentation, accessed July 20, 2026, https://prezi.com/erws83lz1h1x/immigration-what-would-jesus-do/.

56 Em Griffin, "Anxiety/Uncertainty Management Theory of William Gudykunst," in *A First Look at Communication Theory*, 6th ed. (Boston: McGraw-Hill, 2006), 426–38, https://www.afirstlook.com/docs/anxietyuncertainty.pdf.

57 Alejandro Figueroa, "Springfield Honors Haitian Community at City Hall Flag Ceremony," WYSO, May 19, 2023, https://www.wyso.org/news/2023-05-19/springfield-honors-haitian-community-city-hall-flag-ceremony.

58 Laura Crimaldi, "Haitian Pride Unfurled in Greater Boston as Community Confronts Trump Immigration Push," *Boston Globe*, May 17, 2025, https://www.bostonglobe.com/2025/05/17/metro/greater-boston-haitian-flag-day-celebration-trump-deportation-fears/.

59 MassLive, photo gallery, accessed July 20, 2026, https://www.masslive.com/galleries/5RDBS2UUMJDQTDBL5QATVPF2HU/.

60 Carl Ruby, "I'm Proud of Our City Leaders," Central Christian Church, May 19, 2023, https://www.ccspringfield.org/blog/im-proud-of-our-city-leaders.

61 Natalie Driscoll, "ICYMI: Haitian Flag Day Fair and Festival," Hub Springfield, May 24, 2023, https://hubspringfield.com/haitian-flag-day-052423/.

62 Natalie Driscoll, "ICYMI: Haitian Flag Day Fair and Festival," Hub Springfield, May 24, 2023, https://hubspringfield.com/haitian-flag-day-052423/.

63 sezthem, "Springfield, Ohio, Resolution No. 5844 Welcoming Immigrants," YouTube video, September 25, 2024, https://www.youtube.com/watch?v=UjI2N90CauY.

64 "Springfield, Ohio's 2014 Resolution Welcoming Immigrants," Microsoft Word document, accessed July 20, 2026, https://www.dropbox.com/scl/fi/qr1iw90psi2jnl6ek3vso/Springfield-Ohio-s-2014-Resolution-Welcoming-Immigrants.docx?rlkey=l3cm7729rj3sz3qlbddkz11qq&dl=0.

65 Vicky Forrest, "Citizen Comments at Springfield Commission Reflect National Divide," *Springfield News-Sun*, July 26, 2024, https://www.springfieldnewssun.com/news/citizen-comments-at-springfield-commission-reflect-national-divide/article_18af6889-c874-57d6-a8ec-b0ef5518d4ee.html.

66 City of Springfield, Ohio, "City of Springfield Clarifies Position on Welcoming America Network," October 24, 2025, https://springfieldohio.gov/city-of-springfield-clarifies-position-on-welcoming-america-network/.

67 Global Detroit, "Building an Inclusive and Prosperous Michigan," accessed July 20, 2026, https://globaldetroitmi.org/inclusive-southeast-michigan/.

68 Global Detroit, "Our Story," accessed July 20, 2026, https://globaldetroitmi.org/our-story/.

69 Global Detroit, "Funders," accessed July 20, 2026, https://globaldetroitmi.org/funders/.

70 Welcoming America, "About Welcoming America," accessed July 20, 2026, https://welcomingamerica.org/about/.

71 David M. Lubell, "Building a More Welcoming America," Open Society Foundations, April 26, 2011, https://www.opensocietyfoundations.org/voices/building-more-welcoming-america.

72 Welcoming America, 2019 Annual Report (2020), https://welcomingamerica.org/wp-content/uploads/2021/04/2019_Welcoming_America_Annual_Report.pdf.

73 Welcoming America, Resilience through Welcoming: 2020 Annual Report (2021), https://welcomingamerica.org/wp-content/uploads/2021/07/Welcoming-America-2020-Annual-Report.pdf.

74 Welcoming America, A Year of Fostering Belonging: 2021 Annual Report (2022), https://welcomingamerica.org/wp-content/uploads/2022/09/Welcoming-America-2021-annual-report-for-web.pdf.

75 *The Arab American News*, "Detroit Receives $750K Grant to Aid Undocumented Residents Impacted by COVID-19," July 11, 2020, https://arabamericannews.com/2020/07/11/detroit-receives-750k-grant-to-aid-undocumented-residents-impacted-by-covid-19/.

76 Upwardly Global, Building an Equitable Economy That Includes Immigrants & Refugees: 2020 Annual Report (2020), https://www.upwardlyglobal.org/wp-content/uploads/2022/08/UpGlo-Annual-Report-2020-1.pdf.

77 Carnegie Corporation of New York, "Four Freedoms Fund: A Pioneering Foundation Partnership Advocates for Immigrants," 2008, Center for Strategic Philanthropy and Civil Society, Duke University, https://cspcs.sanford.duke.edu/cspcs-case-study/four-freedoms-fund-a-pioneering-foundation-partnership-advocates-for-immigrants/.

78 Upwardly Global, Expanding Our Impact: 2023 Annual Report (2024), https://www.upwardlyglobal.org/wp-content/uploads/2025/04/UpwardlyGlobal-2023AnnualReport.pdf.
79 ProPublica, "Foundation to Promote Open Society," Nonprofit Explorer, accessed July 20, 2026, https://projects.propublica.org/nonprofits/organizations/263753801.
80 InfluenceWatch, "Arab Community Center for Economic and Social Services (ACCESS)," accessed July 20, 2026, https://www.influencewatch.org/non-profit/arab-community-center-for-economic-and-social-services-access/.

Chapter 5

1 Darvio Morrow, "In Springfield, Migrants Are Taking a Toll on the City's Most Vulnerable," opinion, *Newsweek*, September 13, 2024, https://www.newsweek.com/springfield-migrants-are-taking-toll-citys-most-vulnerable-opinion-1953385.
2 "Newsmax, the Truth About Springfield, Ohio with Glenda Bailey," YouTube video, accessed July 20, 2026, https://www.youtube.com/watch?v=S13RMuW2tvo.
3 TheDC Shorts, "Woman's Comments Cause CHAOS at Springfield City Commission Meeting," YouTube video, October 10, 2024, https://www.youtube.com/watch?v=xzN9Rn16Gz4.
4 Donald J. Trump (@realDonaldTrump), "Happy #CincoDeMayo! The best taco bowls are made in Trump Tower Grill. I love Hispanics!," Twitter post, May 5, 2016, https://x.com/realDonaldTrump/status/728297587418247168.
5 John Burnett and Felix Contreras, "How Mexico Learned to Polka," NPR, March 11, 2015, https://www.npr.org/2015/03/11/392141073/how-mexico-learned-to-polka.
6 Audrey Conklin, "Migrants Wear Biden T-Shirts at US-Mexico Border, Demand Clearer Policies," Fox News, March 3, 2021, https://www.foxnews.com/world/migrants-biden-shirts-us-mexico-border.
7 Pilar Arias and Griff Jenkins, "Migrant at U.S.-Mexico Border Wears Biden-Harris Shirt, Claims Not to Know Who They Are," Fox News, March 7, 2024, https://www.foxnews.com/politics/migrant-us-mexico-border-wears-biden-harris-shirt-claims-not-know-who-they-are.
8 Charles Creitz, "Haitian Migrant Sports 'Biden-Harris' Shirt as Thousands More Converge at Guatemala-Mexico Border," Fox News, September 27, 2021, https://www.foxnews.com/media/haitian-migrant-sports-biden-harris-shirts-as-thousands-more-converge-at-guatemala-mexico-border.
9 U.S. Citizenship and Immigration Services, "Temporary Protected Status," last reviewed or updated May 28, 2026, https://www.uscis.gov/humanitarian/temporary-protected-status.
10 U.S. Citizenship and Immigration Services, "Temporary Protected Status Designated Country: Haiti," accessed July 20, 2026, https://www.uscis.gov/humanitarian/temporary-protected-status/temporary-protected-status-designated-country-haiti.
11 Social Security Administration, Supplemental Nutrition Assistance Program (SNAP) Facts, Publication No. 05-10101 (March 2025), https://www.ssa.gov/pubs/EN-05-10101.pdf.
12 Center on Budget and Policy Priorities, "A Quick Guide to SNAP Eligibility and Benefits," updated October 3, 2025, https://www.cbpp.org/research/food-assistance/a-quick-guide-to-snap-eligibility-and-benefits.
13 Alison Moodie, "Temporary Protected Status, Explained," Boundless, updated July 4, 2025, https://www.boundless.com/immigration-resources/temporary-protected-status.
14 Erik Crew, "Current Status of Employment Authorization of Haitian TPS Holders Pursuant to Court Order in Lesly Miot et al. v. Trump et al., Case No. 25-cv-02471

(D.D.C.)," Haitian Bridge Alliance, February 4, 2026, https://haitianbridgealliance.org/wp-content/uploads/2026/02/2026.02.04_Letters_for_Employers_re_TPS_for_Haiti_HBA_Final.pdf.

15 Social Security Administration, "Apply for Your Social Security Card While Applying for Your Work Permit, Lawful Permanent Residency, or U.S. Naturalization," accessed July 20, 2026, https://www.ssa.gov/ssnvisa/ebe.html.

16 HIAS, Employment Authorization Application Toolkit for Pro Se Applicants, updated January 4, 2023, https://resources.humanrightsfirst.org/wp-content/uploads/2023/02/Pro-Se-EAD-Toolkit-2022.pdf.

17 U.S. Department of Housing and Urban Development, "What Is 'Temporary Protected Status' with Respect to Immigrants from Hostile Countries?," HUD Exchange, accessed July 20, 2026, https://www.hudexchange.info/faqs/4070/what-is-temporary-protected-status-with-respect-to-immigrants-from/.

18 U.S. Citizenship and Immigration Services, Online Request to Be a Supporter and Declaration of Financial Support, Form I-134A, ed. July 11, 2023, https://www.uscis.gov/sites/default/files/document/forms/i-134a.pdf.

19 U.S. Citizenship and Immigration Services, "Humanitarian or Significant Public Benefit Parole for Aliens Outside the United States," last reviewed or updated December 15, 2025, https://www.uscis.gov/humanitarian/humanitarian_parole.

20 U.S. Citizenship and Immigration Services, "Family Reunification Parole Processes," last reviewed or updated January 27, 2026, https://www.uscis.gov/FRP.

21 U.S. Citizenship and Immigration Services, Online Request to Be a Supporter and Declaration of Financial Support, Form I-134A, ed. July 11, 2023, https://www.uscis.gov/sites/default/files/document/forms/i-134a.pdf.

22 U.S. Citizenship and Immigration Services, "FAQs on the Effect of Changes to Parole and Temporary Protected Status (TPS) for SAVE Agencies," updated July 10, 2026, https://www.uscis.gov/save/current-user-agencies/guidance/faqs-on-the-effect-of-changes-to-parole-and-temporary-protected-status-tps-for-save-agencies.

23 U.S. Citizenship and Immigration Services, "Temporary Protected Status Designated Country: Haiti," last reviewed or updated February 4, 2025, https://www.uscis.gov/humanitarian/temporary-protected-status/temporary-protected-status-designated-country-haiti.

24 U.S. Citizenship and Immigration Services, "Deferred Enforced Departure (DED) and Temporary Protected Status (TPS) Live Engagement Questions and Answers," May 24, 2021, https://www.uscis.gov/sites/default/files/document/outreach-engagements/Temporary_Protected_Status_and_Deferred_Enforced_Departure_for_Venezuela-Questions_and_Answers.pdf.

25 Vicky Forrest, "Citizen Comments at Springfield Commission Reflect National Divide," *Springfield News-Sun*, July 26, 2024, https://www.springfieldnewssun.com/news/citizen-comments-at-springfield-commission-reflect-national-divide/JQIFDAQBHFAIPCDC3KJVMVDPDU/.

26 Charles Creitz, "Haitian Migrant Sports 'Biden-Harris' Shirt as Thousands More Converge at Guatemala-Mexico Border," Fox News, September 27, 2021, https://www.foxnews.com/media/haitian-migrant-sports-biden-harris-shirts-as-thousands-more-converge-at-guatemala-mexico-border.

27 Tanya Broder, Ben D'Avanzo, Sarah Krieger, and Matthew Lopas, "Overview of Immigrant Eligibility for Federal Programs," National Immigration Law Center, January 1, 2026, https://www.nilc.org/resources/overview-immeligfedprograms/.

28 Administration for Children and Families, Office of Family Assistance, "Temporary Assistance for Needy Families (TANF)," accessed July 20, 2026, https://acf.gov/ofa/programs/temporary-assistance-needy-families-tanf.

29 Clark County Department of Job & Family Services, Haitian Entrant Benefits in Clark County, Ohio Fact Sheet, updated September 17, 2024, https://www.clarkcountyohio.gov/DocumentCenter/View/8118/Clark-County-Ohio-Benefits-Fact-Sheet?bidId=.

30 Garson O'Toole, "Quote Origin: It Is Difficult to Get a Man to Understand Something When His Salary Depends Upon His Not Understanding It," Quote Investigator, November 30, 2017, updated August 17, 2024, https://quoteinvestigator.com/2017/11/30/salary/.

31 Internal Revenue Service, "Work Opportunity Tax Credit," last reviewed or updated June 26, 2026, https://www.irs.gov/businesses/small-businesses-self-employed/work-opportunity-tax-credit.

32 Emily Corwin, "A Tax Credit Was Meant to Help Marginalized Workers Get Permanent Jobs. Instead It's Subsidizing Temp Work," *ProPublica*, August 23, 2022, https://www.propublica.org/article/work-opportunity-tax-credit-temp-permanent-employment.

33 Oscar El Blue Independent Media, "Canoe Capsized, 3 Are Missing," YouTube video, accessed July 20, 2026, https://www.youtube.com/watch?v=tM9Y1-TK9Ss.

34 Oscar El Blue Independent Media, "Canoe Capsized, 3 Are Missing," YouTube video, accessed July 20, 2026, https://www.youtube.com/watch?v=tM9Y1-TK9Ss.

35 Redacted, "He's EXPOSING the Hidden U.S. Child Concentration Camps Used for Trafficking," YouTube video, 33:12, September 10, 2023, https://www.youtube.com/watch?v=N3FYvsqCpGM.

36 U.S. Department of Homeland Security, "DHS Leads Efforts to Rescue Child Victims of Sex and Labor Trafficking," July 25, 2025, https://www.dhs.gov/news/2025/07/25/dhs-leads-efforts-rescue-child-victims-sex-and-labor-trafficking.

37 U.S. Department of Homeland Security, "DHS Leads Efforts to Rescue Child Victims of Sex and Labor Trafficking," July 25, 2025, https://www.dhs.gov/news/2025/07/25/dhs-leads-efforts-rescue-child-victims-sex-and-labor-trafficking.

38 Aldgra Fredly, "Border Czar Homan Says More Than 145,000 Illegal Immigrant Children Located," *The Epoch Times*, January 31, 2026, updated February 3, 2026, https://www.theepochtimes.com/us/border-czar-homan-says-more-than-145000-illegal-immigrant-children-located-5979019.

39 Redacted, "He's EXPOSING the Hidden U.S. Child Concentration Camps Used for Trafficking," YouTube video, 33:12, September 10, 2023, https://www.youtube.com/watch?v=N3FYvsqCpGM.

40 America's Future, "Where Did the Children Go: An Exposé Special—Whistleblowers Reveal the Truth," accessed July 20, 2026, https://www.americasfuture.net/where-did-the-children-go/.

41 Tara Lee Rodas, testimony before the U.S. House Judiciary Subcommittee on Immigration Integrity, Security, and Enforcement, "The Biden Border Crisis: Exploitation of Unaccompanied Alien Children," April 26, 2023, https://judiciary.house.gov/sites/evo-subsites/republicans-judiciary.house.gov/files/evo-media-document/rodas-testimony.pdf.

42 U.S. Department of Homeland Security, "100 Days of the Most Secure Border in American History," April 28, 2025, https://www.dhs.gov/news/2025/04/28/100-days-most-secure-border-american-history.

43 U.S. Customs and Border Protection, "Border Crossings Once Again at a Record Low in November 2025," December 4, 2025, https://www.cbp.gov/newsroom/national-media-release/border-crossings-once-again-record-low-november-2025.

44 Wikipedia contributors, "Staples Easy Button," Wikipedia, The Free Encyclopedia, last modified June 13, 2026, https://en.wikipedia.org/wiki/Staples_Easy_Button.

45 U.S. Congress, House, Committee on Homeland Security, Trafficked, Exploited, and Missing: Migrant Children Victims of the Biden-Harris Administration, joint hearing before the Subcommittee on Border Security and Enforcement and the Subcommittee on Oversight, Investigations, and Accountability, 118th Cong., 2nd sess., November 19, 2024, Serial No. 118-83, https://www.congress.gov/event/118th-congress/house-event/LC74263/text.

46 Christian Heiens (@ChristianHeiens), X post, April 15, 2026, https://x.com/christianheiens/status/2044571761115599144.

Chapter 6

1 Aristotle, *The Politics*, trans. Benjamin Jowett, bk. 5, pt. 11, sec. 4, ContextUS, accessed July 20, 2026, https://contextus.org/Aristotle%2C_The_Politics%2C_Book_Five%2C_Part_Eleven.4?lang=en&with=all&lang2=en.

2 Jessica Orozco et al., "Springfield Staffing Firm Responds to Allegations of Busing, Exploiting Haitians," *Springfield News-Sun*, updated September 28, 2024, https://www.springfieldnewssun.com/news/springfield-staffing-firm-responds-to-allegations-of-busing-exploiting-haitians/article_ce8a1a4c-fbe6-5dc5-8948-8e2c68fb3537.html.

3 Clark County Board of Elections, "About Us," accessed May 1, 2026, https://www.boe.ohio.gov/clark/about-us/.

4 Nick Johnson, "Springfield, Ohio Is Under a Migration Invasion. Is Your Town Next?," YouTube video, 55:20, September 17, 2024, https://www.youtube.com/watch?v=DOuNn-PI9j0.

5 "Ten Enterprises LLC," Bizapedia, accessed July 20, 2026, https://www.bizapedia.com/oh/ten-enterprises-llc.html.

6 "Searching for a Home? These Are the Top 20 U.S. Housing Markets," *USA Today*, April 15, 2021, https://www.usatoday.com/story/money/2021/04/15/home-near-me-here-were-top-20-u-s-housing-markets-march-2021/7218326002/.

7 Stephen Starr, "Overcharged for Substandard Housing: Untold Story of Haitians in Springfield," *The Guardian*, October 1, 2024, https://www.theguardian.com/us-news/2024/oct/01/haitians-springfield-ohio-housing.

8 Fox News, "Asra Nomani," accessed July 20, 2026, https://www.foxnews.com/person/n/asra-nomani.

9 Asra Q. Nomani, "Exclusive: In a Game of 'Springfieldopoly,' 'King George' Built an Empire with Estimated Revenues of $180M, and Feds and State AG Now Expand Human Trafficking Probe into Alleged Identity Theft and Tax Fraud," *Jewish Journal*, September 28, 2024, https://jewishjournal.com/commentary/opinion/375369/exclusive-in-a-game-of-springfieldopoly-king-george-built-an-empire-with-estimated-revenues-of-.

10 Asra Q. Nomani, "Exclusive: Feds and State AG Investigate an Alleged Human Trafficking Empire Run in Springfield, Ohio, for Years by 'King George,'" *Jewish Journal*, September 18, 2024, https://jewishjournal.com/commentary/opinion/375011/feds-and-state-ag-investigate-an-alleged-human-trafficking-empire-run-in-springfield-ohio/.

11 Nomani, Asra Q. "Exclusive: Feds and State AG Investigate an Alleged Human Trafficking Empire Run in Springfield, Ohio, for Years by 'King George.'" *Jewish Journal*, September 18, 2024. https://jewishjournal.com/commentary/opinion/375011/feds-and-state-ag-investigate-an-alleged-human-trafficking-empire-run-in-springfield-ohio/.

12 Asra Q. Nomani, "Exclusive: In a Game of 'Springfieldopoly,' 'King George' Built an Empire with Estimated Revenues of $180M, and Feds and State AG Now Expand Human Trafficking Probe into Alleged Identity Theft and Tax Fraud," *Jewish Journal*,

September 28, 2024, https://jewishjournal.com/commentary/opinion/375369/exclusive-in-a-game-of-springfieldopoly-king-george-built-an-empire-with-estimated-revenues-of-180m-and-feds-and-state-ag-now-expand-human-trafficking-probe-int/.

13 Office of Ohio Governor Mike DeWine, "Governor DeWine Announces New Traffic Safety Program in Springfield, Provides Updates on Area Health, Education Initiatives," December 5, 2024, https://governor.ohio.gov/media/news-and-media/governor-dewine-announces-new-traffic-safety-program-in-springfield-provides-updates-on-area-health-education-initiatives.

14 Life in Christ Community Church, "Pastors and Staff," accessed July 20, 2026, https://lifeinchristcommunitychurch.org/staff/.

15 Asra Q. Nomani, "Exclusive: In a Game of 'Springfieldopoly,' 'King George' Built an Empire with Estimated Revenues of $180M, and Feds and State AG Now Expand Human Trafficking Probe into Alleged Identity Theft and Tax Fraud," *Jewish Journal*, September 28, 2024, https://jewishjournal.com/commentary/opinion/375369/exclusive-in-a-game-of-springfieldopoly-king-george-built-an-empire-with-estimated-revenues-of-180m-and-feds-and-state-ag-now-expand-human-trafficking-probe-int/.

Chapter 7

1 Jessica Orozco, "Springfield Leaders Reject Recent Wild Haitian Rumors, Focus on Few Key Problems," *Springfield News-Sun*, September 10, 2024, https://www.springfieldnewssun.com/politics/springfield-leaders-reject-recent-wild-haitian-rumors-focus-on-few-key-problems/article_d29a2edd-8098-5a90-b90f-6f324d14bdb5.html.

2 WHIO Staff, "Driver Hospitalized after Driving off I-70 into Freezing Pond in Clark County," WHIO-TV 7, March 17, 2026, https://www.whio.com/news/local/troopers-investigate-car-into-pond-i-70-behind-loves/W5MJIDVQLNCPDNFARQTW3NCDUA/.

3 WHIO Staff, "Driver Hospitalized after Driving off I-70 into Freezing Pond in Clark County," WHIO-TV 7, March 17, 2026, https://www.whio.com/news/local/troopers-investigate-car-into-pond-i-70-behind-loves/W5MJIDVQLNCPDNFARQTW3NCDUA/.

4 Majority Haitian (@MajorityHaitian), X post, September 20, 2025, https://x.com/MajorityHaitian/status/1969353614846996791.

5 Springfield Police Division, Rules and Regulations & Manual of Procedures, rev. July 7, 2021, https://springfieldohio.gov/wp-content/uploads/2021/11/Rules-and-Regulations_v07072021.pd.

6 Springfield Police Division, Rules and Regulations & Manual of Procedures, rev. July 7, 2021, https://springfieldohio.gov/wp-content/uploads/2021/11/Rules-and-Regulations_v07072021.pd.

7 Brooke Spurlock, "Clark County Sheriff Talks Current Jail Conditions Related to Overcapacity, Disrepair," *Springfield News-Sun*, July 29, 2025, https://www.springfieldnewssun.com/news/clark-county-sheriff-talks-current-jail-conditions-related-to-overcapacity-disrepair/article_fd39cd76-e807-523a-9c0b-c2f34fcc9c1c.html.

8 Lauren Steen, "Clark County Positions $108M Public Safety Center as Long-Term Public Investment," *Dayton Business Journal*, January 2, 2026, https://www.bizjournals.com/dayton/news/2026/01/02/clark-county-public-safety-center-2026.html.

9 Clark County, Ohio, Clark County, Ohio Haitian Influx: Frequently Asked Questions, updated September 25, 2024, https://www.clarkcountyohio.gov/DocumentCenter/View/8133/Clark-County-Ohio-Haitian-Influx-FAQs.

10 Clark County, Ohio, Clark County, Ohio Haitian Influx: Frequently Asked Questions, updated September 25, 2024, https://www.clarkcountyohio.gov/DocumentCenter/View/8133/Clark-County-Ohio-Haitian-Influx-FAQs.

11 Ann Block and Erin Quinn, "The Impact of Crimes on Eligibility for Temporary Protected Status" (Immigrant Legal Resource Center, March 2023), https://www.ilrc.org/sites/default/files/2023-03/%20the%20impact%20of%20crimes%20on%20eligibility%20for%20TPS%20FINAL.pdf.

12 African American Health Equity Task Force, Buffalo Center for Health Equity, and UB Community Health Equity Research Institute, "Statement on Anti-Racism and Health Equity," June 2020, https://www.buffalo.edu/content/dam/www/inclusion/docs/Comm%20Health%20Equity.pdf.

13 Investigative News Service, "Springfield, Ohio Has Been Covering Up Race of Murderers, Records Show," October 18, 2024, https://investigativenews.substack.com/p/springfield-ohio-has-been-covering.

14 Springfield Police Division, Rules & Regulations, rev. July 7, 2021, https://springfieldohio.gov/wp-content/uploads/2021/11/Rules-and-Regulations_v07072021.pdf.

15 Setys001 (@Setys001), X post, September 10, 2024, https://x.com/Setys001/status/1833645592960008470.

16 "Stop the Influx Into Springfield, Ohio," Facebook group, accessed July 20, 2026, https://www.facebook.com/groups/1894983897588392.

17 "Springfield, Ohio: Are You Not Entertained?," private Facebook group, accessed July 29, 2026, https://www.facebook.com/groups/1023076210648934.

18 Alex Kasprak, "No Evidence Haitian Immigrants Are Eating Ducks, Geese or Pets in Springfield, Ohio," Snopes, September 9, 2024, https://www.snopes.com/fact-check/cats-ducks-haitians-springfield/.

19 "Springfield Pet-Eating Hoax," Wikipedia, last modified July 19, 2026, https://en.wikipedia.org/wiki/Springfield_pet-eating_hoax.

20 Maria Ramirez Uribe and Amy Sherman, "'They're Eating the Pets': Trump, Vance Earn PolitiFact's Lie of the Year for Claims about Haitians," PolitiFact, December 17, 2024, https://www.politifact.com/article/2024/dec/17/theyre-eating-the-pets-trump-vance-earn-politifact/.

21 Riley Hoffman, "READ: Harris-Trump Presidential Debate Transcript," ABC News, September 10, 2024, https://abcnews.com/Politics/harris-trump-presidential-debate-transcript/story?id=113560542.

22 Gustaf Kilander, "First Trump Said Haitian Migrants in Ohio Were 'Eating the Pets.' Now He Says They're 'Destroying America,'" Yahoo News, September 20, 2024, https://www.yahoo.com/news/first-trump-said-haitian-migrants-020821337.html.

23 U.S. Census Bureau, "QuickFacts: Springfield City, Ohio," accessed July 20, 2026, https://www.census.gov/quickfacts/fact/table/springfieldcityohio/AFN120222.

24 World Population Review, "Springfield, Ohio Population 2026," accessed July 20, 2026, https://worldpopulationreview.com/us-cities/ohio/springfield.

25 Catherine E. Shoichet, "'Why Springfield?' How a Small Ohio City Became Home for Thousands of Haitians," CNN, September 19, 2024, https://www.cnn.com/2024/09/19/us/springfield-ohio-haitians-immigration-cec.

26 Lauren Caggiano, "What Would the Termination of Haitian TPS Mean for Springfield's Economy?," Hub Springfield, March 20, 2026, https://hubspringfield.com/what-could-the-potential-termination-of-haitian-tps-mean-for-springfields-economy/.

27 Wedly Cazy, "TPS Limbo Puts Financial Strain on Springfield's Haitians, Slows Down Their Businesses," *The Haitian Times*, March 16, 2026, https://haitiantimes.com/2026/03/16/tps-uncertainty-springfield-haitian-community-economic-impact/.

28 Clark County, Ohio, Clark County, Ohio Haitian Influx: Frequently Asked Questions, updated September 25, 2024, https://www.clarkcountyohio.gov/DocumentCenter/View/8133/Clark-County-Ohio-Haitian-Influx-FAQs.

29 Jasmine Garsd, "How Springfield, Ohio, Took Center Stage in the Election Immigration Debate," NPR, August 12, 2024, https://www.npr.org/2024/08/12/nx-s1-5055784/immigration-vance-trump-migration-president-migrants-election-ohio.

30 Josiane Valsaint, "I'm a Haitian TPS Holder. Over 330,000 of Us Hold Our Breath as Congress Decides Our Future," *The Guardian*, July 31, 2026, https://www.theguardian.com/commentisfree/2026/jul/31/haitian-temporary-protected-status-us-trump.

31 Aaron Reichlin-Melnick, "Immigrants Are Making Ohio Great. Let's Talk About That," American Immigration Council, September 17, 2024, https://www.americanimmigrationcouncil.org/blog/immigrants-are-making-ohio-great-lets-talk-about-that/.

32 Clark County–Springfield Transportation Coordinating Committee, CONNECT Clark County: Comprehensive Plan (March 2018), https://springfieldohio.gov/wp-content/uploads/2020/12/CCC-Comprehensive-Plan.pdf.

33 Clark County–Springfield Transportation Coordinating Committee, CONNECT Clark County: Comprehensive Plan (March 2018), https://springfieldohio.gov/wp-content/uploads/2020/12/CCC-Comprehensive-Plan.pdf.

34 Clark County–Springfield Transportation Coordinating Committee, CONNECT Clark County: Comprehensive Plan (March 2018), https://springfieldohio.gov/wp-content/uploads/2020/12/CCC-Comprehensive-Plan.pdf.

35 Clark County–Springfield Transportation Coordinating Committee, CONNECT Clark County: Comprehensive Plan (March 2018), https://springfieldohio.gov/wp-content/uploads/2020/12/CCC-Comprehensive-Plan.pdf.

36 EXPAND Greater Springfield, "Springfield Welcomes Topre America Ohio," May 6, 2023, http://www.expandgreaterspringfield.com/site-selection/industrial-and-corporate-parks/p/item/730/springfield-welcomes-topre-america-ohio.

37 DevelopOhio, "Auto Supplier Plans Additional $73M Investment, 204 Jobs in Springfield," April 23, 2018, https://www.bricker.com/DevelopOhio/Auto-supplier-plans-additional-73M-investment-204-jobs-in-Springfield.

38 EXPAND Greater Springfield, "History," accessed July 20, 2026, http://www.expandgreaterspringfield.com/about/history.

39 IMPLAN, The Economic Impact of JobsOhio Projects 2011–21: Update, prepared for JobsOhio, May 2025, https://www.jobsohio.com/images/implan/jo_11-year_impact_study_2011-2021_final_version_2025_update.pdf.

40 Champaign Economic Partnership, "Rittal," accessed July 20, 2026, https://www.cepohio.com/news/category/rittal.

41 Google Maps, "1475 Upper Valley Pike, Springfield, OH 45504," accessed July 20, 2026, https://www.google.com/maps?daddr=1475+Upper+Valley+Pike,+Springfield,+OH+45504.

42 Gabe's, "Gabe's Opens Its Largest Distribution Center in Clark County, Ohio; Ribbon Cutting April 4," GlobeNewswire, March 29, 2023, https://www.globenewswire.com/news-release/2023/03/29/2637186/0/en/GABE-S-OPENS-ITS-LARGEST-DISTRIBUTION-CENTER-IN-CLARK-COUNTY-OHIO-RIBBON-CUTTING-APRIL-4.html.

43 Donald J. Trump, "Remarks at the Joint Systems Manufacturing Center in Lima, Ohio," March 20, 2019, The American Presidency Project, https://www.presidency.ucsb.edu/documents/remarks-the-joint-systems-manufacturing-center-lima-ohio.

44 Donald J. Trump, "Trump Campaign Press Release—President Trump Is Fighting for Ohio Workers and Families," The American Presidency Project, September 21, 2020, https://www.presidency.ucsb.edu/documents/trump-campaign-press-release-president-trump-fighting-for-ohio-workers-and-families.

45 JobsOhio, "Ohio Attracting Foreign Direct Investment from Manufacturers," February 25, 2022, https://www.jobsohio.com/newsroom/news-press/ohio-attracting-foreign-direct-investment-from-international-manufacturers.

46 Kyle Koehler, "Rep. Kyle Koehler Applauds Local Job Creation," March 20, 2018, https://www.votekoehler.com/news/rep-kyle-koehler-applauds-local-job-creation.

47 Media Matters Staff, "PBS NewsHour Highlights the Positive Impact of Migrant Workers in Springfield, Ohio," Media Matters for America, September 10, 2024, https://www.mediamatters.org/pbs/pbs-newshour-highlights-positive-impact-migrant-workers-springfield-ohio.

48 Omar Jimenez, Caitlin Stephen Hu, and Matthew Reynard, "Springfield Haitians Weigh Their Future as Trump Threatens Deportations," ABC7 New York, October 13, 2024, https://abc7ny.com/post/haitian-migrants-springfield-ohio-weigh-future-donald-trump-threatens-deportations/15424464/.

49 Omar Jimenez, Caitlin Stephen Hu, and Matthew Reynard, "Springfield Haitians Weigh Their Future as Trump Threatens Deportations," ABC7 New York, October 13, 2024, https://abc7ny.com/post/haitian-migrants-springfield-ohio-weigh-future-donald-trump-threatens-deportations/15424464/.

50 Robert Cherry, "A Deeper Look into Haitian Immigrants in Springfield," American Enterprise Institute, October 10, 2024, https://www.aei.org/op-eds/a-deeper-look-into-haitian-immigrants-in-springfield.

51 Robert Cherry, "A Deeper Look into Haitian Immigrants in Springfield," American Enterprise Institute, October 10, 2024, https://www.aei.org/op-eds/a-deeper-look-into-haitian-immigrants-in-springfield.

52 Stephen Starr, "Overcharged for Substandard Housing: Untold Story of Haitians in Springfield," *The Guardian*, October 1, 2024, https://www.theguardian.com/us-news/2024/oct/01/haitians-springfield-ohio-housing.

53 Eli Burgett, "Haitian Migrants Face Uncertain Future as Springfield Braces for Economic Impact," Dayton 24/7 Now, July 29, 2025, https://dayton247now.com/news/local/haitian-migrants-face-uncertain-future-as-springfield-braces-for-economic-impact.

54 Eli Burgett, "Haitian Migrants Face Uncertain Future as Springfield Braces for Economic Impact," Dayton 24/7 Now, July 29, 2025, https://dayton247now.com/news/local/haitian-migrants-face-uncertain-future-as-springfield-braces-for-economic-impact.

55 Howard Schneider, "How Haitian Immigrants Fueled Springfield's Growth," Reuters, September 11, 2024, https://www.reuters.com/world/us/haitian-immigrants-fueled-springfields-growth-now-us-presidential-debate-2024-09-11/.

56 Greater Springfield Partnership, "Haitian Immigration Statement," accessed July 20, 2026, https://www.greaterspringfield.com/haitian-immigration-statement.

57 Omar Jimenez, Caitlin Stephen Hu, and Matthew Reynard, "Springfield Haitians Weigh Their Future as Trump Threatens Deportations," ABC7 New York, October 13, 2024, https://abc7ny.com/post/haitian-migrants-springfield-ohio-weigh-future-donald-trump-threatens-deportations/15424464/.

58 Shay Frank, "DeWine: Businesses Worry about Losing Haitian Employees to Deportation," WYSO, May 20, 2025, https://www.wyso.org/news/2025-05-20/dewine-business-worry-about-losing-haitian-employees-to-deportation.

59 Clark County, Ohio, Clark County, Ohio Haitian Influx: Frequently Asked Questions, updated September 25, 2024, https://www.clarkcountyohio.gov/DocumentCenter/View/8133/Clark-County-Ohio-Haitian-Influx-FAQs.

60 Lauren Caggiano, "What Would the Termination of Haitian TPS Mean for Springfield's Economy?," Hub Springfield, March 20, 2026, https://hubspringfield.com/what-could-the-potential-termination-of-haitian-tps-mean-for-springfields-economy/.

61 City of Springfield, Ohio, "Immigration FAQs," accessed July 20, 2026, https://springfieldohio.gov/immigration-faqs/.

62 City of Springfield, Ohio, "Immigration FAQs," accessed July 20, 2026, https://springfieldohio.gov/immigration-faqs/.

63 Policy Matters Ohio, "Revoking Temporary Protected Status for Haitian Immigrants Will Further Destabilize Springfield's Economy," February 3, 2026, https://policymattersohio.org/news/2026/02/03/revoking-temporary-protected-status-for-haitian-immigrants-will-further-destabilize-springfields-economy/.

64 Stephen Starr, "Haitians Helped Boost Springfield's Economy—Now They're Fleeing in Fear of Trump," *The Guardian*, October 28, 2025, https://www.theguardian.com/us-news/2025/oct/28/springfield-ohio-economy-haitians-trump-immigration.

65 Topre America Corporation–Ohio, "Overhead Crane Operator—C Shift," job posting, Indeed, accessed July 20, 2026, https://www.indeed.com/q-topre-jobs-l-springfield,-oh-jobs.html?sort=date&vjk=d92c6c4afe3575e3.

66 Haitian Bridge Alliance, "Haitian Bridge Alliance Calls DHS Decision to End TPS for Haiti Dangerous, Premature, and Morally Unacceptable," November 26, 2025, https://haitianbridgealliance.org/haitian-bridge-alliance-calls-dhs-decision-to-end-tps-for-haiti-dangerous-premature-and-morally-unacceptable/.

67 Lauren Caggiano, "What Would the Termination of Haitian TPS Mean for Springfield's Economy?," Hub Springfield, March 20, 2026, https://hubspringfield.com/what-could-the-potential-termination-of-haitian-tps-mean-for-springfields-economy/.

68 EXPAND Greater Springfield, "PrimeOhio II Industrial Park," accessed July 20, 2026, http://www.expandgreaterspringfield.com/site-selection/industrial-and-corporate-parks/p/item/728/primeohio-ii-industrial-park.

69 Lauren Caggiano, "What Would the Termination of Haitian TPS Mean for Springfield's Economy?," Hub Springfield, March 20, 2026, https://hubspringfield.com/what-could-the-potential-termination-of-haitian-tps-mean-for-springfields-economy/.

70 Howard Schneider, "How Haitian Immigrants Fueled Springfield's Growth," Reuters, September 11, 2024, https://www.reuters.com/world/us/haitian-immigrants-fueled-springfields-growth-now-us-presidential-debate-2024-09-11/.

71 Wedly Cazy, "As Haitian TPS End Date Nears, Fear, Frustration and Fortitude Spread in Springfield," *The Haitian Times*, January 30, 2026, https://haitiantimes.com/2026/01/30/springfield-haitian-tps-economic-impact/.

72 Wise, "US Dollars to Haitian Gourdes Exchange Rate Today," accessed July 20, 2026, https://wise.com/gb/currency-converter/usd-to-htg-rate.

73 WorldData.info, "Haiti: Country Data and Statistics," last modified July 2026, accessed July 20, 2026, https://www.worlddata.info/america/haiti/index.php.

74 Wedly Cazy, "TPS Limbo Puts Financial Strain on Springfield's Haitians, Slows Down Their Businesses," *The Haitian Times*, March 16, 2026, https://haitiantimes.com/2026/03/16/tps-uncertainty-springfield-haitian-community-economic-impact/.

75 Wedly Cazy, "As Haitian TPS End Date Nears, Despair and Frustration Spread in Springfield," *The Haitian Times*, January 30, 2026, https://haitiantimes.com/2026/01/30/springfield-haitian-tps-economic-impact/.

76 Clark County, Ohio, Clark County, Ohio Haitian Influx: Frequently Asked Questions, updated September 25, 2024, https://www.clarkcountyohio.gov/DocumentCenter/View/8133/Clark-County-Ohio-Haitian-Influx-FAQs?bidId=.

77 Beatrice Dain and Jeanne Batalova, "Haitian Immigrants in the United States," Migration Information Source, Migration Policy Institute, November 8, 2023, https://www.migrationpolicy.org/journal/spotlight/haitian-immigrants-united-states.

78 Cornelius Frolik, "Springfield Has the Worst Job Losses in Ohio: Haiti TPS Ending Could Make It Worse," *Springfield News-Sun*, February 2, 2026, https://www.springfieldnewssun.com/news/springfield-has-the-worst-job-losses-in-ohio-haiti-tps-ending-could-make-it-worse/article_576bf1e9-99fd-5133-85e0-4fc284b0e65d.html.

79 Manuel Orozco and Elisabeth Burgess, "A Commitment Amidst Shared Hardship: Haitian Transnational Migrants and Remittances," *Journal of Black Studies* 42, no. 2 (March 2011): 225–46, https://www.jstor.org/stable/41151337.

80 U.S. Bureau of Economic Analysis, "Total Gross Domestic Product for Springfield, OH (MSA) (Discontinued)," FRED, Federal Reserve Bank of St. Louis, updated December 4, 2024, accessed July 20, 2026, https://fred.stlouisfed.org/series/NGMP44220.

81 Stephen Starr, "Haitians Helped Boost Springfield's Economy—Now They're Fleeing in Fear of Trump," *The Guardian*, October 28, 2025, https://www.theguardian.com/us-news/2025/oct/28/springfield-ohio-economy-haitians-trump-immigration.

82 Lauren Caggiano, "What Would the Termination of Haitian TPS Mean for Springfield's Economy?," Hub Springfield, March 20, 2026, https://hubspringfield.com/what-could-the-potential-termination-of-haitian-tps-mean-for-springfields-economy/.

83 Lauren Caggiano, "What Would the Termination of Haitian TPS Mean for Springfield's Economy?," Hub Springfield, March 20, 2026, https://hubspringfield.com/what-could-the-potential-termination-of-haitian-tps-mean-for-springfields-economy/.

84 Lauren Caggiano, "What Would the Termination of Haitian TPS Mean for Springfield's Economy?," Hub Springfield, March 20, 2026, https://hubspringfield.com/what-could-the-potential-termination-of-haitian-tps-mean-for-springfields-economy/.

85 Clark County, Ohio, Clark County, Ohio Haitian Influx: Frequently Asked Questions, updated September 25, 2024, https://www.clarkcountyohio.gov/DocumentCenter/View/8133/Clark-County-Ohio-Haitian-Influx-FAQs.

86 Parker Perry, "Burchett Defeats Longtime Incumbent Clark County Sheriff," *Dayton Daily News*, November 9, 2016, https://www.daytondailynews.com/burchett-defeats-longtime-incumbent-clark-county-sheriff/article_5ac8c89c-daab-5fea-a1df-2f27813f90a5.html.

87 Alex Oliveira, "Fatal Accidents in Springfield, Ohio, Jumped Four-Fold Last Year—as Residents Say Migrants Unfamiliar with US Rules," *New York Post*, September 15, 2024, https://nypost.com/2024/09/15/us-news/fatal-accidents-in-springfield-ohio-jumped-four-fold-last-year/.

88 Lydia Bice, "Ohio BMV Addresses Rumors about Haitian Drivers in Springfield," Dayton 24/7 Now, September 12, 2024, https://dayton247now.com/news/local/bmv-addresses-rumors-about-haitian-drivers-in-springfield.

89 Lydia Bice, "Ohio BMV Addresses Rumors about Haitian Drivers in Springfield," Dayton 24/7 Now, September 12, 2024, https://dayton247now.com/news/local/bmv-addresses-rumors-about-haitian-drivers-in-springfield.

90 Lydia Bice, "Ohio BMV Addresses Rumors about Haitian Drivers in Springfield," Dayton 24/7 Now, September 12, 2024, https://dayton247now.com/news/local/bmv-addresses-rumors-about-haitian-drivers-in-springfield.

91 Empty Pockets Garage, James, "Springfield, Ohio: The Truth on Traffic Violations & How It Keeps Happening," YouTube video, accessed July 20, 2026, https://www.youtube.com/watch?v=n9z-cE-UoZo.

92 The Heartland Beat, "On the Fear of Accountability," October 6, 2024, Substack, https://heartlandbeat.substack.com/p/on-the-fear-of-accountability.

93 Glenn Beck, "EXCLUSIVE: Springfield, Ohio Locals SPEAK OUT on Migrant Crisis," Facebook video, September 11, 2024, https://www.facebook.com/watch/?v=909344057765093.

94 Candace Hathaway, "Exclusive: 'They Have Decided to Go Silent': Springfield Police Cut Radio Access as Springfield Descends into 'Absolute Turmoil,' Says Ohio Police Chief," *Blaze Media*, September 25, 2024, https://www.theblaze.com/news/springfield-descends-into-absolute-turmoil-says-ohio-police-chief.

95 Clark County, Ohio, Clark County, Ohio Haitian Influx: Frequently Asked Questions, updated September 25, 2024, https://www.clarkcountyohio.gov/DocumentCenter/View/8133/Clark-County-Ohio-Haitian-Influx-FAQs.

96 WSYX ABC 6, "Despite Migration Surge, Springfield Reported Fewer Crashes Last Year over Past Years," YouTube video, September 14, 2024, https://www.youtube.com/watch?v=9jNA8n_oghU.

97 Ohio House Finance Committee, "Substitute House Bill 54 Amendment Summary," February 25, 2025, https://search-prod.lis.state.oh.us/api/v2/general_assembly_136/committees/cmte_h_finance_1/meetings/cmte_h_finance_1_2025-02-25-1030_84/submissions/hb54.sub.bill.summary.pdf.

98 Karen Kasler, "DeWine Signs Ohio's Transportation Budget at the Finish Line; All Items Pass Through without Vetoes," The Statehouse News Bureau, April 1, 2025, https://www.statenews.org/government-politics/2025-04-01/dewine-signs-ohios-transportation-budget-at-the-finish-line-all-items-pass-through-without-vetoes.

99 Phil Plummer, "Representative Plummer Votes in Support of House Transportation Budget," Ohio House of Representatives, February 27, 2025, https://ohiohouse.gov/members/phil-plummer/news/representative-plummer-votes-in-support-of-house-transportation-budget-128145.

100 Ohio General Assembly, "House Bill 434: Exempt Military Driver's License Applicants from Driver's Ed," 136th General Assembly, effective November 25, 2025, https://www.legislature.ohio.gov/legislation/136/hb434.

101 Jessica Orozco, "Closed BMV Location Failed to Meet Six Requirements, State Says," *Springfield News-Sun*, September 25, 2025, https://www.springfieldnewssun.com/news/closed-bmv-location-failed-to-meet-six-requirements-state-says/article_af7e531a-74c5-5779-b035-ff7a85b5d862.html.

102 Carlos Mathis, "Deputy Registrar Resigns; Ohio BMV Location 'Temporarily Closed,'" WDTN, September 25, 2025, https://www.wdtn.com/news/ohio-bmv-location-temporary-closed-in-springfield/.

103 Jessica Orozco, "Closed BMV Location Failed to Meet Six Requirements, State Says," *Springfield News-Sun*, September 25, 2025, https://www.springfieldnewssun.com/news/closed-bmv-location-failed-to-meet-six-requirements-state-says/article_af7e531a-74c5-5779-b035-ff7a85b5d862.html.

104 WHIO Staff, "Car Crashes into Garage in Springfield," WHIO-TV 7, August 28, 2023, https://www.whio.com/news/car-crashes-into-garage-springfield/ec1c94af-3366-404f-95a6-a83784ebd642/.

105 Walter Curt, "Clark County Catastrophe: The Human Cost of Biden's Lax Immigration Policies," *The W.C. Dispatch*, August 30, 2023, https://www.wcdispatch.com/p/clark-county-catastrophe-the-human.

106 Walter Curt, "Clark County Catastrophe: The Human Cost of Biden's Lax Immigration Policies," *The W.C. Dispatch*, August 30, 2023, https://www.wcdispatch.com/p/clark-county-catastrophe-the-human.

107 Jessica Orozco, "Crash Reconstruction Expert Details Fatal School Bus Crash in Trial of Minivan Driver," *Springfield News-Sun*, May 1, 2024, https://www.springfieldnewssun.com/news/crash-reconstruction-expert-details-fatal-school-bus-crash-in-trial-of-minivan-driver/article_f31f95f0-bcfc-5db4-9925-039f3ab3ae18.html.

108 John Binder, "Illegal Alien, Freed into U.S. from Southern Border, Charged with Killing 11-Year-Old Aiden Clark," Breitbart News, August 28, 2023, https://www.breitbart.com/politics/2023/08/28/illegal-alien-freed-southern-border-charged-killing-11-year-old-aiden-clark/.

109 Neil Munro, "Springfield, Ohio: Residents Say Haitian Migrants Crashing Cars, Spiking Insurance, Eating Ducks from Parks," Breitbart News, September 9, 2024, https://www.breitbart.com/immigration/2024/09/09/bidens-migrants-in-springfield-ohio-car-crashes-civic-chaos-and-nazis/.

110 Bethany Bruner, "Ohio Jury Convicts Man Who Caused First Day of School Bus Crash That Killed 11-Year-Old," *The Columbus Dispatch*, May 1, 2024, https://www.dispatch.com/story/news/courts/2024/05/01/ohio-school-bus-crash-death-haitian-immigrant-manslaughter/73531021007/.

111 Germania Rodriguez Poleo, "Father of Ohio Boy Killed by Haitian Migrant in Springfield Crash Speaks Out," *Daily Mail*, September 11, 2024, https://www.dailymail.com/news/article-13838621/father-springfield-boy-killed-haitin-migrant-crash-shocking-remarks.html.

112 Isabelle Hanson, "Clark County Community Honors, Remembers Student Who Died in Bus Crash," ABC 6 On Your Side, August 23, 2023, https://abc6onyourside.com/news/local/clark-county-community-honors-remembers-student-who-died-in-bus-crash.

113 Stephen Starr, "How a Child's Death Caused an Ohio City to Turn on Its Haitian Community," Al Jazeera, December 12, 2023, https://www.aljazeera.com/features/2023/12/12/how-a-childs-death-caused-an-ohio-city-to-turn-on-its-haitian-community.

114 Empty Pockets Garage, James, "Haitian Invasion, Springfield, Ohio: Corrupt N.G.O.'s in the Name of Religion," YouTube video, January 11, 2026, https://www.youtube.com/watch?v=uXxD6MVyYbY.

115 "Aiden James Clark Obituary," Littleton & Rue Funeral Home and Crematory, accessed July 20, 2026, https://www.littletonandrue.com/obituaries/Aiden-James-Clark?obId=28788238.

116 Brooke Spurlock, "Woman Crossing Road Killed in Morning Crash in Springfield Twp.," *Springfield News-Sun*, December 1, 2023, https://www.springfieldnewssun.com/news/woman-crossing-road-killed-in-morning-crash-in-springfield-twp/article_af4c7ede-913d-512a-aeb1-b15579533896.html.

117 Jackson Lytle & Lewis Life Celebration Center, "Kathy Lynn Heaton Obituary," accessed July 20, 2026, https://www.jacksonlytle.com/obituaries/kathy-heaton.

118 Mia Cathell, "The Haitian Horror Story No One's Talking About," Townhall, September 19, 2024, https://townhall.com/tipsheet/miacathell/2024/09/19/deadly-driving-haitians-n2644772.

119 Jack Morphet, Alex Oliveira, and Joe Durbin, "Influx of Wild-Driving Haitian Migrants Turning Streets of Springfield, Ohio, into Combat Zone: 'Eight to 10 Accidents a Day Here,'" *New York Post*, September 12, 2024, https://nypost.com/2024/09/12/us-news/influx-of-wild-driving-haitian-migrants-turning-streets-of-springfield-ohio-into-combat-zone/.

120 Mia Cathell, "The Haitian Horror Story No One's Talking About," Townhall, September 19, 2024, https://townhall.com/tipsheet/miacathell/2024/09/19/deadly-driving-haitians-n2644772.

121 Mia Cathell, "The Haitian Horror Story No One's Talking About," Townhall, September 19, 2024, https://townhall.com/tipsheet/miacathell/2024/09/19/deadly-driving-haitians-n2644772.

122 Sarah Nickles, "Standing with Amanda Gipson Through Recovery," GoFundMe, March 3, 2026, https://www.gofundme.com/f/standing-with-amanda-gipson-through-recovery.

123 Pearl Lewandowski, "Truck Driver Pleads Not Guilty in I-75 Crash That Killed Lima Father and Son," Your Hometown Stations, March 12, 2026, https://www.hometownstations.com/news/allen_county/truck-driver-pleads-not-guilty-in-i-75-crash-that-killed-lima-father-and-son/article_a4fa3de2-2ef3-4d6c-8b18-26355871622b.html.

124 Pearl Lewandowski, "Truck Driver Pleads Not Guilty in I-75 Crash That Killed Lima Father and Son," Your Hometown Stations, March 12, 2026, https://www.hometownstations.com/news/allen_county/truck-driver-pleads-not-guilty-in-i-75-crash-that-killed-lima-father-and-son/article_a4fa3de2-2ef3-4d6c-8b18-26355871622b.html.

125 Empty Pockets Garage, James, "Haitian Invasion, Non-Citizen Truck Driver Caused Tragedy for a Family in Ohio," YouTube video, March 22, 2026, https://www.youtube.com/watch?v=Yy1QbjbfKJw.

126 Empty Pockets Garage, James, "Haitian Invasion, Non-Citizen Truck Driver Caused Tragedy for a Family in Ohio," YouTube video, March 22, 2026, https://www.youtube.com/watch?v=Yy1QbjbfKJw.

127 Tal Axelrod, "GOP Gov. DeWine Defends Haitian Immigrants: 'They Came to Springfield to Work,'" ABC News, September 15, 2024, https://abcnews.com/Politics/gop-gov-dewine-defends-haitian-immigrants-springfield-work/story?id=113690058.

128 Clark County, Ohio, Clark County, Ohio Haitian Influx: Frequently Asked Questions, updated September 25, 2024, https://www.clarkcountyohio.gov/DocumentCenter/View/8133/Clark-County-Ohio-Haitian-Influx-FAQs.

129 Clark County, Ohio, Clark County, Ohio Haitian Influx: Frequently Asked Questions, updated September 25, 2024, https://www.clarkcountyohio.gov/DocumentCenter/View/8133/Clark-County-Ohio-Haitian-Influx-FAQs.

130 RentData.org, "Springfield Fair Market Rent: FY 2021 Springfield, OH MSA Rental Data," accessed July 20, 2026, https://www.rentdata.org/springfield-oh-msa/2021.

131 RentData.org, "Springfield Fair Market Rent: FY 2025 Springfield, OH MSA Rental Data," accessed July 20, 2026, https://www.rentdata.org/springfield-oh-msa/2025.

132 Fox Business, "Illegal Immigrant Influx Strangles Housing Supply and Punishes US Families," YouTube video, December 10, 2025, https://www.youtube.com/watch?v=jjCct-uC7vc.

133 Stephen Starr, "Overcharged for Substandard Housing: Untold Story of Haitians in Springfield," *The Guardian*, October 1, 2024, https://www.theguardian.com/us-news/2024/oct/01/haitians-springfield-ohio-housing.

134 Stephen Starr, "Overcharged for Substandard Housing: Untold Story of Haitians in Springfield," *The Guardian*, October 1, 2024, https://www.theguardian.com/us-news/2024/oct/01/haitians-springfield-ohio-housing.

135 Miriam Jordan, "How an Ohio Town Landed in the Middle of the Immigration Debate," *New York Times*, September 3, 2024, https://www.nytimes.com/2024/09/03/us/springfield-ohio-school-bus-crash-haiti-immigrants.html.

136 Better Business Bureau, "Garlind Properties L.L.C. Customer Reviews," accessed July 20, 2026, https://www.bbb.org/us/oh/springfield/profile/property-management/garlind-properties-llc-0322-1440102680/customer-reviews.

137 Stephen Starr, "Overcharged for Substandard Housing: Untold Story of Haitians in Springfield," *The Guardian*, October 1, 2024, https://www.theguardian.com/us-news/2024/oct/01/haitians-springfield-ohio-housing.

138 Stephen Starr, "Overcharged for Substandard Housing: Untold Story of Haitians in Springfield," *The Guardian*, October 1, 2024, https://www.theguardian.com/us-news/2024/oct/01/haitians-springfield-ohio-housing.

139 Jasmine Garsd, "How Springfield, Ohio, Took Center Stage in the Election Immigration Debate," NPR, August 12, 2024, https://www.npr.org/2024/08/12/nx-s1-5055784/immigration-vance-trump-migration-president-migrants-election-ohio.

140 City of Springfield, Ohio, "Rental Property Registration," accessed July 20, 2026, https://springfieldohio.gov/city_services/rental-property-registration/.

141 Holly Souther, "Explosion in Springfield Apartment Building Injures 3," *Springfield News-Sun*, April 8, 2023, https://www.springfieldnewssun.com/news/explosion-in-springfield-apartment-building-injures-3/article_61e267d0-f56d-5b52-8b1d-51de97cccc7c.html.

142 Sydney Dawes, "Woman Hospitalized in Springfield Explosion Dies," *Springfield News-Sun*, April 10, 2023, https://www.springfieldnewssun.com/news/woman-hospitalized-in-springfield-explosion-dies/article_38f38daa-b8a9-5a5b-94c2-4781c34f6a98.html.

143 Jessica Orozco, "Baby Injured in Springfield Townhome Explosion Released from Hospital," *Springfield News-Sun*, April 25, 2023, https://www.springfieldnewssun.com/news/baby-injured-in-springfield-townhome-explosion-released-from-hospital/article_6e51e009-219a-5539-8d96-1274ed063061.html.

144 Holly Souther, "Explosion in Springfield Apartment Building Injures 3," *Springfield News-Sun*, April 8, 2023, https://www.springfieldnewssun.com/news/explosion-in-springfield-apartment-building-injures-3/article_61e267d0-f56d-5b52-8b1d-51de97cccc7c.html.

145 Jessica Orozco, "Springfield Group Aids Families Affected by Deadly Townhome Explosion," *Springfield News-Sun*, April 26, 2023, https://www.springfieldnewssun.com/news/springfield-group-aids-families-affected-by-deadly-townhome-explosion/article_e8a2c617-9d31-56ea-9708-a2e72b270ab7.html.

146 Jessica Orozco, "Springfield Group Aids Families Affected by Deadly Townhome Explosion," *Springfield News-Sun*, April 26, 2023, https://www.springfieldnewssun.com/news/springfield-group-aids-families-affected-by-deadly-townhome-explosion/article_e8a2c617-9d31-56ea-9708-a2e72b270ab7.html.

147 Asra Q. Nomani, "Exclusive: In a Game of 'Springfieldopoly,' 'King George' Built an Empire with Estimated Revenues of $180M, and Feds and State AG Now Expand Human Trafficking Probe into Alleged Identity Theft and Tax Fraud," *Jewish Journal*, September 28, 2024, https://jewishjournal.com/commentary/opinion/375369/exclusive-in-a-game-of-springfieldopoly-king-george-built-an-empire-with-estimated-revenues-of-180m-and-feds-and-state-ag-now-expand-human-trafficking-probe-int/.

148 Alicia Victoria Lozano and Corky Siemaszko, "Baseless Rumors about Haitian Immigrants Threaten to Unravel Springfield, Ohio," *NBC News*, September 15, 2024, https://www.nbcnews.com/news/us-news/baseless-rumors-haitian-immigrants-threaten-unravel-springfield-ohio-rcna170513.

149 Isaac Saul, "The Haitian Immigrant Controversy in Ohio," Tangle, September 12, 2024, https://www.readtangle.com/springfield-ohio-immigration-haiti-cats/.

150 Sarah Spohn, "New Melody Parks Housing Development Pays Homage to Historic Melody Cruise-In Theatre," Hub Springfield, February 22, 2024, https://hubspringfield.com/New-Melody-Parks-housing-development-pays-homage-to-historic-Melody-Cruise-In-Theatre-022224/.

151 U.S. Census Bureau, "Springfield City, Clark County, Ohio," Census Bureau Profile, accessed July 20, 2026, https://data.census.gov/profile/Springfield_city,_Clark_County,_Ohio?g=060XX00US3902374118.

152 "'My Rent Is So High': With Prices Hitting the Roof, Renters Making Hard Choices," *Springfield News-Sun*, accessed July 20, 2026, https://www.springfieldnewssun.com/local/my-rent-is-so-high-with-prices-hitting-the-roof-renters-making-hard-choices/article_104833b3-e842-5497-9043-20d86483afbb.html.

153 Stephen Starr, "Overcharged for Substandard Housing: Untold Story of Haitians in Springfield," *The Guardian*, October 1, 2024, https://www.theguardian.com/us-news/2024/oct/01/haitians-springfield-ohio-housing.

154 Corey Daniels, "Special Report: Renting Apartments to Haitians Is Big Business for Springfield Mayor Rob Rue, Others," The Project for a New American Government, September 18, 2024, https://newamericangovernment.org/special-report-renting-apartments-to-haitians-is-big-business-for-springfield-mayor-rob-rue-others/.

155 Lauren Caggiano, "What Would the Termination of Haitian TPS Mean for Springfield's Economy?," Hub Springfield, March 20, 2026, https://hubspringfield.com/what-could-the-potential-termination-of-haitian-tps-mean-for-springfields-economy/.

156 Jessica Orozco, "Tax Revenue Flat, Springfield Projects Slow Growth in 2026," *Springfield News-Sun*, June 27, 2025, https://www.springfieldnewssun.com/news/tax-revenue-flat-springfield-projects-slow-growth-in-2026/article_b3246377-d86b-535c-bc33-e9a644d08ced.html.

157 Hasan Karim, "Springfield Expected to Generate $45.2M in Income Tax Revenue for 2023," *Springfield News-Sun*, June 27, 2022, https://www.springfieldnewssun.com/news/springfield-expected-to-generate-45-2m-in-income-tax-revenue-for-2023/article_d6f183e5-1495-5731-be47-fb4192750e31.html.

158 City of Springfield, Ohio, "City Manager's 2026 Preliminary Budget," December 16, 2025, https://springfieldohio.gov/city-managers-2026-preliminary-budget/.

159 Clark County, Ohio, 2023 Annual Report (Springfield, OH: Clark County, Ohio, 2024), https://www.clarkcountyohio.gov/DocumentCenter/View/7948/Clark-County-Ohio-Annual-Report-2024.

160 Asra Q. Nomani, "Exclusive: In a Game of 'Springfieldopoly,' 'King George' Built an Empire with Estimated Revenues of $180M, and Feds and State AG Now Expand Human Trafficking Probe into Alleged Identity Theft and Tax Fraud," *Jewish Journal*, September 28, 2024, https://jewishjournal.com/commentary/opinion/375369/exclusive-in-a-game-of-springfieldopoly-king-george-built-an-empire-with-estimated-revenues-of-180m-and-feds-and-state-ag-now-expand-human-trafficking-probe-int/.

161 Clark County Department of Job & Family Services, Haitian Entrant Benefits in Clark County, Ohio Fact Sheet, updated September 17, 2024, https://www.clarkcountyohio.gov/DocumentCenter/View/8118/Clark-County-Ohio-Benefits-Fact-Sheet.

162 Ohio Department of Job and Family Services, Caseload Summary Statistics Report: July 2024 (July 2024), https://dam.assets.ohio.gov/image/upload/jfs.ohio.gov/PRC/CaseloadSummaryReportJuly2024.pdf.

163 Jon Husted (@JonHusted), "UPDATE: In Springfield (Clark County) the Latest Numbers Show 4,324 Haitian Refugees Receiving Either TANF, SNAP or Refugee Cash Assistance," X, September 10, 2024, https://x.com/JonHusted/status/1833559343335121365.

164 Clark County Board of Commissioners, Clark County, Ohio Haitian Influx: Frequently Asked Questions, updated September 25, 2024, https://www.clarkcountyohio.gov/DocumentCenter/View/8133/Clark-County-Ohio-Haitian-Influx-FAQs.

165 Jessica Orozco, "Clark State Gets $250K Grant to Expand English as a Second Language Classes," *Springfield News-Sun*, August 5, 2024, https://www.springfieldnewssun.com/news/clark-state-gets-250k-grant-to-expand-english-as-a-second-language-classes/article_5bf8834f-3da5-5536-b89c-de37f9899064.html.

166 Clark County Board of Commissioners, Clark County, Ohio Haitian Influx: Frequently Asked Questions, updated September 25, 2024, https://www.clarkcountyohio.gov/DocumentCenter/View/8133/Clark-County-Ohio-Haitian-Influx-FAQs.

167 Clark County Board of Commissioners, Clark County, Ohio Haitian Influx: Frequently Asked Questions, updated September 25, 2024, https://www.clarkcountyohio.gov/DocumentCenter/View/8133/Clark-County-Ohio-Haitian-Influx-FAQs.

168 City of Springfield, Ohio, "Current State and Federal Funding Reductions and Increases," accessed July 21, 2026, https://springfieldohio.gov/current-state-and-federal-funding-reductions-and-increases.

169 City of Springfield, Ohio, "Current State and Federal Funding Reductions and Increases," accessed July 21, 2026, https://springfieldohio.gov/current-state-and-federal-funding-reductions-and-increases/.

170 Ohio Secretary of State, "Secretary LaRose Reminds Elections Officials to Be Vigilant After Investigation Uncovers Illegal Voter Registration Forms," September 12, 2024, archived September 13, 2024, at the Internet Archive's Wayback Machine, https://web.archive.org/web/20240913053733/, https://www.ohiosos.gov/media-center/press-releases/2024/2024-09-12/.

171 Vicki (@NoWarningShot_), "Black Fork Strategies, an Ohio-Based Progressive Organization That Touts Itself as 'Building Long-Term Progressive Power,' Has Been Identified by Hamilton County Elections Officials . . .," X, July 28, 2024, https://x.com/NoWarningShot_/status/1817516954908794902.

172 Paula Bolyard, "Haitian Voter Fraud Uncovered in Springfield, Ohio," PJ Media, September 12, 2024, https://pjmedia.com/paula-bolyard/2024/09/12/breaking-ohio-sos-uncovers-fake-haitian-voter-registrations-springfield-n4932487.

173 Claudia Lauer and Alanna Durkin Richer, "FBI Searches Office of Ohio Group That Supports Voter Registration Efforts," AP News, June 12, 2026, https://apnews.com/article/fbi-ohio-voter-registration-investigation-4b241d64db0478c6a5852aa20d3e138f.

174 Andrew Tobias, "FBI Asked Elections Officials about Firm Linked to Ohio Progressive Group More Than a Year before Raid," Signal Ohio, June 16, 2026, https://signalohio.org/fbi-questioned-cuyahoga-elections-officials-about-voter-registration/.

175 Majority Haitian (@MajorityHaitian), "Springfield, Ohio—@RealTomHoman @realDonaldTrump MORE HAITIANS ARE ARRIVING DAILY. 1322 S. Limestone St., 45505 Is a PROCESSING CENTER. From a Post on Facebook," X, May 14, 2025, 5:38 p.m., https://x.com/MajorityHaitian/status/1922768456191021248.

176 J. D. Vance (@JDVance), "In the Last Several Weeks, My Office Has Received Many Inquiries from Actual Residents of Springfield Who've Said Their Neighbors' Pets or Local Wildlife Were Abducted by Haitian Migrants. . . .," X, September 10, 2024, 9:58 a.m., https://x.com/JDVance/status/1833505359513661762.

177 Clark County Combined Health District, Reportable Infectious Diseases in Clark County, Ohio, report created August 26, 2024, https://ccchd.com/wp-content/uploads/2024/09/Clark-County-Reportable-Infectious-Disease-Data-2013-to-2023.pdf.

178 Clark County Combined Health District, 2024 Annual Communicable Disease Report (2025), https://ccchd.com/wp-content/uploads/2025/04/Annual-CD-Report-2024.pdf.

179 Clark County Combined Health District, HIV and AIDS Data Summary: Ohio & Clark County, 2018 to 2022, updated September 11, 2024, https://ccchd.com/wp-content/uploads/2024/09/Ohio-and-Clark-County-HIV-AIDS-Data-2018-to-2022.pdf.

180 Clark County Combined Health District, 2023 Annual Communicable Disease Report, January 18, 2024, revised November 15, 2024, https://ccchd.com/wp-content/uploads/2024/11/REVISED-Annual-CD-Report-2023_Anna-Jean-Sauter.pdf.

181 Clark County Combined Health District, 2024 Annual Communicable Disease Report (2025), https://ccchd.com/wp-content/uploads/2025/04/Annual-CD-Report-2024.pdf.

182 Clark County Combined Health District, 2023 Annual Communicable Disease Report, January 18, 2024, revised November 15, 2024, https://ccchd.com/wp-content/uploads/2024/11/REVISED-Annual-CD-Report-2023_Anna-Jean-Sauter.pdf.

183 Clark County Board of Commissioners, Clark County, Ohio Haitian Influx: Frequently Asked Questions, updated September 25, 2024, https://www.clarkcountyohio.gov/DocumentCenter/View/8133/Clark-County-Ohio-Haitian-Influx-FAQs.

184 Clark County Combined Health District, YouTube channel, accessed July 21, 2026, https://www.youtube.com/@clarkcountycombinedhealthd6107/videos.

185 Clark County Combined Health District, "Health Equity & Cultural Literacy," accessed July 21, 2026, https://ccchd.com/health-equity-cultural-literacy/.

186 Clark County Combined Health District, Notes about: Food and Culture of Haiti, current as of March 24, 2023, https://ccchd.com/wp-content/uploads/2023/03/The-Food-and-Culture-of-Haiti_draft-03.22.2023.pdf.

187 Clark County Combined Health District, Notes about: Food and Culture of Haiti, current as of March 24, 2023, https://ccchd.com/wp-content/uploads/2023/03/The-Food-and-Culture-of-Haiti_draft-03.22.2023.pdf.

188 Clark County Combined Health District, Notes about: Food and Culture of Haiti, current as of March 24, 2023, https://ccchd.com/wp-content/uploads/2023/03/The-Food-and-Culture-of-Haiti_draft-03.22.2023.pdf.

189 Clark County Combined Health District, Notes about: Food and Culture of Haiti, current as of March 24, 2023, https://ccchd.com/wp-content/uploads/2023/03/The-Food-and-Culture-of-Haiti_draft-03.22.2023.pdf.

190 Anthony Karabanow, "Typhoid Fever in Haiti," The CRUDEM Foundation, accessed July 21, 2026, https://crudem.org/typhoid-fever-in-haiti/.

191 Clark County Combined Health District, Notes about: Haitian Beliefs about Death, May 30, 2023, https://ccchd.com/wp-content/uploads/2023/05/Haiti-and-Death.pdf.

192 Clark County Combined Health District, Notes about: Haitian Beliefs about Death, May 30, 2023, https://ccchd.com/wp-content/uploads/2023/05/Haiti-and-Death.pdf.

193 Clark County Combined Health District, Notes about: Haitian Beliefs about Death, May 30, 2023, https://ccchd.com/wp-content/uploads/2023/05/Haiti-and-Death.pdf.

194 Clark County Combined Health District, Notes about: Haitian Beliefs about Death, May 30, 2023, https://ccchd.com/wp-content/uploads/2023/05/Haiti-and-Death.pdf.

195 Clark County Combined Health District, Notes about: Haitian Beliefs about Death, May 30, 2023, https://ccchd.com/wp-content/uploads/2023/05/Haiti-and-Death.pdf.

196 Clark County Combined Health District, Notes about: Haitian Beliefs about Death, May 30, 2023, https://ccchd.com/wp-content/uploads/2023/05/Haiti-and-Death.pdf.

197 Clark County Combined Health District, Notes about: Haitian Beliefs about Death, May 30, 2023, https://ccchd.com/wp-content/uploads/2023/05/Haiti-and-Death.pdf.

198 Clark County Combined Health District, Notes about: Haitian Beliefs about Death, May 30, 2023, https://ccchd.com/wp-content/uploads/2023/05/Haiti-and-Death.pdf.

199 Gino Del Guercio, "The Secrets of Haiti's Living Dead," Harvard Magazine, October 31, 2017, https://www.harvardmagazine.com/faculty-community/are-zombies-real.

200 Jessica Orozco, "Cook Stepping Down as Clark County Health Commissioner Next Year Rather than Cut Services," *Springfield News-Sun*, January 11, 2026, https://www.springfieldnewssun.com/news/cook-stepping-down-as-clark-county-health-commissioner-next-year-rather-than-cut-services/article_3cf5caeb-35ea-5d8a-b0ad-326004761943.html.

201 Clark County Board of Commissioners, *Clark County, Ohio Haitian Influx: Frequently Asked Questions*, updated September 25, 2024, https://www.clarkcountyohio.gov/DocumentCenter/View/8133/Clark-County-Ohio-Haitian-Influx-FAQs.

202 Nevin Smith, "Clark County Combined Health District's Four-Pillar Plan for 2026," *Hub Springfield*, January 29, 2026, https://hubspringfield.com/clark-county-combined-health-districts-four-pillar-plan-for-2026/.

203 Clark County Combined Health District, Clark County Community Health Improvement Plan, 2026–2028 (February 17, 2026), https://ccchd.com/wp-content/uploads/2026/02/FINAL-Clark-County-Community-Health-Improvemet.pdf.

204 Clark County Combined Health District, Board of Health Meeting Packet, October 20, 2022, https://ccchd.com/wp-content/uploads/2022/10/102022-BOH-Packet-1.pdf.

205 Clark County Combined Health District, Clark County Board of Health Regular Monthly Meeting Packet, January 16, 2025, https://ccchd.com/wp-content/uploads/2025/01/011625-BOH-Packet.pdf.

206 Clark County Combined Health District, Clark County Board of Health Regular Monthly Meeting Packet, March 20, 2025, https://ccchd.com/wp-content/uploads/2025/03/032025-BOH-Packet.pdf.

207 Clark County Combined Health District, Clark County Board of Health Regular Monthly Meeting Packet, January 15, 2026, https://ccchd.com/wp-content/uploads/2026/01/011526-BOH-Packet-2.pdf.

208 Clark County Combined Health District, Clark County Board of Health Regular Monthly Meeting Packet, January 15, 2026, https://ccchd.com/wp-content/uploads/2026/01/011526-BOH-Packet-2.pdf.

209 Clark County Board of Commissioners, Clark County, Ohio Haitian Influx: Frequently Asked Questions, updated September 25, 2024, https://www.clarkcountyohio.gov/DocumentCenter/View/8133/Clark-County-Ohio-Haitian-Influx-FAQs.

210 Darvio Morrow, "In Springfield, Migrants Are Taking a Toll on the City's Most Vulnerable," *Newsweek*, September 13, 2024, https://www.newsweek.com/springfield-migrants-are-taking-toll-citys-most-vulnerable-opinion-1953385.

211 Brooke Spurlock, "Springfield Schools Face Influx of Non-English-Speaking Students," *Springfield News-Sun*, September 11, 2023, https://www.springfieldnewssun.com/news/springfield-schools-face-influx-of-non-english-speaking-students/article_6b332a6f-9b2d-5ab0-9c85-09313452ce2b.html.

212 Jessica Orozco and Sydney Dawes, "Are Haitians Fleeing Springfield? What Our Reporting Found," *Springfield News-Sun*, April 18, 2025, updated May 30, 2026, https://www.springfieldnewssun.com/news/are-haitians-fleeing-springfield-what-our-reporting-found/article_bc0bf3ea-b872-5797-886f-4b07ef504b75.html.

213 PolitiFact, "PolitiFact: Trump said each Haitian student in Springfield 'will have a private interpreter.' That's False," WOSU Public Media, September 26, 2024, https://www.wosu.org/politics-government/2024-09-26/politifact-trump-said-every-haitian-student-in-springfield-will-have-a-private-interpreter-thats-false.

214 Jon Husted (@JonHusted), "UPDATE: In Springfield (Clark County) the latest numbers show 4,324 Haitian refugees receiving either TANF, SNAP or Refugee Cash Assistance (Federal Funding) . . .," X, September 10, 2024, https://x.com/JonHusted/status/1833559343335121365.

215 Isaac Saul, "The Haitian Immigrant Controversy in Ohio," Tangle, September 12, 2024, https://www.readtangle.com/springfield-ohio-immigration-haiti-cats/.

216 Brooke Spurlock, "Springfield's Non-English Speaking Student Population Increased by 630 Last 5 Years," *Springfield News-Sun*, February 12, 2024, updated May 29, 2026, https://www.springfieldnewssun.com/news/springfield-s-non-english-speaking-student-population-increased-by-630-last-5-years/article_09560bd4-f102-5564-894e-69c287463315.html.

217 PolitiFact, "PolitiFact: Trump said each Haitian student in Springfield 'will have a private interpreter.' That's False," WOSU Public Media, September 26, 2024, https://www.wosu.org/politics-government/2024-09-26/politifact-trump-said-every-haitian-student-in-springfield-will-have-a-private-interpreter-thats-false.

218 PolitiFact, "PolitiFact: Trump said each Haitian student in Springfield 'will have a private interpreter.' That's False," WOSU Public Media, September 26, 2024, https://www.wosu.org/politics-government/2024-09-26/politifact-trump-said-every-haitian-student-in-springfield-will-have-a-private-interpreter-thats-false.

219 Gustaf Kilander, "First Trump said Haitian migrants in Ohio were 'eating the pets'. Now he says they're 'destroying America'," Yahoo News, September 20, 2024, https://www.yahoo.com/news/first-trump-said-haitian-migrants-020821337.html.

220 "More Bomb Threats in Springfield, Despite No Criminal Charges, Raising More Questions," The Ohio Register, February 9, 2026, https://www.theohioregister.com/more-bomb-threats-in-springfield-despite-no-criminal-charges-raising-more-questions/.

221 City of Springfield, Ohio v. The Blood Tribe, No. 3:25-cv-00033 (S.D. Ohio Feb. 6, 2025) (complaint and civil cover sheet), CourtListener, https://www.courtlistener.com/docket/69619730/1/1/city-of-springfield-ohio-v-the-blood-tribe/.

222 *City of Springfield, Ohio v. The Blood Tribe*, No. 3:25-cv-00033 (S.D. Ohio Feb. 6, 2025) (complaint), CourtListener, https://www.courtlistener.com/docket/69619730/1/city-of-springfield-ohio-v-the-blood-tribe/.

223 Yael Grauer, "How to Remove Your Contact Info From Online People-Search Sites," Consumer Reports, updated October 5, 2024, https://www.consumerreports.org/electronics/personal-information/how-to-delete-your-information-from-people-search-sites-a6926856917.

224 Chris Stewart, "How People Finding Websites Get Your Information, What You Can Do to Protect Yourself," abc15.com, accessed July 21, 2026, https://www.abc15.com/news/national/how-people-finding-websites-get-your-information-what-you-can-do-to-protect-yourself.

225 "Bitcoin Price Chart 2022," Bitbo, accessed July 21, 2026, https://charts.bitbo.io/price/2022.

226 "Bitcoin Price Chart 2025," Bitbo, accessed July 21, 2026, https://charts.bitbo.io/price/2025.

227 Ann Coulter (@AnnCoulter), "Liberals act as if the only reason anyone would want to revoke Haitians 'temporary' (15 yrs) protected status is because we HATE Haitians . . .," X, April 16, 2026, https://x.com/anncoulter/status/2044821272132047052.

228 Jon Husted (@JonHusted), "Springfield, Ohio Haitian Immigrants overwhelming Springfield, Ohio have made the national news . . .," X, September 9, 2024, https://x.com/JonHusted/status/1833214746817904961.

229 Jon Husted (@JonHusted), "UPDATE: In Springfield (Clark County) the latest numbers show 4,324 Haitian refugees receiving either TANF, SNAP or Refugee Cash Assistance (Federal Funding) . . . ," X, September 10, 2024, https://x.com/JonHusted/status/1833559343335121365.

230 TheDC Shorts, "Woman's Comments Cause CHAOS at Springfield City Commission Meeting . . . ," YouTube video, October 10, 2024, https://www.youtube.com/watch?v=xzN9Rn16Gz4.

231 _Darke County Sheriff's Office, "UPDATE: On June 21, 2026, a rear-seat passenger from the Honda CR-V, Wilnack Saintilma, 30, of Springfield, succumbed to his injuries at Miami Valley Hospital," Facebook post, June 24, 2026, https://www.facebook.com/DarkeCountySheriff/posts/1436718988489361/.

232 Littleton & Rue Funeral Home and Crematory, "[Funeral Service for Wilnack Saintilma]," Facebook video, accessed July 29, 2026, https://www.facebook.com/littletonandrue/videos/1325113983132938.

233 "1 Dead, Several Injured after Crash on SR-41 in Clark Co.," WDTN, July 22, 2026, https://www.wdtn.com/traffic/1-dead-several-injured-after-crash-on-sr-41-in-clark-co/.

234 WHIO, "Pierre Georges, 36, of Springfield Died on Scene," Facebook post, accessed July 28, 2026, https://www.facebook.com/whionews/posts/1355644003414731/.

Chapter 8

1 DataRepublican (@DataRepublican), "After spending too much time on the award search tool, I'm starting to wonder if we've had a UBI system all along for one political party—just disguised as grants," X, January 28, 2025, https://x.com/DataRepublican/status/1884300100656324988.

2 Empty Pockets Garage, "Haitian Invasion, Springfield, Ohio. Corrupt N.G.O's in the name of religion," YouTube video, January 11, 2026, https://www.youtube.com/watch?v=uXxD6MVyYbY.

3 Internal Revenue Service, "Exempt Organizations Business Master File Extract – Ohio (eo_oh.csv)," CSV file, n.d., accessed July 21, 2026, https://www.irs.gov/pub/irs-soi/eo_oh.csv.

4 Census Reporter, "Clark County, OH," https://censusreporter.org/profiles/05000US39023-clark-county-oh/ (ACS 2024 1-year estimates).

5 Jack Windsor, "On Springfield, DeWine and TPS Revocations . . . ," Facebook, June 26, 2026, https://www.facebook.com/100053501239023/posts/1542111824248844/.

6 Empty Pockets Garage, "Mondays with James & Jimmy. Following the money looking into N.G.O.s," YouTube video, April 13, 2026, https://www.youtube.com/watch?v=JKfVRc8zxqY.

7 Devlin Barrett, "Justice Dept. Charges Prominent Civil Rights Group With Financial Crimes," *New York Times*, April 21, 2026, https://www.nytimes.com/2026/04/21/us/politics/southern-poverty-law-center-doj-investigation.html.

8 Charles Creitz, "SPLC Saw Revenue Surge After Charlottesville Rally as DOJ Alleges Informant Ties," Fox News, April 23, 2026, https://www.foxnews.com/politics/splc-saw-revenue-surge-after-charlottesville-rally-doj-alleges-informant-ties.

9 Bob Moser, "The Reckoning of Morris Dees and the Southern Poverty Law Center," *The New Yorker*, March 21, 2019, https://www.newyorker.com/news/news-desk/the-reckoning-of-morris-dees-and-the-southern-poverty-law-center.

10 Jeff Pinkleton, LinkedIn profile, https://www.linkedin.com/in/jeffpinkleton/.

11 "What is The Gathering?," The Gathering of the Miami Valley, n.d., https://gatheringmv.org/what-is-the-gathering/.

12 Asra Q. Nomani, "Exclusive: In a Game of 'Springfieldopoly,' 'King George' Built an Empire with Estimated Revenues of $180M, and Feds and State AG Now Expand Human Trafficking Probe into Alleged Identity Theft and Tax Fraud," *Jewish Journal*, September 28, 2024, https://jewishjournal.com/commentary/opinion/375369/exclusive-in-a-game-of-springfieldopoly-king-george-built-an-empire-with-estimated-revenues-of-180m-and-feds-and-state-ag-now-expand-human-trafficking-probe-int/.

13 Asra Q. Nomani, "Exclusive: In a Game of 'Springfieldopoly,' 'King George' Built an Empire with Estimated Revenues of $180M, and Feds and State AG Now Expand Human Trafficking Probe into Alleged Identity Theft and Tax Fraud," *Jewish Journal*, September 28, 2024, https://jewishjournal.com/commentary/opinion/375369/exclusive-in-a-game-of-springfieldopoly-king-george-built-an-empire-with-estimated-revenues-of-180m-and-feds-and-state-ag-now-expand-human-trafficking-probe-int/.

14 Asra Q. Nomani, "Exclusive: In a Game of 'Springfieldopoly,' 'King George' Built an Empire with Estimated Revenues of $180M, and Feds and State AG Now Expand Human Trafficking Probe into Alleged Identity Theft and Tax Fraud," *Jewish Journal*, September 28, 2024, https://jewishjournal.com/commentary/opinion/375369/exclusive

-in-a-game-of-springfieldopoly-king-george-built-an-empire-with-estimated-revenues-of-180m-and-feds-and-state-ag-now-expand-human-trafficking-probe-int/.

15 Greater Springfield Partnership, "Haitian Immigration Statement," n.d., https://www.greaterspringfield.com/haitian-immigration-statement.

16 Jessica Orozco, "Haitian Coalition Becomes 'CommUnity Connection Coalition,' Expands Mission," *Springfield News-Sun*, January 31, 2026, updated April 3, 2026, https://www.springfieldnewssun.com/news/haitian-coalition-becomes-community-connection-coalition-expands-mission/article_4b5df17d-ff51-5f38-95db-59a345fd65d7.html.

17 Jessica Orozco, "Haitian Coalition Becomes 'CommUnity Connection Coalition,' Expands Mission," *Springfield News-Sun*, January 31, 2026, updated April 3, 2026, https://www.springfieldnewssun.com/news/haitian-coalition-becomes-community-connection-coalition-expands-mission/article_4b5df17d-ff51-5f38-95db-59a345fd65d7.html.

18 Brooke Spurlock and Stephen Starr, "What Springfield's Haitian Immigrants Need," *Springfield News-Sun*, September 20, 2024, https://www.springfieldnewssun.com/ohio/what-springfield-s-haitian-immigrants-need/article_714a7881-6b65-5260-be0f-0ce1fd4885a0.html.

19 Asra Q. Nomani, "Exclusive: In a Game of 'Springfieldopoly,' 'King George' Built an Empire with Estimated Revenues of $180M, and Feds and State AG Now Expand Human Trafficking Probe into Alleged Identity Theft and Tax Fraud," *Jewish Journal*, September 28, 2024, https://jewishjournal.com/commentary/opinion/375369/exclusive-in-a-game-of-springfieldopoly-king-george-built-an-empire-with-estimated-revenues-of-180m-and-feds-and-state-ag-now-expand-human-trafficking-probe-int/.

20 "Bryan Heck L," GovSalaries, accessed July 21, 2026, https://govsalaries.com/heck-bryan-l-178904737.

21 "Bryan Heck," GovSalaries, accessed July 21, 2026, https://govsalaries.com/heck-bryan-210247457.

22 OpenSpringfield, "Employee Compensation," accessed July 21, 2026, https://openspringfield.org/payroll.

23 Jeff Skinner, "Ohio State Auditor Reviewing Expenditures by Springfield City Officials," *The Ohio Register*, November 24, 2025, https://www.theohioregister.com/ohio-state-auditor-reviewing-expenditures-by-springfield-city-officials/.

24 City of Springfield, Ohio, City Commission Agenda, February 15, 2022, https://springfieldohio.gov/wp-content/uploads/2022/02/February-15-Agenda.pdf.

25 City of Springfield, Ohio, City Commission Agenda, February 15, 2022, https://springfieldohio.gov/wp-content/uploads/2022/02/February-15-Agenda.pdf.

26 City of Springfield, Ohio, City Commission Agenda, February 15, 2022, https://springfieldohio.gov/wp-content/uploads/2022/02/February-15-Agenda.pdf.

27 City of Springfield, Ohio, City Commission Agenda, February 15, 2022, https://springfieldohio.gov/wp-content/uploads/2022/02/February-15-Agenda.pdf.

28 City of Springfield, Ohio, City Commission Agenda, February 15, 2022, https://spring-fieldohio.gov/wp-content/uploads/2022/02/February-15-Agenda.pdf.

29 City of Springfield, Ohio, City Commission Agenda, February 15, 2022, https://springfieldohio.gov/wp-content/uploads/2022/02/February-15-Agenda.pdf.

30 City of Springfield, Ohio, City Commission Agenda, February 15, 2022, https://springfieldohio.gov/wp-content/uploads/2022/02/February-15-Agenda.pdf.

31 WKEF Staff. "Unanimous Vote Puts Springfield City Manager Bryan Heck on Administrative Leave." Dayton 24/7 Now, July 29, 2026. https://dayton247now.com/news/local/unanimous-vote-puts-springfield-city-manager-bryan-heck-on-administrative-leave.

32 Carl Ruby, "Civil Disobedience for Such a Time as This," Central Christian Church, April 9, 2025, https://www.ccspringfield.org/blog/civil-disobedience-for-such-a-time-as-this.

33 Jessica Orozco, "Springfield G92, Pastor Reject Social Media Rumors about Help for Haitians," *Springfield News-Sun*, February 13, 2026, https://www.springfieldnewssun.com/news/springfield-g92-pastor-reject-social-media-rumors-about-help-for-haitians/article_5f69fc6f-c2ae-5974-a62d-728900ff8f94.html.

34 Springfield G92, "Springfield G92 Love Thy Neighbor," Facebook video, accessed July 21, 2026, https://www.facebook.com/watch/?v=541342562336598.

35 G92, "Events," accessed July 21, 2026, https://springfieldg92.org/events/.

36 LeAnne Marie McPherson, "G92 Grants $50K to Support Haitian Immigrants and Others in Need in Springfield," WDTN, May 27, 2026, https://www.wdtn.com/news/g92-grants-50k-to-support-haitian-immigrants-and-others-in-need-in-springfield/.

37 UNDIVIDED, "UNDIVIDED," accessed July 21, 2026, https://undivided.us/.

38 WBNS 10TV, "Community Leaders Brace to Defend Haitians in Springfield, Ohio, against Deportation," YouTube video, July 30, 2025, https://www.youtube.com/watch?v=n1L4BVLcFDc.

39 Obed Lamy and Julie Carr Smyth, "Ohio City Whose Haitian Migrants Were Disparaged by Trump Braces to Defend Them against Deportation," *The Intelligencer*, August 3, 2025, https://www.theintelligencer.net/news/top-headlines/2025/08/ohio-city-whose-haitian-migrants-were-disparaged-by-trump-braces-to-defend-them-against-deportation/.

40 Amanda Becker, "The Original 'Wine Moms' Are in Ohio. They're Mobilizing to Support Haitians in Springfield," *Ohio Capital Journal*, February 16, 2026, https://ohiocapitaljournal.com/2026/02/16/the-original-wine-moms-are-in-ohio-theyre-mobilizing-to-support-haitians-in-springfield/.

41 Indivisible Springfield Ohio, accessed July 21, 2026, https://indivisiblespringfieldoh.com/.

42 "Indivisible Springfield Ohio," Action Network, accessed July 21, 2026, https://actionnetwork.org/groups/indivisible-springfield-ohio.

43 Indivisible, "Find a Group," accessed July 21, 2026, https://indivisible.org/get-involved/find-a-group/?keywords=springfield%2C+oh.

44 "The Indivisible Project (Indivisible)," InfluenceWatch, accessed July 21, 2026, https://www.influencewatch.org/non-profit/the-indivisible-project-indivisible/.

45 Alese Underwood, "Springfield Advocates Walk for Peace," Spectrum News 1, January 20, 2026, https://spectrumnews1.com/oh/columbus/news/2026/01/20/springfield-advocates-walk-for-peace.

46 Amanda Becker, "Fear, Faith and Preparation as ICE Closes In on an Ohio Community," *The 19th*, January 28, 2026, https://19thnews.org/2026/01/ice-churches-children-springfield-ohio/.

47 Mary McCarty, "Checking In on Springfield's Haitian Community," *Cincinnati Magazine*, January 13, 2026, https://www.cincinnatimagazine.com/article/checking-in-on-springfields-haitian-community/.

48 Rocking Horse Community Health Center, "Complete Health & Wellness Services for Our Community," accessed July 21, 2026, https://rockinghorsecenter.org/.

49 Jessica Orozco, "Haitian Immigrant Patients More Than Triple at Springfield's Rocking Horse Health Center," *Springfield News-Sun*, May 14, 2023, https://www.springfieldnewssun.com/news/haitian-immigrant-patients-more-than-triple-at-springfield-s-rocking-horse-health-center/article_cfe8e565-8330-5c92-acb8-a22462538c8b.html.

50 Stephanie Armour, "Happening in Springfield: New Immigrants Offer Economic Promise, Health System Challenges," *Ohio Capital Journal*, October 14, 2024, https://ohiocapitaljournal.com/2024/10/14/happening-in-springfield-new-immigrants-offer-economic-promise-health-system-challenges/.

51 Stephanie Armour, "Haitian Immigrants in Springfield Bring Economic Promise, Public Health Challenges," *Healthbeat*, October 10, 2024, https://www.healthbeat.org/2024/10/10/haitian-immigrants-in-springfield-ohio-bring-economic-promise-but-face-health-challenges/.

52 Vicky Forrest, "Crowd Questions Springfield Leaders on Immigration Issues after Bus Crash," *Springfield News-Sun*, August 30, 2023, https://www.springfieldnewssun.com/news/crowd-questions-springfield-leaders-on-immigration-issues-after-bus-crash/article_ff342079-cbfa-504e-8ce6-27acd04daba9.html.

53 Cause IQ, "Rocking Horse Community Health Center," accessed July 21, 2026, https://www.causeiq.com/organizations/rocking-horse-community-health-center,311593544/.

54 Advocates for Basic Legal Equality, "Home," accessed July 21, 2026, https://www.ablelaw.org/.

55 Ohio Access to Justice Foundation, "Legal Aid Lawyer Profile: Katie Kersh, Advocates for Basic Legal Equality," September 30, 2021, https://www.ohiojusticefoundation.org/legal-aid-lawyer-profile-katie-kersh-advocates-for-basic-legal-equality.

56 Advocates for Basic Legal Equality, "Serving Springfield's Haitian Community," updated February 2, 2026, https://www.ablelaw.org/areas-of-impact/serving-springfields-haitian-community/.

57 Haitian Support Center, "About Us," accessed July 21, 2026, https://haitiansupportcenter.org/about-us/.

58 Candid, "Haitian Community Help & Support Center," GuideStar, accessed July 21, 2026, https://www.guidestar.org/profile/93-4819144.

59 Kathryn Mobley, "Haitian Support Center Co-Founder Reacts after Judge Lets TPS Continue for Now," WYSO, February 3, 2026, https://www.wyso.org/news/2026-02-03/haitian-support-center-co-founder-reacts-after-judge-lets-tps-continue-for-now.

60 Haitian Support Center, "About Us," accessed July 21, 2026, https://haitiansupportcenter.org/about-us/.

61 Kathryn Mobley, "Springfield Neighbors United Rallies around City's Haitians, Other Immigrants," WYSO, January 30, 2025, https://www.wyso.org/news/2025-01-30/springfield-neighbors-united-rally-around-citys-haitians-other-immigrants.

62 Marian Stewart, "Springfield Neighbors United: Stand With Us for Immigration Justice," Faith Choice Ohio, February 3, 2026, https://www.faithchoiceohio.org/blog/springfield-neighbors-united-stand-with-us-for-immigration-justice.

63 G92, "Get Involved," accessed July 21, 2026, https://springfieldg92.org/get-involved/.

64 Haitian Support Center, "About Us," accessed July 21, 2026, https://haitiansupportcenter.org/about-us/.

65 Emily Belz, "Rebuilding Broken Walls with the Nehemiah Foundation," *Christianity Today*, September/October 2025, https://www.christianitytoday.com/2025/09/rebuilding-broken-walls-nehemiah-foundation/.

66 Amanda Becker, "Fear, Faith and Preparation as ICE Closes In on an Ohio Community," *The 19th*, January 28, 2026, https://19thnews.org/2026/01/ice-churches-children-springfield-ohio/.

67 Nehemiah Foundation, "Haitian Community Help & Support Center," August 13, 2024, https://nehemiahfoundation.org/churches/haitian-community-help-support-center/.

68 Pedro Gonzalez, "In Rose City, the Dream Has Wilted," *Chronicles*, November 15, 2024, https://chroniclesmagazine.org/society-culture/in-rose-city-the-dream-has-wilted/.

69 Andrew Long-Higgins and David Long-Higgins, "A Pastoral Letter of Support for Our Haitian Siblings in Springfield," United Church of Christ, September 18, 2024, https://www.ucc.org/a-pastoral-letter-of-support-for-our-haitian-siblings-in-springfield/.

70 Brooke Spurlock, "Springfield Foundation Awards $834K in Grants to Clark County Nonprofits," *Springfield News-Sun*, February 5, 2024, https://www.springfieldnewssun.com/news/springfield-foundation-awards-834k-in-grants-to-clark-county-nonprofits/article_4923110b-dcca-5458-8a19-c5a7d8a84282.html.

71 WYSO, "Haitians in the Heartland," accessed July 21, 2026, https://www.wyso.org/haitians-in-the-heartland.

72 Haitian Community Alliance, "Haitian Community Alliance (HCA): Uniting for Empowerment, Safety, and Progress in Springfield," archived February 11, 2026, Internet Archive, Wayback Machine, https://web.archive.org/web/20260211011710/https://haitiancommunityalliance.org/.

73 Jessica Orozco, "Churches May Help House Thousands of Springfield Children Left Behind If TPS Expires," *Springfield News-Sun*, February 9, 2026, https://www.springfieldnewssun.com/news/churches-may-help-house-thousands-of-springfield-children-left-behind-if-tps-expires/article_74d1b599-5e81-5198-9822-c4e9041d6746.html.

74 Theresa Hice-Fromille, "How One Ohio Town Is Resisting the Threat of an ICE Raid," ZNetwork, April 30, 2026, https://znetwork.org/znetarticle/how-one-ohio-town-is-resisting-the-threat-of-an-ice-raid/.

75 Society of St. Vincent de Paul–Springfield Region, "Neighbors Helping Neighbors," accessed July 21, 2026, https://svdpspfld.org/.

76 Amanda Becker, "The Ohio Grandma Racing to Help Haitian Parents Protect Children as More Deportations Near," *The 19th*, December 15, 2025, https://19thnews.org/2025/12/springfield-ohio-haitian-family-separation/.

77 Howard Schneider, "How Haitian Immigrants Fueled Springfield's Growth," Reuters, September 11, 2024, https://www.reuters.com/world/us/haitian-immigrants-fueled-springfields-growth-now-us-presidential-debate-2024-09-11/.

78 Su Casa Hispanic Center, "Catholic Charities Springfield Office Is Now Open!," Hispanic Chamber Cincinnati USA, July 31, 2024, https://business.hispanicchambercincinnati.com/news/details/catholic-charities-springfield-office-is-now-open.

79 Springfield 2051, "Making History Now," accessed July 21, 2026, https://springfield2051.com/.

80 Springfield 2051, "Advisory Group," accessed July 21, 2026, https://springfield2051.com/advisory-group/.

81 Future iQ, "Springfield 2051—Making History Now Project (2025–2026)," accessed July 21, 2026, https://future-iq.com/project/springfield2051-2025-2026/.

82 Mike Frazier, "What Will Springfield Look Like in 25 Years? 'Springfield 2051' Is Building a Roadmap," WYSO, April 5, 2026, https://www.wyso.org/news/2026-04-05/what-will-springfield-look-like-in-25-years-springfield-2051-is-building-a-roadmap.

83 Jeff Skinner, "Public Private Partnership Gives Update on Springfield 2051 Project, Leading to New Questions," The Ohio Register, May 5, 2026, https://www.theohioregister.com/public-private-partnership-gives-update-on-springfield-2051-project-leading-to-new-questions/.

84 Laura A. Bischoff, "Ohio Gov. Mike DeWine and Haiti: What Ties Does He Have?," *The Columbus Dispatch*, February 3, 2026, 2:24 a.m. ET, https://www.dispatch.com/story/news/politics/2026/02/03/ohio-gov-mike-dewine-haiti-what-ties-does-he-have-dewine-family-foundation-tom-hagan/88431011007/.

85 Grantmakers.io, "DeWine Family Foundation Inc.," accessed July 21, 2026, https://www.grantmakers.io/profiles/v1/311483132-dewine-family-foundation-inc/?page=1.

86 American Immigration Lawyers Association, "Presidential Executive Order on Enhancing State and Local Involvement in Refugee Resettlement," October 1, 2019, AILA Doc. No. 19092706, https://www.aila.org/library/trump-eo-state-local-refugee-resettlement.

87 Karen Kasler, "Gov. DeWine Tells President Trump: Refugees Are Welcome in Ohio," WOSU 89.7 NPR News, December 31, 2019, 3:17 p.m. EST, https://www.wosu.org/news/2019-12-31/gov-dewine-tells-president-trump-refugees-are-welcome-in-ohio.
88 Karen Kasler, "Gov. DeWine Tells President Trump: Refugees Are Welcome in Ohio," WOSU 89.7 NPR News, December 31, 2019, 3:17 p.m. EST, https://www.wosu.org/news/2019-12-31/gov-dewine-tells-president-trump-refugees-are-welcome-in-ohio.
89 Jo Ingles, "Gov. Mike DeWine Remembers Pope Francis as a Compassionate World Leader," WOUB Public Media, April 22, 2025, https://woub.org/2025/04/22/dewine-remembers-pope-francis/.
90 U.S. Department of State, Office of International Religious Freedom, 2018 Report on International Religious Freedom: Haiti (Washington, DC: U.S. Department of State, 2019), https://www.state.gov/wp-content/uploads/2019/05/HAITI-2018-INTERNATIONAL-RELIGIOUS-FREEDOM-REPORT.pdf.

Chapter 9

1 Gino Del Guercio, "The Secrets of Haiti's Living Dead," *Harvard Magazine*, October 31, 2017, https://www.harvardmagazine.com/2017/10/are-zombies-real.
2 Ohio History Connection, "Fort Hill Earthworks & Nature Preserve," accessed July 21, 2026, https://www.ohiohistory.org/visit/browse-historical-sites/fort-hill-earthworks-nature-preserve/.
3 Ohio History Connection, "Ancient DNA from the Ohio Hopewell," June 22, 2006, https://www.ohiohistory.org/ancient-dna-from-the-ohio-hopewell/.
4 "Ancient DNA from Siberian Boy Links Europe and America," BBC News, November 20, 2013, https://www.bbc.com/news/science-environment-25020958.
5 Emilee Dehmer, "The Curious Case of Elkmont, Tennessee: The Ghost Town of the Smoky Mountains," Tennessee State Museum, December 13, 2020, https://tnmuseum.org/Stories/posts/the-curious-case-of-elkmont-tennessee-the-ghost-town-of-the-smoky-mountains.
6 Patrick Aftoora Orsagos, Mike Catalini, and Julie Carr Smyth, "Ohio Father Forbids Trump and Others from Invoking His Son's Death in Immigration Debate," *PBS NewsHour*, September 12, 2024, 8:50 p.m. EDT, https://www.pbs.org/newshour/politics/ohio-father-forbids-trump-and-others-from-invoking-his-sons-death-in-immigration-debate.
7 Kathryn Mobley, "A Clark County School Bus Crash Left Her Afraid. So Her Father Became the District's New Driver," WYSO, April 2, 2025, 1:24 p.m. EDT, https://www.wyso.org/news/2025-04-02/a-clark-county-school-bus-crash-left-her-afraid-so-her-father-became-the-districts-new-driver.
8 Empty Pockets Garage, James, "Haitian Invasion, Springfield, Ohio: Corrupt N.G.O.'s in the Name of Religion," YouTube video, streamed live January 11, 2026, https://www.youtube.com/watch?v=uXxD6MVyYbY.
9 Clark County, Ohio, Clark County, Ohio Haitian Influx: Frequently Asked Questions, updated September 25, 2024, 3:00 p.m., https://www.clarkcountyohio.gov/DocumentCenter/View/8133/Clark-County-Ohio-Haitian-Influx-FAQs.
10 Mark Edwin Sanders for Clark County Commissioner, Facebook post, accessed July 21, 2026, https://www.facebook.com/permalink.php?story_fbid=pfbid0VvvijXyQvtiimWwPcGG9Z9bYTSHxsKQthyKrCuVzEmKP28ymju2EG9L1Z11QAU7l&id=61586394565214.
11 TheEagleEyes, "Springfield Ohio Citizen Stating Migrants Are Eating Domesticated Animals," YouTube video, October 3, 2024, https://www.youtube.com/watch?v=kpzhBzEhzIk.

12 Lenovo, "What Is AutoCorrect? How Does It Work & Can I Use It Offline?," accessed July 21, 2026, https://www.lenovo.com/us/en/glossary/auto-correct/.

13 Victorine Bih Takwe, "This Is How Cameroonians Speak French and English," YouTube Short, April 24, 2024, https://www.youtube.com/shorts/9-jL5iYrdYU.

14 Four Paws Forever, "Welcome with Love, Guide with Patience," accessed July 21, 2026, https://fourpawsforever.org/.

15 Wikipedia contributors, "Dog Meat," Wikipedia, last modified July 20, 2026, 8:19 p.m. UTC, https://en.wikipedia.org/w/index.php?title=Dog_meat&oldid=1365182376.

16 BBC Newsbeat, "The Countries Where People Still Eat Cats and Dogs for Dinner," BBC News, April 12, 2017, https://www.bbc.com/news/newsbeat-39577557.

17 Associated Press, "President Trump Signs the Farm Bill Making Dog and Cat Meat Illegal in the United States," WRDW, December 21, 2018, 6:15 a.m. EST, https://www.wrdw.com/content/news/President-Trump-Signs-the-Farm-Bill-Making-Dog-and-Cat-Meat-Illegal-in-the-United-States-503308841.html.

18 Rogue Art Historian, "Haitian Culture, Vodou and Animal Sacrifice," The Rogue Art Historian, September 17, 2024, https://roguearthistorian.substack.com/p/haitian-culture-vodou-and-animal.

19 Monir Ghaedi, "Fact Check: Disinformation Targets Haitian Migrants," DW, September 13, 2024, https://www.dw.com/en/fact-check-how-the-stigmatization-of-haitian-vodou-led-to-a-disinformation-campaign/a-70200764.

20 International Orthodox Christian Charities, "IOCC and MTI Deliver Critical Medical Aid to Suffering Haitians," ReliefWeb, January 21, 2010, https://reliefweb.int/report/haiti/iocc-and-mti-deliver-critical-medical-aid-suffering-haitians.

21 isitmeyourelooking4x, "Things You See While Driving in CBUS," Reddit post, r/Columbus, July 28, 2024, https://www.reddit.com/r/Columbus/comments/1eebh9o/things_you_see_while_driving_in_cbus/.

22 Mark Feuerborn, "Strange Columbus Photo's Connection to Claims about Haitian Immigrants in Springfield," NBC4i, September 10, 2024, https://www.nbc4i.com/news/local-news/columbus/strange-columbus-photos-connection-to-claims-about-haitians-in-springfield/.

23 "Woman Sentenced in Case That Sparked Springfield Cat-Eating Rumours," BBC News, December 4, 2024, https://www.bbc.com/news/articles/cy890gpqw1po.

24 TMZ Staff, "Ohio Wildlife Officials Give Context for Photo of Man Holding 2 Geese," TMZ, September 13, 2024, updated September 13, 2024, https://www.tmz.com/2024/09/13/ohio-wildlife-officials-give-context-man-geese-picture/.

25 WHIO Staff, "Dayton Police 'Strongly Refutes' New Social Media Video Claiming Migrants Ate Cats," WHIO-TV 7, September 14, 2024, 6:41 p.m. EDT, https://www.whio.com/news/local-news/columbus/strange-columbus-photos-connection-to-claims-about-haitians-in-springfield/.

26 Taylor Hansen (@TaylerUSA), "A Haitian Is Caught on Video Chopping an Animal Apart with a Machete in Public," X, October 8, 2024, https://x.com/TaylerUSA/status/1843515880732537157.

27 TBS NEWS DIG Powered by JNN, "「移民がペットを食べている」トランプ氏"差別発言"に揺れる街、異例の激戦　米大統領選【報道特集】" [""Immigrants Are Eating Pets': Town Shaken by Trump's 'Discriminatory Remarks' amid an Unusually Close U.S. Presidential Election"], YouTube video, premiered November 3, 2024, https://www.youtube.com/watch?v=Gkx1hpETS80.

28 Sophia T. Dog (@SophiaTDog1), X post, May 4, 2026, https://x.com/SophiaTDog1/status/2051357102174543918.

29 Agent Texes (@Agenttexes), X post, May 4, 2026, https://x.com/Agenttexes/status/2051357856969150862.
30 Layla Is Ready (@Layla_Is_Ready), X post, May 4, 2026, https://x.com/Layla_Is_Ready/status/2051408482058797147.
31 Nezzar (@NezzarLLS121219), X post, May 4, 2026, https://x.com/NezzarLLS121219/status/2051416815444820049.
32 acabforever6 (@acabforever6), X post, May 4, 2026, https://x.com/acabforever6/status/2051336494271607221.
33 Sara (@sara_doesnt), X post, May 4, 2026, 7:02 a.m. EDT, https://x.com/sara_doesnt/status/2051256030382707027.
34 Marius (@Marius233387891), X post, May 4, 2026, https://x.com/Marius233387891/status/2051343539477631143.
35 Dub2Dope (@Dub2Dope), X post, May 4, 2026, 11:48 a.m. EDT, https://x.com/Dub2Dope/status/2051328235565350939.
36 Tamra (@tamthebarista), X post, May 4, 2026, 1:22 p.m. EDT, https://x.com/tamthebarista/status/2051351848477454743.
37 Joshua Lisec, So Good They Call You a Fake: Command Attention, Monetize Your Talent Stack, and Become the Uncontested Authority in Your Niche (LisecGhostwriting.com, 2023), Kindle ed., https://www.amazon.com/Good-They-Call-You-Fake-ebook/dp/B0C4WN1KKH.
38 Brandon Gill (@realBrandonGill), "You can call me any name you want. I just want my children to grow up in a country that they recognize," X post, May 6, 2026, 10:18 a.m. EDT, https://x.com/realBrandonGill/status/2052030296845959493.
39 Alicia Victoria Lozano, "'It Just Exploded': Springfield Woman Claims She Never Meant to Spark False Rumors about Haitians," NBC News, September 13, 2024, https://www.nbcnews.com/news/us-news/-just-exploded-springfield-woman-says-never-meant-spark-rumors-haitian-rcna171099.
40 Kevin Williams, "Ohio Woman Says She Regrets Sharing False Rumor About Haitians on Facebook," *New York Times*, September 17, 2024, 6:35 p.m. ET, https://www.nytimes.com/2024/09/17/us/springfield-haitians-pets-facebook-rumor.html.
41 Alicia Victoria Lozano, "'It Just Exploded': Springfield Woman Claims She Never Meant to Spark False Rumors about Haitians," NBC News, September 13, 2024, https://www.nbcnews.com/news/us-news/-just-exploded-springfield-woman-says-never-meant-spark-rumors-haitian-rcna171099.
42 Sam Howard and Jack Brewster, "Triple Hearsay: Original Sources of the Claim That Haitians Eat Pets in Ohio Admit No First-Hand Knowledge," NewsGuard's Reality Check, September 12, 2024, https://www.newsguardrealitycheck.com/p/origins-haitians-eating-pets-claim.
43 Sam Howard and Jack Brewster, "Triple Hearsay: Original Sources of the Claim That Haitians Eat Pets in Ohio Admit No First-Hand Knowledge," NewsGuard's Reality Check, September 12, 2024, https://www.newsguardrealitycheck.com/p/origins-haitians-eating-pets-claim.
44 John E. Reid and Associates, Inc., "About," accessed July 21, 2026, https://reid.com/abou.
45 John E. Reid and Associates, Inc., "Leaving the Room during an Interrogation," September 1, 2014, https://reid.com/resources/investigator-tips/leaving-the-room-during-an-interrogation.
46 Elon Musk (@elonmusk), X post, September 12, 2024, 6:24 a.m. EDT, https://x.com/elonmusk/status/1834176196797722907.
47 Elon Musk (@elonmusk), X post, September 12, 2024, 6:24 a.m. EDT, https://x.com/elonmusk/status/1834176196797722907.

48 Grace L., "Elon Stirs Controversy with TikTok Post on Haitian Culture and Trump's Claim: 'They're Eating Your Pets,'" Baller Alert, September 13, 2024, https://balleralert.com/elon-stirs-controversy-with-tiktok-post-on-haitian-culture-and-trumps-claim-theyre-eating-your-pets/.

49 LikeChrisss (@LikeChrisss), X post, September 12, 2024, 8:21 a.m. EDT, https://x.com/LikeChrisss/status/1834205792842461560.

50 1804_Jon (@1804_Jon), X post, September 12, 2024, 8:00 a.m. EDT, https://x.com/1804_Jon/status/1834200479846309994.

51 Elon Musk (@elonmusk), X post, September 12, 2024, 6:24 a.m. EDT, archived September 12, 2024, Ghostarchive, https://ghostarchive.org/archive/qneP4.

52 Meus (@MeusHernst), X post, September 15, 2024, 4:09 a.m. EDT, https://x.com/MeusHernst/status/1835229373009453506.

53 Meus (@MeusHernst), X post, September 12, 2024, 8:25 a.m. EDT, https://x.com/MeusHernst/status/1834206620449906866.

54 Meus (@MeusHernst), X post, September 26, 2024, 10:07 p.m. EDT, https://x.com/MeusHernst/status/1839486961343459829.

55 OI World Desk, "Watch: Haitian President's UN Speech Goes Viral after Water Pitcher Mishap," *The Times of India*, September 27, 2024, 1:08 p.m. IST, https://timesofindia.indiatimes.com/world/rest-of-world/watch-haitian-presidents-un-speech-goes-viral-after-water-pitcher-mishap/articleshow/113730819.cms.

56 Briefly by NewJ, "Haitian President Edgard Leblanc Fils Became an Internet Sensation after a Lighthearted Mishap during His UN General Assembly Speech," Facebook video, accessed July 21, 2026, https://www.facebook.com/watch/?v=1711683376334618.

57 Chronicles of a Zoe, "The Truth About Voodoo Sacrifices in Haitian Culture," YouTube video, July 7, 2023, https://www.youtube.com/watch?v=D0Q9Dhx5tSk.

58 Chronicles of a Zoe, YouTube channel, accessed July 21, 2026, https://www.youtube.com/@ChroniclesofaZoe.

59 Former Farm and Dairy Reporters, "Goat Dairy Designed around Success," *Farm and Dairy*, August 16, 2001, https://www.farmanddairy.com/news/goat-dairy-designed-around-success/1302.html.

60 Chronicles of a Zoe, "The Truth About Voodoo Sacrifices in Haitian Culture," YouTube video, July 7, 2023, https://www.youtube.com/watch?v=D0Q9Dhx5tSk.

61 Mike Dash, "The Trial That Gave Vodou a Bad Name," *Smithsonian Magazine*, May 29, 2013, https://www.smithsonianmag.com/history/the-trial-that-gave-vodou-a-bad-name-83801276.

62 Mike Dash, "The Trial That Gave Vodou a Bad Name," *Smithsonian Magazine*, May 29, 2013, https://www.smithsonianmag.com/history/the-trial-that-gave-vodou-a-bad-name-83801276.

63 Joseph J. Williams, Voodoos and Obeahs: Phases of West India Witchcraft (New York: Lincoln Mac Veagh, Dial Press, 1932), 75, https://books.google.co.uk/books?id=GSSO7fuOGY0C&pg=PA75.

64 Laënnec Hurbon, "The Bizoton Affair," An Island Luminous: An Interactive History of Haiti, Florida International University, accessed July 21, 2026, https://islandluminous.fiu.edu/part05-slide10.html.

65 U.S. Department of State, Office of the Historian, "U.S. Invasion and Occupation of Haiti, 1915–34," Milestones in the History of U.S. Foreign Relations, accessed July 21, 2026, https://history.state.gov/milestones/1914-1920/haiti.

66 David J. Ulbrich, "Stability or Disruption: The U.S. Marine Occupation and the Voodoo Trials in Haiti, 1926–30," Marine Corps History 5, no. 2 (Winter 2019): 21–38, https://doi.org/10.35318/mch.2019050202.

67 David J. Ulbrich, "Stability or Disruption: The U.S. Marine Occupation and the Voodoo Trials in Haiti, 1926–30," Marine Corps History 5, no. 2 (Winter 2019): 21–38, https://www.usmcu.edu/Portals/218/MCH_Winter%202019_v5_n2_web.pdf.

68 Republic of Haiti, Code pénal, accessed July 21, 2026, https://www.oas.org/juridico/PDFs/mesicic4_hti_penal.pdf.

69 Juliann Jenson, "Abuse of Corpse Crimes in Other States," memorandum, Colorado Legislative Council Staff, February 21, 2020, https://content.leg.colorado.gov/sites/default/files/abuse_of_corpse_crimes-interestedperson.pdf.

70 Erika Bourguignon, "The Persistence of Folk Belief: Some Notes on Cannibalism and Zombis in Haiti," *Journal of American Folklore* 72, no. 283 (January–March 1959): 36–46, https://www.jstor.org/stable/538386.

71 Chronicles of a Zoe, "The Truth About Voodoo Sacrifices in Haitian Culture," YouTube video, July 7, 2023, https://www.youtube.com/watch?v=D0Q9Dhx5tSk.

72 City of Miami, "The History of Haiti and the Haitian Revolution," Haitian Bicentennial, archived August 9, 2007, Internet Archive, Wayback Machine, https://web.archive.org/web/20070809214616/http://www.ci.miami.fl.us/haiti2004/history.htm.

73 Kurt Caz, "Voodoo in Haiti Gone Wrong!," YouTube video, August 26, 2021, https://www.youtube.com/watch?v=JlXKXhln7OA.

74 firedrops, "I'm an Anthropologist Who Studies Haitian Vodou. AMA!," Reddit post, r/Anthropology, May 9, 2014, https://www.reddit.com/r/Anthropology/comments/254xy7/im_an_anthropologist_who_studies_haitian_vodou_ama/.

75 firedrops, "I'm an Anthropologist Who Studies Haitian Vodou. AMA!," Reddit post, r/Anthropology, May 9, 2014, https://www.reddit.com/r/Anthropology/comments/254xy7/im_an_anthropologist_who_studies_haitian_vodou_ama/.

76 [deleted], "Now That Some Time Has Passed . . . Can We Unpack the 'Eating the Dogs and Cats' Situation," Reddit post, r/haiti, April 6, 2026, https://www.reddit.com/r/haiti/comments/1sedjrw/now_that_some_time_has_passedcan_we_unpack_the/.

77 zombigoutesel, comment on "Now That Some Time Has Passed . . . Can We Unpack the 'Eating the Dogs and Cats' Situation," Reddit, April 6, 2026, https://www.reddit.com/r/haiti/comments/1sedjrw/comment/oepajph/.

78 [deleted], "[Deleted by User]," Reddit post, r/haiti, April 6, 2026, https://www.reddit.com/r/haiti/comments/1sedjrw/deleted_by_user/.

79 Technical_Success918, comment on "[Deleted by User]," Reddit, April 6, 2026, 7:38 p.m. EDT, https://www.reddit.com/r/haiti/comments/1sedjrw/comment/oepg24v/.

80 Unusual_Newspaper_46, comment on "[Deleted by User]," Reddit, April 6, 2026, 8:11 p.m. EDT, https://www.reddit.com/r/haiti/comments/1sedjrw/comment/oepm3qm/.

81 LowForsaken4782, comment on "[Deleted by User]," Reddit, April 7, 2026, 7:34 a.m. EDT, https://www.reddit.com/r/haiti/comments/1sedjrw/comment/oes89ce/.

82 [deleted], "Haitian Food Taboos," Reddit post, r/haiti, February 18, 2023, 6:16 p.m. EST, https://www.reddit.com/r/haiti/comments/115v3pf/haitian_food_taboos/.

83 zombigoutesel, comment on "Haitian Food Taboos," Reddit, February 18, 2023, 7:00 p.m. EST, https://www.reddit.com/r/haiti/comments/115v3pf/comment/j93m2li.

84 Tim Deagan, "A Haitian Pet Store," *LiveJournal*, April 12, 2005, https://timdeagan.livejournal.com/2102.html.

85 Wikipedia, s.v. "Kathleen A. Deagan," last modified March 25, 2026, https://en.wikipedia.org/wiki/Kathleen_A._Deagan.

86 Tim Deagan, "A Haitian Pet Store," *LiveJournal*, April 12, 2005, https://timdeagan.livejournal.com/2102.html.

87 Tim Deagan, "A Haitian Pet Store," *LiveJournal*, April 12, 2005, https://timdeagan.livejournal.com/2102.html.

88 Tim Deagan, "A Haitian Pet Store," *LiveJournal*, April 12, 2005, https://timdeagan.livejournal.com/2102.html.

89 Tim Deagan, "A Haitian Pet Store," *LiveJournal*, April 12, 2005, https://timdeagan.livejournal.com/2102.html.

90 TikTok, "ayoitsdamenace," TikTok Discover, accessed July 21, 2026, https://www.tiktok.com/discover/ayoitsdamenace.

91 I Meme Therefore I Am (@ImMeme0), X post, September 12, 2024, 3:25 a.m. EDT, https://x.com/ImMeme0/status/1834131118750113953.

92 I Meme Therefore I Am (@ImMeme0), X post, September 12, 2024, 3:25 a.m. EDT, https://x.com/ImMeme0/status/1834131118750113953.

93 Stephanie Stock (@OAMFStephanie), X post, September 12, 2024, 9:22 a.m. EDT, https://x.com/OAMFStephanie/status/1834221086642237487.

94 Ford Boss Me – Auto / Politics / Family, "Eating the Cats? Haitian Family Interview—Says Yes It's True We Eat Cats but Not Dogs," YouTube video, October 8, 2024, https://www.youtube.com/watch?v=3PELqwZaM3w.

95 Ford Boss Me – Auto / Politics / Family, "Eating the Cats? Haitian Family Interview—Says Yes It's True We Eat Cats but Not Dogs," YouTube video, October 8, 2024, https://www.youtube.com/watch?v=3PELqwZaM3w.

96 Huguens Morency, "Do Haitians Eat Cats? The Real Cultural Truth Explained," Haitian Report, last updated March 19, 2026, https://www.haitianreport.com/2019/03/does-haitian-eat-cats.html.

97 Huguens Morency, "Do Haitians Eat Cats? The Real Cultural Truth Explained," Haitian Report, last updated March 19, 2026, https://www.haitianreport.com/2019/03/does-haitian-eat-cats.html.

98 Google, search results for "Huguens Morency," accessed July 21, 2026, https://www.google.com/search?q=Huguens+MORENCY.

99 Huguens Morency, "Do Haitians Eat Cats? The Real Cultural Truth Explained," Haitian Report, last updated March 19, 2026, https://www.haitianreport.com/2019/03/does-haitian-eat-cats.html.

100 Tim Hains, "Springfield, Ohio Residents Air Grievances about Wave of Haitian Migrants: 'Who Is Getting Paid to Bring Them over Here?,'" RealClearPolitics, September 9, 2024, https://www.realclearpolitics.com/video/2024/09/09/full_replay_residents_of_springfield_ohio_speak_about_wave_of_haitian_migrants_at_city_commission_meeting.html.

101 Voice 7, "Addressing Misinformation with Anthony Harris: A Conversation on the Harmful Claims Impacting Springfield's Haitian Community," YouTube video, streamed live September 18, 2024, https://www.youtube.com/watch?v=WiBB_XAKDec.

102 Voice 7, "Addressing Misinformation with Anthony Harris: A Conversation on the Harmful Claims Impacting Springfield's Haitian Community," YouTube video, streamed live September 18, 2024, https://www.youtube.com/watch?v=WiBB_XAKDec.

103 Thick Shelled Egg (@ThickShelledEgg), X post, September 12, 2024, 6:32 a.m. EDT, https://x.com/ThickShelledEgg/status/1834178337570259097.

104 Phil Plummer, "Representative Plummer Votes in Support of House Transportation Budget," Ohio House of Representatives, February 27, 2025, https://ohiohouse.gov/members/phil-plummer/news/representative-plummer-votes-in-support-of-house-transportation-budget-128145.

105 Surf Dayton, "Buck Creek," accessed July 21, 2026, https://www.surfdayton.com/buck-creek.

106 Darvio Morrow (@DTheKingpin), X post, September 12, 2024, 7:37 p.m. EDT, https://x.com/dthekingpin/status/1834375821324177845.

107 Darvio Morrow, "In Springfield, Migrants Are Taking a Toll on the City's Most Vulnerable," *Newsweek*, September 13, 2024, https://www.newsweek.com/springfield-migrants-are-taking-toll-citys-most-vulnerable-opinion-1953385.

108 Natasha Phillips, photograph of Old Reid Park, Google Maps, July 2017, https://www.google.com/maps/place/Old+Reid+Park/@39.9429962,-83.7555271,3a,75y,90t/data=!3m7!1e2!3m5!1sCIHM0ogKEICAgICE8JvDWQ!2e10!3e12!7i3232!8i2424.

109 Cap'n Berreh, photograph of Old Reid Park, Google Maps, August 2020, https://www.google.com/maps/place/Old+Reid+Park/@39.942565,-83.7550929,3a,75y,90t/data=!3m7!1e2!3m5!1sCIHM0ogKEICAgICC1MatCA!2e10!3e12!7i4032!8i1960.

110 Jessicae Stacy, photograph of Old Reid Park, Google Maps, April 2022, https://www.google.com/maps/place/Old+Reid+Park/@39.942565,-83.7550929,3a,75y,90t/data=!3m7!1e2!3m5!1sCIHM0ogKEICAgIC2kviV0gE!2e10!3e12!7i3000!8i4000.

111 Jessicae Stacy, photograph of Old Reid Park, Google Maps, April 2022, https://www.google.com/maps/place/Old+Reid+Park/@39.942565,-83.7550929,3a,75y/data=!3m8!1e2!3m6!1sCIHM0ogKEICAgIC2kvjHGw!2e10!3e12!7i3000!8i4000.

112 Jessicae Stacy, photograph of Old Reid Park, Google Maps, April 2022, https://www.google.com/maps/place/Old+Reid+Park/@39.9429962,-83.7555271,3a,75y,90t/data=!3m7!1e2!3m5!1sCIHM0ogKEICAgIC2kviVMg!2e10!3e12!7i3000!8i4000.

113 Amanda Miller, photograph of Old Reid Park, Google Maps, August 2022, https://www.google.com/maps/place/Old+Reid+Park/@39.9482241,-83.755436,3a,75y,90t/data=!3m7!1e2!3m5!1sCIHM0ogKEICAgIDukZ_fGg!2e10!3e12!7i2543!8i2336.

114 Gretchen Barger, photograph of Old Reid Park, Google Maps, March 2023, https://www.google.com/maps/place/Old+Reid+Park/@39.942565,-83.7550929,3a,94.3y,90t/data=!3m7!1e2!3m5!1sCIHM0ogKEICAgICR2I3D3wE!2e10!3e12!7i1080!8i720.

115 Shelley Ward, photograph of Old Reid Park, Google Maps, February 2026, https://www.google.com/maps/place/Old+Reid+Park/@39.942565,-83.7550929,3a,75y/data=!3m8!1e2!3m6!1sCIABIhBYsZyxtsgtDoZn3VNgJhE7!2e10!3e12!6shttps:%2F%2Flh3.googleusercontent.com%2Fgps-cs-s%2FAPNQkAHmErrTM2NZCOCmzlQGdZLHMxe51wu-xVZ1wYbjNMDuD3fFPHBmd8yUds4Ka4Kf-_v5til4HYPYIICzjoPJBCaLHAACMb4YqdpFR490U1o7WNqplluVVpX-g9qWV9mSVKnROIWRHA3XwXqB%3Dw203-h152-k-no!7i4000!8i3000.

116 Regina Crum (@regina_crum), "Snyder Park Normally Has a Ton of White Ducks. The White Ducks Are Missing," Threads post, September 11, 2024, https://www.threads.com/@regina_crum/post/C_ymjPnvnf-.

117 Jessica Orozco, "Parks Staff: Snyder Park 'Don't Eat the Ducks' Sign Was Posted by Someone Else," *Springfield News-Sun*, September 13, 2024, https://www.springfieldnewssun.com/news/parks-staff-snyder-park-don-t-eat-the-ducks-sign-was-posted-by-someone-else/article_cd507413-a791-5867-b888-40e15466758c.html.

118 Josh Sweigart and Jessica Orozco, "Are Haitian Migrants Stealing Geese in Springfield Parks? Here's What We Know," *Dayton Daily News*, September 13, 2024, archived September 14, 2024, Internet Archive, Wayback Machine, https://web.archive.org/web/20240914000500/https://www.daytondailynews.com/local/are-haitian-migrants-stealing-geese-in-springfield-parks-heres-what-we-know/VVEXS7XEDBEEXNVKBRPAQXRBJA/.

119 Juliann Ventura, "Small Springfield College Moves Classes Online, Cancels Athletic Events Due to Bomb Threats," *The Hill*, September 17, 2024, https://thehill.com/campaign-issues/education/4885533-small-springfield-college-moves-classes-online-cancels-athletic-events-due-to-bomb-threats/.

120 Springfield Police Division, "8.26.24 Warder at Water," police report, August 26, 2024, uploaded by The Federalist, Scribd, https://www.scribd.com/embeds/767911174/content?start_page=1&view_mode=scroll&access_key=key-FgAt6C3w3O2whVVHFZH.

121 FDRLST, "EXCLUSIVE: Police Audio Confirm Haitian Goose-Hunting in Ohio: 'They All Had Geese in Their Hands,'" Rumble video, September 10, 2024, https://rumble.com/v5eglea-exclusive-police-audio-confirm-haitian-goose-hunting-in-ohio-they-all-had-g.html.

122 Alex Kasprak, "No, 'Police Audio' Doesn't Confirm Reports of 'Haitian Goose-Hunting' in Springfield, Ohio," Snopes, September 13, 2024, https://www.snopes.com/fact-check/police-audio-haitian-geese/.

123 Mid-Ohio Waterfowl Rescue, Facebook page, accessed July 21, 2026, https://www.facebook.com/p/Mid-Ohio-Waterfowl-Rescue-100064727826979/.

124 Charity Navigator, "Mid Ohio Waterfowl Rescue," accessed July 21, 2026, https://www.charitynavigator.org/ein/852438240.

125 Brittany Chain, "I'm a Duck Rescuer in Ohio—Since the Springfield Migrants 'Eating Pets' Rumors Started, My Phone's Been Ringing off the Hook," *Daily Mail*, September 12, 2024, https://www.dailymail.com/news/article-13843271/ohio-duck-rescue-phone-haitian-migrants-springfield-pet-eating-rumors.html.

126 Mid-Ohio Waterfowl Rescue, "I Deleted the Post about the Ducks in Springfield," Facebook post, September 12, 2024, https://www.facebook.com/permalink.php?story_fbid=pfbid09EnS3hVh1jY5rs26hGxxwsKGNJoUyvpJDJxeXd7QnbEekQ9x5ERgF6ozcmZqXeCcl&id=100064727826979.

127 Mid-Ohio Waterfowl Rescue, "I Deleted the Post about the Ducks in Springfield," Facebook post, September 12, 2024, https://www.facebook.com/permalink.php?story_fbid=pfbid09EnS3hVh1jY5rs26hGxxwsKGNJoUyvpJDJxeXd7QnbEekQ9x5ERgF6ozcmZqXeCcl&id=100064727826979.

128 Mid-Ohio Waterfowl Rescue, "I Deleted the Post about the Ducks in Springfield," Facebook post, September 12, 2024, https://www.facebook.com/permalink.php?story_fbid=pfbid09EnS3hVh1jY5rs26hGxxwsKGNJoUyvpJDJxeXd7QnbEekQ9x5ERgF6ozcmZqXeCcl&id=100064727826979.

129 Mid-Ohio Waterfowl Rescue, "I Deleted the Post about the Ducks in Springfield," Facebook post, September 12, 2024, https://www.facebook.com/permalink.php?story_fbid=pfbid09EnS3hVh1jY5rs26hGxxwsKGNJoUyvpJDJxeXd7QnbEekQ9x5ERgF6ozcmZqXeCcl&id=100064727826979.

130 Dinesh D'Souza (@DineshDSouza), X post, April 21, 2026, 12:16 p.m. EDT, https://x.com/dineshdsouza/status/2046624244050677866.

131 Chronicles of a Zoe, "The Truth About Voodoo Sacrifices in Haitian Culture," YouTube video, July 7, 2023, https://www.youtube.com/watch?v=D0Q9Dhx5tSk.

Chapter 10

1 Lauren Jade Hill, "Anthony Bourdain: My First Trip to Vietnam Changed My Life," *Condé Nast Traveler*, September 26, 2014, https://www.cntraveler.com/stories/2014-09-26/anthony-bourdain-my-first-trip-to-vietnam-changed-my-life.

2 Joshua Lisec (@JoshuaLisec), X post, April 4, 2026, 2:33 p.m. EDT, https://x.com/JoshuaLisec/status/2040497967518327009.

3 Michael Brun, "After John Legend Spoke Up in Support of Haitian Immigrants in His Hometown of Springfield, Ohio," Facebook video, November 8, 2024, https://www.facebook.com/watch/?v=1851050178638906.

4 [Untitled menu picture], Yelp, accessed July 21, 2026, https://s3-media0.fl.yelpcdn.com/bphoto/fhIJmcDC7JH2-yQHW9N9LQ/o.jpg.

5 Jen Balduf and Marshall Gorby, "Springfield Haitian Restaurant Draws Crowds; Manager Says, 'We Came Here to Work,'" *Springfield News-Sun*, September 15, 2024, https://www.springfieldnewssun.com/news/springfield-haitian-restaurant-draws-crowds-manager-says-we-came-here-to-work/article_243757d1-b25e-5fcd-91f4-e693e17ece40.html.

6 Caitlin Stephen Hu and Omar Jimenez, "Fear and Frustration in Ohio City as Political Debate Seizes on Growing Haitian Population," CNN, September 12, 2024, https://www.cnn.com/2024/09/12/politics/springfield-ohio-migrants-jd-vance.

7 Jérôme Sessini, "U.S. Focus: The Haitian Community in Ohio," Magnum Photos, December 17, 2024, https://www.magnumphotos.com/newsroom/u-s-focus-the-haitian-community-in-ohio/.

8 Jérôme Sessini, "U.S. Focus: The Haitian Community in Ohio," Magnum Photos, December 17, 2024, https://www.magnumphotos.com/newsroom/u-s-focus-the-haitian-community-in-ohio/.

9 Jérôme Sessini, "U.S. Focus: The Haitian Community in Ohio," Magnum Photos, December 17, 2024, https://www.magnumphotos.com/newsroom/u-s-focus-the-haitian-community-in-ohio/.

10 Jerome Sessini, "What's Really Happening in Springfield, Ohio," *The Nation*, January 2025, https://www.thenation.com/article/world/magnum-ehrp-springfield-ohio/.

11 Jérôme Sessini, "U.S. Focus: The Haitian Community in Ohio," Magnum Photos, December 17, 2024, https://www.magnumphotos.com/newsroom/u-s-focus-the-haitian-community-in-ohio/.

12 First Diversity Staffing, "About Us," accessed April 14, 2026, https://www.firstdiversity.com/about-4.

13 Majority Haitian (@MajorityHaitian), X post, September 9, 2025, 8:00 a.m. EDT, https://x.com/MajorityHaitian/status/1965384914477744399.

14 Majority Haitian (@MajorityHaitian), X post, September 9, 2025, 8:00 a.m. EDT, https://x.com/MajorityHaitian/status/1965384914477744399/photo/1.

15 Majority Haitian (@MajorityHaitian), X post, September 9, 2025, 8:00 a.m. EDT, https://x.com/MajorityHaitian/status/1965384914477744399/photo/2.

16 Dan Bazile, "Haitian Restaurant Receives Support from Near and Far in Springfield, Ohio," Spectrum News 1, September 26, 2024, https://spectrumnews1.com/oh/columbus/news/2024/09/26/haitian-restaurant-receives-support-from-near-and-far-in-springfield--ohio-.

17 "Springfield, Ohio Has Been Covering Up Race of Murderers, Records Show," Investigative News Service, October 18, 2024, https://investigativenews.substack.com/p/springfield-ohio-has-been-covering.

18 Caitlin Stephen Hu and Omar Jimenez, "Fear and Frustration in Ohio City as Political Debate Seizes on Growing Haitian Population," CNN, September 12, 2024, https://www.cnn.com/2024/09/12/politics/springfield-ohio-migrants-jd-vance.

19 "Clark County Municipal Court Cases," *Springfield News-Sun*, December 3, 2025, https://www.springfieldnewssun.com/crime/clark-county-municipal-court-cases/article_8888e581-0f04-558f-a0c2-d790d40a7a65.htm.

20 "Louis, Rosena JN | 2026-01-22 19:19:00 Clark County, Ohio Booking," *Busted Newspaper*, January 22, 2026, https://bustednewspaper.com/ohio/louis-rosena-jn/20260122-191900/.

21 "Clark County Municipal Court Cases," *Springfield News-Sun*, January 26, 2026, https://www.springfieldnewssun.com/crime/clark-county-municipal-court-cases/article_d26fc57b-4d22-58d2-9d3f-ba4dbcce6acc.html.

22 "Clark County Municipal Court Cases," *Springfield News-Sun*, March 18, 2026, https://www.springfieldnewssun.com/crime/clark-county-municipal-court-cases/article_13489458-3c5d-5334-a325-d288120f8360.html.

23 Majority Haitian (@MajorityHaitian), X post, March 23, 2026, 12:46 p.m. EDT, https://x.com/MajorityHaitian/status/2036122412840796277.

24 Brooke Spurlock, "Clark County Sheriff Talks Current Jail Conditions Related to Overcapacity, Disrepair," *Springfield News-Sun*, July 29, 2025, https://www.springfieldnewssun.com/news/clark-county-sheriff-talks-current-jail-conditions-related-to-overcapacity-disrepair/article_fd39cd76-e807-523a-9c0b-c2f34fcc9c1c.html.

25 "Clark County Municipal Court Cases," *Springfield News-Sun*, December 5, 2025, https://www.springfieldnewssun.com/crime/clark-county-municipal-court-cases/article_40dcfc24-0106-59f9-aa3e-736d61d0f338.html.

26 "Clark County Municipal Court Cases," *Springfield News-Sun*, March 31, 2025, https://www.springfieldnewssun.com/crime/clark-county-municipal-court-cases/article_323fc6a2-631f-53ab-a270-e7817458dbfd.html.

27 Staff, "Clark County Municipal Court Cases," *Springfield News-Sun*, July 12, 2017, archived July 12, 2017, Internet Archive, Wayback Machine, https://web.archive.org/web/20170712183114/http://www.springfieldnewssun.com/news/local/clark-county-municipal-court-cases/hoYGE5mBtzaW2a6C9XVmQO.

Chapter 11

1 Rep. Brandon Gill (@RepBrandonGill), X post, May 4, 2026, 7:20 p.m. EDT, https://x.com/repbrandongill/status/2051441974675128755.

2 Jake Offenhartz, "Secret Tunnel in NYC Synagogue Leads to Brawl between Police and Worshippers," Associated Press, January 9, 2024, republished by AOL, https://www.aol.com/news/secret-tunnel-nyc-synagogue-leads-182815811.html.

3 Jake Offenhartz, "Secret Tunnel in NYC Synagogue Leads to Brawl between Police and Worshippers," Associated Press, January 9, 2024, republished by AOL, https://www.aol.com/news/secret-tunnel-nyc-synagogue-leads-182815811.html.

4 Never Happened, "We Don't Do That in America," YouTube Short, accessed July 21, 2026, https://www.youtube.com/shorts/43N3CXPj1js.

5 Cornelius Frolik and Jessica Orozco, "Springfield Shares Flock Camera Data with ICE-Affiliated Agencies, Blocks Immigration Searches," *Dayton Daily News*, June 25, 2026, https://www.daytondailynews.com/local/springfield-shares-flock-camera-data-with-ice-affiliated-agencies-blocks-immigration-searches/article_c467ca92-6038-5e37-8658-297dacc9d728.html.

6 Sergio R. Bustos, "South Florida Lawmakers Want Trump Administration to Halt Flow of Illegal Weapons to Haiti from US," WLRN Public Media, August 1, 2025, 7:45 p.m. EDT, https://www.wlrn.org/americas/2025-08-01/south-florida-lawmakers-want-trump-administration-to-halt-flow-of-illegal-weapons-to-haiti-from-us.

7 Mark Schwendau, "Springfield Gun Sales Girl Turns Whistleblower," The Thinking Conservative, September 22, 2024, modified December 29, 2024, https://www.thethinkingconservative.com/springfield-gun-sales-girl-turns-whistleblower/.

8 Fellowship of the Martyrs, "Springfield, Ohio: Selling Weapons to Immigrants," YouTube video, 3:32, September 16, 2024, https://www.youtube.com/watch?v=z6BejxSb9jY.

9 Fellowship of the Martyrs, "Springfield, Ohio: Selling Weapons to Immigrants," YouTube video, 3:32, September 16, 2024, https://www.youtube.com/watch?v=z6BejxSb9jY.

10 Fellowship of the Martyrs, "Update on Libby, Whistleblower Gun Store Employee in Springfield, Ohio," YouTube video, September 22, 2024, https://www.youtube.com/watch?v=_H9D31YVTXY.

11 Majority Haitian (@MajorityHaitian), "Exactly. Listen to this grandmother talking about Springfield High School & why she transferred her granddaughter to a different school. Adult Haitian men are in class with teenage girls," X, January 28, 2025, 12:28 p.m., https://x.com/MajorityHaitian/status/1884292479899558060.
12 Ohio Rev. Code § 3313.64, "Entitlement to Attend School; District of Attendance," effective September 30, 2025, https://codes.ohio.gov/ohio-revised-code/section-3313.64.
13 Majority Haitian (@MajorityHaitian), "Exactly. Listen to this grandmother talking about Springfield High School & why she transferred her granddaughter to a different school. Adult Haitian men are in class with teenage girls," X, January 28, 2025, 12:28 p.m., https://x.com/MajorityHaitian/status/1884292479899558060.
14 Nick Johnson, "Springfield, Ohio Is Under a Migration Invasion. Is Your Town Next?," YouTube video, September 17, 2024, https://www.youtube.com/watch?v=DOuNn-PI9j0.

Chapter 12

1 Hillsong UNITED, "Oceans (Where Feet May Fail)," Oceans, BMG Rights Management (US) LLC, 2013, YouTube Music, https://music.youtube.com/watch?v=c4n8cqcCouk.
2 "Community," Corinth Presbyterian Church, April 20 2026, https://www.corinthpresbyteriandayton.org/community/.
3 "Facebook Live Video," Corinth Presbyterian Church, Facebook, accessed April 6, 2026, https://www.facebook.com/watch/live/?ref=watch_permalink&v=951115227394651.
4 Central Christian Church, "What Is the Denominational Background of Central Christian Church?," position paper, accessed July 21, 2026, https://s3.amazonaws.com/media.cloversites.com/24/24c7fb29-0f9d-48cc-bfc8-7f57e6134280/documents/Denominational_Background.pdf.
5 Central Christian, "Think. Believe. Act.," accessed July 21, 2026, https://www.ccspringfield.org/.
6 "Facebook Live Video," Corinth Presbyterian Church, Facebook, accessed April 6, 2026, https://www.facebook.com/watch/live/?ref=watch_permalink&v=951115227394651.
7 "Matthew 22:21," Bible Gateway, accessed July 21, 2026, https://www.biblegateway.com/verse/en/Matthew%2022%3A21.
8 John 18:38 (New International Version), Bible Gateway, accessed July 21, 2026, https://www.biblegateway.com/passage/?search=John%2018%3A38&version=NIV.
9 Matthew 27:25 (New International Version), Bible Gateway, accessed July 21, 2026, https://www.biblegateway.com/verse/en/Matthew%2027%3A25.
10 "Facebook Live Video," Corinth Presbyterian Church, Facebook, accessed April 6, 2026, https://www.facebook.com/watch/live/?ref=watch_permalink&v=951115227394651.
11 Hillsong UNITED, "Oceans (Where Feet May Fail)," Oceans, BMG Rights Management (US) LLC, 2013, YouTube Music, https://music.youtube.com/watch?v=c4n8cqcCouk.
12 Janet Ward Schofield, "Realistic Group Conflict Theory," in *Encyclopedia of Group Processes and Intergroup Relations*, ed. John M. Levine and Michael A. Hogg (Thousand Oaks, CA: SAGE Publications, 2010), 682–85, https://sk.sagepub.com/ency/edvol/processes/chpt/realistic-group-conflict-theory.
13 Tom Hand, "Americana Corner: The Battle of Piqua," *Bryan County News*, April 4, 2024, https://www.bryancountynews.com/opinion/americana-corner-battle-piqua.
14 Enon Community Historical Society, "Adena Mound," accessed July 21, 2026, https://enonhistoricalsociety.com/historical-sites/adena-mound/.
15 "Osmond Cheres Obituary," *Springfield News-Sun*, April 5, 2026, Legacy.com, https://www.legacy.com/us/obituaries/dayton/name/osmond-cheres-obituary?id=61180946.
16 Central Christian, "Thank You for Joining Us Today!," YouTube video, streamed live April 12, 2026, https://www.youtube.com/watch?v=iOxirbI5_mU.

17 Central Christian, "Thank You for Joining Us Today!," YouTube video, streamed live April 11, 2026, https://www.youtube.com/watch?v=fhzINRgpLNE.
18 Central Christian, "Thank You for Joining Us Today!," YouTube video, streamed live April 12, 2026, https://www.youtube.com/watch?v=iOxirbI5_mU.
19 Central Christian, "Thank You for Joining Us Today!," YouTube video, streamed live April 12, 2026, https://www.youtube.com/watch?v=iOxirbI5_mU.
20 Central Christian, "Thank You for Joining Us Today!," YouTube video, streamed live April 12, 2026, https://www.youtube.com/watch?v=iOxirbI5_mU.
21 Central Christian, "Thank You for Joining Us Today!," YouTube video, streamed live April 12, 2026, https://www.youtube.com/watch?v=iOxirbI5_mU.
22 1 Corinthians 15:14 (New International Version), Bible Gateway, accessed July 21, 2026, https://www.biblegateway.com/verse/en/1%20Corinthians%2015%3A14.
23 Central Christian, "Thank You for Joining Us Today!," YouTube video, streamed live April 12, 2026, https://www.youtube.com/watch?v=iOxirbI5_mU.
24 "Facebook Live Video," Corinth Presbyterian Church, Facebook, accessed April 6, 2026, https://www.facebook.com/watch/live/?ref=watch_permalink&v=951115227394651.
25 Nottawaseppi Huron Band of the Potawatomi, "1795 Treaty of Greenville: First Recognition as Sovereign Entity," May 10, 2022, https://nhbp-nsn.gov/timeline/1795/.
26 "Chief Leather Lips," Touring Ohio, accessed July 21, 2026, https://touring-ohio.com/history/leatherlips.html.
27 Dublin Historical Society, "Chief Leatherlips," accessed July 21, 2026, https://dublinohiohistory.org/history/historical-people/chief-leatherlips/.
28 "King of the Black People Peter Griffin Template," PNG image, Imgflip, accessed July 28, 2026, https://imgflip.com/memetemplate/179887627/King-of-the-black-people-peter-griffin.

Chapter 13

1 Barack Obama, "Remarks by the President at the Summit on Countering Violent Extremism," speech delivered at the U.S. Department of State, Washington, DC, February 19, 2015, 10:33 a.m. EST, Obama White House Archives, https://obamawhitehouse.archives.gov/the-press-office/2015/02/19/remarks-president-summit-countering-violent-extremism-february-19-2015.
2 "Home," Out To Pastor, accessed July 21, 2026, https://www.outtopastor.com/.
3 "Home," Out To Pastor, accessed July 21, 2026, https://www.outtopastor.com/.
4 Human Events Staff, "Jack Posobiec: Amazon Has Crossed a Line in Apparent Removal of Camp of the Saints," Human Events, April 20, 2026, https://humanevents.com/2026/04/20/jack-posobiec-amazon-has-crossed-a-line-in-apparent-removal-of-camp-of-the-saints.
5 Jean Raspail, The Camp of the Saints, trans. Ethan Rundell, with an introduction by Nathan Pinkoski (Vauban Books, 2025), Amazon product page, accessed July 21, 2026, https://www.amazon.com/Camp-Saints-Jean-Raspail/dp/B0FG4MJS8K.
6 Francis X. Maier, "In the Camp of the Saints," *The Catholic Thing*, February 11, 2026, reproduced by the Ethics and Public Policy Center, https://eppc.org/publication/in-the-camp-of-the-saints/.
7 Office of Congresswoman Ayanna Pressley, "Breaking: House Passes Pressley-Led Measure to Extend Temporary Protected Status for Haiti, Now Heads to Senate," press release, April 16, 2026, https://pressley.house.gov/2026/04/16/breaking-house-passes-pressley-led-measure-to-extend-temporary-protected-status-for-haiti-now-heads-to-senate/.

8 Alexander Bolton, "GOP Sen. Katie Britt: House-Passed Bill to Extend Haitian Refugee Status DOA in Senate," *The Hill*, April 17, 2026, 12:43 p.m. EDT, https://thehill.com/homenews/senate/5836545-britt-rebukes-moderate-republicans/.

9 Jean Raspail, *The Camp of the Saints*, trans. Ethan Rundell, with an introduction by Nathan Pinkoski (Vauban Books, 2025), Amazon product page, accessed July 21, 2026, https://www.amazon.com/Camp-Saints-Jean-Raspail/dp/B0FG4MJS8K.

10 Trump War Room (@TrumpWarRoom), "I don't know of a single homeless Haitian in this town—because they all got vouchers! Americans are losing their homes because Kamala is . . .," X, September 12, 2024, https://x.com/TrumpWarRoom/status/1834237576112218248.

11 The White House, "At USAID, Waste and Abuse Runs Deep," February 3, 2025, https://www.whitehouse.gov/releases/2025/02/at-usaid-waste-and-abuse-runs-deep/.

12 Emma Colton, "'Sesame Street in Iraq': USAID's 'Wasteful and Dangerous' Spending Exposed by Senator," Fox News, February 5, 2025, 3:19 p.m. EST, https://www.foxnews.com/politics/sesame-street-iraq-usaids-wasteful-dangerous-spending-exposed-senator.

13 Andrew Mark Miller, Aubrie Spady, and Deirdre Heavey, "'Wasteful and Dangerous': DOGE's Top Five Most Shocking Revelations," Fox News, February 15, 2025, 10:00 a.m. EST, https://www.foxnews.com/politics/wasteful-dangerous-doges-top-5-most-shocking-revelations.

14 Caitlin McFall, "White House Flags Top USAID Boondoggles under Elon Musk's Microscope," Fox News, February 4, 2025, 2:39 p.m. EST, https://www.foxnews.com/world/top-usaid-projects-under-elon-musks-microscope.

15 Jessica Orozco, "Springfield Anticipates Leaner 2026 Budget, Avoids Deficit Spending," *Springfield News-Sun*, January 22, 2026, https://www.springfieldnewssun.com/news/springfield-anticipates-leaner-2026-budget-avoids-deficit-spending/article_188fe0ca-389a-5422-83e5-d1268d402553.html.

16 Dayton 24/7 Now, "Springfield Community to Voice Concerns on Understaffed Fire Stations," YouTube video, April 21, 2026, https://www.youtube.com/watch?v=NRmrBUBKmTA.

17 City of Springfield, Ohio—Government, "City Commission Meeting, April 21, 2026," YouTube video, streamed live April 21, 2026, https://www.youtube.com/watch?v=feyj732oz0Q.

18 Jessica Orozco and Vicky Forrest, "Haitian Community Center Purchasing Former City Fire Station for Operations," *Springfield News-Sun*, November 4, 2024, https://www.springfieldnewssun.com/news/haitian-community-center-purchasing-former-city-fire-station-for-operations/article_4a81a88d-356b-5381-83da-4898eecf6b12.html.

19 City of Springfield, Ohio—Government, "City Commission Meeting, April 21, 2026," YouTube video, streamed live April 21, 2026, https://www.youtube.com/watch?v=feyj732oz0Q.

20 Joshua Lisec, "What Do the People of Springfield Want?," Facebook post, April 21, 2026, https://www.facebook.com/story.php?story_fbid=10226736195149387&id=1784781217.

21 City of Springfield, Ohio—Government, "City Commission Meeting, April 21, 2026," YouTube video, streamed live April 21, 2026, https://www.youtube.com/watch?v=feyj732oz0Q.

22 Jessica Orozco, "New Haitian Community Alliance Aims to Unify Springfield, Empower Haitian People," *Springfield News-Sun*, October 7, 2024, https://www.springfieldnewssun.com/news/new-haitian-community-alliance-aims-to-unify-springfield-empower-haitian-people/article_687e5bf6-b6c2-5ef1-870b-00255d5cafc1.html.

23 Jessica Orozco, "New Haitian Community Alliance Aims to Unify Springfield, Empower Haitian People," *Springfield News-Sun*, October 7, 2024, https://www

.springfieldnewssun.com/news/new-haitian-community-alliance-aims-to-unify-springfield-empower-haitian-people/article_687e5bf6-b6c2-5ef1-870b-00255d5cafc1.html.

24 Jeff Skinner, "Payen Gun Case Quietly Closed," *The Ohio Register*, October 5, 2025, https://www.theohioregister.com/payen-gun-case-quietly-closed/.

25 Huo Jingnan, Audrey Nguyen, and Jude Joffe-Block, "How Influencers Flocked to Springfield Chasing Debunked Rumors and Attention," NPR, September 20, 2024, 9:42 a.m. EDT, republished by WHQR, https://www.whqr.org/national/2024-09-20/how-influencers-flocked-to-springfield-chasing-debunked-rumors-and-attention.

26 "Ohio City Whose Haitian Migrants Were Disparaged by Trump Braces to Defend Them against Deportation," Associated Press, July 31, 2025, republished by TribLIVE, https://triblive.com/news/world/ohio-city-whose-haitian-migrants-were-disparaged-by-trump-braces-to-defend-them-against-deportation/.

27 Jeff Skinner, "Payen Gun Case Quietly Closed," *The Ohio Register*, October 5, 2025, https://www.theohioregister.com/payen-gun-case-quietly-closed/.

28 "The Gulag Archipelago, 1918–1956 Quotes," Goodreads, accessed July 22, 2026, https://www.goodreads.com/work/quotes/17436547-v-vii.

29 Ohio Rev. Code § 2923.12, "Carrying Concealed Weapons," effective March 27, 2013, https://codes.ohio.gov/assets/laws/revised-code/authenticated/29/2923/2923.12/3-27-2013/2923.12-3-27-2013.pdf.

30 Jeff Skinner, "Payen Gun Case Quietly Closed," *The Ohio Register*, October 5, 2025, https://www.theohioregister.com/payen-gun-case-quietly-closed/.

31 Jeff Skinner, "Payen Gun Case Quietly Closed," *The Ohio Register*, October 5, 2025, https://www.theohioregister.com/payen-gun-case-quietly-closed/.

32 Notre Dame Catholic Church, Facebook page, accessed July 22, 2026, https://www.facebook.com/notredamecc/.

33 Vicky Forrest, "Springfield City Meeting a Mix of Angry Outbursts, Increased Calls for Unity," *Springfield News-Sun*, September 26, 2024, https://www.springfieldnewssun.com/news/springfield-city-meeting-a-mix-of-angry-outbursts-increased-calls-for-unity/article_bdf5c1a5-822d-5698-95d1-00e0f8381296.html.

34 Defense Manpower Data Center, "Persian Gulf War," Defense Casualty Analysis System, accessed July 22, 2026, https://dcas.dmdc.osd.mil/dcas/app/conflictCasualties/gulf.

35 Max Greenwood and Jacqueline Charles, "Trump Campaign's False Claims about Haitians Eating Pets in Ohio Stoke Immigration Fears," *Miami Herald*, updated October 23, 2024, 9:34 a.m., https://www.miamiherald.com/news/nation-world/world/americas/haiti/article292238615.html.

36 Stephen Starr, "'Used as a Pawn': How the US Election Has Poisoned Springfield, Ohio," *The Guardian*, September 30, 2024, 7:00 a.m. EDT, https://www.theguardian.com/us-news/2024/sep/30/springfield-ohio-republicans-haitian-immigrants-lies.

37 WBNS 10TV, "Haitian Migrants in Ohio Turn to Faith amid Deportation Fears," YouTube video, January 27, 2025, https://www.youtube.com/watch?v=s6L1byZzEWM.

38 Dan Grossman, "Haitian Immigrants Hopeful Springfield, Ohio, Will Rise above Political Turmoil," *Scripps News*, September 24, 2024, https://www.scrippsnews.com/us-news/haitian-immigrants-hopeful-springfield-ohio-will-rise-above-political-turmoil.

39 "Haitian Immigrants Hopeful Springfield, Ohio, Will Rise above Political Turmoil," Haitian Community Alliance, September 24, 2024, https://haitiancommunityalliance.org/hca/haitian-immigrants-hopeful-springfield-ohio-will-rise-above-political-turmoil-haitian-community-alliance/.

40 Kathryn Mobley and Kaitlin Schroeder, "'I'm Really Scared for My Kids Right Now.' Political Spotlight, Threats Rattle Springfield," WYSO, September 13, 2024, 2:50 p.m.

EDT, republished by Ideastream Public Media, https://www.ideastream.org/2024-09-13/im-really-scared-for-my-kids-right-now-political-spotlight-threats-rattle-springfield.

41 Lauren Shows, "Celebrate Unity, Haitian Independence," *Yellow Springs News*, January 2, 2025, https://ysnews.com/news/2025/01/celebrate-unity-haitian-independence.

42 "Gov. DeWine Says Springfield Is 'Moving Forward' 8 Months after False Claims," WBNS-10TV, May 19, 2025, https://www.10tv.com/article/news/local/dewine-says-springfield-is-moving-forward-after-controversy/530-703f7484-9597-4c78-abbc-c9e7df641abd.

43 James Phillips, "How to Write a Military Character Letter," YouTube video, March 15, 2019, https://www.youtube.com/watch?v=dikUEMOMnOc.

44 Gregory Bereiter, The U.S. Navy in Operation Enduring Freedom, 2001–2002 (Naval History and Heritage Command, 2016), https://www.history.navy.mil/research/library/online-reading-room/title-list-alphabetically/u/us-navy-operation-enduring-freedom-2001-2002.html.

45 Wikipedia, s.v. "Operation Southern Watch," last modified July 8, 2026, https://en.wikipedia.org/wiki/Operation_Southern_Watch.

46 Vicky Forrest, "Springfield City Meeting a Mix of Angry Outbursts, Increased Calls for Unity," *Springfield News-Sun*, September 26, 2024, https://www.springfieldnewssun.com/news/springfield-city-meeting-a-mix-of-angry-outbursts-increased-calls-for-unity/article_bdf5c1a5-822d-5698-95d1-00e0f8381296.html.

47 Jared M. Huff, Yevgeniya K. Pinelis, and Jennie W. Wenger, Adjusting First-Term Contract Lengths in the Navy: Implications and Recommendations, report no. DRM-2013-U-004794-Final (CNA, July 2013), https://apps.dtic.mil/sti/tr/pdf/ADA589140.pdf.

48 Chrissa Loukas, "'I Don't Think Immigration Is the Problem. I Think Criminality Is the Problem': Springfield Haitian Leader Sends Message to Trump," Spectrum News 1, January 21, 2025, 5:30 a.m. ET, https://spectrumnews1.com/oh/columbus/news/2025/01/21/springfield-haitian-leader-president-trump.

49 Obed Manuel, "Bomb Threats Followed Trump's False Claims about Springfield. Some Haitians May Leave," NPR, September 19, 2024, 5:29 p.m., republished by Oregon Public Broadcasting, https://www.opb.org/article/2024/09/19/bomb-threats-followed-trump-s-false-claims-about-springfield-some-haitians-may-leave/.

50 Spectrum News Staff, "Ohio Haitian TPS Holders Keep Status after Judge Blocks End to Protection," Spectrum News 1, February 3, 2026, 8:09 a.m. EST, https://spectrumnews1.com/oh/columbus/news/2026/02/03/ohio-haitian-community-tps-pause.

51 Chrissa Loukas, "'I Don't Think Immigration Is the Problem. I Think Criminality Is the Problem': Springfield Haitian Leader Sends Message to Trump," Spectrum News 1, January 21, 2025, 5:30 a.m. ET, https://spectrumnews1.com/oh/columbus/news/2025/01/21/springfield-haitian-leader-president-trump.

52 Chrissa Loukas, "'I Don't Think Immigration Is the Problem. I Think Criminality Is the Problem': Springfield Haitian Leader Sends Message to Trump," Spectrum News 1, January 21, 2025, 5:30 a.m. ET, https://spectrumnews1.com/oh/columbus/news/2025/01/21/springfield-haitian-leader-president-trump.

53 Office of Congresswoman Sheila Cherfilus-McCormick, "Congresswoman Sheila Cherfilus-McCormick, Only Member of Congress of Haitian Descent," press release, accessed July 22, 2026, https://cherfilus-mccormick.house.gov/media/press-releases/congresswoman-sheila-cherfilus-mccormick-only-member-congress-haitian-descent.

54 Jesse Scheckner, "South Florida Democratic Congresswomen to Host 3 Events on Impacts of Donald Trump's 'Big, Ugly Law,'" Florida Politics, August 26, 2025, https://floridapolitics.com/archives/753337-south-florida-democratic-congresswomen-to-host-3-events-on-impacts-of-donald-trumps-big-ugly-law/.

55 Anthony Man, "'Florida's in a Crisis.' Broward Democrats Sound Alarm about Trump, DeSantis Policies," *South Florida Sun Sentinel*, August 30, 2025, https://www.sun-sentinel.com/2025/08/30/floridas-in-a-crisis-broward-democrats-sound-alarm-about-trump-desantis-policies/.

56 NBC 6 South Florida, "One-on-One with Rep. Sheila Cherfilus-McCormick," YouTube video, August 3, 2022, https://www.youtube.com/watch?v=qhgXbyW0ATw.

57 Emgage PAC, "Sheila Cherfilus-McCormick," endorsement profile, accessed July 22, 2026, https://emgagepac.org/endorsements/sheila-cherfilus-mccormick/.

58 Ming S. Zhao, "Power Women: Sheila Cherfilus-McCormick on How to Successfully Navigate Work, Love and Life as a Powerful Woman," *Authority Magazine*, October 15, 2021, Medium, https://medium.com/authority-magazine/power-women-sheila-cherfilus-mccormick-on-how-to-successfully-navigate-work-love-and-life-as-a-a264831c576b.

59 Josh Christenson, "Rep. Sheila Cherfilus-McCormick Resigns from Congress Just Minutes before House Ethics Committee Was to Sanction Florida Dem," *New York Post*, April 21, 2026, https://nypost.com/2026/04/21/us-news/rep-sheila-cherfilus-mccormick-resigns-from-congress-just-minutes-before-house-ethics-committee-was-to-sanction-florida-dem/.

60 Majority Haitian (@MajorityHaitian), "BREAKING SPRINGFIELD OHIO: Illegal Haitian nightclub, security guards in bulletproof vests, strippers, alcohol sales & no liquor license," X, August 31, 2025, 10:57 p.m., https://x.com/MajorityHaitian/status/1962349139078889706.

61 Albert Pike (@AlbertPike1809), X post, September 1, 2025, 1:17 a.m., https://x.com/AlbertPike1809/status/1962384184762368352.

62 Majority Haitian (@MajorityHaitian), "BREAKING SPRINGFIELD OHIO: Illegal Haitian nightclub licensed as convenience store. Prostitution? Drug sales? CASH & credit cards!," X, August 31, 2025, 11:18 p.m., https://x.com/MajorityHaitian/status/1962354229571457041.

63 Ohio Department of Commerce, Division of Liquor Control, "Permit Class Types," April 13, 2021, https://com.ohio.gov/divisions-and-programs/liquor-control/new-permit-info/guides-and-resources/permit-class-types.

64 Ohio Department of Commerce, Division of Liquor Control, "Searchable Liquor Control Information," Power BI dashboard, accessed July 22, 2026, https://app.powerbigov.us/view?r=eyJrIjoiMTNiNDYzMDYtZGVhZC00ZmY3LWExOTctNzU5NzE5ZjAzMmMyIiwidCI6IjUwZjhmY2M0LTk0ZDgtNGYwNy04NGViLTM2ZWQ1N2M3YzhhMiJ9.

65 Ohio Department of Commerce, Division of Liquor Control, "Permit Class Types," April 13, 2021, https://com.ohio.gov/divisions-and-programs/liquor-control/new-permit-info/guides-and-resources/permit-class-types.

66 Majority Haitian (@MajorityHaitian), "Springfield, Ohio—Looks like the illegal Haitian nightclub in the O'Connor's plaza is still planning on a big Haitian rave tonight," X, September 6, 2025, 11:21 a.m., https://x.com/MajorityHaitian/status/1964348327983489180.

67 Clark County Auditor, "Parcel 3400600003122023," property record for 1935 S. Yellow Springs St., Springfield, OH, accessed July 22, 2026, https://clarkcountyauditor.org/Parcel?Parcel=3400600003122023.

68 "Six People Shot at Celebration of Life in Springfield; Venue Owner Talks about Rebuilding after Tragedy," WDTN, June 2, 2021, https://www.wdtn.com/news/local-news/six-people-shot-at-celebration-of-life-in-springfield-venue-owner-talks-about-rebuilding-after-tragedy/.

69 Ohio Investigative Unit, "Establishments and Bring Your Own Beverages," accessed July 22, 2026, https://oiu.ohio.gov/law-enforcement-resources/resources/establishments-and-bring-your-own-beverages.

70 Jeff Skinner, "Citizen Action Forces Police Shutdown of Haitian Samedi Rave," *The Ohio Register*, September 7, 2025, https://www.theohioregister.com/citizen-action-forces-police-shutdown-of-haitian-samedi-rave/.

71 "Event Promotional Image," Eventbrite, accessed April 21, 2026, https://www.eventbrite.com/e/_next/image?url=https%3A%2F%2Fimg.evbuc.com%2Fhttps%253A%252F%252Fcdn.evbuc.com%252Fimages%252F1104405233%252F220575299035%252F1%252Foriginal.20250825-151413%3Fcrop%3Dfocalpoint%26fit%3Dcrop%26w%3D1880%26auto%3Dformat%252Ccompress%26q%3D75%26sharp%3D10%26fp-x%3D0.497814020681%26fp-y%3D0.808365758755%26s%3De804d3cb49afe17dd2926acecb77d1d1&w=1880&q=75.

72 Springfield Navigators (@springfieldnavigators), "CLIENT SPOLIGHT: CMS Caribbean Market, LLC, 2113 Park Rd., Springfield, Ohio," Instagram post, April 24, 2023, https://www.instagram.com/p/CrbU5BSMpRU/.

73 Google Maps, "The Hill Lounge, 2113 Park Rd., Springfield, OH 45504," accessed July 22, 2026, https://www.google.com/maps?daddr=2113+Park+Rd,+Springfield,+OH+45504.

74 The Hill Lounge, "Harmonik Live in Springfield, OH," promotional image, Eventbrite, accessed July 22, 2026, https://www.eventbrite.com/e/_next/image?url=https%3A%2F%2Fimg.evbuc.com%2Fhttps%253A%252F%252Fcdn.evbuc.com%252Fimages%-252F1115699763%252F220575299035%252F1%252Foriginal.20250905-191335%3Fcrop%3Dfocalpoint%26fit%3Dcrop%26w%3D1880%26auto%3Dformat%252Ccompress%26q%3D75%26sharp%3D10%26fp-x%3D0.493371212121%26fp-y%3D0.643055555556%26s%3D07ba469d1e94be81f626e269aa7dd945&w=1880&q=75.

75 The Hill Lounge, "Harmonik Live Concert in Springfield Ohio at The State (September 27)," Eventbrite, event held September 27–28, 2025, https://www.eventbrite.com/e/harmonik-live-concert-in-springfield-ohio-at-the-state-september-27-tick-ets-1628513982159.

76 Jeff Skinner, "Citizen Action Forces Police Shutdown of Haitian Samedi Rave," *The Ohio Register*, September 7, 2025, https://www.theohioregister.com/citizen-action-forces-police-shutdown-of-haitian-samedi-rave/.

77 The Hill Lounge, "The Hill Lounge Opens in Springfield with Grand Celebration on July 4th," June 21, 2025, https://thehilllounge.com/general/the-hill-lounge-opens-in-springfield-with-grand-celebration-on-july-4th.

78 Ohio Department of Commerce, Division of Liquor Control, "Liquor Control Information," accessed July 22, 2026, https://com.ohio.gov/divisions-and-programs/liquor-control/renewal-existing-permit-info/guides-and-resources/liquor-control-information.

79 Ohio Department of Commerce, Division of Liquor Control, "Searchable Liquor Control Information," Power BI dashboard, accessed July 22, 2026, https://app.powerbigov.us/view?r=eyJrIjoiMTNiNDYzMDYtZGVhZC00ZmY3LWExOTctN-zU5NzE5ZjAzMmMyIiwidCI6IjUwZjhmY2M0LTk0ZDgtNGYwNy04NGViLTM2ZWQ1N2M3YzhhMiJ9.

80 Ohio Secretary of State, "Domestic Limited Liability Company Certificate of Amendment or Restatement: CMS Caribbean Market, LLC," changing the company name to CMS & Event Center, LLC, document ID 202524800802, electronically filed September 5, 2025, https://bizimage.ohiosos.gov/api/image/pdf/202524800802.

81 Jeff Skinner, "Citizen Action Forces Police Shutdown of Haitian Samedi Rave," *The Ohio Register*, September 7, 2025, https://www.theohioregister.com/citizen-action-forces-police-shutdown-of-haitian-samedi-rave/.

82 Springfield, Ohio, Codified Ordinances § 1311.21, "Endorsements on Certificates of Use and Occupancy," Ordinance 08-353, passed December 9, 2008, amended by Ordinance 19-289, passed December 10, 2019, https://codelibrary.amlegal.com/codes/springfield/latest/springfield_oh/0-0-0-16602.

83 Mark Ackerman, "They Aren't Licensed Casinos. So Why Are These Gaming Centers Paying Out Cash?," News 5 Cleveland, November 22, 2021, https://www.news5cleveland.com/news/local-news/investigations/they-arent-licensed-casinos-so-why-are-these-gaming-centers-paying-out-cash.

84 "Star Wars: Episode VII The Force Awakens," Wookieepedia, Fandom, accessed July 22, 2026, https://starwars.fandom.com/wiki/Star_Wars:_Episode_VII_The_Force_Awakens.

85 Walter Curt (@wcdispatch), "Everyday at Springfield Walmart this is the case. I am convinced it's why Walmart started offering discounted home delivery in the area," X, May 4, 2026, 12:44 p.m., https://x.com/wcdispatch/status/2051342163317764548.

86 Joshua Lisec, "I Went to Springfield's Walmart Yesterday. Haitians with Carts Piled 1.5X Full," Facebook post, May 3, 2026, https://www.facebook.com/joshlisec/posts/pfbid0XcePzuZNYjHSi71Q6Nn7Zj521EtxQzdtocpaZgrwQAf3RMKrWNiT6NE9XFvVAEjGl.

87 Joshua Lisec, "I Went to Springfield's Walmart Yesterday. Haitians with Carts Piled 1.5X Full," Facebook post, May 3, 2026, https://www.facebook.com/joshlisec/posts/pfbid0XcePzuZNYjHSi71Q6Nn7Zj521EtxQzdtocpaZgrwQAf3RMKrWNiT6NE9XFvVAEjGl.

Chapter 14

1 StarTalk, "What Is Schrödinger's Cat? | Neil deGrasse Tyson Explains," YouTube video, May 31, 2022, https://www.youtube.com/watch?v=keiFzYJbfdw.

2 William Brangham (@wbrangham), "I Think in General, the Haitians Who Come to Springfield Are Here to Work," Instagram post, September 5, 2024, https://www.instagram.com/p/C_iowDpO5-P/.

3 Brooke Spurlock, "Clark County Sees More Overdoses, First Responders Use More Narcan," *Springfield News-Sun*, April 22, 2023, https://www.springfieldnewssun.com/news/clark-county-sees-more-overdoses-first-responders-use-more-narcan/article_8472b5b5-605e-585c-b94c-a7e0bff253b0.html.

4 Alison Ringhiser and Caleb Clayton, "Opioid Crisis in Ohio," Critical Questions, no. 29 (Ohio Northern University Institute for Civics and Public Policy, September 25, 2023), https://digitalcommons.onu.edu/cgi/viewcontent.cgi?article=1028&context=critical_questions.

5 Clark County Substance Abuse, Treatment, and Support Task Force, Theory of Change to Overcome the Opioid Crisis, Ohio Department of Mental Health and Addiction Services, accessed July 22, 2026, https://dam.assets.ohio.gov/image/upload/collectiveimpact.mha.ohio.gov/funded-communities/clark/6-Clark_Theory_of_Change.pdf.

6 Case Western Reserve University, Begun Center for Violence Prevention Research and Education, "Overdose Crisis: Ohio Cities Among Worst in Nation," data brief, January 2025, https://ccbh.net/wp-content/uploads/2025/01/OverdoseCrisisOhioCitiesAmongWorstInNation_01.08.2025.pdf.

7 Case Western Reserve University, Begun Center for Violence Prevention Research and Education, "Overdose Crisis: Ohio Cities Among Worst in Nation," data brief, January 2025, https://ccbh.net/wp-content/uploads/2025/01/OverdoseCrisisOhioCitiesAmongWorstInNation_01.08.2025.pdf.

8 Alison Ringhiser and Caleb Clayton, "Opioid Crisis in Ohio," Critical Questions, no. 29 (Ohio Northern University Institute for Civics and Public Policy, September 25, 2023), https://digitalcommons.onu.edu/cgi/viewcontent.cgi?article=1028&context=critical_questions.

9 Rep. Don Bacon (@RepDonBacon), "Removing TPS Status for Haitians Living in the United States Would Cost 350,000 Workers Their Ability to Work," X, April 15, 2026, 6:52 p.m., https://x.com/repdonbacon/status/2044549535985193241.

10 Brandon Gill (@realBrandonGill), "65% of Haitian Non-Citizen Households Are on Welfare," X, April 15, 2026, 7:20 p.m., https://x.com/realbrandongill/status/2044556407165300790.

11 Robert Cherry, "A Deeper Look into Haitian Immigrants in Springfield," American Enterprise Institute, October 10, 2024, https://www.aei.org/op-eds/a-deeper-look-into-haitian-immigrants-in-springfield/.

12 Steven A. Camarota and Karen Zeigler, Non-Citizen Use of Welfare by Region and Country of Birth: High Levels Driven by Lack of Education, Not Unwillingness to Work (Center for Immigration Studies, March 18, 2026), https://cis.org/Report/NonCitizen-Use-Welfare-Region-and-Country-Birth.

13 CID Latinoamérica–Gallup de Panamá (@cid_gallup), "According to CID Gallup's Latest Survey Conducted in May 2025, 64% of . . .," Instagram Reel, June 21, 2025, https://www.instagram.com/reel/DLK3w8ktAj-/.

14 Jireh Sánchez, "Encuesta revela 88.3 % de dominicanos respaldan aumento deportaciones de haitianos," ("Poll reveals 88.3% of Dominicans support increased deportations of Haitians."), RDÉ Digital, February 20, 2025, https://rdedigital.com/encuesta-revela-88-3-de-dominicanos-respaldan-aumento-deportaciones-de-haitianos/.

15 Josh Sweigart, "'Deport Them All,' 'Defund ICE': Some in Springfield Welcome Possible ICE Surge, While Others Recoil," *Springfield News-Sun*, February 2, 2026, https://www.springfieldnewssun.com/news/deport-them-all-defund-ice-some-in-springfield-welcome-possible-ice-surge-while-others-recoil/article_ff5a6c98-8c7b-5667-93af-635c80a120b4.html.

16 Springfield 2051, "Springfield 2051 | Making History Now," accessed July 22, 2026, https://springfield2051.com/.

17 Danae King, "Haitians Bring Growth, Challenges and Unwanted Attention to Springfield," The Columbus Dispatch, February 17, 2026, 3:05 p.m. ET, https://www.dispatch.com/story/news/regional/2026/02/17/springfield-residents-say-haitian-population-growth-brought-challenges/88530100007/.

18 Amazon, "Rich Baris: Books, Biography, Latest Update," accessed July 22, 2026, https://www.amazon.com/stores/author/B00CWNBMAU.

19 U.S. Department of Homeland Security, "Haitian Illegal Alien Violently Kills Innocent Mother by Repeatedly Hitting Her with a Hammer Outside Gas Station in Fort Myers," press release, April 7, 2026, https://www.dhs.gov/news/2026/04/07/haitian-illegal-alien-violently-kills-innocent-mother-repeatedly-hitting-her-hammer.

20 Chip Roy (@chiproytx), "I've heard my colleagues talk about Haitians fleeing danger. You know who else was fleeing danger?," X post, April 16, 2026, 1:45 p.m., https://x.com/chiproytx/status/2044834608110334124.

21 The Truth Wire (@TheTruthWireX), "A Haitian illegal alien brutally murdered an innocent woman with a hammer at a gas station," X post, April 8, 2026, 6:52 a.m., https://x.com/TheTruthWireX/status/2041831445740539966.

22 Elon Musk (@elonmusk), "The Biden administration actively flew illegals into America with no vetting of their violent criminal past into America and paid for

their flights via NGOs," X post, April 12, 2026, 6:26 a.m., https://x.com/elonmusk/status/2043274481666511164.

23 Joseph de Maistre, *The Generative Principle of Political Constitutions: Studies on Sovereignty, Religion, and Enlightenment*, ed. and trans. Jack Lively (1965; repr., London: Routledge, 2017), 125, Scribd, https://www.scribd.com/document/833147906/Joseph-de-Maistre-Jack-Lively-The-Generative-Principle-of-Political-Constitutions-Studies-on-Sovereignty-Religion-and-Enlightenment-1965-Routle.

24 Rob Henderson, "How the Luxury Beliefs of an Educated Elite Erode Society," Rob Henderson's Newsletter, February 25, 2024, https://www.robkhenderson.com/p/how-the-luxury-beliefs-of-an-educated.

25 Rod Dreher, "Immigration as Culture War," *The American Conservative*, April 4, 2013, https://www.theamericanconservative.com/peter-hitchens-immigration-britain/.

26 Adam Waytz et al., "Ideological Differences in the Expanse of the Moral Circle," *Nature Communications* 10 (September 26, 2019): fig. 5, article 4389, https://doi.org/10.1038/s41467-019-12227-0.

27 Adam Waytz et al., "Ideological Differences in the Expanse of the Moral Circle," *Nature Communications* 10 (September 26, 2019): article 4389, https://doi.org/10.1038/s41467-019-12227-0.

28 City of Springfield, Ohio–Government, "Global Education Peace Network Juneteenth Celebration," YouTube video, streamed live June 20, 2020, https://www.youtube.com/watch?v=jx2wdH7hoGI.

29 Galatians 3:28 (New International Version), Bible Gateway, accessed July 22, 2026, https://www.biblegateway.com/passage/?search=Galatians%203%3A28&version=NIV.

30 Matthew 2 (New King James Version), Bible Gateway, accessed July 22, 2026, https://www.biblegateway.com/passage/?search=Matthew%202&version=NKJV.

31 Jeff Louderback, "Springfield Residents Vent Frustration at City Leaders over Haitian Immigrant Surge," *The Santa Clarita Valley Signal*, September 20, 2024, https://signalscv.com/2024/09/springfield-residents-vent-frustration-at-city-leaders-over-haitian-immigrant-surge/.

32 Charlie Kirk (@charliekirk11), "You're trolling, but to answer the bad faith question, NO. I posted about this in detail, but of course you don't reference that," X post, September 1, 2025, 8:26 p.m., https://x.com/charliekirk11/status/1962673529524232355.

33 Luke Garrett, "Vance Defends Spreading Claims That Haitian Migrants Are Eating Pets," NPR, September 15, 2024, https://www.npr.org/2024/09/15/nx-s1-5113140/vance-false-claims-haitian-migrants-pets.

34 JD Vance (@JDVance), "In the last several weeks, my office has received many inquiries from actual residents of Springfield who've said their neighbors' pets or local wildlife were abducted by Haitian migrants," X post, last modified September 10, 2024, 9:58 a.m., https://x.com/JDVance/status/1833505359513661762.

35 Jessica Orozco, Josh Sweigart, Aimee Hancock, and Lynn Hulsey, "Springfield Staffing Firm Responds to Allegations of Busing, Exploiting Haitians," *Springfield News-Sun*, September 28, 2024, https://www.springfieldnewssun.com/news/springfield-staffing-firm-responds-to-allegations-of-busing-exploiting-haitians/article_ce8a1a4c-fbe6-5dc5-8948-8e2c68fb3537.html.

Chapter 15

1 Matthew Malone, "Aleksandr Solzhenitsyn: A Witness to Truth in Darkness," Word on Fire, June 13, 2024, https://www.wordonfire.org/articles/aleksandr-solzhenitsyn-a-witness-to-truth-in-darkness/.

2 Jasmine Garsd, "How Springfield, Ohio, Took Center Stage in the Election Immigration Debate," NPR, August 12, 2024, https://www.npr.org/2024/08/12/nx-s1-5055784/immigration-vance-trump-migration-president-migrants-election-ohio.

3 Jason Bartlett (@Jason2bartlett), "I'm just a white South African having a lovely, peaceful and safe weekend on my farm in Alabama. God is God," X post, April 17, 2026, 5:43 p.m., https://x.com/Jason2bartlett/status/2045256902020411843.

4 Wikipedia, s.v. "White South Africans," last modified July 10, 2026, 1:59 a.m. UTC, https://en.wikipedia.org/wiki/White_South_Africans.

5 Mithil Aggarwal, "How a Land Law Sparked Elon Musk's Accusations of 'Genocide' against His Home Country," NBC News, February 10, 2025, https://www.nbcnews.com/news/world/south-africa-racist-white-farmers-trump-musk-genocide-ramaphosa-rcna190749.

6 Jack Posobiec and Joshua Lisec, *Unhumans: The Secret History of Communist Revolutions (and How to Crush Them)*, foreword by Stephen K. Bannon (War Room Books, 2024), https://www.amazon.com/Unhumans-Secret-History-Communist-Revolutions/dp/1648210856.

7 Taya Bass (@travelingflying), "South African man: 'In South Africa, if you're White, you have a target on your back,'" X post, April 18, 2026, 3:00 p.m., https://x.com/travelingflying/status/2045578107281932601.

8 Taya Bass (@travelingflying), "South African man: 'In South Africa, if you're White, you have a target on your back,'" X post, April 18, 2026, 3:00 p.m., https://x.com/travelingflying/status/2045578107281932601.

9 Associated Press, "Hillside of White Crosses Fuels Misleading Story about South Africa Farm Killings," YouTube video, June 16, 2025, https://www.youtube.com/watch?v=Z_4B0t-ey5M.

10 Melo (@POFFADER), "Your father killed Black people in South Africa. You are always quick to divide or to speak for White people," X post, April 11, 2026, 10:20 a.m., https://x.com/POFFADER/status/2042970968100913288.

11 Elon Musk (@elonmusk), "Yeah, because they broke into his house in South Africa and tried to kill him and my kid sister, you stupid asshole," X post, April 11, 2026, 2:54 p.m., https://x.com/elonmusk/status/2043039890036949476.

12 Majority Haitian (@MajorityHaitian), X profile, accessed April 22, 2026, https://x.com/MajorityHaitian.

13 Thomas Paine, "I Prefer Peace. But If Trouble Must Come, Let It Come in My Time," BrainyQuote, accessed July 22, 2026, https://www.brainyquote.com/quotes/thomas_paine_400961.

14 Brandon Gill (@realBrandonGill), "65% of Haitian non-citizen households are on welfare. They are draining our resources, making America weaker and poorer," X post, April 15, 2026, 7:20 p.m., https://x.com/realbrandongill/status/2044556407165300790.

15 Danae King, "Haitians Bring Growth, Challenges and Unwanted Attention to Springfield," *The Columbus Dispatch*, February 17, 2026, 3:05 p.m. ET, https://www.dispatch.com/story/news/regional/2026/02/17/springfield-residents-say-haitian-population-growth-brought-challenges/88530100007/.

16 Kajsa Ekholm Friedman and Jonathan Friedman, "Getting Ready for the Dark Ages? Preppers, Populists and Climate Prophets: The Disintegration of Global Hegemony, PC Hysteria, and the Deplorable Ugliness of Decline," in *Extremism, Society, and the State*, ed. Giacomo Loperfido (New York: Berghahn Books, 2021), 25, fig. 1.2, https://www.researchgate.net/figure/Mean-in-group-bias-by-race-ethnicity-created-by-the-authors_fig2_381037290.

Chapter 16

1 Eric Schmitt (@SenEricSchmitt), "America is not a strip mall with an airport attached. We are not some global economic zone," X post, April 22, 2026, 1:06 p.m., https://x.com/senericschmitt/status/2046998982287565277.

2 Jessica Orozco, "Springfield Police Chief: No Evidence That Shooting of Haitian Father Was Related to Race," *Springfield News-Sun*, July 8, 2026, https://www.springfieldnewssun.com/local/crime/springfield-police-chief-no-evidence-that-shooting-of-haitian-father-was-related-to-race/article_7d9b949d-aede-5409-bb40-d6281b40681c.html.

3 "Federal Judge Calls Out the Racism of Trump Admin's Plan to End TPS for Haitians," *Mother Jones*, February 3, 2026, https://www.motherjones.com/politics/2026/02/temporary-protected-status-kristi-noem-ana-reyes-ruling/.

4 Maria Ramirez Uribe, "'I Am Afraid': The Aftermath of Springfield, Ohio, Misinformation on Haitians Who Live There," Poynter, September 16, 2024, https://www.poynter.org/fact-checking/2024/springfield-ohio-impact-haitian-immigrants/.

5 Miot v. Trump, No. 25-cv-02471 (ACR), memorandum opinion, ECF No. 124 (D.D.C. February 2, 2026), https://storage.courtlistener.com/recap/gov.uscourts.dcd.283214/gov.uscourts.dcd.283214.124.0_1.pdf.

6 Breitbart News (@BreitbartNews), "Justices Sonia Sotomayor and Ketanji Brown Jackson Invoke Trump's Comments on 'Sh*thole Countries' and 'They're Eating the Dogs,'" X post, April 29, 2026, 11:12 a.m., https://x.com/breitbartnews/status/2049507126955901141.

7 Damita Menezes and Ali Bradley, "Trump on Springfield Haitian Migrants: 'They Have to Be Removed,'" NewsNation, October 2, 2024, https://www.newsnationnow.com/politics/2024-election/trump-springfield-haitian-migrants-removed/.

8 Joseph R. Biden Jr., "What They Are Saying: Biden Administration Re-designates Haiti for Temporary Protected Status," May 23, 2021, The American Presidency Project, https://www.presidency.ucsb.edu/documents/what-they-are-saying-biden-administration-re-designates-haiti-for-temporary-protected.

9 Royce Murray, "Ninth Circuit Court Allows Trump's Plan to End Temporary Protected Status to Go Forward," American Immigration Council, September 14, 2020, https://www.americanimmigrationcouncil.org/blog/tps-ramos-decision/.

10 Royce Murray, "Ninth Circuit Court Allows Trump's Plan to End Temporary Protected Status to Go Forward," American Immigration Council, September 14, 2020, https://www.americanimmigrationcouncil.org/blog/tps-ramos-decision/.

11 Damita Menezes and Ali Bradley, "Trump on Springfield Haitian Migrants: 'They Have to Be Removed,'" NewsNation, October 2, 2024, https://www.newsnationnow.com/politics/2024-election/trump-springfield-haitian-migrants-removed/.

12 "As Haitian TPS End Date Nears, Despair and Frustration Spread in Springfield," *The Haitian Times*, January 30, 2026, https://haitiantimes.com/2026/01/30/springfield-haitian-tps-economic-impact/.

13 National Immigration Forum, "Temporary Protected Status (TPS): Fact Sheet," July 13, 2026, https://forumtogether.org/article/temporary-protected-status-fact-sheet/.

14 Camilo Montoya-Galvez, "Judge Blocks DHS from Ending Deportation Protections for 350,000 Haitians One Day before They Were Set to Lapse," CBS News, updated February 2, 2026, 9:04 p.m. EST, https://www.msn.com/en-us/news/us/judge-blocks-dhs-from-ending-deportation-protections-for-350000-haitians/ar-AA1Vx9oW.

15 Camilo Montoya-Galvez, "Judge Delays Termination of Legal Status for Immigrants from Honduras, Nepal and Nicaragua," CBS News, updated August 1, 2025, 6:48 p.m. EDT, https://www.cbsnews.com/news/judge-delays-termination-of-legal-status-for-immigrants-from-honduras-nepal-and-nicaragua/.

16 Camilo Montoya-Galvez, "Judge Delays Termination of Legal Status for Immigrants from Honduras, Nepal and Nicaragua," CBS News, updated August 1, 2025, 6:48 p.m. EDT, https://www.cbsnews.com/news/judge-delays-termination-of-legal-status-for-immigrants-from-honduras-nepal-and-nicaragua/.

17 Noem v. National TPS Alliance, 606 U.S. ___ (2025), No. 25A326, slip op. (U.S. October 3, 2025), https://www.supremecourt.gov/opinions/24pdf/25a326_3ebh.pdf.

18 6 U.S.C. § 557 (2024), https://uscode.house.gov/view.xhtml?req=granuleid:USC-prelim-title6-section557&num=0&edition=prelim.

19 8 U.S.C. § 1254a (2024), https://uscode.house.gov/view.xhtml?req=granuleid:USC-prelim-title8-section1254a&num=0&edition=prelim.

20 8 U.S.C. § 1254a (2024), https://uscode.house.gov/view.xhtml?req=granuleid:USC-prelim-title8-section1254a&num=0&edition=prelim.

21 5 U.S.C. § 706 (2024), https://uscode.house.gov/view.xhtml?req=granuleid:USC-prelim-title5-section706&num=0&edition=prelim.

22 Don Bacon (@RepDonBacon), "I Will Vote My Christian and American Values. You've Convinced Me Now to Look at Venezuela and El Salvador TPS," X post, April 16, 2026, 11:31 a.m., https://x.com/RepDonBacon/status/2044800973755785522.

23 Auron MacIntyre (@AuronMacIntyre), "Just a GOP congressman casually threatening to flood the country with immigrants to punish Americans," X post, April 16, 2026, 4:39 p.m., https://x.com/auronmacintyre/status/2044878290628866095.

24 Gabe Guidarini (@GabeGuidarini), "There's a reason Ohio is the most frequently targeted state for mass-importation of foreign nationals like Haitians and Somalis," X post, December 28, 2025, 6:43 p.m., https://x.com/GabeGuidarini/status/2005424455527350751.

25 "Moreno, Jordan among Speakers at 'Meet the Candidates,'" *Sidney Daily News*, September 4, 2024, https://www.sidneydailynews.com/2024/09/04/bernie-moreno-jim-jordan-mike-carey-speak-at-republican-event/.

26 Maria Ramirez Uribe, "What's Next for Immigrants with TPS Status after Supreme Court Ruling?," PBS NewsHour, July 9, 2026, https://www.pbs.org/newshour/politics/whats-next-for-immigrants-with-tps-status-after-supreme-court-ruling.

27 Jeff Skinner, "Supreme Court Upholds Termination of Haitian TPS, Clearing Path for Deportations," *The Ohio Register*, June 25, 2026, https://www.theohioregister.com/supreme-court-upholds-termination-of-haitian-tps-clearing-path-for-deportations.

28 Megan Henry, "Ohio Cities Brace for Impact of Supreme Court Allowing Trump to Take Legal Status Away from Haitians," *Ohio Capital Journal*, June 25, 2026, https://ohiocapitaljournal.com/2026/06/25/ohio-cities-brace-for-impact-of-supreme-court-allowing-trump-to-take-legal-status-away-from-haitians/.

29 Megan Henry, "Ohio Cities Brace for Impact of Supreme Court Allowing Trump to Take Legal Status Away from Haitians," *Ohio Capital Journal*, June 25, 2026, https://ohiocapitaljournal.com/2026/06/25/ohio-cities-brace-for-impact-of-supreme-court-allowing-trump-to-take-legal-status-away-from-haitians/.

30 Joshua Lisec (@JoshuaLisec), "LIVE BREAKING NEWS: Springfield's pro-Haitian activists lead a protest at City Hall tonight, claim 'no moral justification' for ending TPS for the city's Haitians," X video post, June 25, 2026, 7:05 p.m., https://x.com/JoshuaLisec/status/2070282353012818258/video/1.

31 "Rally in Support of Haitian TPS," photograph, *Dayton Daily News*, accessed July 29, 2026, https://www.daytondailynews.com/rally-in-support-of-haitian-tps/image_2a624166-938e-56a9-afa2-309d0a882ec6.html.

32 Cornelius Frolik, "Haiti TPS: Many Haitians Want Asylum. Most Won't Get It," *Dayton Daily News*, July 7, 2026, https://www.daytondailynews.com/local/haiti-tps-many

-haitians-want-asylum-most-won-t-get-it/article_a7fffd69-50be-58e9-9099-d2e665f6c204.html.

33 Connor Steffen, "Springfield Haitian Immigrants Get 2-Week TPS Work Permit Extension as Legal Battles Continue," WCPO 9, July 10, 2026, 3:24 p.m., https://www.wcpo.com/news/local-news/springfield-haitian-immigrants-get-2-week-tps-work-permit-extension-as-legal-battles-continue.

34 Julian Jackson, "Haitians in Springfield Now Face Expired Driver's Licenses, Work Permits," WDTN, July 6, 2026, https://www.wdtn.com/as-seen-on-2-news/haitians-springfield-ohio-temporary-protected-status-drivers-license/.

35 State of the Union (@CNNSOTU), "Republican Gov. Mike DeWine on Trump Administration Plan to Deport Haitians: 'It Is Not in the United States's Interest, Certainly Not in Ohio's Interest,'" X video post, June 28, 2026, 9:52 a.m., https://x.com/CNNSOTU/status/2071230271848874102.

36 Neil Munro, "Ohio Gov. Mike DeWine: Americans Are 'Other People' in Migration Politics, 'Haitians Came There to Work,'" *Breitbart*, July 31, 2026, https://www.breitbart.com/immigration/2026/07/31/ohio-gov-mike-dewine-americans-are-other-people-in-migration-politics-haitians-came-there-to-work/.

37 Bernie Moreno (@berniemoreno), "Average Home Price in Springfield, Ohio, in 2022: $140,000; 2026: $220,000," X post, June 28, 2026, 2:14 p.m., https://x.com/berniemoreno/status/2071296110715363618.

38 Jeff Skinner, "Supreme Court Upholds Termination of Haitian TPS, Clearing Path for Deportations," *The Ohio Register*, June 25, 2026, https://www.theohioregister.com/supreme-court-upholds-termination-of-haitian-tps-clearing-path-for-deportations.

39 Connor Steffen, "Springfield Haitian Immigrants Get 2-Week TPS Work Permit Extension as Legal Battles Continue," WCPO 9, July 10, 2026, 3:24 p.m., https://www.wcpo.com/news/local-news/springfield-haitian-immigrants-get-2-week-tps-work-permit-extension-as-legal-battles-continue.

40 Ohio Immigrant Alliance, Facebook post, June 26, 2026, https://www.facebook.com/OhioImmigrantAlliance/posts/pfbid02eehLChB3fP5gYUE9TgibZ1YouFBABDKfPdqhHFfqYHYMSHjFqMQ8Pm4TFbYZqTUVl.

41 Julian Jackson, "Haitians in Springfield Now Face Expired Driver's Licenses, Work Permits," WDTN, July 6, 2026, https://www.wdtn.com/as-seen-on-2-news/haitians-springfield-ohio-temporary-protected-status-drivers-license/.

42 Julian Jackson, "Haitians in Springfield Now Face Expired Driver's Licenses, Work Permits," WDTN, July 6, 2026, https://www.wdtn.com/as-seen-on-2-news/haitians-springfield-ohio-temporary-protected-status-drivers-license/.

43 Human Events (@HumanEvents), "Joshua Lisec Tells Jack Posobiec That 80% of Haitians in Springfield, Ohio, Have Not Self-Deported: 'The People Have Had Enough,'" X video post, July 20, 2026, 3:11 p.m., https://x.com/HumanEvents/status/2079282955554275701.

44 Yvena Jean Francois Radio Yvena TV, "Grand Opening Lantern Bar Restaurant Springfield, OH," Facebook video, accessed July 29, 2026, https://www.facebook.com/watch/?v=2570206476831533.

45 Sarah Donaldson, "Sen. Moreno Says Haitians in Ohio Should Have Self-Deported Already," The Statehouse News Bureau, January 29, 2026, 5:20 p.m., https://www.statenews.org/government-politics/2026-01-29/sen-moreno-says-haitians-in-ohio-should-have-self-deported-already.

46 Jeff Skinner, "Supreme Court Upholds Termination of Haitian TPS, Clearing Path for Deportations," *The Ohio Register*, June 25, 2026, https://www.theohioregister.com/supreme-court-upholds-termination-of-haitian-tps-clearing-path-for-deportations.
47 Julian Jackson, "Haitians in Springfield Now Face Expired Driver's Licenses, Work Permits," WDTN, July 6, 2026, https://www.wdtn.com/as-seen-on-2-news/haitians-springfield-ohio-temporary-protected-status-drivers-license/.
48 Jessica Orozco, "'Why Can't We Do for Our Own, Too?': Springfield Residents Question Support for Haitians," *Springfield News-Sun*, accessed July 22, 2026, https://www.springfieldnewssun.com/local/why-can-t-we-do-for-our-own-too-springfield-residents-question-support-for-haitians/article_0b88740f-ae9c-52b6-bf1b-46ed4341e95a.html.
49 Jessica Orozco, "'Why Can't We Do for Our Own, Too?': Springfield Residents Question Support for Haitians," *Springfield News-Sun*, accessed July 22, 2026, https://www.springfieldnewssun.com/local/why-can-t-we-do-for-our-own-too-springfield-residents-question-support-for-haitians/article_0b88740f-ae9c-52b6-bf1b-46ed4341e95a.html.
50 Jessica Orozco, "'Why Can't We Do for Our Own, Too?': Springfield Residents Question Support for Haitians," *Springfield News-Sun*, accessed July 22, 2026, https://www.springfieldnewssun.com/local/why-can-t-we-do-for-our-own-too-springfield-residents-question-support-for-haitians/article_0b88740f-ae9c-52b6-bf1b-46ed4341e95a.html.
51 Jessica Orozco, "Springfield Faith Leader: Haitians Face 'Existential Fear' over Potential Deportations to Gang-Run Country," *Springfield News-Sun*, July 28, 2026, https://www.springfieldnewssun.com/local/springfield-faith-leader-haitians-face-existential-fear-over-potential-deportations-to-gang-run-country/article_83daab5a-d8c2-5ac5-a838-e1535d3989df.html.
52 Jessica Orozco, "'Why Can't We Do for Our Own, Too?': Springfield Residents Question Support for Haitians," *Springfield News-Sun*, accessed July 22, 2026, https://www.springfieldnewssun.com/local/why-can-t-we-do-for-our-own-too-springfield-residents-question-support-for-haitians/article_0b88740f-ae9c-52b6-bf1b-46ed4341e95a.html.
53 Empty Pockets Garage, James, "Springfield, Ohio Had It's Town Hall Meeting Tonight," YouTube video, streamed live July 21, 2026, https://www.youtube.com/watch?v=ducpNFtIoU0.
54 City of Springfield, Ohio—Government, "City Commission Meeting, July 28, 2026," YouTube video, streamed live July 28, 2026, https://www.youtube.com/watch?v=vds7X_a1yrQ.
55 George Shillcock, "Ohio Pastors Aiding Haitians Say ICE Will Use 'Carrot and Stick' Approach after End of TPS," WOSU 89.7 NPR News, July 28, 2026, 3:38 p.m. EDT, https://www.wosu.org/politics-government/2026-07-28/ohio-pastors-aiding-haitians-say-ice-will-use-carrot-and-stick-approach-after-end-of-tps.
56 Newsmax Wires, "Homan to Newsmax: ICE Surge Operation Coming to New York," Newsmax, July 20, 2026, https://www.newsmax.com/newsmax-tv/tom-homan-ice-new-york/2026/07/20/id/1263489/.
57 "Minority Health Fair," Facebook event, April 25, 2026, 10:00 a.m.–1:00 p.m., https://www.facebook.com/events/1700-clifton-ave-springfield-oh-45505-4008-united-states/minority-health-fair/1546818936533333/.
58 larosenbrgr, "Newsmax, the Truth About Springfield, Ohio with Glenda Bailey," YouTube video, September 20, 2024, https://www.youtube.com/watch?v=S13RMuW2tvo.
59 "Matthew 13:12," Bible Hub, accessed July 22, 2026, https://biblehub.com/matthew/13-12.htm.
60 Empty Pockets Garage, James, "Haitian Invasion, Springfield, Ohio 06/28/26," YouTube livestream, June 28, 2026, https://www.youtube.com/watch?v=BsyuHqiS_vQ.

61 "Little Boxes," Wikipedia, accessed July 22, 2026, https://en.wikipedia.org/wiki/Little_Boxes.
62 United Nations Population Division, Replacement Migration: Is It a Solution to Declining and Ageing Populations?, ESA/P/WP.160 (New York: United Nations, March 21, 2000), https://www.un.org/development/desa/pd/sites/www.un.org.development.desa.pd/files/unpd-egm_200010_un_2001_replacementmigration.pdf.
63 United Nations Population Division, Replacement Migration: Is It a Solution to Declining and Ageing Populations?, ESA/P/WP.160 (New York: United Nations, March 21, 2000), https://www.un.org/development/desa/pd/sites/www.un.org.development.desa.pd/files/unpd-egm_200010_un_2001_replacementmigration.pdf.
64 *Alt-Right: Age of Rage*, Netflix, 2018, https://www.netflix.com/title/80998786.
65 Political Stuff, "2018 SPLC Senior Fellow Mark Potok Tracking Decline of White Population in US," YouTube video, April 22, 2026, https://www.youtube.com/watch?v=M111nYwH3D8.
66 Cats without Borders (@russ62960450), "Let's Be Honest: It Was a Countdown and Represented the Telos (or at Least an Important Success Metric) of the SPLC," X post, April 22, 2026, 8:37 a.m., https://x.com/russ62960450/status/2046931285726159030.
67 Ms. Muck Raker (@muck.raking.media), "Evidence from a 2010 SPLC Video and Photos Shows Mark Potok's Office Wall with Notes Tracking Declining Non-Hispanic White U.S. Population," Instagram reel, accessed July 22, 2026, https://www.instagram.com/reel/DPWdHHxDcB7/.
68 Dr Manhattva (@Manhattva), "One of the Most Disturbing Things I've Ever Seen," X post, April 22, 2026, 12:28 p.m., https://x.com/Manhattva/status/2046989654751420440.
69 "SPLC's Mark Potok Keeps a Paper Tracking the Decline of the White Population in His Office," Reddit post, r/conspiracy, April 22, 2026, 8:47 p.m., https://www.reddit.com/r/conspiracy/comments/1st3oly/splcs_mark_potok_keeps_a_paper_tracking_the/.

Acknowledgements

1 A. O. Scott, "'Angels & Demons': Mayhem at the Vatican," *Rutland Herald*, May 15, 2009, https://www.rutlandherald.com/news/angels-demons-mayhem-at-the-vatican/article_f03d9a71-415c-5677-bec2-67169e69630e.html.

INDEX